Node.js Complete Reference Guide

Discover a more sustainable way of writing software with high levels of reusability and collaboration using Node.js

Valentin Bojinov
David Herron
Diogo Resende

BIRMINGHAM - MUMBAI

Node.js Complete Reference Guide

First published: December 2018

Production reference: 1181218

Published by Packt Publishing Ltd.
Livery Place
35 Livery Street
Birmingham
B3 2PB, UK.

ISBN 978-1-78995-211-7

www.packtpub.com

Contributors

About the authors

Valentin Bojinov studied computer science at the Technological School of Electronic Systems in Sofia, Bulgaria, a college within the Technical University of Sofia. He holds a B.Sc. in telecommunication and information engineering. Valentin is an expert in Java, SOAP, RESTful web services, and B2B integration. He specializes B2B Integration and Service Oriented Architecture and currently works as an Senior Integration Consultant in an UK consultancy company Estafet Limited.

David Herron is a software engineer in Silicon Valley, working on projects from an X.400 e-mail server to assist launching the OpenJDK project, to Yahoo's Node.js application-hosting platform, and applications to monitor solar power array performance. David writes about electric vehicles, environmental issues, and green technology on LongTailPipe, and about other topics, including Node.js, Drupal, and Doctor Who on TechSparx. Using Node.js he developed AkashaCMS.

Diogo Resende is a developer with more than 15 years of experience, working with Node.js almost from the beginning. His computer education and experience in many industry and telecommunication projects have given him a wider background knowledge of other architecture components that influence the overall performance.

Packt is searching for authors like you

If you're interested in becoming an author for Packt, please visit `authors.packtpub.com` and apply today. We have worked with thousands of developers and tech professionals, just like you, to help them share their insight with the global tech community. You can make a general application, apply for a specific hot topic that we are recruiting an author for, or submit your own idea.

Table of Contents

Preface

Machine learning is becoming more and more transformational to businesses every passing day. Machine Learning with Node.js Complete Reference Guide takes you through rudimentary knowledge of JavaScript and server-side development to create, maintain, deploy, and test your own Node.js applications.

You will begin by learning how to use the HTTP Server and Client objects, store data with both SQL and MongoDB databases, and unit test applications with Mocha 5.x, and functionally test them with Puppeteer 1.1.x. Then, you will learn to create scalable and rich RESTful applications on the Node.js platform and write a simple HTTP request handler with self-descriptive URLs. You will learn to set accurate HTTP status codes, study how to keep your applications backward-compatible and explore some authentication techniques to secure your application. Then, you will study how Node.js has emerged as a strong candidate for developing microservices.

With this Learning Path, you will be able to use the best practices and create efficient microservices.

This Learning Path includes content from the following Packt products:

- RESTful Web API Design with Node.js 10, Third Edition by Valentin Bojinov
- Node.js Web Development, Fourth Edition by David Herron
- Hands-On Microservices with Node.js by Diogo Resende

Who this book is for

Node.js Complete Reference Guide is designed for web developers who have a rudimentary understanding of JavaScript and web application development, are keen to enrich their development skills to create RESTful applications, and want utilize their skills to build microservices.

What this book covers

Chapter 1, *About Node.js*, introduces you to the Node.js platform. It covers its uses, the technological architecture choices in Node.js, its history, the history of server-side JavaScript, why JavaScript should be liberated from the browser, and important recent advances in the JavaScript scene.

Chapter 2, *Setting up Node.js*, goes over setting up a Node.js developer environment. This includes installing Node.js on Windows, macOS, and Linux. Important tools are covered, including the npm and yarn package management systems and Babel, which is used for transpiling modern JavaScript into a form that's runnable on older JavaScript implementations.

Chapter 3, *Node.js Modules*, explores the module as the unit of modularity in Node.js applications. We dive deep into understanding and developing Node.js modules and using npm to maintain dependencies. We learn about the new module format, ES6 Modules, that should supplant the CommonJS module format currently used in Node.js, and are natively supported in Node.js 10.x.

Chapter 4, *HTTP Servers and Clients*, starts exploring web development with Node.js. We develop several small webserver and client applications in Node.js. We use the Fibonacci algorithm to explore the effects of heavy-weight, long-running computations on a Node.js application. We also learn several mitigation strategies, and have our first experience with developing REST services.

Chapter 5, *Your First Express Application*, begins the section on developing a note-taking application. The first step is getting a basic application running.

Chapter 6, *Implementing the Mobile-First Paradigm*, uses Bootstrap V4 to implement responsive web design. We take a look at integrating a popular icon set so that we can have pictorial buttons, and go over compiling a custom Bootstrap theme.

Chapter 7, *Data Storage and Retrieval*, ensures that we don't lose our notes when we restart the application. We explore several database engines and a method to enable easily switching between them at will.

Chapter 8, *Multiuser Authentication the Microservice Way*, adds user authentication to the note-taking application. Both logged-in and anonymous users can access the application, with varying capabilities based on role. Authentication is supported both for locally stored credentials and for using OAuth against Twitter.

`Chapter 9`, *Dynamic Client/Server Interaction with Socket.IO*, lets our users talk with each other in real time. JavaScript code will run in both the browser and the server, with Socket.IO providing the plumbing needed for real-time event exchange. Users will see
notes change as they're edited by other users and can leave messages/comments for others.

`Chapter 10`, *Deploying Node.js Applications*, helps us understand Node.js application deployment. We look at both traditional Linux service deployment using an /etc/init script and using Docker for both local development and deployment on cloud hosting services.

`Chapter 11`, *Unit Testing and Functional Testing*, takes a look at three test development models: unit testing, REST testing, and functional testing. We'll use the popular Mocha and Chai frameworks for the first two, and Puppeteer for the third. Puppeteer uses a headless version of Chrome to support running tests. Docker is used to facilitate setting up and tearing down test environments.

`Chapter 12`, *REST – What You Did Not Know*, gives you a brief introduction to the history of REST and how it couples with the HTTP protocol.

`Chapter 13`, *Building a Typical Web API*, takes you through structuring your application using human-readable URL and URI parameters. You will get to develop a read-only RESTful service application, using the filesystem for storage.

`Chapter 14`, *Using NoSQL Databases*, showcases how to use the MongoDB NoSQL database, and explains the foundation of document data stores.

`Chapter 15`, *Restful API Design Guidelines*, explains that there are a number of prerequisites that a RESTful API should meet.

`Chapter 16`, *Implementing a Full Fledged RESTful Service*, focuses on implementing a production-ready RESTful service that uses NoSQL to store its data. You will get to learn how to handle binary data and how to version an API while it evolves.

`Chapter 17`, *Consuming a RESTful API*, showcases a sample frontend client that serves as a consumption reference implementation.

`Chapter 18`, *Securing the Application*, covers restricting access to your data by choosing an appropriate authentication approach. You'll then be able to protect data leakage with transport layer security.

`Chapter` 19, The *Age of Microservices*, covers the evolution of computing and how development has changed and shifted from paradigm to paradigm depending on processing capacity and user demand, ultimately resulting in the age of microservices.

`Chapter` 20, *Modules and Toolkits*, introduces you to some modules that help you create a microservice, detailing different full toolkits approaches, such as Hydra and Seneca.

`Chapter` 21, *Building a Microservice*, covers the development of a simple microservice using Seneca and Hydra.

`Chapter` 22, *State*, covers the development of our microservice: from using the server filesystem to moving to a more structured database service, such as MySQL.

`Chapter` 23, *Testing*, covers the mocking of services.

`Chapter` 24, *Design Patterns*, enumerates some of the most common architectural design patterns and reviews the continuous integration and deployment loop used throughout the book.

To get the most out of this book

The execution of the code examples provided in this Learning Path requires Node.js running on POSIX-like operating systems, various UNIX derivatives (Solaris, for example) or workalikes (Linux, macOS, and so on), as well as on Microsoft Windows. It can
run on machines both large and small, including the tiny ARM devices such as the Raspberry Pi microscale embeddable computer for DIY software/hardware projects.

Because many Node.js packages are written in C or C++, you must have a C compiler (such as GCC), Python 2.7 (or later), and the node-gyp package. If you plan to use encryption in your networking code, you will also need the OpenSSL cryptographic library. The modern UNIX derivatives almost certainly come with these, and Node.js's configure script, used when installing from source, will detect their presence. If you need to install them, Python is available at `http://python.org` and OpenSSL is available at `http://openssl.org`.

Download the example code files

You can download the example code files for this book from your account at
`www.packt.com`. If you purchased this book elsewhere, you can visit
`www.packt.com/support` and register to have the files emailed directly to you.

You can download the code files by following these steps:

1. Log in or register at `www.packt.com`.
2. Select the **SUPPORT** tab.
3. Click on **Code Downloads & Errata**.
4. Enter the name of the book in the **Search** box and follow the onscreen
   instructions.

Once the file is downloaded, please make sure that you unzip or extract the folder
using the latest version of:

- WinRAR/7-Zip for Windows
- Zipeg/iZip/UnRarX for Mac
- 7-Zip/PeaZip for Linux

The code bundle for the book is also hosted on GitHub at `https://github.com/`
`PacktPublishing/Node.js-Complete-Reference-Guide`. In case there's an update to
the code, it will be updated on the existing GitHub repository.

We also have other code bundles from our rich catalog of books and videos available
at `https://github.com/PacktPublishing/`. Check them out!

Conventions used

There are a number of text conventions used throughout this book.

`CodeInText`: Indicates code words in text, database table names, folder names,
filenames, file extensions, pathnames, dummy URLs, user input, and Twitter handles.
Here is an example: "The `EventEmitter` object is defined in the events module of
Node.js."

A block of code is set as follows:

```
if (anotherNote instanceof Note) {
  ... it's a Note, so act on it as a Note
}
```

Any command-line input or output is written as follows:

```
$ npm update express
$ npm update
```

Bold: Indicates a new term, an important word, or words that you see onscreen. For example, words in menus or dialog boxes appear in the text like this. Here is an example: "If you need something different, click on the **DOWNLOADS** link in the header for all possible downloads: "

Warnings or important notes appear like this.

Tips and tricks appear like this.

Get in touch

Feedback from our readers is always welcome.

General feedback: If you have questions about any aspect of this book, mention the book title in the subject of your message and email us at customercare@packtpub.com.

Errata: Although we have taken every care to ensure the accuracy of our content, mistakes do happen. If you have found a mistake in this book, we would be grateful if you would report this to us. Please visit www.packt.com/submit-errata, selecting your book, clicking on the Errata Submission Form link, and entering the details.

Piracy: If you come across any illegal copies of our works in any form on the Internet, we would be grateful if you would provide us with the location address or website name. Please contact us at `copyright@packt.com` with a link to the material.

If you are interested in becoming an author: If there is a topic that you have expertise in and you are interested in either writing or contributing to a book, please visit `authors.packtpub.com`.

Reviews

Please leave a review. Once you have read and used this book, why not leave a review on the site that you purchased it from? Potential readers can then see and use your unbiased opinion to make purchase decisions, we at Packt can understand what you think about our products, and our authors can see your feedback on their book. Thank you!

For more information about Packt, please visit `packt.com`.

About Node.js

Node.js is an exciting new platform for developing web applications, application servers, any sort of network server or client, and general purpose programming. It is designed for extreme scalability in networked applications through an ingenious combination of server-side JavaScript, asynchronous I/O, and asynchronous programming. It is built around JavaScript anonymous functions, and a single execution thread event-driven architecture.

While only a few years old, Node.js has quickly grown in prominence and it's now playing a significant role. Companies, both small and large, are using it for large-scale and small-scale projects. PayPal, for example, has converted many services from Java to Node.js.

The Node.js architecture departs from a typical choice made by other application platforms. Where threads are widely used to scale an application to fill the CPU, Node.js eschews threads because of their inherent complexity. It's claimed that with single-thread event-driven architectures, memory footprint is low, throughput is high, the latency profile under load is better, and the programming model is simpler. The Node.js platform is in a phase of rapid growth, and many are seeing it as a compelling alternative to the traditional web application architectures using Java, PHP, Python, or Ruby on Rails.

At its heart, it is a standalone JavaScript engine with extensions making it suitable for general purpose programming and with a clear focus on application server development. Even though we're comparing Node.js to application server platforms, it is not an application server. Instead, Node.js is a programming run-time akin to Python, Go, or Java SE. While there are web application frameworks and application servers written in Node.js, it is simply a system to execute JavaScript programs.

It is implemented around a non-blocking I/O event loop and a layer of file and network I/O libraries, all built on top of the V8 JavaScript engine (from the Chrome web browser). The rapid performance and feature improvements implemented in Chrome quickly flow through to the Node.js platform. Additionally, a team of folks are working on a Node.js implementation that runs on top of Microsoft's ChakraCore JavaScript engine (from the Edge web browser). That would give the Node.js community greater flexibility by not being reliant on one JavaScript engine provider. Visit `https://github.com/nodejs/node-chakracore` to take a look at the project.

The Node.js I/O library is general enough to implement any sort of server executing any TCP or UDP protocol, whether it's **domain name system** (**DNS**), HTTP, **internet relay chat** (**IRC**), or FTP. While it supports developing internet servers or clients, its biggest use case is in regular websites, in place of technology such as an Apache/PHP or Rails stack, or to complement existing websites. For example, adding real-time chat or monitoring existing websites can be easily done with the Socket. IO library for Node.js. Its lightweight, high-performance nature often sees Node.js used as a **glue** service.

A particularly intriguing combination is deploying small services using Docker into cloud hosting infrastructure. A large application can be divided into what's now called microservices that are easily deployed at scale using Docker. The result fits agile project management methods since each microservice can be easily managed by a small team that collaborates at the boundary of their individual API.

This book will give you an introduction to Node.js. We presume the following:

- You already know how to write software
- You are familiar with JavaScript
- You know something about developing web applications in other languages

We will cover the following topics in this chapter:

- An introduction to Node.js
- Why you should use Node.js
- The architecture of Node.js
- Performance, utilization, and scalability with Node.js
- Node.js, microservice architecture, and testing
- Implementing the Twelve-Factor App model with Node.js

We will dive right into developing working applications and recognize that often the best way to learn is by rummaging around in working code.

The capabilities of Node.js

Node.js is a platform for writing JavaScript applications outside web browsers. This is not the JavaScript we are familiar with in web browsers! For example, there is no DOM built into Node.js, nor any other browser capability.

Beyond its native ability to execute JavaScript, the bundled modules provide capabilities of this sort:

- Command-line tools (in shell script style)
- An interactive-terminal style of program that is **Read-Eval-Print Loop (REPL)**
- Excellent process control functions to oversee child processes
- A buffer object to deal with binary data
- TCP or UDP sockets with comprehensive event-driven callbacks
- DNS lookup
- An HTTP, HTTPS and HTTP/2 client/server layered on top of the TCP library filesystem access
- Built-in rudimentary unit testing support through assertions

The network layer of Node.js is low level while being simple to use. For example, the HTTP modules allow you to write an HTTP server (or client) using a few lines of code. This is powerful, but it puts you, the programmer, very close to the protocol requests and makes you implement precisely those HTTP headers that you should return in request responses.

Typical web application developers don't need to work at a low level of the HTTP or other protocols. Instead, we tend to be more productive, working with higher-level interfaces. For example, PHP coders assume that Apache (or other HTTP servers) is already there providing the HTTP protocol, and that they don't have to implement the HTTP server portion of the stack. By contrast, a Node.js programmer does implement an HTTP server to which their application code is attached.

To simplify the situation, the Node.js community has several web application frameworks, such as Express, providing the higher-level interfaces required by typical programmers. You can quickly configure an HTTP server with baked-in capabilities such as sessions, cookies, serving static files, and logging, letting developers focus on their business logic. Other frameworks provide OAuth 2 support, or focus on REST APIs, and so on.

Node.js is not limited to web service application development. The community around Node.js has taken it in many other directions,

Build tools: Node.js has become a popular choice for developing command-line tools used in software development, or communicating with service infrastructure. Grunt and Gulp are widely used by frontend developers to build assets for websites. Babel is widely used for transpiling modern ES-2016 code to run on older browsers. Popular CSS optimizers and processors, such as PostCSS, are written in Node.js. Static website generation systems such as Metalsmith, Punch, and AkashaCMS, run at the command line and generate website content that you upload to a web server.

Web UI testing: Puppeteer gives you control over a headless-Chrome web browser instance. With it, you can develop Node.js scripts controlling a modern full-featured web browser. Typical use cases involve web scraping and testing web applications.

Desktop applications: Both Electron and **node-webkit** (**NW.js**) are frameworks for developing desktop applications for Windows, macOS, and Linux. These frameworks utilize a large chunk of Chrome, wrapped by Node.js libraries, to develop desktop applications using web UI technologies. Applications are written with modern HTML5, CSS3, and JavaScript, and can utilize leading-edge web frameworks, such as Bootstrap, React, or AngularJS. Many popular applications have been built using Electron, including the Slack desktop client application, the Atom and Microsoft Visual Code programming editors, the Postman REST client, the GitKraken GIT client, and Etcher, which makes it incredibly easy to burn OS images to flash drives to run on single-board computers.

Mobile applications: The Node.js for Mobile Systems project lets you develop smartphone or tablet computer applications using Node.js, for both iOS and Android. Apple's App Store rules preclude incorporating a JavaScript engine with JIT capabilities, meaning that normal Node.js cannot be used in an iOS application. For iOS application development, the project uses Node.js-on-ChakraCore to skirt around the App Store rules. For Android application development the project uses regular Node.js on Android. At the time of writing, the project is in an early stage of development, but it looks promising.

Internet of Things (**IoT**): Reportedly, it is a very popular language for Internet-of-Things projects, and Node.js does run on most ARM-based single-board computers. The clearest example is the NodeRED project. It offers a graphical programming environment, letting you draw programs by connecting blocks together. It features hardware-oriented input and output mechanisms, for example, to interact with **General Purpose I/O** (**GPIO**) pins on Raspberry Pi or Beaglebone single-board computers.

Server-side JavaScript

Quit scratching your head already! Of course you're doing it, scratching your head and mumbling to yourself, "What's a browser language doing on the server?" In truth, JavaScript has a long and largely unknown history outside the browser. JavaScript is a programming language, just like any other language, and the better question to ask is "Why should JavaScript remain trapped inside browsers?".

Back in the dawn of the web age, the tools for writing web applications were at a fledgling stage. Some were experimenting with Perl or TCL to write CGI scripts, and the PHP and Java languages had just been developed. Even then, JavaScript saw use on the server side. One early web application server was Netscape's LiveWire server, which used JavaScript. Some versions of Microsoft's ASP used JScript, their version of JavaScript. A more recent server-side JavaScript project is the RingoJS application framework in the Java universe. Java 6 and Java 7 were both shipped with the Rhino JavaScript engine. In Java 8, Rhino was dropped in favor of the newer Nashorn JavaScript engine.

In other words, JavaScript outside the browser is not a new thing, even if it is uncommon.

Why should you use Node.js?

Among the many available web application development platforms, why should you choose Node.js? There are many stacks to choose from; what is it about Node.js that makes it rise above the others? We will see in the following sections.

Popularity

Node.js is quickly becoming a popular development platform with adoption by plenty of big and small players. One of those is PayPal, who are replacing their incumbent Java-based system with one written in Node.js. For PayPal's blog post about this, visit
`https://www.paypal-engineering.com/2013/11/22/node-js-at-paypal/`. Other large Node.js adopters include Walmart's online e-commerce platform, LinkedIn, and eBay.

According to NodeSource, Node.js usage is growing rapidly (visit `https://nodesource.com/node-by-numbers`). The measures include increasing bandwidth for downloading Node.js releases, increasing activity in Node.js-related GitHub projects, and more.

It's best to not just follow the crowd because the crowd claims their software platform does cool things. Node.js does some cool things, but more important is its technical merit.

JavaScript at all levels of the stack

Having the same programming language on the server and client has been a long-time dream on the web. This dream dates back to the early days of Java, where Java applets were to be the frontend to server applications written in Java, and JavaScript was originally envisioned as a lightweight scripting language for those applets. Java never fulfilled its hype as a client-side programming language, for various reasons. We ended up with JavaScript as the principle in-browser, client-side language, rather than Java. Typically, the frontend JavaScript developers were in a different language universe than the server-side team, who was likely to be coding in PHP, Java, Ruby, or Python.

Over time, in-browser JavaScript engines became incredibly powerful, letting us write ever-more complex browser-side applications. With Node.js, we may finally be able to implement applications with the same programming language on the client and server by having JavaScript at both ends of the web, in the browser and server.

A common language for frontend and backend offers several potential benefits:

- The same programming staff can work on both ends of the wire
- Code can be migrated between server and client more easily
- Common data formats (JSON) exist between server and client
- Common software tools exist for server and client
- Common testing or quality reporting tools for server and client
- When writing web applications, view templates can be used on both sides

The JavaScript language is very popular due to its ubiquity in web browsers. It compares favorably against other languages while having many modern, advanced language concepts. Thanks to its popularity, there is a deep talent pool of experienced JavaScript programmers out there.

Leveraging Google's investment in V8

To make Chrome a popular and excellent web browser, Google invested in making V8 a super-fast JavaScript engine. Google, therefore, has a huge motivation to keep on improving V8. V8 is the JavaScript engine for Chrome, and it can also be executed standalone. Node.js is built on top of the V8 JavaScript engine.

As Node.js becomes more important to the V8 team, there's a potential synergy of faster V8 performance wins as more people focus on V8 improvements.

Leaner, asynchronous, event-driven model

We'll get into this later. The Node.js architecture, a single execution thread, an ingenious event-oriented asynchronous-programming model, and a fast JavaScript engine, has less overhead than thread-based architectures.

Microservice architecture

A new sensation in software development is the microservice idea. Microservices are focused on splitting a large web application into small, tightly-focused services that can be easily developed by small teams. While they aren't exactly a new idea, they're more of a reframing of old client-server computing models, the microservice pattern fits well with agile project management techniques, and gives us more granular application deployment.

Node.js is an excellent platform for implementing microservices. We'll get into this later.

Node.js is stronger for having survived a major schism and hostile fork

During 2014 and 2015, the Node.js community faced a major split over policy, direction, and control. The **io.js** project was a hostile fork driven by a group who wanted to incorporate several features and change who's in the decision-making process. The end result was a merge of the Node.js and io.js repositories, an independent Node.js foundation to run the show, and the community is working together to move forward in a common direction.

A concrete result of healing that rift is the rapid adoption of
new ECMAScript language features. The V8 engine is adopting those new features
quickly to advance the state of web development. The Node.js team, in turn, is
adopting those features as quickly as they show up in V8, meaning that Promises and
`async` functions are quickly becoming a reality for Node.js programmers.

The bottom line is that the Node.js community not only survived the io.js fork, but the
community and the platform it nurtures grew stronger as a result.

Threaded versus event-driven architecture

Node.js's blistering performance is said to be because of its asynchronous event-
driven architecture, and its use of the V8 JavaScript engine. That's a nice thing to say,
but what's the rationale for the statement?

The V8 JavaScript engine is among the fastest JavaScript implementations. As a result,
Chrome is widely used not just to view website content, but to run complex
applications. Examples include Gmail, the Google GSuite applications (Docs, Slides,
and so on), image editors such as Pixlr, and drawing applications such as draw.io and
Canva. Both Atom and Microsoft's Visual Studio Code are excellent IDE's that just
happen to be implemented in Node.js and Chrome using Electron. That these
applications exist and are happily used by a large number of people is testament to
V8's performance. Node.js benefits from V8 performance improvements.

The normal application server model uses blocking I/O to retrieve data, and it uses
threads for concurrency. Blocking I/O causes threads to wait on results. That causes a
churn between threads as the application server starts and stops the threads to handle
requests. Each suspended thread (typically waiting on an I/O operation to finish)
consumes a full stack trace of memory, increasing memory consumption overhead.
Threads add complexity to the application server as well as server overhead.

Node.js has a single execution thread with no waiting on I/O or context switching. Instead, there is an event loop looking for events and dispatching them to handler functions. The paradigm is that any operation that would block or otherwise take time to complete must use the asynchronous model. These functions are to be given an anonymous function to act as a handler callback, or else (with the advent of ES2015 promises), the function would return a Promise. The handler function, or Promise, is invoked when the operation is complete. In the meantime, control returns to the event loop, which continues dispatching events.

At the Node.js interactive conference in 2017, IBM's Chris Bailey made a case for Node.js being an excellent choice for highly scalable microservices. Key performance characteristics are I/O performance, measured in transactions per second, startup time, because that limits how quickly your service can scale up to meet demand, and memory footprint, because that determines how many application instances can be deployed per server. Node.js excels on all those measures; with every subsequent release each, is either improving or remaining fairly steady. Bailey presented figures comparing Node.js to a similar benchmark written in Spring Boot showing Node.js to perform much better. To view his talk, see `https://www.youtube.com/watch?v=Fbhhc4jtGW4`.

To help us wrap our heads around why this would be, let's return to Ryan Dahl, the creator of Node.js, and the key inspiration leading him to create Node.js. In his **Cinco de NodeJS** presentation in May 2010, `https://www.youtube.com/watch?v=M-sc73Y-zQA`, Dahl asked us what happens while executing a line of code such as this:

```
result = query('SELECT * from db');
// operate on the result
```

Of course, the program pauses at that point while the database layer sends the query to the database, which determines the result and returns the data. Depending on the query, that pause can be quite long; well, a few milliseconds, which is an eon in computer time. This pause is bad because that execution thread can do nothing while waiting for the result to arrive. If your software is running on a single-threaded platform, the entire server would be blocked and unresponsive. If instead, your application is running on a thread-based server platform, a thread context switch is required to satisfy any other requests that arrive. The greater the number of outstanding connections to the server, the greater the number of thread context switches. Context switching is not free because more threads require more memory per thread state and more time for the CPU to spend on thread management overhead.

Simply using an asynchronous, event-driven I/O, Node.js removes most of this overhead while introducing very little of its own.

Using threads to implement concurrency often comes with admonitions such as these: *expensive and error-prone, the error-prone synchronization primitives of Java,* or *designing concurrent software can be complex and error prone.* The complexity comes from the access to shared variables and various strategies to avoid deadlock and competition between threads. The *synchronization primitives of Java* are an example of such a strategy, and obviously many programmers find them difficult to use. There's the tendency to create frameworks such as `java.util.concurrent` to tame the complexity of threaded concurrency, but some might argue that papering over complexity does not make things simpler.

Node.js asks us to think differently about concurrency. Callbacks fired asynchronously from an event loop are a much simpler concurrency model—simpler to understand, simpler to implement, simpler to reason about, and simpler to debug and maintain.

Ryan Dahl points to the relative access time of objects to understand the need for asynchronous I/O. Objects in memory are more quickly accessed (in the order of nanoseconds) than objects on disk or objects retrieved over the network (milliseconds or seconds). The longer access time for external objects is measured in zillions of clock cycles, which can be an eternity when your customer is sitting at their web browser ready to move on if it takes longer than two seconds to load the page.

In Node.js, the query discussed previously will read as follows:

```
query('SELECT * from db', function (err, result) {
    if (err) throw err; // handle errors
    // operate on result
});
```

The programmer supplies a function that is called (hence the name *callback function*) when the result (or error) is available. Instead of a thread context switch, this code returns almost immediately to the event loop. That event loop is free to handle other requests. The Node.js runtime keeps track of the stack context leading to this callback function, and eventually an event will fire causing this callback function to be called.

Advances in the JavaScript language are giving us new options to implement this idea. The equivalent code looks like so when used with ES2015 Promise's:

```
query('SELECT * from db')
.then(result => {
    // operate on result
})
.catch(err => {
    // handle errors
});
```

The following with an ES-2017 `async` function:

```
try {
    var result = await query('SELECT * from db');
    // operate on result
} catch (err) {
    // handle errors
}
```

All three of these code snippets perform the same query written earlier. The difference is that the query does not block the execution thread, because control passes back to the event loop. By returning almost immediately to the event loop, it is free to service other requests. Eventually, one of those events will be the response to the query shown previously, which will invoke the callback function.

With the callback or Promise approach, the `result` is not returned as the result of the function call, but is provided to a callback function that will be called later. The order of execution is not one line after another, as it is in synchronous programming languages. Instead, the order of execution is determined by the order of the callback function execution.

When using an `async` function, the coding style LOOKS like the original synchronous code example. The `result` is returned as the result of the function call, and errors are handled in a natural manner using `try/catch`. The `await` keyword integrates asynchronous results handling without blocking the execution thread. A lot is buried under the covers of the `async/await` feature, and we'll be covering this model extensively throughout the book.

Commonly, web pages bring together data from dozens of sources. Each one has a query and response as discussed earlier. Using asynchronous queries, each query can happen in parallel, where the page construction function can fire off dozens of queries—no waiting, each with their own callback—and then go back to the event loop, invoking the callbacks as each is done. Because it's in parallel, the data can be collected much more quickly than if these queries were done synchronously one at a time. Now, the reader on the web browser is happier because the page loads more quickly.

Performance and utilization

Some of the excitement over Node.js is due to its throughput (the requests per second it can serve). Comparative benchmarks of similar applications, for example, Apache, show that Node.js has tremendous performance gains.

One benchmark going around is this simple HTTP server (borrowed from `https://nodejs.org/en/`), which simply returns a `Hello World` message directly from memory:

```
var http = require('http');
http.createServer(function (req, res) {
  res.writeHead(200, {'Content-Type': 'text/plain'});
  res.end('Hello World\n');
}).listen(8124, "127.0.0.1");
console.log('Server running at http://127.0.0.1:8124/');
```

This is one of the simpler web servers that you can build with Node.js. The `http` object encapsulates the HTTP protocol, and its `http.createServer` method creates a whole web server, listening on the port specified in the `listen` method. Every request (whether a `GET` or `POST` on any URL) on that web server calls the provided function. It is very simple and lightweight. In this case, regardless of the URL, it returns a simple `text/plain` that is the `Hello World` response.

Ryan Dahl showed a simple benchmark (`https://www.youtube.com/watch?v=M-sc73Y-zQA`) that returned a 1-megabyte binary buffer; Node.js gave 822 req/sec, while Nginx gave 708 req/sec, for a 15% improvement over Nginx. He also noted that Nginx peaked at four megabytes memory, while Node.js peaked at 64 megabytes.

The key observation was that Node.js, running an interpreted JIT-compiled high-level language, was about as fast as Nginx, built of highly optimized C code, while running similar tasks. That presentation was in May 2010, and Node.js has improved hugely since then, as shown in Chris Bailey's talk that we referenced earlier.

Yahoo! search engineer Fabian Frank published a performance case study of a real-world search query suggestion widget implemented with Apache/PHP and two variants of Node.js stacks (http://www.slideshare.net/FabianFrankDe/nodejs-performance-case-study). The application is a pop-up panel showing search suggestions as the user types in phrases, using a JSON-based HTTP query. The Node.js version could handle eight times the number of requests per second with the same request latency. Fabian Frank said both Node.js stacks scaled linearly until CPU usage hit 100%. In another presentation (http://www.slideshare.net/FabianFrankDe/yahoo-scale-nodejs), he discussed how Yahoo! Axis is running on Manhattan + Mojito and the value of being able to use the same language (JavaScript) and framework (YUI/YQL) on both frontend and backend.

LinkedIn did a massive overhaul of their mobile app using Node.js for the server-side to replace an old Ruby on Rails app. The switch let them move from 30 servers down to three, and allowed them to merge the frontend and backend team because everything was written in JavaScript. Before choosing Node.js, they'd evaluated Rails with Event Machine, Python with Twisted, and Node.js, choosing Node.js for the reasons that we just discussed. For a look at what LinkedIn did, see http://arstechnica.com/information-technology/2012/10/a-behind-the-scenes-look-at-linkedins-mobile-engineering/.

Most existing advice on Node.js performance tips tends to have been written for older V8 versions that used the CrankShaft optimizer. The V8 team has completely dumped CrankShaft, and it has a new optimizer called TurboFan. For example, under CrankShaft, it was slower to use `try/catch`, `let/const`, generator functions, and so on. Therefore, common wisdom said to not use those features, which is depressing because we want to use the new JavaScript features because of how much it has improved the JavaScript language. Peter Marshall, an Engineer on the V8 team at Google, gave a talk at Node.js Interactive 2017 claiming that, under TurboFan, you should just write natural JavaScript. With TurboFan, the goal is for across-the-board performance improvements in V8. To view the presentation, see https://www.youtube.com/watch?v=YqOhBezMx1o.

A truism about JavaScript is that it's no good for heavy computation work, because of the nature of JavaScript. We'll go over some ideas related to this in the next section. A talk by Mikola Lysenko at Node.js Interactive 2016 went over some issues with numerical computing in JavaScript, and some possible solutions. Common numerical computing involves large numerical arrays processed by numerical algorithms that you might have learned in Calculus or Linear Algebra classes. What JavaScript lacks is multi-dimensional arrays, and access to certain CPU instructions. The solution he presented is a library to implement multi-dimensional arrays in JavaScript, along with another library full of numerical computing algorithms. To view the presentation, see `https://www.youtube.com/watch?v=1ORaKEzlnys`.

The bottom line is that Node.js excels at event-driven I/O throughput. Whether a Node.js program can excel at computational programs depends on your ingenuity in working around some limitations in the JavaScript language. A big problem with computational programming is that it prevents the event loop from executing and, as we will see in the next section, that can make Node.js look like a poor candidate for anything.

Is Node.js a cancerous scalability disaster?

In October 2011, software developer and blogger Ted Dziuba wrote a blog post (since pulled from his blog) titled *Node.js is a cancer*, calling it a *scalability disaster*. The example he showed for proof is a CPU-bound implementation of the Fibonacci sequence algorithm. While his argument was flawed, he raised a valid point that Node.js application developers have to consider the following: where do you put the heavy computational tasks?

A key to maintaining high throughput of Node.js applications is ensuring that events are handled quickly. Because it uses a single execution thread, if that thread is bogged down with a big calculation, Node.js cannot handle events, and event throughput will suffer.

The Fibonacci sequence, serving as a stand-in for heavy computational tasks, quickly becomes computationally expensive to calculate, especially for a naïve implementation such as this:

```
const fibonacci = exports.fibonacci = function(n) {
    if (n === 1 || n === 2) return 1;
    else return fibonacci(n-1) + fibonacci(n-2);
}
```

Yes, there are many ways to calculate fibonacci numbers more quickly. We are showing this as a general example of what happens to Node.js when event handlers are slow, and not to debate the best ways to calculate mathematics functions. Consider this server:

```
const http = require('http');
const url  = require('url');

const fibonacci = // as above

http.createServer(function (req, res) {
  const urlP = url.parse(req.url, true);
  let fibo;
  res.writeHead(200, {'Content-Type': 'text/plain'});
  if (urlP.query['n']) {
    fibo = fibonacci(urlP.query['n']);
    res.end('Fibonacci '+ urlP.query['n'] +'='+ fibo);
  } else {
    res.end('USAGE: http://127.0.0.1:8124?n=## where ## is the
Fibonacci number desired');
  }
}).listen(8124, '127.0.0.1');
console.log('Server running at http://127.0.0.1:8124');
```

For sufficiently large values of n (for example, 40), the server becomes completely unresponsive because the event loop is not running, and instead this function is blocking event processing because it is grinding through the calculation.

Does this mean that Node.js is a flawed platform? No, it just means that the programmer must take care to identify code with long-running computations and develop solutions. These include rewriting the algorithm to work with the event loop, or rewriting the algorithm for efficiency, or integrating a native code library, or foisting computationally expensive calculations on to a backend server.

A simple rewrite dispatches the computations through the event loop, letting the server continue to handle requests on the event loop. Using callbacks and closures (anonymous functions), we're able to maintain asynchronous I/O and concurrency promises:

```
const fibonacciAsync = function(n, done) {
    if (n === 0) return 0;
    else if (n === 1 || n === 2) done(1);
    else if (n === 3) return 2;
    else {
        process.nextTick(function() {
            fibonacciAsync(n-1, function(val1) {
```

```
                process.nextTick(function() {
                    fibonacciAsync(n-2, function(val2) {
                    done(val1+val2); }); });
                });
            });
        });
    }
}
```

Because this is an asynchronous function, it necessitates a small refactoring of the server:

```
const http = require('http');
const url  = require('url');

const fibonacciAsync = // as above

http.createServer(function (req, res) {
   let urlP = url.parse(req.url, true);
   res.writeHead(200, {'Content-Type': 'text/plain'});
   if (urlP.query['n']) {
     fibonacciAsync(urlP.query['n'], fibo => {
        res.end('Fibonacci '+ urlP.query['n'] +'='+ fibo);
     });
   } else {
      res.end('USAGE: http://127.0.0.1:8124?n=## where ## is the
Fibonacci number desired');
   }
}).listen(8124, '127.0.0.1'); console.log('Server running at
http://127.0.0.1:8124');
```

Dziuba's valid point wasn't expressed well in his blog post, and it was somewhat lost in the flames following that post. Namely, that while Node.js is a great platform for I/O-bound applications, it isn't a good platform for computationally intensive ones.

Later in this book, we'll explore this example a little more deeply.

Server utilization, the business bottom line, and green web hosting

The striving for optimal efficiency (handling more requests per second) is not just about the geeky satisfaction that comes from optimization. There are real business and environmental benefits. Handling more requests per second, as Node.js servers can do, means the difference between buying lots of servers and buying only a few servers. Node.js potentially lets your organization do more with less.

Roughly speaking, the more servers you buy, the greater the cost, and the greater the environmental impact of having those servers. There's a whole field of expertise around reducing costs and the environmental impact of running web server facilities, to which that rough guideline doesn't do justice. The goal is fairly obvious—fewer servers, lower costs, and a reduced environmental impact through utilizing more efficient software.

Intel's paper, *Increasing Data Center Efficiency with Server Power Measurements* (`https:/`
`/www.intel.com/content/dam/doc/white-paper/intel-it-data-center-`
`efficiency-server-power-paper.pdf`), gives an objective framework for understanding efficiency and data center costs. There are many factors, such as buildings, cooling systems, and computer system designs. Efficient building design, efficient cooling systems, and efficient computer systems (data center efficiency, data center density, and storage density) can lower costs and environmental impact. But you can destroy those gains by deploying an inefficient software stack compelling you to buy more servers than you would if you had an efficient software stack. Alternatively, you can amplify gains from data center efficiency with an efficient software stack that lets you decrease the number of servers required.

This talk about efficient software stacks isn't just for altruistic environmental purposes. This is one of those cases where being green can help your business bottom line.

Embracing advances in the JavaScript language

The last couple of years have been an exciting time for JavaScript programmers. The TC-39 committee that oversees the ECMAScript standard has added many new features, some of which are syntactic sugar, but several of which have propelled us into a whole new era of JavaScript programming. By itself, the `async/await` feature promises us a way out of what's called Callback Hell, or the situation we find ourselves in when nesting callbacks within callbacks. It's such an important feature that it should necessitate a broad rethinking of the prevailing callback-oriented paradigm in Node.js and the rest of the JavaScript ecosystem.

Refer back a few pages to this:

```
query('SELECT * from db', function (err, result) {
    if (err) throw err; // handle errors
    // operate on result
});
```

This was an important insight on Ryan Dahl's part, and is what propelled Node.js's popularity. Certain actions take a long time to run, such as database queries, and should not be treated the same as operations that quickly retrieve data from memory. Because of the nature of the JavaScript language, Node.js had to express this asynchronous coding construct in an unnatural way. The results do not appear at the next line of code, but instead appear within this callback function. Further, errors have to be handled in an unnatural way, inside that callback function.

The convention in Node.js is that the first parameter to a callback function is an error indicator, and the subsequent parameters are the results. This is a useful convention that you'll find all across the Node.js landscape. However, it complicates working with results and errors because both land in an inconvenient location — that callback function. The natural place for errors and results to land is on the subsequent line(s) of code.

We descend further into **callback hell** with each layer of callback function nesting. The seventh layer of callback nesting is more complex than the sixth layer of callback nesting. Why? If nothing else, it's that the special considerations for error handling become ever more complex as callbacks are nested more deeply.

```
var results = await query('SELECT * from db');
```

Instead, ES2017 async functions return us to this very natural expression of programming intent. Results and errors land in the correct location, while preserving the excellent event-driven asynchronous programming model that made Node.js great. We'll see later in the book how this works.

The TC-39 committee added many more new features to JavaScript, such as:

- An improved syntax for Class declarations making object inheritance and getter/setter functions very natural.
- A new module format that is standardized across browsers and Node.js.
- New methods for strings, such as the template string notation.
- New methods for collections and arrays — for example, operations for `map`/`reduce`/`filter`.
- The `const` keyword to define variables that cannot be changed, and the `let` keyword to define variables whose scope is limited to the block in which they're declared, rather than hoisted to the front of the function.
- New looping constructs, and an iteration protocol that works with those new loops.
- A new kind of function, the arrow function, which is lighter weight meaning less memory and execution time impact
- The Promise object represents a result that is promised to be delivered in the future. By themselves, Promises can mitigate the callback hell problem, and they form part of the basis for `async` functions.
- Generator functions are an intriguing way to represent asynchronous iteration over a set of values. More importantly, they form the other half of the basis for async functions.

You may see the new JavaScript described as ES6 or ES2017. What's the preferred name to describe the version of JavaScript that is being used?

ES1 through ES5 marked various phases of JavaScript's development. ES5 was released in 2009, and is widely implemented in modern browsers. Starting with ES6, the TC-39 committee decided to change the naming convention because of their intention to add new language features every year. Therefore, the language version name now includes the year, hence ES2015 was released in 2015, ES2016 was released in 2016, and ES2017 was released in 2017.

Deploying ES2015/2016/2017/2018 JavaScript code

The pink elephant in the room is that, because of how JavaScript is delivered to the world, we cannot just start using the latest ES2017 features. In frontend JavaScript, we are limited by the fact that old browsers are still in use. Internet Explorer version 6 has fortunately been almost completely retired, but there are still plenty of old browsers installed on older computers that are still serving a valid role for their owners. Old browsers mean old JavaScript implementations, and if we want our code to work, we need it to be compatible with old browsers.

Using code rewriting tools such as Babel, some of the new features can be retrofitted to function on some of the older browsers. Frontend JavaScript programmers can adopt (some of) the new features at the cost of a more complex build toolchain, and the risk of bugs introduced by the code rewriting process. Some may wish to do that, while others will prefer to wait a while.

The Node.js world doesn't have this problem. Node.js has rapidly adopted ES2015/2016/2017 features as quickly as they were implemented in the V8 engine. With Node.js 8, we can now use async functions as a native feature, and most of the ES2015/2016 features became available with Node.js version 6. The new module format is now supported in Node.js version 10.

In other words, while frontend JavaScript programmers can argue that they must wait a couple of years before adopting ES2015/2016/2017 features, Node.js programmers have no need to wait. We can simply use the new features without needing any code rewriting tools.

Node.js, the microservice architecture, and easily testable systems

New capabilities, such as cloud deployment systems and Docker, make it possible to implement a new kind of service architecture. Docker makes it possible to define server process configuration in a repeatable container that's easy to deploy by the millions into a cloud hosting system. It lends itself best to small single-purpose service instances that can be connected together to make a complete system. Docker isn't the only tool to help simplify cloud deployments; however, its features are well attuned to modern application deployment needs.

Some have popularized the microservice concept as a way to describe this kind of system. According to the `microservices.io` website, a microservice consists of a set of narrowly focused, independently deployable services. They contrast this with the monolithic application deployment pattern where every aspect of the system is integrated into one bundle (such as a single WAR file for a Java EE app server). The microservice model gives developers much needed flexibility.

Some advantages of microservices are as follows:

- Each microservice can be managed by a small team
- Each team can work on its own schedule, so long as the service API compatibility is maintained
- Microservices can be deployed independently, such as for easier testing
- It's easier to switch technology stack choices

Where does Node.js fit in with this? Its design fits the microservice model like a glove:

- Node.js encourages small, tightly focused, single-purpose modules
- These modules are composed into an application by the excellent npm package management system
- Publishing modules is incredibly simple, whether via the NPM repository or a Git URL

Node.js and the Twelve-Factor app model

Throughout this book, we'll call out aspects of the **Twelve-Factor App** model, and ways to implement those ideas in Node.js. This model is published on `http://12factor.net`, and is a set of guidelines for application deployment in the modern cloud computing era. It's not that the Twelve-Factor App model is the be-all and end-all of application architecture paradigms. It's a set of useful ideas, clearly birthed after many late nights spent debugging complex applications, which offer useful ideas that could save us all a lot of effort by having easier-to-maintain and more reliable systems.

The guidelines are straightforward, and once you read them, they will seem like pure common sense. As a best practice, the Twelve-Factor App model is a compelling strategy for delivering the kind of fluid self-contained cloud-deployed applications called for by our current computing environment.

Summary

You learned a lot in this chapter. Specifically, you saw that JavaScript has a life outside web browsers and you learned about the difference between asynchronous and blocking I/O. We then covered the attributes of Node.js and where it fits in the overall web application platform market and threaded versus asynchronous software. Lastly, we saw the advantages of fast event-driven asynchronous I/O, coupled with a language with great support for anonymous closures.

Our focus in this book is real-world considerations of developing and deploying Node.js applications. We'll cover as many aspects as we can of developing, refining, testing, and deploying Node.js applications.

Now that we've had this introduction to Node.js, we're ready to dive in and start using it. In Chapter 2, *Setting up Node.js*, we'll go over setting up a Node.js environment, so let's get started.

2
Setting up Node.js

Before getting started with using Node.js, you must set up your development environment. In the following chapters, we'll use this for development and for non-production deployment.

In this chapter, we will cover the following topics:

- How to install Node.js from source and prepackaged binaries on Linux, macOS, or Windows
- How to install **Node Package Manager** (**NPM**) and some popular tools
- The Node.js module system
- Node.js and JavaScript language improvements from the ECMAScript committee

So let's get on with it.

System requirements

Node.js runs on POSIX-like operating systems, various UNIX derivatives (Solaris, for example) or workalikes (Linux, macOS, and so on), as well as on Microsoft Windows. It can run on machines both large and small, including the tiny ARM devices such as the Raspberry Pi microscale embeddable computer for DIY software/hardware projects.

Node.js is now available via package management systems, limiting the need to compile and install from source.

Because many Node.js packages are written in C or C++, you must have a C compiler (such as GCC), Python 2.7 (or later), and the `node-gyp` package. If you plan to use encryption in your networking code, you will also need the OpenSSL cryptographic library. The modern UNIX derivatives almost certainly come with these, and Node.js's configure script, used when installing from source, will detect their presence. If you need to install them, Python is available at `http://python.org` and OpenSSL is available at `http://openssl.org`.

Installing Node.js using package managers

The preferred method for installing Node.js, now, is to use the versions available in package managers, such as `apt-get`, or MacPorts. Package managers simplify your life by helping to maintain the current version of the software on your computer, ensuring to update dependent packages as necessary, all by typing a simple command such as `apt-get update`. Let's go over this first.

Installing on macOS with MacPorts

The MacPorts project (`http://www.macports.org/`) has for years been packaging a long list of open source software packages for macOS, and they have packaged Node.js. After you have installed MacPorts using the installer on their website, installing Node.js is pretty much this simple:

```
$ port search nodejs npm
. . .
nodejs6 @6.12.0 (devel, net)
    Evented I/O for V8 JavaScript

nodejs7 @7.10.1 (devel, net)
    Evented I/O for V8 JavaScript

nodejs8 @8.9.1 (devel, net)
    Evented I/O for V8 JavaScript

nodejs9 @9.2.0 (devel, net)
    Evented I/O for V8 JavaScript

Found 6 ports.
--
```

```
npm4 @4.6.1 (devel)
    node package manager

npm5 @5.5.1 (devel)
    node package manager

Found 4 ports.

$ sudo port install nodejs8 npm5
.. long log of downloading and installing prerequisites and Node
$ which node
/opt/local/bin/node
$ node --version
v8.9.1
```

Installing on macOS with Homebrew

Homebrew is another open source software package manager for macOS, which
some say is the perfect replacement for MacPorts. It is available through their home
page at `http://brew.sh/`. After installing Homebrew using the instructions on their
website and ensuring that Homebrew is correctly set up, use the following:

```
$ brew update
... long wait and lots of output
$ brew search node
==> Searching local taps...

node ✔ libbitcoin-node node-build node@6 nodeenv
leafnode llnode node@4 nodebrew nodenv
==> Searching taps on GitHub...
caskroom/cask/node-profiler
==> Searching blacklisted, migrated and deleted formulae...
```

Then, install it this way:

```
$ brew install node
...
==> Installing node
==> Downloading
https://homebrew.bintray.com/bottles/node-8.9.1.el_capitan.bottle.tar.
gz
######################################################################
## 100.0%
==> Pouring node-8.9.1.el_capitan.bottle.tar.gz
==> Caveats
Bash completion has been installed to:
```

```
    /usr/local/etc/bash_completion.d
==> Summary
  /usr/local/Cellar/node/8.9.1: 5,012 files, 49.6MB
```

Once installed this way, the Node.js command can be run as follows:

```
$ node --version
v8.9.1
```

Installing on Linux, *BSD, or Windows from package management systems

Node.js is now available through most of the package management systems.
Instructions on the Node.js website currently list packaged versions of Node.js for a
long list of Linux, as well as FreeBSD, OpenBSD, NetBSD, macOS, and even
Windows. Visit `https://nodejs.org/en/download/package-manager/` for more
information.

For example, on Debian and other Debian-based Linux distro's (such as Ubuntu), use
the following commands:

```
# curl -sL https://deb.nodesource.com/setup_10.x | sudo -E bash -
# sudo apt-get install -y nodejs
# sudo apt-get install -y build-essential
```

To download other Node.js versions (this example shows version 10.x), modify the
URL to suit.

Installing Node.js in the Windows Subsystem for Linux (WSL)

The **Windows Subsystem for Linux (WSL)** lets you install Ubuntu, openSUSE, or
SUSE Linux Enterprise on Windows. All three are available via the Store built into
Windows 10. You may need to update your Windows for the installation to work.

Once installed, the Linux-specific instructions will install Node.js within the Linux
subsystem.

To install the WSL, see `https://msdn.microsoft.com/en-us/commandline/wsl/`
`install-win10`.

Opening an administrator-privileged PowerShell on Windows

Some of the commands you'll run while installing tools on Windows are to be executed in a PowerShell window with elevated privileges. We mention this because the process of enabling the WSL includes a command to be run in such a PowerShell window.

The process is simple:

1. In the Start menu, enter **PowerShell** in the applications search box.
2. The resultant menu will list **PowerShell**.
3. Right-click the **PowerShell** entry.
4. The context menu that comes up will have an entry **Run as Administrator**. Click on that.

The resultant command window will have administrator privileges, and the title bar will say **Administrator: Windows PowerShell**.

Installing the Node.js distribution from nodejs.org

The `https://nodejs.org/en/` website offers built-in binaries for Windows, macOS, Linux, and Solaris. We can simply go to the website, click on the **Install** button, and run the installer. For systems with package managers, such as the ones we've just discussed, it's preferable to use the package management system. That's because you'll find it easier to stay up-to-date with the latest version. But, that doesn't serve all people because:

- Some will prefer to install a binary rather than deal with the package manager
- Their chosen system doesn't have a package management system
- The Node.js implementation in their package management system is out-of-date

Simply go to the Node.js website and you'll see something like the following screenshot. The page does its best to determine your OS and supply the appropriate download. If you need something different, click on the **DOWNLOADS** link in the header for all possible downloads:

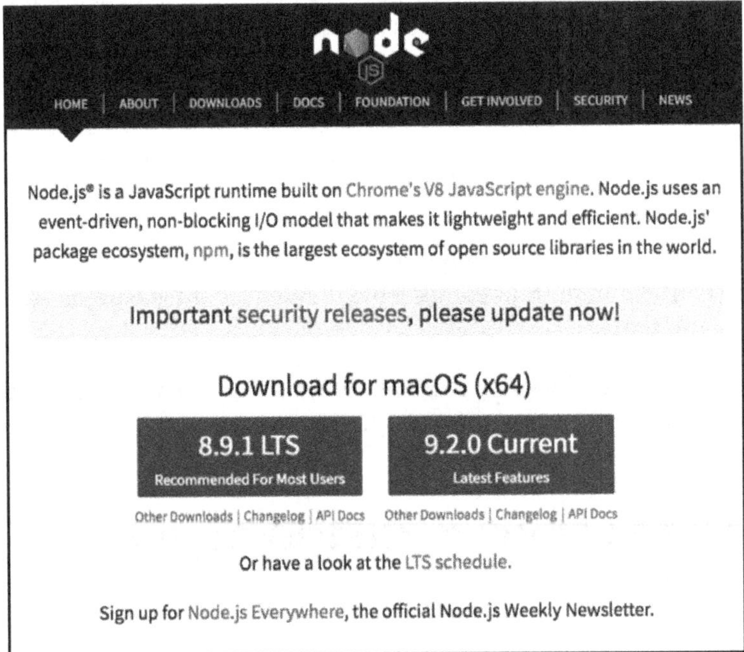

For macOS, the installer is a `PKG` file giving the typical installation process. For Windows, the installer simply takes you through the typical Install Wizard process.

Once finished with the installer, you have command-line tools, such as `node` and `npm`, with which you can run Node.js programs. On Windows, you're supplied with a version of the Windows command shell preconfigured to work nicely with Node.js.

Installing from source on POSIX-like systems

Installing the prepackaged Node.js distributions is the preferred installation method. However, installing Node.js from source is desirable in a few situations:

- It can let you optimize the compiler settings as desired
- It can let you cross-compile, say, for an embedded ARM system
- You might need to keep multiple Node.js builds for testing
- You might be working on Node.js itself

Now that you have the high-level view, let's get our hands dirty mucking around in some build scripts. The general process follows the usual `configure`, `make`, and `make install` routine that you may already have performed with other open source software packages. If not, don't worry, we'll guide you through the process.

> The official installation instructions are in the `README.md` contained within the source distribution
> at `https://github.com/nodejs/node/blob/master/README.md`.

Installing prerequisites

There are three prerequisites: a C compiler, Python, and the OpenSSL libraries. The Node.js compilation process checks for their presence and will fail if the C compiler or Python is not present. The specific method of installing these is dependent on your operating system.

These sorts of commands will check for their presence:

```
$ cc --version
Apple LLVM version 7.0.2 (clang-700.1.81)
Target: x86_64-apple-darwin15.3.0
Thread model: posix
$ python
Python 2.7.11 (default, Jan  8 2016, 22:23:13)
[GCC 4.2.1 Compatible Apple LLVM 7.0.2 (clang-700.1.81)] on darwin
Type "help", "copyright", "credits" or "license" for more information.
>>>
```

See this for details: `https://github.com/nodejs/node/blob/master/BUILDING.md`.

The Node.js build tools do not support Python 3.x.

Installing developer tools on macOS

Developer tools (such as GCC) are an optional installation on macOS. Fortunately, they're easy to acquire.

You start with Xcode, which is available for free through the Mac App Store. Simply search for Xcode and click on the **Get** button. Once you have Xcode installed, open a Terminal window and type the following:

```
$ xcode-select --install
```

This installs the Xcode command-line tools:

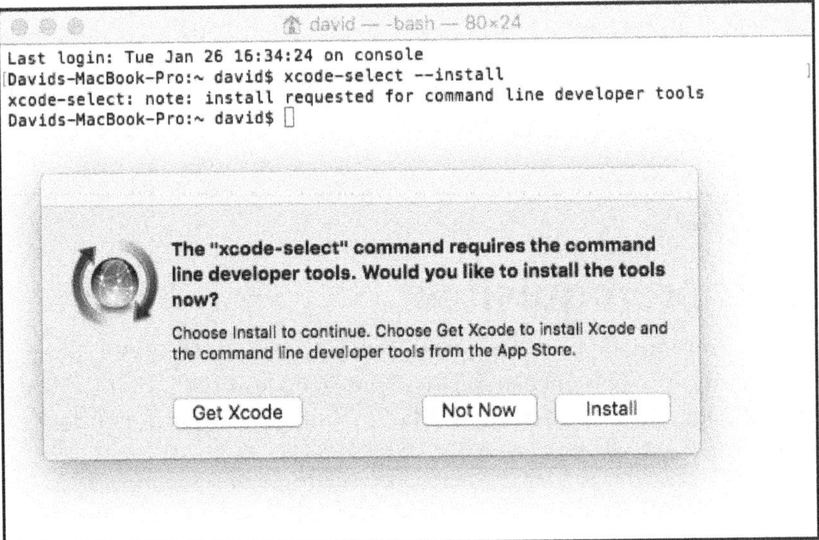

For additional information, visit
`http://osxdaily.com/2014/02/12/install-command-line-tools-mac-os-x/`.

Installing from source for all POSIX-like systems

Compiling Node.js from source follows this process:

1. Download the source from
2. `http://nodejs.org/download`. Configure the source for building using `./configure`.
3. Run `make`, then `make install`.

The source bundle can be downloaded with your browser, or as follows, substituting your preferred version:

```
$ mkdir src
$ cd src
$ wget https://nodejs.org/dist/v10.0.0/node-v10.0.0.tar.gz
$ tar xvfz node-v10.0.0.tar.gz
$ cd node-v10.0.0
```

Now we configure the source so that it can be built. This is just like many other open source packages, and there are a long list of options to customize the build:

```
$ ./configure --help
```

To cause the installation to land in your home directory, run it this way:

```
$ ./configure --prefix=$HOME/node/10.0.0
..output from configure
```

If you're going to install multiple Node.js versions side by side, it's useful to put the version number in the path like this. That way, each version will sit in a separate directory. It's a simple matter of switching between Node.js versions by changing the `PATH` variable appropriately:

```
# On bash shell:
$ export PATH=${HOME}/node/VERSION-NUMBER/bin:${PATH}
# On csh
$ setenv PATH ${HOME}/node/VERSION-NUMBER/bin:${PATH}
```

A simpler way to install multiple Node.js versions is the `nvm` script described later.

If you want to install Node.js in a system-wide directory, simply leave off the `--prefix` option and it will default to installing in `/usr/local`.

After a moment, it'll stop and will likely have successfully configured the source tree for installation in your chosen directory. If this doesn't succeed, the error messages that are printed will describe what needs to be fixed. Once the configure script is satisfied, you can go on to the next step.

With the configure script satisfied, you compile the software:

```
$ make
.. a long log of compiler output is printed
$ make install
```

If you are installing into a system-wide directory, do the last step this way instead:

```
$ make
$ sudo make install
```

Once installed, you should make sure that you add the installation directory to your PATH variable as follows:

```
$ echo 'export PATH=$HOME/node/10.0.0/bin:${PATH}' >>~/.bashrc
$ . ~/.bashrc
```

Alternatively, for csh users, use this syntax to make an exported environment variable:

```
$ echo 'setenv PATH $HOME/node/10.0.0/bin:${PATH}' >>~/.cshrc
$ source ~/.cshrc
```

This should result in some directories, as follows:

```
$ ls ~/node/10.0.0/
bin    include    lib    share
$ ls ~/node/10.0.0/bin
```

Installing from source on Windows

The BUILDING.md document referenced previously has instructions. One uses the build tools from Visual Studio, or else the full Visual Studio 2017 product:

- Visual Studio 2017: https://www.visualstudio.com/downloads/
- Build tools: https://www.visualstudio.com/downloads/#build-tools-for-visual-studio-2017

Three additional tools are required:

- Git for Windows: `http://git-scm.com/download/win`
- Python: `https://www.python.org/`
- OpenSSL: `https://www.openssl.org/source/` and `https://wiki.openssl.org/index.php/Binaries`

Then, run the included `.\vcbuild` script to perform the build.

Installing multiple Node.js instances with nvm

Normally, you won't install multiple versions of Node.js and doing so adds complexity to your system. But if you are hacking on Node.js itself, or are testing your software against different Node.js releases, you may want to have multiple Node.js installations. The method to do so is a simple variation on what we've already discussed.

Earlier, while discussing building Node.js from source, we noted that one can install multiple Node.js instances in separate directories. It's only necessary to build from source if you need a customized Node.js build, and most folks will be satisfied with pre-built Node.js binaries. They, too, can be installed into separate directories.

To switch between Node.js versions is simply a matter of changing the `PATH` variable (on POSIX systems), as follows, using the directory where you installed Node.js:

```
$ export PATH=/usr/local/node/VERSION-NUMBER/bin:${PATH}
```

It starts to be a little tedious to maintain this after a while. For each release, you have to set up Node.js, NPM, and any third-party modules you desire in your Node.js installation. Also, the command shown to change your `PATH` is not quite optimal. Inventive programmers have created several version managers to simplify managing multiple Node.js/NPM releases and providing commands to change your `PATH` the smart way:

- Node version manager: `https://github.com/tj/n`
- Node version manager: `https://github.com/creationix/nvm`

Both maintain multiple simultaneous versions of Node and let you easily switch between versions. Installation instructions are available on their respective websites.

For example, with nvm, you can run commands like these:

```
$ nvm ls
...
          v6.0.0
          v6.1.0
          v6.2.2
          v6.3.1
          v6.4.0

            ...
         v6.11.2
          v7.0.0
          v7.1.0
         v7.10.0
          v8.0.0
          v8.1.3
          v8.2.1
          v8.5.0
          v8.9.1
          v8.9.3
          v9.2.0
          v9.4.0
          v9.5.0
         v9.10.1
         v9.11.1
      -> v10.0.0
      -> system
node -> stable (-> v8.9.1) (default)
stable -> 8.9 (-> v8.9.1) (default)
iojs -> N/A (default)
$ nvm use 10
Now using node v10.0.0 (npm v5.6.0)
$ node --version
v10.0.0
$ nvm use v4.2
Now using node v4.2.0 (npm v2.14.7)
$ node --version
v4.2.0
$ nvm install 9
Downloading
https://nodejs.org/dist/v9.2.0/node-v9.2.0-darwin-x64.tar.xz...
###############################################################################
## 100.0%
WARNING: checksums are currently disabled for node.js v4.0 and later
Now using node v9.2.0 (npm v5.5.1)
```

```
$ node --version
v9.2.0
$ which node
/Users/david/.nvm/versions/node/v9.2.0/bin/node
$ /usr/local/bin/node --version
v8.9.1
$ /opt/local/bin/node --version
v8.9.1
```

This demonstrates that you can have a system-wide Node.js installed, keep multiple private Node.js versions managed by nvm, and switch between them as needed. When new Node.js versions are released, they are simple to install with nvm even if the official packaged version for your OS doesn't immediately update.

Installing nvm on Windows

Unfortunately, nvm does not support Windows. Fortunately, a couple of Windows-specific clones of the nvm concept exist:

- https://github.com/coreybutler/nvm-windows
- https://github.com/marcelklehr/nodist

Another route is to use the WSL. Because in WSL you're interacting with a Linux command line, you can use nvm itself.

Many of the examples in this book were tested using the nvm-windows application. There are slight behavior differences, but it acts largely the same as nvm for Linux and macOS. The biggest change is the version number specifier in the nvm use and nvm install commands.

With nvm for Linux and macOS one can type a simple version number, like nvm use 8, and it will automatically substitute the latest release of the named Node.js version. With nvm-windows the same command acts as if you typed "nvm use 8.0.0". In other words, with nvm-windows you must use the exact version number. Fortunately, the list of supported versions is easily available using the "nvm list available" command.

Native code modules and node-gyp

While we won't discuss native code module development in this book, we do need to make sure that they can be built. Some modules in the NPM repository are native code, and they must be compiled with a C or C++ compiler to build the corresponding `.node` files (the `.node` extension is used for binary native-code modules).

The module will often describe itself as a wrapper for some other library. For example, the `libxslt` and `libxmljs` modules are wrappers around the C/C++ libraries of the same name. The module includes the C/C++ source code, and when installed, a script is automatically run to do the compilation with `node-gyp`.

The `node-gyp` tool is a cross-platform command-line tool written in Node.js for compiling native add-on modules for Node.js. We've mentioned native code modules several times, and it is this tool that compiles them for use with Node.js.

You can easily see this in action by running these commands:

```
$ mkdir temp
$ cd temp
$ npm install libxmljs libxslt
```

This is done in a temporary directory, so you can delete it afterward. If your system does not have the tools installed to compile native code modules, you'll see error messages. Otherwise, you'll see in the output a `node-gyp` execution, followed by many lines of text obviously related to compiling C/C++ files.

The `node-gyp` tool has prerequisites similar to those for compiling Node.js from source. Namely, a C/C++ compiler, a Python environment, and other build tools such as Git. For Unix/macOS/Linux systems those are easy to come by. For Windows, you should install:

- Visual Studio Build Tools: `https://www.visualstudio.com/downloads/#build-tools-for-visual-studio-2017`
- Git for Windows: `http://git-scm.com/download/win`
- Python for Windows: `https://www.python.org/`

Normally, you won't need to worry about installing `node-gyp`. That's because it is installed behind the scenes as part of NPM. That's done so that NPM can automatically build native code modules.

Its GitHub repository contains documentation
at `https://github.com/nodejs/node-gyp`.

Reading the `node-gyp` documentation, in its repository, will give you a clearer
understanding of the compilation prerequisites discussed previously, as well as of
developing native code modules.

Node.js versions policy and what to use

We just threw around so many different Node.js version numbers in the previous
section that you may have become confused over which version to use. This book is
targeting Node.js version 10.x, and it's expected that everything we'll cover is
compatible with Node.js 10.x and any subsequent release.

Starting with Node.js 4.x, the Node.js team is following a dual-track approach. The
even-numbered releases (4.x, 6.x, 8.x, and so on) are what they're calling **Long Term
Support (LTS)**, while the odd-numbered releases (5.x, 7.x, 9.x, and so on) are where
current new feature development occurs. While the development branch is kept
stable, the LTS releases are positioned as being for production use and will receive
updates for several years.

At the time of writing, Node.js 8.x is the current LTS release; Node.js 9.x was just
released and will eventually become Node.js 10.x, which in turn will eventually
become the LTS release. For complete details about the release schedule, refer to
`https://github.com/nodejs/LTS/`.

A major impact of each new Node.js release, beyond the usual performance
improvements and bug fixes, is bringing in the latest V8 JavaScript engine release. In
turn, this means bringing in more of the ES-2015/2016/2017 features as the V8 team
implements those features. In Node.js 8.x, `async/await` functions arrived, and in
Node.js 10.x support for the standard ES6 module format has arrived.

A practical consideration is whether a new Node.js release will break your code. New
language features are always being added as V8 catches up with ECMA Script, and
the Node.js team sometimes makes breaking changes in the Node.js API. If you've
tested on one Node.js version, will it work on an earlier version? Will a Node.js
change break some assumptions we made?

The NPM Package Manager helps us ensure that our packages execute on the correct Node.js version. This means that we can specify in the `package.json` file, which we'll explore in `Chapter 3`, *Node.js Modules*, the compatible Node.js versions for a package.

We can add an entry to `package.json` as follows:

```
engines: {
  "node": ">=6.x"
}
```

This means exactly what it implies—that the given package is compatible with Node.js version 6.x or later.

Of course, your development machine(s) could have several Node.js versions installed. You'll need the version your software is declared to support, plus any later versions you wish to evaluate.

Editors and debuggers

Since Node.js code is JavaScript, any JavaScript-aware editor will be useful. Unlike some other languages that are so complex that an IDE with code completion is a necessity, a simple programming editor is perfectly sufficient for Node.js development.

Two editors are worth calling out because they are written in Node.js: Atom and Microsoft Visual Studio Code.

Atom (`https://atom.io/`) bills itself as a hackable editor for the 21st century. It is extendable by writing Node.js modules using the Atom API, and the configuration files are easily editable. In other words, it's hackable in the same way plenty of other editors have been, going back to Emacs, meaning one writes a software module to add capabilities to the editor. The Electron framework was invented in order to build Atom, and Electron is a super easy way to build desktop applications using Node.js.

Microsoft Visual Studio Code (https://code.visualstudio.com/) is also a hackable editor—well, the home page says extensible and customizable, which means the same thing—that is also open source, and is also implemented in Electron. But it's not a hollow me-too editor, aping Atom while adding nothing of its own. Instead, Visual Studio Code is a solid programmers editor in its own right, bringing interesting functionality to the table.

As for debuggers, there are several interesting choices. Starting with Node.js 6.3, the inspector protocol made it possible to use the Google Chrome debugger. Visual Studio Code has a built-in debugger that also uses the inspector protocol.

For a full list of debugging options and tools, see https://nodejs.org/en/docs/guides/debugging-getting-started/.

Running and testing commands

Now that you've installed Node.js, we want to do two things—verify that the installation was successful, and familiarize you with the command-line tools.

Node.js's command-line tools

The basic installation of Node.js includes two commands, node and npm. We've already seen the node command in action. It's used either for running command-line scripts or server processes. The other, npm, is a package manager for Node.js.

The easiest way to verify that your Node.js installation works is also the best way to get help with Node.js. Type the following command:

```
$ node --help
Usage: node [options] [ -e script | script.js | - ] [arguments]
       node inspect script.js [arguments]

Options:
  -v, --version print Node.js version
  -e, --eval script evaluate script
  -p, --print evaluate script and print result
  -c, --check syntax check script without executing
  -i, --interactive always enter the REPL even if stdin
                           does not appear to be a terminal
  -r, --require module to preload (option can be repeated)
  - script read from stdin (default; interactive mode if a tty)
  --inspect[=[host:]port] activate inspector on host:port
```

```
                                      (default: 127.0.0.1:9229)
    --inspect-brk[=[host:]port]
                                      activate inspector on host:port
                                      and break at start of user script
    --inspect-port=[host:]port
                                      set host:port for inspector

  ... many more options
  Environment variables:
  NODE_DEBUG ','-separated list of core modules
                                that should print debug information
  NODE_DISABLE_COLORS set to 1 to disable colors in the REPL
  NODE_EXTRA_CA_CERTS path to additional CA certificates
                                file
  NODE_ICU_DATA data path for ICU (Intl object) data
                                (will extend linked-in data)
  NODE_NO_WARNINGS set to 1 to silence process warnings
  NODE_NO_HTTP2 set to 1 to suppress the http2 module
  NODE_OPTIONS set CLI options in the environment
                                via a space-separated list
  NODE_PATH ':'-separated list of directories
                                prefixed to the module search path
  NODE_PENDING_DEPRECATION set to 1 to emit pending deprecation
                                warnings
  NODE_REPL_HISTORY path to the persistent REPL history
                                file
  NODE_REDIRECT_WARNINGS write warnings to path instead of
                                stderr
  OPENSSL_CONF load OpenSSL configuration from file

  Documentation can be found at https://nodejs.org/
```

Note that there are options for both Node.js and V8 (not shown in the previous command line). Remember that Node.js is built on top of V8; it has its own universe of options that largely focus on details of bytecode compilation or garbage collection and heap algorithms. Enter `node --v8-options` to see the full list of them.

On the command line, you can specify options, a single script file, and a list of arguments to that script. We'll discuss script arguments further in the next section, *Running a simple script with Node.js*.

Running Node.js with no arguments plops you into an interactive JavaScript shell:

```
$ node
> console.log('Hello, world!');
Hello, world!
undefined
```

Any code you can write in a Node.js script can be written here. The command interpreter gives a good Terminal-oriented user experience and is useful for interactively playing with your code. You do play with your code, don't you? Good!

Running a simple script with Node.js

Now, let's see how to run scripts with Node.js. It's quite simple; let's start by referring to the help message shown previously. The command-line pattern is just a script filename and some script arguments, which should be familiar to anyone who has written scripts in other languages.

Creating and editing Node.js scripts can be done with any text editor that deals with plain text files, such as VI/VIM, Emacs, Notepad++, Atom, Visual Studio Code, Jedit, BB Edit, TextMate, or Komodo. It's helpful if it's a programmer-oriented editor, if only for the syntax coloring.

For this and other examples in this book, it doesn't truly matter where you put the files. However, for the sake of neatness, you can start by making a directory named `node-web-dev` in the home directory of your computer, and inside that creating one directory per chapter (for example, `chap02` and `chap03`).

First, create a text file named `ls.js` with the following content:

```js
const fs = require('fs');
const util = require('util');
const fs_readdir = util.promisify(fs.readdir);

(async () => {
  const files = await fs_readdir('.');
  for (let fn of files) {
    console.log(fn);
  }
})().catch(err => { console.error(err); });
```

Next, run it by typing the following command:

```
$ node ls.js
ls.js
```

This is a pale cheap imitation of the Unix `ls` command (as if you couldn't figure that out from the name). The `readdir` function is a close analog to the Unix `readdir` system call (type `man 3 readdir` in a Terminal window to learn more) and is used to list the files in a directory.

We have written this using an inline `async` function, the `await` keyword, and an ES2015 `for..of` loop. Using `util.promisify`, we can convert any callback-oriented function so it returns a Promise, so that the Promise plays well with the `await` keyword.

By default `fs` module functions use the callback paradigm, as does most Node.js modules. But within `async` functions it is more convenient if functions instead return promises. Using `util.promisify` we can make it so.

This script is hardcoded to list files in the current directory. The real `ls` command takes a directory name, so let's modify the script a little.

Command-line arguments land in a global array named `process.argv`. Therefore we can modify `ls.js`, copying it as `ls2.js`, as follows to see how this array works:

```js
const fs = require('fs');
const util = require('util');
const fs_readdir = util.promisify(fs.readdir);

(async () => {
  var dir = '.';
  if (process.argv[2]) dir = process.argv[2];
  const files = await fs_readdir(dir);
  for (let fn of files) {
    console.log(fn);
  }
})().catch(err => { console.error(err); });
```

You can run it as follows:

```
$ pwd
/Users/David/chap02
$ node ls2 ..
chap01
chap02
$ node ls2
app.js
ls.js
ls2.js
```

We simply checked if a command-line argument was present, if `(process.argv[2])` If it was, we overrode the value of the `dir` variable, `dir = process.argv[2]`, and we then used that as the `readdir` argument.

If you give it a non-existent directory pathname, an error will be thrown and printed using the `catch` clause. That looks like so:

```
$ node ls2.js /nonexistent
{ Error: ENOENT: no such file or directory, scandir '/nonexistent'
  errno: -2,
  code: 'ENOENT',
  syscall: 'scandir',
  path: '/nonexistent' }
```

Conversion to async functions and the Promise paradigm

In the previous section we discussed the `util.promisify` and its ability to convert a callback-oriented function into one that returns a Promise. The latter play well within async functions and therefore it is preferable for functions to return a Promise.

To be more precise, `util.promisify` is to be given a function that uses the error-first-callback paradigm. The last argument of such functions is a callback function whose first argument is interpreted as an error indicator, hence the phrase error-first-callback. What `util.promisify` returns is another function that returns a Promise.

The Promise serves the same purpose as the error-first-callback. If an error is indicated, the Promise resolves to the rejected status, while if success is indicated the Promise resolves to a success status. As we see in these examples, within an `async` function the Promise is handled very nicely.

The Node.js ecosystem has a large body of functions using the error-first-callback. The community has begun a conversion process where functions will return a Promise, and possibly also take an error-first-callback for API compatibility.

One of the new features in Node.js 10 is an example of such a conversion. Within the `fs` module is a submodule, named `fs.promises`, with the same API but producing Promise objects. We could rewrite the previous example as so:

```
const fs = require('fs').promises;
(async () => {
 var dir = '.';
 if (process.argv[2]) dir = process.argv[2];
 const files = await fs.readdir(dir);
```

```
    for (let fn of files) {
        console.log(fn);
    }
})().catch(err => { console.error(err); });
```

As you can see, the functions in the `fs.promises` module returns a Promise without requiring a callback function. The new program, which you can save as `ls2-promises.js`, is run as so:

```
$ node ls2-promises.js
(node:40329) ExperimentalWarning: The fs.promises API is experimental
app.js
ls.js
ls2-promises.js
ls2.js
```

The API is currently in an experimental state and therefore we're shown this warning.

Another choice is a 3rd party module, `fs-extra`. This module has an extended API beyond the standard `fs` module. On the one hand its functions return a Promise if no callback function is provided, or else invokes the callback. In addition it includes several useful functions.

In the rest of this book we will be using `fs-extra` because of those additional functions. For documentation of the module, see: `https://www.npmjs.com/package/fs-extra`.

Launching a server with Node.js

Many scripts that you'll run are server processes. We'll be running lots of these scripts later on. Since we're still in the dual mode of verifying the installation and familiarizing you with using Node.js, we want to run a simple HTTP server. Let's borrow the simple server script on the Node.js home page (`http://nodejs.org`).

Create a file named `app.js` containing the following:

```
const http = require('http');
http.createServer(function (req, res) {
    res.writeHead(200, {'Content-Type': 'text/plain'});
    res.end('Hello, World!\n');
}).listen(8124, '127.0.0.1');
console.log('Server running at http://127.0.0.1:8124');
```

Run it as follows:

```
$ node app.js
Server running at http://127.0.0.1:8124
```

This is the simplest of web servers you can build with Node.js. If you're interested in how it works, flip forward to Chapter 4, *HTTP Servers and Clients*; Chapter 5, *Your First Express Application*; and Chapter 6, *Implementing the Mobile-First Paradigm*. For the moment, just visit http://127.0.0.1:8124 in your browser to see the **Hello, World!** message:

A question to ponder is why this script did not exit when ls.js did exit. In both cases, execution of the script reaches the end of the script; the Node.js process does not exit in app.js, while in ls.js it does.

The reason is the presence of active event listeners. Node.js always starts up an event loop, and in app.js, the listen function creates an event listener that implements the HTTP protocol. This event listener keeps app.js running until you do something such as typing *Ctrl* + *C* in the Terminal window. In ls.js, there is nothing that creates a long-running event listener, so when ls.js reaches the end of its script, the node process will exit.

NPM – the Node.js package manager

Node.js by itself is a pretty basic system, being a JavaScript interpreter with a few interesting asynchronous I/O libraries. One of the things that makes Node.js interesting is the rapidly growing ecosystem of third-party modules for Node.js.

At the center of that ecosystem is NPM. While Node.js modules can be downloaded as source and assembled manually for use with Node.js programs, that's tedious and it's difficult to implement a repeatable build process. NPM gives us a simpler way; NPM is the de facto standard package manager for Node.js and it greatly simplifies downloading and using these modules. We will talk about NPM at length in the next chapter.

The sharp-eyed will have noticed that npm is already installed via all the installation methods discussed previously. In the past, npm was installed separately, but today it is bundled with Node.js.

Now that we have npm installed, let's take it for a quick spin. The **hexy** program is a utility for printing hex dumps of files. That's a very 1970 thing to do, but is still extremely useful. It serves our purpose right now in giving us something to quickly install and try out:

```
$ npm install -g hexy
/opt/local/bin/hexy ->
/opt/local/lib/node_modules/hexy/bin/hexy_cmd.js
+ hexy@0.2.10
added 1 package in 1.107s
```

Adding the -g flag makes the module available globally, irrespective of the present-working-directory of your command shell. A global install is most useful when the module provides a command-line interface. When a package provides a command-line script, npm sets that up. For a global install, the command is installed correctly for use by all users of the computer.

Depending on how Node.js is installed for you, that may need to be run with sudo:

```
$ sudo npm install -g hexy
```

Once it is installed, you'll be able to run the newly-installed program this way:

```
$ hexy --width 12 ls.js
00000000: 636f 6e73 7420 6673 203d 2072 const.fs.=.r
0000000c: 6571 7569 7265 2827 6673 2729 equire('fs')
00000018: 3b0a 636f 6e73 7420 7574 696c ;.const.util
00000024: 203d 2072 6571 7569 7265 2827 .=.require('
00000030: 7574 696c 2729 3b0a 636f 6e73 util');.cons
0000003c: 7420 6673 5f72 6561 6464 6972 t.fs_readdir
00000048: 203d 2075 7469 6c2e 7072 6f6d .=.util.prom
00000054: 6973 6966 7928 6673 2e72 6561 isify(fs.rea
00000060: 6464 6972 293b 0a0a 2861 7379 ddir);..(asy
0000006c: 6e63 2028 2920 3d3e 207b 0a20 nc.().=>.{..
00000078: 2063 6f6e 7374 2066 696c 6573 .const.files
```

```
00000084: 203d 2061 7761 6974 2066 735f  .=.await.fs_
00000090: 7265 6164 6469 7228 272e 2729  readdir('.')
0000009c: 3b0a 2020 666f 7220 2866 6e20  ;...for.(fn.
000000a8: 6f66 2066 696c 6573 2920 7b0a  of.files).{.
000000b4: 2020 2020 636f 6e73 6f6c 652e  ....console.
000000c0: 6c6f 6728 666e 293b 0a20 207d  log(fn);...}
000000cc: 0a7d 2928 292e 6361 7463 6828  .})().catch(
000000d8: 6572 7220 3d3e 207b 2063 6f6e  err.=>.{.con
000000e4: 736f 6c65 2e65 7272 6f72 2865  sole.error(e
000000f0: 7272 293b 207d 293b           rr);.});
```

Again, we'll be doing a deep dive into NPM in the next chapter. The `hexy` utility is both a Node.js library and a script for printing out these old-style hex dumps.

Node.js, ECMAScript 2015/2016/2017, and beyond

In 2015, the ECMAScript committee released a long-awaited major update of the JavaScript language. The update brought in many new features to JavaScript, such as Promises, arrow functions, and Class objects. The language update set the stage for improvements. since that should dramatically improve our ability to write clean, understandable JavaScript code.

The browser makers are adding those much-needed features, meaning the V8 engine is adding those features as well. These features are making their way into Node.js starting with version 4.x.

To learn about the current status of ES-2015 in Node.js, visit `https://nodejs.org/en/docs/es6/`.

By default, only the ES-2015/2016/2017 features that V8 considers stable are enabled by Node.js. Further features can be enabled with command-line options. The almost-complete features are enabled with the `--es_staging` option. The website documentation gives more information.

The Node green website (`http://node.green/`) has a table listing the status of a long list of features in Node.js versions.

The ES2017 language spec is published at:
`https://www.ecma-international.org/publications/standards/Ecma-262.htm`.

The TC-39 committee does its work on GitHub `https://github.com/tc39`.

The ES-2015 features make a big improvement in the JavaScript language. One feature, the `Promise` class, should mean a fundamental rethinking of common idioms in Node.js programming. In ES-2017, a pair of new keywords, `async` and `await`, will simplify writing asynchronous code in Node.js, and it should encourage the Node.js community to further rethink the common idioms of the platform.

There's a long list of new JavaScript features, but let's quickly go over two of them that we'll use extensively.

The first is a lighter-weight function syntax called the arrow function:

```
fs.readFile('file.txt', 'utf8', (err, data) => {
    if (err) ...; // do something with the error
    else ...;    // do something with the data
});
```

This is more than the syntactic sugar of replacing the `function` keyword with the fat arrow. Arrow functions are lighter-weight as well as being easier to read. The lighter weight comes at the cost of changing the value of `this` inside the arrow function. In regular functions, `this` has a unique value inside the function. In an arrow function, `this` has the same value as the scope containing the arrow function. This means that, when using an arrow function, we don't have to jump through hoops to bring `this` into the callback function because `this` is the same at both levels of the code.

The next feature is the `Promise` class, which is used for deferred and asynchronous computations. Deferred code execution to implement asynchronous behavior is a key paradigm for Node.js, and it requires two idiomatic conventions:

- The last argument to an asynchronous function is a callback function, which is called when an asynchronous execution is to be performed
- The first argument to the callback function is an error indicator

While convenient, these conventions resulted in multilayer code pyramids that can be difficult to understand and maintain:

```
doThis(arg1, arg2, (err, result1, result2) => {
    if (err) ...;
    else {
        // do some work
```

```
doThat(arg2, arg3, (err2, results) => {
    if (err2) ...;
    else {
        doSomethingElse(arg5, err => {
            if (err) .. ;
            else ..;
        });
    }
  });
}
});
```

Depending on how many steps are required for a specific task, a code pyramid can get quite deep. Promises will let us unravel the code pyramid and improve reliability, because error handling is more straightforward and easily captures all errors.

A `Promise` class is created as follows:

```
function doThis(arg1, arg2) {
    return new Promise((resolve, reject) => {
        // execute some asynchronous code
        if (errorIsDetected) return reject(errorObject);
        // When the process is finished call this:
        resolve(result1, result2);
    });
}
```

Rather than passing in a callback function, the caller receives a `Promise` object. When properly utilized, the preceding pyramid can be coded as follows:

```
doThis(arg1, arg2)
.then(result => {
  // This can receive only one value, hence to
  // receive multiple values requires an object or array
  return doThat(arg2, arg3);
})
.then((results) => {
  return doSomethingElse(arg5);
})
.then(() => {
  // do a final something
})
.catch(err => {
  // errors land here
});
```

This works because the `Promise` class supports chaining if a `then` function returns a `Promise` object.

The `async`/`await` feature implements the promise of the Promise class to simplify asynchronous coding. This feature becomes active within an `async` function:

```
async function mumble() {
    // async magic happens here
}
```

An `async` arrow function is as follows:

```
const mumble = async () => {
    // async magic happens here
};
```

It's used as so:

```
async function doSomething(arg1, arg2, arg3, arg4, arg5) {
    var { result1, result2 } = await doThis(arg1, arg2);
    var results = await doThat(arg2, arg3);
    await doSomethingElse(arg5);
    // do a final something
    return finalResult;
}
```

Isn't this a breath of fresh air compared to the nested structure we started with?

The `await` keyword is used with a Promise. It automatically waits for the Promise to resolve. If the Promise resolves successfully then the value is returned, and if it resolves with an error then that error is thrown. Both handling results and throwing errors are handled in the natural manner.

This example also shows another ES2015 feature: destructuring. The fields of an object can be extracted using the following:

```
var { value1, value2 } = {
    value1: "Value 1", value2: "Value 2", value3: "Value3"
};
```

We have an object with three fields, but extract only two of the fields.

Using Babel to use experimental JavaScript features

The Babel transpiler (`http://babeljs.io/`) is a great way to use cutting-edge JavaScript features on older implementations. The word **transpile** means Babel rewrites JavaScript code into other JavaScript code, specifically to rewrite ES-2015 or ES-2016 features to older JavaScript code. Babel converts JavaScript source to an abstract syntax tree, then manipulates that tree to rewrite the code using older JavaScript features, and then writes that tree to a JavaScript source code file.

Put another way, Babel rewrites JavaScript code into JavaScript code, applying desired transformations such as converting ES2015/2016 features into ES5 code that can run in a web browser.

Many use Babel to experiment with new JavaScript feature proposals working their way through the TC-39 committee. Others use Babel to use new JavaScript features in projects on JavaScript engines that do not support those features.

The Node Green website makes it clear that Node.js supports pretty much all of the ES2015/2016/2017 features. Therefore, as a practical matter, we no longer need to use Babel for Node.js projects.

For web browsers, there is a much longer time lag between a set of ECMAScript features and when we can reliably use those features in browser-side code. It's not that the web browser makers are slow in adopting new features, because the Google, Mozilla, and Microsoft teams are proactive about adopting the latest features. Apple's Safari team seems slow to adopt new features, unfortunately. What's slower, however, is the penetration of new browsers into the fleet of computers in the field.

Therefore, modern JavaScript programmers need to familiarize themselves with Babel.

We're not ready to show example code for these features, but we can go ahead and document the setup of the Babel tool. For further information on setup documentation, visit `http://babeljs.io/docs/setup/`, and then click on the CLI button.

To get a brief introduction to Babel, we'll use it to transpile the scripts we saw earlier to run on Node.js 6.x. In those scripts we used async functions, which are not supported in Node.js 6.x.

In the directory containing `ls.js` and `ls2.js`, type these commands:

```
$ npm install babel-cli \
        babel-plugin-transform-es2015-modules-commonjs \
        babel-plugin-transform-async-to-generator
```

This installs the Babel software, along with a couple of transformation plugins. Babel has a plugin system so that you enable the transformations required by your project. Our primary goal in this example is converting the `async` functions shown earlier into Generator functions. Generators are a new sort of function introduced with ES2015, which form the foundation for implementation of `async` functions.

Because Node.js 6.x does not have `util.promisify`, we need to make one substitution:

```
// const fs_readdir = util.promisify(fs.readdir);
const fs_readdir = dir => {
    return new Promise((resolve, reject) => {
        fs.readdir(dir, (err, fileList) => {
            if (err) reject(err);
            else resolve(fileList);
        });
    });
};
```

This structure is more or less what the `util.promisify` function does.

Next, create a file named `.babelrc` containing the following:

```
{
  "plugins": [
    "transform-es2015-modules-commonjs",
    "transform-async-to-generator"
  ]
}
```

This file instructs Babel to use the named transformation plugins that we installed earlier.

Because we installed `babel-cli`, a `babel` command is installed such that we can type the following:

```
$ ./node_modules/.bin/babel --help
```

To transpile your code, run the following command:

```
$ ./node_modules/.bin/babel ls2.js -o ls2-babel.js
```

This command transpiles the named file, producing a new file. The new file is as follows:

```javascript
'use strict';

function _asyncToGenerator(fn) { return function () { var gen =
fn.apply(this, arguments); return new Promise(function (resolve,
reject) { function step(key, arg) { try { var info = gen[key](arg);
var value = info.value; } catch (error) { reject(error); return; } if
(info.done) { resolve(value); } else { return
Promise.resolve(value).then(function (value) { step("next", value); },
function (err) { step("throw", err); }); } } return step("next"); });
}; }

const fs = require('fs');
const util = require('util');
// const fs_readdir = util.promisify(fs.readdir);

const fs_readdir = dir => {
 return new Promise((resolve, reject) => {
   fs.readdir(dir, (err, fileList) => {
      if (err) reject(err);
      else resolve(fileList);
   });
 });
};

_asyncToGenerator(function* () {
 var dir = '.';
 if (process.argv[2]) dir = process.argv[2];
 const files = yield fs_readdir(dir);
 for (let fn of files) {
     console.log(fn);
 }
})().catch(err => {
 console.error(err);
});
```

This code isn't meant to be easy to read by humans. Instead, it's meant that you edit the original source file, and then convert it for your target JavaScript engine. The main thing to notice is that the transpiled code uses a Generator function in place of the `async` function, and the `yield` keyword in place of the `await` keyword. The `_asyncToGenerator` function implements functionality similar to async functions.

The transpiled script is run as follows:

```
$ node ls2-babel
.babelrc
app.js
babel
ls.js
ls2-babel.js
ls2.js
node_modules
```

In other words, it runs the same as the `async` version, but on an older Node.js release.

Summary

You learned a lot in this chapter about installing Node.js, using its command-line tools, and running a Node.js server. We also breezed past a lot of details that will be covered later in the book, so be patient.

Specifically, we covered downloading and compiling the Node.js source code, installing Node.js either for development use in your home directory or for deployment in system directories and installing NPM—the de facto standard package manager used with Node.js. We also saw how to run Node.js scripts or Node.js servers. We then took a look at the new features in ES-2015/2016/2017. Finally, we saw how to use Babel to implement those features in your code.

Now that we've seen how to set up the basic system, we're ready to start working on implementing applications with Node.js. First, you must learn the basic building blocks of Node.js applications and modules, which we will cover in the next chapter.

Node.js Modules

Before writing Node.js applications, you must learn about Node.js modules and packages. Modules and packages are the building blocks for breaking down your application into smaller pieces.

In this chapter, we will cover the following topics:

- Defining a module
- The CommonJS and ES2015 module specifications
- Using ES2015/2016/2017 coding practices in Node.js
- Using the ES6 module format in Node.js code
- Understanding how Node.js finds modules
- The npm package management system

So, let's get on with it.

Defining a module

Modules are the basic building blocks for constructing Node.js applications. A Node.js module encapsulates functions, hiding details inside a well-protected container, and exposing an explicitly-declared list of functions.

There are two module formats that we must consider:

- The traditional Node.js format based on the CommonJS standard has been used since Node.js was created.
- With ES2015/2016 a new format, ES6 Modules, has been defined with a new `import` keyword. ES6 modules will be (or is) supported in all JavaScript implementations.

Because ES6 modules are now the standard module format, the Node.js **Technical Steering Committee** (**TSC**) is committed to first-class support for ES6 modules.

We have already seen modules in action in the previous chapter. Every JavaScript file we use in Node.js is itself a module. It's time to see what they are and how they work. We'll start with CommonJS modules and then quickly bring in ES6 modules.

In the `ls.js` example in Chapter 2, *Setting up Node.js*, we wrote the following code to pull in the `fs` module, giving us access to its functions:

```
const fs = require('fs');
```

The `require` function searches for the named module, loading the module definition into the Node.js runtime, and making its functions available. In this case, the `fs` object contains the code (and data) exported by the `fs` module. The `fs` module is part of the Node.js core and provides filesystem functions.

By declaring `fs` as `const`, we have a little bit of assurance against making coding mistakes that would modify the object holding the module reference.

In every Node.js module, the `exports` object within the module is the interface exported to other code. Anything assigned to a field of the `exports` object is available to other pieces of code, and everything else is hidden. By the way, this object is actually `module.exports`. The `exports` object is an alias for `module.exports`.

The `require` function and `module.exports` objects both come from the CommonJS specification. ES6 modules have similar concepts, but a different implementation.

Let's look at a brief example of this before diving into the details. Ponder over the `simple.js` module:

```
var count = 0;
exports.next = function() { return ++count; };
exports.hello = function() {
  return "Hello, world!";
};
```

We have one variable, `count`, which is not attached to the `exports` object, and a function, `next`, which is attached. Now, let's use it:

```
$ node
> const s = require('./simple');
undefined
> s.hello();
'Hello, world!'
```

```
> s.next();
1
> s.next();
2
> s.next();
3
> console.log(s.count);
undefined
undefined
>
```

The `exports` object in the module is the object that is returned by
`require('./simple')`. Therefore, each call to `s.next` calls the `next` function in
`simple.js`. Each returns (and increments) the value of the local variable, `count`. An
attempt to access the private field, `count`, shows it's unavailable from outside the
module.

To reiterate the rule:

- Anything (functions or objects) assigned as a field of `exports` (as known
  as `module.exports`) is available to other code outside the module
- Objects not assigned to `exports` are not available to code outside the
  module, unless the module exports those objects via another mechanism

This is how Node.js solves the global object problem of browser-based JavaScript. The
variables that look like they're global variables are only global to the module
containing that variable. These variables are not visible to any other code.

Now that we've got a taste for modules, let's take a deeper look.

CommonJS and ES2015 module formats

Node.js's module implementation is strongly inspired by, but not identical to, the
CommonJS module specification. The differences between them might only be
important if you need to share code between Node and other CommonJS systems.

Among the changes in ES2015 is a standard module format meant for use
everywhere. It has some interesting features, and by existing everywhere it should
advance the state of JavaScript. Since it is incompatible with the CommonJS/Node.js
module system, adopting ES2015 modules in Node.js means reworking our practices
and accepted norms.

As a practical matter, Node.js programmers will be dealing with both module formats for some time during a transition period. Our long-term goal should be to adopt ES2015 modules across the board. The Node.js platform is slated to bring in support for ES2015 modules in Node.js 10. As of Node.js 8.5, the feature is available by setting a command-line flag.

CommonJS/Node.js module format

We've already seen a couple of examples of this module format, with the `simple.js` example, and the programs we examined in Chapter 2, *Setting up Node.Js*. So let's take a closer look.

CommonJS modules are stored in files with the extension `.js`.

Loading a CommonJS module is a synchronous operation. That means that when the `require('modulename')` function call returns, the module has been located and completely read into memory and is ready to go. The module is cached in memory so that subsequent `require('modulename')` calls return immediately, and all return the exact same object.

Node.js modules provide a simple encapsulation mechanism to hide implementation details while exposing an API. Modules are treated as if they were written as follows:

```
(function() { ... contents of module file ... })();
```

Thus, everything within the module is contained within an anonymous private namespace context. This is how the global object problem is resolved; everything in a module that looks global is actually contained within this private context.

Objects and functions can be exposed from a CommonJS module by means of two free variables Node.js inserts into this private context: `module` and `exports`:

- The `module` object contains several fields that you might find useful. Refer to the online Node.js documentation for details.
- The `exports` object is an alias of the `module.exports` field. This means that the following two lines of code are equivalent:

```
exports.funcName = function(arg, arg1) { ... };
module.exports.funcName = function(arg, arg2) { .. };
```

Your code can break the alias between the two if you do this:

```
exports = function(arg, arg1) { ... };
```

Do not do that, because `exports` will no longer be equivalent to `module.exports`. If your intent is to assign a single object or function to be what's returned by `require`, do this instead:

```
module.exports = function(arg, arg1) { ... };
```

Some modules do export a single function because that's how the module author envisioned delivering the desired functionality.

> The Node.js package format is derived from the CommonJS module system (`http://commonjs.org`). When developed, the CommonJS team aimed to fill a gap in the JavaScript ecosystem. At that time, there was no standard module system, making it trickier to package JavaScript applications. The `require` function, the `exports` object, and other aspects of Node.js modules come directly from the CommonJS `Modules/1.0` spec.

ES6 module format

ES6 modules are a new module format designed for all JavaScript environments. While Node.js has had a good module system for its whole existence, browser-side JavaScript has not. That left the browser-side community with either relying on the `<script>` tag, or using non-standardized solutions. For that matter, traditional Node.js modules were never standardized, outside of the CommonJS effort. Therefore, ES6 modules stand to be a big improvement for the entire JavaScript world, by getting everyone on the same page with a common module format and mechanisms.

The side effect is that the Node.js community needs to start looking at, learning about, and adopting the ES2015 module format.

ES6 modules are referred to by Node.js with the extension `.mjs`. When it came to implementing the new module format, the Node.js team determined that they could not support both CommonJS and ES6 modules with the `.js` extension. The `.mjs` extension was decided as the solution, and you may see tongue-in-cheek references to *Michael Jackson Script* for this file extension.

One interesting detail is that ES6 modules load asynchronously. This may not have an impact on Node.js programmers, except that this is part of the rationale behind requiring the new `.mjs` extension.

Create a file named `simple2.mjs` in the same directory as the `simple.js` example that we looked at earlier:

```
var count = 0;
export function next() { return ++count; }
function squared() { return Math.pow(count, 2); }
export function hello() {
    return "Hello, world!";
}
export default function() { return count; }
export const meaning = 42;
export let nocount = -1;
export { squared };
```

ES6 items exported from a module are declared with the `export` keyword. This keyword can be put in front of any top-level declaration, such as variable, function, or class declarations:

```
export function next() { .. }
```

The effect of this is similar to the following:

```
module.exports.next = function() { .. }
```

The intent of both is essentially the same: to make a function, or other object, available to code outside the module. A statement such as `export function next()` is a named export, meaning the exported thing has a name, and that code outside the module uses that name to access the object. As we see here, named `exports` can be functions or objects, and they may also be class definitions.

Using `export default` can be done once per module, and is the `default` export from the module. The `default` export is what code outside the module accesses when using the module object itself, rather than when using one of the exports from the module.

You can also declare something, such as the `squared` function, and then export it later.

Now let's see how to use this ES2015 module. Create a `simpledemo.mjs` file with the following:

```
import * as simple2 from './simple2.mjs';

console.log(simple2.hello());
console.log(`${simple2.next()} ${simple2.squared()}`);
console.log(`${simple2.next()} ${simple2.squared()}`);
```

```
console.log(`${simple2.default()} ${simple2.squared()}`);
console.log(`${simple2.next()} ${simple2.squared()}`);
console.log(`${simple2.next()} ${simple2.squared()}`);
console.log(`${simple2.next()} ${simple2.squared()}`);
console.log(simple2.meaning);
```

The `import` statement does what it means: it imports objects exported from a
module. This version of the `import` statement is most similar to a traditional Node.js
`require` statement, meaning that it creates an object through which you access the
objects exported from the module.

This is how the code executes:

```
$ node --experimental-modules simpledemo.mjs
(node:63937) ExperimentalWarning: The ESM module loader is
experimental.
Hello, world!
1 1
2 4
2 4
3 9
4 16
5 25
42
```

As of Node.js 8.5, the new module format is available behind an option flag as shown
here. You're also presented with this nice warning that it's an experimental feature.
Accessing the `default` export is accomplished by accessing the field named
`default`. Accessing an exported value, such as the `meaning` field, is done without
parentheses because it is a value and not a function.

Now to see a different way to import objects from a module, create another file,
named `simpledemo2.mjs`, containing the following:

```
import {
    default as simple, hello, next
} from './simple2.mjs';
console.log(hello());
console.log(next());
console.log(next());
console.log(simple());
console.log(next());
console.log(next());
console.log(next());
```

In this case, each imported object is its own thing rather than being attached to another object. Instead of writing `simple2.next()`, you simply write `next()`. The `as` clause is a way to declare an alias, if nothing else so you can use the default export. We already used an `as` clause earlier, and it can be used in other instances where you wish to provide an alias for the value being exported or imported.

Node.js modules can be used from ES2015 `.mjs` code. Create a file named `ls.mjs`, containing the following:

```
import _fs from 'fs';
const fs = _fs.promises;
import util from 'util';

(async () => {
  const files = await fs.readdir('.');
  for (let fn of files) {
    console.log(fn);
  }
}) ().catch(err => { console.error(err); });
```

You cannot, however, `require` an ES2015 module into regular Node.js code. The lookup algorithm for ES2015 modules is different, and as we mentioned earlier, ES2015 modules are loaded asynchronously.

Another wrinkle is handling the `fs.promises` submodule. We are using that submodule in the example, but how? This `import` statement does not work:

```
import { promises as fs } from 'fs';
```

This fails as so:

```
$ node --experimental-modules ls.mjs
(node:45186) ExperimentalWarning: The ESM module loader is
experimental.
file:///Volumes/Extra/book-4th/chap03/ls.mjs:1
import { promises as fs } from 'fs';
         ^^^^^^^^
SyntaxError: The requested module 'fs' does not provide an export
named 'promises'
  at ModuleJob._instantiate (internal/modules/esm/module_job.js:89:21)
```

That leaves us with this construct:

```
import _fs from 'fs';
const fs = _fs.promises;
```

Executing the script gives the following:

```
$ node --experimental-modules ls.mjs
(node:65359) ExperimentalWarning: The ESM module loader is
experimental.
(node:37671) ExperimentalWarning: The fs.promises API is experimental
ls.mjs
module1.js
module2.js
simple.js
simple2.mjs
simpledemo.mjs
simpledemo2.mjs
```

The last thing to note about ES2015 module code is that `import` and `export` statements must be top-level code. Even putting an `export` inside a simple block like this:

```
{
    export const meaning = 42;
}
```

Results in an error:

```
$ node --experimental-modules badexport.mjs
(node:67984) ExperimentalWarning: The ESM module loader is
experimental.
SyntaxError: Unexpected token export
  at ModuleJob.loaders.set [as moduleProvider]
(internal/loader/ModuleRequest.js:32:13)
  at <anonymous>
```

While there are a few more details about ES2015 modules, these are their most important attributes.

JSON modules

Node.js supports using `require('/path/to/file-name.json')` to import a JSON file. It is equivalent to this code:

```
const fs = require('fs');
module.exports = JSON.parse(
        fs.readFileSync('/path/to/file-name.json', 'utf8'));
```

That is, the JSON file is read synchronously, and the text is parsed as JSON. The resultant object is available as the object exported from the module. Create a file named `data.json`, containing the following:

```
{
    "hello": "Hello, world!",
    "meaning": 42
}
```

Now create a file named `showdata.js`, containing the following:

```
const util = require('util');
const data = require('./data');
console.log(util.inspect(data));
```

It will execute as follows:

```
$ node showdata.js
{ hello: 'Hello, world!', meaning: 42 }
```

The `util.inspect` function is a useful way to present an object in an easy-to-read fashion.

Supporting ES6 modules on older Node.js versions

While support for ES6 modules arrived as an experimental feature in Node.js 8.5, there are two ways to use these modules on earlier Node.js implementations.

One method is to use the Babel transpiler to rewrite ES6 code so it can execute on older Node.js versions. For an example, see `https://blog.revillweb.com/using-es2015-es6-modules-with-babel-6-3ffc0870095b`.

The better method is the `esm` package in the Node.js registry. Simply do the following:

```
$ nvm install 6
Downloading and installing node v6.14.1...
Downloading
https://nodejs.org/dist/v6.14.1/node-v6.14.1-darwin-x64.tar.xz...
############################################################################
## 100.0%
Computing checksum with shasum -a 256
Checksums matched!
Now using node v6.14.1 (npm v3.10.10)
$ nvm use 6
Now using node v6.14.1 (npm v3.10.10)
```

```
$ npm install esm
... npm output
$ node --require esm simpledemo.mjs
Hello, world!
1 1
2 4
2 4
3 9
4 16
5 25
42
```

To use this module, one simply invokes `require('esm')` once, and ES6 modules are retrofitted into Node.js. The `--require` flag automatically loads the named module. Without rewriting the code, we can selectively use the esm module with this the command-line option.

This example demonstrates retrofitting ES6 modules into older Node.js releases. To successfully execute the `ls.mjs` example we must have support for `async/await` functions, and arrow functions. Since Node.js 6.x does not support either, the `ls.mjs` example will fail, and will necessitate rewriting such code:

```
$ node --version
v6.14.1
$ node -r esm ls.mjs
/Users/David/chap03/ls.mjs:5
(async () => {
     ^

SyntaxError: Unexpected token (
  at exports.runInThisContext (vm.js:53:16)
  at Module._compile (module.js:373:25)
```

For more information, see:
`https://medium.com/web-on-the-edge/es-modules-in-node-today-32cff914e4b`.
That article describes an older release of the `esm` module, at the time named `@std/esm`.

Demonstrating module-level encapsulation

A key attribute of modules is encapsulation. The objects that are not exported from the module are private to the module, and cannot be accessed from code outside the module. To reiterate, modules are treated as if they were written as follows:

```
(function() { ... contents of module file ... }) ();
```

This JavaScript idiom defines an anonymous private scope. Anything declared within that scope cannot be accessed by code outside the scope. That is, unless some code makes object references available to other code outside this private scope. That's what the `module.exports` object does: it is a mechanism for the module author to expose object references from the module. Other code can then access resources inside the module in a controlled fashion.

The top-level variables inside a module look like they exist in the global scope. Instead of being truly Global, they're safely private to the module and are completely inaccessible to other code.

Let's take a look at a practical demonstration of that encapsulation. Create a file named `module1.js`, containing the following:

```
const A = "value A";
const B = "value B";
exports.values = function() {
    return { A: A, B: B };
}
```

Then, create a file named `module2.js`, containing the following:

```
const util = require('util');
const A = "a different value A";
const B = "a different value B";
const m1 = require('./module1');
console.log(`A=${A} B=${B} values=${util.inspect(m1.values())}`);
console.log(`${m1.A} ${m1.B}`);
const vals = m1.values();
vals.B = "something completely different";
console.log(util.inspect(vals));
console.log(util.inspect(m1.values()));
```

Then, run it as follows (you must have Node.js already installed):

```
$ node module2.js
A=a different value A B=a different value B values={ A: 'value A', B:
'value B' }
undefined undefined
{ A: 'value A', B: 'something completely different' }
{ A: 'value A', B: 'value B' }
```

This artificial example demonstrates encapsulation of the values in `module1.js` from those in `module2.js`. The `A` and `B` values in `module1.js` don't overwrite `A` and `B` in `module2.js` because they're encapsulated within `module1.js`. The `values` function in `module1.js` does allow code in `module2.js` access to the values; however, `module2.js` cannot directly access those values. We can modify the object `module2.js` received from `module1.js`. But doing so does not change the values within `module1.js`.

Finding and loading CommonJS and JSON modules using require

We have talked about several types of modules: CommonJS, JSON, ES2015, and native code modules. All but the ES2015 modules are loaded using the `require` function. That function has a very powerful and flexible algorithm for locating modules within a directory hierarchy. This algorithm, coupled with the npm package management system, gives the Node.js platform a lot of power and flexibility.

File modules

The CommonJS and ES2015 modules we've just looked at are what the Node.js documentation describes as a **file module**. Such modules are contained within a single file, whose filename ends with `.js`, `.mjs`, `.json`, or `.node`. The latter are compiled from C or C++ source code, or even other languages such as Rust, while the former are of course written in JavaScript or JSON.

We've already looked at several examples of using these modules, as well as the difference between the CommonJS format traditionally used in Node.js, and the new ES2015 modules that are now supported.

Modules baked into Node.js binary

Some modules are pre-compiled into the Node.js binary. These are the core Node.js modules documented on the Node.js website at `https://nodejs.org/api/index.html`.

They start out as source code within the Node.js build tree. The build process compiles them into the binary so that the modules are always available.

Directories as modules

A module can contain a whole directory structure full of stuff. Stuff here is a technical term referring to internal file modules, data files, template files, documentation, tests, assets, and more. Once stored within a properly constructed directory structure, Node.js will treat these as a module that satisfies a `require('moduleName')` call.

This may be a little confusing because the word *module* is being overloaded with two meanings. In some cases, a module is a file, and in other cases, a module is a directory containing one or more file modules.

In most cases, a directory-as-module contains a `package.json` file. This file contains data about the module (known as package) that Node.js uses while loading the module. The Node.js runtime recognizes these two fields:

```
{ name: "myAwesomeLibrary",
  main: "./lib/awesome.js" }
```

If this `package.json` file is in a directory named `awesomelib`, then `require('./awesomelib')` will load the file module in `./awesomelib/lib/awesome.js`.

If there is no `package.json`, then Node.js will look for either `index.js` or `index.node`. In such a case, `require('./awesomelib')` will load the file module in `./awesomelib/index.js`.

In either case, the directory module can easily contain other file modules. The module that's initially loaded would simply use `require('./anotherModule')` one or more times to load other, private modules.

The npm package management system can recognize a lot more data in
the `package.json` file. That includes the package name, its author, the home page
URL, the issue-queue URL, package dependencies, and more. We'll go over this later.

Module identifiers and pathnames

Generally speaking, the module name is a pathname, but with the file extension
removed. Earlier, when we wrote `require('./simple')`, Node.js knew to add `.js`
to the filename and load in `simple.js`. Similarly, Node.js would
recognize `simple.json` or `simple.node` as the filename legitimately
satisfying `require('./simple')`.

There are three types of module identifiers: relative, absolute, and top-level:

- **Relative module identifiers**: These begin with `./` or `../` and absolute
  identifiers begin with `/`. The module name is identical with POSIX
  filesystem semantics. The resultant pathname is interpreted relative to the
  location of the file being executed. That is, a module identifier beginning
  with `./` is looked for in the current directory, whereas one starting with
  `../` is looked for in the parent directory.
- **Absolute module identifiers**: These begin with `/` and are, of course, looked
  for in the root of the filesystem, but this is not a recommended practice.
- **Top-level module identifiers**: These begin with none of those strings and
  are just the module name, or else `module-name/path/to/module`. These
  must be stored in a `node_modules` directory, and the Node.js runtime has
  a nicely flexible algorithm for locating the correct `node_modules` directory:
  - In the case of `module-name/path/to/module` specifiers,
    what will be loaded is a module `path/to/module` within the
    top-level module named `module-name`
  - The baked-in modules are specified using top-level module
    names

The search begins in the directory containing the file calling `require()`. If that
directory contains a `node_modules` directory, which then contains either a matching
directory module or a matching file module, then the search is satisfied. If the local
`node_modules` directory does not contain a suitable module, it tries again in the
parent directory, and it will continue upward in the filesystem until it either finds a
suitable module or it reaches the root directory.

That is, with a `require` call in `/home/david/projects/notes/foo.js`, the following directories will be consulted:

- `/home/david/projects/notes/node_modules`
- `/home/david/projects/node_modules`
- `/home/david/node_modules`
- `/home/node_modules`
- `/node_modules`

If the module is not found through this search, there are global folders in which modules can be located. The first is specified in the `NODE_PATH` environment variable. This is interpreted as a colon-delimited list of absolute paths similar to the `PATH` environment variable. On Windows, the elements of `NODE_PATH` are of course separated by semicolons. Node.js will search those directories for a matching module.

The `NODE_PATH` approach is not recommended, because of surprising behavior which can happen if people are unaware that this variable must be set. If a specific module located in a specific directory referenced in `NODE_PATH` is required for proper function, and the variable is not set, the application will likely fail. As the Twelve-Factor Application model suggests, it is best for all dependencies to be explicitly declared, and with Node.js that means listing all dependencies in the `package.json` so that npm or yarn can manage the dependencies.

This variable was implemented before the module resolution algorithm just described was finalized. Because of that algorithm, `NODE_PATH` is largely unnecessary.

There are three additional locations that can hold modules:

- `$HOME/.node_modules`
- `$HOME/.node_libraries`
- `$PREFIX/lib/node`

In this case, $HOME is what you expect, the user's home directory, and $PREFIX is the directory where Node.js is installed.

Some are beginning to recommend against using global modules. The rationale is the desire for repeatability and deployability. If you've tested an app, and all its code is conveniently located within a directory tree, you can copy that tree for deployment to other machines. But, what if the app depended on some other file that was magically installed elsewhere on the system? Will you remember to deploy such files?

An example of application directory structure

Let's take a look at the filesystem structure of a typical Node.js Express application:

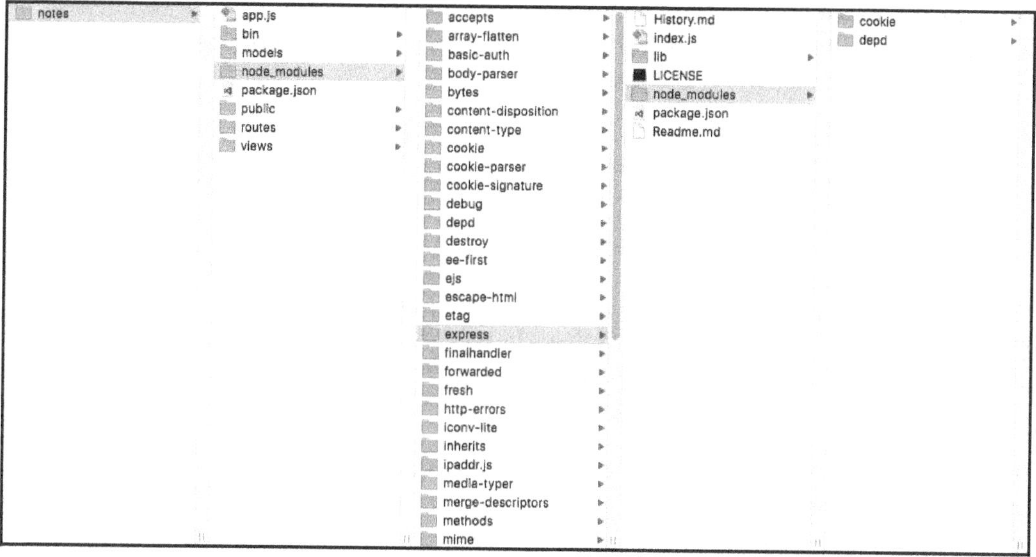

This is an Express application (we'll start using Express in Chapter 5, *Your First Express Application*) containing a few modules installed in the node_modules directory. One of those, Express, has its own node_modules directory containing a couple of modules.

For `app.js` to load `models-sequelize/notes.js`, it uses the following `require` call:

```
const notesModel = require('./models-sequelize/notes');
```

This is a relative module identifier, where the pathname is resolved relative to the directory containing the file making the reference.

Use the following code to do the reverse in `models-sequelize/notes.js`:

```
const app = require('../app');
```

Again, this is a relative module identifier, this time resolved relative to the subdirectory containing `models-sequelize/notes.js`.

Any reference to a top-level module identifier will first look in the `node_modules` directory shown here. This directory is populated from the dependencies listed in the `package.json`, as we'll see in a few pages:

```
const express = require('express');
const favicon = require('serve-favicon');
const logger = require('morgan');
const cookieParser = require('cookie-parser');
const bodyParser = require('body-parser');
```

All of these are typical modules included in an Express application. Most of them are readily visible in the screenshot shown earlier. What's loaded is the main file in the corresponding subdirectory of `node_modules`, for example, `node_modules/express/index.js`.

But the application cannot directly reference the dependencies of the Express module that are in its internal `node_modules` directory. The module search algorithm only moves upward in the filesystem; it does not descend into subsidiary directory trees.

One side effect of the upward search direction is the handling of conflicting dependencies.

Suppose two modules (modules A and B) listed a dependency on the same module (C)? In the normal case, the two dependencies on module C could be handled by the same instance of that module. As we'll see in a few pages, npm's dependency list in `package.json` can use loose or precise version number references. Depending on the current version number for module C, modules A and B may, or may not, be in agreement as to which version to use. If they do not agree, npm can arrange the module installation such that both module A and B get the version of module C they depend on, without either stepping on the other. If both are agreeable with the same module C instance, only one copy will be installed, but if they disagree then npm will install two copies. The two copies will be located such that the module search algorithm will cause each module to find the correct version of module C.

Let's try a concrete example to clarify what was just said. In the screenshot earlier, you see two instances of the `cookie` module. We can use npm to query for all references to this module:

```
$ npm ls cookie
notes@0.0.0 /Users/David/chap05/notes
├──┬ cookie-parser@1.3.5
│  └── cookie@0.1.3
└──┬ express@4.13.4
   └── cookie@0.1.5
```

This says the `cookie-parser` module depends on version 0.1.3 of `cookie`, while Express depends on version 0.1.5. How does npm avoid problems with these two conflicting versions? By putting one inside the `node_modules` directory inside the `express` module. This way, when *Express* refers to this module, it will use the `0.1.5` instance in its own `node_modules` directory, while the `cookie-parser` module will use the `0.1.3` instance in the top-level `node_modules` directory.

Finding and loading ES6 modules using import

The `import` statement is used to load ES6 modules, and it only works inside an ES6 module. Because ES6 modules are loaded asynchronously, the `require()` statement cannot load ES6 modules. As we said earlier, ES6 modules are recognized by Node.js by the `.mjs` extension. The ECMAScript TC-39 committee has (or plans to) officially register that file extension with the recognized authorities so that regular tools will recognize both file extensions as JavaScript.

The module specifier one hands to the `import` statement is interpreted as a URL. For the time being, Node.js will only accept `file:` URL because of the security implications of loading modules over the Internet. Because it's a URL, some characters such as `:`, `?`, `#`, or `%` must receive special treatment. For example:

```
import './foo?search';
import './foo#hash';
```

These are valid module specifiers where `?search` and `#hash` have the sort of meaning you'd expect in a URL. So long as Node.js only supports `file:` URL for `import` statements, we cannot make use of that feature, but we have to keep it in mind and avoid using these strings in module URL.

One can install custom module loader hooks that could conceivably use those URL parts for some purpose.

The module search algorithm is similar to what we described for `require`. If the specifier begins with `./`, `../`, or `/`, the specifier is interpreted as a pathname. Otherwise, it is interpreted as a top-level module similar to the `require` statement, with one big difference. The `import` statement will not search for a global module. This is frowned on, but if one must use a global module, that can be accomplished with a symbolic link.

For documentation, see `https://nodejs.org/api/esm.html`.

Hybrid CommonJS/Node.js/ES6 module scenarios

We've gone over the format for CommonJS/Node.js modules, the format for ES6 modules, and the algorithm for locating and importing both. The last thing to cover is those hybrid situations where our code will use both module formats at the same time.

As a practical matter, ES6 modules are very new to the Node.js platform, and therefore we have a large body of existing code written as CommonJS/Node.js modules. Many tools in the Node.js market have implementation dependencies on the CommonJS format. This means we'll be facing situations where ES6 modules will need to use CommonJS modules, and vice versa:

- CommonJS module loads other CommonJS modules with `require()`

- CommonJS module cannot load ES6 modules—except for two methods:
    - Dynamic import, also known as `import()`, can load an ES6 module as an asynchronous operation
    - The `@std/esm` package supplies a `require()` function with one that can load ES6 modules as an asynchronous operation
- ES6 modules load other ES6 modules with `import`, with the full semantics of the `import` statement
- ES6 modules load CommonJS modules using `import`

Therefore, out of the box, three of the scenarios are directly supported. The fourth is supported with a workaround module.

When an ES6 module loads a CommonJS module, its `module.exports` object is exposed as the `default` export of the module. This means your code uses this pattern:

```
import cjsModule from 'common-js-module';
...
cjsModule.functionName();
```

This is extremely similar to using a CommonJS module in another CommonJS module. You are simply transliterating the `require()` call into an `import` statement.

Dynamic imports with import()

ES6 modules do not cover all the requirements to fully replace Node.js/CommonJS modules. One of the missing capabilities is being addressed with the Dynamic Import feature currently on its way through the TC-39 committee.

Support for dynamic imports landed in Node.js 9.7. See the documentation at:
`https://github.com/tc39/proposal-dynamic-import`.

We'll use dynamic imports to solve an issue in Chapter 7, *Data Storage and Retrieval,* about dynamically choosing the module to load. In normal usage of the `require()` statement, can use a simple string literal to specify the module name. But it is also possible to use a string literal to compute the module name, like so:

```
// Node.js dynamically determined module loading
const moduleName = require(`../models/${process.env.MODEL_NAME}`);
```

We used this technique in earlier editions of this book to dynamically choose between several implementations of the same model API. The ES6 `import` statement does not support anything but a simple string literal, and therefore cannot compute the module specifier like this example.

With dynamic imports, we have an `import()` function where the module specifier is a regular string, letting us make a similar dynamic choice of module. Unlike the `require()` function, which is synchronous, `import()` is asynchronous, and returns a Promise. Hence, it's not a direct replacement for `require()` in that it's not terribly useful as a top-level function. You'll see how to use it in Chapter 7, *Data Storage and Retrieval.*

Perhaps the most important feature it brings is that CommonJS modules can use `import()` to load an ES6 module.

The import.meta feature

Another new feature, `import.meta`, is making its way through the TC-39 committee, and is being implemented for Node.js 10.x. It is an object existing within the scope of an ES6 module providing some metadata about the module. See `https://github.com/tc39/proposal-import-meta`.

A partial implementation, supporting just `import.meta.url`, has landed in the Node.js source. Its use requires the `--harmony-import-meta` command-line flag. The content of `import.meta.url` is a fully qualified `file:` URL for the current module, such as `file:///Users/david/chap10/notes/app.mjs`.

Where this becomes important is that ES6 modules do not support the `__dirname`, `__filename`, and other global variables used historically in Node.js modules. The `__dirname` variable is routinely used to read in resource data from files sitting in the package directory. It is intended that for such cases, one parses the directory name out of `import.meta.url`.

npm - the Node.js package management system

As described in `Chapter2`, *Setting up Node.js*, npm is a package management and distribution system for Node.js. It has become the de facto standard for distributing modules (packages) for use with Node.js. Conceptually, it's similar to tools such as `apt-get` (Debian), `rpm/yum` (Red Hat/Fedora), `MacPorts` (macOS), `CPAN` (Perl), or `PEAR` (PHP). Its purpose is publishing and distributing Node.js packages over the Internet using a simple command-line interface. With npm, you can quickly find packages to serve specific purposes, download them, install them, and manage packages you've already installed.

The `npm` application extends on the package format for Node.js, which in turn is largely based on the CommonJS package specification. It uses the same `package.json` file that's supported natively by Node.js, but with additional fields to build in additional functionality.

The npm package format

An npm package is a directory structure with a `package.json` file describing the package. This is exactly what was referred to earlier as a directory module, except that npm recognizes many more `package.json` tags than Node.js does. The starting point for npm's `package.json` are the CommonJS Packages/1.0 specification. The documentation for npm's `package.json` implementation is accessed using the following command:

```
$ npm help json
```

A basic `package.json` file is as follows:

```
{ "name": "packageName",
  "version": "1.0",
  "main": "mainModuleName",
  "modules": {
   "mod1": "lib/mod1",
   "mod2": "lib/mod2"
  }
}
```

The file is in JSON format, which, as a JavaScript programmer, you should be familiar with.

The most important tags are `name` and `version`. The name will appear in URLs and command names, so choose one that's safe for both. If you desire to publish a package in the public `npm` repository, it's helpful to check whether a particular name is already being used at `http://npmjs.com` or with the following command:

```
$ npm search packageName
```

The `main` tag is treated the same as we discussed in the previous section on directory modules. It defines which file module will be returned when invoking `require('packageName')`. Packages can contain many modules within themselves and they can be listed in the `modules` list.

Packages can be bundled as tar-gzip archives (tarballs), especially to send them over the internet.

A package can declare dependencies on other packages. That way, npm can automatically install other modules required by the module being installed. Dependencies are declared as follows:

```
"dependencies": {
    "foo" : "1.0.0 - 2.x.x",
    "bar" : ">=1.0.2 <2.1.2"
 }
```

The `description` and `keyword` fields help people find the package when searching in an npm repository (`https://www.npmjs.com/`). Ownership of a package can be documented in the `homepage`, `author`, or `contributors` fields:

```
"description": "My wonderful package that walks dogs",
"homepage": "http://npm.dogs.org/dogwalker/",
"author": "dogwhisperer@dogs.org"
```

Some npm packages provide executable programs meant to be in the user's PATH. These are declared using the bin tag. It's a map of command names to the script that implements that command. The command scripts are installed into the directory containing the node executable using the name given:

```
bin: {
    'nodeload.js': './nodeload.js',
    'nl.js': './nl.js'
},
```

The directories tag describes the package directory structure. The lib directory is automatically scanned for modules to load. There are other directory tags for binaries, manuals, and documentation:

```
directories: { lib: './lib', bin: './bin' },
```

The script tags are script commands run at various events in the life cycle of the package. These events include install, activate, uninstall, update, and more. For more information about script commands, use the following command:

```
$ npm help scripts
```

We've already used the scripts feature when showing how to set up Babel. We'll use these later for automating the build, test, and execution processes.

This was only a taste of the npm package format; see the documentation (npm help json) for more.

Finding npm packages

By default, npm modules are retrieved over the internet from the public package registry maintained on http://npmjs.com. If you know the module name, it can be installed simply by typing the following:

```
$ npm install moduleName
```

But what if you don't know the module name? How do you discover the interesting modules? The website http://npmjs.com publishes a searchable index of the modules in that registry.

The npm package also has a command-line search function to consult the same index:

```
[MacBook-Pro-4:notes david$ npm search mp3
NAME                    | DESCRIPTION           | AUTHOR         | DATE         | VERSION    | KEYWORDS
mp3                     | An MP3 decoder for_   | =devongovett   | 2014-06-17 | 0.1.0      | audio av aurora.js aurora decode
file-type               | Detect the file_      | =mifi_         | 2017-11-22 | 7.3.0      | mime file type archive image img pic picture flash photo vid
mp3-duration            | Get the duration of_  | =ddsol         | 2017-10-16 | 1.1.0      | mp3 duration length file audio
is-mp3                  | Check if a_           | =hemanth       | 2017-05-02 | 1.1.3      | mp3 type detect check is binary buffer uint8array
browser-id3-writer      | Pure JS library for_  | =egoroof       | 2017-07-06 | 4.0.0      | browser nodejs writer id3 mp3 audio tag library
transloadit             | Node.js SDK for_      | =kvz =tim-kos  | 2017-10-16 | 1.10.2     | transloadit encoding transcoding video audio mp3
audio-decode            | Decode audio data_    | =dfcreative_   | 2017-06-19 | 1.3.1      | audiojs audio dsp decode codec mp3 wav web-audio
id3-parser              | A pure JavaScript_    | =creeper       | 2017-10-26 | 1.5.1      | id3 id3 parser id3 tag id3v2 id3v1 mp3 metadata mp3
audio-type              | Detect the audio_     | =dfcreative_   | 2016-04-23 | 1.0.2      | audio sound wav mp3 flac type detect check is binary buffer
handbrake-js            | Handbrake for_        | =75lb          | 2017-05-26 | 2.2.2      | handbrake encode transcode video mp4 m4v avi h.264 h.265 vp8
npmdoc-youtube-mp3      | #### basic api_       | =npmdoc        | 2017-04-26 | 2017.4._   | documentation youtube-mp3
npmtest-youtube-mp3     | #### basic test_      | =npmtest2      | 2017-04-25 | 2017.4._   | coverage test youtube-mp3
jsmediatags             | Media Tags Reader_    | =aadsm         | 2017-10-27 | 3.8.1      | ID3 tags mp3 audio mp4
hypem resolver          | Resolve a hypem_      | =feedm3        | 2016-03-05 | 1.2.5      | hypem soundcloud mp3 converter
soundcloud-mp3          | Guess the mp3_        | =olizilla      | 2015-06-17 | 1.0.0      |
mp3-to-video            | Create video from_    | =slorenzo      | 2016-10-05 | 1.0.3      | mp3 convert video ffmpeg
music-metadata          | Streaming music_      | =borewit       | 2017-10-25 | 0.8.7      | tag tags MusicBrainz Discogs Picard IDd3 ID3v1 ID3v2 m4a mp3
react-cassette-player   | Simple ReactJS_       | =chadpaulson   | 2016-04-10 | 1.1.2      | react-component svg html5 audio html5 audio mp3 ogg wav medi
media-library           | a media library_      | =guillaume86   | 2016-01-05 | 1.2.4      | media mp3 audio library id3 music
amrToMp3                | 微信amr音频转mp3模块    | =traveller     | 2016-10-06 | 1.0.7      | amr amr to mp3 wechat amr
```

Of course, upon finding a module, it's installed as follows:

```
$ npm install acoustid
```

After installing a module, you may want to see the documentation, which would be on the module's website. The `homepage` tag in `package.json` lists that URL. The easiest way to look at the `package.json` file is with the `npm view` command, as follows:

```
$ npm view akasharender
...
{ name: 'akasharender',
  description: 'Rendering support for generating static HTML websites
  or EPUB eBooks',
  'dist-tags': { latest: '0.6.15' },
  versions:
   [ '0.0.1',
   ...
  author: 'David Herron <david@davidherron.com>
  (http://davidherron.com)',
  repository: { type: 'git', url:
  'git://github.com/akashacms/akasharender.git' },
  homepage: 'http://akashacms.com/akasharender/toc.html',
  ...
}
```

You can use `npm view` to extract any tag from `package.json`, like the following, which lets you view just the `homepage` tag:

```
$ npm view akasharender homepage
http://akashacms.org/akasharender/toc.html
```

Other fields in the `package.json` can be viewed by simply giving the desired tag name.

Other npm commands

The main `npm` command has a long list of subcommands for specific package management operations. These cover every aspect of the life cycle of publishing packages (as a package author), and downloading, using, or removing packages (as an npm consumer).

You can view the list of these commands just by typing `npm` (with no arguments). If you see one you want to learn more about, view the help information:

```
$ npm help <command>
The help text will be shown on your screen.
Or, see the website: http://docs.npmjs.com
```

Installing an npm package

The `npm install` command makes it easy to install packages upon finding the one of your dreams, as follows:

```
$ npm install express
/home/david/projects/notes/
- express@4.13.4
...
```

The named module is installed in `node_modules` in the current directory. The specific version installed depends on any version number listed on the command line, as we see in the next section.

Installing a package by version number

Version number matching in npm is powerful and flexible. The same sort of version specifiers used in `package.json` dependencies can also be used with the `npm install` command:

```
$ npm install package-name@tag
$ npm install package-name@version
$ npm install package-name@version-range
```

The last two are what they sound like. You can specify `express@4.16.2` to target a precise version, or `express@">4.1.0 < 5.0"` to target a range of Express V4 versions.

The version match specifiers include these choices:

- **Exact version match**: 1.2.3
- **At least version N**: >1.2.3
- **Up to version N**: <1.2.3
- **Between two releases**: >=1.2.3 <1.3.0

The `@tag` attribute is a symbolic name such as `@latest`, `@stable`, or `@canary`. The package owner assigns these symbolic names to specific version numbers, and can reassign them as desired. The exception is `@latest`, which is updated whenever a new release of the package is published.

For more documentation, run these commands: `npm help json` and `npm help npm-dist-tag`.

Global package installs

In some instances you want to install a module globally, so that it can be used from any directory. For example, the Grunt or Gulp build tools are widely useful, and conceivably you will find it useful if these tools are installed globally. Simply add the `-g` option:

```
$ npm install -g grunt-cli
```

If you get an error, and you're on a Unix-like system (Linux/Mac), you may need to run this with `sudo`:

```
$ sudo npm install -g grunt-cli
```

A global install is most important for those packages which install executable commands. We'll get into this shortly.

If a local package install lands in `node_modules`, where does a global package install land? On a Unix-like system it lands in `PREFIX/lib/node_modules`, and on Windows it lands in `PREFIX/node_modules`. In this case PREFIX means the directory where Node.js is installed. You can inspect the location of this directory like so:

```
$ npm config get prefix
/Users/david/.nvm/versions/node/v8.9.1
```

The algorithm used by Node.js for the `require` function automatically searches this directory for packages if the package is not found elsewhere.

Remember that ES6 modules do not support global packages.

Avoiding global module installation

Some in the Node.js community now frown on installing a package globally. One rationale exists in the Twelve Factor model. Namely, a software project is more reliable if all its dependencies are explicitly declared. If a build tool such as Grunt is required, but is not explicitly declared in `package.json`, the users of the application would have to receive instructions to install Grunt, and they would have to follow those instructions.

Users being users, they might skip over the instructions, fail to install the dependency, and then complain the application doesn't work. Surely most of us have done that once or twice.

It's recommended to avoid this potential problem by installing everything locally via one mechanism—the `npm install` command.

Maintaining package dependencies with npm

As we mentioned earlier, the `npm install` command by itself installs the packages listed in the `dependencies` section of `package.json`. This is easy and convenient. Simply by listing all the dependencies, it's quick and easy to install the dependencies required for using the package. What happens is npm looks in `package.json` for the `dependencies` or `devDependencies` field, and it will automatically install the mentioned packages.

You can manage the dependencies manually by editing `package.json`. Or you can use npm to assist you with editing the dependencies. You can add a new dependency like so:

```
$ npm install akasharender --save
```

In response, npm will add a `dependencies` tag to `package.json`:

```
"dependencies": {
    "akasharender": "^0.6.15"
}
```

Now, when your application is installed, npm will automatically also install that package along with any `dependencies` listed by that package.

The `devDependencies` are modules used during development. That field is initialized the same as above, but with the `--save-dev` flag.

By default, when an npm install is run, modules listed in both `dependencies` and `devDependencies` are installed. Of course, the purpose for having two lists is to not install the `devDependencies` in some cases:

```
$ npm install --production
```

This installs only the modules listed in `dependencies` and none of the `devDependencies` modules.

In the Twelve-Factor application model, it's suggested that we explicitly identify the dependencies required by the application. This way we can reliably build our application, knowing that we've tested against a specific set of dependencies that we've carefully identified. By installing exactly the dependencies against which the application has been tested, we have more confidence in the application. On the Node.js platform, npm gives us this dependencies section, including a flexible mechanism to declare compatible package versions by their version number.

Automatically updating package.json dependencies

With npm@5 (also known as npm version 5), one change was that it's no longer required to add `--save` to the `npm install` command. Instead, npm by default acts as if you ran the command with `--save`, and will automatically add the dependency to your `package.json`. This is meant to simplify using npm, and it is arguably more convenient that npm now does this. At the same time it can be very surprising and inconvenient for npm to go ahead and modify `package.json` for you. The behavior can be disabled by using the `--no-save` flag. This behavior can be permanently disabled using the following:

```
$ npm config set save false
```

The `npm config` command supports a long list of settable options for tuning behavior of npm. See `npm help config` for the documentation, and `npm help 7 config` for the list of options.

Fixing bugs by updating package dependencies

Bugs exist in every piece of software. An update to the Node.js platform may break an existing package, as might an upgrade to packages used by the application. Your application may trigger a bug in a package it uses. In these and other cases, fixing the problem might be as simple as updating a package dependency to a later (or earlier) version.

First identify whether the problem exists in the package or in your code. After determining it's a problem in another package, investigate whether the package maintainers have already fixed the bug. Is the package hosted on GitHub or another service with a public issue queue? Look for an open issue on this problem. That investigation will tell you whether to update the package dependency to a later version. Sometimes, it will tell you to revert to an earlier version; for example, if the package maintainer introduced a bug that doesn't exist in an earlier version.

Sometimes, you will find that the package maintainers are unprepared to issue a new release. In such a case, you can fork their repository and create a patched version of their package.

One approach to fixing this problem is **pinning** the package version number to one that's known to work. You might know that version 6.1.2 was the last release against which your application functioned, and that starting with version 6.2.0 your application breaks. Hence, in `package.json`:

```
"dependencies": {
    "module1": "6.1.2"
}
```

This freezes your dependency to the specific version number. You're free, then, to take your time updating your code to work against later releases of that module. Once your code is updated, or the upstream project is updated, change the dependency appropriately.

Another approach is to host a version of the package somewhere outside of the npm repository. This is covered in a later section.

Packages that install commands

Some packages install command-line programs. A side effect of installing such packages is a new command that you can type at the shell prompt or use in shell scripts. An example is the hexy program that we briefly used in Chapter 2, *Setting up Node.js*. Another example is the widely used Grunt or Gulp build tools.

The `package.json` file in such packages specifies the command-line tools that are installed. The command can be installed to one of two places:

- **Global Install**: It is installed either to a directory such as `/usr/local`, or to the `bin` directory where Node.js was installed. The `npm bin -g` command tells you the absolute pathname for this directory.
- **Local Install**: To `node_modules/.bin` in the package where the module is being installed. The `npm bin` command tells you the absolute pathname for this directory.

To run the command, simply type the command name at a shell prompt. Except there's a little bit of configuration required to make that simple.

Configuring the PATH variable to handle commands installed by modules

Typing the full pathname is not a user-friendly requirement to execute the command. We want to use the commands installed by modules, and we want a simple process for doing so. Meaning, we must add an appropriate value in the PATH variable, but what is it?

For global package installations, the executable lands in a directory that is probably already in your PATH variable, like /usr/bin or /usr/local/bin. Local package installations are what require special handling. The full path for the node_modules/.bin directory varies for each project, and obviously it won't work to add the full path for every node_modules/.bin directory to your PATH.

Adding ./node_modules/.bin to the PATH variable (or, on Windows, .\node_modules\.bin) works great. Any time your shell is in the root of a Node.js project, it will automatically find locally-installed commands from Node.js packages.

How we do this depends on the command shell you use, and your operating system.

On a Unix-like system the command shells are bash and csh. Your PATH variable would be set up in one of these ways:

```
$ export PATH=./node_modules/.bin:${PATH}      # bash
$ setenv PATH ./node_modules/.bin:${PATH}      # csh
```

The next step is adding the command to your login scripts so the variable is always set. On bash, add the corresponding line to your ~/.bashrc, and on csh add it to your ~/.cshrc.

Configuring the PATH variable on Windows

On Windows, this task is handled through a system-wide settings panel:

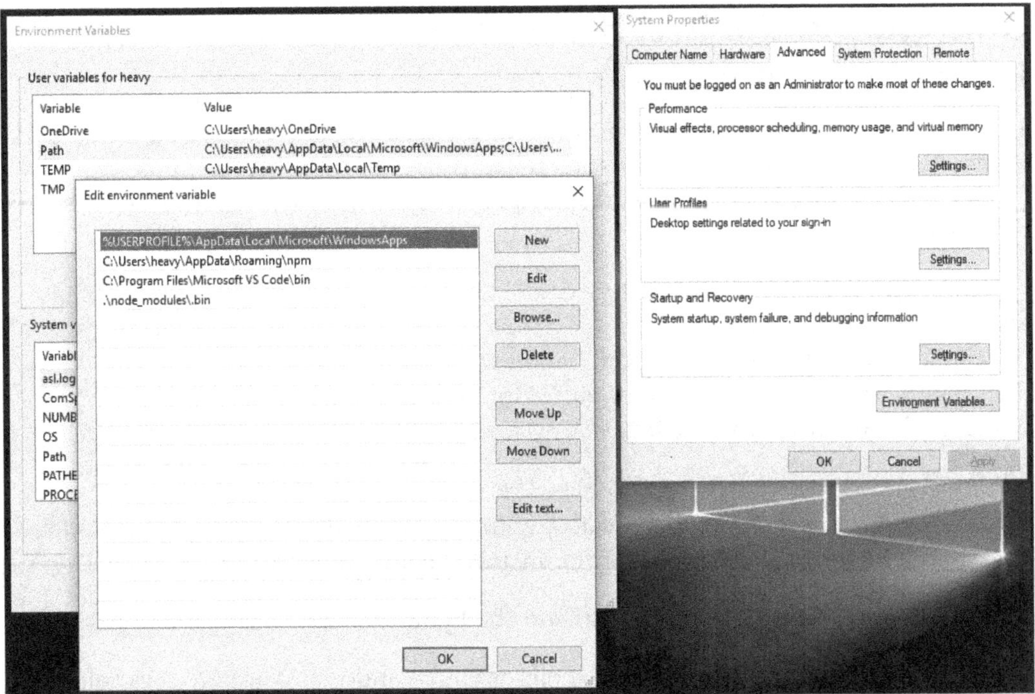

This pane of the **System Properties** panel is found by searching for PATH in the
Windows Settings screen. Click on the **Environment Variables** button, then select
the **Path** variable, and finally click on the **Edit** button. In the screen here click the **New**
button to add an entry to this variable, and enter `.\node_modules\.bin` as shown.
You'll have to restart any open command shell windows. Once you do, the effect will
be as shown previously.

Avoiding modifications to the PATH variable

What if you don't want to add these variables to your PATH at all times? The `npm-path` module may be of interest. This is a small program that computes the correct
PATH variable for your shell and operating system. See the package at `https://www.npmjs.com/package/npm-path`.

Updating outdated packages you've installed

The coder codes, updating their package, leaving you in their dust unless you keep up.

To find out if your installed packages are out of date, use the following command:

```
$ npm outdated
```

The report shows the current npm packages, the currently-installed version, as well as the current version in the npm repository. Updating the outdated packages is very simple:

```
$ npm update express
$ npm update
```

Installing packages from outside the npm repository

As awesome as the npm repository is, we don't want to push everything we do through their service. This is especially true for internal development teams who cannot publish their code for all the world to see. While you can rent or install a private npm repository, there's another way. Packages can be installed from other locations. Details about this are in `npm help package.json` in the `dependencies` section. Some examples are:

- **URL**: You can specify any URL that downloads a tarball, that is, a `.tar.gz` file. For example, GitHub or GitLab repositories can easily export tarball URL. Simply go to the **Releases** tab to find them.
- **Git URL**: Similarly, any Git repository can be accessed with the right URL. For example:

  ```
  $ npm install git+ssh://user@hostname:project.git#tag --save
  ```

- **GitHub Shortcut**: For GitHub repositories you can list just the repository specifier, such as `expressjs/express`. A tag or a commit can be referenced using `expressjs/express#tag-name`.
- **Local filesystem**: You can install from a local directory using a URL like this: `file:../../path/to/dir`.

Initializing a new npm package

If you want to create a new package, you can create the `package.json` file by hand or you can get npm's help. The `npm init` command leads you through a little dialog to get starting values for the `package.json` file.

Once you get through the questions, the `package.json` file is written to disk.

Expect to have to edit that file considerably before publishing to the npm repository. A few fields help give a good impression to folks looking at the package listing on `npmjs.com`:

- Link to the home page, and issue queue URL
- Keywords, so it can be linked with other similar packages
- A good description that helps folks understand the purpose
- A good `README.md` file so folks can read some documentation right away

Declaring Node.js version compatibility

It's important that your Node.js software runs on the correct version of Node.js. The primary reason being when new features are added to the platform. You'll want to use those new features, whether it is the async functions added in 8.x or the ES Modules supported added in 10.x. We need a way to declare the Node.js version required to run our software.

This dependency is declared in `package.json` using the `engines` tag:

```
"engines": {
    "node": ">= 8.x"
}
```

This, of course, uses the same version number matching scheme discussed earlier.

Publishing an npm package

All those packages in the npm repository came from people like you with an idea of a better way of doing something. It is very easy to get started with publishing packages. Online docs can be found at `https://docs.npmjs.com/getting-started/publishing-npm-packages`.

You first use the `npm adduser` command to register yourself with the npm repository. You can also sign up with the website. Next, you log in using the `npm login` command.

Finally, while sitting in the package root directory, use the `npm publish` command. Then, stand back so that you don't get stampeded by the crush of thronging fans. Or, maybe not. There are almost 600,000 packages in the repository, with almost 400 packages added every day. To get yours to stand out, you will require some marketing skill, which is another topic beyond the scope of this book.

Explicitly specifying package dependency version numbers

One feature of the Twelve-Factor methodology is step two, explicitly declaring your dependencies. We've already touched on this, but it's worth reiterating and to seeing npm makes this easy to accomplish.

Step one of the Twelve-Factor methodology is ensuring that your application code is checked into a source code repository. You probably already know this, and even have the best of intentions to ensure that everything is checked in. With Node.js, each module should have its own repository rather than putting every single last piece of code in one repository.

Each module can then progress on its own timeline. A breakage in one module is easy to back out by changing the version dependency in `package.json`.

This gets us to Twelve-Factor step two. There are two aspects of this step, one of which is the package versioning that we discussed previously. The next is explicitly declaring version numbers, which can be declared in `dependencies` and `devDependencies` sections of `package.json`. This ensures that everyone on the team is on the same page, developing against the same versions of the same modules. When it's time to deploy to testing, staging, or production servers, and the deployment script runs `npm install` or `npm update`, the code will use a known version of the module that everyone tested against.

The lazy way of declaring dependencies is putting `*` in the version field. That uses the latest version in the npm repository. Maybe this will work, until one day the maintainers of that package introduce a bug. You'll type `npm update`, and all of a sudden your code doesn't work. You'll head over to the GitHub site for the package, look in the issue queue, and possibly see that others have already reported the problem you're seeing. Some of them will say that they've pinned on the previous release until this bug is fixed. What that means is their `package.json` file does not depend on `*` for the latest version, but on a specific version number before the bug was created.

Don't do the lazy thing, do the smart thing.

The other aspect of explicitly declaring dependencies is to not implicitly depend on global packages. Earlier, we said that some in the Node.js community caution against installing modules in the global directories. This might seem like an easy shortcut to sharing code between applications. Just install it globally, and you don't have to install the code in each application.

But, doesn't that make deployment harder? Will the new team member be instructed on all the special files to install here and there to make the application run? Will you remember to install that global module on all destination machines?

For Node.js, that means listing all the module dependencies in `package.json`, and then the installation instructions are simply `npm install`, followed perhaps by editing a configuration file.

The Yarn package management system

As powerful as npm is, it is not the only package management system for Node.js. Because the Node.js core team does not dictate a package management system, the Node.js community is free to roll up their sleeves and develop any system they feel best. That the vast majority of us use npm is a testament to its value and usefulness. But there is a competitor.

Yarn (see `https://yarnpkg.com/en/`) is a collaboration between engineers at Facebook, Google, and several other companies. They proclaim that Yarn is ultra fast, ultra-secure (by using checksums of everything), and ultra reliable (by using a `yarn-lock.json` file to record precise dependencies).

Instead of running their own package repository, Yarn runs on top of npm's package repository at `npmjs.com`. This means that the Node.js community is not forked by Yarn, but enhanced by having an improved package management tool.

The npm team responded to Yarn in npm@5 (also known as npm version 5) by improving performance, and by introducing a `package-lock.json` file to improve reliability. The npm team have announced additional improvements in npm@6.

Yarn has become very popular and is widely recommended over npm. They perform extremely similar functions, and the performance is not that different to npm@5. The command-line options are worded differently. An important benefit Yarn brings to the Node.js community is that competition between Yarn and npm seems to be breeding faster advances in Node.js package management.

To get you started, these are the most important commands:

- `yarn add`: Adds a package to use in your current package
- `yarn init`: Initializes the development of a package
- `yarn install`: Installs all the dependencies defined in a `package.json` file
- `yarn publish`: Publishes a package to a package manager
- `yarn remove`: Removes an unused package from your current package

Running `yarn` by itself does the `yarn install` behavior. There are several other commands in Yarn, and `yarn help` will list them all.

Summary

You learned a lot in this chapter about modules and packages for Node.js.

Specifically, we covered implementing modules and packages for Node.js, managing installed modules and packages, and saw how Node.js locates modules.

Now that you've learned about modules and packages, we're ready to use them to build applications, which is the topic of the next chapter.

HTTP Servers and Clients

4

Now that you've learned about Node.js modules, it's time to put this knowledge to work by building a simple Node.js web application. In this chapter, we'll keep to a simple application, enabling us to explore three different application frameworks for Node.js. In later chapters, we'll build some more complex applications, but before we can walk, we must learn to crawl.

We will cover the following topics in this chapter:

- EventEmitters
- Listening to HTTP events and the HTTP Server object
- HTTP request routing
- ES2015 template strings
- Building a simple web application with no frameworks
- The Express application framework
- Express middleware functions
- How to deal with computationally intensive code
- The HTTP Client object
- Creating a simple REST service with Express

Sending and receiving events with EventEmitters

EventEmitters are one of the core idioms of Node.js. If Node.js's core idea is an event-driven architecture, emitting events from an object is one of the primary mechanisms of that architecture. An EventEmitter is an object that gives notifications—events—at different points in its life cycle. For example, an HTTP Server object emits events concerning each stage of the startup/shutdown of the Server object, and as HTTP requests are made from HTTP clients.

Many core Node.js modules are EventEmitters, and EventEmitters are an excellent
skeleton to implement asynchronous programming. EventEmitters have nothing to
do with web application development, but they are so much part of the Node.js
woodwork that you may skip over their existence.

In this chapter, we'll work with the HTTPServer and HTTPClient objects. Both are
subclasses of the `EventEmitter` class, and rely on it to send events for each step of
the HTTP protocol.

JavaScript classes and class inheritance

Before getting started on the `EventEmitter` class, we need to take a look at another
of the ES2015 features: classes. The JavaScript language has always had objects, and a
concept of a class hierarchy, but nothing so formal as in other languages. The ES2015
class object builds on the existing prototype-based inheritance model, but with a
syntax looking very much like class definitions in other languages.

For example, consider this class we'll be using later in the book:

```
class Note {
    constructor(key, title, body) {
        this._key = key;
        this._title = title;
        this._body = body;
    }
    get key() { return this._key; }
    get title() { return this._title; }
    set title(newTitle) { return this._title = newTitle; }
    get body() { return this._body; }
    set body(newBody) { return this._body = newBody; }
}
```

Once you've defined the class, you can export the class definition to other modules:

```
module.exports.Note = class Note { .. }    # in CommonJS modules
export class Note { .. }                   # in ES6 modules
```

The functions marked with `get` or `set` keywords are getters and setters, used like so:

```
var aNote = new Note("key", "The Rain in Spain", "Falls mainly on the
plain");
var key = aNote.key;
var title = aNote.title;
aNote.title = "The Rain in Spain, which made me want to cry with joy";
```

New instances of a class are created with `new`. You access a getter or setter function as if it is a simple field on the object. Behind the scenes, the getter/setter function is invoked.

The preceding implementation is not the best because the `_title` and `_body` fields are publicly visible, and there is no data hiding or encapsulation. We'll go over a better implementation later.

One tests whether a given object is of a certain class by using the `instanceof` operator:

```
if (anotherNote instanceof Note) {
    ... it's a Note, so act on it as a Note
}
```

Finally, you declare a subclass using the `extends` operator, similar to what's done in other languages:

```
class LoveNote extends Note {
    constructor(key, title, body, heart) {
        super(key, title, body);
        this._heart = heart;
    }
    get heart() { return this._heart; }
    set heart(newHeart) { return this._heart = newHeart; }
}
```

In other words, the `LoveNote` class has all the fields of `Note`, plus this new field named `heart`.

The EventEmitter Class

The `EventEmitter` object is defined in the events module of Node.js. Directly using the `EventEmitter` class means performing `require('events')`. In most cases, you'll be using an existing object that uses `EventEmitter` internally and you won't require this module. But there are cases where needs dictate implementing an `EventEmitter` subclass.

Create a file named `pulser.js` containing the following code:

```
const EventEmitter = require('events');

class Pulser extends EventEmitter {
    start() {
```

```
        setInterval(() => {
            console.log(`${new Date().toISOString()} >>>> pulse`);
            this.emit('pulse');
            console.log(`${new Date().toISOString()} <<<< pulse`);
        }, 1000);
    }
}
module.exports = Pulser;
```

This defines a `Pulser` class, which inherits from `EventEmitter`. In older Node.js releases, this would require using `util.inherits`, but the new class object makes subclassing much simpler.

Another thing to examine is how `this.emit` in the callback function refers to the Pulser object. Before the ES2015 arrow function, when our callbacks used a regular `function`, `this` would not have referred to the `Pulser` object. Instead, it would have referred to some other object related to the `setInterval` function. Because it is an arrow function, the `this` inside the arrow function is the same `this` as in the outer function.

If you needed to use a `function` rather than an arrow function, this trick would work:

```
class Pulser extends EventEmitter {
    start() {
        var self = this;
        setInterval(function() {
            self.emit(...);
        });
    }
}
```

What's different is the assignment of `this` to `self`. The value of `this` inside the function is different, but the value of `self` remains the same in every enclosed scope. This widely-used trick is less necessary now that we have arrow functions.

If you want a simple EventEmitter, but with your own class name, the body of the extended class can be empty:

```
class HeartBeat extends EventEmitter {}
const beatMaker = new HeartBeat();
```

The purpose of the `Pulser` class is sending a timed event, once a second, to any listeners. The `start` method uses `setInterval` to kick off repeated callback execution, scheduled for every second, calling `emit` to send the `pulse` events to any listeners.

Now, let's see how to use the `Pulser` object. Create a new file, called `pulsed.js`, containing:

```js
const Pulser = require('./pulser');

// Instantiate a Pulser object
const pulser = new Pulser();
// Handler function
pulser.on('pulse', () => {
    console.log(`${new Date().toISOString()} pulse received`);
});
// Start it pulsing
pulser.start();
```

Here, we create a `Pulser` object and consume its `pulse` events. Calling `pulser.on('pulse')` sets up connections for the `pulse` events to invoke the callback function. It then calls the `start` method to get the process going.

Enter this into a file and name the file `pulsed.js`. When you run it, you should see the following output:

```
$ node pulsed.js
2017-12-03T06:24:10.272Z >>>> pulse
2017-12-03T06:24:10.275Z pulse received
2017-12-03T06:24:10.276Z <<<< pulse
2017-12-03T06:24:11.279Z >>>> pulse
2017-12-03T06:24:11.279Z pulse received
2017-12-03T06:24:11.279Z <<<< pulse
2017-12-03T06:24:12.281Z >>>> pulse
2017-12-03T06:24:12.281Z pulse received
2017-12-03T06:24:12.282Z <<<< pulse
```

That gives you a little practical knowledge of the `EventEmitter` class. Let's now look at its operational theory.

The EventEmitter theory

With the `EventEmitter` class, your code emits events that other code can receive. It's a way of connecting two separated sections of your program, kind of like how quantum entanglement means two electrons can communicate with each other from any distance. Seems simple enough.

The event name can be anything that makes sense to you, and you can define as many event names as you like. Event names are defined simply by calling `.emit` with the event name. There's nothing formal to do and no registry of event names. Simply making a call to `.emit` is enough to define an event name.

 By convention, the event name `error` indicates errors.

An object sends events using the `.emit` function. Events are sent to any listeners that have registered to receive events from the object. The program registers to receive an event by calling that object's `.on` method, giving the event name and an event handler function.

There is no central distribution point for all events. Instead, each instance of an `EventEmitter` object manages its own set of listeners and distributes its events to those listeners.

Often, it is required to send data along with an event. To do so, simply add the data as arguments to the `.emit` call, as follows:

```
this.emit('eventName', data1, data2, ..);
```

When the program receives that event, the data appears as arguments to the callback function. Your program would listen to such an event as follows:

```
emitter.on('eventName', (data1, data2, ...theArgs) => {
  // act on event
});
```

There is no handshaking between event receivers and the event sender. That is, the event sender simply goes on with its business, and it gets no notifications about any events received, any action taken, or any error that occurred.

In this example, we used another of the ES2015 features, the `rest` operator, shown
here as `...theArgs`. The *rest* operator catches any number of remaining function
parameters into an array. Since `EventEmitter` can pass along any number of
parameters, and the `rest` operator can automatically receive any number of
parameters, it's a match made in heaven, or else in the TC-39 committee.

HTTP server applications

The HTTP server object is the foundation of all Node.js web applications. The object
itself is very close to the HTTP protocol, and its use requires knowledge of that
protocol. In most cases, you'll be able to use an application framework such as
Express that hides the HTTP protocol details, allowing the programmer to focus on
business logic.

We already saw a simple HTTP server application in `Chapter 2`, *Setting up Node.js*,
which is as follows:

```javascript
const http = require('http');
http.createServer((req, res) => {
  res.writeHead(200, {'Content-Type': 'text/plain'});
  res.end('Hello, World!\n');
}).listen(8124, '127.0.0.1');
console.log('Server running at http://127.0.0.1:8124');
```

The `http.createServer` function creates an `http.Server` object. Because it is an
`EventEmitter`, this can be written in another way to make that fact explicit:

```javascript
const http = require('http');
const server = http.createServer();
server.on('request', (req, res) => {
  res.writeHead(200, {'Content-Type': 'text/plain'});
  res.end('Hello, World!\n');
});
server.listen(8124, '127.0.0.1');
console.log('Server running at http://127.0.0.1:8124');
```

The `request` event takes a function, which receives `request` and `response` objects.
The `request` object has data from the web browser, while the `response` object is
used to gather the data to be sent in the response. The `listen` function causes the
server to start listening and arranging to dispatch an event for every request arriving
from a web browser.

Now, let's look at something more interesting with different actions based on the
URL.

Create a new file, named `server.js`, containing the following code:

```javascript
const http = require('http');
const util = require('util');
const url  = require('url');
const os   = require('os');

const server = http.createServer();
server.on('request', (req, res) => {
    var requrl = url.parse(req.url, true);
    if (requrl.pathname === '/') {
        res.writeHead(200, {'Content-Type': 'text/html'});
        res.end(
`<html><head><title>Hello, world!</title></head>
<body><h1>Hello, world!</h1>
<p><a href='/osinfo'>OS Info</a></p>
</body></html>`);
    } else if (requrl.pathname === "/osinfo") {
        res.writeHead(200, {'Content-Type': 'text/html'});
        res.end(
`<html><head><title>Operating System Info</title></head>
<body><h1>Operating System Info</h1>
<table>
<tr><th>TMP Dir</th><td>${os.tmpdir()}</td></tr>
<tr><th>Host Name</th><td>${os.hostname()}</td></tr>
<tr><th>OS Type</th><td>${os.type()} ${os.platform()} ${os.arch()}
${os.release()}</td></tr>
<tr><th>Uptime</th><td>${os.uptime()}
${util.inspect(os.loadavg())}</td></tr>
<tr><th>Memory</th><td>total: ${os.totalmem()} free:
${os.freemem()}</td></tr>
<tr><th>CPU's</th><td><pre>${util.inspect(os.cpus())}</pre></td></tr>
<tr><th>Network</th><td><pre>${util.inspect(os.networkInterfaces())}</
pre></td></tr>
</table>
</body></html>`);
    } else {
        res.writeHead(404, {'Content-Type': 'text/plain'});
        res.end("bad URL "+ req.url);
    }
});

server.listen(8124);
console.log('listening to http://localhost:8124');
```

To run it, type the following command:

```
$ node server.js
listening to http://localhost:8124
```

This application is meant to be similar to PHP's `sysinfo` function. Node's `os` module is consulted to provide information about the server. This example can easily be extended to gather other pieces of data about the server:

```
Operating System Info

TMP Dir    /var/folders/ts/58kmwr_92sl4m8sprnm67l0c0000gn/T
Host Name  MacBook-Pro-4
OS Type    Darwin darwin x64 15.6.0
Uptime     263939 [ 5.52587890625, 4.009765625, 3.3779296875 ]
Memory     total: 17179869184 free: 338968576

          [ { model: 'Intel(R) Core(TM) i7-3520M CPU @ 2.90GHz',
              speed: 2900,
              times: { user: 58440130, nice: 0, sys: 35335240, idle: 78521300, irq: 0 } },
            { model: 'Intel(R) Core(TM) i7-3520M CPU @ 2.90GHz',
              speed: 2900,
              times: { user: 37769340, nice: 0, sys: 16522590, idle: 118003860, irq: 0 } },
   CPU's    { model: 'Intel(R) Core(TM) i7-3520M CPU @ 2.90GHz',
              speed: 2900,
              times: { user: 58006180, nice: 0, sys: 28342820, idle: 85946820, irq: 0 } },
            { model: 'Intel(R) Core(TM) i7-3520M CPU @ 2.90GHz',
              speed: 2900,
              times: { user: 38607110, nice: 0, sys: 16825270, idle: 116863400, irq: 0 } } ]
          { lo0:
             [ { address: '::1',
                 netmask: 'ffff:ffff:ffff:ffff:ffff:ffff:ffff:ffff',
                 family: 'IPv6',
                 mac: '00:00:00:00:00:00',
                 scopeid: 0,
                 internal: true,
                 cidr: '::1/128' },
               { address: '127.0.0.1',
                 netmask: '255.0.0.0',
                 family: 'IPv4',
                 mac: '00:00:00:00:00:00',
```

A central part of any web application is the method of routing requests to request handlers. The `request` object has several pieces of data attached to it, two of which are useful for routing requests: the `request.url` and `request.method` fields.

In `server.js`, we consult the `request.url` data to determine which page to show, after parsing (using `url.parse`) to ease the digestion process. In this case, we can do a simple comparison of the `pathname` to determine which handler method to use.

Some web applications care about the HTTP verb (GET, DELETE, POST, and so on)
used and must consult the `request.method` field of the `request` object. For
example, POST is frequently used for FORM submissions.

The `pathname` portion of the request URL is used to dispatch the request to the
correct handler. While this routing method, based on simple string comparison, will
work for a small application, it'll quickly become unwieldy. Larger applications will
use pattern matching to use part of the request URL to select the request handler
function and other parts to extract request data out of the URL. We'll see this in action
while looking at Express later in the *Getting started with Express* section.

A search for a URL match in the npm repository turns up several promising packages
that could be used to implement request matching and routing. A framework like
Express has this capability already baked in and tested.

If the request URL is not recognized, the server sends back an error page using a 404
result code. The result code informs the browser about the status of the request,
where a 200 code means everything is fine, and a 404 code means the requested page
doesn't exist. There are, of course, many other HTTP response codes, each with their
own meaning.

ES2015 multiline and template strings

The previous example showed two of the new features introduced with ES2015,
multiline and template strings. The feature is meant to simplify our life while creating
text strings.

The existing string representations use single quotes and double quotes. Template
strings are delimited with the backtick character that's also known as the **grave
accent**:

```
`template string text`
```

Before ES2015, one way to implement a multiline string was this construct:

```
["<html><head><title>Hello, world!</title></head>",
 "<body><h1>Hello, world!</h1>",
 "<p><a href='/osinfo'>OS Info</a></p>",
 "</body></html>"]
.join('\n')
```

Yes, that was the code used in the same example in previous versions of this book. This is what we can do with ES2015:

```
`<html><head><title>Hello, world!</title></head>
<body><h1>Hello, world!</h1>
<p><a href='/osinfo'>OS Info</a></p>
</body></html>`
```

This is more succinct and straightforward. The opening quote is on the first line, the closing quote on the last line, and everything in between is part of our string.

The real purpose of the template strings feature is supporting strings where we can easily substitute values directly into the string. Most other programming languages support this ability, and now JavaScript does too.

Pre-ES2015, a programmer could have written code like this:

```
[ ...
   "<tr><th>OS Type</th><td>{ostype} {osplat} {osarch}
{osrelease}</td></tr>"
   ... ].join('\n')
.replace("{ostype}", os.type())
.replace("{osplat}", os.platform())
.replace("{osarch}", os.arch())
.replace("{osrelease}", os.release())
```

Again, this is extracted from the same example in previous versions of this book. With template strings, this can be written as follows:

```
`...<tr><th>OS Type</th><td>${os.type()} ${os.platform()} ${os.arch()}
${os.release()}</td></tr>...`
```

Within a template string, the part within the `${ .. }` brackets is interpreted as an expression. It can be a simple mathematical expression, a variable reference, or, as in this case, a function call.

The last thing to mention is a matter of indentation. In normal coding, one indents a long argument list to the same level as the containing function call. But, for these multiline string examples, the text content is flush with column zero. What's up?

This may impede the readability of your code, so it's worth weighing code readability against another issue: excess characters in the HTML output. The blanks we would use to indent the code for readability will become part of the string and will be output in the HTML. By making the code flush with column zero, we don't add excess blanks to the output at the cost of some code readability.

This approach also carries a security risk. Have you verified the data is safe? That it will not form the basis of a security attack? In this case, we're dealing with simple strings and numbers coming from a safe data source. Therefore this code is as safe as the Node.js runtime. What about user-supplied content, and the risk that a nefarious user might supply insecure content implanting some kind of malware into target computers?

For this and many other reasons, it is often safer to use an external template engine. Applications like Express make it easy to do so.

HTTP Sniffer – listening to the HTTP conversation

The events emitted by the HTTPServer object can be used for additional purposes beyond the immediate task of delivering a web application. The following code demonstrates a useful module that listens to all the HTTP Server events. It could be a useful debugging tool, which also demonstrates how HTTP server objects operate.

Node.js's HTTP Server object is an `EventEmitter` and the HTTP Sniffer simply listens to every server event, printing out information pertinent to each event.

What we're about to do is:

1. Create a module, `httpsniffer`, that prints information about HTTP requests.
2. Add that module to the `server.js` script we just created.
3. Rerun that server to view a trace of HTTP activity.

Create a file named `httpsniffer.js` containing the following code:

```js
const util = require('util');
const url  = require('url');

const timestamp = () => { return new Date().toISOString(); }

exports.sniffOn = function(server) {
  server.on('request', (req, res) => {
    console.log(`${timestamp()} e_request`);
    console.log(`${timestamp()} ${reqToString(req)}`);
  });
  server.on('close', errno => { console.log(`${timestamp()} e_close
${errno}`); });
```

```javascript
  server.on('checkContinue', (req, res) => {
    console.log(`${timestamp()} e_checkContinue`);
    console.log(`${timestamp()} ${reqToString(req)}`);
    res.writeContinue();
  });
  server.on('upgrade', (req, socket, head) => {
    console.log(`${timestamp()} e_upgrade`);
    console.log(`${timestamp()} ${reqToString(req)}`);
  });
  server.on('clientError', () => { console.log(`${timestamp()}
  e_clientError`); });
};

const reqToString = exports.reqToString = (req) => {
  var ret=`req ${req.method} ${req.httpVersion} ${req.url}` +'\n';
  ret += JSON.stringify(url.parse(req.url, true)) +'\n';
  var keys = Object.keys(req.headers);
  for (var i = 0, l = keys.length; i < l; i++) {
    var key = keys[i];
    ret += `${i} ${key}: ${req.headers[key]}` +'\n';
  }
  if (req.trailers) ret += util.inspect(req.trailers) +'\n';
  return ret;
};
```

That was a lot of code! But the key to it is the `sniffOn` function. When given an
HTTP Server object, it uses the `.on` function to attach listener functions that print data
about each emitted event. It gives a fairly detailed trace of HTTP traffic on an
application.

In order to use it, simply insert this code just before the `listen` function in
`server.js`:

```javascript
require('./httpsniffer').sniffOn(server);
server.listen(8124);
console.log('listening to http://localhost:8124');
```

With this in place, run the server as we did earlier. You can visit
`http://localhost:8124/` in your browser and see the following console output:

```
$ node server.js
listening to http://localhost:8124
2017-12-03T19:21:33.162Z request
2017-12-03T19:21:33.162Z request GET 1.1 /
{"protocol":null,"slashes":null,"auth":null,"host":null,"port":null,"h
ostname":null,"hash":null,"search":"","query":{},"pathname":"/","path"
:"/","href":"/"}
```

```
0 host: localhost:8124
1 upgrade-insecure-requests: 1
2 accept:
text/html,application/xhtml+xml,application/xml;q=0.9,*/*;q=0.8
3 user-agent: Mozilla/5.0 (Macintosh; Intel Mac OS X 10_11_6)
AppleWebKit/604.3.5 (KHTML, like Gecko) Version/11.0.1 Safari/604.3.5
4 accept-language: en-us
5 accept-encoding: gzip, deflate
6 connection: keep-alive
{}

2017-12-03T19:21:42.154Z request
2017-12-03T19:21:42.154Z request GET 1.1 /osinfo
{"protocol":null,"slashes":null,"auth":null,"host":null,"port":null,"h
ostname":null,"hash":null,"search":"","query":{},"pathname":"/osinfo",
"path":"/osinfo","href":"/osinfo"}
0 host: localhost:8124
1 connection: keep-alive
2 upgrade-insecure-requests: 1
3 accept:
text/html,application/xhtml+xml,application/xml;q=0.9,*/*;q=0.8
4 user-agent: Mozilla/5.0 (Macintosh; Intel Mac OS X 10_11_6)
AppleWebKit/604.3.5 (KHTML, like Gecko) Version/11.0.1 Safari/604.3.5
5 referer: http://localhost:8124/
6 accept-language: en-us
7 accept-encoding: gzip, deflate
{}
```

You now have a tool for snooping on HTTPServer events. This simple technique prints a detailed log of event data. The pattern can be used for any `EventEmitter` object. You can use this technique as a way to inspect the actual behavior of `EventEmitter` objects in your program.

Web application frameworks

The HTTPServer object is very close to the HTTP protocol. While this is powerful in the same way that driving a stick shift car gives you low-level control over the driving experience, typical web application programming is better done at a higher level. Does anybody use assembly language to write web applications? It's better to abstract away the HTTP details and concentrate on your application.

The Node.js developer community has developed quite a few application frameworks to help with different aspects of abstracting away HTTP protocol details. Of them, Express is the most popular, and Koa (`http://koajs.com/`) should be considered because it was developed by the same team and has fully integrated support for `async` functions.

The ExpressJS Wiki has a list of frameworks built on top of ExpressJS, or tools that work with it. This includes template engines, middleware modules, and more. The ExpressJS Wiki is located at `https://github.com/expressjs/express/wiki`.

One reason to use a web framework is that they often provide the best practices used in web application development for over 20 years. The usual best practices include the following:

- Providing a page for bad URLs (the 404 page)
- Screening URLs and forms for any injected scripting attacks
- Supporting the use of cookies to maintain sessions
- Logging requests for both usage tracking and debugging
- Authentication
- Handling static files, such as images, CSS, JavaScript, or HTML
- Providing cache control headers to caching proxies
- Limiting things such as page size or execution time

Web frameworks help you invest your time in the task without getting lost in the details of implementing HTTP protocol. Abstracting away details is a time-honored way for programmers to be more efficient. This is especially true when using a library or framework providing prepackaged functions that take care of the details.

Getting started with Express

Express is perhaps the most popular Node.js web app framework. It's so popular that it's part of the MEAN Stack acronym. MEAN refers to MongoDB, ExpressJS, AngularJS, and Node.js. Express is described as being Sinatra-like, referring to a popular Ruby application framework, and that it isn't an opinionated framework, meaning the framework authors don't impose their opinions about structuring an application. This means Express is not at all strict about how your code is structured; you just write it the way you think is best.

You can visit the home page for Express at `http://expressjs.com/`.

Shortly, we'll implement a simple application to calculate Fibonacci numbers using Express, and in later chapters, we'll do quite a bit more with Express. We'll also explore how to mitigate the performance problems from computationally intensive code we discussed earlier.

As of writing this book, Express 4.16 is the current version, and Express 5 is in Alpha testing. According to the ExpressJS website, there are very few differences between Express 4 and Express 5.

Let's start by installing the express-generator. While we can just start writing some code, the express-generator provides a blank starting application. We'll take that and modify it.

Install it using the following commands:

```
$ mkdir fibonacci
$ cd fibonacci
$ npm install express-generator@4.x
```

This is different from the suggested installation method on the Express website, which was to use the -g tag for a global install. We're also using an explicit version number to ensure compatibility. As of writing this book, `express-generator@5.x` does not exist. When it does exist, one should be able to use the 5.x version with the following instructions.

Earlier, we discussed how many now recommend against installing modules globally. In the Twelve-Factor model, it's strongly recommended to not install global dependencies, and that's what we're doing.

The result is that an `express` command is installed in the `./node_modules/.bin` directory:

```
$ ls node_modules/.bin/
express
```

Run the `express` command like so:

```
$ ./node_modules/.bin/express --help

  Usage: express [options] [dir]

  Options:
    -h, --help          output usage information
    -V, --version       output the version number
    -e, --ejs           add ejs engine support (defaults to jade)
```

```
    --hbs               add handlebars engine support
-H, --hogan             add hogan.js engine support
-c, --css <engine>      add stylesheet <engine> support
(less|stylus|compass|sass) (defaults to plain css)
    --git               add .gitignore
-f, --force             force on non-empty directory
```

We probably don't want to type ./node_modules/.bin/express every time we run the express-generator application or, for that matter, any of the other applications that provide command-line utilities. Refer back to the discussion in Chapter 3, *Node.js Modules* about adding that directory to the PATH variable.

Now that you've installed express-generator in the fibonacci directory, use it to set up the blank framework application:

```
$ ./node_modules/.bin/express --view=hbs --git .
destination is not empty, continue? [y/N] y

   create : .
   create : ./package.json
   create : ./app.js
   create : ./.gitignore
   create : ./public
   create : ./routes
   create : ./routes/index.js
   create : ./routes/users.js
   create : ./views
   create : ./views/index.hbs
   create : ./views/layout.hbs
   create : ./views/error.hbs
   create : ./bin
   create : ./bin/www
   create : ./public/javascripts
   create : ./public/images
   create : ./public/stylesheets
   create : ./public/stylesheets/style.css

install dependencies:
  $ cd . && npm install

run the app:
  $ DEBUG=fibonacci:* npm start

  $ npm uninstall express-generator
  added 83 packages and removed 5 packages in 4.104s
```

This created a bunch of files for us, which we'll walk through in a minute. The `node_modules` directory still has the `express-generator` module, which is now not useful. We can just leave it there and ignore it, or we can add it to the `devDependencies` of the `package.json` it generated. Alternatively, we can uninstall it as shown here.

The next thing to do is run the blank application in the way we're told. The command shown, `npm start`, relies on a section of the supplied `package.json` file:

```
"scripts": {
    "start": "node ./bin/www"
},
```

The `npm` tool supports scripts that are ways to automate various tasks. We'll use this capability throughout the book to do various things. When the Twelve-Factor Application model suggests automating all your administrative tasks, the `npm` scripts feature is an excellent mechanism to do so. Most `npm` scripts are run with the `npm run scriptName` command, but the `start` command is explicitly recognized by `npm` and can be run as shown previously.

The steps are:

1. Install the dependencies `npm install`.
2. Start the application using `npm start`.
3. Optionally modify `package.json` to always run with debugging.

To install the dependencies, and run the application, type these commands:

```
$ npm install
$ DEBUG=fibonacci:* npm start

> fibonacci@0.0.0 start /Users/David/chap04/fibonacci
> node ./bin/www

  fibonacci:server Listening on port 3000 +0ms
```

Setting the `DEBUG` variable this way turns on some debugging output, which includes this message about listening on port 3000. Otherwise, we aren't told this information. This syntax is what's used in the Bash shell to run a command with an environment variable. If you get an error try running just "`npm start`" then read the next section.

We can modify the supplied `npm start` script to always run the app with debugging enabled. Change the `scripts` section to the following:

```
"scripts": {
    "start": "DEBUG=fibonacci:* node ./bin/www"
},
```

Since the output says it is listening on port `3000`, we direct our browser to `http://localhost:3000/` and see the following output:

Setting environment variables in Windows cmd.exe command line

If you're on Windows the previous example may have failed with an error that DEBUG is not a known command. The problem is that the Windows shell, the `cmd.exe` program, does not support the Bash command-line structure.

Adding `VARIABLE=value` at the beginning of a command-line is specific to some shells, like Bash, on Linux and macOS. It sets that environment variable only for the command-line being executed, and is a very convenient way to temporarily override environment variables for a specific command.

Clearly a solution is required if your `package.json` is to be usable across different operating systems.

The best solution appears to be the `cross-env` package in the npm repository, see: `https://www.npmjs.com/package/cross-env` With this package installed, commands in the `scripts` section in `package.json` can set environment variables just as in Bash on Linux/macOS. The usage looks like so:

```
"scripts": {
    "start": "cross-env DEBUG=fibonacci:* node ./bin/www"
},
"dependencies": {

    ...
    "cross-env": "5.1.x"
}
```

Then the command is executed as so:

```
C:\Users\david\Documents\chap04\fibonacci>npm install
... output from installing packages
C:\Users\david\Documents\chap04\fibonacci>npm run start

> fibonacci@0.0.0 start C:\Users\david\Documents\chap04\fibonacci
> cross-env DEBUG=fibonacci:* node ./bin/www

fibonacci:server Listening on port 3000 +0ms
GET / 304 90.597 ms - -
GET /stylesheets/style.css 304 14.480 ms - -
GET /fibonacci 200 84.726 ms - 503
GET /stylesheets/style.css 304 4.465 ms - -
GET /fibonacci?fibonum=22 500 1069.049 ms - 327
GET /stylesheets/style.css 304 2.601 ms - -
```

Walking through the default Express application

We have a working, blank Express application; let's look at what was generated for us. We're doing this to familiarize ourselves with Express before diving in to start coding our `Fibonacci` application.

Because we used the `--view=hbs` option, this application is set up to use the `Handlebars.js` template engine. Handlebars was built on top of Mustache, and was originally designed for use in the browser; for more information see its homepage at `http://handlebarsjs.com/`. The version shown here has been packaged for use with Express, and is documented at `https://github.com/pillarjs/hbs`.

Generally speaking, a template engine makes it possible to insert data into generated web pages. The ExpressJS Wiki has a list of template engines for Express `https://github.com/expressjs/express/wiki#template-engines`.

The `views` directory contains two files, `error.hbs` and `index.hbs`. The `hbs` extension is used for Handlebars files. Another file, `layout.hbs`, is the default page layout. Handlebars has several ways to configure layout templates and even partials (snippets of code which can be included anywhere).

The `routes` directory contains the initial routing setup, that is, the code to handle specific URLs. We'll modify these later.

The `public` directory will contain assets that the application doesn't generate, but are simply sent to the browser. What's initially installed is a CSS file, `public/stylesheets/style.css`.

The `package.json` file contains our dependencies and other metadata.

The `bin` directory contains the `www` script that we saw earlier. That's a Node.js script, which initializes the HTTPServer objects, starts it listening on a TCP port, and calls the last file we'll discuss, `app.js`. These scripts initialize Express, hook up the routing modules, and do other things.

There's a lot going on in the `www` and `app.js` scripts, so let's start with the application initialization. Let's first take a look at a couple of lines in `app.js`:

```
var express = require('express');
...
var app = express();
...
module.exports = app;
```

This means that `app.js` is a module that exports the object returned by the `express` module. It doesn't start the HTTP server object, however.

Now, let's turn to the `www` script. The first thing to see is that it starts with this line:

```
#!/usr/bin/env node
```

This is a Unix/Linux technique to make a command script. It says to run the following as a script using the `node` command. In other words, we have Node.js code and we're instructing the operating system to execute that code using the Node.js runtime:

```
$ ls -l bin/www
-rwx------  1 david  staff  1595 Feb  5  1970 bin/www
```

We can also see that the script was made executable by `express-generator`.

It calls the `app.js` module as follows:

```
var app = require('../app');
...
var port = normalizePort(process.env.PORT || '3000');
app.set('port', port);
...
var server = http.createServer(app);
...
server.listen(port);
server.on('error', onError);
server.on('listening', onListening);
```

We see where port `3000` comes from; it's a parameter to the `normalizePort` function. We also see that setting the `PORT` environment variable will override the default port `3000`. And finally, we see that the HTTP Server object is created here, and is told to use the application instance created in `app.js`. Try running the following command:

```
$ PORT=4242 DEBUG=fibonacci:* npm start
```

The application now tells you that it's listening on port `4242`, where you can ponder the meaning of life.

The `app` object is next passed to `http.createServer()`. A look in the Node.js documentation tells us this function takes a `requestListener`, which is simply a function that takes the `request` and `response` objects we've seen previously. Therefore, the `app` object is such a function.

Finally, the `www` script starts the server listening on the port we specified.

Let's now walk through `app.js` in more detail:

```
app.set('views', path.join(__dirname, 'views'));
app.set('view engine', 'hbs');
```

This tells Express to look for templates in the `views` directory and to use the EJS templating engine.

The `app.set` function is used for setting application properties. It'll be useful to browse the API documentation as we go through (`http://expressjs.com/en/4x/api.html`).

Next is a series of `app.use` calls:

```
app.use(logger('dev'));
app.use(bodyParser.json());
app.use(bodyParser.urlencoded({ extended: false }));
app.use(cookieParser());
app.use(express.static(path.join(__dirname, 'public')));

app.use('/', routes);
app.use('/users', users);
```

The `app.use` function mounts middleware functions. This is an important piece of Express jargon we will discuss shortly. At the moment, let's say that middleware functions are executed during the processing of routes. This means all the features named here are enabled in `app.js`:

- Logging is enabled using the Morgan request logger. Visit `https://www.npmjs.com/package/morgan` for its documentation.
- The `body-parser` module handles parsing HTTP request bodies. Visit `https://www.npmjs.com/package/body-parser` for its documentation.
- The `cookie-parser` module is used to parse HTTP cookies. Visit `https://www.npmjs.com/package/cookie-parser` for its documentation.
- A static file web server is configured to serve the asset files in the `public` directory.
- Two router modules, `routes` and `users`, to set up which functions handle which URLs.

The Express middleware

Let's round out the walkthrough of `app.js` by discussing what middleware functions do for our application. We have an example at the end of the script:

```
app.use(function(req, res, next) {
  var err = new Error('Not found');
  err.status = 404;
  next(err);
});
```

The comment says *catch 404 and forward to error handler*. As you probably know, an HTTP 404 status means the requested resource was not found. We need to tell the user their request wasn't satisfied, and maybe show them a picture of a flock of birds pulling a whale out of the ocean. This is the first step in doing so. Before getting to the last step of reporting this error, you must learn how middleware works.

We do have a middleware function right in front of us. Refer to its documentation at `http://expressjs.com/en/guide/writing-middleware.html`.

Middleware functions take three arguments. The first two, `request` and `response`, are equivalent to the `request` and `response` of the Node.js HTTP request object. However, Express expands the objects with additional data and capabilities. The last, `next`, is a callback function controlling when the request-response cycle ends, and it can be used to send errors down the middleware pipeline.

The incoming request gets handled by the first middleware function, then the next, then the next, and so on. Each time the request is to be passed down the chain of middleware functions, the `next` function is called. If `next` is called with an error object, as shown here, an error is being signaled. Otherwise, the control simply passes to the next middleware function in the chain.

What happens if `next` is not called? The HTTP request will hang because no response has been given. A middleware function gives a response when it calls functions on the `response` object, such as `res.send` or `res.render`.

For example, consider the inclusion of `app.js`:

```
app.get('/', function(req, res) { res.send('Hello World!'); });
```

This does not call `next`, but instead calls `res.send`. This is the correct method of ending the request-response cycle, by sending a response (`res.send`) to the request. If neither `next` nor `res.send` is called, the request never gets a response.

Hence, a middleware function does one of the following four things:

- Executes its own business logic. The request logger middleware shown earlier is an example.
- Modifies the request or response objects. Both the `body-parser` and `cookie-parser` do so, looking for data to add to the `request` object.
- Calls `next` to proceed to the next middleware function or else signals an error.
- Sends a response, ending the cycle.

The ordering of middleware execution depends on the order they're added to the `app` object. The first added is executed first, and so on.

Middleware and request paths

We've seen two kinds of middleware functions so far. In one, the first argument is the handler function. In the other, the first argument is a string containing a URL snippet, and the second argument is the handler function.

What's actually going on is `app.use` has an optional first argument: the path the middleware is mounted on. The path is a pattern match against the request URL, and the given function is triggered if the URL matches the pattern. There's even a method to supply named parameters in the URL:

```
app.use('/user/profile/:id', function(req, res, next) {
    userProfiles.lookup(req.params.id, (err, profile) => {
        if (err) return next(err);
        // do something with the profile
        // Such as display it to the user
        res.send(profile.display());
    });
});
```

This path specification has a pattern, `:id`, and the value will land in `req.params.id`. In this example, we're suggesting a user profiles service, and that for this URL we want to display information about the named user.

Another way to use a middleware function is on a specific HTTP request method. With `app.use`, any request will be matched, but in truth, GET requests are supposed to behave differently to POST requests. You call `app.METHOD` where METHOD matches one of the HTTP request verbs. That is, `app.get` matches the GET method, `app.post` matches POST, and so on.

Finally, we get to the `router` object. This is a kind of middleware used explicitly for routing requests based on their URL. Take a look at `routes/users.js`:

```
var express = require('express');
var router = express.Router();
router.get('/', function(req, res, next) {
  res.send('respond with a resource');
});
module.exports = router;
```

We have a module whose `exports` object is a router. This router has only one route, but it can have any number of routes you think is appropriate.

Back in `app.js`, this is added as follows:

```
app.use('/users', users);
```

All the functions we discussed for the `app` object apply to the `router` object. If the request matches, the router is given the request for its own chain of processing functions. An important detail is that the request URL prefix is stripped when the request is passed to the router instance.

You'll notice that the `router.get` in `users.js` matches `'/'` and that this router is mounted on `'/users'`. In effect, that `router.get` matches `/users` as well, but because the prefix was stripped, it specifies `'/'` instead. This means a router can be mounted on different path prefixes without having to change the router implementation.

Error handling

Now, we can finally get back to the generated `app.js`, the **404 Error page not found**, and any other errors the application might want to show to the user.

A middleware function indicates an error by passing a value to the `next` function call. Once Express sees an error, it will skip any remaining non-error routing, and it will only pass it to error handlers instead. An error handler function has a different signature than what we saw earlier.

In `app.js`, which we're examining, this is our error handler:

```
app.use(function(err, req, res, next) {
  res.status(err.status || 500);
  res.render('error', {
    message: err.message,
    error: {}
  });
});
```

Error handler functions take four parameters, with `err` added to the familiar `req`, `res`, and `next`. For this handler, we use `res.status` to set the HTTP response status code, and we use `res.render` to format an HTML response using the `views/error.hbs` template. The `res.render` function takes data, rendering it with a template to produce HTML.

This means any error in our application will land here, bypassing any remaining middleware functions.

Calculating the Fibonacci sequence with an Express application

The Fibonacci numbers are the integer sequence: *0, 1, 1, 2, 3, 5, 8, 13, 21, 34, ...*

Each entry in the list is the sum of the previous two entries in the list. The sequence was invented in 1202 by Leonardo of Pisa, who was also known as Fibonacci. One method to calculate entries in the Fibonacci sequence is the recursive algorithm we showed earlier. We will create an Express application that uses the Fibonacci implementation and then explore several methods to mitigate performance problems in computationally intensive algorithms.

Let's start with the blank application we created in the previous step. We had you name that application *Fibonacci* for a reason. We were thinking ahead.

In `app.js`, make the following changes to the top portion of the file:

```
const express = require('express');
const hbs = require('hbs');
const path = require('path');
const favicon = require('serve-favicon');
const logger = require('morgan');
const cookieParser = require('cookie-parser');
const bodyParser = require('body-parser');
```

```
const index = require('./routes/index');
const fibonacci = require('./routes/fibonacci');

const app = express();

// view engine setup
app.set('views', path.join(__dirname, 'views'));
app.set('view engine', 'hbs');
hbs.registerPartials(path.join(__dirname, 'partials'));

// uncomment after placing your favicon in /public
//app.use(favicon(path.join(__dirname, 'public', 'favicon.ico')));
app.use(logger('dev'));
app.use(bodyParser.json());
app.use(bodyParser.urlencoded({ extended: false }));
app.use(cookieParser());
app.use(express.static(path.join(__dirname, 'public')));

app.use('/', index);
app.use('/fibonacci', fibonacci);
```

Most of this is what `express-generator` gave us. The `var` statements have been
changed to `const`, for that little teensy bit of extra comfort. We explicitly imported
the `hbs` module so we could do some configuration. And we imported a router
module for Fibonacci, which we'll see in a minute.

For the `Fibonacci` application, we don't need to support users, and therefore deleted
that routing module. The `fibonacci` module, which we'll show next, serves to query
a number for which we'll calculate the Fibonacci number.

In the top-level directory, create a file, `math.js`, containing this extremely simplistic
Fibonacci implementation:

```
exports.fibonacci = function(n) {
    if (n === 0) return 0;
    else if (n === 1 || n === 2) return 1;
    else return exports.fibonacci(n-1) + exports.fibonacci(n-2);
};
```

In the `views` directory, look at the file named `layout.hbs` which `express-
generator` created:

```
<!DOCTYPE html>
<html>
  <head>
    <title>{{title}}</title>
    <link rel='stylesheet' href='/stylesheets/style.css' />
```

```
    </head>
    <body>
      {{{body}}}
    </body>
  </html>
```

This file contains the structure we'll use for HTML pages. Going by the Handlebars syntax, we see that `{{title}}` appears within the HTML `title` tag. It means when we call `res.render`, we should supply a `title` attribute. The `{{{body}}}` tag is where the view template content lands.

Change `views/index.hbs` to just contain the following:

```
<h1>{{title}}</h1>
{{> navbar}}
```

This serves as the front page of our application. It will be inserted in place of `{{{body}}}` in `layout.hbs`. The marker, `{{> navbar}}`, refers to a partial named `navbar`. Earlier, we configured a directory named `partials` to hold partials. Now let's create a file, `partials/navbar.html`, containing:

```
<div class='navbar'>
<p><a href='/'>home</a> | <a href='/fibonacci'>Fibonacci's</a></p>
</div>
```

This will serve as a navigation bar that's included on every page.

Create a file, `views/fibonacci.hbs`, containing the following code:

```
<h1>{{title}}</h1>
{{> navbar}}
{{#if fiboval}}
  <p>Fibonacci for {{fibonum}} is {{fiboval}}</p>
  <hr/>
{{/if}}
<p>Enter a number to see its' Fibonacci number</p>
<form name='fibonacci' action='/fibonacci' method='get'>
<input type='text' name='fibonum' />
<input type='submit' value='Submit' />
</form>
```

> Remember that the files in `views` are templates into which data is rendered. They serve the View aspect of the **Model-View-Controller (MVC)** paradigm, hence the directory name.

In the `routes` directory, delete the `user.js` module. It is generated by the Express framework, but we will not use it in this application.

In `routes/index.js`, change the router function to the following:

```
/* GET home page. */
router.get('/', function(req, res, next) {
  res.render('index', { title: "Welcome to the Fibonacci Calculator"
});
});
```

The anonymous object passed to `res.render` contains the data values we provide to the layout and view templates.

Then, finally, in the `routes` directory, create a file named `fibonacci.js` containing the following code:

```
const express = require('express');
const router = express.Router();

const math = require('../math');
router.get('/', function(req, res, next) {
  if (req.query.fibonum) {
    // Calculate directly in this server
    res.render('fibonacci', {
      title: "Calculate Fibonacci numbers",
      fibonum: req.query.fibonum,
      fiboval: math.fibonacci(req.query.fibonum)
    });
  } else {
    res.render('fibonacci', {
      title: "Calculate Fibonacci numbers",
      fiboval: undefined
    });
  }
});

module.exports = router;
```

The `package.json` is already set up so we can use `npm start` to run the script and always have debugging messages enabled. And now we're ready to do so:

```
$ npm start
> fibonacci@0.0.0 start /Users/david/chap04/fibonacci
> DEBUG=fibonacci:* node ./bin/www
fibonacci:server Listening on port 3000 +0ms
```

As it suggests, you can visit `http://localhost:3000/` and see what we have:

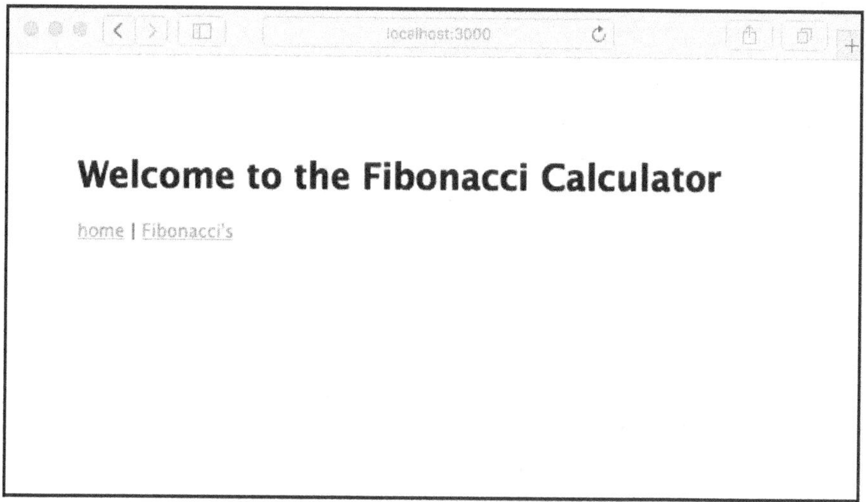

This page is rendered from the `views/index.hbs` template. Simply click on the **Fibonacci's** link to go to the next page, which is of course rendered from the `views/fibonacci.hbs` template. On that page, you'll be able to enter a number, click on the **Submit** button, and get an answer (hint: pick a number below `40` if you want your answer in a reasonable amount of time):

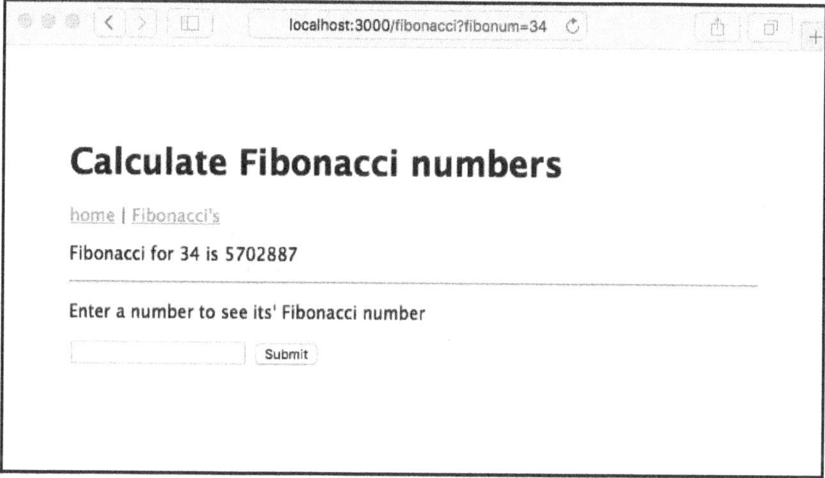

Let's walk through the application to discuss how it works.

There are two routes in `app.js`: the route for `/`, which is handled by `routes/index.js`, and the route for `/fibonacci`, which is handled by `routes/fibonacci.js`.

The `res.render` function renders the named template using the provided data values and emits the result as an HTTP response. For the home page of this application, the rendering code (`routes/index.js`) and template (`views/index.hbs`) aren't much, and it is on the Fibonacci page where all the action is happening.

The `views/fibonacci.hbs` template contains a form in which the user enters a number. Because it is a GET form, when the user clicks on the **Submit** button, the browser will issue an HTTP GET on the `/fibonacci` URL. What distinguishes one GET on `/fibonacci` from another is whether the URL contains a query parameter named `fibonum`. When the user first enters the page, there is no `fibonum` and hence nothing to calculate. After the user has entered a number and clicked on **Submit**, there is a `fibonum` and something to calculate.

Express automatically parses the query parameters, making them available as `req.query`. That means `routes/fibonacci.js` can quickly check whether there is a `fibonum`. If there is, it calls the `fibonacci` function to calculate the value.

Earlier, we asked you to enter a number less than 40. Go ahead and enter a larger number, such as 50, but go take a coffee break because this is going to take a while to calculate. Or proceed on to reading the next section where we start to discuss use of computationally intensive code.

Computationally intensive code and the Node.js event loop

This Fibonacci example is purposely inefficient to demonstrate an important consideration for your applications. What happens to the Node.js event loop when running long computations? To see the effect, open two browser windows, each opened to the Fibonacci page. In one, enter the number 55 or greater, and in the other, enter 10. Note that the second window freezes, and if you leave it running long enough, the answer will eventually pop up in both windows. What's happening is the Node.js event loop is blocked from processing events because the Fibonacci algorithm is running and does not ever yield to the event loop.

Since Node.js has a single execution thread, processing requests depend on request handlers quickly returning to the event loop. Normally, the asynchronous coding style ensures that the event loop executes regularly.

This is true even for requests that load data from a server halfway around the globe, because the asynchronous I/O is non-blocking and control is quickly returned to the event loop. The naïve Fibonacci function we chose doesn't fit into this model because it's a long-running blocking operation. This type of event handler prevents the system from processing requests and stops Node.js from doing what it's meant to do, namely to be a blisteringly fast web server.

In this case, the long-response-time problem is obvious. Response time quickly escalates to the point where you can take a vacation to Tibet and perhaps get reincarnated as a llama in Peru during the time it takes to respond with the Fibonacci number!

To see this more clearly, create a file named `fibotimes.js` containing the following code:

```
const math = require('./math');
const util = require('util');

for (var num = 1; num < 80; num++) {
    let now = new Date().toISOString();
    console.log(`${now} Fibonacci for ${num} =
${math.fibonacci(num)}`);
}
```

Now run it. You will get the following output:

```
$ node fibotimes.js
2017-12-10T23:04:42.342Z Fibonacci for 1 = 1
2017-12-10T23:04:42.345Z Fibonacci for 2 = 1
2017-12-10T23:04:42.345Z Fibonacci for 3 = 2
2017-12-10T23:04:42.345Z Fibonacci for 4 = 3
2017-12-10T23:04:42.345Z Fibonacci for 5 = 5
...
2017-12-10T23:04:42.345Z Fibonacci for 10 = 55
2017-12-10T23:04:42.345Z Fibonacci for 11 = 89
2017-12-10T23:04:42.345Z Fibonacci for 12 = 144
2017-12-10T23:04:42.345Z Fibonacci for 13 = 233
2017-12-10T23:04:42.345Z Fibonacci for 14 = 377
...
2017-12-10T23:04:44.072Z Fibonacci for 40 = 102334155
2017-12-10T23:04:45.118Z Fibonacci for 41 = 165580141
2017-12-10T23:04:46.855Z Fibonacci for 42 = 267914296
```

```
2017-12-10T23:04:49.723Z Fibonacci for 43 = 433494437
2017-12-10T23:04:54.218Z Fibonacci for 44 = 701408733
...
2017-12-10T23:06:07.531Z Fibonacci for 48 = 4807526976
2017-12-10T23:07:08.056Z Fibonacci for 49 = 7778742049
^C
```

This quickly calculates the first 40 or so members of the Fibonacci sequence, but after the 40th member, it starts taking a couple of seconds per result and quickly degrades from there. It is untenable to execute code of this sort on a single-threaded system that relies on a quick return to the event loop. A web service containing such code would give poor performance to the users.

There are two general ways to solve this problem in Node.js:

- **Algorithmic refactoring**: Perhaps, like the Fibonacci function we chose, one of your algorithms is suboptimal and can be rewritten to be faster. Or, if not faster, it can be split into callbacks dispatched through the event loop. We'll look at one such method in a moment.
- **Creating a backend service**: Can you imagine a backend server dedicated to calculating Fibonacci numbers? Okay, maybe not, but it's quite common to implement backend servers to offload work from frontend servers, and we will implement a backend Fibonacci server at the end of this chapter.

Algorithmic refactoring

To prove that we have an artificial problem on our hands, here is a much more efficient `Fibonacci` function:

```
exports.fibonacciLoop = function(n) {
    var fibos = [];
    fibos[0] = 0;
    fibos[1] = 1;
    fibos[2] = 1;
    for (var i = 3; i <= n; i++) {
        fibos[i] = fibos[i-2] + fibos[i-1];
    }
    return fibos[n];
}
```

If we substitute a call to `math.fibonacciLoop` in place of `math.fibonacci`, the `fibotimes` program runs much faster. Even this isn't the most efficient implementation; for example, a simple prewired lookup table is much faster at the cost of some memory.

Edit `fibotimes.js` as follows and rerun the script. The numbers will fly by so fast your head will spin:

```
for (var num = 1; num < 8000; num++) {
    let now = new Date().toISOString();
    console.log(`${now} Fibonacci for ${num} =
${math.fibonacciLoop(num)}`);
}
```

Some algorithms aren't so simple to optimize and still take a long time to calculate the result. In this section, we're exploring how to handle inefficient algorithms, and therefore will stick with the inefficient Fibonacci implementation.

It is possible to divide the calculation into chunks and then dispatch the computation of those chunks through the event loop. Add the following code to `math.js`:

```
exports.fibonacciAsync = function(n, done) {
    if (n === 0) done(undefined, 0);
    else if (n === 1 || n === 2) done(undefined, 1);
    else {
        setImmediate(() => {
            exports.fibonacciAsync(n-1, (err, val1) => {
                if (err) done(err);
                else setImmediate(() => {
                    exports.fibonacciAsync(n-2, (err, val2) => {
                        if (err) done(err);
                        else done(undefined, val1+val2);
                    });
                });
            });
        });
    }
};
```

This converts the `fibonacci` function from asynchronous function to a traditional callback-oriented asynchronous function. We're using `setImmediate` at each stage of the calculation to ensure the event loop executes regularly and that the server can easily handle other requests while churning away on a calculation. It does nothing to reduce the computation required; this is still the silly, inefficient Fibonacci algorithm. All we've done is spread the computation through the event loop.

In `fibotimes.js`, we can use this:

```js
const math = require('./math');
const util = require('util');

(async () => {
    for (var num = 1; num < 8000; num++) {
        await new Promise((resolve, reject) => {
            math.fibonacciAsync(num, (err, fibo) => {
                if (err) reject(err);
                else {
                    let now = new Date().toISOString();
                    console.log(`${now} Fibonacci for ${num} =
                    ${fibo}`);
                    resolve();
                }
            })
        })
    }
})().catch(err => { console.error(err); });
```

This version of `fibotimes.js` executes the same, we simply type `node fibotimes`. However, using `fibonacciAsync` will require changes in the server.

Because it's an asynchronous function, we will need to change our router code. Create a new file, named `routes/fibonacci-async1.js`, containing the following:

```js
const express = require('express');
const router = express.Router();

const math = require('../math');

router.get('/', function(req, res, next) {
  if (req.query.fibonum) {
    // Calculate using async-aware function, in this server
    math.fibonacciAsync(req.query.fibonum, (err, fiboval) => {
      res.render('fibonacci', {
        title: "Calculate Fibonacci numbers",
        fibonum: req.query.fibonum,
        fiboval: fiboval
      });
    });
  } else {
    res.render('fibonacci', {
      title: "Calculate Fibonacci numbers",
      fiboval: undefined
    });
  }
```

```
});

    module.exports = router;
```

This is the same as earlier, just rewritten for an asynchronous Fibonacci calculation.

In `app.js`, make this change to the application wiring:

```
// const fibonacci = require('./routes/fibonacci');
const fibonacci = require('./routes/fibonacci-async1');
```

With this change, the server no longer freezes when calculating a large Fibonacci number. The calculation of course still takes a long time, but at least other users of the application aren't blocked.

You can verify this by again opening two browser windows in the application. Enter 60 in one window, and in the other start requesting smaller Fibonacci numbers. Unlike with the original `fibonacci` function, using `fibonacciAsync` allows both windows to give answers, though if you really did enter 60 in the first window you might as well take that three-month vacation to Tibet:

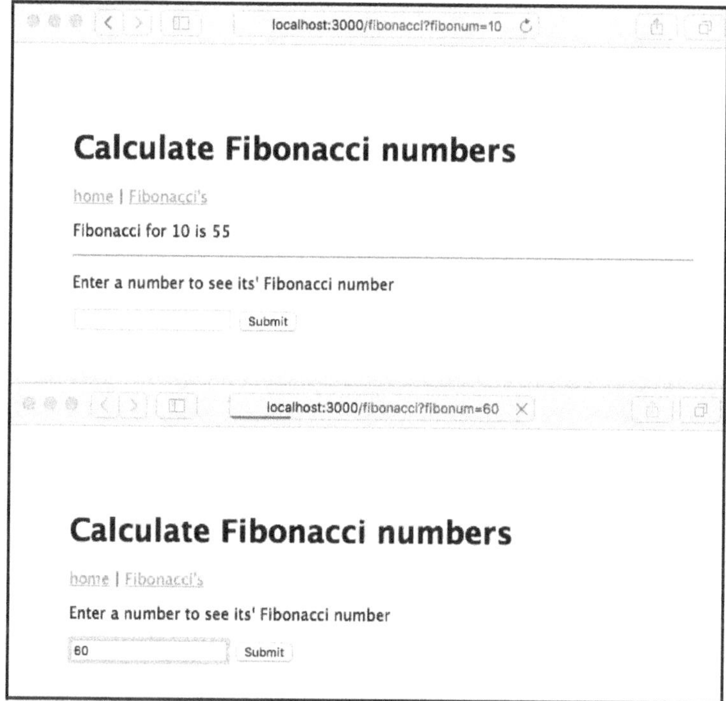

It's up to you, and your specific algorithms, to choose how to best optimize your code and to handle any long-running computations you may have.

Making HTTP Client requests

The next way to mitigate computationally intensive code is to push the calculation to a backend process. To explore that strategy, we'll request computations from a backend Fibonacci server, using the HTTP Client object to do so. However, before we look at that, let's first talk in general about using the HTTP Client object.

Node.js includes an HTTP Client object, useful for making HTTP requests. It has the capability to issue any kind of HTTP request. In this section, we'll use the HTTP Client object to make HTTP requests similar to calling a **Representational State Transfer (REST)** web service.

Let's start with some code inspired by the `wget` or `curl` commands to make HTTP requests and show the results. Create a file named `wget.js` containing this code:

```
const http = require('http');
const url = require('url');
const util = require('util');

const argUrl = process.argv[2];
const parsedUrl = url.parse(argUrl, true);

// The options object is passed to http.request
// telling it the URL to retrieve
const options = {
  host: parsedUrl.hostname,
  port: parsedUrl.port,
  path: parsedUrl.pathname,
  method: 'GET'
};

if (parsedUrl.search) options.path += "?"+parsedUrl.search;

const req = http.request(options);
// Invoked when the request is finished
req.on('response', res => {
  console.log('STATUS: ' + res.statusCode);
  console.log('HEADERS: ' + util.inspect(res.headers));
  res.setEncoding('utf8');
  res.on('data', chunk => { console.log('BODY: ' + chunk); });
  res.on('error', err => { console.log('RESPONSE ERROR: ' + err); });
```

```
});
// Invoked on errors
req.on('error', err => { console.log('REQUEST ERROR: ' + err); });
req.end();
```

You can run the script as follows:

```
$ node wget.js http://example.com
STATUS: 200
HEADERS: { 'accept-ranges': 'bytes',
  'cache-control': 'max-age=604800',
  'content-type': 'text/html',
  date: 'Sun, 10 Dec 2017 23:40:44 GMT',
  etag: '"359670651"',
  expires: 'Sun, 17 Dec 2017 23:40:44 GMT',
  'last-modified': 'Fri, 09 Aug 2013 23:54:35 GMT',
  server: 'ECS (rhv/81A7)',
  vary: 'Accept-Encoding',
  'x-cache': 'HIT',
  'content-length': '1270',
  connection: 'close' }
BODY: <!doctype html>
<html>
...
```

There's more in the printout, namely the HTML of the page at
`http://example.com/`. The purpose of `wget.js` is to make an HTTP request and
show you voluminous details of the response. An HTTP request is initiated with the
`http.request` method, as follows:

```
var http = require('http');
var options = {
  host: 'example.com',
  port: 80,
  path: null,
  method: 'GET'
};
var request = http.request(options);
request.on('response', response => {
  ...
});
```

The `options` object describes the request to make, and the `callback` function is called when the response arrives. The `options` object is fairly straightforward, with the `host`, `port`, and `path` fields specifying the URL being requested. The `method` field must be one of the HTTP verbs (`GET`, `PUT`, `POST`, and so on). You can also provide a `headers` array for the headers in the HTTP request. For example, you might need to provide a cookie:

```
var options = {
   headers: { 'Cookie': '.. cookie value' }
};
```

The `response` object is itself an `EventEmitter`, which emits the `data` and `error` events. The `data` event is called as data arrives, and the `error` event is, of course, called on errors.

The request object is a `WritableStream`, which is useful for HTTP requests containing data, such as `PUT` or `POST`. This means the `request` object has a `write` function that writes data to the requester. The data format in an HTTP request is specified by the standard **Multipurpose Internet Mail Extensions (MIME)** originally created to give us better email. Around 1992, the WWW community worked with the MIME standard committee which was developing a format for multi-part, multi-media-rich electronic mail. Receiving fancy-looking email is so commonplace today that one might not be aware that email used to be plain text. MIME-types were developed to describe the format of each piece of data, and the WWW community adopted this for use on the web. HTML forms will post with a Content-Type of `multipart/form-data`, for example.

Calling a REST backend service from an Express application

Now that we've seen how to make HTTP client requests, we can look at how to make a REST query inside an Express web application. What that effectively means is to make an HTTP `GET` request to a backend server, which responds with the Fibonacci number represented by the URL. To do so, we'll refactor the `Fibonacci` application to make a Fibonacci server that is called from the application. While this is overkill for calculating Fibonacci numbers, it lets us look at the basics of implementing a multitier application stack in Express.

Inherently, calling a REST service is an asynchronous operation. That means calling the REST service will involve a function call to initiate the request and a callback function to receive the response. REST services are accessed over HTTP, so we'll use the HTTP client object to do so.

Implementing a simple REST server with Express

While Express has a powerful templating system, making it suitable for delivering HTML web pages to browsers, it can also be used to implement a simple REST service. The parameterized URLs we showed earlier (`/user/profile/:id`) can act like parameters to a REST call. And Express makes it easy to return data encoded in JSON.

Now, create a file named `fiboserver.js` containing this code:

```
const math  = require('./math');
const express = require('express');
const logger = require('morgan');
const app = express();
app.use(logger('dev'));
app.get('/fibonacci/:n', (req, res, next) => {
    math.fibonacciAsync(Math.floor(req.params.n), (err, val) => {
        if (err) next('FIBO SERVER ERROR ' + err);
        else res.send({ n: req.params.n, result: val });
    });
});
app.listen(process.env.SERVERPORT);
```

This is a stripped-down Express application that gets right to the point of providing a Fibonacci calculation service. The one route it supports handles the Fibonacci computation using the same functions we've already worked with.

This is the first time we've seen `res.send` used. It's a flexible way to send responses which can take an array of header values (for the HTTP response header), and an HTTP status code. As used here, it automatically detects the object, formats it as JSON text, and sends it with the correct `Content-Type`.

In `package.json`, add this to the `scripts` section:

```
"server": "SERVERPORT=3002 node ./fiboserver"
```

This automates launching our Fibonacci service.

> Note that we're specifying the TCP/IP port via an environment
> variable and using that variable in the application. This is another
> aspect of the Twelve-Factor application model: to put configuration
> data in the environment.

Now, let's run it:

```
$ npm run server
> fibonacci@0.0.0 server /Users/David/chap04/fibonacci
> SERVERPORT=3002 node ./fiboserver
```

Then, in a separate command window, we can use the `curl` program to make some
requests against this service:

```
$ curl -f http://localhost:3002/fibonacci/10
{"n":"10","result":55}
$ curl -f http://localhost:3002/fibonacci/11
{"n":"11","result":89}
$ curl -f http://localhost:3002/fibonacci/12
{"n":"12","result":144}
```

Over in the window where the service is running, we'll see a log of `GET` requests and
how long each took to process:

```
$ npm run server

> fibonacci@0.0.0 server /Users/David/chap04/fibonacci
> SERVERPORT=3002 node ./fiboserver

GET /fibonacci/10 200 0.393 ms - 22
GET /fibonacci/11 200 0.647 ms - 22
GET /fibonacci/12 200 0.772 ms - 23
```

Now, let's create a simple client program, `fiboclient.js`, to programmatically call
the Fibonacci service:

```
const http = require('http');
[
  "/fibonacci/30", "/fibonacci/20", "/fibonacci/10",
  "/fibonacci/9", "/fibonacci/8", "/fibonacci/7",
  "/fibonacci/6", "/fibonacci/5", "/fibonacci/4",
  "/fibonacci/3", "/fibonacci/2", "/fibonacci/1"
].forEach(path => {
    console.log(`${new Date().toISOString()} requesting ${path}`);
    var req = http.request({
```

```
        host: "localhost",
        port: process.env.SERVERPORT,
        path: path,
        method: 'GET'
    }, res => {
        res.on('data', chunk => {
            console.log(`${new Date().toISOString()} BODY: ${chunk}`);
        });
    });
    req.end();
});
```

Then, in `package.json`, add this to the `scripts` section:

```
"scripts": {
  "start": "node ./bin/www",
  "server": "SERVERPORT=3002 node ./fiboserver" ,
  "client": "SERVERPORT=3002 node ./fiboclient"
}
```

Then run the *client* app:

```
$ npm run client

> fibonacci@0.0.0 client /Users/David/chap04/fibonacci
> SERVERPORT=3002 node ./fiboclient

2017-12-11T00:41:14.857Z requesting /fibonacci/30
2017-12-11T00:41:14.864Z requesting /fibonacci/20
2017-12-11T00:41:14.865Z requesting /fibonacci/10
2017-12-11T00:41:14.865Z requesting /fibonacci/9
2017-12-11T00:41:14.866Z requesting /fibonacci/8
2017-12-11T00:41:14.866Z requesting /fibonacci/7
2017-12-11T00:41:14.866Z requesting /fibonacci/6
2017-12-11T00:41:14.866Z requesting /fibonacci/5
2017-12-11T00:41:14.866Z requesting /fibonacci/4
2017-12-11T00:41:14.866Z requesting /fibonacci/3
2017-12-11T00:41:14.867Z requesting /fibonacci/2
2017-12-11T00:41:14.867Z requesting /fibonacci/1
2017-12-11T00:41:14.884Z BODY: {"n":"9","result":34}
2017-12-11T00:41:14.886Z BODY: {"n":"10","result":55}
2017-12-11T00:41:14.891Z BODY: {"n":"6","result":8}
2017-12-11T00:41:14.892Z BODY: {"n":"7","result":13}
2017-12-11T00:41:14.893Z BODY: {"n":"8","result":21}
2017-12-11T00:41:14.903Z BODY: {"n":"3","result":2}
2017-12-11T00:41:14.904Z BODY: {"n":"4","result":3}
2017-12-11T00:41:14.905Z BODY: {"n":"5","result":5}
2017-12-11T00:41:14.910Z BODY: {"n":"2","result":1}
```

```
2017-12-11T00:41:14.911Z BODY: {"n":"1","result":1}
2017-12-11T00:41:14.940Z BODY: {"n":"20","result":6765}
2017-12-11T00:41:18.200Z BODY: {"n":"30","result":832040}
```

We're building our way toward adding the REST service to the web application. At this point, we've proved several things, one of which is the ability to call a REST service in our program.

We also inadvertently demonstrated an issue with long-running calculations. You'll notice the requests were made from the largest to the smallest, but the results appeared in a very different order. Why? It's because of the processing time for each request, and the inefficient algorithm we're using. The computation time increases enough to ensure that the larger request values require enough processing time to reverse the order.

What happens is that `fiboclient.js` sends all its requests right away, and then each one waits for the response to arrive. Because the server is using `fibonacciAsync`, it will work on calculating all responses simultaneously. The values that are quickest to calculate are the ones that will be ready first. As the responses arrive in the client, the matching response handler fires, and in this case, the result prints to the console. The results will arrive when they're ready and not a millisecond sooner.

Refactoring the Fibonacci application for REST

Now that we've implemented a REST-based server, we can return to the `Fibonacci` application, applying what we've learned to improve it. We will lift some of the code from `fiboclient.js` and transplant it into the application to do this. Create a new file, `routes/fibonacci-rest.js`, with the following code:

```
const express = require('express');
const router = express.Router();
const http = require('http');
const math = require('../math');

router.get('/', function(req, res, next) {
  if (req.query.fibonum) {
    var httpreq = http.request({
      host: "localhost",
      port: process.env.SERVERPORT,
      path: "/fibonacci/"+Math.floor(req.query.fibonum),
      method: 'GET'
```

```
    });
    httpreq.on('response', response => {
      response.on('data', chunk => {
        var data = JSON.parse(chunk);
        res.render('fibonacci', {
          title: "Calculate Fibonacci numbers",
          fibonum: req.query.fibonum,
          fiboval: data.result
        });
      });
      response.on('error', err => { next(err); });
    });
    httpreq.on('error', err => { next(err); });
    httpreq.end();
  } else {
    res.render('fibonacci', {
      title: "Calculate Fibonacci numbers",
      fiboval: undefined
    });
  }
});

module.exports = router;
```

In `app.js`, make this change:

```
const index = require('./routes/index');
// const fibonacci = require('./routes/fibonacci');
// const fibonacci = require('./routes/fibonacci-async1');
// const fibonacci = require('./routes/fibonacci-await');
const fibonacci = require('./routes/fibonacci-rest');
```

Then, in `package.json`, change the `scripts` entry to the following:

```
"scripts": {
  "start": "DEBUG=fibonacci:* node ./bin/www",
  "startrest": "DEBUG=fibonacci:* SERVERPORT=3002 node ./bin/www",
  "server": "DEBUG=fibonacci:* SERVERPORT=3002 node ./fiboserver" ,
  "client": "DEBUG=fibonacci:* SERVERPORT=3002 node ./fiboclient"
},
```

How can we have the same value for SERVERPORT for all three `scripts` entries? The
answer is that the variable is used differently in different places. In `startrest`, that
variable is used in `routes/fibonacci-rest.js` to know at which port the REST
service is running. Likewise, in `client`, `fiboclient.js` uses that variable for the
same purpose. Finally, in `server`, the `fiboserver.js` script uses the SERVERPORT
variable to know which port to listen on.

In `start` and `startrest`, no value is given for `PORT`. In both cases, `bin/www` defaults to `PORT=3000` if it is not specified.

In one command window, start the backend server, and in the other, start the application. Open a browser window as before, and make a few requests. You should see output similar to this:

```
$ npm run server

> fibonacci@0.0.0 server /Users/David/chap04/fibonacci
> DEBUG=fibonacci:* SERVERPORT=3002 node ./fiboserver

GET /fibonacci/34 200 21124.036 ms - 27
GET /fibonacci/12 200 1.578 ms - 23
GET /fibonacci/16 200 6.600 ms - 23
GET /fibonacci/20 200 33.980 ms - 24
GET /fibonacci/28 200 1257.514 ms - 26
```

The output like this for the application:

```
$ npm run startrest

> fibonacci@0.0.0 startrest /Users/David/chap04/fibonacci
> DEBUG=fibonacci:* SERVERPORT=3002 node ./bin/www

  fibonacci:server Listening on port 3000 +0ms
GET /fibonacci?fibonum=34 200 21317.792 ms - 548
GET /stylesheets/style.css 304 20.952 ms - -
GET /fibonacci?fibonum=12 304 109.516 ms - -
GET /stylesheets/style.css 304 0.465 ms - -
GET /fibonacci?fibonum=16 200 83.067 ms - 544
GET /stylesheets/style.css 304 0.900 ms - -
GET /fibonacci?fibonum=20 200 221.842 ms - 545
GET /stylesheets/style.css 304 0.778 ms - -
GET /fibonacci?fibonum=28 200 1428.292 ms - 547
GET /stylesheets/style.css 304 19.083 ms - -
```

Because we haven't changed the templates, the screen will look exactly as it did earlier.

We may run into another problem with this solution. The asynchronous implementation of our inefficient Fibonacci algorithm may cause the Fibonacci service process to run out of memory. In the Node.js FAQ, `https://github.com/nodejs/node/wiki/FAQ`, it's suggested to use the `--max_old_space_size` flag. You'd add this in `package.json` as follows:

```
"server": "SERVERPORT=3002 node ./fiboserver --max_old_space_size
5000",
```

However, the FAQ also says that if you're running into maximum memory space problems, your application should probably be refactored. This gets back to our point several pages ago that there are several approaches to addressing performance problems, one of which is the algorithmic refactoring of your application.

Why go to the trouble of developing this REST server when we could just directly use `fibonacciAsync`?

We can now push the CPU load for this heavyweight calculation to a separate server. Doing so would preserve CPU capacity on the frontend server so it can attend to web browsers. GPU co-processors are now widely used for numerical computing and can be accessed via a simple network API. The heavy computation can be kept separate, and you can even deploy a cluster of backend servers sitting behind a load balancer, evenly distributing requests.

What we've demonstrated is that it's possible to implement simple multitier REST services in a few lines of Node.js and Express.

Some RESTful modules and frameworks

Here are a few available packages and frameworks to assist your REST-based projects:

- Restify (`>http://restify.com/`): This offers both client-side and server-side frameworks for both ends of REST transactions. The server-side API is similar to Express.
- Loopback (`http://loopback.io/`): This is an offering from StrongLoop, the current sponsor of the Express project. It offers a lot of features and is, of course, built on top of Express.

Summary

You learned a lot in this chapter about Node's HTTP support, implementing web applications, and REST service implementation.

Now we can move on to implementing a more complete application: one for taking notes. We will use the Notes application for several upcoming chapters as a vehicle to explore the Express application framework, database access, deployment to cloud services or on your own server, and user authentication.

In the next chapter, we will build the basic infrastructure.

5
Your First Express Application

Now that we've got our feet wet building an Express application for Node.js, let's work on an application that performs a useful function. The application we'll build will keep a list of notes, and it will let us explore some aspects of a real application.

In this chapter, we'll only build the basic infrastructure of the application, and in the later chapters, we'll extend the application considerably.

The topics covered in this chapter includes

- Using Promises and async functions in Express router functions
- Applying the MVC paradigm to Express applications
- Building an Express application
- JavaScript Class definitions
- Implementing the CRUD paradigm
- Handlebars templates

Promises, async functions, and Express router functions

Before we get into developing our application, we must take a deeper look at a pair of new ES-2015/2016/2017 features that collectively revolutionize JavaScript programming: The `Promise` class and `async` functions. Both are used for deferred and asynchronous computation and can make intensely nested callback a thing of the past:

- A `Promise` represents an operation that hasn't completed yet but is expected to be completed in the future. We've seen Promises in use. The `.then` or `.catch` functions are invoked when the promised result (or error) is available.
- *Generator* functions are a new kind of function that can be paused and resumed, and can return results from the middle of the function.
- Those two features were mixed with another, the iteration protocol, along with some new syntax, to create `async` functions.

The magic of `async` functions is that we can write asynchronous code as if it's synchronous code. It's still asynchronous code, meaning long-running request handlers won't block the event loop. The code looks like the synchronous code we'd write in other languages. One statement follows another, the errors are thrown as exceptions, and the results land on the next line of code. Promise and `async` functions are so much of an improvement that it's extremely compelling for the Node.js community to switch paradigms, meaning rewriting legacy callback-oriented APIs.

Over the years, several other approaches have been used to manage asynchronous code, and you may come across code using these other techniques. Before the `Promise` object was standardized, at least two implementations were available: Bluebird (`http://bluebirdjs.com/`) and Q (`https://www.npmjs.com/package/q`). Use of a non-standard Promise library should be carefully considered, since there is value in maintaining compatibility with the standard Promise object.

The **Pyramid of Doom** is named after the shape the code takes after a few layers of nesting. Any multistage process can quickly escalate to code nested 15 levels deep. Consider the following example:

```
router.get ('/path/to/something', (req, res, next) => {
  doSomething(arg1, arg2, (err, data1) => {
    if (err) return next(err);
    doAnotherThing(arg3, arg2, data1, (err2, data2) => {
      if (err2) return next(err2);
      somethingCompletelyDifferent(arg1, arg42, (err3, data3) => {
        if (err3) return next(err3);
        doSomethingElse((err4, data4) => {
          if (err4) return next(err4);
          res.render('page', { data });
        });
      });
    });
  });
});
```

Rewriting this as an `async` function will make this much clearer. To get there, we need to examine the following ideas:

- Using Promises to manage asynchronous results
- Generator functions and Promises
- `async` functions

We generate a Promise this way:

```javascript
exports.asyncFunction = function(arg1, arg2) {
  return new Promise((resolve, reject) => {
    // perform some task or computation that's asynchronous
    // for any error detected:
    if (errorDetected) return reject(dataAboutError);
    // When the task is finished
    resolve(theResult);
  });
};
```

Note that `asyncFunction` is an asynchronous function, but it does not take a callback. Instead, it returns a `Promise` object, and the asynchronous code is executed within a callback passed to the `Promise` class.

Your code must indicate the status of the asynchronous operation via the `resolve` and `reject` functions. As implied by the function names, `reject` indicates an error occurred and `resolve` indicates a success result. Your caller then uses the function as follows:

```javascript
asyncFunction(arg1, arg2)
.then((result) => {
    // the operation succeeded
    // do something with the result
    return newResult;
})
.catch(err => {
    // an error occurred
});
```

The system is fluid enough that the function passed in a `.then` can return something, such as another Promise, and you can chain the `.then` calls together. The value returned in a `.then` handler (if any) becomes a new Promise object, and in this way you can construct a chain of `.then` and `.catch` calls to manage a sequence of asynchronous operations.

A sequence of asynchronous operations would be implemented as a chain of `.then` functions, as we will see in the next section.

Promises and error handling

Promise objects can be in one of three states:

- **Pending**: This is the initial state, neither fulfilled nor rejected
- **Fulfilled**: This is the final state where it executed successfully and produced a result
- **Rejected**: This is the final state where execution failed

Consider this code segment similar to the one we'll use later in this chapter:

```
notes.read(req.query.key)
.then(note => { return filterNote(note); })
.then(note => { return swedishChefSpeak(note); })
.then(note => {
    res.render('noteview', {
        title: note ? note.title : "",
        notekey: req.query.key,
        note: note
    });
})
.catch(err => { next(err); });
```

There are several places where errors can occur in this little bit of code. The `notes.read` function has several possible failure modes: the `filterNote` function might want to raise an alarm if it detects a cross-site scripting attack. The Swedish chef could be on strike. There could be a failure in `res.render` or the template being used. But we have only one way to catch and report errors. Are we missing something?

The `Promise` class automatically captures errors, sending them down the chain of operations attached to the `Promise`. If the `Promise` class has an error on its hands, it skips over the `.then` functions and will instead invoke the first `.catch` function it finds. In other words, using instances of Promise provides a higher assurance of capturing and reporting errors. With the older convention, error reporting was trickier, and it was easy to forget to add correct error handling.

Flattening our asynchronous code

The problem being addressed is that asynchronous coding in JavaScript results in the Pyramid of Doom. To explain, let's reiterate the example Ryan Dahl gave as the primary Node.js idiom:

```
db.query('SELECT ..etc..', function(err, resultSet) {
    if (err) {
        // Instead, errors arrive here
    } else {
        // Instead, results arrive here
    }
});
// We WANT the errors or results to arrive here
```

The goal was to avoid blocking the event loop with a long operation. Deferring the processing of results or errors using callback functions was an excellent solution and is the founding idiom of Node.js. The implementation of callback functions led to this pyramid-shaped problem. Namely, that results and errors land in the callback. Rather than delivering them to the next line of code, the errors and results are buried.

Promises help flatten the code so that it no longer takes a pyramidal shape. They also capture errors, ensuring delivery to a useful location. But those errors and results are still buried inside an anonymous function and do not get delivered to the next line of code.

Further, using Promises results in a little bit of boilerplate code that obscures the programmers intent. It's less boilerplate than with regular callback functions, but the boilerplate is still there.

Fortunately, the ECMAScript committee kept working on the problem.

Promises and generators birthed async functions

Generators and the associated Iteration Protocol are a large topic, which we will briefly cover.

The Iteration Protocol is what's behind the new `for..of` loop, and some other new looping constructs. These constructs can be used with anything producing an iterator. For more about both, see `https://developer.mozilla.org/en-US/docs/Web/JavaScript/Reference/Iteration_protocols`.

A generator is a kind of function which can be stopped and started using the `yield` keyword. Generators produce an iterator whose values are whatever is given to the yield statement. For more on this, see `https://developer.mozilla.org/en-US/docs/Web/JavaScript/Reference/Global_Objects/Generator`.

Consider this:

```
$ cat gen.js
function* gen() {
    yield 1;
    yield 2;
    yield 3;
    yield 4;
}
for (let g of gen()) {
   console.log(g);
}
$ node gen.js
1
2
3
4
```

The `yield` statement causes a generator function to pause and to provide the value given to the next call on its `next` function. The `next` function isn't explicitly seen here, but is what controls the loop, and is part of the iteration protocol. Instead of the loop, try calling `gen().next()` several times:

```
var geniter = gen();
console.log(geniter.next());
console.log(geniter.next());
console.log(geniter.next());
```

You'll see this:

```
$ node gen.js
{ value: 1, done: false }
{ value: 2, done: false }
{ value: 3, done: false }
```

The Iteration protocol says the iterator is finished when `done` is `true`. In this case, we didn't call it enough to trigger the end state of the iterator.

Where generators became interesting is when used with functions that return a Promise. The Promise is what's made available through the iterator. The code consuming the iterator can wait on the Promise to get its value. A series of asynchronous operations could be inside the generator and invoked in an iterable fashion.

With the help of an extra function, a generator function along with Promise-returning asynchronous functions can be a very nice way to write asynchronous code. We saw an example of this in Chapter 2, *Setting up Node.js*, while exploring Babel. Babel has a plugin to rewrite `async` functions into a generator along with a helper function, and we took a look at the transpiled code and the helper function. The `co` library (`https:/ /www.npmjs.com/package/co`) is a popular helper function for implementing asynchronous coding in generators. Create a file named `2files.js`:

```
const fs = require('fs-extra');
const co = require('co');
const util = require('util');
co(function* () {
  var texts = [
    yield fs.readFile('hello.txt', 'utf8'),
    yield fs.readFile('goodbye.txt', 'utf8')
  ];
  console.log(util.inspect(texts));
});
```

Then run it like so:

```
$ node 2files.js
[ 'Hello, world!\n', 'Goodbye, world!\n' ]
```

Normally, `fs.readFile` sends its result to a callback function, and we'd build a little pyramid-shaped piece of code to perform this task. The `fs-extra` module contains implementations of all functions from the built-in `fs` module but changed to return a Promise instead of a callback function. Therefore, each `fs.readFile` shown here is returning a Promise that's resolved when the file content is fully read into memory. What `co` does is it manages the dance of waiting for the Promise to be resolved (or rejected), and returns the value of the Promise. Therefore, with two suitable text files we have the result shown from executing `2files.js`.

The important thing is that the code is very clean and readable. We aren't caught up in boilerplate code required to manage asynchronous operations. The intent of the programmer is pretty clear.

`async` functions take that same combination of generators and Promises and define a standardized syntax in the JavaScript language. Create a file named `2files-async.js`:

```
const fs    = require('fs-extra');
const util  = require('util');
async function twofiles() {
    var texts = [
        await fs.readFile('hello.txt', 'utf8'),
        await fs.readFile('goodbye.txt', 'utf8')
    ];
    console.log(util.inspect(texts));
}
twofiles().catch(err => { console.error(err); });
```

Then run it like so:

```
$ node 2files-async.js
[ 'Hello, world!\n', 'Goodbye, world!\n' ]
```

Clean. Readable. The intent of the programmer is clear. No dependency on an add-on library, with syntax built-in to the JavaScript language. Most importantly, everything is handled in a natural way. Errors are indicated naturally by throwing exceptions. The results of an asynchronous operation naturally appear as the result of the operation, with the `await` keyword facilitating the delivery of that result.

To see the real advantage, let's return to the Pyramid of Doom example from earlier:

```
router.get('/path/to/something', async (req, res, next) => {
    try {
        let data1 = await doSomething(req.query.arg1, req.query.arg2);
        let data2 = await doAnotherThing(req.query.arg3,
req.query.arg2,
        data1);
        let data3 = await somethingCompletelyDifferent(req.query.arg1,
req.query.arg42);
        let data4 = await doSomethingElse();
        res.render('page', { data1, data2, data3, data4 });
    } catch(err) {
        next(err);
    }
});
```

Other than the `try/catch`, this example became very clean compared to its form as a callback pyramid. All the asynchronous callback boilerplate is erased, and the intent of the programmer shines clearly.

Why was the `try`/`catch` needed? Normally, an `async` function catches thrown errors, automatically reporting them correctly. But since this example is within an Express router function, we're limited by its capabilities. Express doesn't know how to recognize an `async` function, and therefore it does not know to look for the thrown errors. Instead, we're required to `catch` them and call `next(err)`.

This improvement is only for code executing inside an `async` function. Code outside an `async` function still requires callbacks or Promises for asynchronous coding. Further, the return value of an `async` function is a Promise.

Refer to the official specification of `async` functions at `https://tc39.github.io/ecmascript-asyncawait/` for details.

Express and the MVC paradigm

Express doesn't enforce an opinion on how you should structure the Model, View, and Controller modules of your application, or whether you should follow any kind of MVC paradigm at all. As we learned in the previous chapter, the blank application created by the Express Generator provides two aspects of the MVC model:

- The `views` directory contains template files, controlling the display portion, corresponding to the View.
- The `routes` directory contains code implementing the URLs recognized by the application and coordinating the response to each URL. This corresponds to the controller.

This leaves you wondering where to put code corresponding to the model. Models hold the application data, changing it as instructed by the controller and supplying data requested by View code. At a minimum, the Model code should be in separate modules from the Controller code. This is to ensure a clean separation of concerns, for example, to ease the unit testing of each.

The approach we'll use is to create a `models` directory as a sibling of the `views` and `routes` directories. The `models` directory will hold modules for storing the notes and related data. The API of the modules in the `models` directory will provide functions to create, read, update, or delete data items **Create, Read, Update**, and **Delete** or **Destroy (CRUD** model) and other functions necessary for the View code to do its thing.

The CRUD model (create, read, update, destroy) is the four basic operations of persistent data storage. The `Notes` application is structured as a CRUD application to demonstrate implementing each of these operations.

We'll use functions named `create`, `read`, `update`, and `destroy` to implement each of the basic operations.

We're using the verb `destroy` rather than `delete`, because `delete` is a reserved word in JavaScript.

Creating the Notes application

Let's start creating the *Notes* application as before, by using the Express generator to give us a starting point:

```
$ mkdir notes
$ cd notes
$ npm install express-generator@4.x
$ ./node_modules/.bin/express --view=hbs --git .
destination is not empty, continue? [y/N] y

   create : .
   create : ./package.json
   create : ./app.js
   create : ./.gitignore
   create : ./public
   create : ./routes
   create : ./routes/index.js
   create : ./routes/users.js
   create : ./views
   create : ./views/index.hbs
   create : ./views/layout.hbs
   create : ./views/error.hbs
   create : ./bin
   create : ./bin/www
   create : ./public/stylesheets
   create : ./public/stylesheets/style.css

install dependencies:
   $ cd . && npm install

run the app:
   $ DEBUG=notes:* npm start
```

```
      create : ./public/javascripts
      create : ./public/images
$ npm install
added 82 packages and removed 5 packages in 97.188s
$ npm uninstall express-generator
up to date in 8.325s
```

If you wish, you can run `npm start` and view the blank application in your browser. Instead, let's move on to setting up the code.

Your first Notes model

Create a directory named `models`, as a sibling of the `views` and `routes` directories.

Then, create a file named `Note.js` in that directory, and put this code in it:

```
const _note_key = Symbol('key');
const _note_title = Symbol('title');
const _note_body = Symbol('body');

module.exports = class Note {
    constructor(key, title, body) {
        this[_note_key] = key;
        this[_note_title] = title;
        this[_note_body] = body;
    }

    get key() { return this[_note_key]; }
    get title() { return this[_note_title]; }
    set title(newTitle) { this[_note_title] = newTitle; }
    get body() { return this[_note_body]; }
    set body(newBody) { this[_note_body] = newBody; }
};
```

This defines a new class, `Note`, for use within our `Notes` application. The intent is to hold data related to notes being exchanged between users of our application.

Understanding ES-2015 class definitions

This sort of object class definition is new to JavaScript with ES-2015. It simplifies defining classes over previous methods and brings JavaScript class definitions closer to the syntax in other languages. Under the hood, JavaScript classes still use prototype-based inheritance, but with a simpler syntax, and the coder doesn't even have to think about the object prototype.

We can reliably determine whether an object is a note with the `instanceof` operator:

```
$ node
> const Note = require('./Note');
> typeof Note
'function'
> const aNote = new Note('foo', 'The Rain In Spain', 'Falls mainly on
the plain');
> var notNote = {}
> notNote instanceof Note
false
> aNote instanceof Note
true
> typeof aNote
'object'
```

This shows us the clearest method to identify an object is with the `instanceof` operator. The `typeof` operator informs us `Note` is a function (because of the prototype-based inheritance behind the scenes), and that an instance of the `Note` class is an object. With instance of, we can easily determine whether an object is an instance of a given class.

With the Note class, we have used `Symbol` instances to provide a small measure of data hiding. JavaScript classes don't provide a data-hiding mechanism—you can't label a field `private` as you can in Java, for example. It's useful to know how to hide implementation details. This is an important attribute of object-oriented programming, because it's useful to have the freedom to change the implementation at will. And there's the issue of controlling which code can manipulate the object's fields.

First, we declared getter and setter functions to provide access to the values. We went over normal getter/setter usage in `Chapter 4`, *HTTP Servers and Clients*.

Access to a getter-based field is by using the name of the property, and not by calling a function - `aNote.title` and not `aNote.title()`. It looks like you're accessing an object property by assigning a value or accessing the value. In actuality, the function defined in the class is executed on every access. You can define a read-only property by only implementing a getter, and no setter, as we did with the `key` field.

There are significant differences between the preceding and simply defining anonymous objects:

```
{
    key: 'foo', title: 'The Rain in Spain',
    body: 'Falls mainly on the plain'
}
```

We write code like that in JavaScript all the time. It's easy, it's quick, and it's a very fluid way to share data between functions. But there's no measure of hiding implementation details, and no clear identification of object type.

In the `Note` class, we could have used this `constructor` method:

```
class Note {
  constructor(key, title, body) {
      this.key = key;
      this.title = title;
      this.body = body;
  }
}
```

That's effectively the same as the anonymous object, in that no details have been hidden and no control is implemented in terms of which code can do what to object instances. The only advantage over an anonymous object is using the `instanceof` operator to identify object instances.

The method we chose uses the Symbol class, which is also new with ES-2015. A Symbol is an opaque object with two main use cases:

- Generating unique keys to use as property fields—as in the previous `Note` class
- Symbolic identifiers that you can use for concepts like COLOR_RED

You define a Symbol through a factory method that generates `Symbol` instances:

```
> let symfoo = Symbol('foo')
```

Each time you invoke the Symbol factory method, a new and unique instance is created. For example, `Symbol('foo') === Symbol('foo')` is `false`, as is `symfoo === Symbol('foo')`, because a new instance is created on each side of the equality operator. However, `symfoo === symfoo` is true, because they are the same instance.

What this means in practice is that if we try a direct approach to access a field, it fails:

```
> aNote[Symbol('title')]
undefined
```

Remember that each time we use the Symbol factory method we get a new instance. The new instance of `Symbol('title')` is not the same instance used within the `Note.js` module.

The bottom line is that using `Symbol` objects for the fields provides a small measure of implementation hiding.

Filling out the in-memory Notes model

Create a file named `notes-memory.js` in the `models` directory, with this code:

```js
const Note = require('./Note');

var notes = [];

exports.update = exports.create = async function(key, title, body) {
    notes[key] = new Note(key, title, body);
    return notes[key];
};

exports.read = async function(key) {
    if (notes[key]) return notes[key];
    else throw new Error(`Note ${key} does not exist`);
};

exports.destroy = async function(key) {
    if (notes[key]) {
        delete notes[key];
    } else throw new Error(`Note ${key} does not exist`);
};

exports.keylist = async function() { return Object.keys(notes); };
exports.count = async function() { return notes.length; };
exports.close = async function() { }
```

This is a simple in-memory data store that's fairly self-explanatory. The `key` for each Note instance is used as the index to an array, which in turn holds the Note instance. Simple, fast, and easy to implement. It does not support any long-term data persistence. Any data stored in this model will disappear when the server is killed.

We have used `async` functions because in the future we'll be storing data in the file system or in databases. Therefore, we need an asynchronous API.

The `create` and `update` functions are being handled by the same function. At this stage of the Notes application, the code for both these functions can be exactly the same because they perform the exact same operation. Later, when we add database support to Notes, the `create` and `update` functions will need to be different. For example, in a SQL data model, `create` would be implemented with an `INSERT INTO` command, while `update` would be implemented with an `UPDATE` command.

The Notes home page

We're going to modify the starter application to support creating, editing, updating, viewing, and deleting notes. Let's start by fixing up the home page. It should show a list of notes, and the top navigation bar should link to an **ADD Note** page so that we can always add a new note.

While we will be modifying the generated `app.js`, it needs no modification to support the home page. These lines of code are related to the home page:

```
const index = require('./routes/index');
..
app.use('/', index);
```

Additionally, to support Handlebars templates `app.js` requires these changes:

```
const hbs = require('hbs');
...
app.set('view engine', 'hbs');
hbs.registerPartials(path.join(__dirname, 'partials'));
```

We'll put Handlebars `partials` in a directory, `partials`, which is a sibling to the `views` directory. Change `routes/index.js` to this:

```
const express = require('express');
const router = express.Router();
const notes = require('../models/notes-memory');

/* GET home page. */
router.get('/', async (req, res, next) => {
  let keylist = await notes.keylist();
  let keyPromises = keylist.map(key => {
    return notes.read(key)
  });
  let notelist = await Promise.all(keyPromises);
  res.render('index', { title: 'Notes', notelist: notelist });
});

module.exports = router;
```

This gathers data about the notes that we'll be displaying on the home page. By default, we'll show a simple table of note titles. We do need to talk about the technique.

The `Promise.all` function executes an array of Promises. The Promises are evaluated in parallel, allowing our code to potentially make parallel requests to a service. This should execute more quickly than making the requests one at a time sequentially.

We could have written a simple `for` loop like so:

```
let keylist = await notes.keylist();
let notelist = [];
for (key of keylist) {
    let note = await notes.read(keylist);
    notelist.push({ key: note.key, title: note.title });
}
```

While simpler to read, the notes are retrieved one at a time with no opportunity to overlap `read` operations.

The Promise array is constructed using the `map` function. With `map`, one iterates over an array to produce a new array. In this case, the new array contains the Promises generated by the `notes.read` function calls.

Because we wrote `await Promise.all`, the `notelist` array will be completely filled with the correct data once all the Promises succeed. If any Promise fails—is rejected, in other words—an exception will be thrown instead. What we've done is enqueue a list of asynchronous operations and neatly waited for them all to finish.

The `notelist` array is then passed into the `view` templates we're about to write.

Start with `views/layout.hbs`, containing:

```
<!DOCTYPE html>
<html>
 <head>
 <title>{{title}}</title>
 <link rel='stylesheet' href='/stylesheets/style.css' />
 </head>
  <body>
  {{> header }}
  {{{body}}}
  </body>
</html>
```

This is the generated file, with the addition of a partial for the page header. We already declared `partials` to live in the `partials` directory. Create `partials/header.hbs`, containing:

```
<header>
 <h1>{{ title }}</h1>
  <div class='navbar'>
  <p><a href='/'>Home</a> | <a href='/notes/add'>ADD Note</a></p>
  </div>
</header>
```

Change `views/index.hbs` to this:

```
{{#each notelist}}
<ul>
  <li>{{ key }}:
  <a href="/notes/view?key={{ key }}">{{ title }}</a>
  </li>
</ul>
{{/each}}
```

This simply steps through the array of note data and formats a simple listing. Each item links to the `/notes/view` URL with a `key` parameter. We have yet to look at that code, but this URL will obviously display the note. Another thing of note is that no HTML for the list is generated if the `notelist` is empty.

There's of course a whole lot more that could be put into this. For example, it's easy to add jQuery support to every page just by adding the appropriate `script` tags here.

We now have enough written to run the application; let's view the home page:

```
$ DEBUG=notes:* npm start

> notes@0.0.0 start /Users/David/chap05/notes
> node ./bin/www

  notes:server Listening on port 3000 +0ms
GET / 200 87.300 ms - 308
GET /stylesheets/style.css 200 27.744 ms - 111
```

If we visit `http://localhost:3000`, we will see the following page:

Because there aren't any notes (yet), there's nothing to show. Clicking on the **Home** link just refreshes the page. Clicking on the **ADD Note** link throws an error because we haven't (yet) implemented that code. This shows that the provided error handler in `app.js` is performing as expected.

Adding a new note – create

Now, let's look at creating notes. Because the application doesn't have a route configured for the `/notes/add` URL, we must add one. To do that, we need a controller for the notes.

In `app.js`, make the following changes.

Comment out these lines:

```
// var users = require('./routes/users');
..
// app.use('/users', users);
```

At this stage, the `Notes` application does not support users, and these routes are not required. That will change in a future chapter.

What we really need to do is add code for the `notes` controller:

```
// const users = require('./routes/users');
const notes  = require('./routes/notes');
..
// app.use('/users', users);
app.use('/notes', notes);
```

Now, we'll add a Controller module containing the `notes` router. Create a file named `routes/notes.js`, with this content:

```
const util = require('util');
const express = require('express');
const router = express.Router();
const notes = require('../models/notes-memory');

// Add Note.
router.get('/add', (req, res, next) => {
    res.render('noteedit', {
        title: "Add a Note",
        docreate: true,
        notekey: "", note: undefined
    });
});

module.exports = router;
```

The resulting `/notes/add` URL corresponds to the link in `partials/header.hbs`.

In the `views` directory, add a template named `noteedit.hbs`, containing the following:

```
<form method='POST' action='/notes/save'>
<input type='hidden' name='docreate' value='<%=
                docreate ? "create" : "update"%>'>
<p>Key:
{{#if docreate }}
    <input type='text' name='notekey' value=''/>
{{else}}
    {{#if note }}{{notekey}}{{/if}}
    <input type='hidden' name='notekey'
        value='{{#if note }}{{notekey}}{{/if}}'/>
{{/if}}
</p>
<p>Title: <input type='text' name='title'
        value='{{#if note }}{{note.title}}{{/if}}' /></p>
<br/><textarea rows=5 cols=40 name='body' >
    {{#if note }}{{note.body}}{{/if}}
    </textarea>
<br/><input type='submit' value='Submit' />
</form>
```

We'll be reusing this template to support both editing notes and creating new ones.

Notice that the `note` and `notekey` objects passed to the template are empty in this case. The template detects this condition and ensures the input areas are empty. Additionally, a flag, `docreate`, is passed in so that the form records whether it is being used to create or update a note. At this point, we're adding a new note, so no note object exists. The template code is being written defensively to not throw errors.

This template is a form that will POST its data to the /notes/save URL. If you were to run the application at this time, it would give you an error message because no route is configured for that URL.

To support the `/notes/save` URL, add this to `routes/notes.js`:

```
// Save Note (update)
router.post('/save', async (req, res, next) => {
    var note;
    if (req.body.docreate === "create") {
        note = await notes.create(req.body.notekey,
                req.body.title, req.body.body);
    } else {
        note = await notes.update(req.body.notekey,
                req.body.title, req.body.body);
    }
    res.redirect('/notes/view?key='+ req.body.notekey);
});
```

Because this URL will also be used for both creating and updating notes, it needs to detect the `docreate` flag and call the appropriate model operation.

The model returns a Promise for both `notes.create` and `notes.update`. Of course, we must call the corresponding Model function based on the `docreate` flag.

This is a `POST` operation handler. Because of the `bodyParser` middleware, the form data is added to the `req.body` object. The fields attached to `req.body` correspond directly to elements in the HTML form.

Now, we can run the application again and use the **Add a Note** form:

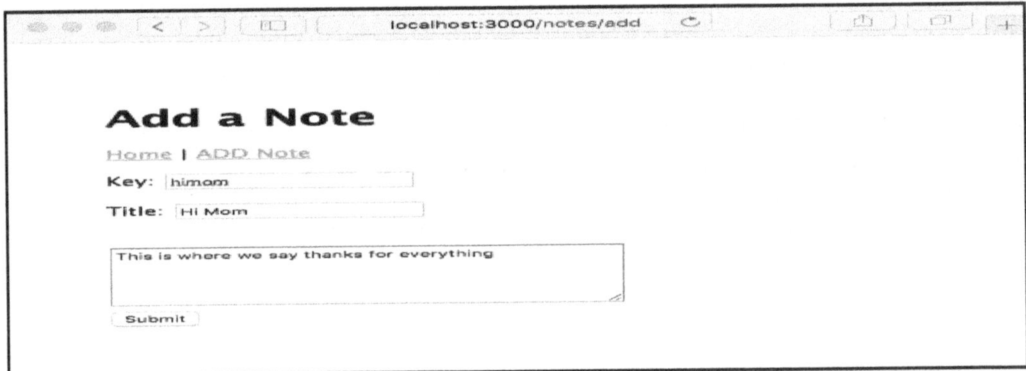

But upon clicking on the **Submit** button, we get an error message. There isn't anything, yet, implementing the `/notes/view` URL.

You can modify the URL in the location box to revisit `http://localhost:3000`, and you'll see something like the following screenshot on the home page:

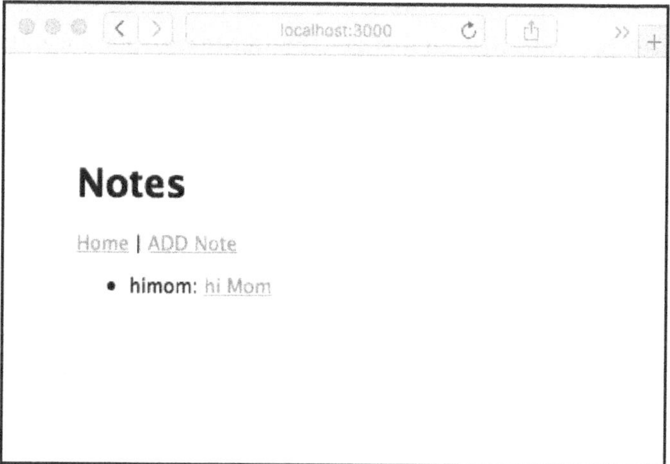

The note is actually there; we just need to implement `/notes/view`. Let's get on with that.

Viewing notes – read

Now that we've looked at how to create notes, we need to move on to reading them. This means implementing controller logic and view templates for the `/notes/view` URL.

To `routes/notes.js`, add this router function:

```
// Read Note (read)
router.get('/view', async (req, res, next) => {
    var note = await notes.read(req.query.key);
    res.render('noteview', {
        title: note ? note.title : "",
        notekey: req.query.key, note: note
    });
});
```

Because this route is mounted on a router handling `/notes`, this route handles `/notes/view`.

If `notes.read` successfully reads the note, it is rendered with the `noteview` template. If something goes wrong, we'll instead display an error to the user through Express.

To the `views` directory, add the `noteview.hbs` template, referenced by this code:

```
{{#if note}}<h3>{{ note.title }}</h3>{{/if}}
{{#if note}}<p>{{ note.body }}</p>{{/if}}
<p>Key: {{ notekey }}</p>
{{#if notekey }}
    <hr/>
    <p><a href="/notes/destroy?key={{notekey}}">Delete</a>
     | <a href="/notes/edit?key={{notekey}}">Edit</a></p>
{{/if}}
```

This is straightforward: taking data out of the note object and displaying using HTML. At the bottom are two links, one to `/notes/destroy` to delete the note and the other to `/notes/edit` to edit it.

The code for neither of these exists at the moment. But that won't stop us from going ahead and executing the application:

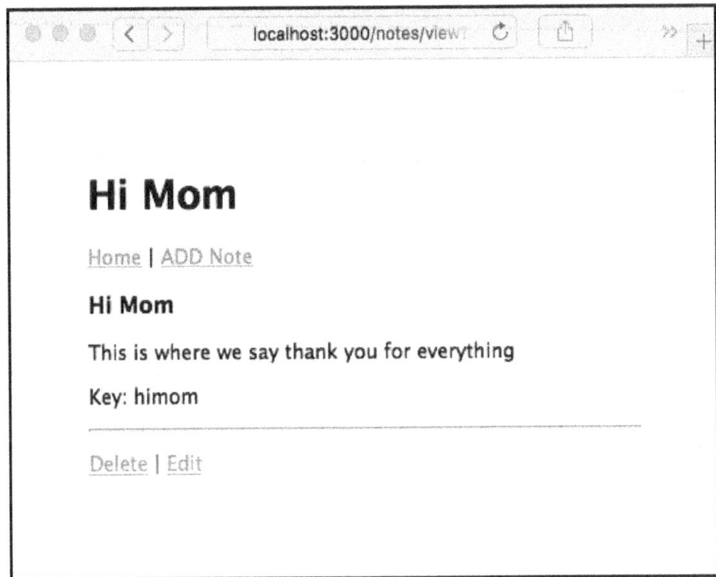

As expected, with this code, the application correctly redirects to `/notes/view`, and we can see our handiwork. Also, as expected, clicking on either the **Delete** or **Edit** links will give you an error, because the code hasn't been implemented.

Editing an existing note – update

Now that we've looked at the `create` and `read` operations, let's look at how to update or edit a note.

To `routes/notes.js`, add this router function:

```
// Edit note (update)
router.get('/edit', async (req, res, next) => {
    var note = await notes.read(req.query.key);
    res.render('noteedit', {
        title: note ? ("Edit " + note.title) : "Add a Note",
        docreate: false,
        notekey: req.query.key, note: note
    });
});
```

We're reusing the `noteedit.ejs` template, because it can be used for both `create` and `update`/`edit` operations. Notice that we pass `false` for `docreate`, informing the template that it is to be used for editing.

In this case, we first retrieve the note object and then pass it through to the template. This way, the template is set up for editing rather than note creation. When the user clicks on the **Submit** button, we'll end up in the same `/notes/save` route handler shown in the preceding screenshot. It already does the right thing: calling the `notes.update` method in the model rather than `notes.create`.

Because that's all we need do, we can go ahead and rerun the application:

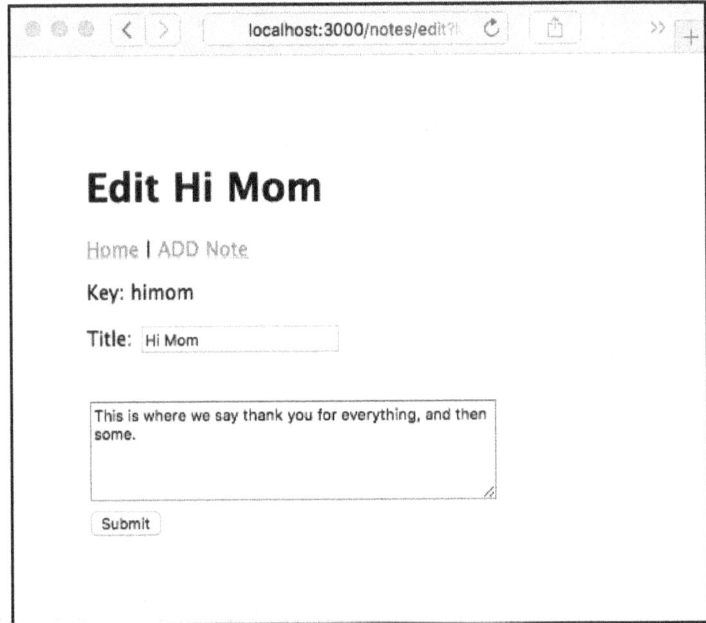

Click on the **Submit** button here, and you will be redirected to the /notes/view screen and will then be able to read the newly edited note. Back to the /notes/view screen: we've just taken care of the **Edit** link, but the **Delete** link still produces an error.

Deleting notes – destroy

Now, let's look at how to implement the /notes/destroy URL to delete notes.

To routes/notes.js, add the following router function:

```
// Ask to Delete note (destroy)
router.get('/destroy', async (req, res, next) => {
    var note = await notes.read(req.query.key);
    res.render('notedestroy', {
        title: note ? note.title : "",
        notekey: req.query.key, note: note
    });
});
```

Destroying a note is a significant step if only because there's no trash can to retrieve it from if we make a mistake. Therefore, we want to ask the user whether they're sure they want to delete that note. In this case, we retrieve the note and then render the following page, displaying a question to ensure they do want to delete the note.

To the `views` directory, add a `notedestroy.hbs` template:

```
<form method='POST' action='/notes/destroy/confirm'>
<input type='hidden' name='notekey' value='{{#if
note}}{{notekey}}{{/if}}'>
<p>Delete {{note.title}}?</p>
<br/><input type='submit' value='DELETE' />
<a href="/notes/view?key={{#if note}}{{notekey}}{{/if}}">Cancel</a>
</form>
```

This is a simple form, asking the user to confirm by clicking on the button. The **Cancel** link just sends them back to the `/notes/view` page. Clicking on the **Submit** button generates a `POST` request on the `/notes/destroy/confirm` URL.

That URL needs a request handler. Add this code to `routes/notes.js`:

```
// Really destroy note (destroy)
router.post('/destroy/confirm', async (req, res, next) => {
    await notes.destroy(req.body.notekey);
    res.redirect('/');
});
```

This calls the `notes.destroy` function in the model. If it succeeds, the browser is redirected to the home page. If not, an error message is shown to the user. Rerunning the application, we can now view it in action:

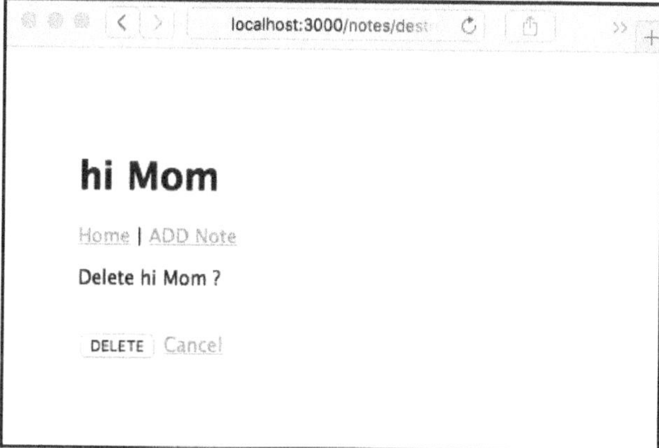

Now that everything is working in the application, you can click on any button or link and keep all the notes you want.

Theming your Express application

The Express team has done a decent job of making sure Express applications look okay out of the gate. Our Notes application won't win any design awards, but at least it isn't ugly. There's a lot of ways to improve it, now that the basic application is running. Let's take a quick look at theming an Express application. In Chapter 6, *Implementing the Mobile-First Paradigm*, we'll take a deeper dive, focusing on that all-important goal of addressing the mobile market.

If you're running the *Notes* application using the recommended method, `npm start`, a nice log of activity is being printed in your console window. One of those is the following:

```
GET /stylesheets/style.css 304 0.702 ms - -
```

This is due to this line of code that we put in `layout.hbs`:

```
<link rel='stylesheet' href='/stylesheets/style.css' />
```

This file was autogenerated for us by the Express Generator at the outset and dropped inside the `public` directory. The `public` directory is managed by the Express static file server, using this line in `app.js`:

```
app.use(express.static(path.join(__dirname, 'public')));
```

Let's open `public/stylesheets/style.css` and take a look:

```css
body {
  padding: 50px;
  font: 14px "Lucida Grande", Helvetica, Arial, sans serif;
}

a {
  color: #00B7FF;
}
```

Something that leaps out is that the application content has a lot of white space at the top and left-hand sides of the screen. The reason is that `body` tags have the `padding: 50px` style. Changing it is quick business.

Since there is no caching in the Express static file server, we can simply edit the CSS file and reload the page, and the CSS will be reloaded as well. It's possible to turn on cache-control headers and ETags generation, as you would do for a production website. Look in the online Express documentation for details.

It involves a little bit of work:

```css
body {
  padding: 5px;
  ..
}
..
header {
    background: #eeeeee;
    padding: 5px;
}
```

As a result, we'll have this:

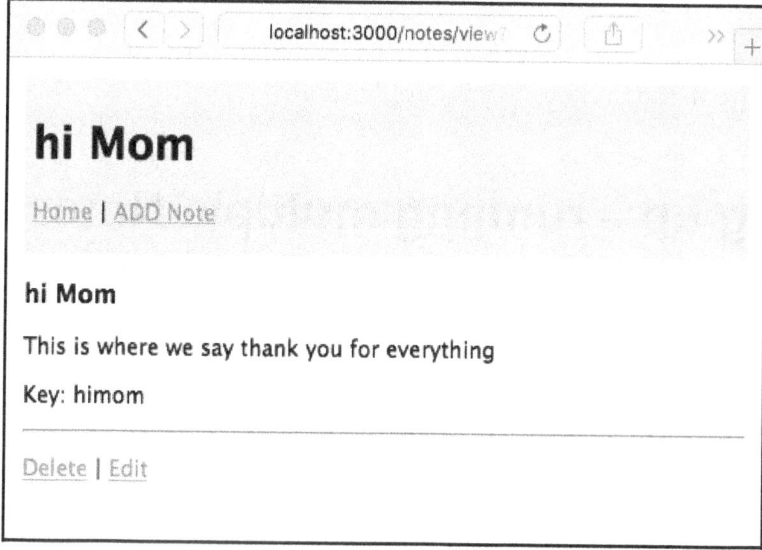

We're not going to win any design awards with this either, but there's the beginning of some branding and theming possibilities.

Generally speaking, the way we've structured the page templates, applying a site-wide theme is just a matter of adding appropriate code to `layout.hbs` along with appropriate stylesheets and other assets. Many of the modern theming frameworks, such as Twitter's Bootstrap, serve up CSS and JavaScript files out of a CDN server, making it incredibly easy to incorporate into a site design.

For jQuery, refer to `http://jquery.com/download/`.

Google's Hosted Libraries service provides a long list of libraries, hosted on Google's CDN infrastructure. Refer to `https://developers.google.com/speed/libraries/`.

While it's straightforward to use third-party CDNs to host these assets, it's safer to host them yourself. Not only do you take responsibility for bandwidth consumption of your application, but you're certain of not being affected by any outages of third-party services. As reliable as Google might be, their service can go down, and if that means jQuery and Bootstrap doesn't load, your customer will think your site is broken. But if those files are loaded from the same server as your application, the reliability of delivering those files will exactly equal the reliability of your application.

In `Chapter 6`, *Implementing the Mobile-First Paradigm*, we will look at a simple method to add those front-end libraries to your application.

Scaling up – running multiple Notes instances

Now that we've got ourselves a running application, you'll have played around a bit and created, read, updated, and deleted many notes.

Suppose for a moment this isn't a toy application, but one that is interesting enough to draw a million users a day. Serving a high load typically means adding servers, load balancers, and many other things. A core part is to have multiple instances of the application running at the same time to spread the load.

Let's see what happens when you run multiple instances of the Notes application at the same time.

The first thing is to make sure the instances are on different ports. In `bin/www`, you'll see that setting the `PORT` environment variable controls the port being used. If the `PORT` variable is not set, it defaults to `http://localhost:3000`, or what we've been using all along.

Let's open up `package.json` and add these lines to the `scripts` section:

```
"scripts": {
    "start": "DEBUG=notes:* node ./bin/www",
    "server1": "DEBUG=notes:* PORT=3001 node ./bin/www",
    "server2": "DEBUG=notes:* PORT=3002 node ./bin/www" },
```

The `server1` script runs on `PORT` `3001`, while the `server2` script runs on `PORT` `3002`. Isn't it nice to have all this documented in one place?

Then, in one command window, run this:

```
$ npm run server1

> notes@0.0.0 server1 /Users/David/chap05/notes
> DEBUG=notes:* PORT=3001 node ./bin/www

  notes:server Listening on port 3001 +0ms
```

In another command window, run this:

```
$ npm run server2

> notes@0.0.0 server2 /Users/David/chap05/notes
> DEBUG=notes:* PORT=3002 node ./bin/www

  notes:server Listening on port 3002 +0ms
```

This gives us two instances of the Notes application. Use two browser windows to visit `http://localhost:3001` and `http://localhost:3002`. Enter a couple of notes, and you might see something like this:

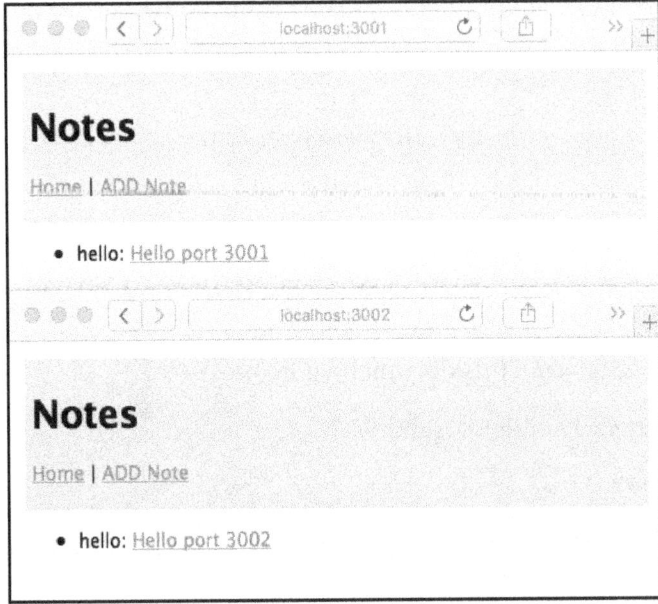

After editing and adding some notes, your two browser windows could look like the preceding screenshot. The two instances do not share the same data pool. Each is instead running in its own process and memory space. You add a note in one, and it does not show in the other screen.

Additionally, because the model code does not persist data anywhere, the notes are not saved. You might have written the greatest Node.js programming book of all time, but as soon as the application server restarts, it's gone.

Typically, you run multiple instances of an application to scale performance. That's the old *throw more servers at it* trick. For this to work, the data of course must be shared, and each instance must access the same data source. Typically, this involves a database. And when it comes to user identity information, it might even entail armed guards.

Hold on—we'll get to database implementation shortly. Before that, we'll cover mobile-first development.

Summary

We've come a long way in this chapter.

We started with the Pyramid of Doom and how the `Promise` object and `async` functions can help us a tame asynchronous code. We'll be using these techniques all through this book.

We quickly moved on to writing the foundation of a real application with Express. At the moment, it keeps its data in memory, but it has the basic functionality of what will become a note-taking application supporting real-time collaborative commenting on the notes.

In the next chapter, we'll dip our toes in the water of responsive, mobile-friendly web design. Due to the growing popularity of mobile computing devices, it's become necessary to address mobile devices first before desktop computer users. In order to reach those millions of users a day, the Notes application users need a good user experience when using their smartphone.

In following chapters, we'll keep growing the capabilities of the Notes application, starting with database storage models.

6
Implementing the Mobile-First Paradigm

Now that our first Express application is usable, we act on the mantra of this age of software development: mobile-first. Mobile devices, whether they be smartphones, tablet computers, automobile dashboards, refrigerator doors, or bathroom mirrors, are taking over the world.

Another issue is mobile-first indexing, meaning that search engines are starting to preference indexing the mobile version of a website. Search engines so far concentrated on indexing the desktop version of websites, but the growing popularity of mobile devices means search engine results are skewed away from what folks are using. Google says it is not fair to mobile users if the search result, which was derived from the desktop version, does not match the mobile version of a website. For Google's take, including technical tips on the markup to use, see `http://webmasters.googleblog.com/2017/12/getting-your-site-ready-for-mobile.html`.

The primary considerations in designing for mobiles are the small screen sizes, the touch-oriented interaction, that there's no mouse, and the somewhat different user interface expectations. With the *Notes* application, our user interface needs are modest, and the lack of a mouse doesn't make any difference to us.

In this chapter, we won't do much Node.js development. Instead, we'll:

- Modify the templates for better mobile presentation
- Edit CSS and SASS files to customize the style
- Learn about Bootstrap 4, a popular framework for responsive UI design

By doing so, we'll dip our toes in the water of what it means to be a full stack web engineer.

Problem – the Notes app isn't mobile friendly

Let's start by quantifying the problem. We need to explore how well (or not) the application behaves on a mobile device. This is simple to do:

1. Start the *Notes* application. Determine the IP address of the host system.
2. Using your mobile device, connect to the service using the IP address, and browse around the *Notes* application, putting it through its paces, noting any difficulties.

Another way to approach this is to use your desktop browser, resizing it to be very narrow. The Chrome DevTools also includes a mobile device emulator. Either way, you can mimic the small screen size of a smartphone on your desktop.

To see a real user interface problem on a mobile screen, edit `views/noteedit.ejs` and change this line:

```
<br/><textarea rows=5 cols=80 name='body' >
    {{#if note }}{{note.body}}{{/if}}
    </textarea>
```

What's changed is the `cols=80` parameter. We want this `textarea` element to be overly large so that you can experience how a non-responsive web app appears on a mobile device. View the application on a mobile device and you'll see something like one of the screens in this screenshot:

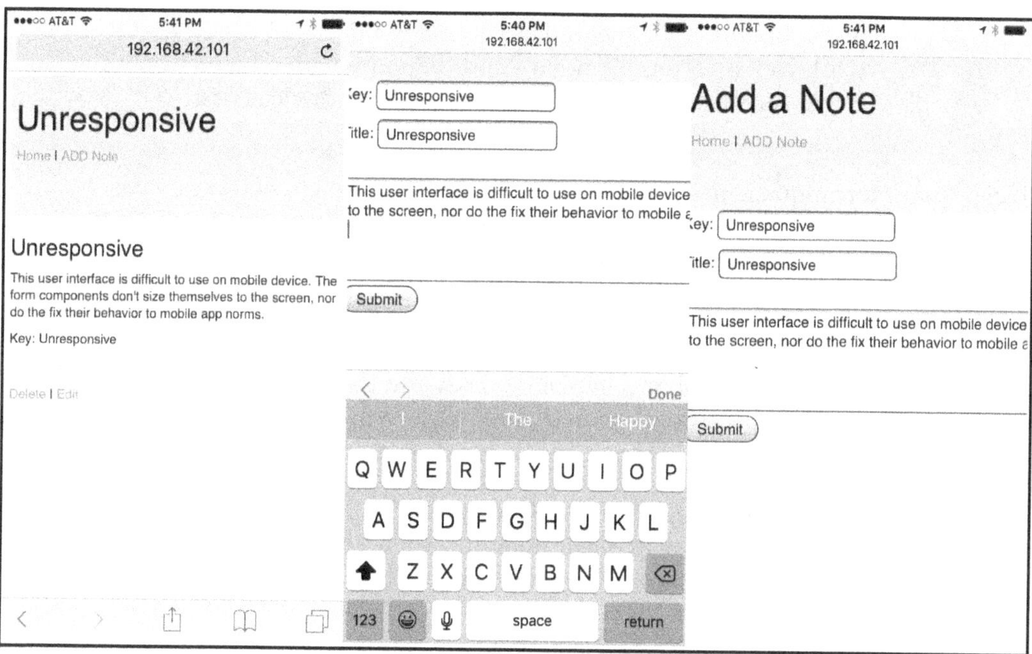

Viewing a note works well on an iPhone 6, but the screen for editing/adding a note is not good. The text entry area is so wide that it runs off the side of the screen. Even though interaction with FORM elements work well, it's clumsy. In general, browsing the *Notes* application gives an acceptable mobile user experience that doesn't suck and won't make our users give rave reviews.

Mobile-first paradigm

Mobile devices have a smaller screen, are generally touch oriented, and have different user experience expectations than a desktop computer.

To accommodate smaller screens, we use **responsive web design** techniques. This means designing the application to accommodate the screen size and ensuring websites provide optimal viewing and interaction across a wide range of devices. Techniques include changing font sizes, rearranging elements on the screen, using collapsible elements that open when touched, and resizing images or videos to fit available space. This is called **responsive** because the application responds to device characteristics by making these changes.

By mobile-first, we mean that you design the application first to work well on a mobile device and then move on to devices with larger screens. It's about prioritizing mobile devices first.

The primary technique is using media queries in stylesheets to detect device characteristics. Each media query section targets a range of devices, using CSS declaration to appropriately restyle content.

Let's consult a concrete example. The **Twenty Twelve** theme for Wordpress has a straightforward responsive design implementation. It's not built with any framework, so you can see clearly how the mechanism works, and the stylesheet is small enough to be easily digestible. Refer to its source code in the Wordpress repository at `https://themes.svn.wordpress.org/twentytwelve/1.9/style.css`.

The stylesheet starts with a number of **resets**, where the stylesheet overrides some typical browser style settings with clear defaults. Then, the bulk of the stylesheet defines styling for mobile devices. Toward the bottom of the stylesheet is a section labeled **Media queries** where, for certain sized screens, the styles defined for mobile devices are overridden to work on devices with larger screens.

It does this with the following two media queries:

```css
@media screen and (min-width: 600px) { /* Screens above 600px width */
}
@media screen and (min-width: 960px) { /* Screens above 960px width */
}
```

The first segment of the stylesheet configures the page layout for all devices. Next, for any browser viewport at least `600px` wide, reconfigure the page to display on the larger screen. Then, for any browser viewport at least `960px` wide, reconfigure it again. The stylesheet has a final media query to cover print devices.

These widths are what's called a **breakpoint**. Those threshold viewport widths are where the design changes itself around. You can see breakpoints in action by going to any responsive website, then resizing the browser window. Watch how the design jumps at certain sizes. Those are the breakpoints chosen by the author of that website.

There's a wide range of differing opinions about the best strategy to choose your breakpoints. Do you target specific devices or do you target general characteristics? The Twenty Twelve theme did fairly well on mobile devices using only two viewport-size media queries. The CSS-Tricks blog has posted an extensive list of specific media queries for every known device, which is available at `https://css-tricks.com/snippets/css/media-queries-for-standard-devices/`.

We should at least target these devices:

- **Small**: This includes iPhone 5 SE.
- **Medium**: This can refer to tablet computers or the larger smartphones.
- **Large**: This includes larger tablet computers or the smaller desktop computers.
- **Extra-large**: This refers to larger desktop computers and other large screens.
- **Landscape/portrait**: You may want to create a distinction between landscape mode and portrait mode. Switching between the two of course changes viewport width, possibly pushing it past a breakpoint. However, your application may need to behave differently in the two modes.

Enough with the theory; let's get back to our code.

Using Twitter Bootstrap on the Notes application

Bootstrap is a mobile-first framework consisting of HTML5, CSS3, and JavaScript code providing a comprehensive set of world class, responsive web design components. It was developed by engineers at Twitter and then released to the world in August 2011.

The framework includes code to retrofit modern features onto older browsers, a responsive 12-column grid system, and a long list of components (some using JavaScript) for building web applications and websites. It's meant to provide a strong foundation on which to build your application.

Refer to `http://getbootstrap.com` for more details.

Setting it up

The first step is to duplicate the code you created in the previous chapter. If, for example, you created a directory named `chap05/notes`, then create one named `chap06/notes` from the content of `chap05/notes`.

Now, we need to go about adding Bootstrap's code in the *Notes* application. The Bootstrap website suggests loading the required CSS and JavaScript files out of the Bootstrap (and jQuery) public CDN. While that's easy to do, we won't do this for two reasons:

- It violates the principle of keeping all dependencies local to the application and not relying on global dependencies
- It prevents us from generating a custom theme

Instead, we'll install a local copy of Bootstrap. There are several ways to install Bootstrap. For example, the Bootstrap website offers a downloadable TAR/GZIP archive (tarball). The better approach is an automated dependency management tool.

The most straightforward choice is using Bootstrap (`https://www.npmjs.com/package/bootstrap`), popper.js (`https://www.npmjs.com/package/popper.js`), and jQuery (`https://www.npmjs.com/package/jquery`) packages in the npm repository. These packages provide no Node.js modules, and instead are frontend code distributed through npm.

We install the packages using the following command:

```
$ npm install bootstrap@4.1.x --save
npm notice created a lockfile as package-lock.json. You should commit
this file.
npm WARN bootstrap@4.1.0 requires a peer of jquery@1.9.1 - 3 but none
is installed. You must install peer dependencies yourself.
npm WARN bootstrap@4.1.0 requires a peer of popper.js@^1.14.0 but none
is installed. You must install peer dependencies yourself.

+ bootstrap@4.1.0
added 1 package in 1.026s

$ npm install jquery@1.9.x --save
+ jquery@1.9.1
$ npm install popper.js@1.14.x --save
+ popper.js@1.14.0
```

As we see here, when we install Bootstrap, it helpfully tells us the corresponding versions of jQuery and `popper.js` to use. Therefore, we dutifully install those versions. What's most important is to see what got downloaded:

```
$ ls node_modules/bootstrap/dist/*
... directory contents
$ ls node_modules/jquery/
... directory contents
$ ls node_modules/popper.js/dist
... directory contents
```

Within each of these directories are the CSS and JavaScript files that are meant to be used in the browser. More importantly, these files are located in a given directory whose pathname is known—specifically, the directories we just inspected. Let's see how to configure our Express app to use those three packages on the browser side.

Adding Bootstrap to application templates

On the Bootstrap website, they give a recommended HTML structure. We'll be interpolating from their recommendation to use Bootstrap code provided through the CDN to instead use the local copies of Bootstrap, jQuery, and Popper that we just installed. Refer to the **Getting started** page at `http://getbootstrap.com/docs/4.0/getting-started/introduction/`.

What we'll do is modify `views/layout.hbs` to match their recommended template:

```html
<!doctype html>
<html lang="en">
  <head>
    <title>{{title}}</title>
    <meta charset="utf-8">
    <meta name="viewport"
        content="width=device-width, initial-scale=1, shrink-to-
        fit=no">

    <link rel="stylesheet"
    href="/assets/vendor/bootstrap/css/bootstrap.min.css">
    <link rel='stylesheet' href='/assets/stylesheets/style.css' />
  </head>
<body>
  {{> header }}
  {{{body}}}
  <!-- jQuery first, then Popper.js, then Bootstrap JS -->
  <script src="/assets/vendor/jquery/jquery.min.js"></script>
  <script src="/assets/vendor/popper.js/popper.min.js"></script>
```

```
<script
src="/assets/vendor/bootstrap/js/bootstrap.min.js"></script>
  </body>
</html>
```

This is largely the template shown on the Bootstrap site, incorporating the previous content of `views/layout.hbs`. Our own stylesheet is loaded following the Bootstrap stylesheet, giving us the opportunity to override anything in Bootstrap we want to change. What's different is that instead of loading Bootstrap, `popper.js`, and jQuery packages from their respective CDNs, we use the path `/assets/vendor/product-name` instead.

 This is the same as recommended on the Bootstrap website except the URLs point to our own site rather than relying on the public CDN.

This `/assets/vendor` URL is not currently recognized by the `Notes` application. To add this support, edit `app.js` to add these lines:

```
app.use(express.static(path.join(__dirname, 'public')));
app.use('/assets/vendor/bootstrap', express.static(
  path.join(__dirname, 'node_modules', 'bootstrap', 'dist')));
app.use('/assets/vendor/jquery', express.static(
  path.join(__dirname, 'node_modules', 'jquery')));
app.use('/assets/vendor/popper.js', express.static(
  path.join(__dirname, 'node_modules', 'popper.js', 'dist')));
```

Within the `public` directory, we have a little house-keeping to do. When `express-generator` set up the initial project, it generated `public/images`, `public/javascripts`, and `public/stylesheets` directories. We want each to be within the `/assets` directory, so do this:

```
$ mkdir public/assets
$ mv public/images/ public/javascripts/ public/stylesheets/
public/assets/
```

We now have our asset files, including Bootstrap, `popper.js`, and jQuery, all available to the `Notes` application under the `/assets` directory. The page layout refers to these assets and should give us the default Bootstrap theme:

```
$ npm start
> notes@0.0.0 start /Users/David/chap06/notes
> DEBUG=notes:* node ./bin/www
```

```
    notes:server Listening on port 3000 +0ms
GET / 200 306.660 ms - 883
GET /stylesheets/style.css 404 321.057 ms - 2439
GET /assets/stylesheets/style.css 200 160.371 ms - 165
GET /assets/vendor/bootstrap/js/bootstrap.min.js 200 157.459 ms -
50564
GET /assets/vendor/popper.js/popper.min.js 200 769.508 ms - 18070
GET /assets/vendor/jquery/jquery.min.js 200 777.988 ms - 92629
GET /assets/vendor/bootstrap/css/bootstrap.min.css 200 788.028 ms -
127343
```

The on-screen differences are minor, but this is the proof necessary that the CSS and JavaScript files for Bootstrap are being loaded. We have accomplished the first major goal—using a modern, mobile-friendly framework to implement a mobile-first design.

Alternative layout frameworks

Bootstrap isn't the only JavaScript/CSS framework providing a responsive layout and useful components. We're using Bootstrap in this project because of its popularity. These frameworks are worthy of a look:

- Pure.css (`https://purecss.io/`): A responsive CSS framework with an emphasis on a small code footprint.
- Picnic CSS (`https://picnicss.com/`): A responsive CSS framework emphasizing small size and beauty.
- Shoelace (`https://shoelace.style/`): A CSS framework emphasizing using future CSS, meaning it uses CSS constructs at the leading edge of CSS standardization. Since most browsers don't support those features, cssnext (`http://cssnext.io/`) is used to retrofit that support. Shoelace uses a grid layout system based on Bootstrap's grid.
- PaperCSS (`https://www.getpapercss.com/`): An informal CSS framework which looks like it was hand drawn.
- Foundation (`https://foundation.zurb.com/`): Self-described as the most advanced responsive frontend framework in the world.
- Base (`http://getbase.org/`): A lightweight modern CSS framework.

HTML5 Boilerplate (`https://html5boilerplate.com/`) is an extremely useful basis from which to code the HTML and other assets. It contains the current best practices for the HTML code in web pages, as well as tools to normalize CSS support and configuration files for several web servers.

Flexbox and CSS Grids

Other new technologies impacting web application development are two new CSS layout methodologies. The CSS3 committee has been working on several fronts, including page layout.

In the distant past, we used nested HTML tables for page layout. That is a bad memory that we don't have to revisit. More recently, we've been using a box model using DIVs, and even at times using absolute or relative placement techniques. All these techniques have been suboptimal in several ways, some more than others.

One popular layout technique is to divide the horizontal space into columns and assign a certain number of columns to each thing on the page. With some frameworks, we can even have nested DIVs, each with their own set of columns. Bootstrap 3, and other modern frameworks, used that layout technique.

The two new CSS layout methodologies, Flexbox (`https://en.wikipedia.org/wiki/CSS_flex-box_layout`) and CSS Grids (`https://developer.mozilla.org/en-US/docs/Web/CSS/CSS_Grid_Layout`), are a significant improvement over all previous methodologies. We are mentioning these technologies because they're both worthy of attention. Both are somewhat early in their adoption curve—they've been standardized by committees and adopted in the latest browsers, but of course there are a lot of old browsers in the field.

With Bootstrap 4, the Bootstrap team chose to go with Flexbox. Therefore, under the hood are Flexbox CSS constructs.

Mobile-first design for the Notes application

We've learned about the basics of responsive design and Bootstrap, and we hooked the Bootstrap framework into our application. Now we're ready to launch a redesign of the application so that it works well on mobile devices.

Laying the Bootstrap grid foundation

Bootstrap uses a 12-column grid system to control layout, giving applications a responsive mobile-first foundation on which to build. It automatically scales components as the viewport changes size or shape. The method relies on <div> elements with classes to describe the role each <div> plays in the layout.

The basic layout pattern is as follows:

```
<div class="container-fluid">
  <div class="row">
    <div class="col-sm-3">Column 1 content</div> <!-- 25% -->
    <div class="col-sm-9">Column 2 content</div> <!-- 75% -->
  </div>
  <div class="row">
    <div class="col-sm-3">Column 1 content</div> <!-- 25% -->
    <div class="col-sm-6">Column 2 content</div> <!-- 50% -->
    <div class="col-sm-3">Column 3 content</div> <!-- 25% -->
  </div>
</div>
```

The outermost layer is the `.container` or `.container-fluid` element. Containers provide a means to center or horizontally pad the content. Containers marked as `.container-fluid` act as if they have `width: 100%`, meaning they expand to fill the horizontal space.

A `.row` is what it sounds like, a `"row"`. Technically, a row is a wrapper for columns. Containers are wrappers for rows, and rows are wrappers for columns, and columns contain the stuff displayed to our users. Got that?

Columns are marked with variations of the `.col` class. With the basic column class, `.col`, the columns divide equally into the available space. You can specify a numerical column count to assign different widths to each column. Bootstrap supports up to 12 numbered columns, hence each row in the example adds up to 12 columns.

You can also specify a breakpoint to which the column applies:

- Using `col-xs` targets extra-small devices (smartphones, <576px)
- Using `col-sm` targets small devices (>= 576px)
- Using `col-md` targets medium devices (>= 768px)
- Using `col-lg` targets large devices (>= 992px)
- Using `col-xl` targets extra-large devices (>= 1200px)

Specifying a breakpoint, for example `col-sm`, means that it applies to devices matching that breakpoint, or larger. Hence, in the example shown earlier, the column definitions applied to `col-sm`, `col-md`, `col-lg`, and `col-xl` devices, but not to `col-xs` devices.

The column count is appended to the class name. That means using `col-#` when not targeting a breakpoint, for example, `col-4`, or `col-{breakpoint}-#` when targeting a breakpoint, for example, `col-md-4`. If the columns add up to more than 12, the columns beyond the twelfth column wrap around to become a new row. The word `auto` can be used instead of a numerical column count to size the column to the natural width of its content.

It's possible to mix and match to target multiple breakpoints:

```
<div class="container-fluid">
  <div class="row">
    <div class="col-xs-9 col-md-3 col-lg-6">Column 1 content</div>
    <div class="col-xs-3 col-md-9 col-lg-6">Column 2 content</div>
  </div>
  ...
</div>
```

This declares three different layouts, one for extra-small devices, another for medium devices, and the last for large devices. This gives us enough to start modifying the `Notes` application. The grid system can do a lot more. For details, see the documentation: `http://getbootstrap.com/docs/4.0/layout/grid/`.

Responsive page structure for the Notes application

We structured each of the page layouts as follows:

```
<!DOCTYPE html>
<html>
<head> .. headerStuff </head>
<body>
.. pageHeader
.. main content
.. bottomOfPageStuff
</body>
</html>
```

The page content therefore has two visible rows: the header and the main content. At the bottom of the page are invisible things like the JavaScript files for Bootstrap and jQuery.

No change is required in `views/layout.hbs`. One might think the `container-fluid` wrapper would be in that file, with the rows and columns specified in the other templates. Instead, we'll do it in the templates to give us the most layout freedom.

Using icon libraries and improving visual appeal

The world around us isn't constructed of words, but instead things. Hence, a pictorial style, as icons, should help computer software to be more comprehensible. Giving a good user experience should make our users reward us with more likes in the app store.

There are several icon libraries that can be used in a website. The Bootstrap team has a curated list at `http://getbootstrap.com/docs/4.1/extend/icons/`. For this project, we'll use Feather Icons (`https://feathericons.com/`) and its conveniently available npm package, `https://www.npmjs.com/package/feather-icons`.

In `package.json`, add this to the dependencies:

```
"feather-icons": ">=4.5.x"
```

Then run `npm install` to download the new package. You can then inspect the downloaded package and see that `./node_modules/feather-icons/dist/feather.js` contains browser-side code, making it easy to use the icons.

We make that directory available by mounting it in `app.js`, just as we did for Bootstrap and jQuery libraries. Add this code to `app.js`:

```
app.use('/assets/vendor/feather-icons', express.static(
    path.join(__dirname, 'node_modules', 'feather-icons', 'dist')));
```

Going by the documentation, we must put this at the bottom of `views/layout.hbs` to enable `feather-icons` support:

```
<script src="/assets/vendor/feather-icons/feather.js"></script>
<script>
   feather.replace();
</script>
```

To use one of the icons, use a `data-feather` attribute specifying one of the icon names, like so:

```
<i data-feather="circle"></i>
```

What's important is the `data-feather` attribute, which the Feather Icons library uses to identify the SVG file to use. The Feather Icons library completely replaces the element where it found the `data-feather` attribute. Therefore, if you want the icon to be a clickable link, it's necessary to wrap the icon definition with an <a> tag, rather than adding `data-feather` to the <a> tag. The next section shows an example.

Responsive page header navigation bar

The header section we designed before contains a page title and a little navigation bar. Bootstrap has several ways to spiff this up, and even give us a responsive navigation bar which neatly collapses to a menu on small devices.

In `views/pageHeader.ejs`, make this change:

```
<header class="page-header">
<h1>{{ title }}</h1>
<nav class="navbar navbar-expand-md navbar-dark bg-dark">
   <a class="navbar-brand" href='/'><i data-feather="home"></i></a>
    <button class="navbar-toggler" type="button"
       data-toggle="collapse" data-target="#navbarSupportedContent"
```

```
         aria-controls="navbarSupportedContent"
         aria-expanded="false" aria-label="Toggle navigation">
         <span class="navbar-toggler-icon"></span>
      </button>
      <div class="collapse navbar-collapse" id="navbarSupportedContent">
         <div class="navbar-nav col">
         {{#if breadcrumb}}
         <a class="nav-item nav-link" href='{{breadcrumb.url}}'>
         {{breadcrumb.title}}</a>
         {{/if}}
         </div>
         <a class="nav-item nav-link btn btn-light col-auto"
                    href='/notes/add'>ADD Note</a>
      </div>
   </nav>
   </header>
```

Adding `class="page-header"` informs Bootstrap this is, well, the page header. Within that we have the `<h1>` header as before, giving the page title, and then a responsive Bootstrap `navbar`.

By default the `navbar` is expanded—meaning the components inside the `navbar` are visible—because of the `navbar-expand-md` class. This `navbar` is using a `navbar-toggler` button which governs the responsiveness of the `navbar`. By default, this button is hidden and the body of the `navbar` is visible. If the screen is small enough, the `navbar-toggler` is switched so it's visible, the body of the `navbar` is invisible, and when clicking on the now-visible `navbar-toggler`, a menu drops down containing the body of the `navbar`:

We chose the feather icons *home* icon because it says go home. It's intended that the middle portion of the `navbar` will contain a breadcrumb as we navigate around the *Notes* application.

The **ADD Note** button is glued to the right-hand-side with a little Flexbox magic. The container is a Flexbox, meaning we can use the Bootstrap classes to control the space consumed by each item. The breadcrumb area is empty in this case, but the `<div>` that would contain it is there and declared with `class="col"`, meaning that it takes up a column unit. The **ADD Note** button is, on the other hand, declared with `class="col-auto"`, meaning it takes up only the room required for itself. It is the empty breadcrumb area that will expand to fill the space, while the **ADD Note** button fills only its own space, and is therefore pushed over to the side.

Because it's the same application, the functionality all works; we're simply working on the presentation. We've added a few notes but the presentation of the list on the front page leaves a lot to be desired. The small size of the title is not very touch-friendly, since it doesn't present a large target area for a fingertip. And can you explain why the `notekey` value has to be displayed on the home page?

Improving the Notes list on the front page

The current home page has a simple text list that's not terribly touch-friendly and showing the *key* at the front of the line might be inexplicable to the user. Let's fix this.

Edit `views/index.hbs` and make this change:

```
<div class="container-fluid">
  <div class="row">
    <div class="col-12 btn-group-vertical" role="group">
      {{#each notelist}}
      <a class="btn btn-lg btn-block btn-outline-dark"
         href="/notes/view?key={{ key }}">{{ title }}</a>
      {{/each}}
    </div>
  </div>
</div>
```

The first change is to switch away from using a list and to use a vertical button group. By making the text links look and behave like buttons, we're improving the user interface, especially its touch friendliness. We chose the `btn-outline-dark` button style because it looks good in the user interface. We use large buttons (`btn-lg`) that fill the width of the container (`btn-block`).

We eliminated showing the notekey to the user. This information doesn't add anything to the user experience:

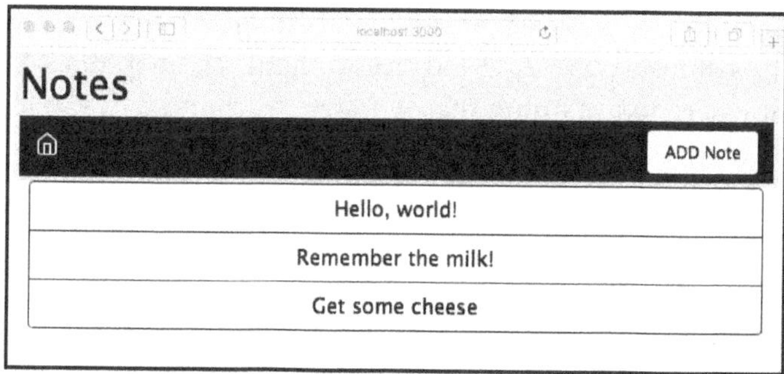

This is beginning to take shape, with a decent-looking home page that handles resizing very nicely and is touch friendly.

There's still something more to do with this, since the header area is taking up a fair amount of space. We should always feel free to rethink a plan as we look at intermediate results. Earlier, we created one design for the header area, but on reflection that design looks to be too large. The intention had been to insert a breadcrumb just to the right of the home icon, and to leave the `<h1>` title at the top of the header area. But this is taking up vertical space and we can tighten up the header and possibly improve the appearance.

Edit `partials/header.hbs` and replace it with the following:

```
<header class="page-header">
<nav class="navbar navbar-expand-md navbar-dark bg-dark">
  <a class="navbar-brand" href='/'><i data-feather="home"></i></a>
  <button class="navbar-toggler" type="button"
        data-toggle="collapse" data-target="#navbarSupportedContent"
        aria-controls="navbarSupportedContent"
        aria-expanded="false"
        aria-label="Toggle navigation">
    <span class="navbar-toggler-icon"></span>
  </button>
  <div class="collapse navbar-collapse" id="navbarSupportedContent">
    <span class="navbar-text col">{{ title }}</span>
    <a class="nav-item nav-link btn btn-light col-auto"
href='/notes/add'>ADD Note</a>
  </div>
</nav>
</header>
```

This removes the <h1> tag at the top of the header area, immediately tightening the presentation.

Within the `navbar-collapse` area, we've replaced what had been intended as the breadcrumb, with a simple `navbar-text` component. To keep the **ADD Note** button glued to the right, we're maintaining the `class="col"` and `class="col-auto"` settings:

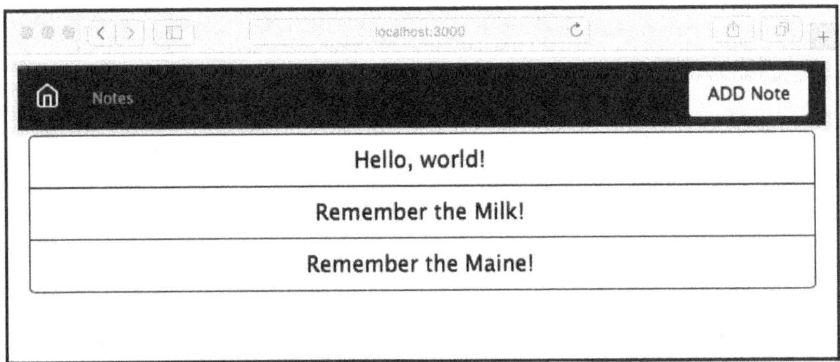

Which header area design is better? That's a good question. Since beauty is in the eye of the beholder, both designs are probably equally good. What we have demonstrated is the ease with which we can update the design by editing the template files.

Cleaning up the Note viewing experience

Viewing a Note isn't bad, but the user experience can be improved. The user does not need to see the notekey, for example. Additionally, Bootstrap has nicer-looking buttons we can use.

In `views/noteview.hbs`, make these changes:

```
<div class="container-fluid">
    <div class="row"><div class="col-xs-12">
        {{#if note}}<h3>{{ note.title }}</h3>{{/if}}
        {{#if note}}<p>{{ note.body }}</p>{{/if}}
        <p>Key: {{ notekey }}</p>
    </div></div>
    {{#if notekey }}
        <div class="row"><div class="col-xs-12">
        <div class="btn-group">
            <a class="btn btn-outline-dark"
                href="/notes/destroy?key={{notekey}}"
```

```
            role="button">Delete</a>
        <a class="btn btn-outline-dark"
            href="/notes/edit?key={{notekey}}"
            role="button">Edit</a>
    </div>
    </div></div>
  {{/if}}
</div>
```

We have declared two rows, one for the Note, and another for buttons to act on the Note. Both are declared to consume all 12 columns, and therefore take up the full available width. The buttons are again contained within a button group:

Do we really need to show the notekey to the user? We'll leave it there, but that's an open question for the user experience team. Otherwise, we've improved the note-reading experience.

Cleaning up the add/edit note form

The next major glaring problem is the form for adding and editing notes. As we said earlier, it's easy to get the text input area to overflow a small screen. On the other hand, Bootstrap has extensive support for making nice-looking forms that work well on mobile devices.

Change the form in views/noteedit.hbs to this:

```
<form method='POST' action='/notes/save'>
  <div class="container-fluid">
    {{#if docreate}}
      <input type='hidden' name='docreate' value="create">
    {{else}}
```

```
      <input type='hidden' name='docreate' value="update">
  {{/if}}
  <div class="form-group row align-items-center">
    <label for="notekey" class="col-1 col-form-label">Key</label>
    {{#if docreate }}
      <div class="col">
        <input type='text' class="form-control"
               placeholder="note key" name='notekey' value=''/>
      </div>
    {{else}}
      {{#if note }}
        <span class="input-group-text">{{notekey}}</span>
      {{/if}}
      <input type='hidden' name='notekey'
             value='{{#if note }}{{notekey}}{{/if}} '/>
    {{/if}}
  </div>

  <div class="form-group row">
    <label for="title" class="col-1 col-form-label">Title</label>
    <div class="col">
      <input type="text" class="form-control"
             id='title' name='title' placeholder="note title"
             value='{{#if note }}{{note.title}}{{/if}}'>
    </div>
  </div>

  <div class="form-group row">
    <textarea class="form-control" name='body'
              rows="5">{{#if note }}{{note.body}}{{/if}}</textarea>
  </div>
  <button type="submit" class="btn btn-default">Submit</button>
  </div>
</form>
```

There's a lot going on here. What we've done is reorganize the `form` so Bootstrap can do the right things with it. The first thing to note is that we have several instances of this:

```
<div class="form-group row"> .. </div>
```

These are contained within a `container-fluid`, meaning that we've set up three rows in the form.

Bootstrap uses `form-group` elements to add structure to forms, and to encourage proper use of `<label>` elements, along with other form elements. It's good practice to use a `<label>` with every `<input>` to improve assistive behavior in the browser, rather than if you simply left some dangling text.

Every form element has `class="form-control"`. Bootstrap uses this to identify the controls so it can add styling and behavior.

By default, Bootstrap formats `form-group` elements so the `label` appears on another line from the input control. Note that we've added `class="col-1"` to the labels and `class="col"` to the `<div>` wrapping the input. This declares two columns, the first consuming one column unit and the other consuming the remainder.

The `placeholder='key'` attribute puts sample text in an otherwise empty text input element. It disappears as soon as the user types something and is an excellent way to prompt the user with what's expected.

Finally, we changed the **Submit** button to be a Bootstrap button. These look nice, and Bootstrap makes sure that they work great:

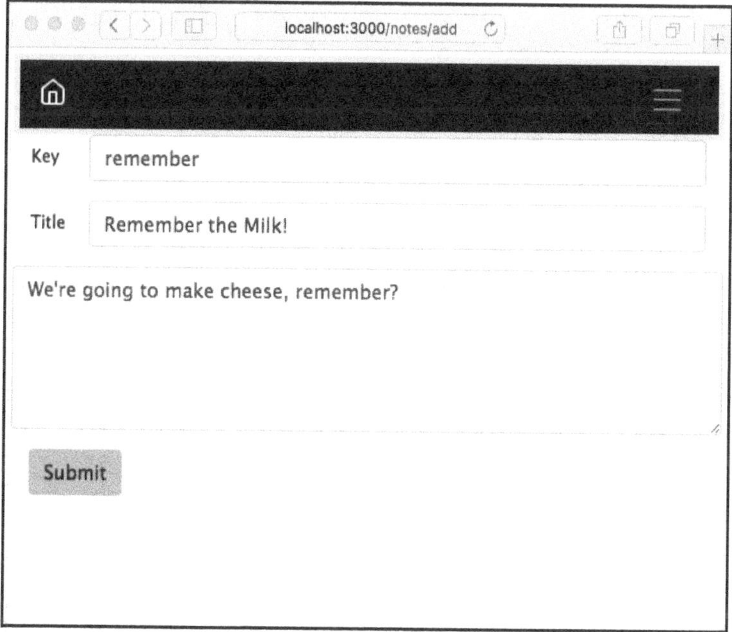

The result looks good and works well on the iPhone. It automatically sizes itself to whatever screen it's on. Everything behaves nicely. In this screenshot, we've resized the window small enough to cause the navbar to collapse. Clicking on the so-called hamburger icon on the right (the three horizontal lines) causes the navbar contents to pop up as a menu.

Cleaning up the delete-note window

The window used to verify the desire to delete a Note doesn't look bad, but it can be improved.

Edit `views/notedestroy.hbs` to contain the following:

```
<form method='POST' action='/notes/destroy/confirm'>
  <div class="container-fluid">
    <input type='hidden' name='notekey' value='{{#if
note}}{{notekey}}{{/if}}'>
    <p class="form-text">Delete {{note.title}}?</p>
    <div class="btn-group">
      <button type="submit" value='DELETE'
              class="btn btn-outline-dark">DELETE</button>
      <a class="btn btn-outline-dark"
              href="/notes/view?key={{#if note}}{{notekey}}{{/if}}"
              role="button">
        Cancel</a>
    </div>
  </div>
</form>
```

We've reworked everything to use Bootstrap form goodness. The question about deleting the Note is wrapped with `class="form-text"` so that Bootstrap can display this properly.

The buttons are wrapped with `class="btn-group"` as before. The buttons have exactly the same styling as on other screens, giving a consistent look across the application:

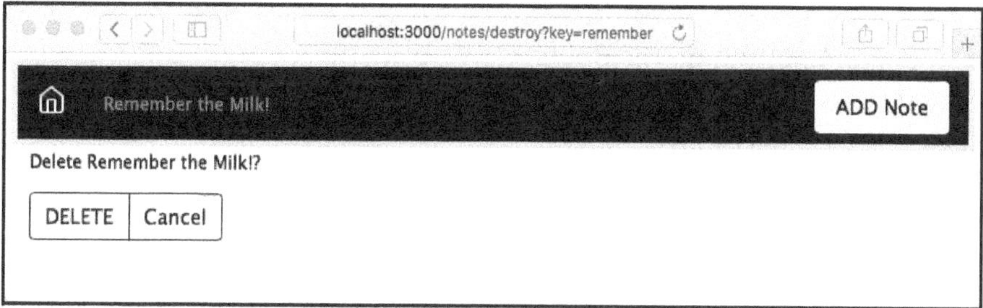

There is an issue that the title text in the navbar does not use the word `Delete`. In `routes/notes.js`, we can make this change:

```
// Ask to Delete note (destroy)
router.get('/destroy', async (req, res, next) => {
  var note = await notes.read(req.query.key);
  res.render('notedestroy', {
    title: note ? `Delete ${note.title}` : "",
    notekey: req.query.key, note: note
  });
});
```

What we've done is changed the `title` parameter passed to the template. We'd done this in the `/notes/edit` route handler and seemingly missed doing so in this handler.

Building a customized Bootstrap

One reason to use Bootstrap is that you can easily build a customized version. Stylesheets are built using SASS, which is one of the CSS preprocessors to simplify CSS development. In Bootstrap's code, one file (`scss/_variables.scss`) contains variables used throughout the rest of Bootstrap's `.scss` files. Change one variable and it can automatically affect the rest of Bootstrap.

Earlier, we overrode a couple of Bootstrap behaviors with our custom CSS file,
`public/stylesheets/style.css`. This is an easy way to change a couple of
specific things, but it doesn't work for large-scale changes to Bootstrap. Serious
Bootstrap customization requires generating a customized Bootstrap build.

The official documentation on the Bootstrap website (`http://getbootstrap.com/
docs/4.1/getting-started/build-tools/`) is useful for reference on the build
process.

If you've followed the directions given earlier, you have a directory, `chap06/notes`,
containing the `Notes` application source code. Create a directory
named `chap06/notes/theme`, within which we'll set up a custom Bootstrap build
process.

As students of the Twelve Factor Application model, we'll be using
a `package.json` in that directory to automate the build process. There isn't any
Node.js code involved; npm is also a convenient tool to automate the software build
processes.

To start, download the Bootstrap source tree from `https://github.com/twbs/
bootstrap`. While the Bootstrap npm package includes SASS source files, it isn't
sufficient to build Bootstrap, and therefore one must download the source tree. What
we do is navigate to the GitHub repository, click on the **Releases** tab, and select the
URL for the most recent release.

With `theme/package.json` containing this `scripts` section:

```
{
  "scripts": {
    "download": "wget -O -
https://github.com/twbs/bootstrap/archive/v4.1.0.tar.gz | tar xvfz -",
    "postdownload": "cd bootstrap-4.1.0 && npm install"
  }
}
```

Type this command:

```
$ npm run download
```

This downloads the tar-gzip (tarball) archive from the Bootstrap repository and immediately unpacks it. If you are on Windows, it will be easiest to run that script in Windows Subsystem for Linux to execute these commands. After downloading and unpacking the archive, the `postdownload` step runs `npm install` in the directory. The Bootstrap team uses their `package.json`, not only to track all the dependencies required to build Bootstrap, but to drive the build process.

The `npm install` for Bootstrap will take a long time, so be patient.

This much only installs the tools necessary to build Bootstrap. Building the Bootstrap documentation requires installing additional Ruby-based tools (Jekyll and some plugins).

To build Bootstrap, let's add the following lines to the `scripts` section in our `theme/package.json`:

```
"scripts": {
...
  "build": "cd bootstrap-4.1.0 && npm run dist",
  "watch": "cd bootstrap-4.1.0 && npm run watch"
...
}
```

Obviously you'll need to adjust the directory name as the Bootstrap project issues new releases. In the Bootstrap source tree, running `npm run dist` builds Bootstrap, while `npm run watch` sets up an automated process to scan for changed files and rebuilds Bootstrap upon changing any file. By adding these lines to our `theme/package.json`, we can start this in the terminal and it automatically reruns the build as needed.

Now run a build with this command:

```
$ npm run build
```

The built files land in the `theme/bootstrap-4.1.0/dist` directory. The content of that directory will match the contents of the corresponding npm package.

In case it hasn't been obvious all along—there are Bootstrap version numbers embedded in these URLs and file or directory names. As new Bootstrap releases are issued, you must adjust the pathnames to match the current version number.

Before proceeding, let's take a look around the Bootstrap source tree. The `scss`
directory contains the SASS source that will be compiled into the Bootstrap CSS files.
To generate a customized Bootstrap build will require a few modifications in that
directory.

The `bootstrap-4.1.0/scss/bootstrap.scss` file contains `@import` directives to
pull in all Bootstrap components. The
file `bootstrap-4.1.0/scss/_variables.scss` contains definitions used in the
remainder of the Bootstrap SASS source. Editing, or overriding, these values will
change the look of websites using the resulting Bootstrap build.

For example, these definitions determine the main color values:

```scss
$white: #fff !default;
$gray-100: #f8f9fa !default;
. . .
$gray-800: #343a40 !default;
. . .
$blue: #007bff !default;
. . .
$red: #dc3545 !default;
$orange: #fd7e14 !default;
$yellow: #ffc107 !default;
$green: #28a745 !default;
. . .
$primary: $blue !default;
$secondary: $gray-600 !default;
$success: $green !default;
$info: $cyan !default;
$warning: $yellow !default;
$danger: $red !default;
$light: $gray-100 !default;
$dark: $gray-800 !default;
```

These are similar to CSS statements. The `!default` attribute designates these values
as the default. Any `!default` values can be overridden without editing
`_values.scss`.

Create a file, `theme/_custom.scss`, containing the following:

```scss
$white: #fff !default;
$gray-900: #212529 !default;
$body-bg: $gray-900 !default;
$body-color: $white !default;
```

This reverses the values for the `$body-bg` and `$body-color` settings in
`_variables.scss`. The Notes app will now use white text on a dark background,
rather than the default white background with dark text. Because these declarations
do not use `!default`, they'll override the values in `_variables.scss`.

Then make a copy of `scss/bootstrap.scss` in the theme directory and modify it,
like so:

```
@import "custom";
@import "functions";
@import "variables";
...
```

We're importing the `_custom.scss` file we just created. Finally, add this line to the
`scripts` section of `theme/package.json`:

```
"prebuild": "cp _custom.scss bootstrap.scss bootstrap-4.1.0/scss",
```

With that in place, before building Bootstrap these two files will be copied in place.
Next, rebuild Bootstrap:

```
$ npm run build

> @ prebuild /Users/David/chap06/notes/theme
> cp _custom.scss bootstrap.scss bootstrap-4.1.0/scss

> @ build /Users/David/chap06/notes/theme
> cd bootstrap-4.1.0 && npm run dist
...
```

While that's building, let's modify `notes/app.js` to mount the build directory:

```
// app.use('/assets/vendor/bootstrap', express.static(
// path.join(__dirname, 'node_modules', 'bootstrap', 'dist')));
app.use('/assets/vendor/bootstrap', express.static(
    path.join(__dirname, 'theme', 'bootstrap-4.1.0', 'dist')));
```

What we've done is switch from the Bootstrap in `node_modules` to what we just built
in the `theme` directory. The Bootstrap version number shows up here, so this must
also be updated as new Bootstrap releases are adopted.

Then reload the application, and you'll see the following:

To get exactly this, you may need to make a change in the templates. The Button elements we used earlier have the `btn-outline-dark` class, which works well on a light background. The background is now dark and these buttons need to use light coloring.

To change the buttons, in `views/index.hbs` make this change:

```
<a class="btn btn-lg btn-block btn-outline-light"
    href="/notes/view?key={{ key }}"> {{ title }} </a>
```

Make a similar change in `views/noteview.hbs`:

```
<a class="btn btn-outline-light" href="/notes/destroy?key={{notekey}}"
    role="button"> Delete </a>
<a class="btn btn-outline-light" href="/notes/edit?key={{notekey}}"
    role="button"> Edit </a>
```

That's cool, we can now rework the Bootstrap color scheme any way we want. Don't show this to your user experience team, because they'll throw a fit. We did this to prove the point that we can edit `_custom.scss` and change the Bootstrap theme.

Pre-built custom Bootstrap themes

If all this is too complicated for you, several websites provide pre-built Bootstrap themes, or else simplified tools to generate a Bootstrap build. To get our feet wet, let's download a theme from Bootswatch (`https://bootswatch.com/`). This is both a collection of free and open source themes and a build system for generating custom Bootstrap themes (`https://github.com/thomaspark/bootswatch/`).

Let's use the **Minty** theme from Bootswatch to explore the needed changes. You can download the theme from the website or add the following to the `scripts` section of `package.json`:

```
"dl-minty": "mkdir -p minty && npm run dl-minty-css && npm run dl-minty-min-css",
"dl-minty-css": "wget https://bootswatch.com/4/minty/bootstrap.css -O minty/bootstrap.css",
"dl-minty-min-css": "wget
https://bootswatch.com/4/minty/bootstrap.min.css -O
minty/bootstrap.min.css"
```

This will download the prebuilt CSS files for our chosen theme. In passing, notice that the Bootswatch website offers `_variables.scss` and `_bootswatch.scss` files which should be usable with a workflow similar to what we implemented in the previous section. The GitHub repository matching the Bootswatch website has a complete build procedure for building custom themes.

Perform the download:

```
$ npm run dl-minty

> notes@0.0.0 dl-minty /Users/David/chap06/notes
> mkdir -p minty && npm run dl-minty-css && npm run dl-minty-min-css

> notes@0.0.0 dl-minty-css /Users/David/chap06/notes
> wget https://bootswatch.com/4/minty/bootstrap.css -O
minty/bootstrap.css

> notes@0.0.0 dl-minty-min-css /Users/David/chap06/notes
> wget https://bootswatch.com/4/minty/bootstrap.min.css -O
minty/bootstrap.min.css
```

In `app.js` we will need to change the Bootstrap mounts to separately mount the JavaScript and CSS files. Use the following:

```
// app.use('/assets/vendor/bootstrap', express.static(
// path.join(__dirname, 'node_modules', 'bootstrap', 'dist')));
// app.use('/assets/vendor/bootstrap', express.static(
// path.join(__dirname, 'theme', 'bootstrap-4.0.0', 'dist')));
app.use('/assets/vendor/bootstrap/js', express.static(
  path.join(__dirname, 'node_modules', 'bootstrap', 'dist', 'js')));
app.use('/assets/vendor/bootstrap/css', express.static(
  path.join(__dirname, 'minty')));
```

Instead of one mount for `/vendor/bootstrap`, we now have two mounts for each of the subdirectories. Simply make the `/vendor/bootstrap/css` mount point to a directory containing the CSS files you downloaded from the theme provider.

Because Minty is a light-colored theme, the buttons need to use the dark style. We had earlier changed the buttons to use a light style because of the dark background. We must now switch from `btn-outline-light` back to `btn-outline-dark`. In `partials/header.hbs`, the color scheme requires a change to the navbar content:

```
<div class="collapse navbar-collapse" id="navbarSupportedContent">
 <span class="navbar-text text-dark col">{{ title }}</span>
 <a class="nav-item nav-link btn btn-dark col-auto"
href='/notes/add'>ADD Note</a>
</div>
```

We selected `text-dark` and `btn-dark` classes to provide some contrast against the background.

Re-run the application and you'll see something like this:

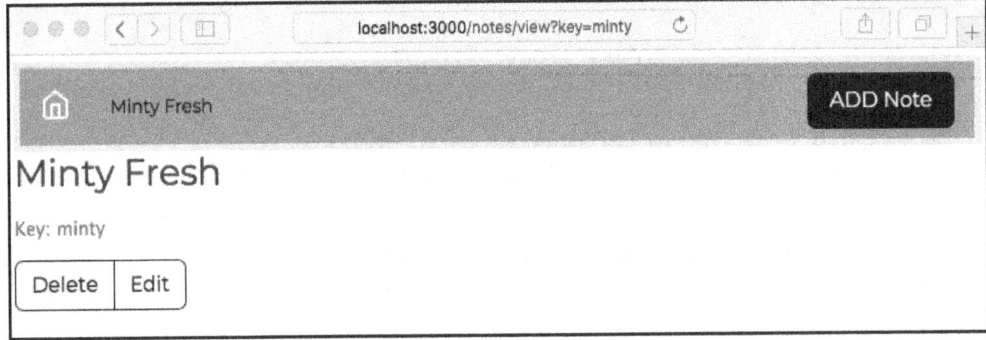

Summary

The possibilities for using Bootstrap are endless. While we covered a lot of material, we only touched the surface, and we could have done much more to the *Notes* application.

You learned what the Twitter Bootstrap framework can do. Bootstrap's goal is to make mobile-responsive development easy. We used Bootstrap to make great improvements to the way the `Notes` app looks and feels. We customized Bootstrap, dipping our toes into generating a custom theme.

Now, we want to get back to writing Node.js code. We left off `Chapter 5`, *Your First Express Application*, with the problem of persistence so that the *Notes* application can be stopped and restarted without losing our notes. In `Chapter 7`, *Data Storage and Retrieval*, we'll dive into using databases to store our data.

To give ourselves some experience with the ES6 Module format, we'll rewrite the *Notes* application accordingly.

Data Storage and Retrieval

7

In the previous two chapters, we built a small and somewhat useful application for storing notes, and then made it work on mobile devices. While the application works reasonably well, it doesn't store those notes anywhere on a long-term basis, meaning the notes are lost when you stop the server and, if you run multiple instances of Notes, each instance has its own set of notes. The typical next step is to introduce a database tier.

In this chapter, we will look at database support in Node.js, so the user sees the same set of notes for any Notes instance accessed, and to reliably store notes for long-term retrieval.

We'll start with the *Notes* application code used in the previous chapter. We started with a simple, in-memory data model using an array to store the notes, and then made it mobile friendly. In this chapter, we will:

- Discover logging operational and debugging information
- Begin using the ES6 module format
- Implement data persistence for Notes objects using several database engines

Let's get started!

The first step is to duplicate the code from the previous chapter. For instance, if you were working in `chap06/notes`, duplicate that to be `chap07/notes`.

Data storage and asynchronous code

By definition, external data storage systems require asynchronous code in the Node.js architecture. The access time to retrieve data from disk, from another process, or from a database, always takes sufficient time to require deferred execution.

The existing `Notes` data model is an in-memory data store. In theory, in-memory data access does not require asynchronous code and therefore, the existing model module could have used regular functions rather than `async` functions.

We knew that Notes must move to using databases, and would require an asynchronous API to access Notes data. For that reason, the existing Notes model API uses `async` functions so that in this chapter, we can persist Note data to databases.

Logging

Before we get into databases, we have to address one of the attributes of a high-quality software system: managing logged information, including normal system activity, system errors, and debugging information. Logs give us an insight into the behavior of the system. How much traffic is it getting? If it's a website, which pages are people hitting the most? How many errors occur and of what kind? Do attacks occur? Are malformed requests being sent?

Log management is also an issue. Log rotation means regularly moving the log file out of the way, to start with a fresh log file. You should process logged data to produce reports. A high priority on screening for security vulnerabilities is a must.

The Twelve Factor application model suggests simply sending logging information to the console, and then some other software system captures that output and directs it to a logging service. Following their advice can reduce system complexity by having fewer things that can break. In a later chapter, we'll use PM2 for that purpose.

Let's first complete a tour of information logging as it stands right now in Notes.

When we used the Express Generator to initially create the *Notes* application, it configured an activity logging system using `morgan`:

```
const logger = require('morgan');
..
app.use(logger('dev'));
```

This is what prints the requests on the Terminal window. Visit `https://github.com/expressjs/morgan` for more information.

Internally, Express uses the **Debug** package for debugging traces. You can turn these on using the DEBUG environment variable. We should try to use this package in our application code. For more information, visit
`https://www.npmjs.com/package/debug`.

Finally, the application might generate uncaught exceptions. The uncaughtException error needs to be captured, logged, and dealt with appropriately.

Request logging with Morgan

The Morgan package has two general areas for configuration:

- Log format
- Log location

As it stands, Notes uses the dev format, which is described as a concise status output meant for developers. This can be used to log web requests as a way to measure website activity and popularity. The Apache log format already has a large ecosystem of reporting tools and, sure enough, Morgan can produce log files in this format.

To change the format, simply change this line in app.js:

```
app.use(logger(process.env.REQUEST_LOG_FORMAT || 'dev'));
```

Then run *Notes* as follows:

```
$ REQUEST_LOG_FORMAT=common npm start
> notes@0.0.0 start /Users/david/chap07/notes
> node ./bin/www
::1 - - [12/Feb/2016:05:51:21 +0000] "GET / HTTP/1.1" 304 -
::1 - - [12/Feb/2016:05:51:21 +0000] "GET
/vendor/bootstrap/css/bootstrap.min.css HTTP/1.1" 304 -
::1 - - [12/Feb/2016:05:51:21 +0000] "GET /stylesheets/style.css
HTTP/1.1" 304 -
::1 - - [12/Feb/2016:05:51:21 +0000] "GET
/vendor/bootstrap/js/bootstrap.min.js HTTP/1.1" 304 -
```

To revert to the previous logging output, simply do not set this environment variable. If you've looked at Apache access logs, this logging format will look familiar. The ::1 notation at the beginning of the line is IPV6 notation for the localhost, which you may be more familiar with as 127.0.0.1.

We can declare victory on request logging and move on to debugging messages. However, let's look at logging this to a file directly. While it's possible to capture stdout through a separate process, Morgan is already installed in Notes and it does provide the capability to direct its output to a file.

The Morgan documentation suggests this:

```
// create a write stream (in append mode)
var accessLogStream = fs.createWriteStream(__dirname + '/access.log',
{flags: 'a'})

// setup the logger
app.use(morgan('combined', {stream: accessLogStream}));
```

But this has a problem; it's impossible to perform log rotation without killing and restarting the server. Instead, we'll use their rotating-file-stream package.

First, install the package:

```
$ npm install rotating-file-stream --save
```

Then we add this code to app.js:

```
const fs = require('fs-extra');
...
const rfs = require('rotating-file-stream');
var logStream;
// Log to a file if requested
if (process.env.REQUEST_LOG_FILE) {
  (async () => {
    let logDirectory = path.dirname(process.env.REQUEST_LOG_FILE);
    await fs.ensureDir(logDirectory);
    logStream = rfs(process.env.REQUEST_LOG_FILE, {
        size: '10M',      // rotate every 10 MegaBytes written
        interval: '1d',   // rotate daily
        compress: 'gzip'  // compress rotated files
    });
  })().catch(err => { console.error(err); });
}
..
app.use(logger(process.env.REQUEST_LOG_FORMAT || 'dev', {
    stream: logStream ? logStream : process.stdout
}));
```

Here, we're using an environment variable, REQUEST_LOG_FILE, to control whether to send the log to stdout or to a file. The log can go into a directory, and the code will automatically create that directory if it doesn't exist. By using rotating-file-stream (https://www.npmjs.com/package/rotating-file-stream), we're guaranteed to have log file rotation with no extra systems required.

The fs-extra module is being used because it adds Promise-based functions to the fs module (https://www.npmjs.com/package/fs-extra). In this case, fs.ensureDir checks if the named directory structure exists and, if not, the directory path is created.

Debugging messages

You can generate quite a detailed trace of what Express does by running *Notes* this way:

```
$ DEBUG=express:* npm start
```

This is pretty useful if you want to debug Express. But, we can use this in our own code as well. It is similar to inserting console.log statements, but without having to remember to comment out the debugging code.

It is very simple to enable debugging in a module:

```
const debug = require('debug')('module-name');
..
debug('some message');
..
debug(`got file ${fileName}`);
```

Capturing stdout and stderr

Important messages can be printed to process.stdout or process.stderr, which can be lost if you don't capture that output. The Twelve Factor model suggests using a system facility to capture these output streams. With Notes, we'll use PM2 for that purpose, which we'll cover in Chapter 10, *Deploying Node.js Applications*.

The logbook module (https://github.com/jpillora/node-logbook) offers some useful capabilities in term of not only capturing process.stdout and process.stderr, but sending that output to useful places.

Uncaught exceptions

Uncaught exceptions is another area where important information can be lost. This is easy to fix in the *Notes* application:

```
const error = require('debug')('notes:error');

process.on('uncaughtException', function(err) {
  error("I've crashed!!! - "+ (err.stack || err));
});

..
if (app.get('env') === 'development') {
  app.use(function(err, req, res, next) {
    // util.log(err.message);
    res.status(err.status || 500);
    error((err.status || 500) +' '+ error.message);
    res.render('error', {
      message: err.message,
      error: err
    });
  });
}

..
app.use(function(err, req, res, next) {
  // util.log(err.message);
  res.status(err.status || 500);
  error((err.status || 500) +' '+ error.message);
  res.render('error', {
    message: err.message,
    error: {}
  });
});
```

The `debug` package has a convention we're following. For an application with several modules, all debugger objects should use the naming pattern `app-name:module-name`. In this case, we used `notes:error` that will be used for all error messages. We could also use `notes:memory-model` or `notes:mysql-model` for debugging different models.

While we were setting up the handler for uncaught exceptions, it is also a good idea to add error logging into the error handlers.

Unhandled Promise rejections

Using Promise and `async` functions automatically channels errors in a useful direction. Errors will cause a Promise to flip into a *rejected* state, which must eventually be handled in a `.catch` method. Since we're all human, we're bound to forget to ensure that all code paths handle their rejected Promise's.

Currently, Node.js prints the following warning if it detects an unhandled Promise rejection:

```
(node:4796) UnhandledPromiseRejectionWarning: Unhandled promise
rejection
```

The warning goes on to say that the default handler for unhandled Promise rejection has been deprecated and that such Promise rejections will crash the Node process rather than print this message. The built-in `process` module does emit an event in this case, so it's easy enough to add a handler:

```
import util from 'util';
...
process.on('unhandledRejection', (reason, p) => {
  error(`Unhandled Rejection at: ${util.inspect(p)} reason:
${reason}`);
});
```

At the minimum, we can print an error message such as the following:

```
notes:error Unhandled Rejection at: Promise {
  notes:error <rejected> TypeError: model(...).keylist is not a
function
  ... full stack trace
} reason: TypeError: model(...).keylist is not a function +3s
```

Using the ES6 module format

We wrote the *Notes* application using CommonJS modules, the traditional Node.js module format. While the application could continue using that format, the JavaScript community has chosen to switch to ES6 modules in both browser and Node.js code, and therefore it's important to switch ES6 modules so we can all get on board with a common module format. Let's rewrite the application using ES6 modules, and then write ES6 modules for anything new we add.

The changes required are large to replace `require` statements with `import` statements, and renaming files from `foo.js` to `foo.mjs`. Let's get started.

Rewriting app.js as an ES6 module

Let's start with `app.js`, changing its name to `app.mjs`:

```
$ mv app.js app.mjs
```

Change the block of `require` statements at the top to the following:

```
import fs from 'fs-extra';
import url from 'url';
import express from 'express';
import hbs from 'hbs';
import path from 'path';
import util from 'util';
import favicon from 'serve-favicon';
import logger from 'morgan';
import cookieParser from 'cookie-parser';
import bodyParser from 'body-parser';
import DBG from 'debug';
const debug = DBG('notes:debug');
const error = DBG('notes:error');
import { router as index } from './routes/index';
// const users = require('./routes/users');
import { router as notes } from './routes/notes';

// Workaround for lack of __dirname in ES6 modules
const __dirname = path.dirname(new URL(import.meta.url).pathname);

const app = express();

import rfs from 'rotating-file-stream';
```

Then, at the bottom of the script, make this change:

```
export default app;
```

Let's talk a little about the workaround mentioned here. There were several global variables automatically injected by Node.js into CommonJS modules. Those variables are not supported by ES6 modules. The critical variable for *Notes* is `__dirname`, which is used in `app.mjs` in several places. The code change shown here includes a workaround based on a brand new JavaScript feature that is available starting in Node.js 10.x, the `import.meta.url` variable.

The `import.meta` object is meant to inject useful information into an ES6 module. As the name implies, the `import.meta.url` variable contains the URL describing where the module was loaded from. For Node.js, at this time, ES6 modules can only be loaded from a `file://` URL on the local filesystem. That means, if we extract the `pathname` of that URL, we can easily calculate the directory containing the module, as shown here.

Why this solution? Why not use a pathname beginning with `./`? The answer is that a `./` filename is evaluated relative to the process's current working directory. That directory is usually different from the directory containing the Node.js module being executed. Therefore it is more than convenient that the Node.js team has added the `import.meta.url` feature.

The pattern followed in most cases is this change:

```
const moduleName = require('moduleName');   // in CommonJS modules
import moduleName from 'moduleName';        // in ES6 modules
```

Remember that Node.js uses the same module lookup algorithm in both ES6 and CommonJS modules. A Node.js `require` statement is synchronous, meaning that by the time `require` finishes, it has executed the module and is returning its `module.exports`. By contrast, an ES6 module is asynchronous, meaning the module may not have finished loading, and you can import just the required bits of the module.

Most of the module imports shown here are for regular Node.js modules installed in the `node_modules` directory, most of which are CommonJS modules. The rule for using `import` with a CommonJS module is that the `module.exports` object is treated as if it were the default export. The `import` statement shown earlier name the default export (or the `module.exports` object) as shown in the `import` statement. For a CommonJS module imported this way, you then use it as you would in a CommonJS context, `moduleName.functionName()`.

The usage of the `debug` module is effectively the same, but is coded differently. In the CommonJS context, we're told to use that module as follows:

```
const debug = require('debug')('notes:debug');
const error = require('debug')('notes:error');
```

In other words, the `module.exports` of this module is a function, which we immediately invoke. There isn't a syntax for ES6 modules to use the `debug` module in that fashion. Therefore, we had to break it apart as shown, and explicitly call that function.

The final point of discussion is the `import` of the two router modules. It was first attempted to have those modules export the `router` as the default value, but Express threw an error in that case. Instead, we'll rewrite these modules to export `router` as a named export and then use that named export as shown here.

Rewriting bin/www as an ES6 module

Remember that `bin/www` is a script used to launch the application. It is written as a CommonJS script, but because `app.mjs` is now an ES6 module, `bin/www` also must be rewritten as an ES6 module. A CommonJS module cannot, at the time of writing, import an ES6 module.

Change the filename:

```
$ mv bin/www bin/www.mjs
```

Then, at the top, change the `require` statements to `import` statements:

```
import app from '../app.mjs';
import DBG from 'debug';
const debug = DBG('notes:server-debug');
const error = DBG('notes:server-error');
import http from 'http';
```

We've already discussed everything here except that `app.mjs` exports its app object as the default export. Therefore, we use it as shown here.

Rewriting models code as ES6 modules

The models directory contains two modules: `Note.js` defines the `Note` class, and `notes-memory.js` contains an in-memory data model. Both are easy to convert to ES6 modules.

Change the filenames:

```
$ cd models
$ mv Note.js Note.mjs
$ mv notes-memory.js notes-memory.mjs
```

In `Note.mjs`, simply make the following change:

```
export default class Note {
    ...
}
```

This makes the `Note` class the default export.

Then, in `notes-memory.mjs`, make the following change:

```
import Note from './Note';

var notes = [];

async function crupdate(key, title, body) {
  notes[key] = new Note(key, title, body);
  return notes[key];
}

export function create(key, title, body) { return crupdate(key, title,
body); }
export function update(key, title, body) { return crupdate(key, title,
body); }

export async function read(key) {
  if (notes[key]) return notes[key];
  else throw new Error(`Note ${key} does not exist`);
}

export async function destroy(key) {
  if (notes[key]) {
    delete notes[key];
  } else throw new Error(`Note ${key} does not exist`);
}
```

```
export async function keylist() { return Object.keys(notes); }
export async function count() { return notes.length; }
export async function close() { }
```

This is a straightforward transliteration of assigning functions to `module.exports` to using named exports.

By defining the `Note` class as the default export of the `Note.mjs` module, it `imports` nicely into any module using that class.

Rewriting router modules as ES6 modules

The `routes` directory contains two router modules. As it stands, each router module creates a `router` object, adds route functions to that object, and then assigns it to the `module.exports` field. That suggests we should export the `router` as the default export, but as we said earlier, that didn't work out right. Instead, we'll export `router` as a named export.

Change the filenames:

```
$ cd routes
$ mv index.js index.mjs
$ mv notes.js notes.mjs
```

Then, at the top of each, change the `require` statement block to the following:

```
import util from 'util';
import express from 'express';
import * as notes from '../models/notes-memory';

export const router = express.Router();
```

It will be the same in both files. Then, at the bottom of each file, delete the line assigning `router` to `module.exports`.

Let's turn to `app.mjs` and change how the router modules are imported.

Because `router` is a named export, by default you'd import the `router` object, in `app.mjs`, as follows:

```
import { router } from './routes/index';
```

But then we'd have a conflict since both modules define a `router` object. Instead, we changed the name of this object using an `as` clause:

```
import { router as index } from './routes/index';
import { router as notes } from './routes/notes';
```

The `router` object from each module is hence given a suitable name.

Storing notes in the filesystem

The filesystem is an often overlooked database engine. While filesystems don't have the sort of query features supported by database engines, they are a reliable place to store files. The notes schema is simple enough that the filesystem can easily serve as its data storage layer.

Let's start by adding a function to `Note.mjs`:

```
export default class Note {
    ...
    get JSON() {
        return JSON.stringify({
          key: this.key, title: this.title, body: this.body
        });
    }

    static fromJSON(json) {
        var data = JSON.parse(json);
        var note = new Note(data.key, data.title, data.body);
        return note;
    }
}
```

`JSON` is a getter, which means it gets the value of the object. In this case, the `note.JSON` attribute/getter, no parentheses, will simply give us the JSON representation of the Note. We'll use this later for writing to JSON files.

`fromJSON` is a static function, or factory method, to aid in constructing `Note` objects if we have a JSON string. The difference is that `JSON` is associated with an instance of the `Note` class, while `fromJSON` is associated with the class itself. The two can be used as follows:

```
const note = new Note("key", "title", "body");
const json = note.JSON;       // produces JSON text
const newnote = Note.fromJSON(json); // produces new Note instance
```

Now, let's create a new module, `models/notes-fs.mjs`, to hold the filesystem model:

```
import fs from 'fs-extra';
import path from 'path';
import util from 'util';
import Note from './Note';
import DBG from 'debug';
const debug = DBG('notes:notes-fs');
const error = DBG('notes:error-fs');

async function notesDir() {
    const dir = process.env.NOTES_FS_DIR || "notes-fs-data";
    await fs.ensureDir(dir);
    return dir;
}

function filePath(notesdir, key) { return path.join(notesdir,
`${key}.json`); }

async function readJSON(notesdir, key) {
    const readFrom = filePath(notesdir, key);
    var data = await fs.readFile(readFrom, 'utf8');
    return Note.fromJSON(data);
}
```

The `notesDir` function will be used throughout `notes-fs` to ensure that the directory exists. To make this simple, we're using the `fs-extra` module because it adds Promise-based functions to the `fs` module (`https://www.npmjs.com/package/fs-extra`). In this case, `fs.ensureDir` verifies whether the named directory structure exists, and, if not, the directory path is created.

The environment variable, `NOTES_FS_DIR`, configures a directory within which to store notes. We'll have one file per note and store the note as JSON. If no environment variable is specified, we'll fall back on using `notes-fs-data` as the directory name.

Because we're adding another dependency:

```
$ npm install fs-extra --save
```

The filename for each data file is the `key` with `.json` appended. That gives one limitation that filenames cannot contain the `/` character, so we test for that using the following code:

```
async function crupdate(key, title, body) {
    var notesdir = await notesDir();
    if (key.indexOf('/') >= 0)
        throw new Error(`key ${key} cannot contain '/'`);
    var note = new Note(key, title, body);
    const writeTo = filePath(notesdir, key);
    const writeJSON = note.JSON;
    await fs.writeFile(writeTo, writeJSON, 'utf8');
    return note;
}

export function create(key, title, body) { return crupdate(key, title,
body); }
export function update(key, title, body) { return crupdate(key, title,
body); }
```

As is the case with the `notes-memory` module, the `create` and `update` functions use the exact same code. The `notesDir` function is used to ensure that the directory exists, then we create a `Note` object, and then write the data to a file.

Notice how the code is very straightforward because of the `async` function. We aren't checking for errors because they'll be automatically caught by the `async` function and bubble out to our caller:

```
export async function read(key) {
    var notesdir = await notesDir();
    var thenote = await readJSON(notesdir, key);
    return thenote;
}
```

Using `readJSON`, read the file from the disk. It already generates the `Note` object, so all we have to do is return that object:

```
export async function destroy(key) {
    var notesdir = await notesDir();
    await fs.unlink(filePath(notesdir, key));
}
```

The `fs.unlink` function deletes our file. Because this module uses the filesystem, deleting the file is all that's necessary to delete the `note` object:

```
export async function keylist() {
    var notesdir = await notesDir();
    var filez = await fs.readdir(notesdir);
    if (!filez || typeof filez === 'undefined') filez = [];
    var thenotes = filez.map(async fname => {
        var key = path.basename(fname, '.json');
        var thenote = await readJSON(notesdir, key);
        return thenote.key;
    });
    return Promise.all(thenotes);
}
```

The contract for `keylist` is to return a Promise that will resolve to an array of keys for existing note objects. Since they're stored as individual files in the `notesdir`, we have to read every file in that directory to retrieve its key.

`Array.map` constructs a new array from an existing array, namely the array of filenames returned by `fs.readdir`. Each entry in the constructed array is the `async` function, which reads the Note, returning the `key`:

```
export async function count() {
    var notesdir = await notesDir();
    var filez = await fs.readdir(notesdir);
    return filez.length;
}

export async function close() { }
```

Counting the number of notes is simply a matter of counting the number of files in `notesdir`.

Dynamic import of ES6 modules

Before we start modifying the router functions, we have to consider how to account for multiple models. We currently have two modules for our data model, `notes-memory` and `notes-fs`, and we'll be implementing several more by the end of this chapter. We will need a simple method to select between the model being used.

There are several possible ways to do this. For example, in a CommonJS module, it's possible to do the following:

```
const path  = require('path');
const notes = require(process.env.NOTES_MODEL
                ? path.join('..', process.env.NOTES_MODEL)
                : '../models/notes-memory');
```

This lets us set an environment variable, `NOTES_MODEL`, to select the module to use for the data model.

This approach does not work with the regular `import` statement, because the module name in an `import` statement cannot be such an expression. The Dynamic Import feature now in Node.js does offer a mechanism similar to the snippet just shown.

Dynamic import is an `import()` function that returns a Promise that will resolve to the imported module. As a function-returning-a-Promise, `import()` won't be useful as top-level code in the module. But, consider this:

```
var NotesModule;

async function model() {
   if (NotesModule) return NotesModule;
   NotesModule = await import(`../models/notes-
${process.env.NOTES_MODEL}`);
   return NotesModule;
}

export async function create(key, title, body) {
    return (await model()).create(key, title, body);
}
export async function update(key, title, body) {
    return (await model()).update(key, title, body);
}
export async function read(key) { return (await model()).read(key); }
export async function destroy(key) { return (await
model()).destroy(key); }
export async function keylist() { return (await model()).keylist(); }
export async function count() { return (await model()).count(); }
export async function close() { return (await model()).close(); }
```

Save that module in a file, `models/notes.mjs`. This module implements the same API as we'll use for all Notes model modules. The `model()` function is the key to dynamically selecting a notes model implementation based on an environment variable.

This is an `async` function and therefore its return value is a Promise. The value of that Promise is the selected module, as loaded by `import()`. Because `import()` returns a Promise, we use `await` to know whether it loaded correctly.

Every API method follows this pattern:

```
export async function methodName(args) {
    return (await model()).methodName(args);
}
```

Because `model()` returns a Promise, it's most succinct to use an `async` function and use `await` to resolve the Promise. Once the Promise is resolved, we simply call the `methodName` function and go about our business. Otherwise, those API method functions would be as follows:

```
export function methodName(args) {
    return model().then(notes => { return notes.methodName(args); });
}
```

The two implementations are equivalent, and it's clear which is the more succinct.

With all this `await`ing on Promise's returned from `async` functions, it's worth discussing the overhead. The worst case is on the first call to `model()`, because the selected notes model has not been loaded. The first time around, the call flow goes as follows:

- The API method calls `model()`, which calls `import()`, then `await`'s the module to finish loading
- The API method `await`'s the Promise returned from `model()`, getting the module object, and it then calls the API function
- The caller is also using `await` to receive the final result

The first time around, the time is dominated by waiting on `import()` to finish loading the module. On subsequent calls, the module has already been loaded and the first step is to simply form a resolved Promise containing the module. The API method can then quickly get on with delegating to the actual API method.

To use this, in `routes/index.mjs`, and in `routes/notes.mjs`, we make this change:

```
import util from 'util';
import express from 'express';
import * as notes from '../models/notes';

export const router = express.Router();
```

Running the Notes application with filesystem storage

In `package.json`, add this to the `scripts` section:

```
"start-fs": "DEBUG=notes:* NOTES_MODEL=fs node --experimental-modules
./bin/www.mjs",
```

 When you put these entries in `package.json`, make sure that you use correct JSON syntax. In particular, if you leave a comma at the end of the `scripts` section, it will fail to parse and npm will throw up an error message.

With this code in place, we can now run the *Notes* application as follows:

```
$ DEBUG=notes:* npm run start-fs
> notes@0.0.0 start-fs /Users/david/chap07/notes
> NOTES_MODEL=models/notes-fs node --experimental-modules ./bin/www.mjs
  notes:server Listening on port 3000 +0ms
  notes:fs-model keylist dir=notes-fs-data files=[  ] +4s
```

Then we can use the application at `http://localhost:3000` as before. Because we did not change any template or CSS files, the application will look exactly as you left it at the end of `Chapter 6`, *Implementing the Mobile-First Paradigm.*

Because debugging is turned on for `notes:*`, we'll see a log of whatever the *Notes* application is doing. It's easy to turn this off simply by not setting the `DEBUG` variable.

You can now kill and restart the *Notes* application and see the exact same notes. You can also edit the notes at the command line using regular text editors such as `vi`. You can now start multiple servers on different ports and see exactly the same notes:

```
"server1": "NOTES_MODEL=fs PORT=3001 node --experimental-
modules ./bin/www.mjs",
"server2": "NOTES_MODEL=fs PORT=3002 node --experimental-
modules ./bin/www.mjs",
```

Then you start `server1` and `server2` in separate command windows as we did in *Chapter 5*, *Your First Express Application*. Then, visit the two servers in separate browser windows, and you will see that both browser windows show the same notes.

The final check is to create a note where the key has a / character. Remember that the key is used to generate the filename where we store the note, and therefore the key cannot contain a / character. With the browser open, click on **ADD Note** and enter a note, ensuring that you use a / character in the `key` field. On clicking the **Submit** button, you'll see an error saying that this isn't allowed.

Storing notes with the LevelUP data store

To get started with actual databases, let's look at an extremely lightweight, small-footprint database engine: **LevelUP**. This is a Node.js-friendly wrapper around the LevelDB engine developed by Google, which is normally used in web browsers for local data persistence. It is a non-indexed, NoSQL data store designed originally for use in browsers. The Node.js module, Level, uses the LevelDB API, and supports multiple backends, including `LevelDOWN`, which integrates the C++ LevelDB database into Node.js.

Visit `https://www.npmjs.com/package/level` for information on the module. The `level` package automatically sets up the `levelup` and `leveldown` packages.

To install the database engine, run this command:

```
$ npm install level@2.1.x --save
```

Then, start creating the `models/notes-level.mjs` module:

```
import fs from 'fs-extra';
import path from 'path';
import util from 'util';
import Note from './Note';
import level from 'level';
```

```
import DBG from 'debug';
const debug = DBG('notes:notes-level');
const error = DBG('notes:error-level');

var db;

async function connectDB() {
    if (typeof db !== 'undefined' || db) return db;
    db = await level(
        process.env.LEVELDB_LOCATION || 'notes.level', {
            createIfMissing: true,
            valueEncoding: "json"
    });
    return db;
}
```

The `level` module gives us a `db` object through which to interact with the database. We're storing that object as a global within the module for ease of use. If the `db` object is set, we can just return it immediately. Otherwise, we open the database using `createIfMissing` to go ahead and create the database if needed.

The location of the database defaults to `notes.level` in the current directory. The environment variable `LEVELDB_LOCATION` can be set, as the name implies, to specify the database location:

```
async function crupdate(key, title, body) {
    const db = await connectDB();
    var note = new Note(key, title, body);
    await db.put(key, note.JSON);
    return note;
}

export function create(key, title, body) {
    return crupdate(key, title, body);
}

export function update(key, title, body) {
    return crupdate(key, title, body);
}
```

Calling db.put either creates a new database entry, or replaces an existing one.
Therefore, both update and create are set to be the same function. We convert the
Note to JSON so it can be easily stored in the database:

```
export async function read(key) {
    const db = await connectDB();
    var note = Note.fromJSON(await db.get(key));
    return new Note(note.key, note.title, note.body);
}
```

Reading a Note is easy: just call db.get and it retrieves the data, which must be
decoded from the JSON representation.

Notice that db.get and db.put did not take a callback function, and that we use
await to get the results value. The functions exported by level can take a callback
function, in which the callback will be invoked. Alternatively, if no callback function
is provided, the level function will instead return a Promise for compatibility with
async functions:

```
export async function destroy(key) {
    const db = await connectDB();
    await db.del(key);
}
```

The db.destroy function deletes a record from the database:

```
export async function keylist() {
    const db = await connectDB();
    var keyz = [];
    await new Promise((resolve, reject) => {
        db.createKeyStream()
        .on('data', data => keyz.push(data))
        .on('error', err => reject(err))
        .on('end', () => resolve(keyz));
    });
    return keyz;
}

export async function count() {
    const db = await connectDB();
    var total = 0;
    await new Promise((resolve, reject) => {
        db.createKeyStream()
        .on('data', data => total++)
        .on('error', err => reject(err))
        .on('end', () => resolve(total));
    });
}
```

```
        return total;
    }

    export async function close() {
        var _db = db;
        db = undefined;
        return _db ? _db.close() : undefined;
    }
```

The createKeyStream function uses an event-oriented interface similar to the Streams API. It will stream through every database entry, emitting events as it goes. A data event is emitted for every key in the database, while the end event is emitted at the end of the database, and the error event is emitted on errors. The effect is that there's no simple way to present this as a simple Promise. Instead, we invoke createKeyStream, let it run its course, collecting data as it goes. We have to wrap it inside a Promise object, and call resolve on the end event.

Then we add this to package.json in the scripts section:

```
"start-level": "DEBUG=notes:* NOTES_MODEL=level node --experimental-
modules ./bin/www.mjs",
```

Finally, you can run the *Notes* application:

```
$ DEBUG=notes:* npm run start-level
> notes@0.0.0 start /Users/david/chap07/notes
> node ./bin/www
  notes:server Listening on port 3000 +0ms
```

The printout in the console will be the same, and the application will also look the same. You can put it through its paces and see that everything works correctly.

Since level does not support simultaneous access to a database from multiple instances, you won't be able to use the multiple *Notes* application scenario. You will, however, be able to stop and restart the application at will without losing any notes.

Storing notes in SQL with SQLite3

To get started with more normal databases, let's see how to use SQL from Node.js. First, we'll use SQLite3, a lightweight, simple-to-set-up database engine eminently suitable for many applications.

To learn about that database engine, visit `http://www.sqlite.org/`.

To learn about the Node.js module, visit `https://github.com/mapbox/node-sqlite3/wiki/API` or `https://www.npmjs.com/package/sqlite3`.

The primary advantage of SQLite3 is that it doesn't require a server; it is a self-contained, no-set-up-required SQL database.

The first step is to install the module:

```
$ npm install sqlite3@3.x --save
```

SQLite3 database schema

Next, we need to make sure that our database is configured. We're using this SQL table definition for the schema (save this as `models/schema-sqlite3.sql`):

```sql
CREATE TABLE IF NOT EXISTS notes (
    notekey VARCHAR(255),
    title VARCHAR(255),
    body TEXT
);
```

How do we initialize this schema before writing some code? One way is to ensure that the `sqlite3` package is installed through your operating system package management system, such as using `apt-get` on Ubuntu/Debian, and MacPorts on macOS. Once it's installed, you can run the following command:

```
$ sqlite3 chap07.sqlite3
SQLite version 3.21.0 2017-10-24 18:55:49
Enter ".help" for usage hints.
sqlite> CREATE TABLE IF NOT EXISTS notes (
   ...> notekey VARCHAR(255),
   ...> title VARCHAR(255),
   ...> body TEXT
   ...> );
sqlite> .schema notes
```

```
CREATE TABLE notes (
    notekey VARCHAR(255),
    title VARCHAR(255),
    body TEXT
);
sqlite> ^D
$ ls -l chap07.sqlite3
-rwx------ 1 david staff 8192 Jan 14 20:40 chap07.sqlite3
```

While we can do that, the Twelve Factor application model says we must automate any administrative processes in this way. To that end, we should instead write a little script to run an SQL operation on SQLite3 and use that to initialize the database.

Fortunately, the `sqlite3` command offers us a way to do this. Add the following to the `scripts` section of `package.json`:

```
"sqlite3-setup": "sqlite3 chap07.sqlite3 --init models/schema-
sqlite3.sql",
```

Run the setup script:

```
$ npm run sqlite3-setup
> notes@0.0.0 sqlite3-setup /Users/david/chap07/notes
> sqlite3 chap07.sqlite3 --init models/schema-sqlite3.sql
-- Loading resources from models/schema-sqlite3.sql
SQLite version 3.10.2 2016-01-20 15:27:19
Enter ".help" for usage hints.
sqlite> .schema notes
CREATE TABLE notes (
    notekey VARCHAR(255),
    title   VARCHAR(255),
    body    TEXT
);
sqlite> ^D
```

We could have written a small Node.js script to do this, and it's easy to do so. However, by using the tools provided by the package, we have less code to maintain in our own project.

SQLite3 model code

Now, we can write code to use this database in the *Notes* application.

Create `models/notes-sqlite3.mjs` file:

```js
import util from 'util';
import Note from './Note';
import sqlite3 from 'sqlite3';
import DBG from 'debug';
const debug = DBG('notes:notes-sqlite3');
const error = DBG('notes:error-sqlite3');

var db; // store the database connection here

async function connectDB() {
    if (db) return db;
    var dbfile = process.env.SQLITE_FILE || "notes.sqlite3";
    await new Promise((resolve, reject) => {
        db = new sqlite3.Database(dbfile,
            sqlite3.OPEN_READWRITE | sqlite3.OPEN_CREATE,
            err => {
                if (err) return reject(err);
                resolve(db);
            });
    });
    return db;
}
```

This serves the same purpose as the `connectDB` function in `notes-level.mjs`: to manage the database connection. If the database is not open, it'll go ahead and do so, and even make sure that the database file is created (if it doesn't exist). But if it is already open, it is immediately returned:

```js
export async function create(key, title, body) {
    var db = await connectDB();
    var note = new Note(key, title, body);
    await new Promise((resolve, reject) => {
        db.run("INSERT INTO notes ( notekey, title, body) "+
            "VALUES ( ?, ? , ? );", [ key, title, body ], err => {
                if (err) return reject(err);
                resolve(note);
            });
    });
    return note;
}

export async function update(key, title, body) {
    var db = await connectDB();
    var note = new Note(key, title, body);
    await new Promise((resolve, reject) => {
        db.run("UPDATE notes "+
```

```
                "SET title = ?, body = ? WHERE notekey = ?",
                [ title, body, key ], err => {
                    if (err) return reject(err);
                    resolve(note);
            });
        });
        return note;
    }
```

These are our `create` and `update` functions. As promised, we are now justified in defining the Notes model to have separate functions for `create` and `update` operations, because the SQL statement for each is different.

Calling `db.run` executes an SQL query, giving us the opportunity to insert parameters into the query string.

The `sqlite3` module uses a parameter substitution paradigm that's common in SQL programming interfaces. The programmer puts the SQL query into a string, and then places a question mark in each place where the aim is to insert a value into the query string. Each question mark in the query string has to match a value in the array provided by the programmer. The module takes care of encoding the values correctly so that the query string is properly formatted, while preventing SQL injection attacks.

The `db.run` function simply runs the SQL query it is given, and does not retrieve any data. Because the `sqlite3` module doesn't produce any kind of Promise, we have to wrap function calls in a `Promise` object:

```
export async function read(key) {
  var db = await connectDB();
  var note = await new Promise((resolve, reject) => {
    db.get("SELECT * FROM notes WHERE notekey = ?", [key], (err,row)
  => {
            if (err) return reject(err);
            const note = new Note(row.notekey, row.title, row.body);
            resolve(note);
        });
    });
    return note;
  }
```

To retrieve data using the `sqlite3` module, you use the `db.get`, `db.all`, or `db.each` functions. The `db.get` function used here returns only the first row of the result set. The `db.all` function returns all rows of the result set at once, which can be a problem for available memory if the result set is large. The `db.each` function retrieves one row at a time, while still allowing processing of the entire result set.

For the *Notes* application, using `db.get` to retrieve a note is sufficient because there is only one note per `notekey`. Therefore, our `SELECT` query will return at most one row anyway. But what if your application will see multiple rows in the result set? We'll see what to do about that in a minute.

By the way, this `read` function has a bug in it. See if you can spot the error. We'll read more about this in Chapter 11, *Unit Testing and Functional Testing*, when our testing efforts uncover the bug:

```
export async function destroy(key) {
    var db = await connectDB();
    return await new Promise((resolve, reject) => {
        db.run("DELETE FROM notes WHERE notekey = ?;", [key], err => {
            if (err) return reject(err);
            resolve();
        });
    });
}
```

To destroy a note, we simply execute the DELETE FROM statement:

```
export async function keylist() {
    var db = await connectDB();
    var keyz = await new Promise((resolve, reject) => {
        var keyz = [];
        db.all("SELECT notekey FROM notes", (err, rows) => {
            if (err) return reject(err);
            resolve(rows.map(row => row.notekey ));
        });
    });
    return keyz;
}
```

The `db.all` function retrieves all rows of the result set.

The contract for this function is to return an array of note keys. The `rows` object is an array of results from the database that contains the data we are to return, but in a different format. Therefore, we use the `map` function to convert the array into the format required to fulfill the contract:

```
export async function count() {
    var db = await connectDB();
    var count = await new Promise((resolve, reject) => {
        db.get("select count(notekey) as count from notes", (err, row)
        => {
            if (err) return reject(err);
            resolve(row.count);
```

```
            });
        });
        return count;
    }

    export async function close() {
        var _db = db;
        db = undefined;
        return _db ? new Promise((resolve, reject) => {
                _db.close(err => {
                    if (err) reject(err);
                    else resolve();
                });
            }) : undefined;
    }
```

We can simply use SQL to count the number of notes for us. In this case, `db.get` returns a row with a single column, `count`, which is the value we want to return.

Running Notes with SQLite3

Finally, we're ready to run the *Notes* application with SQLite3. Add the following code to the `scripts` section of `package.json`:

```
"start-sqlite3": "SQLITE_FILE=chap07.sqlite3 NOTES_MODEL=sqlite3 node
--experimental-modules ./bin/www.mjs",
```

Run the *Notes* application:

```
$ DEBUG=notes:* npm run start-sqlite3
> notes@0.0.0 start-sqlite3 /Users/david/chap07/notes
> SQLITE_FILE=chap07.sqlite3 NOTES_MODEL=models/notes-sqlite3 node
./bin/www.mjs
  notes:server Listening on port 3000 +0ms
  notes:sqlite3-model Opened SQLite3 database chap07.sqlite3 +5s
```

You can now browse the application at `http://localhost:3000`, and run it through its paces as before.

Because SQLite3 supports simultaneous access from multiple instances, you can run the multiserver example by adding this to the `scripts` section of `package.json`:

```
"server1-sqlite3": "SQLITE_FILE=chap07.sqlite3 NOTES_MODEL=sqlite3
PORT=3001 node ./bin/www.mjs",
"server2-sqlite3": "SQLITE_FILE=chap07.sqlite3 NOTES_MODEL=sqlite3
PORT=3002 node ./bin/www.mjs",
```

Then, run each of these in separate command Windows, as before.

Because we still haven't made any changes to the View templates or CSS files, the application will look the same as before.

Of course, you can use the `sqlite` command, or other SQLite3 client applications, to inspect the database:

```
$ sqlite3 chap07.sqlite3
SQLite version 3.10.2 2016-01-20 15:27:19
Enter ".help" for usage hints.
sqlite> select * from notes;
hithere|Hi There||ho there what there
himom|Hi Mom||This is where we say thanks
```

Storing notes the ORM way with Sequelize

There are several popular SQL database engines, such as PostgreSQL, MySQL (`https://www.npmjs.com/package/mysql`), and MariaDB (`https://www.npmjs.com/package/mariasql`). Corresponding to each are Node.js client modules similar in nature to the `sqlite3` module that we just used. The programmer is close to the SQL, which can be good in the same way that driving a stick shift car is fun. But what if we want a higher-level view of the database so that we can think in terms of objects rather than rows of a database table? **Object Relation Mapping (ORM)** systems provide such a higher-level interface and even offer the ability to use the same data model with several databases.

The **Sequelize** module (`http://www.sequelizejs.com/`) is Promise-based, offers strong, well-developed ORM features, and can connect with SQLite3, MySQL, PostgreSQL, MariaDB, and MSSQL. Because Sequelize is Promise-based, it will fit naturally with the Promise-based application code we're writing.

A prerequisite to most SQL database engines is having access to a database server. In the previous section, we skirted around that issue by using SQLite3, which requires no database server setup. While it's possible to install a database server on your laptop, we want to avoid the complexity of doing so, and will use Sequelize to manage an SQLite3 database. We'll also see that it's simply a matter of a configuration file to run the same Sequelize code against a hosted database such as MySQL.

In `Chapter 10`, *Deploying Node.js Applications*, we'll learn how to use Docker to easily set up any service, including database servers, on our laptop and deploy the exact same configuration to a live server. Most web hosting providers offer MySQL or PostgreSQL as part of the service.

Before we start on the code, let's install two modules:

```
$ npm install sequelize@4.31.x --save
$ npm install js-yaml@3.10.x --save
```

The first obviously installs the Sequelize package. The second, `js-yaml`, is installed so that we can implement a YAML-formatted file to store the Sequelize connection configuration. YAML is a human-readable *data serialization language*, which simply means YAML is an easy-to-use text file format to describe data objects. Perhaps the best place to learn about YAML is its Wikipedia page at `https://en.wikipedia.org/wiki/YAML`.

Sequelize model for the Notes application

Let's create a new file, `models/notes-sequelize.mjs`:

```
import fs from 'fs-extra';
import util from 'util';
import jsyaml from 'js-yaml';
import Note from './Note';
import Sequelize from 'sequelize';
import DBG from 'debug';
const debug = DBG('notes:notes-sequelize');
const error = DBG('notes:error-sequelize');

var SQNote;
var sequlz;

async function connectDB() {
  if (typeof sequlz === 'undefined') {
    const YAML = await
fs.readFile(process.env.SEQUELIZE_CONNECT, 'utf8');
    const params = jsyaml.safeLoad(YAML, 'utf8');
```

```
        sequlz = new Sequelize(params.dbname, params.username,
                                params.password, params.params);
    }
    if (SQNote) return SQNote.sync();
    SQNote = sequlz.define('Note', {
        notekey: { type: Sequelize.STRING, primaryKey: true, unique:
        true },
        title: Sequelize.STRING,
        body: Sequelize.TEXT
    });
    return SQNote.sync();
}
```

The database connection is stored in the `sequlz` object, and is established by reading a configuration file (we'll go over this file later), and instantiating a Sequelize instance. The data model, `SQNote`, describes our object structure to Sequelize so that it can define corresponding database table(s). If `SQNote` is already defined, we simply return it, otherwise we define and return `SQNote`.

The Sequelize connection parameters are stored in a YAML file we specify in the `SEQUELIZE_CONNECT` environment variable. The line `new Sequelize(..)` opens the database connection. The parameters obviously contain any needed database name, username, password, and other options required to connect with the database.

The line `sequlz.define` is where we define the database schema. Instead of defining the schema as the SQL command to create the database table, we're giving a high-level description of the fields and their characteristics. Sequelize maps the object attributes into columns in tables.

We're telling Sequelize to call this schema Note, but we're using a `SQNote` variable to refer to that schema. That's because we already defined Note as a class to represent notes. To avoid a clash of names, we'll keep using the `Note` class, and use SQNote to interact with Sequelize about the notes stored in the database.

Online documentation can be found at the following locations:
Sequelize class: `http://docs.sequelizejs.com/en/latest/api/sequelize/`.
Defining
models: `http://docs.sequelizejs.com/en/latest/api/model/`.

Add these functions to `models/notes-sequelize.mjs`:

```
export async function create(key, title, body) {
    const SQNote = await connectDB();
    const note = new Note(key, title, body);
```

```
    await SQNote.create({ notekey: key, title: title, body: body });
    return note;
}

export async function update(key, title, body) {
    const SQNote = await connectDB();
    const note = await SQNote.find({ where: { notekey: key } })
    if (!note) { throw new Error(`No note found for ${key}`); } else {
        await note.updateAttributes({ title: title, body: body });
        return new Note(key, title, body);
    }
}
```

There are several ways to create a new object instance in Sequelize. The simplest is to call an object's `create` function (in this case, `SQNote.create`). That function collapses together two other functions, `build` (to create the object), and `save` (to write it to the database).

Updating an object instance is a little different. First, we must retrieve its entry from the database using the `find` operation. The `find` operation is given an object specifying the query. Using `find`, we retrieve one instance, whereas the `findAll` operation retrieves all matching instances.

For documentation on Sequelize queries, visit
`http://docs.sequelizejs.com/en/latest/docs/querying/`.

Like most or all other Sequelize functions, `SQNote.find` returns a Promise. Therefore, inside an `async` function, we `await` the result of the operation.

The update operation requires two steps, the first being to `find` the corresponding object to read it in from the database. Once the instance is found, we can update its values simply with the `updateAttributes` function:

```
export async function read(key) {
    const SQNote = await connectDB();
    const note = await SQNote.find({ where: { notekey: key } })
    if (!note) { throw new Error(`No note found for ${key}`); } else {
        return new Note(note.notekey, note.title, note.body);
    }
}
```

To read a note, we use the `find` operation again. There is the possibility of an empty result, and we have to throw an error to match.

The contract for this function is to return a `Note` object. That means taking the fields retrieved using Sequelize and using that to create a `Note` object:

```
export async function destroy(key) {
    const SQNote = await connectDB();
    const note = await SQNote.find({ where: { notekey: key } })
    return note.destroy();
}
```

To destroy a note, we use the `find` operation to retrieve its instance, and then call its `destroy()` method:

```
export async function keylist() {
    const SQNote = await connectDB();
    const notes = await SQNote.findAll({ attributes: [ 'notekey' ] });
    return notes.map(note => note.notekey);
}
```

Because the `keylist` function acts on all `Note` objects, we use the `findAll` operation. We query for the `notekey` attribute on all notes. We're given an array of objects with a field named `notekey`, and we use the `.map` function to convert this into an array of the note keys:

```
export async function count() {
    const SQNote = await connectDB();
    const count = await SQNote.count();
    return count;
}

export async function close() {
    if (sequlz) sequlz.close();
    sequlz = undefined;
    SQNote = undefined;
}
```

For the `count` function, we can just use the `count()` method to calculate the needed result.

Configuring a Sequelize database connection

Sequelize supports the same API on several SQL database engines. The database connection is initialized using parameters on the Sequelize constructor. The Twelve Factor Application model suggests that configuration data such as this should be kept outside the code and injected using environment variables or a similar mechanism. What we'll do is use a YAML-formatted file to store the connection parameters, specifying the filename with an environment variable.

The Sequelize library does not define any such file for storing connection parameters. But it's simple enough to develop such a file. Let's do so.

The API for the Sequelize constructor is: `constructor(database: String, username: String, password: String, options: Object)`.

In the `connectDB` function, we wrote the constructor as follows:

```
sequlz = new Sequelize(params.dbname, params.username,
params.password, params.params);
```

This file, named `models/sequelize-sqlite.yaml`, provides with us a simple mapping that looks like this for an SQLite3 database:

```
dbname: notes
username:
password:
params:
    dialect: sqlite
    storage: notes-sequelize.sqlite3
```

The YAML file is a direct mapping to the Sequelize constructor parameters. The `dbname`, `username`, and `password` fields in this file correspond directly to the connection credentials, and the `params` object gives additional parameters. There are many, many, possible attributes to use in the `params` field, and you can read about them in the Sequelize documentation at `http://docs.sequelizejs.com/manual/installation/usage.html`.

The `dialect` field tells Sequelize what kind of database to use. For an SQLite database, the database filename is given in the `storage` field.

Let's first use SQLite3, because no further setup is required. After that, we'll get adventurous and reconfigure our Sequelize module to use MySQL.

If you already have a different database server available, it's simple to create a corresponding configuration file. For a plausible MySQL database on your laptop, create a new file, such as `models/sequelize-mysql.yaml`, containing something like the following code:

```
dbname: notes
username: .. user name
password: .. password
params:
    host: localhost
    port: 3306
    dialect: mysql
```

This is straightforward. The `username` and `password` must correspond to the database credentials, while `host` and `port` will specify where the database is hosted. Set the database `dialect` and other connection information, and you're good to go.

To use MySQL, you will need to install the base MySQL driver so that Sequelize can use MySQL:

```
$ npm install mysql@2.x --save
```

Running with Sequelize against other databases it supports, such as PostgreSQL, is just as simple. Just create a configuration file, install the Node.js driver, and install/configure the database engine.

Running the Notes application with Sequelize

Now we can get ready to run the *Notes* application using Sequelize. We can run this against both SQLite3 and MySQL, but let's start with SQLite. Add this entry to the `scripts` entry in `package.json`:

```
"start-sequelize": "SEQUELIZE_CONNECT=models/sequelize-sqlite.yaml
NOTES_MODEL=sequelize node  --experimental-modules ./bin/www.mjs"
```

Then run it as follows:

```
$ DEBUG=notes:* npm run start-sequelize
> notes@0.0.0 start-sequelize /Users/david/chap07/notes
> SEQUELIZE_CONNECT=models/sequelize-sqlite.yaml NOTES_MODEL=sequelize
node --experimental-modules ./bin/www.mjs
  notes:server Listening on port 3000 +0ms
```

As before, the application looks exactly the same because we've not changed the View templates or CSS files. Put it through its paces and everything should work.

With Sequelize, multiple *Notes* application instances is as simple as adding these lines to the `scripts` section of `package.json`, and then starting both instances as before:

```
"server1-sequelize": "SEQUELIZE_CONNECT=models/sequelize-sqlite.yaml
NOTES_MODEL=sequelize PORT=3001 node --experimental-modules
./bin/www.mjs",
"server2-sequelize": "SEQUELIZE_CONNECT=models/sequelize-sqlite.yaml
NOTES_MODEL=sequelize PORT=3002 node --experimental-modules
./bin/www.mjs",
```

You will be able to start both instances, use separate browser windows to visit both instances, and see that they show the same set of notes.

To reiterate using the Sequelize-based model on a given database server:

1. Install and provision the database server instance, or else get the connection parameters for an already-provisioned database server.
2. Install the corresponding Node.js driver.
3. Write a YAML configuration file corresponding to the connection parameters.
4. Create new `scripts` entries in `package.json` to automate starting Notes against that database.

Storing notes in MongoDB

MongoDB is widely used with Node.js applications, a sign of which is the popular MEAN acronym: MongoDB (or MySQL), Express, Angular, and Node.js. MongoDB is one of the leading NoSQL databases. It is described as a *scalable, high-performance, open source, document-oriented database*. It uses JSON-style documents with no predefined, rigid schema and a large number of advanced features. You can visit their website for more information and documentation at `http://www.mongodb.org`.

Documentation on the Node.js driver for MongoDB can be found at `https://www.npmjs.com/package/mongodb` and `http://mongodb.github.io/node-mongodb-native/`.

Mongoose is a popular ORM for MongoDB (`http://mongoosejs.com/`). In this section, we'll use the native MongoDB driver instead, but Mongoose is a worthy alternative.

You will need a running MongoDB instance. The `compose.io`
(`https://www.compose.io/`) and `ScaleGrid.io` (`https://scalegrid.io/`) hosted
service providers offer hosted MongoDB services. Nowadays, it is straightforward to
host MongoDB as a Docker container as part of a system built of other Docker
containers. We'll do this in `Chapter 11`, *Unit Testing and Functional Testing*.

It's possible to set up a temporary MongoDB instance for testing on, say, your laptop.
It is available in all the operating system package management systems, and the
MongoDB website has instructions
(`https://docs.mongodb.org/manual/installation/`).

Once installed, it's not necessary to set up MongoDB as a background service. Instead,
you can run a couple of simple commands to get a MongoDB instance running in the
foreground of a command window, which you can kill and restart any time you like.

In one command window, run the following:

```
$ mkdir data
$ mongod --dbpath data
```

In another command window, you can test it as follows:

```
$ mongo
MongoDB shell version: 3.0.8
connecting to: test
Welcome to the MongoDB shell.
For interactive help, type "help".
For more comprehensive documentation, see
   http://docs.mongodb.org/
Questions? Try the support group
   http://groups.google.com/group/mongodb-user
> db.foo.save({ a: 1});
WriteResult({ "nInserted" : 1 })
> db.foo.find();
{ "_id" : ObjectId("56o0o98673f65b7988a96a77"), "a" : 1 }
>
bye
```

This saves a *document* in the collection named `foo`. The second command finds all
documents in `foo`, printing them out for you. The `_id` field is added by MongoDB
and serves as a document identifier. This is useful for testing and debugging. For a
real deployment, your MongoDB server must be properly installed on a server. See
the MongoDB documentation for these instructions.

MongoDB model for the Notes application

Now that you've proved you have a working MongoDB server, let's get to work.

Installing the Node.js driver is as simple as running the following command:

```
$ npm install mongodb@3.x --save
```

Now create a new file, `models/notes-mongodb.mjs`:

```
import util from 'util';
import Note from './Note';
import mongodb from 'mongodb';
const MongoClient = mongodb.MongoClient;
import DBG from 'debug';
const debug = DBG('notes:notes-mongodb');
const error = DBG('notes:error-mongodb');

var client;

async function connectDB() {
    if (!client) client = await
MongoClient.connect(process.env.MONGO_URL);
    return {
        db: client.db(process.env.MONGO_DBNAME),
        client: client
    };
}
```

The `MongoClient` class is used to connect with a MongoDB instance. The required URL, which will be specified through an environment variable, uses a straightforward format: `mongodb://localhost/`. The database name is specified via another environment variable.

Documentation for the corresponding objects can be found at `http://mongodb.github.io/node-mongodb-native/2.2/api/MongoClient.html` for MongoClient and `http://mongodb.github.io/node-mongodb-native/2.2/api/Db.html` for Db

This creates the database client, and then opens the database connection. Both objects are returned from `connectDB` in an anonymous object. The general pattern for MongoDB operations is as follows:

```
(async () => {
  const client = await MongoClient.connect(process.env.MONGO_URL);
  const db = client.db(process.env.MONGO_DBNAME);
```

```
    // perform database operations using db object
    client.close();
}) ();
```

Therefore, our model methods require both `client` and `db` objects, because they will use both. Let's see how that's done:

```
export async function create(key, title, body) {
    const { db, client } = await connectDB();
    const note = new Note(key, title, body);
    const collection = db.collection('notes');
    await collection.insertOne({ notekey: key, title, body });
    return note;
}

export async function update(key, title, body) {
    const { db, client } = await connectDB();
    const note = new Note(key, title, body);
    const collection = db.collection('notes');
    await collection.updateOne({ notekey: key }, { $set: { title, body
} });
    return note;
}
```

We retrieve `db` and `client` into individual variables using a destructuring assignment.

MongoDB stores all documents in collections. A *collection* is a group of related documents, and a collection is analogous to a table in a relational database. This means creating a new document or updating an existing one starts by constructing it as a JavaScript object, and then asking MongoDB to save that object to the database. MongoDB automatically encodes the object into its internal representation.

The `db.collection` method gives us a `Collection` object with which we can manipulate the named collection. See its documentation at `http://mongodb.github. io/node-mongodb-native/2.2/api/Collection.html`.

As the method name implies, `insertOne` inserts one document into the collection. Likewise, the `updateOne` method first finds a document (in this case, by looking up the document with the matching `notekey` field), and then changes fields in the document as specified.

You'll see that these methods return a Promise. The `mongodb` driver supports both callbacks and Promises. Many methods will invoke the callback function if one is provided, otherwise it returns a Promise that will deliver the results or errors. And, of course, since we're using `async` functions, the `await` keyword makes this so clean.

Further documentation can be found at the following links:
Insert: `https://docs.mongodb.org/getting-started/node/insert/`.

Update: `https://docs.mongodb.org/getting-started/node/updat e/`.

Next, let's look at reading a note from MongoDB:

```
export async function read(key) {
    const { db, client } = await connectDB();
    const collection = db.collection('notes');
    const doc = await collection.findOne({ notekey: key });
    const note = new Note(doc.notekey, doc.title, doc.body);
    return note;
}
```

The `mongodb` driver supports several variants of `find` operations. In this case, the *Notes* application ensures that there is exactly one document matching a given key. Therefore, we can use the `findOne` method. As the name implies, `findOne` will return the first matching document.

The argument to `findOne` is a query descriptor. This simple query looks for documents whose `notekey` field matches the requested `key`. An empty query will, of course, match all documents in the collection. You can match against other fields in a similar way, and the query descriptor can do much more. For documentation on queries, visit `https://docs.mongodb.org/getting-started/node/query/`.

The `insertOne` method we used earlier also took the same kind of query descriptor.

In order to satisfy the contract for this function, we create a `Note` object and then return it to the caller. Hence, we create a Note using the data retrieved from the database:

```
export async function destroy(key) {
    const { db, client } = await connectDB();
    const collection = db.collection('notes');
    await collection.findOneAndDelete({ notekey: key });
}
```

One of the `find` variants is `findOneAndDelete`. As the name implies, it finds one document matching the query descriptor, and then deletes that document:

```
export async function keylist() {
    const { db, client } = await connectDB();
    const collection = db.collection('notes');
    const keyz = await new Promise((resolve, reject) => {
        var keyz = [];
        collection.find({}).forEach(
            note => { keyz.push(note.notekey); },
            err => {
                if (err) reject(err);
                else resolve(keyz);
            }
        );
    });
    return keyz;
}
```

Here, we're using the base `find` operation and giving it an empty query so that it matches every document. What we're to return is an array containing the `notekey` for every document.

All of the `find` operations return a `Cursor` object. The documentation can be found at `http://mongodb.github.io/node-mongodb-native/2.1/api/Cursor.html`.

The Cursor object is, as the name implies, a pointer into a result set from a query. It has a number of useful functions related to operating on a result set. For example, you can skip the first few items in the results, or limit the size of the result set, or perform the `filter` and `map` operations.

The `Cursor.forEach` method takes two callback functions. The first is called on every element in the result set. In this case, we can use that to record just the `notekey` in an array. The second callback is called after all elements in the result set have been processed. We use this to indicate success or failure, and to return the `keyz` array.

Because `forEach` uses this pattern, it does not have an option for supplying a Promise, and we have to create the Promise ourselves, as shown here:

```
export async function count() {
    const { db, client } = await connectDB();
    const collection = db.collection('notes');
    const count = await collection.count({});
    return count;
}
```

```
export async function close() {
    if (client) client.close();
    client = undefined;
}
```

The `count` method takes a query descriptor and, as the name implies, counts the number of matching documents.

Running the Notes application with MongoDB

Now that we have our MongoDB model, we can get ready to run *Notes* with it.

By now you know the drill; add this to the `scripts` section of `package.json`:

```
"start-mongodb": "MONGO_URL=mongodb://localhost/ MONGO_DBNAME=chap07
NOTES_MODEL=mongodb node --experimental-modules ./bin/www.mjs",
```

The `MONGO_URL` environment variable is the URL to connect with your MongoDB database.

You can start the *Notes* application as follows:

```
$ DEBUG=notes:* npm run start-mongodb
> notes@0.0.0 start-mongodb /Users/david/chap07/notes
> MONGO_URL=mongodb://localhost/ MONGO_DBNAME=chap07
NOTES_MODEL=mongodb node --experimental-modules ./bin/www
  notes:server Listening on port 3000 +0ms
```

You can browse the application at `http://localhost:3000` and put it through its paces. You can kill and restart the application, and your notes will still be there.

Add this to the `scripts` section of `package.json`:

```
"server1-mongodb": "MONGO_URL=mongodb://localhost/ MONGO_DBNAME=chap07
NOTES_MODEL=mongodb PORT=3001 node --experimental-modules
./bin/www.mjs",
"server2-mongodb": "MONGO_URL=mongodb://localhost/ MONGO_DBNAME=chap07
NOTES_MODEL=mongodb PORT=3002 node --experimental-modules
./bin/www.mjs",
```

You will be able to start two instances of the *Notes* application, and see that both share the same set of notes.

Summary

In this chapter, we went through a real whirlwind of different database technologies. While we looked at the same seven functions over and over, it's useful to be exposed to the various data storage models and ways of getting things done. Even so, we only touched the surface of options for accessing databases and data storage engines from Node.js.

By abstracting the model implementations correctly, we were able to easily switch data storage engines while not changing the rest of the application. We did skip around the issue of setting up database servers. As promised, we'll get to that in Chapter 10, *Deploying Node.js Applications*, when we explore production deployment of Node.js applications.

By focusing the model code on the purpose of storing data, both the models and the application should be easier to test. The application can be tested with a mock data module that provides known predictable notes that can be checked predictably. We'll look at this in more depth in Chapter 11, *Unit Testing and Functional Testing*.

In the next chapter, we'll focus on authenticating our users using OAuth2.

8
Multiuser Authentication the Microservice Way

Now that our Notes application can save its data in a database, we can think about the next phase of making this a real application, namely authenticating our users.

It's so natural to log in to a website to use its services. We do it every day, and we even trust banking and investment organizations to secure our financial information through login procedures on a website. HTTP is a stateless protocol, and a web application cannot tell much about one HTTP request versus another. Because HTTP is stateless, HTTP requests do not natively know whether the user driving the web browser is logged in, the user's identity, or even whether the HTTP request was initiated by a human being.

The typical method for user authentication is to send a cookie to the browser containing a token to carry user identity. The cookie needs to contain data identifying the browser and whether that browser is logged in. The cookie will then be sent with every request, letting the application track which user account is associated with the browser.

With Express, the best way to do this is with the `express-session` middleware. It stores data as a cookie and looks for that data on every browser request. It is easy to configure, but is not a complete solution for user authentication. There are several add-on modules that handle user authentication, and some even support authenticating users against third-party websites, such as Facebook or Twitter.

One package appears to be leading the pack in user authentication – Passport (`http://passportjs.org/`). It supports a long list of services against which to authenticate, making it easy to develop a website that lets users sign up with credentials from another website, for example, Twitter. Another, express-authentication (`https://www.npmjs.com/package/express-authentication`), bills itself as the opinionated alternative to Passport.

We will use Passport to authenticate users against both a locally stored user credentials database and using OAuth2 to authenticate against a Twitter account. We'll also take this as an opportunity to explore REST-based microservice implementation with Node.js.

In this chapter, we'll discuss the following three aspects of this phase:

- Creating a microservice to store user profile/authentication data.
- User authentication with a locally stored password.
- Using OAuth2 to support authentication via third-party services. Specifically, we'll use Twitter as a third-party authentication service.

Let's get started!

The first thing to do is duplicate the code used for the previous chapter. For example, if you kept that code in `chap07/notes`, create a new directory, `chap08/notes`.

Creating a user information microservice

We could implement user authentication and accounts by simply adding a user model, and a few routes and views to the existing *Notes* application. While it would be accomplishable, is this what we would do in a real-world production application?

Consider the high value of user identity information, and the super-strong need for robust and reliable user authentication. Website intrusions happen regularly, and it seems the item most frequently stolen is user identities.

Can you design and build a user authentication system with the required level of security? One that is probably safe against all kinds of intruders?

As with so many other software development problems, it's best to use a pre-existing authentication library, preferably one with a long track record, where significant bugs have been fixed already.

Another issue is architectural choices to promote security. Bugs will occur and the talented miscreants will break in. Walling off the user information database is an excellent idea to limit the risk.

Keeping a user information database enables you to authenticate your users, present user profiles, help users connect with each other, and so forth. Those are useful services to offer to website users, but how can you limit the risk that data will fall into the wrong hands?

In this chapter, we'll develop a user authentication microservice. The plan is to eventually segregate that service into a well-protected barricaded area. This mimics an architectural choice made by some sites, to strictly control API and even physical access to the user information database, implementing as many technological barriers as possible against unapproved access.

Microservices are, of course, not a panacea, meaning we shouldn't try to force-fit every application into the microservice box. By analogy, microservices are like the Unix philosophy of small tools each doing one thing well, which we mix/match/combine into larger tools. Another word for this is composability. While we can build a lot of useful software tools with that philosophy, does it work for applications such as Photoshop or LibreOffice? While composing a system out of single-purpose tools is highly flexible, one loses the advantages gained by tight integration of components.

The first question is whether to use a REST-service oriented framework, code the REST application on bare Node.js, or what? You could implement REST services on the built-in `http` module. The advantage of using an application framework is the framework authors will have already baked-in a lot of best practices and bug fixing and security measures. Express, for example, is widely used, very popular, and can easily be used for REST services. There are other frameworks more aligned with developing REST services, and we'll use one of them – Restify (`http://restify.com/`).

The user authentication server will require two modules:

- Using Restify, implementing the REST interface
- A data model using Sequelize to store user data objects in an SQL database

To test the service, we'll write a couple of simple scripts for administering user information in the database. We won't be implementing an administrative user interface in the *Notes* application, and will rely on the scripts to administer the users. As a side effect, we'll have a tool to run a couple of simple tests against the user service.

After this service is functioning correctly, we'll set about modifying the Notes application to access user information from the service, while using Passport to handle authentication.

The first step is creating a new directory to hold the User Information microservice. This should be a sibling directory to the Notes application. If you created a directory named `chap08/notes` to hold the Notes application, then create a directory named `chap08/users` to hold the microservice.

Then run the following commands:

```
$ cd users
$ npm init
.. answer questions
.. name - user-auth-server
$ npm install debug@^2.6.x fs-extra@^5.x js-yaml@^3.10.x \
      restify@^6.3.x restify-clients@^1.5.x sequelize@^4.31.x \
      sqlite3@^3.1.x --save
```

This gets us ready to start coding. We'll use the `debug` module for logging messages, `js-yaml` to read the Sequelize configuration file, `restify` for its REST framework, and `sequelize/mysql/sqlite3` for database access.

User information model

We'll be storing the user information using a Sequelize-based model in an SQL database. As we go through this, ponder a question: should we integrate the database code directly into the REST API implementation? Doing so would reduce the user information microservice to one module, with database queries mingled with REST handlers. By separating the REST service from the data storage model, we have the freedom to adopt other data storage systems besides Sequelize/SQL. Further, the data storage model could conceivably be used in ways other than the REST service.

Create a new file named `users-sequelize.mjs` in `users`, containing the following:

```
import Sequelize from "sequelize";
import jsyaml from 'js-yaml';
import fs from 'fs-extra';
import util from 'util';
import DBG from 'debug';
const log = DBG('users:model-users');
const error = DBG('users:error');

var SQUser;
var sequlz;

async function connectDB() {
    if (SQUser) return SQUser.sync();
    const yamltext = await fs.readFile(process.env.SEQUELIZE_CONNECT,
    'utf8');
    const params = await jsyaml.safeLoad(yamltext, 'utf8');
    if (!sequlz) sequlz = new Sequelize(params.dbname,
params.username,
                              params.password,
```

```
params.params);
// These fields largely come from the Passport / Portable Contacts
schema.
// See http://www.passportjs.org/docs/profile
//
// The emails and photos fields are arrays in Portable Contacts.
// We'd need to set up additional tables for those.
//
// The Portable Contacts "id" field maps to the "username" field
here
if (!SQUser) SQUser = sequlz.define('User', {
    username: { type: Sequelize.STRING, unique: true },
    password: Sequelize.STRING,
    provider: Sequelize.STRING,
    familyName: Sequelize.STRING,
    givenName: Sequelize.STRING,
    middleName: Sequelize.STRING,
    emails: Sequelize.STRING(2048),
    photos: Sequelize.STRING(2048)
});
return SQUser.sync();
}
```

As with our Sequelize-based model for Notes, we use a YAML file to store connection configuration. We're even using the same environment variable, `SEQUELIZE_CONNECT`.

What is the best storage service for user authentication data? By using Sequelize, we have our pick of SQL databases to choose from. While NoSQL databases are all the rage, is there any advantage to using one to store user authentication data? Nope. An SQL server will do the job just fine, and Sequelize allows us the freedom of choice.

It's tempting to simplify the overall system by using the same database instance to store notes and user information, and to use Sequelize for both. But we've chosen to simulate a secured server for user data. That calls for the data to be in separate database instances, preferably on separate servers. A highly secure application deployment might put the user information service on completely separate servers, perhaps in a physically isolated data center, with carefully configured firewalls, and there might even be armed guards at the door.

The user profile schema shown here is derived from the normalized profile provided by Passport; refer to `http://www.passportjs.org/docs/profile` for more information. Passport will harmonize information given by third-party services into a single object definition. To simplify our code, we're simply using the schema defined by Passport:

```
export async function create(username, password, provider, familyName,
givenName, middleName, emails, photos) {
    const SQUser = await connectDB();
    return SQUser.create({
        username, password, provider,
        familyName, givenName, middleName,
        emails: JSON.stringify(emails), photos: JSON.stringify(photos)
    });
}

export async function update(username, password, provider, familyName,
givenName, middleName, emails, photos) {
    const user = await find(username);
    return user ? user.updateAttributes({
        password, provider,
        familyName, givenName, middleName,
        emails: JSON.stringify(emails),
        photos: JSON.stringify(photos)
    }) : undefined;
}
```

Our `create` and `update` functions take user information and either add a new record or update an existing record:

```
export async function find(username) {
    const SQUser = await connectDB();
    const user = await SQUser.find({ where: { username: username } });
    const ret = user ? sanitizedUser(user) : undefined;
    return ret;
}
```

This lets us look up a user information record, and we return a sanitized version of that data.

Remember that Sequelize returns a `Promise` object. Because this is executed inside an `async` function, the `await` keyword will resolve the Promise, causing any error to be thrown or results to be provided as the return value. In turn, async functions return a `Promise` to the caller.

Because we're segregating the user data from the rest of the Notes application, we want to return a sanitized object rather than the actual SQUser object. What if there was some information leakage because we simply sent the SQUser object back to the caller? The sanitizedUser function, shown later, creates an anonymous object with exactly the fields we want exposed to the other modules:

```
export async function destroy(username) {
    const SQUser = await connectDB();
    const user = await SQUser.find({ where: { username: username } });
    if (!user) throw new Error('Did not find requested '+ username +'
to delete');
    user.destroy();
}
```

This lets us support deleting user information. We do this as we did for the Notes Sequelize model, by first finding the user object and then calling its destroy method:

```
export async function userPasswordCheck(username, password) {
    const SQUser = await connectDB();
    const user = await SQUser.find({ where: { username: username } });
    if (!user) {
        return { check: false, username: username, message: "Could not
        find user" };
    } else if (user.username === username && user.password ===
password) {
        return { check: true, username: user.username };
    } else {
        return { check: false, username: username, message: "Incorrect
        password" };
    }
}
```

This lets us support the checking of user passwords. The three conditions to handle are as follows:

- Whether there's no such user
- Whether the passwords matched
- Whether they did not match

The object we return lets the caller distinguish between those cases. The check field indicates whether to allow this user to be logged in. If check is false, there's some reason to deny their request to log in, and the message is what should be displayed to the user:

```
export async function findOrCreate(profile) {
    const user = await find(profile.id);
    if (user) return user;
    return await create(profile.id, profile.password,
profile.provider,
                profile.familyName, profile.givenName,
profile.middleName,
                profile.emails, profile.photos);
}
```

This combines two actions in one function: first, to verify whether the named user exists and, if not, to create that user. Primarily, this will be used while authenticating against third-party services:

```
export async function listUsers() {
    const SQUser = await connectDB();
    const userlist = await SQUser.findAll({});
    return userlist.map(user => sanitizedUser(user));
}
```

List the existing users. The first step is using findAll to give us the list of the users as an array of SQUser objects. Then we sanitize that list so we don't expose any data that we don't want exposed:

```
export function sanitizedUser(user) {
    var ret = {
        id: user.username, username: user.username,
        provider: user.provider,
        familyName: user.familyName, givenName: user.givenName,
        middleName: user.middleName,
        emails: JSON.parse(user.emails),
        photos: JSON.parse(user.photos)
    };
    try {
        ret.emails = JSON.parse(user.emails);
    } catch(e) { ret.emails = []; }
    try {
        ret.photos = JSON.parse(user.photos);
    } catch(e) { ret.photos = []; }
    return ret;
}
```

This is our utility function to ensure we expose a carefully controlled set of information to the caller. With this service, we're emulating a secured user information service that's walled off from other applications. As we said earlier, this function returns an anonymous sanitized object where we know exactly what's in the object.

It's very important to decode the JSON string we put into the database. Remember that we stored the `emails` and `photos` data using `JSON.stringify` in the database. Using `JSON.parse`, we decode those values, just like adding hot water to instant coffee produces a drinkable beverage.

A REST server for user information

We are building our way towards integrating user information and authentication into the Notes application. The next step is to wrap the user data model we just created into a REST server. After that, we'll create a couple of scripts so that we can add some users, perform other administrative tasks, and generally verify that the service works. Finally, we'll extend the Notes application with login and logout support.

In the `package.json` file, change the `main` tag to the following line of code:

```
"main": "user-server.mjs",
```

Then create a file named `user-server.mjs`, containing the following code:

```
import restify from 'restify';
import util from 'util';

import DBG from 'debug';
const log = DBG('users:service');
const error = DBG('users:error');

import * as usersModel from './users-sequelize';

var server = restify.createServer({
    name: "User-Auth-Service",
    version: "0.0.1"
});

server.use(restify.plugins.authorizationParser());
server.use(check);
server.use(restify.plugins.queryParser());
server.use(restify.plugins.bodyParser({
```

```
        mapParams: true
}));
```

The `createServer` method can take a long list of configuration options. These two may be useful for identifying information.

As with Express applications, the `server.use` calls initialize what Express would call middleware functions, but which Restify calls handler functions. These are callback functions whose API is `function (req, res, next)`. As with Express, these are the request and response objects, and `next` is a function which, when called, carries execution to the next handler function.

Unlike Express, every handler function must call the `next` function. In order to tell Restify to stop processing through handlers, the `next` function must be called as `next(false)`. Calling `next` with an `error` object also causes the execution to end, and the error is sent back to the requestor.

The handler functions listed here do two things: authorize requests and handle parsing parameters from both the URL and the `post` request body. The `authorizationParser` function looks for HTTP basic auth headers. The `check` function is shown later and emulates the idea of an API token to control access.

Refer to `http://restify.com/docs/plugins-api/` for more information on the built-in handlers available in Restify.

Add this to `user-server.mjs`:

```
// Create a user record
server.post('/create-user', async (req, res, next) => {
    try {
        var result = await usersModel.create(
                req.params.username, req.params.password,
            req.params.provider,
                req.params.familyName, req.params.givenName,
            req.params.middleName,
                req.params.emails, req.params.photos);
        res.send(result);
        next(false);
    } catch(err) { res.send(500, err); next(false); }
});
```

As for Express, the `server.VERB` functions let us define the handlers for specific HTTP actions. This route handles a POST on `/create-user`, and, as the name implies, this will create a user by calling the `usersModel.create` function.

As a `POST` request, the parameters arrive in the body of the request rather than as URL parameters. Because of the `mapParams` flag on the `bodyParams` handler, the arguments passed in the HTTP body are added to `req.params`.

We simply call `usersModel.create` with the parameters sent to us. When completed, the `result` object should be a `user` object, which we send back to the requestor using `res.send`:

```
// Update an existing user record
server.post('/update-user/:username', async (req, res, next) => {
    try {
        var result = await usersModel.update(
            req.params.username, req.params.password,
        req.params.provider,
            req.params.familyName, req.params.givenName,
        req.params.middleName,
            req.params.emails, req.params.photos);
        res.send(usersModel.sanitizedUser(result));
        next(false);
    } catch(err) { res.send(500, err); next(false); }
});
```

The `/update-user` route is handled in a similar way. However, we have put the `username` parameter on the URL. Like Express, Restify lets you put named parameters in the URL like as follows. Such named parameters are also added to `req.params`.

We simply call `usersModel.update` with the parameters sent to us. That, too, returns an object we send back to the caller with `res.send`:

```
// Find a user, if not found create one given profile information
server.post('/find-or-create', async (req, res, next) => {
    log('find-or-create '+ util.inspect(req.params));
    try {
        var result = await usersModel.findOrCreate({
            id: req.params.username, username: req.params.username,
            password: req.params.password, provider:
            req.params.provider,
            familyName: req.params.familyName, givenName:
            req.params.givenName,
            middleName: req.params.middleName,
            emails: req.params.emails, photos: req.params.photos
```

```
        });
        res.send(result);
        next(false);
    } catch(err) { res.send(500, err); next(false); }
});
```

This handles our `findOrCreate` operation. We simply delegate this to the model code, as done previously.

As the name implies, we'll look to see whether the named user already exists and, if so, simply return that user, otherwise it will be created:

```
// Find the user data (does not return password)
server.get('/find/:username', async (req, res, next) => {
    try {
        var user = await usersModel.find(req.params.username);
        if (!user) {
            res.send(404, new Error("Did not find "+
            req.params.username));
        } else {
            res.send(user);
        }
        next(false);
    } catch(err) { res.send(500, err); next(false); }
});
```

Here, we support looking up the user object for the provided `username`.

If the user was not found, then we return a 404 status code because it indicates a resource that does not exist. Otherwise, we send the object that was retrieved:

```
// Delete/destroy a user record
server.del('/destroy/:username', async (req, res, next) => {
    try {
        await usersModel.destroy(req.params.username);
        res.send({});
        next(false);
    } catch(err) { res.send(500, err); next(false); }
});
```

This is how we delete a user from the Notes application. The `DEL` HTTP verb is meant to be used to delete things on a server, making it the natural choice for this functionality:

```
// Check password
server.post('/passwordCheck', async (req, res, next) => {
    try {
        await usersModel.userPasswordCheck(
                    req.params.username, req.params.password);
        res.send(check);
        next(false);
    } catch(err) { res.send(500, err); next(false); }
});
```

This is another aspect of keeping the password solely within this server. The password check is performed by this server, rather than in the Notes application. We simply call the `usersModel.userPasswordCheck` function shown earlier and send back the object it returns:

```
// List users
server.get('/list', async (req, res, next) => {
    try {
        var userlist = await usersModel.listUsers();
        if (!userlist) userlist = [];
        res.send(userlist);
        next(false);
    } catch(err) { res.send(500, err); next(false); }
});
```

Then, finally, if required, we send a list of Notes application users back to the requestor. In case no list of users is available, we at least send an empty array:

```
server.listen(process.env.PORT, "localhost", function() {
    log(server.name +' listening at '+ server.url);
});

// Mimic API Key authentication.

var apiKeys = [ {
    user: 'them',
    key: 'D4ED43C0-8BD6-4FE2-B358-7C0E230D11EF'
} ];

function check(req, res, next) {
    if (req.authorization) {
        var found = false;
        for (let auth of apiKeys) {
```

```
            if (auth.key   === req.authorization.basic.password
              && auth.user === req.authorization.basic.username) {
                  found = true;
                  break;
              }
        }
        if (found) next();
        else {
              res.send(401, new Error("Not authenticated"));
              next(false);
        }
    } else {
          res.send(500, new Error('No Authorization Key'));
          next(false);
    }
}
```

As with the Notes application, we listen to the port named in the PORT environment variable. By explicitly listening only on `localhost`, we'll limit the scope of systems that can access the user authentication server. In a real deployment, we might have this server behind a firewall with a tight list of host systems allowed to have access.

This last function, `check`, implements authentication for the REST API itself. This is the handler function we added earlier.

It requires the caller to provide credentials on the HTTP request using the basic auth headers. The `authorizationParser` handler looks for this and gives it to us on the `req.authorization.basic` object. The `check` function simply verifies that the named user and password combination exists in the local array.

This is meant to mimic assigning an API key to an application. There are several ways of doing so; this is just one.

This approach is not limited to just authenticating using HTTP basic auth. The Restify API lets us look at any header in the HTTP request, meaning we could implement any kind of security mechanism we like. The `check` function could implement some other security method, with the right code.

Because we added `check` with the initial set of `server.use` handlers, it is called on every request. Therefore, every request to this server must provide the HTTP basic auth credentials required by this check.

This strategy is good if you want to control access to every single function in your API. For the user authentication service, that's probably a good idea. Some REST services in the world have certain API functions that are open to the world and others protected by an API token. To implement that, the `check` function should not be configured among the `server.use` handlers. Instead, it should be added to the appropriate route handlers as follows:

```
server.get('/request/url', authHandler, (req, res, next) => {
    ..
});
```

Such an `authHandler` would be coded similarly to our `check` function. A failure to authenticate is indicated by sending an error code and using `next(false)` to end the routing function chain.

We now have the complete code for the user authentication server. It defines several request URLs, and for each, the corresponding function in the user model is called.

Now we need a YAML file to hold the database credentials, so create `sequelize-sqlite.yaml`, containing the following code:

```
dbname: users
username:
password:
params:
    dialect: sqlite
    storage: users-sequelize.sqlite3
```

Since this is Sequelize, it's easy to switch to other database engines simply by supplying a different configuration file. Remember that the filename of this configuration file must appear in the `SEQUELIZE_CONNECT` environment variable.

Finally, `package.json` should look as follows:

```
{
  "name": "user-auth-server",
  "version": "0.0.1",
  "description": "",
  "main": "user-server.js",
  "scripts": {
    "start": "DEBUG=users:* PORT=3333 SEQUELIZE_CONNECT=sequelize-
sqlite.yaml node --experimental-modules user-server"
  },
  "author": "",
  "license": "ISC",
  "engines": {
```

```
      "node": ">=8.9"
    },
    "dependencies": {
      "debug": "^2.6.9",
      "fs-extra": "^5.x",
      "js-yaml": "^3.10.x",
      "mysql": "^2.15.x",
      "restify": "^6.3.x",
      "restify-clients": "^1.5.x",
      "sqlite3": "^3.1.x",
      "sequelize": "^4.31.x"
    }
}
```

We configure this server to listen on port 3333 using the database credentials we just gave and with debugging output for the server code.

You can now start the user authentication server:

```
$ npm start
> user-auth-server@0.0.1 start /Users/david/chap08/users
> DEBUG=users:* PORT=3333 SEQUELIZE_CONNECT=sequelize-mysql.yaml node
user-server
   users:server User-Auth-Service listening at http://127.0.0.1:3333
+0ms
```

But we don't have any way to interact with this server, yet.

Scripts to test and administer the user authentication server

To give ourselves assurance that the user authentication server works, let's write a couple of scripts to exercise the API. Because we're not going to take the time to write an administrative backend to the Notes application, these scripts will let us add and delete users who are allowed access to Notes. These scripts will live within the user authentication server package directory.

The Restify package supports coding REST servers. For the REST clients, we're using a companion library, restify-clients, which has been spun out of Restify.

Create a file named `users-add.js`, containing the following code:

```js
'use strict';

const util = require('util');
const restify = require('restify-clients');

var client = restify.createJsonClient({
  url: 'http://localhost:'+process.env.PORT,
  version: '*'
});

client.basicAuth('them', 'D4ED43C0-8BD6-4FE2-B358-7C0E230D11EF');

client.post('/create-user', {
    username: "me", password: "w0rd", provider: "local",
    familyName: "Einarrsdottir", givenName: "Ashildr", middleName: "",
    emails: [], photos: []
},
(err, req, res, obj) => {
    if (err) console.error(err.stack);
    else console.log('Created '+ util.inspect(obj));
});
```

This is the basic structure of a Restify client. We create the `Client` object – we have a choice between the `JsonClient`, as used here, the `StringClient`, and the `HttpClient`. The HTTP `basicAuth` credentials are easy to set, as shown here.

Then we make the request, in this case a `POST` request on `/create-user`. Because it is a `POST` request, the object we specify here is formatted by Restify into HTTP POST body parameters. As we saw earlier, the server has the `bodyParser` handler function configured, which converts those body parameters into the `req.param` object.

In the Restify client, as for the Restify server, we use the various HTTP methods by calling `client.METHOD`. Because it is a `POST` request, we use `client.post`. When the request finishes, the callback function is invoked.

Before running these scripts, start the authentication server in one window using the following command:

```
$ npm start
```

Now run the test script using the following command:

```
$ PORT=3333 node users-add.js
Created { id: 1, username: 'me', password: 'w0rd', provider: 'local',
  familyName: 'Einarrsdottir', givenName: 'Ashildr',
  middleName: '',
  emails: '[]', photos: '[]',
  updatedAt: '2016-02-24T02:34:41.661Z',
  createdAt: '2016-02-24T02:34:41.661Z' }
```

We can inspect our handiwork using the following command:

```
$ sqlite3 users-sequelize.sqlite3
SQLite version 3.10.2 2016-01-20 15:27:19
Enter ".help" for usage hints.
sqlite> .schema users
CREATE TABLE `Users` (`id` INTEGER PRIMARY KEY AUTOINCREMENT,
`username` VARCHAR(255) UNIQUE, `password` VARCHAR(255), `provider`
VARCHAR(255), `familyName` VARCHAR(255), `givenName` VARCHAR(255),
`middleName` VARCHAR(255), `emails` VARCHAR(2048), `photos`
VARCHAR(2048), `createdAt` DATETIME NOT NULL, `updatedAt` DATETIME NOT
NULL, UNIQUE (`username`));
sqlite> select * from users;
2|me|w0rd|local|Einarrsdottir|Ashildr||[]||[]|2018-01-21 05:34:56.629
+00:00|2018-01-21 05:34:56.629 +00:00
sqlite> ^D
```

Now let's write a script, `users-find.js`, to look up a given user:

```
'use strict';

const util = require('util');
const restify = require('restify-clients');

var client = restify.createJsonClient({
  url: 'http://localhost:'+process.env.PORT,
  version: '*'
});

client.basicAuth('them', 'D4ED43C0-8BD6-4FE2-B358-7C0E230D11EF');

client.get('/find/'+ process.argv[2],
(err, req, res, obj) => {
    if (err) console.error(err.stack);
    else console.log('Found '+ util.inspect(obj));
});
```

This simply calls the `/find` URL, specifying the `username` that the user supplies as a command-line argument. Note that the `get` operation does not take an object full of parameters. Instead, any parameters would be added to the URL.

It's run as follows:

```
$ PORT=3333 node users-find.js me
Found { username: 'me', provider: 'local',
  familyName: 'Einarrsdottir', givenName: 'Ashildr',
  middleName: '',
  emails: '[]', photos: '[]' }
```

Similarly, we can write scripts against the other REST functions. But we need to get on with the real goal of integrating this into the Notes application.

Login support for the Notes application

Now that we have proved that the user authentication service is working, we can set up the Notes application to support user logins. We'll be using Passport to support login/logout, and the authentication server to store the required data.

Among the available packages, Passport stands out for simplicity and flexibility. It integrates directly with the Express middleware chain, and the Passport community has developed hundreds of so-called Strategy modules to handle authentication against a long list of third-party services. See `http://www.passportjs.org/` for information and documentation.

Accessing the user authentication REST API

The first step is to create a user data model for the Notes application. Rather than retrieving data from data files or a database, it will use REST to query the server we just created. We could have created user model code that directly accesses the database but, for reasons already discussed, we've decided to segregate user authentication into a separate service.

Let us now turn to the Notes application, which you may have stored as `chap08/notes`. We'll be modifying the application, first to access the user authentication REST API, and then to use Passport for authorization and authentication.

For the test/admin scripts that we created earlier, we used the `restify-clients` module. That package is a companion to the `restify` library, where `restify` supports the server side of the REST protocol and `restify-clients` supports the client side. Their names might give away the purpose.

However nice the `restify-clients` library is, it doesn't support a Promise-oriented API, as is required to play well with `async` functions. Another library, `superagent`, does support a Promise-oriented API, plays well in `async` functions, and there is a companion to that package, Supertest, that's useful in unit testing. We'll use Supertest in *Chapter 11, Unit Testing and Functional Testing*, when we talk about unit testing. For documentation, see `https://www.npmjs.com/package/superagent`:

```
$ npm install superagent@^3.8.x
```

Create a new file, `models/users-superagent.mjs`, containing the following code:

```
import request from 'superagent';
import util from 'util';
import url from 'url';
const URL = url.URL;
import DBG from 'debug';
const debug = DBG('notes:users-superagent');
const error = DBG('notes:error-superagent');

function reqURL(path) {
    const requrl = new URL(process.env.USER_SERVICE_URL);
    requrl.pathname = path;
    return requrl.toString();
}
```

The `reqURL` function replaces the `connectXYZZY` functions that we wrote in earlier modules. With `superagent`, we don't leave a connection open to the service, but open a new connection on each request. The common thing to do is to formulate the request URL. The user is expected to provide a base URL, such as `http://localhost:3333/`, in the USER_SERVICE_URL environment variable. This function modifies that URL, using the new WHATWG URL support in Node.js, to use a given URL path:

```
export async function create(username, password,
            provider, familyName, givenName, middleName,
            emails, photos) {
    var res = await request
        .post(reqURL('/create-user'))
        .send({
            username, password, provider,
```

```
            familyName, givenName, middleName, emails, photos
        })
        .set('Content-Type', 'application/json')
        .set('Acccept', 'application/json')
        .auth('them', 'D4ED43C0-8BD6-4FE2-B358-7C0E230D11EF');
    return res.body;
}


export async function update(username, password,
        provider, familyName, givenName, middleName,
        emails, photos) {
    var res = await request
        .post(reqURL(`/update-user/${username}`))
        .send({
            username, password, provider,
            familyName, givenName, middleName, emails, photos
        })
        .set('Content-Type', 'application/json')
        .set('Acccept', 'application/json')
        .auth('them', 'D4ED43C0-8BD6-4FE2-B358-7C0E230D11EF');
    return res.body;
}
```

These are our `create` and `update` functions. In each case, they take the data provided, construct an anonymous object, and `POST` it to the server.

The `superagent` library uses an API style where one chains together method calls to construct a request. The chain of method calls can end in a `.then` or `.end` clause, either of which take a callback function. But leave off both, and it will return a Promise.

All through this library, we'll use the `.auth` clause to set up the required authentication key.

These anonymous objects are a little different than usual. We're using a new ES-2015 feature here that we haven't discussed so far. Rather than specifying the object fields using the `fieldName:` `fieldValue` notation, ES-2015 gives us the option to shorten this when the variable name used for `fieldValue` matches the desired `fieldName`. In other words, we can just list the variable names, and the field name will automatically match the variable name.

In this case, we've purposely chosen variable names for the parameters to match field names of the object with parameter names used by the server. By doing so, we can use this shortened notation for anonymous objects, and our code is a little cleaner by using consistent variable names from beginning to end:

```
export async function find(username) {
    var res = await request
        .get(reqURL(`/find/${username}`))
        .set('Content-Type', 'application/json')
        .set('Acccept', 'application/json')
        .auth('them', 'D4ED43C0-8BD6-4FE2-B358-7C0E230D11EF');
    return res.body;
}
```

Our `find` operation lets us look up user information:

```
export async function userPasswordCheck(username, password) {
    var res = await request
        .post(reqURL(`/passwordCheck`))
        .send({ username, password })
        .set('Content-Type', 'application/json')
        .set('Acccept', 'application/json')
        .auth('them', 'D4ED43C0-8BD6-4FE2-B358-7C0E230D11EF');
    return res.body;
}
```

We're sending the request to check passwords to the server.

A point about this method is useful to note. It could have taken the parameters in the URL, instead of the request body as is done here. But since request URL are routinely logged to files, putting the username and password parameters in the URL means user identity information would be logged to files and part of activity reports. That would obviously be a very bad choice. Putting those parameters in the request body not only avoids that bad result, but if an HTTPS connection to the service were used, the transaction would be encrypted:

```
export async function findOrCreate(profile) {
    var res = await request
        .post(reqURL('/find-or-create'))
        .send({
            username: profile.id, password: profile.password,
            provider: profile.provider,
            familyName: profile.familyName,
            givenName: profile.givenName,
            middleName: profile.middleName,
            emails: profile.emails, photos: profile.photos
        })
```

```
        .set('Content-Type', 'application/json')
        .set('Acccept', 'application/json')
        .auth('them', 'D4ED43C0-8BD6-4FE2-B358-7C0E230D11EF');
    return res.body;
}
```

The `findOrCreate` function either discovers the user in the database, or creates a
new user. The `profile` object will come from Passport, but take careful note of what
we do with `profile.id`. The Passport documentation says it will provide the
username in the `profile.id` field. But we want to store it as `username`, instead:

```
export async function listUsers() {
    var res = await request
        .get(reqURL('/list'))
        .set('Content-Type', 'application/json')
        .set('Acccept', 'application/json')
        .auth('them', 'D4ED43C0-8BD6-4FE2-B358-7C0E230D11EF');
    return res.body;
}
```

Finally, we can retrieve a list of users.

Login and logout routing functions

What we've built so far is a user data model, with a REST API wrapping that model to
create our authentication information service. Then, within the Notes application, we
have a module that requests user data from this server. As of yet, nothing in the
Notes application knows that this user model exists. The next step is to create a
routing module for login/logout URLs and to change the rest of Notes to use user
data.

The routing module is where we use `passport` to handle user authentication. The
first task is to install the required modules:

```
$ npm install passport@^0.4.x passport-local@1.x --save
```

The `passport` module gives us the authentication algorithms. To support different
authentication mechanisms, the passport authors have developed several strategy
implementations. The authentication mechanisms, or strategies, correspond to the
various third-party services that support authentication, such as using OAuth2 to
authenticate against services such as Facebook, Twitter, or GitHub.

The `LocalStrategy` authenticates solely using data stored local to the application,
for example, our user authentication information service.

Let's start by creating the routing module, `routes/users.mjs`:

```
import path from 'path';
import util from 'util';
import express from 'express';
import passport from 'passport';
import passportLocal from 'passport-local';
const LocalStrategy = passportLocal.Strategy;
import * as usersModel from '../models/users-superagent';
import { sessionCookieName } from '../app';

export const router = express.Router();

import DBG from 'debug';
const debug = DBG('notes:router-users');
const error = DBG('notes:error-users');
```

This brings in the modules we need for the `/users` router. This includes the two `passport` modules and the REST-based user authentication model.

In `app.mjs`, we will be adding *session* support so our users can log in and log out. That relies on storing a cookie in the browser, and the cookie name is found in this variable exported from `app.mjs`. We'll be using that cookie in a moment:

```
export function initPassport(app) {
  app.use(passport.initialize());
  app.use(passport.session());
}

export function ensureAuthenticated(req, res, next) {
  try {
    // req.user is set by Passport in the deserialize function
    if (req.user) next();
    else res.redirect('/users/login');
  } catch (e) { next(e); }
}
```

The `initPassport` function will be called from `app.mjs`, and it installs the `Passport` middleware into the Express configuration. We'll discuss the implications of this later when we get to `app.mjs` changes, but `Passport` uses sessions to detect whether this HTTP request is authenticated or not. It looks at every request coming into the application, looks for clues about whether this browser is logged in or not, and attaches data to the request object as `req.user`.

The `ensureAuthenticated` function will be used by other routing modules and is to be inserted into any route definition that requires an authenticated logged-in user. For example, editing or deleting a note requires the user to be logged in, and therefore the corresponding routes in `routes/notes.mjs` must use `ensureAuthenticated`. If the user is not logged in, this function redirects them to `/users/login` so that they can do so:

```
outer.get('/login', function(req, res, next) {
  try {
    res.render('login', { title: "Login to Notes", user: req.user, });
  } catch (e) { next(e); }
});

router.post('/login',
  passport.authenticate('local', {
    successRedirect: '/', // SUCCESS: Go to home page
    failureRedirect: 'login', // FAIL: Go to /user/login
  })
);
```

Because this router is mounted on `/users`, all these routes will have `/user` prepended. The `/users/login` route simply shows a form requesting a username and password. When this form is submitted, we land in the second route declaration, with a `POST` on `/users/login`. If `passport` deems this a successful login attempt using `LocalStrategy`, then the browser is redirected to the home page. Otherwise, it is redirected to the `/users/login` page:

```
router.get('/logout', function(req, res, next) {
  try {
    req.session.destroy();
    req.logout();
    res.clearCookie(sessionCookieName);
  res.redirect('/');
  } catch (e) { next(e); }
});
```

When the user requests to log out of Notes, they are to be sent to `/users/logout`. We'll be adding a button to the header template for this purpose. The `req.logout` function instructs Passport to erase their login credentials, and they are then redirected to the home page.

This function deviates from what's in the Passport documentation. There, we are told to simply call `req.logout`. But calling only that function sometimes results in the user not being logged out. It's necessary to destroy the session object, and to clear the cookie, in order to ensure that the user is logged out. The cookie name is defined in `app.mjs`, and we imported `sessionCookieName` for this function:

```
passport.use(new LocalStrategy(
  async (username, password, done) => {
    try {
      var check = await usersModel.userPasswordCheck(username,
      password);
      if (check.check) {
        done(null, { id: check.username, username: check.username });
      } else {
        done(null, false, check.message);
      }
    } catch (e) { done(e); }
  }
));
```

Here is where we define our implementation of `LocalStrategy`. In the callback function, we call `usersModel.userPasswordCheck`, which makes a REST call to the user authentication service. Remember that this performs the password check and then returns an object indicating whether they're logged in or not.

A successful login is indicated when `check.check` is `true`. For this case, we tell Passport to use an object containing the `username` in the session object. Otherwise, we have two ways to tell Passport that the login attempt was unsuccessful. In one case, we use `done(null, false)` to indicate an error logging in, and pass along the error message we were given. In the other case, we'll have captured an exception, and pass along that exception.

You'll notice that Passport uses a callback-style API. Passport provides a `done` function, and we are to call that function when we know what's what. While we use an `async` function to make a clean asynchronous call to the backend service, Passport doesn't know how to grok the Promise that would be returned. Therefore, we have to throw a `try/catch` around the function body to catch any thrown exception:

```
passport.serializeUser(function(user, done) {
  try {
    done(null, user.username);
  } catch (e) { done(e); }
});

passport.deserializeUser(async (username, done) => {
```

```
try {
  var user = await usersModel.find(username);
  done(null, user);
} catch(e) { done(e); }
});
```

The preceding functions take care of encoding and decoding authentication data for
the session. All we need to attach to the session is the `username`, as we did in
`serializeUser`. The `deserializeUser` object is called while processing an
incoming HTTP request and is where we look up the user profile data. Passport will
attach this to the request object.

Login/logout changes to app.js

We have a few changes required in `app.mjs`, some of which we've already touched
on. We did carefully isolate the Passport module dependencies to
`routes/users.mjs`. The changes required in `app.mjs` support the code in
`routes/users.mjs`.

It's now time to uncomment a line we told you to comment out way back in Chapter
5, *Your First Express Application*. The imports for the routing modules will now look as
follows:

```
import { router as index } from './routes/index';
import { router as users, initPassport } from './routes/users';
import { router as notes } from './routes/notes';
```

The User router supports the `/login` and `/logout` URL's as well as using `Passport`
for authentication. We need to call `initPassport` for a little bit of initialization:

```
import session from 'express-session';
import sessionFileStore from 'session-file-store';
const FileStore = sessionFileStore(session);
export const sessionCookieName = 'notescookie.sid';
```

Because `Passport` uses sessions, we need to enable session support in Express, and
these modules do so. The `session-file-store` module saves our session data to
disk so that we can kill and restart the application without losing sessions. It's also
possible to save sessions to databases with appropriate modules. A filesystem session
store is suitable only when all Notes instances are running on the same server
computer. For a distributed deployment situation, you'll need to use a session store
that runs on a network-wide service, such as a database.

We're defining `sessionCookieName` here so it can be used in multiple places. By default, `express-session` uses a cookie named `connect.sid` to store the session data. As a small measure of security, it's useful when there's a published default to use a different non-default value. Any time we use the default value, it's possible that an attacker might know a security flaw depending on that default.

Use the following command to install the modules:

```
$ npm install express-session@1.15.x session-file-store@1.2.x --save
```

Express Session support, including all the various Session Store implementations, is documented on its GitHub project page at `https://github.com/expressjs/session`.

Add this in `app.mjs`:

```
app.use(session({
   store: new FileStore({ path: "sessions" }),
   secret: 'keyboard mouse',
   resave: true,
   saveUninitialized: true,
   name: sessionCookieName
}));
initPassport(app);
```

Here we initialize the session support. The field named `secret` is used to sign the session ID cookie. The session cookie is an encoded string that is encrypted in part using this secret. In the Express Session documentation, they suggest the string `keyboard cat` for the secret. But, in theory, what if Express has a vulnerability, such that knowing this secret can make it easier to break the session logic on your site? Hence, we chose a different string for the secret just to be a little different and perhaps a little more secure.

Similarly, the default cookie name used by `express-session` is `connect.sid`. Here's where we change the cookie name to a non-default name.

The `FileStore` will store its session data records in a directory named `sessions`. This directory will be auto-created as needed:

```
app.use('/', index);
app.use('/users', users);
app.use('/notes', notes);
```

The preceding are the three routers used in the Notes application.

Login/logout changes in routes/index.mjs

This router module handles the home page. It does not require the user to be logged in, but we want to change the display a little if they are logged in:

```
router.get('/', async (req, res, next) => {
  try {
    let keylist = await notes.keylist();
    let keyPromises = keylist.map(key => { return notes.read(key) });
    let notelist = await Promise.all(keyPromises);
    res.render('index', {
      title: 'Notes', notelist: notelist,
      user: req.user ? req.user : undefined
    });
  } catch (e) { next(e); }
});
```

Remember that we ensured that `req.user` has the user profile data, which we did in `deserializeUser`. We simply check for this and make sure to add that data when rendering the views template.

We'll be making similar changes to most of the other route definitions. After that, we'll go over the changes to the view templates in which we use `req.user` to show the correct buttons on each page.

Login/logout changes required in routes/notes.mjs

The changes required here are more significant, but still straightforward:

```
import { ensureAuthenticated } from './users';
```

We need to use the `ensureAuthenticated` function to protect certain routes from being used by users who are not logged in. Notice how ES6 modules let us import just the function(s) we require. Since that function is in the user router module, we need to import it from there:

```
router.get('/add', ensureAuthenticated, (req, res, next) => {
  try {
    res.render('noteedit', {
      title: "Add a Note",
      docreate: true, notekey: "",
      user: req.user, note: undefined
    });
  } catch (e) { next(e); }
});
```

The first thing we added is to call `usersRouter.ensureAuthenticated` in the route definition. If the user is not logged in, they'll redirect to `/users/login`, thanks to that function.

Because we've ensured that the user is authenticated, we know that `req.user` will already have their profile information. We can then simply pass it to the view template.

For the other routes, we need to make similar changes:

```
router.post('/save', ensureAuthenticated, (req, res, next) => {
    ..
});
```

The `/save` route requires only this change to call `ensureAuthenticated` to make sure that the user is logged in:

```
router.get('/view', (req, res, next) => {
    try {
        var note = await notes.read(req.query.key);
        res.render('noteview', {
            title: note ? note.title : "",
            notekey: req.query.key,
            user: req.user ? req.user : undefined,
            note: note
        });
    } catch (e) { next(e); }
});
```

For this route, we don't require the user to be logged in. We do need the user's profile information, if any, sent to the view template:

```
router.get('/edit', ensureAuthenticated, (req, res, next) => {
    try {
        var note = await notes.read(req.query.key);
        res.render('noteedit', {
            title: note ? ("Edit " + note.title) : "Add a Note",
            docreate: false,
            notekey: req.query.key,
            user: req.user ? req.user : undefined,
            note: note
        });
    } catch (e) { next(e); }
});
router.get('/destroy', ensureAuthenticated, (req, res, next) => {
    try {
        var note = await notes.read(req.query.key);
```

```
        res.render('notedestroy', {
            title: note ? `Delete ${note.title}` : "",
            notekey: req.query.key,
            user: req.user ? req.user : undefined,
            note: note
        });
    } catch (e) { next(e); }
});
router.post('/destroy/confirm', ensureAuthenticated, (req, res, next)
=> {
    ..
});
```

For these routes, we require the user to be logged in. In most cases, we need to send the `req.user` value to the view template.

View template changes supporting login/logout

So far, we've created a backend user authentication service, a REST module, to access that service, a router module to handle routes related to logging in and out of the website, and changes in `app.mjs` to use those modules. We're almost ready, but we've got a number of outstanding changes to make in the templates. We're passing the `req.user` object to every template because each one must be changed to accommodate whether the user is logged in or not.

In `partials/header.hbs`, make the following additions:

```
    ...
    {{#if user}}
        <div class="collapse navbar-collapse"
         id="navbarSupportedContent">
            <span class="navbar-text text-dark col">{{ title }}</span>
            <a class="btn btn-dark col-auto" href="/users/logout">
            Log Out <span class="badge badge-light">{{ user.username
}}
        </span></a>
            <a class="nav-item nav-link btn btn-dark col-auto"
        href='/notes/add'>
                                ADD Note</a>
        </div>
    {{else}}
        <div class="collapse navbar-collapse" id="navbarLogIn">
            <a class="btn btn-primary" href="/users/login">Log in</a>
        </div>
    {{/if}}
    ...
```

What we're doing here is controlling which buttons to display at the top of the screen depending on whether the user is logged in or not. The earlier changes ensure that the `user` variable will be `undefined` if the user is logged out, otherwise it will have the user profile object. Therefore, it's sufficient to check the `user` variable as shown here to render different user interface elements.

A logged-out user doesn't get the **ADD Note** button, and gets a **Log in** button. Otherwise, the user gets an **ADD Note** button and a **Log Out** button. The **Log in** button takes the user to `/users/login`, while the **Log Out** button takes them to `/users/logout`. Both of those are handled in `routes/users.js`, and perform the expected function.

The **Log Out** button has a Bootstrap badge component displaying the username. This adds a little visual splotch, in which we'll put the username that's logged in. As we'll see later, it will serve as a visual cue to the user as to their identity.

We need to create `views/login.hbs`:

```
<div class="container-fluid">
  <div class="row">
    <div class="col-12 btn-group-vertical" role="group">

        <form method='POST' action='/users/login'>
        <div class="form-group">
        <label for="username">User name:</label>
        <input class="form-control" type='text' id='username'
               name='username' value='' placeholder='User Name'/>
        </div>
        <div class="form-group">
        <label for="password">Password:</label>
        <input class="form-control" type='password' id='password'
               name='password' value='' placeholder='Password'/>
        </div>
        <button type="submit" class="btn btn-default">Submit</button>
        </form>

    </div>
  </div>
</div>
```

This is a simple form decorated with Bootstrap goodness to ask for the username and password. When submitted, it creates a POST request to /users/login, which invokes the desired handler to verify the login request. The handler for that URL will start the Passport's process to decide whether the user is authenticated or not.

In views/notedestroy.hbs, we want to display a message if the user is not logged in. Normally, the form to cause the note to be deleted is displayed, but if the user is not logged in, we want to explain the situation:

```
<form method='POST' action='/notes/destroy/confirm'>
<div class="container-fluid">
    {{#if user}}
    <input type='hidden' name='notekey' value='{{#if
note}}{{notekey}}{{/if}}'>
    <p class="form-text">Delete {{note.title}}?</p>

    <div class="btn-group">
        <button type="submit" value='DELETE'
                class="btn btn-outline-dark">DELETE</button>
        <a class="btn btn-outline-dark"
           href="/notes/view?key={{#if note}}{{notekey}}{{/if}}"
           role="button">Cancel</a>
    </div>
    {{else}}
    {{> not-logged-in }}
    {{/if}}
</div>
</form>
```

That's straightforward; if the user is logged in, display the form, otherwise display the message in partials/not-logged-in.hbs. We determine our approach based on the user variable.

We could put something like this in partials/not-logged-in.hbs:

```
<div class="jumbotron">
 <h1>Not Logged In</h1>
 <p>You are required to be logged in for this action, but you are not.
 You should not see this message. It's a bug if this message appears.
 </p>
 <p><a class="btn btn-primary" href="/users/login">Log in</a></p>
</div>
```

In `views/noteedit.hbs`, we need a similar change:

```
..
<div class="row"><div class="col-xs-12">
{{#if user}}

..
{{else}}
{{> not-logged-in }}
{{/if}}
</div></div>

..
```

That is, at the bottom we add a segment that, for non-logged-in users, pulls in the `not-logged-in` partial.

The **Bootstrap jumbotron** component makes a nice and large text display that stands out nicely, and will catch the viewer's attention. However, the user should never see this because each of those templates is used only when we've preverified that the user is logged in.

A message such as this is useful as a check against bugs in your code. Suppose that we slipped up and failed to properly ensure that these forms were displayed only to logged-in users. Suppose that we had other bugs that didn't check the form submission to ensure it's requested only by a logged-in user. Fixing the template in this way is another layer of prevention against displaying forms to users who are not allowed to use that functionality.

Running the Notes application with user authentication

Now we're ready to run the Notes application and try our hand at logging in and out.

We need to change the scripts section of `package.json` as follows:

```
"scripts": {
    "start": "DEBUG=notes:* SEQUELIZE_CONNECT=models/sequelize-
sqlite.yaml NOTES_MODEL=sequelize
USER_SERVICE_URL=http://localhost:3333 node --experimental-modules
./bin/www.mjs",
    "dl-minty": "mkdir -p minty && npm run dl-minty-css && npm run dl-
    minty-min-css",
    "dl-minty-css": "wget https://bootswatch.com/4/minty/bootstrap.css
    -O minty/bootstrap.css",
    "dl-minty-min-css": "wget
```

```
https://bootswatch.com/4/minty/bootstrap.min.css -O
minty/bootstrap.min.css"
},
```

In the previous chapters, we built up quite a few combinations of models and databases for running the Notes application. This leaves us with one, configured to use the Sequelize model for Notes, using the SQLite3 database, and to use the new user authentication service that we wrote earlier. We can simplify the `scripts` section by deleting those other configurations. All the other Notes data models are still available just by setting the environment variables appropriately.

The `USER_SERVICE_URL` needs to match the port number that we designated for that service.

In one window, start the user authentication service as follows:

```
$ cd users
$ npm start
> user-auth-server@0.0.1 start /Users/david/chap08/users
> DEBUG=users:* PORT=3333 SEQUELIZE_CONNECT=sequelize-sqlite.yaml node
user-server
  users:server User-Auth-Service listening at http://127.0.0.1:3333
  +0ms
```

Then, in another window, start the Notes application:

```
$ cd notes
$ DEBUG=notes:* npm start
> notes@0.0.0 start /Users/david/chap08/notes
> SEQUELIZE_CONNECT=models/sequelize-sqlite.yaml
NOTES_MODEL=models/notes-sequelize USERS_MODEL=models/users-rest
USER_SERVICE_URL=http://localhost:3333 node ./bin/www
  notes:server Listening on port 3000 +0ms
```

You'll be greeted with the following:

Notice the new button, **Log in**, and the lack of an **ADD Note** button. We're not logged in, and therefore `partials/header.hbs` is rigged to show only the **Log in** button.

Click on the **Log in** button, and you will see the login screen:

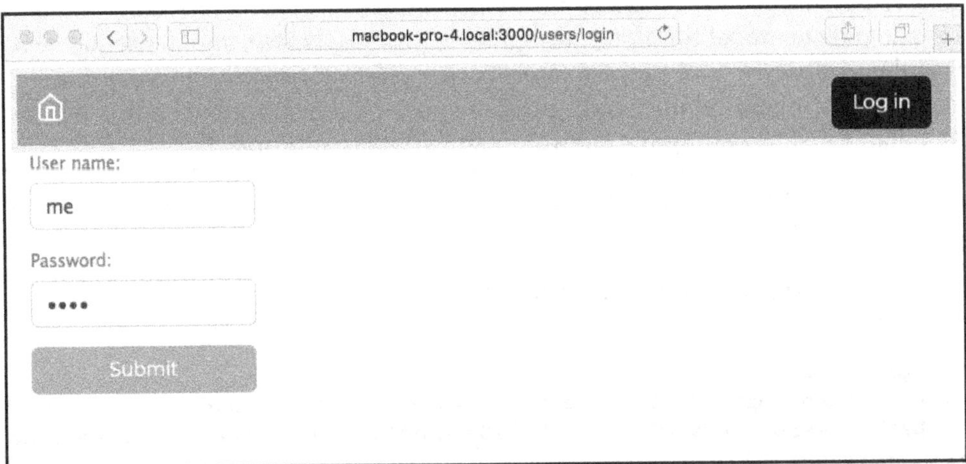

This is our login form from `views/login.hbs`. You can now log in, create a note or three, and you might end up with the following on the home page:

You now have both **Log Out** and **ADD Note** buttons.

You'll notice that the **Log Out** button has the username (**me**) shown. After some thought and consideration, this seemed the most compact way to show whether the user is logged in or not, and which user is logged in. This might drive the user experience team nuts, and you won't know whether this user interfaces design works until it's tested with users, but it's good enough for our purpose at the moment.

Twitter login support for the Notes application

If you want your application to hit the big time, it's a great idea to allow users to register using third-party credentials. Websites all over the internet allow you to log in using Facebook, Twitter, or accounts from other services. Doing so removes hurdles to prospective users signing up for your service. Passport makes it extremely easy to do this.

Supporting Twitter requires installing **TwitterStrategy**, registering a new application with Twitter, and adding a couple of routes into `routes/user.mjs` and a small change in `partials/header.hbs`. Integrating other third-party services requires similar steps.

Registering an application with Twitter

Twitter, as with every other third-party service, uses OAuth to handle authentication and requires an authentication key to write software using their API. It's their service, so you have to play by their rules, of course.

To register a new application with Twitter, go to `https://apps.twitter.com/`. Then you click on the **Create New App** button. Since we haven't deployed the Notes application to a regular server and, more importantly, there isn't a valid domain name for the application, we have to give Twitter the configuration required for testing on our local laptop.

Every service offering OAuth2 authentication has an administrative backend for registering new applications. The common purpose is to describe the application to the service so that the service can correctly recognize the application when requests are made using the authentication tokens. The normal situation is that the application is deployed to a regular server, and is accessed through a domain name such as `MyNotes.info`. We've done neither as of this moment.

At the time of writing, there are four pieces of information requested by the Twitter sign-up process:

- **Name**: This is the application name, and it can be anything you like. It would be good form to use test in the name in case Twitter's staff decide to do some validation.
- **Description**: Descriptive phrase, and again it can be anything you like. Again, it would be good form to, at this time, describe it as a test application.
- **Website**: This would be your desired domain name. Here, the help text helpfully suggests *If you don't have a URL yet, just put a placeholder here but remember to change it later.*
- **Callback URL**: This is the URL to return to after successful authentication. Since we don't have a public URL to supply, this is where we specify a value referring to your laptop. It's been found that `http://localhost:3000` works just fine. macOS users have another option because of the `.local` domain name, which is automatically assigned to their laptop. All along, we could have used a URL similar to this to access the Notes application at `http://MacBook-Pro-2.local:3000/`.

It was found by attempting this procedure with different services that Facebook (and other) services are not lenient about test applications hosted on laptops. At least Twitter is keen for developers to configure a test application on their laptop. Passport's other OAuth-based strategies will work similarly enough to Twitter, so the knowledge we're gaining will transfer to those other authentication strategies.

The last thing to notice is the extremely sensitive nature of the authentication keys. It's bad form to check these into a source code repository or otherwise put them in a place where anybody can access the key.

Twitter does change the signup page from time to time, but it should look something like the following:

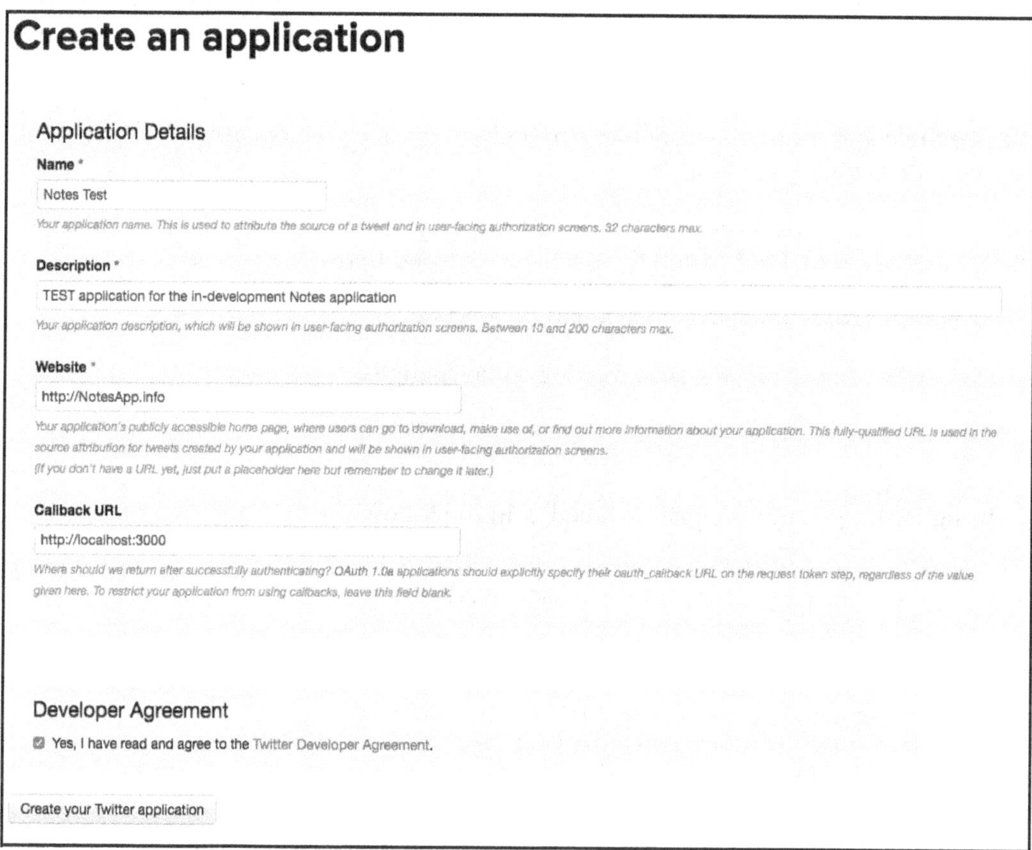

Implementing TwitterStrategy

As with many web applications, we have decided to allow our users to log in using Twitter credentials. The OAuth2 protocol is widely used for this purpose and is the basis for authenticating on one website using credentials maintained by another website.

The application registration process you just followed at `apps.twitter.com` generated for you a pair of API keys, a consumer key, and, consumer secret. These keys are part of the OAuth protocol, and will be supplied by any OAuth service you register with, and the keys should be treated with the utmost care. Think of them as the username and password your service uses to access the OAuth-based service (Twitter et al). The more people who can see these keys, the more likely a miscreant can see them and then cause trouble. Anybody with those secrets can write access the service API as if they are you.

Dozens of Strategy packages for various third-party services are available within the Passport ecosystem. Let's install the package required to use `TwitterStrategy`:

```
$ npm install passport-twitter@1.x --save
```

In `routes/users.mjs`, let's start making some changes:

```
import passportTwitter from 'passport-twitter';
const TwitterStrategy = passportTwitter.Strategy;
```

To bring in the package we just installed, add the following:

```
const twittercallback = process.env.TWITTER_CALLBACK_HOST
      ? process.env.TWITTER_CALLBACK_HOST
      : "http://localhost:3000";

passport.use(new TwitterStrategy({
   consumerKey: process.env.TWITTER_CONSUMER_KEY,
   consumerSecret: process.env.TWITTER_CONSUMER_SECRET,
   callbackURL: `${twittercallback}/users/auth/twitter/callback`
},
async function(token, tokenSecret, profile, done) {
   try {
      done(null, await usersModel.findOrCreate({
         id: profile.username, username: profile.username, password: "",
         provider: profile.provider, familyName: profile.displayName,
         givenName: "", middleName: "",
         photos: profile.photos, emails: profile.emails
      }));
   } catch(err) { done(err); }
}));
```

This registers `TwitterStrategy` with `passport`, arranging to call the user authentication service as users register with the Notes application. This callback function is called when users successfully authenticate using Twitter.

We defined the `usersModel.findOrCreate` function specifically to handle user registration from third-party services such as Twitter. Its task is to look for the user described in the profile object and, if that user does not exist, to autocreate that user account in Notes.

 The `consumerKey` and `consumerSecret` values are supplied by Twitter, after you've registered your application. These secrets are used in the OAuth protocol as proof of identity to Twitter.

The `callbackURL` setting in the `TwitterStrategy` configuration is a holdover from Twitter's OAuth1-based API implementation. In OAuth1, the callback URL was passed as part of the OAuth request. Since `TwitterStrategy` uses Twitter's OAuth1 service, we have to supply the URL here. We'll see in a moment where that URL is implemented in Notes.

The `callbackURL`, `consumerKey`, and `consumerSecret` are all injected using environment variables. It is tempting, because of the convenience, to just put those keys in the source code. But, how widely distributed is your source code? In the Slack API documentation (`https://api.slack.com/docs/oauth-safety`), we're warned *Do not distribute client secrets in email, distributed native applications, client-side JavaScript, or public code repositories.*

In `Chapter 10`, *Deploying Node.js Applications*, we'll put these keys into a Dockerfile. That's not entirely secure because the Dockerfile will also be committed to a source repository somewhere.

It was found while debugging that the profile object supplied by the `TwitterStrategy` did not match the documentation on the `passport` website. Therefore, we have mapped the object actually supplied by `passport` into something that Notes can use:

```
router.get('/auth/twitter', passport.authenticate('twitter'));
```

To start the user logging in with Twitter, we'll send them to this URL. Remember that this URL is really `/users/auth/twitter`, and, in the templates, we'll have to use that URL. When this is called, the passport middleware starts the user authentication and registration process using `TwitterStrategy`.

Once the user's browser visits this URL, the OAuth dance begins. It's called a dance because the OAuth protocol involves carefully designed redirects between several websites. Passport sends the browser over to the correct URL at Twitter, where Twitter asks the user whether they agree to authenticate using Twitter, and then Twitter redirects the user back to your callback URL. Along the way, specific tokens are passed back and forth in a very carefully designed dance between websites.

Once the OAuth dance concludes, the browser lands here:

```
router.get('/auth/twitter/callback',
    passport.authenticate('twitter', { successRedirect: '/',
                        failureRedirect: '/users/login' }));
```

This route handles the callback URL, and it corresponds to the `callbackURL` setting configured earlier. Depending on whether it indicates a successful registration or not, passport will redirect the browser to either the home page or back to the `/users/login` page.

Because `router` is mounted on `/user`, this URL is actually `/user/auth/twitter/callback`. Therefore, the full URL to use in configuring the `TwitterStrategy`, and to supply to Twitter, is `http://localhost:3000/user/auth/twitter/callback`

In the process of handling the callback URL, Passport will invoke the callback function shown earlier. Because our callback uses the `usersModel.findOrCreate` function, the user will be automatically registered if necessary.

We're almost ready, but we need to make a couple of small changes elsewhere in Notes.

In `partials/header.hbs`, make the following changes to the code:

```
. . .
{{else}}
<div class="collapse navbar-collapse" id="navbarLogIn">
    <span class="navbar-text text-dark col"></span>
    <a class="nav-item nav-link btn btn-dark col-auto"
href="/users/login">
                            Log in</a>
    <a class="nav-item nav-link btn btn-dark col-auto"
href="/users/auth/twitter">
    <img width="15px"
src="/assets/vendor/twitter/Twitter_Social_Icon_Rounded_Square_Color.p
ng"/>
        Log in with Twitter</a>
```

```
</div>
{{/if}}
```

This adds a new button that, when clicked, takes the user to `/users/auth/twitter`, which, of course, kicks off the Twitter authentication process.

The image being used is from the official Twitter brand assets page at `https://about.twitter.com/company/brand-assets`. Twitter recommends using these branding assets for a consistent look across all services using Twitter. Download the whole set and then pick one you like. For the URL shown here, place the chosen image in a directory named `public/assets/vendor/twitter`. Notice that we force the size to be small enough for the navigation bar.

With these changes, we're ready to try logging in with Twitter.

Start the Notes application server as done previously:

```
$ npm start

> notes@0.0.0 start /Users/David/chap08/notes
> DEBUG=notes:* SEQUELIZE_CONNECT=models/sequelize-sqlite.yaml
NOTES_MODEL=sequelize USER_SERVICE_URL=http://localhost:3333 node --
experimental-modules ./bin/www.mjs

(node:42095) ExperimentalWarning: The ESM module loader is
experimental.
  notes:server-debug Listening on port 3000 +0ms
```

Then use a browser to visit `http://localhost:3000`:

Notice the new button. It looks about right, thanks to having used the official Twitter branding image. The button is a little large, so maybe you want to consult a designer. Obviously, a different design is required if you're going to support dozens of authentication services.

Clicking on this button takes the browser to `/users/auth/twitter`, which starts Passport running the OAuth2 protocol transactions necessary to authenticate. And then, once you're logged in with Twitter, you'll see something like the following screenshot:

We're now logged in, and notice that our Notes username is the same as our Twitter username. You can browse around the application and create, edit, or delete notes. In fact, you can do this to any note you like, even ones created by others. That's because we did not create any sort of access control or permissions system, and therefore every user has complete access to every note. That's a feature to put on the backlog.

By using multiple browsers or computers, you can simultaneously log in as different users, one user per browser.

You can run multiple instances of the Notes application by doing what we did earlier:

```
"scripts": {
  "start": "SEQUELIZE_CONNECT=models/sequelize-sqlite.yaml
NOTES_MODEL=models/notes-sequelize USERS_MODEL=models/users-rest
USER_SERVICE_URL=http://localhost:3333 node ./bin/www",
  "start-server1": "SEQUELIZE_CONNECT=models/sequelize-sqlite.yaml
NOTES_MODEL=models/notes-sequelize USERS_MODEL=models/users-rest
USER_SERVICE_URL=http://localhost:3333 PORT=3000 node ./bin/www",
  "start-server2": "SEQUELIZE_CONNECT=models/sequelize-sqlite.yaml
NOTES_MODEL=models/notes-sequelize USERS_MODEL=models/users-rest
USER_SERVICE_URL=http://localhost:3333 PORT=3002 node ./bin/www",
  "dl-minty": "mkdir -p minty && npm run dl-minty-css && npm run dl-
minty-min-css",
```

```
    "dl-minty-css": "wget https://bootswatch.com/4/minty/bootstrap.css
-O minty/bootstrap.css",
    "dl-minty-min-css": "wget
https://bootswatch.com/4/minty/bootstrap.min.css -O
minty/bootstrap.min.css"
  },
```

Then, in one command window, run the following command:

```
$ npm run start-server1

> notes@0.0.0 start-server1 /Users/David/chap08/notes
> DEBUG=notes:* SEQUELIZE_CONNECT=models/sequelize-sqlite.yaml
NOTES_MODEL=sequelize USER_SERVICE_URL=http://localhost:3333 PORT=3000
node --experimental-modules ./bin/www.mjs

(node:43591) ExperimentalWarning: The ESM module loader is
experimental.
  notes:server-debug Listening on port 3000 +0ms
```

In another command window, run the following command:

```
$ npm run start-server2

> notes@0.0.0 start-server2 /Users/David/chap08/notes
> DEBUG=notes:* SEQUELIZE_CONNECT=models/sequelize-sqlite.yaml
NOTES_MODEL=sequelize USER_SERVICE_URL=http://localhost:3333 PORT=3002
node --experimental-modules ./bin/www.mjs

(node:43755) ExperimentalWarning: The ESM module loader is
experimental.
  notes:server-debug Listening on port 3002 +0ms
```

As previously, this starts two instances of the Notes server, each with a different value in the PORT environment variable. In this case, each instance will use the same user authentication service. As shown here, you'll be able to visit the two instances at http://localhost:3000 and http://localhost:3002. And, as previously, you'll be able to start and stop the servers as you wish, see the same notes in each, and see that the notes are retained after restarting the server.

Another thing to try is to fiddle with the **session store**. Our session data is being stored in the sessions directory. These are just files in the filesystem, and we can take a look:

```
$ ls -l sessions/
total 32
-rw-r--r-- 1 david wheel 139 Jan 25 19:28 -
```

```
QOS7eX8ZBAfmK9CCV8Xj8v-3DVEtaLK.json
-rw-r--r-- 1 david wheel 139 Jan 25 21:30
T7VT4xt3_e9BiU49OMC6RjbJi6xB7VqG.json
-rw-r--r-- 1 david wheel 223 Jan 25 19:27
ermh-7ijiqY7XXMnA6zPzJvsvsWUghWm.json
-rw-r--r-- 1 david wheel 139 Jan 25 21:23
uKzkXKuJ8uMN_ROEfaRSmvPU7NmBc3md.json
$ cat sessions/T7VT4xt3_e9BiU49OMC6RjbJi6xB7VqG.json
{"cookie":{"originalMaxAge":null,"expires":null,"httpOnly":true,"path"
:"/"},"__lastAccess":1516944652270,"passport":{"user":"7genblogger"}}
```

This is after logging in using a Twitter account; you can see that the Twitter account name is stored here in the session data.

What if you want to clear a session? It's just a file in the filesystem. Deleting the session file erases the session, and the user's browser will be forcefully logged out.

The session will time out if the user leaves their browser idle for long enough. One of the `session-file-store` options, `ttl`, controls the timeout period, which defaults to 3,600 seconds (an hour). With a timed-out session, the application reverts to a logged-out state.

Securely keeping secrets and passwords

We've cautioned several times about the importance of safely handling user identification information. The intention to safely handle that data is one thing, but it is important to follow through and actually do so. While we're using a few good practices so far, as it stands, the Notes application would not withstand any kind of security audit:

- User passwords are kept in clear text in the database
- The authentication tokens for Twitter *et al*, are in the source code in clear text
- The authentication service API key is not a cryptographically secure anything, it's just a cleartext UUID

If you don't recognize the phrase clear text, it simply means unencrypted. Anyone could read the text of user passwords or the authentication tokens. It's best to keep both encrypted to avoid information leakage.

The Notes application stack

Did you notice earlier when we said run the Notes application stack? It's time to explain to the marketing team what's meant by that phrase. They'll perhaps need to put an architecture diagram on marketing brochures and the like. It's also useful for developers like us to take a step back and draw a picture of what we've created, or are planning to create.

Here's the sort of diagram that an engineer might draw to show the marketing team the system design. The marketing team will, of course, hire a graphics artist to clean it up:

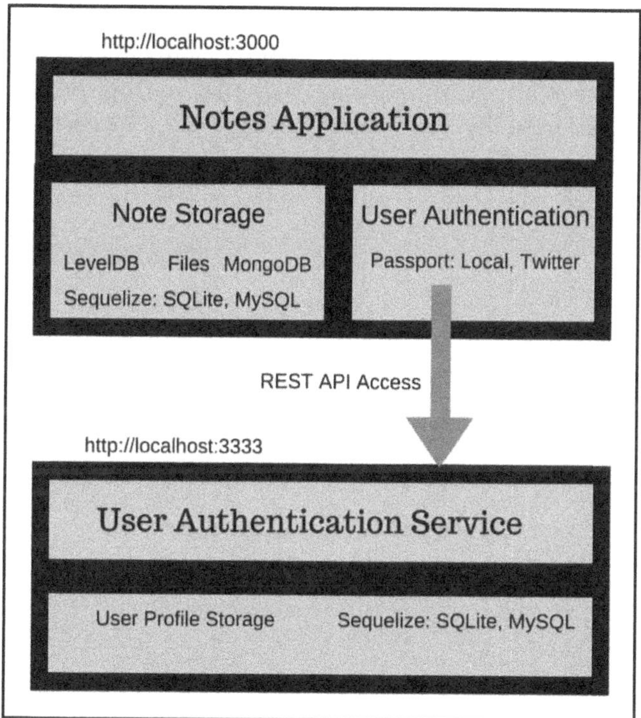

The box labeled Notes Application is the public-facing code implemented by the templates and the router modules. As currently configured, it's visible from our laptop on port 3000. It can use one of several data storage services. It communicates with the backend **User Authentication Service** over port 3333 (as currently configured).

In `Chapter 10`, *Deploying Node.js Applications*, we'll be expanding this picture a bit as we learn how to deploy on a real server.

Summary

You've covered a lot of ground in this chapter, looking at not only user authentication in Express applications, but also microservice development.

Specifically, you covered session management in Express, using Passport for user authentication, including Twitter/OAuth, using router middleware to limit access, creating a REST service with Restify, and when to create a microservice.

In the next chapter, we'll take the *Notes* application to a new level-semi-real-time communication between application users. To do this, we'll write some browser-side JavaScript and explore how the `Socket.io` package can let us send messages between users.

9
Dynamic Client/Server Interaction with Socket.IO

The original design model of the web is similar to the way that mainframes worked in the 1970s. Both old-school dumb terminals, such as the IBM 3270, and web browsers, follow a request-response paradigm. The user sends a request and the far-off computer sends a response screen. While web browsers can show more complex information than old-school dumb terminals, the interaction pattern in both cases is a back and forth of user requests, each resulting in a screen of data sent by the server screen after screen or, in the case of web browsers, page after page.

In case you're wondering what this history lesson is about, that request-response paradigm is evident in the Node.js HTTP Server API, as shown in the following code:

```
http.createServer(function (request, response) {
    ... handle request
}).listen();
```

The paradigm couldn't be more explicit than this. The `request` and the `response` are right there.

The first web browsers were an advancement over text-based user interfaces, with HTML mixing images, and text with varying colors, fonts, and sizes. As CSS came along, HTML improved, iframes allowed embedded media of all kinds, and JavaScript improved, so we have a quite different paradigm. The web browser is still sending requests and receiving a page of data, but that data can be quite complex and, more importantly, JavaScript adds interactivity.

One new technique is keeping an open connection to the server for continual data exchange between server and client. This change in the web application model is called, by some, the real-time web. In some cases, websites keep an open connection to the web browser, with real-time updates to web pages being one goal.

Some observe that traditional web applications can untruthfully display their data; that is, if two people are looking at a page, and one person edits that page, that person's browser will update with the correct copy of the page, while the other browser is not updated. The two browsers show different versions of the page, one of which is untruthful. The second browser can even show a page that no longer exists, if the user at the first browser deletes that page. Some think it would be better if the other person's browser is refreshed to show the new content as soon as the page is edited.

This is one possible role of the real-time web; pages that update themselves as page content changes. All kinds of systems support real-time interactivity between folks on the same website. Whether it's seeing Facebook comments pop up as they're written, or collaboratively edited documents, there's a new interactivity paradigm on the web.

We're about to implement this behavior in the Notes application.

One of the original purposes for inventing Node.js was to support the real-time web. The **Comet** application architecture (Comet is related to AJAX, and both happen to be names of household cleaning products) involves holding the HTTP connection open for a long time, with data flowing back and forth between browser and server over that channel. The term Comet was introduced by Alex Russell in his blog in 2006 (`http://infrequently.org/2006/03/comet-low-latency-data-for-the-browser/`) as a general term for the architectural pattern to implement this real-time, two-way data exchange between client and server. That blog post called for the development of a programming platform very similar to Node.js.

To simplify the task, we'll lean on the `Socket.IO` library (`http://socket.io/`). This library simplifies two-way communication between the browser and server, and can support a variety of protocols with fallback to old-school web browsers.

We'll be covering the following topics:

- Real-time communications in modern web browsers
- The `Socket.IO` library
- Integrating `Socket.IO` with an Express application to support real-time communication
- User experience for real-time communication

Introducing Socket.IO

The aim of `Socket.IO` is to make real-time apps possible in every browser and mobile device. It supports several transport protocols, choosing the best one for the specific browser.

If you were to implement your application with WebSockets, it would be limited to the modern browsers supporting that protocol. Because `Socket.IO` falls back on so many alternate protocols (WebSockets, Flash, XHR, and JSONP), it supports a wide range of web browsers, including some old crufty browsers.

As the application author, you don't have to worry about the specific protocol `Socket.IO` uses in a given browser. Instead, you can implement the business logic and the library takes care of the details for you.

`Socket.IO` requires that a client library make its way into the browser. That library is provided, and is easy to instantiate. You'll be writing code on both the browser side and server side using similar `Socket.IO` APIs at each end.

The model that `Socket.IO` provides is similar to the `EventEmitter` object. The programmer uses the `.on` method to listen for events and the `.emit` method to send them. The emitted events are sent between the browser and the server with the `Socket.IO` library taking care of sending them back and forth.

Information about `Socket.IO` is available at `https://socket.io/`.

Initializing Socket.IO with Express

`Socket.IO` works by wrapping itself around an HTTP Server object. Think back to `Chapter 4`, *HTTP Servers and Clients*, where we wrote a module that hooked into HTTP Server methods so that we could spy on HTTP transactions. The HTTP Sniffer attaches a listener to every HTTP event to print out the events. But what if you used that idea to do real work? Socket.IO uses a similar concept, listening to HTTP requests and responding to specific ones by using the Socket.IO protocol to communicate with client code in the browser.

To get started, let's first make a duplicate of the code from the previous chapter. If you created a directory named `chap08` for that code, create a new directory named `chap09` and copy the source tree there.

We won't make changes to the user authentication microservice, but we will use it for user authentication, of course.

In the Notes source directory, install these new modules:

```
$ npm install socket.io@2.x passport.socketio@3.7.x --save
```

We will incorporate user authentication with the `passport` module, used in Chapter 8, *Multiuser Authentication the Microservice Way*, into some of the real-time interactions we'll implement.

To initialize `Socket.IO`, we must do some major surgery on how the Notes application is started. So far, we used the `bin/www.mjs` script along with `app.mjs`, with each script hosting different steps of launching Notes. `Socket.IO` initialization requires that these steps occur in a different order to what we've been doing. Therefore, we must merge these two scripts into one. What we'll do is copy the content of the `bin/www.mjs` script into appropriate sections of `app.mjs`, and from there, we'll use `app.mjs` to launch Notes.

At the beginning of `app.mjs`, add this to the `import` statements:

```
import http from 'http';
import passportSocketIo from 'passport.socketio';
import session from 'express-session';
import sessionFileStore from 'session-file-store';
const FileStore = sessionFileStore(session);

export const sessionCookieName = 'notescookie.sid';
const sessionSecret = 'keyboard mouse';
const sessionStore = new FileStore({ path: "sessions" });
```

The `passport.socketio` module integrates `Socket.IO` with PassportJS-based user authentication. We'll configure this support shortly. The configuration for session management is now shared between `Socket.IO`, Express, and Passport. These lines centralize that configuration to one place in `app.mjs`, so we can change it once to affect every place it's needed.

Use this to initialize the HTTP Server object:

```
const app = express();

export default app;

const server = http.createServer(app);
import socketio from 'socket.io';
const io = socketio(server);

io.use(passportSocketIo.authorize({
  cookieParser: cookieParser,
  key: sessionCookieName,
  secret: sessionSecret,
  store: sessionStore
}));
```

This moves the `export default app` line from the bottom of the file to this location. Doesn't this location make more sense?

The `io` object is our entry point into the `Socket.IO` API. We need to pass this object to any code that needs to use that API. It won't be enough to simply require the `socket.io` module in other modules because the `io` object is what wraps the `server` object. Instead, we'll be passing the `io` object into whatever modules are to use it.

The `io.use` function installs in `Socket.IO` functions similar to Express middleware. In this case, we integrate Passport authentication into `Socket.IO`:

```
var port = normalizePort(process.env.PORT || '3000');
app.set('port', port);

server.listen(port);
server.on('error', onError);
server.on('listening', onListening);
```

This code is copied from `bin/www.mjs`, and sets up the port to listen to. It relies on three functions that will also be copied into `app.mjs` from `bin/www.mjs`:

```
app.use(session({
  store: sessionStore,
  secret: sessionSecret,
  resave: true,
  saveUninitialized: true,
  name: sessionCookieName
}));
initPassport(app);
```

This changes the configuration of Express session support to match the configuration variables we set up earlier. It's the same variables used when setting up the `Socket.IO` session integration, meaning they're both on the same page.

Use this to initialize `Socket.IO` code in the router modules:

```
app.use('/', index);
app.use('/users', users);
app.use('/notes', notes);

indexSocketio(io);
// notesSocketio(io);
```

This is where we pass the `io` object into modules that must use it. This is so that the Notes application can send messages to the web browsers about changes in Notes. What that means will be clearer in a second. What's required is analogous to the Express router functions, and therefore the code to send/receive messages from `Socket.IO` clients will also be located in the router modules.

We haven't written either of these functions yet (have patience). To support this, we need to make a change in an `import` statement at the top:

```
import { socketio as indexSocketio, router as index } from
'./routes/index';
```

Each router module will export a function named `socketio`, which we'll have to rename as shown here. This function is what will receive the `io` object, and handle any `Socket.IO`-based communications. We haven't written these functions yet.

Then, at the end of `app.mjs`, we'll copy in the remaining code from `bin/www.mjs` so the HTTP Server starts listening on our selected port:

```
function normalizePort(val) {
  var port = parseInt(val, 10);
  if (isNaN(port)) { // named pipe
    return val;
  }
  if (port >= 0) { // port number
    return port;
  }
  return false;
}

/**
 * Event listener for HTTP server "error" event.
 */
```

```
function onError(error) {
  if (error.syscall !== 'listen') { throw error; }

  var bind = typeof port === 'string' ? 'Pipe ' + port : 'Port ' +
  port;

  // handle specific listen errors with friendly messages
  switch (error.code) {
    case 'EACCES':
      console.error(bind + ' requires elevated privileges');
      process.exit(1);
      break;
    case 'EADDRINUSE':
      console.error(bind + ' is already in use');
      process.exit(1);
      break;
    default:
      throw error;
  }
}

/**
 * Event listener for HTTP server "listening" event.
 */

function onListening() {
  var addr = server.address();
  var bind = typeof addr === 'string' ? 'pipe ' + addr : 'port ' +
addr.port;
  debug('Listening on ' + bind);
}
```

Then, in `package.json`, we must start `app.mjs` rather than `bin/www.mjs`:

```
  "scripts": {
    "start": "DEBUG=notes:* SEQUELIZE_CONNECT=models/sequelize-
sqlite.yaml NOTES_MODEL=sequelize
USER_SERVICE_URL=http://localhost:3333 node --experimental-modules
./app",
    "start-server1": "DEBUG=notes:*
SEQUELIZE_CONNECT=models/sequelize-sqlite.yaml NOTES_MODEL=sequelize
USER_SERVICE_URL=http://localhost:3333 PORT=3000 node --experimental-
modules ./app",
    "start-server2": "DEBUG=notes:*
SEQUELIZE_CONNECT=models/sequelize-sqlite.yaml NOTES_MODEL=sequelize
USER_SERVICE_URL=http://localhost:3333 PORT=3002 node --experimental-
modules ./app",
    ...
```

```
},
```

At this point, you can delete `bin/www.mjs` if you like. You can also try starting the server, but it'll fail because the `indexSocketio` function does not exist yet.

Real-time updates on the Notes homepage

The goal we're working towards is for the Notes home page to automatically update the list of notes, as notes are edited or deleted. What we've done so far is to restructure the application startup so that `Socket.IO` is initialized in the Notes application. There's no change of behavior yet, except that it will crash due to a missing function.

The approach is for the Notes model classes to send messages whenever a note is created, updated, or deleted. In the router classes, we'll listen to those messages, then send a list of note titles to all browsers attached to the Notes application.

Where the Notes model so far has been a passive repository of documents, it now needs to emit events to any interested parties. This is the listener pattern and, in theory, there will be code that is interested in knowing when notes are created, edited, or destroyed. At the moment, we'll use that knowledge to update the Notes home page, but there are many potential other uses of that knowledge.

The Notes model as an EventEmitter class

The `EventEmitter` is the class that implements listener support. Let's create a new module, `models/notes-events.mjs`, containing the following:

```
import EventEmitter from 'events';
class NotesEmitter extends EventEmitter {
    noteCreated(note)  { this.emit('notecreated', note); }
    noteUpdate (note)  { this.emit('noteupdate', note); }
    noteDestroy (data) { this.emit('notedestroy', data); }
}

export default new NotesEmitter();
```

This module maintains the listeners to Notes-related events for us. We've created a subclass of `EventEmitter` because it already knows how to manage the listeners. An instance of that object is exported as the default export.

Let's now update `models/notes.mjs` to use `notes-events` to emit events. Because we have a single module, `notes.mjs`, to dispatch calls to the individual Notes models, this module provides a key point at which we can intercept the operations and send events. Otherwise, we'd have to integrate the event-sending code into every Notes model.

```
import _events from './notes-events';
export const events = _events;
```

We need to `import` this module for use here, but also export it so that other modules can also emit Notes events. By doing this, another module that imports Notes can call `notes.events.function` to use the `notes-events` module.

This technique is called **re-exporting**. Sometimes, you need to export a function from module *A* that is actually defined in module *B*. Module *A* therefore imports the function from module *B*, adding it to its exports.

Then we do a little rewriting of these functions:

```
export async function create(key, title, body) {
    const note = await model().create(key, title, body);
    _events.noteCreated(note);
    return note;
}

export async function update(key, title, body) {
    const note = await model().update(key, title, body);
    _events.noteUpdate(note);
    return note;
}

export async function destroy(key) {
    await model().destroy(key);
    _events.noteDestroy({ key });
    return key;
}
```

The contract for the Notes model functions is that they return a `Promise`, and therefore our caller will be using `await` to resolve the `Promise`. There are three steps:

1. Call the corresponding function in the current `model` class, and `await` its result
2. Send the corresponding message to our listeners
3. Return the value, and because this is an `async` function, the value will be received as a `Promise` that fulfills the contract for these functions

Real-time changes in the Notes home page

The Notes model now sends events as Notes are created, updated, or destroyed. For this to be useful, the events must be displayed to our users. Making the events visible to our users means the controller and view portions of the application must consume those events.

Let's start making changes to `routes/index.mjs`:

```
router.get('/', async (req, res, next) => {
  try {
    let notelist = await getKeyTitlesList();
    res.render('index', {
      title: 'Notes', notelist: notelist,
      user: req.user ? req.user : undefined
    });
  } catch (e) { next(e); }
});
```

We need to reuse part of the original routing function, to use it in another function. Therefore, we've pulled code that used to be in this block into a new function, `getKeyTitlesList`:

```
async function getKeyTitlesList() {
  const keylist = await notes.keylist();
  var keyPromises = keylist.map(key => {
    return notes.read(key).then(note => {
      return { key: note.key, title: note.title };
    });
  });
  return Promise.all(keyPromises);
};
```

This portion of the original routing function is now its own function. It generates an array of items containing the `key` and `title` for all existing Notes, using `Promise.all` to manage the process of reading everything.

```
export function socketio(io) {
  var emitNoteTitles = async () => {
    const notelist = await getKeyTitlesList()
    io.of('/home').emit('notetitles', { notelist });
  };
  notes.events.on('notecreated', emitNoteTitles);
  notes.events.on('noteupdate', emitNoteTitles);
  notes.events.on('notedestroy', emitNoteTitles);
};
```

Here is the `socketio` function we discussed while modifying `app.mjs`. We receive the `io` object, then use it to emit a `notestitles` event to all connected browsers.

The `io.of('/namespace')` method restricts whatever follows to the given namespace. In this case, we're emitting a `notestitle` message to the `/home` namespace.

The `io.of` method defines what `Socket.IO` calls a namespace. Namespaces limit the scope of messages sent through `Socket.IO`. The default namespace is `/`, and namespaces look like pathnames, in that they're a series of slash-separated names. An event emitted into a namespace is delivered to any socket listening to that namespace.

The code, in this case, is fairly straightforward. It listens to the events we just implemented, `notecreated`, `noteupdate`, and `notedestroy`. For each of these events, it emits an event, `notetitles`, containing the list of note keys and titles.

That's it!

As Notes are created, updated, and destroyed, we ensure that the homepage will be refreshed to match. The homepage template, `views/index.hbs`, will require code to receive that event and rewrite the page to match.

Changing the homepage and layout templates

`Socket.IO` runs on both client and server, with the two communicating back and forth over the HTTP connection. This requires loading the client JavaScript library into the client browser. Each page of the Notes application in which we seek to implement `Socket.IO` services must load the client library and have custom client code for our application.

Each page in Notes will require a different `Socket.IO` client implementation, since each page has different requirements. This affects how we load JavaScript code in Notes.

Initially, we simply put JavaScript code at the bottom of `layout.hbs`, because every page required the same set of JavaScript modules. But now we've identified the need for a different set of JavaScript on each page. Furthermore, some of the JavaScript needs to be loaded following the JavaScript currently loaded at the bottom of `layout.hbs`. Specifically, jQuery is loaded currently in `layout.hbs`, but we want to use jQuery in the `Socket.IO` clients to perform DOM manipulations on each page. Therefore, some template refactoring is required.

Create a file, `partials/footerjs.hbs`, containing:

```html
<!-- jQuery first, then Popper.js, then Bootstrap JS -->
<script src="/assets/vendor/jquery/jquery.min.js"></script>
<script src="/assets/vendor/popper.js/umd/popper.min.js"></script>
<script src="/assets/vendor/bootstrap/js/bootstrap.min.js"></script>
<script src="/assets/vendor/feather-icons/feather.js"></script>
<script>
  feather.replace()
</script>
```

This had been at the bottom of `views/layout.hbs`. We now need to modify that file as follows:

```html
<body>
    {{> header }}
    {{{body}}}
</body>
```

Then, at the bottom of every template (`error.hbs`, `index.hbs`, `login.hbs`, `notedestroy.hbs`, `noteedit.hbs`, and `noteview.hbs`), add this line:

```handlebars
{{> footerjs}}
```

So far, this hasn't changed what will be loaded in the pages, because `footerjs` contains exactly what was already at the bottom of `layout.hbs`. But it gives us the freedom to load `Socket.IO` client code after the scripts in `footerjs` are loaded.

In `views/index.hbs` add this at the bottom, after the `footerjs` partial:

```
{{> footerjs}}

<script src="/socket.io/socket.io.js"></script>
<script>
$(document).ready(function () {
  var socket = io('/home');
  socket.on('notetitles', function(data) {
    var notelist = data.notelist;
    $('#notetitles').empty();
    for (var i = 0; i < notelist.length; i++) {
      notedata = notelist[i];
      $('#notetitles')
      .append('<a class="btn btn-lg btn-block btn-outline-dark"
      href="/notes/view?key='+
      notedata.key +'">'+ notedata.title +'</a>');
    }
  });
});
</script>
```

The first line is where we load the `Socket.IO` client library. You'll notice that we never set up any Express route to handle the `/socket.io` URL. Instead, the `Socket.IO` library did that for us.

Because we've already loaded jQuery (to support Bootstrap), we can easily ensure that this code is executed once the page is fully loaded using `$(document).ready`.

This code first connects a `socket` object to the `/home` namespace. That namespace is being used for events related to the Notes homepage. We then listen for the `notetitles` events, for which some jQuery DOM manipulation erases the current list of Notes and renders a new list on the screen.

That's it. Our code in `routes/index.mjs` listened to various events from the Notes model, and, in response, sent a `notetitles` event to the browser. The browser code takes that list of note information and redraws the screen.

You might notice that our browser-side JavaScript is not using ES-2015/2016/2017 features. This code would, of course, be cleaner if we were to do so. How can we know whether our visitors use a browser modern enough for those language features? We could use Babel to transpile ES-2015/2016/2017 code into ES5 code capable of running on any browser. However, it may be a useful trade-off to still write ES5 code in the browser.

Running Notes with real-time homepage updates

We now have enough implemented to run the application and see some real-time action.

As you did earlier, start the user information microservice in one window:

```
$ npm start

> user-auth-server@0.0.1 start /Users/david/chap09/users
> DEBUG=users:* PORT=3333 SEQUELIZE_CONNECT=sequelize-sqlite.yaml node
--experimental-modules user-server

(node:11866) ExperimentalWarning: The ESM module loader is
experimental.
  users:service User-Auth-Service listening at http://127.0.0.1:3333
+0ms
```

Then, in another window, start the Notes application:

```
$ npm start

> notes@0.0.0 start /Users/david/chap09/notes
> DEBUG=notes:* SEQUELIZE_CONNECT=models/sequelize-sqlite.yaml
NOTES_MODEL=sequelize USER_SERVICE_URL=http://localhost:3333 node --
experimental-modules ./app

(node:11998) ExperimentalWarning: The ESM module loader is
experimental.
  notes:debug-INDEX Listening on port 3000 +0ms
```

Then, in a browser window, go to `http://localhost:3000` and log in to the Notes application. To see the real-time effects, open multiple browser windows. If you can use Notes from multiple computers, then do that as well.

In one browser window, start creating and deleting notes, while leaving the other browser windows viewing the home page. Create a note, and it should show up immediately on the home page in the other browser windows. Delete a note and it should disappear immediately as well.

Real-time action while viewing notes

It's cool how we can now see real-time changes in a part of the Notes application. Let's turn to the `/notes/view` page to see what we can do. What comes to mind is this functionality:

- Update the note if someone else edits it
- Redirect the viewer to the home page if someone else deletes the note
- Allow users to leave comments on the note

For the first two features, we can rely on the existing events coming from the Notes model. The third feature will require a messaging subsystem, so we'll get to that later in this chapter.

In `routes/notes.mjs`, add this to the end of the module:

```
export function socketio(io) {
    notes.events.on('noteupdate',  newnote => {
        io.of('/view').emit('noteupdate', newnote);
    });
    notes.events.on('notedestroy', data => {
        io.of('/view').emit('notedestroy', data);
    });
};
```

At the top of `app.mjs,` make this change:

```
import { socketio as indexSocketio, router as index } from
'./routes/index';
import { router as users, initPassport } from './routes/users';
import { socketio as notesSocketio, router as notes } from
'./routes/notes';
```

Uncomment that line of code in `app.mjs` because we've now implemented the function we said we'd get to later:

```
indexSocketio(io);
notesSocketio(io);
```

This sets up the Notes application to send `noteupdate` and `notedestroy` messages when notes are updated or destroyed. The destination is the `/view` namespace. We'll need to make a corresponding modification to the note view template so it does the right thing. This means any browser viewing any note in the application will connect to this namespace. Every such browser will receive events about any note being changed, even those notes that are not being viewed. This means that the client code will have to check the key, and only take action if the event refers to the note being displayed.

Changing the note view template for real-time action

As we did earlier, in order to make these events visible to the user, we must not only add client code to the template, `views/noteview.hbs`; we need a couple of small changes to the template:

```
<div class="container-fluid">
    <div class="row"><div class="col-xs-12">
        {{#if note}}<h3 id="notetitle">{{ note.title }}</h3>{{/if}}
        {{#if note}}<div id="notebody">{{ note.body }}</div>{{/if}}
        <p>Key: {{ notekey }}</p>
    </div></div>
    {{#if user }}
    {{#if notekey }}
        <div class="row"><div class="col-xs-12">
        <div class="btn-group">
            <a class="btn btn-outline-dark"
                href="/notes/destroy?key={{notekey}}"
                role="button">Delete</a>
            <a cl e template,  views/noteview.hb
  ass="btn btn-outline-dark"
                href="/notes/edit?key={{notekey}}"
                role="button">Edit</a>
        </div>
        </div></div>
    {{/if}}
    {{/if}}
</div>

{{> footerjs}}
```

```
{{#if notekey }}
<script src="/socket.io/socket.io.js"></script>
<script>
$(document).ready(function () {
    io('/view').on('noteupdate', function(note) {
        if (note.key === "{{ notekey }}") {
            $('h3#notetitle').empty();
            $('h3#notetitle').text(note.title);
            $('#notebody').empty();
            $('#notebody').text(note.body);
        }
    });
    io('/view').on('notedestroy', function(data) {
        if (data.key === "{{ notekey }}") {
            window.location.href = "/";
        }
    });
});
</script>
{{/if}}
```

We connect to the `/view` namespace where the messages are sent. As `noteupdate` or `notedestroy` messages arrive, we check the key to see whether it matches the key for the note being displayed.

A technique is used here that's important to understand. We have mixed JavaScript executed on the server, with JavaScript executed in the browser. We must compare the `notekey` received by the client code against the `notekey` for the note being viewed by this page. The latter `notekey` value is known on the server, while the former is known in the client.

Remember that code within the `{{ .. }}` delimiters is interpreted by the Handlebars template engine on the server. Consider the following:

```
if (note.key === "{{ notekey }}") {
    ..
}
```

This comparison is between the `notekey` value in the browser, which arrived inside the message from the server, and the `notekey` variable on the server. That variable contains the key of the note being displayed. Therefore, in this case, we are able to ensure these code snippets are executed only for the note being shown on the screen.

For the `noteupdate` event, we take the new note content and display it on the screen. For this to work, we had to add `id=` attributes to the HTML so we could use jQuery selectors in manipulating the DOM.

For the `notedestroy` event, we simply redirect the browser window back to the home page. The note being viewed has been deleted, and there's no point the user continuing to look at a note that no longer exists.

Running Notes with real-time updates while viewing a note

At this point, you can now rerun the Notes application and try this out.

Launch the user authentication server and the Notes application as before. Then, in the browser, open multiple windows on the Notes application. This time, have one viewing the home page, and two viewing a note. In one of those windows, edit the note to make a change, and see the text change on both the home page and the page viewing the note.

Then delete the note, and watch it disappear from the home page, and the browser window that had viewed the note is now on the home page.

Inter-user chat and commenting for Notes

This is cool! We now have real-time updates in Notes as we edit delete or create notes. Let's now take it to the next level and implement something akin to inter-user chatting.

It's possible to pivot our Notes application concept and take it in the direction of a social network. In the majority of such networks, users post things (notes, pictures, videos, and so on), and other users comment on those things. Done well, these basic elements can develop a large community of people sharing notes with each other. While the Notes application is kind of a toy, it's not too terribly far from being a basic social network. Commenting the way we will do now is a tiny step in that direction.

On each note page, we'll have an area to display messages from Notes users. Each message will show the username, a timestamp, and their message. We'll also need a method for users to post a message, and we'll also allow users to delete messages.

Each of those operations will be performed without refreshing the screen. Instead, code running inside the web page will send commands to/from the server and take actions dynamically.

Let's get started.

Data model for storing messages

We need to start by implementing a data model for storing messages. The basic fields required are a unique ID, the username of the person sending the message, the namespace the message is sent to, their message, and finally a timestamp for when the message was sent. As messages are received or deleted, events must be emitted from the model so we can do the right thing on the web page.

This model implementation will be written for `Sequelize`. If you prefer a different storage solution, you can , by all means, re-implement the same API on other data storage systems.

Create a new file, `models/messages-sequelize.mjs`, containing the following:

```
import Sequelize from 'sequelize';
import jsyaml from 'js-yaml';
import fs from 'fs-extra';
import util from 'util';
import EventEmitter from 'events';

class MessagesEmitter extends EventEmitter {}

import DBG from 'debug';
const debug = DBG('notes:model-messages');
const error = DBG('notes:error-messages');

var SQMessage;
var sequlz;

export const emitter = new MessagesEmitter();
```

This sets up the modules being used and also initializes the `EventEmitter` interface. We're also exporting the `EventEmitter` as `emitter` so other modules can use it:

```
async function connectDB() {

    if (typeof sequlz === 'undefined') {
        const yamltext = await
        fs.readFile(process.env.SEQUELIZE_CONNECT, 'utf8');
        const params = jsyaml.safeLoad(yamltext, 'utf8');
        sequlz = new Sequelize(params.dbname,
                params.username, params.password, params.params);
    }

    if (SQMessage) return SQMessage.sync();
    SQMessage = sequlz.define('Message', {
        id: { type: Sequelize.INTEGER, autoIncrement: true,
primaryKey:
        true },
        from: Sequelize.STRING,
        namespace: Sequelize.STRING,
        message: Sequelize.STRING(1024),
        timestamp: Sequelize.DATE
    });
    return SQMessage.sync();
}
```

This defines our message schema in the database. We'll use the same database that we used for Notes, but the messages will be stored in their own table.

The `id` field won't be supplied by the caller; instead, it will be autogenerated. Because it is an `autoIncrement` field, each message that's added will be assigned a new `id` number by the database:

```
export async function postMessage(from, namespace, message) {
    const SQMessage = await connectDB();
    const newmsg = await SQMessage.create({
        from, namespace, message, timestamp: new Date()
    });
    var toEmit = {
        id: newmsg.id, from: newmsg.from,
        namespace: newmsg.namespace, message: newmsg.message,
        timestamp: newmsg.timestamp
    };
    emitter.emit('newmessage', toEmit);
}
```

This is to be called when a user posts a new comment/message. We first store it in the database, and then we emit an event saying the message was created:

```
export async function destroyMessage(id, namespace) {
    const SQMessage = await connectDB();
    const msg = await SQMessage.find({ where: { id } });
    if (msg) {
        msg.destroy();
        emitter.emit('destroymessage', { id, namespace });
    }
}
```

This is to be called when a user requests that a message should be deleted. With `Sequelize`, we must first find the message and then delete it by calling its `destroy` method. Once that's done, we emit a message saying the message was destroyed:

```
export async function recentMessages(namespace) {
    const SQMessage = await connectDB();
    const messages = SQMessage.findAll({
        where: { namespace }, order: [ 'timestamp' ], limit: 20
    });
    return messages.map(message => {
        return {
            id: message.id, from: message.from,
            namespace: message.namespace, message: message.message,
            timestamp: message.timestamp
        };
    });
}
```

While this is meant to be called when viewing a note, it is generalized to work for any Socket.IO namespace. It finds the most recent 20 messages associated with the given namespace and returns a cleaned-up list to the caller.

Adding messages to the Notes router

Now that we can store messages in the database, let's integrate this into the Notes router module.

In `routes/notes.mjs`, add this to the `import` statements:

```
import * as messages from '../models/messages-sequelize';
```

If you wish to implement a different data storage model for messages, you'll need to change this `import` statement. You should consider using an environment variable to specify the module name, as we've done elsewhere:

```
// Save incoming message to message pool, then broadcast it
router.post('/make-comment', ensureAuthenticated, async (req, res,
next) => {
    try {
        await messages.postMessage(req.body.from,
            req.body.namespace, req.body.message);
        res.status(200).json({ });
    } catch(err) {
        res.status(500).end(err.stack);
    }
});

// Delete the indicated message
router.post('/del-message', ensureAuthenticated, async (req, res,
next) => {
    try {
        await messages.destroyMessage(req.body.id,
req.body.namespace);
        res.status(200).json({ });
    } catch(err) {
        res.status(500).end(err.stack);
    }
});
```

This pair of routes, `/notes/make-comment` and `/notes/del-message`, is used to post a new comment or delete an existing one. Each calls the corresponding data model function and then sends an appropriate response back to the caller.

Remember that `postMessage` stores a message in the database, and then it turns around and emits that message to other browsers. Likewise, `destroyMessage` deletes the message from the database, then emits a message to other browsers saying that the message has been deleted. Finally, the results from `recentMessages` will reflect the current set of messages in the database.

Both of these will be called by AJAX code in the browser:

```javascript
module.exports.socketio = function(io) {
    io.of('/view').on('connection', function(socket) {
        // 'cb' is a function sent from the browser, to which we
        // send the messages for the named note.
        socket.on('getnotemessages', (namespace, cb) => {
            messages.recentMessages(namespace).then(cb)
            .catch(err => console.error(err.stack));
        });
    });

    messages.emitter.on('newmessage', newmsg => {
        io.of('/view').emit('newmessage', newmsg);
    });
    messages.emitter.on('destroymessage', data => {
        io.of('/view').emit('destroymessage', data);
    });
    ..
};
```

This is the Socket.IO glue code, which we will add to the code we looked at earlier.

The `getnotemessages` message from the browser requests the list of messages for the given Note. This calls the `recentMessages` function in the model. This uses a feature of Socket.IO where the client can pass a callback function, and server-side Socket.IO code can invoke that callback, giving it some data.

We also listen to the `newmessage` and `destroymessage` messages emitted by the messages model, sending corresponding messages to the browser. These are sent using the method described earlier.

Changing the note view template for messages

We need to dive back into `views/noteview.hbs` with more changes so that we can view, create, and delete messages. This time, we will add a lot of code, including using a Bootstrap modal popup to get the message, several AJAX calls to communicate with the server, and, of course, more Socket.IO stuff.

Using a Modal window to compose messages

The Bootstrap framework has a Modal component that serves a similar purpose to Modal dialogs in desktop applications. You pop up the Modal, it prevents interaction with other parts of the web page, you enter stuff into fields in the Modal, and then click a button to make it close.

This new segment of code replaces the existing segment defining the **Edit** and **Delete** buttons, in `views/noteview.hbs`:

```
{{#if user}}
{{#if notekey}}
    <div class="row"><div class="col-xs-12">
    <div class="btn-group">
        <a class="btn btn-outline-dark" href="/notes/destroy?key=
        {{notekey}}"
            role="button">Delete</a>
        <a class="btn btn-outline-dark" href="/notes/edit?key=
        {{notekey}}"
            role="button">Edit</a>
        <button type="button" class="btn btn-outline-dark"
            data-toggle="modal"
            data-target="#notes-comment-modal">Comment</button>
    </div>
    </div></div>

    <div id="noteMessages"></div>
{{/if}}
{{/if}}
```

This adds support for posting comments on a note. The user will see a Modal pop-up window in which they write their comment. We'll show the code for the Modal later.

We added a new button labeled **Comment** that the user will click to start the process of posting a message. This button is connected to the Modal by way of the element ID specified in the `data-target` attribute. The ID will match the outermost `div` wrapping the Modal. This structure of `div` elements and class names are from the Bootstrap website at `http://getbootstrap.com/docs/4.0/components/modal/`.

Let's add the code for the Modal at the bottom of `views/noteview.hbs`.

```
{{> footerjs}}

{{#if notekey}}
{{#if user}}
<div class="modal fade" id="notes-comment-modal" tabindex="-1"
    role="dialog" aria-labelledby="noteCommentModalLabel" aria-
hidden="true">
  <div class="modal-dialog modal-dialog-centered" role="document">
    <div class="modal-content">
      <div class="modal-header">
          <button type="button" class="close" data-dismiss="modal"
aria-
          label="Close">
          <span aria-hidden="true">&times;</span>
          </button>
          <h4 class="modal-title" id="noteCommentModalLabel">Leave a
          Comment</h4>
      </div>
      <div class="modal-body">
        <form method="POST" id="submit-comment" class="well" data-async
            data-target="#rating-modal" action="/notes/make-comment">
          <input type="hidden" name="from" value="{{ user.id }}">
          <input type="hidden" name="namespace" value="/view-
          {{notekey}}">
          <input type="hidden" name="key" value="{{notekey}}">
          <fieldset>
            <div class="form-group">
              <label for="noteCommentTextArea">
              Your Excellent Thoughts, Please</label>
              <textarea id="noteCommentTextArea" name="message"
                    class="form-control" rows="3"></textarea>
            </div>

            <div class="form-group">
              <div class="col-sm-offset-2 col-sm-10">
                <button id="submitNewComment" type="submit" class="btn
                btn-default">
                Make Comment</button>
              </div>
            </div>
          </fieldset>
        </form>
    </div>
  </div>
  </div>
</div>
```

```
{{/if}}
{{/if}}
```

The key portion of this is the HTML form contained within the `div.modal-body` element. It's a straightforward, normal Bootstrap, augmented form with a normal **Submit** button at the bottom. A few hidden `input` elements are used to pass extra information inside the request.

With the HTML set up this way, Bootstrap will ensure that this Modal is triggered when the user clicks on the **Comment** button. The user can close the Modal by clicking on the **Close** button. Otherwise, it's up to us to implement code to handle the form submission using AJAX so that it doesn't cause the page to reload.

Sending, displaying, and deleting messages

Note that these code snippets are wrapped with `{{#if}}` statements, so that certain user interface elements are displayed only to sufficiently privileged users. A user that isn't logged in certainly shouldn't be able to post a message.

Now we have a lot of Socket.IO code to add:

```
{{#if notekey}}
{{#if user}}
<script>
$(document).ready(function () { ... });
{{/if}}
{{/if}}
```

There's another code section to handle the `noteupdate` and `notedestroy` messages. This new section has to do with messages that manage the comments.

We need to handle the form submission for posting a new comment, get the recent messages when first viewing a note, listen for events from the server about new messages or deleted messages, render the messages on the screen, and handle requests to delete a message:

```
$(document).ready(function () {
    io('/view').emit('getnotemessages', '/view-{{notekey}}',
function(msgs) {
        $('#noteMessages').empty();
        if (msgs.length > 0) {
            msgs.forEach(function(newmsg) {
                $('#noteMessages').append(formatMessage(newmsg));
            });
            $('#noteMessages').show();
```

```javascript
                connectMsgDelButton();
        } else $('#noteMessages').hide();
    });
    var connectMsgDelButton = function() {
        $('.message-del-button').on('click', function(event) {
            $.post('/notes/del-message', {
                id: $(this).data("id"),
                namespace: $(this).data("namespace")
            },
            function(response) { });
            event.preventDefault();
        });
    };
    var formatMessage = function(newmsg) {
        return '<div id="note-message-'+ newmsg.id +'" class="card">'
            +'<div class="card-body">'
            +'<h5 class="card-title">'+ newmsg.from +'</h5>'
            +'<div class="card-text">'+ newmsg.message
            +' <small style="display: block">'+ newmsg.timestamp
            +'</small></div>'
            +' <button type="button" class="btn btn-primary message-
            del-button" data-id="'
            + newmsg.id +'" data-namespace="'+ newmsg.namespace +'">'
            +'Delete</button>'
            +'</div>'
            +'</div>';
    };
    io('/view').on('newmessage', function(newmsg) {
        if (newmsg.namespace === '/view-{{notekey}}') {
            $('#noteMessages').prepend(formatMessage(newmsg));
            connectMsgDelButton();
        }
    });
    io('/view').on('destroymessage', function(data) {
        if (data.namespace === '/view-{{notekey}}') {
            $('#noteMessages #note-message-'+ data.id).remove();
        }
    });


    $('form#submit-comment').submit(function(event) {
        // Abort any pending request
        if (request) { request.abort(); }
        var $form = $('form#submit-comment');
        var $target = $($form.attr('data-target'));
        var request = $.ajax({
            type: $form.attr('method'),
            url: $form.attr('action'),
            data: $form.serialize()
```

```
        });
        request.done(function (response, textStatus, jqXHR) { });
        request.fail(function (jqXHR, textStatus, errorThrown) {
            alert("ERROR "+ jqXHR.responseText);
        });
        request.always(function () {
            // Reenable the inputs
            $('#notes-comment-modal').modal('hide');
        });
        event.preventDefault();
    });
});
```

The code within `$('form#submit-comment').submit` handles the form
submission for the comment form. Because we already have jQuery available, we can
use its AJAX support to POST a request to the server without causing a page reload.

Using `event.preventDefault`, we ensure that the default action does not occur. For
the FORM submission, that means the browser page does not reload. What happens
is an HTTP POST is sent to `/notes/make-comment` with a data payload consisting of
the values of the form's `input` elements. Included in those values are three hidden
inputs, `from`, `namespace`, and `key`, providing useful identification data.

If you refer to the `/notes/make-comment` route definition, this calls
`messagesModel.postMessage` to store the message in the database. That function
then posts an event, `newmessage`, which our server-side code forwards to any
browser that's connected to the namespace. Shortly after that, a `newmessage` event
will arrive in browsers.

The `newmessage` event adds a message block, using the `formatMessage` function.
The HTML for the message is `prepended` to `#noteMessages`.

When the page is first loaded, we want to retrieve the current messages. This is
kicked off with `io('/view').emit('getnotemessages',` ... This function, as
the name implies, sends a `getnotemessages` message to the server. We showed the
implementation of the server-side handler for this message earlier, in
`routes/notes.mjs`.

If you remember, we said that Socket.IO supports the provision of a callback function that is called by the server in response to an event. You simply pass a function as the last parameter to a `.emit` call. That function is made available at the other end of the communication, to be called when appropriate. To make this clear, we have a callback function on the browser being invoked by server-side code.

In this case, the server-side calls our callback function with a list of messages. The message list arrives in the client-side callback function, which displays them in the `#noteMessages` area. It uses jQuery DOM manipulation to erase any existing messages, then renders each message into the messages area using the `formatMessage` function.

The message display template, in `formatMessage`, is straightforward. It uses a Bootstrap `card` to give a nice visual effect. And, there is a button for deleting messages.

In `formatMessage` we created a **Delete** button for each message. Those buttons need an event handler, and the event handler is set up using the `connectMsgDelButton` function. In this case, we send an HTTP POST request to `/notes/del-message`. We again use the jQuery AJAX support to post that HTTP request.

The `/notes/del-message` route in turn calls `messagesModel.destroyMessage` to do the deed. That function then emits an event, `destroymessage`, which gets sent back to the browser. As you see here, the `destroymessage` event handler causes the corresponding message to be removed using jQuery DOM manipulation. We were careful to add an `id=` attribute to every message to make removal easy.

Since the flip side of destruction is creation, we need to have the `newmessage` event handler sitting next to the `destroymessage` event handler. It also uses jQuery DOM manipulation to insert the new message into the `#noteMessages` area.

Running Notes and passing messages

That was a lot of code, but we now have the ability to compose messages, display them on the screen, and delete them, all with no page reloads.

You can run the application as we did earlier, first starting the user authentication server in one command-line window and the Notes application in another:

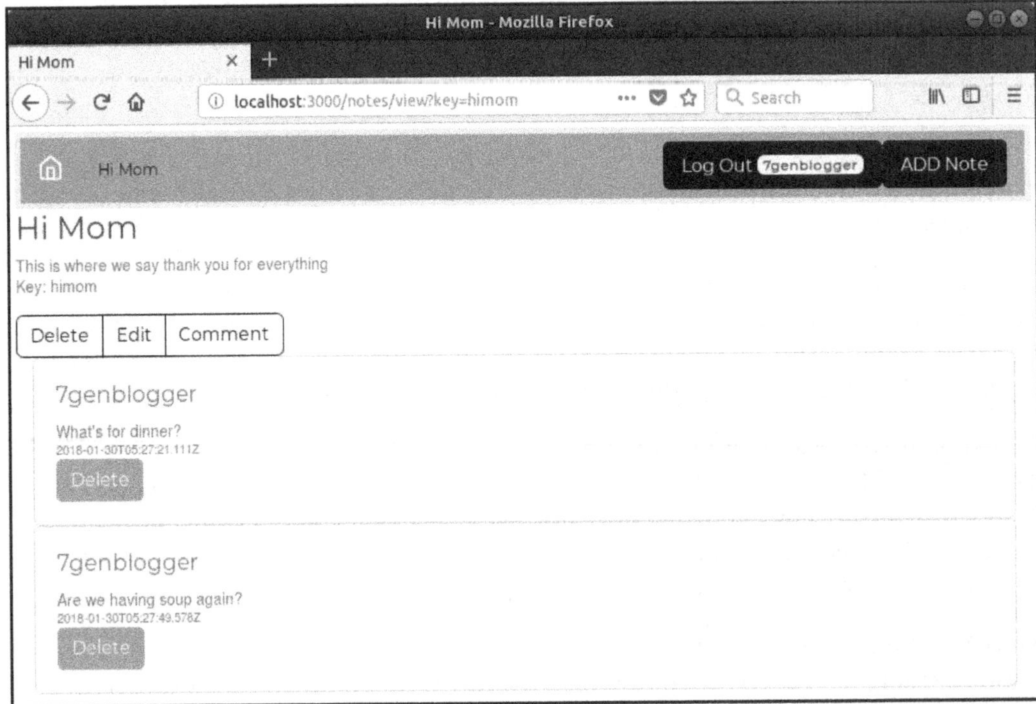

While entering a message, the Modal looks like this:

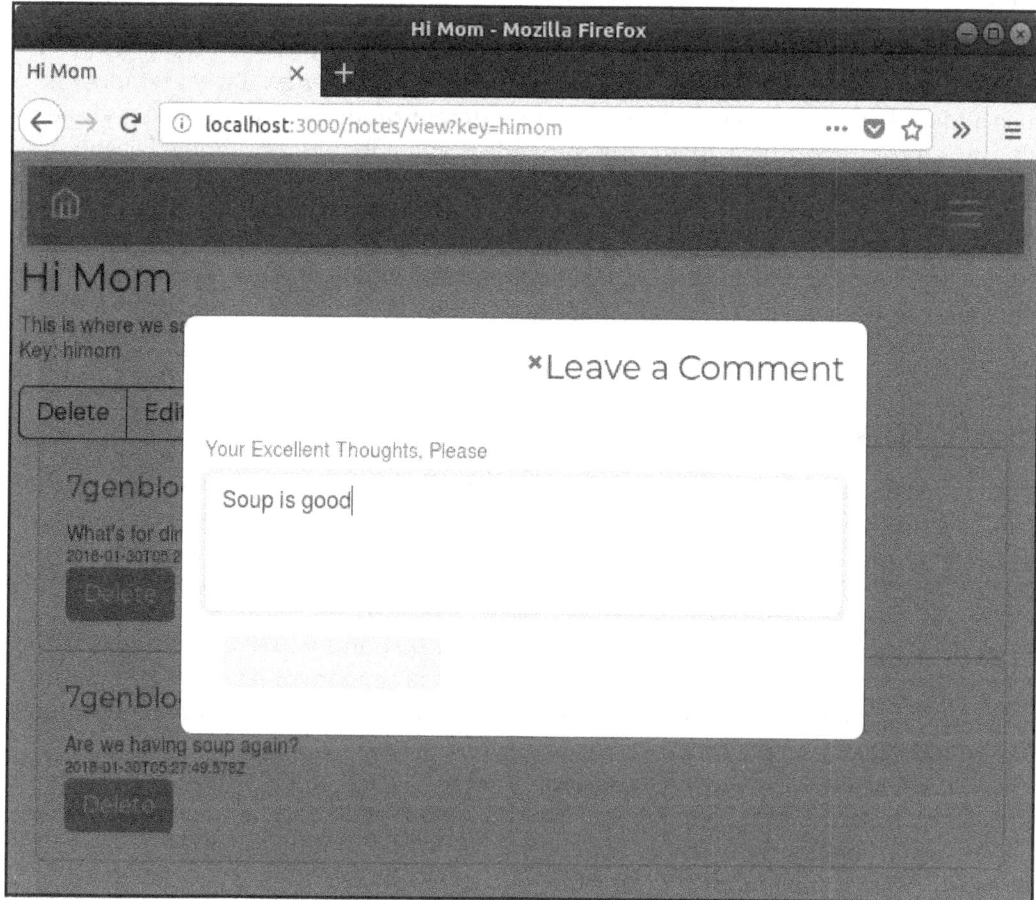

Try this with multiple browser windows viewing the same note or different notes. This way, you can verify that notes show up only on the corresponding note window.

Other applications of Modal windows

We used a Modal and some AJAX code to avoid one page reload due to a form submission. In the Notes application, as it stands, a similar technique could be used when creating a new note, editing existing notes, and deleting existing notes. In each case, we would use a Modal, some AJAX code to handle the form submission, and some jQuery code to update the page without causing a reload.

But wait, that's not all. Consider the sort of dynamic real-time user interface wizardry on the popular social networks. Imagine what events and/or AJAX calls are required.

When you click on an image in Twitter, it pops up, you guessed it, a Modal window to show a larger version of the image. The Twitter **Compose new Tweet** window is also a Modal window. Facebook uses many different Modal windows, such as when sharing a post, reporting a spam post, or while doing a lot of other things Facebook's designers deem to require a pop-up window.

Socket.IO, as we've seen, gives us a rich foundation of events passing between server and client that can build multiuser, multichannel communication experiences for your users.

Summary

While we came a long way in this chapter, maybe Facebook doesn't have anything to fear from the baby steps we took toward converting the Notes application into a social network. This chapter gave us the opportunity to explore some really cool technology for pseudo real-time communication between browser sessions.

Look up the technical definition for the phrase *real time* and you'll see the real-time web is not truly real time. The actual meaning of real time involves software with strict time boundaries that must respond to events within a specified time constraint. Real-time software is typically used in embedded systems to respond to button presses, for applications as diverse as junk food dispensers and medical devices in intensive care units. Eat too much junk food and you could end up in intensive care, and be served by real-time software in both cases. Try and remember the distinction between different meanings for this phrase.

In this chapter, you learned about using Socket.IO for pseudo real-time web experiences, using the `EventEmitter` class to send messages between parts of an application, jQuery, AJAX, and other browser-side JavaScript technologies, while avoiding page reloads while making AJAX calls.

In the next chapter, we will look into Node.js application deployment on real servers. Running code on our laptop is cool, but to hit the big time, the application needs to be properly deployed.

10 Deploying Node.js Applications

Now that the Notes application is fairly complete, it's time to think about how to deploy it to a real server. We've created a minimal implementation of the collaborative note concept that works fairly well. To grow, Notes must escape our laptop and live on a real server. The goal is to look at deployment methods for Node.js applications.

In this chapter, we will cover the following topics:

- Traditional LSB-compliant Node.js deployment
- Using PM2 to improve reliability
- Deployment to a **Virtual Private Server** (**VPS**) provider
- Microservice deployment with Docker (we have four distinct services to deploy)
- Deployment to a Docker hosting provider

The first task is to duplicate the source code from the previous chapter. It's suggested you create a new directory, chap10, as a sibling of the chap09 directory, and copy everything from chap09 to chap10.

Notes application architecture and deployment considerations

Before we get into deploying the Notes application, we need to review its architecture. To deploy the Notes application, we must understand what we're planning to do

We have segmented the services into two groups, as shown in the following diagram:

The user authentication server should be the more secure portion of the system. On our laptop, we weren't able to create the envisioned protective wall around that service, but we're about to implement such protection.

One strategy to enhance security is to expose as few ports as possible. That reduces the so-called attack surface, simplifying our work in hardening the application against security bugs. With the Notes application, we have exactly one port to expose, the HTTP service through which users access the application. The other ports, the two for MySQL servers and the user authentication service port, should be hidden.

Internally, the Notes application needs to access both the Notes database and the user authentication service. That service, in turn, needs to access the user authentication database. As currently envisaged, no service outside the Notes application requires access to either database or to the authentication service.

Implementation of this segmentation requires either two or three subnets, depending on the lengths you wish to go to. The first, FrontNet, contains the Notes application and its database. The second, AuthNet, contains the authentication service and its database. A third possible subnet would contain the Notes and authentication services. The subnet configuration must limit the hosts with access to the subnet, and create a security wall between subnets.

Traditional Linux Node.js service deployment

Traditional Linux/Unix server application deployment uses an **init script** to manage background processes. They are to start every time the system boots and cleanly shut down when the system is halted. While it's a simple model, the specifics of this vary widely from one **operating system (OS)** to another.

A common method is for the `init` process to manage background processes using shell scripts in the `/etc/init.d` directory. Other OSes use other process managers, such as `upstart` or `launchd`.

The Node.js project itself does not include any scripts to manage server processes on any OS. Node.js is more like a construction kit, with the pieces and parts to build servers, and is not a complete polished server framework itself. Implementing a complete web service based on Node.js means creating the scripting to integrate with process management on your OS. It's up to us to develop those scripts.

Web services have to be:

- Reliable: For example, to auto-restart when the server process crashes
- Manageable: Meaning it integrates well with system management practices
- Observable: Meaning the administrator must be able to get status and activity information from the service

To demonstrate what's involved, let's use PM2 to implement background server process management for Notes. PM2 detects the system type and can automatically integrate itself with the process management system. It will create an LSB-style init script (`http://wiki.debian.org/LSBInitScripts`), or other scripts, as required by the process management system on your server.

For this deployment, we'll set up a single Ubuntu 17.10 server. You should provision a **Virtual Private Server (VPS)** from a hosting provider and do all installation and configuration there. Renting a small machine instance from one of the major providers for the time needed to go through this chapter will only cost a couple of dollars.

You can also do the tasks in this section using **VirtualBox** on your laptop. Simply install Debian or Ubuntu as a virtual machine in VirtualBox, then follow the instructions in this section. It won't be quite the same as using a remote VPS hosting provider, but does not require renting a server.

Both the Notes and user authentication services will be on that server, along with a single MySQL instance. While our goal is a strong separation between FrontNet and AuthNet, with two MySQL instances, we won't do so at this time.

Prerequisite – provisioning the databases

The Linux package management system doesn't allow us to install two MySQL instances. Instead, we implement separation in the same MySQL instance by using separate databases with different usernames and access privileges for each database.

The first step is to ensure that MySQL is installed on your server. For Ubuntu, **DigitalOcean** has a fairly good tutorial:
`https://www.digitalocean.com/community/tutorials/how-to-install-mysql-on-ubuntu-14-04`. While the Ubuntu version for that tutorial is old, the instructions are still accurate enough.

The MySQL server must support TCP connections from `localhost`. Edit the configuration file, `/etc/mysql/my.cnf`, to have the following line:

```
bind-address = 127.0.0.1
```

This limits MySQL server connections to the processes on the server. A miscreant would have to break into the server to access your database. Now that our database server is available, let's set up two databases.

In the `chap10/notes/models` directory, create a file named `mysql-create-db.sql` containing the following:

```
CREATE DATABASE notes;
CREATE USER 'notes'@'localhost' IDENTIFIED BY 'notes';
GRANT ALL PRIVILEGES ON notes.* TO 'notes'@'localhost' WITH GRANT
OPTION;
```

In the `chap10/users` directory, create a file named `mysql-create-db.sql` containing the following:

```
CREATE DATABASE userauth;
CREATE USER 'userauth'@'localhost' IDENTIFIED BY 'userauth';
GRANT ALL PRIVILEGES ON userauth.* TO 'userauth'@'localhost' WITH
GRANT OPTION;
```

We can't run those scripts on the server, because the Notes application has not yet been copied to the server. When that's accomplished, we'll run the scripts as:

```
$ mysql -u root -p <chap10/users/mysql-create-db.sql
$ mysql -u root -p <chap10/notes/models/mysql-create-db.sql
```

This will create the two databases, `notes` and `userauth`, with associated usernames and passwords. Each user can access only their associated database. Later, we'll set up Notes and the user authentication service with YAML configuration files to access these databases.

Installing Node.js on Ubuntu

According to the Node.js documentation (`https://nodejs.org/en/download/package-manager/`), the recommended installation method for Debian or Ubuntu Linux distributions is the following:

```
$ curl -sL https://deb.nodesource.com/setup_10.x | sudo -E bash -
$ sudo apt-get update
$ sudo apt-get install -y nodejs build-essential
```

We've seen this before, so substitute the Node.js desired version number in the URL. Installing this way means that as new Node.js releases are issued, upgrades are easily accomplished with the normal package management procedures.

Setting up Notes and user authentication on the server

Before copying the Notes and user authentication code to this server, let's do a little coding to prepare for the move. We know that the Notes and authentication services must access the MySQL instance on `localhost` using the usernames and passwords given earlier.

Using the approach we've followed so far, this means a pair of YAML files for `Sequelize` parameters, and changing environment variables in the `package.json` files to match.

Create a `chap10/notes/models/sequelize-server-mysql.yaml` file containing:

```
dbname: notes
username: notes
password: notes12345
params:
    host: localhost
    port: 3306
    dialect: mysql
```

It was discovered during testing that a simple password such as `notes` was not acceptable to the MySQL server, and that a longer password was required. In `chap10/notes/package.json`, add the following line to the `scripts` section:

```
"on-server": "SEQUELIZE_CONNECT=models/sequelize-server-mysql.yaml
NOTES_MODEL=sequelize USER_SERVICE_URL=http://localhost:3333 PORT=3000
node --experimental-modules ./app",
```

Then create a `chap10/users/sequelize-server-mysql.yaml` file containing the following code the following code:

```
dbname: userauth
username: userauth
password: userauth
params:
    host: localhost
    port: 3306
    dialect: mysql
```

The passwords shown in these configuration files obviously will not pass any security audits.

In `chap10/users/package.json`, add the following line to the `scripts` section:

```
"on-server": "PORT=3333 SEQUELIZE_CONNECT=sequelize-server-mysql.yaml
node  experimental-modules ./user-server",
```

This configures the authentication service to access the databases just created.

Now we need to select a place on the server to install the application code:

```
# ls /opt
```

This empty directory looks to be as good a place as any. Simply upload `chap10/notes` and `chap10/users` to your preferred location. Before uploading, remove the `node_modules` directory in both directories.

That's both to save time on the upload, and because of the simple fact that any native-code modules installed on your laptop will be incompatible with the server.

On your laptop, you might run a command like this:

```
$ rsync --archive --verbose ./ root@159.89.145.190:/opt/
```

Use the actual IP address or domain name assigned to the server being used.

You should end up with something like the following:

```
# ls /opt
notes   users
```

Then, in each directory, run these commands:

```
# rm -rf node_modules
# npm install
```

We're running these commands as `root` rather than a user ID that can use the `sudo` command. The machine offered by the chosen hosting provider (DigitalOcean) is configured so users log in as `root`. Other VPS hosting providers will provide machines where you log in as a regular user and then use `sudo` to perform privileged operations. As you read these instructions, pay attention to the command prompt we show. We've followed the convention where $ is used for commands run as a regular user and # is used for commands run as `root`. If you're running as a regular user, and need to run a `root` command, then run the command with `sudo`.

The simplest way of doing this is to just delete the whole `node_modules` directory and then let `npm install` do its job. Remember that we set up the `PATH` environment variable the following way:

```
# export PATH=./node_modules/.bin:${PATH}
```

You can place this in the login script (`.bashrc`, `.cshrc`, and so on) on your server so it's automatically enabled.

Finally, you can now run the SQL scripts written earlier to set up the database instances:

```
# mysql -u root -p <users/mysql-create-db.sql
# mysql -u root -p <notes/models/mysql-create-db.sql
```

Then you should be able to start up the services by hand to check that everything is working correctly. The MySQL instance has already been tested, so we just need to start the user authentication and Notes services:

```
# cd /opt/users
# DEBUG=users:* npm run on-server

> user-auth-server@0.0.1 on-server /opt/users
> PORT=3333 SEQUELIZE_CONNECT=sequelize-server-mysql.yaml node --
experimental-modules ./user-server

(node:9844) ExperimentalWarning: The ESM module loader is
experimental.
```

Then log in to the server on another Terminal session and run the following:

```
# cd /opt/users/
# PORT=3333 node users-add.js
Created { id: 1, username: 'me', password: 'w0rd', provider: 'local',
  familyName: 'Einarrsdottir', givenName: 'Ashildr', middleName: '',
  emails: '[]', photos: '[]',
  updatedAt: '2018-02-02T00:43:16.923Z', createdAt:
'2018-02-02T00:43:16.923Z' }
# PORT=3333 node users-list.js
List [ { id: 'me', username: 'me', provider: 'local',
    familyName: 'Einarrsdottir', givenName: 'Ashildr', middleName: '',
    emails: '[]', photos: '[]' } ]
```

The preceding command both tests that the backend user authentication service is functioning and gives us a user account we can use to log in. The `users-list` command demonstrates that it works.

You may get an error:

```
users:error /create-user Error: Please install mysql2 package
manually
```

This is generated inside of `Sequelize`. The `mysql2` driver is an alternate MySQL driver, implemented in pure JavaScript, and includes support for returning Promises for smooth usage in `async` functions. If you do get this message, go ahead and install the package and remember to add this dependency to your `package.json`.

Now we can start the Notes service.

```
# cd ../notes
# npm run on-server
```

```
> notes@0.0.0 on-server /opt/notes
> SEQUELIZE_CONNECT=models/sequelize-server-mysql.yaml
NOTES_MODEL=sequelize USER_SERVICE_URL=http://localhost:3333 PORT=3000
node --experimental-modules ./app

(node:9932) ExperimentalWarning: The ESM module loader is
experimental.
```

Then we can use our web browser to connect to the application. Since you probably do not have a domain name associated with this server, Notes can be accessed via the IP address of the server, such as `http://159.89.145.190:3000/`.

In these examples, we're using the IP address of the VPS used to test the instructions in this section. The IP address you use will, of course, be different.

By now, you know that the drill for verifying Notes is working. Create a few notes, open a few browser windows, see that real-time notifications work, and so on. Once you're satisfied that Notes is working on the server, kill the processes and move on to the next section, where we'll set this up to run when the server starts.

Adjusting Twitter authentication to work on the server

The Twitter application we set up for Notes previously won't work because the authentication URL is incorrect for the server. For now, we can log in using the user profile created previously. If you want to see OAuth work with Twitter, go to `apps.twitter.com` and reconfigure the application to use the IP address of your server.

By hosting somewhere other than our laptop, the Twitter `callbackURL` must point to the correct location. The default value was `http://localhost:3000` for use on our laptop. But we now need to use the IP address for the server.
In `notes/package.json`, add the following environment variable to the `on-server` script:

```
TWITTER_CALLBACK_HOST=http://159.89.145.190:3000
```

Use the actual IP address or domain name assigned to the server being used. In a real deployment, we'll have a domain name to use here.

Setting up PM2 to manage Node.js processes

There are many ways to manage server processes, to ensure restarts if the process crashes, and so on. We'll use **PM2** (`http://pm2.keymetrics.io/`) because it's optimized for Node.js processes. It bundles process management and monitoring into one application.

Let's create a directory, `init`, in which to use PM2. The PM2 website suggests you install the tool globally but, as students of the Twelve Factor Application model, we recognize it's best to use explicitly declared dependencies and avoid global unmanaged dependencies.

Create a `package.json` file containing:

```
{
  "name": "pm2deploy",
  "version": "1.0.0",
  "scripts": {
    "start": "pm2 start ecosystem.json",
    "stop": "pm2 stop ecosystem.json",
    "restart": "pm2 restart ecosystem.json",
    "status": "pm2 status",
    "save": "pm2 save",
    "startup": "pm2 startup"
  },
  "dependencies": {
    "pm2": "^2.9.3"
  }
}
```

Install PM2 using `npm install` as usual.

In normal PM2 usage, we launch scripts with `pm2 start script-name.js`. We could make an `/etc/init` script which does that, but PM2 also supports a file named `ecosystem.json` that can be used to manage a cluster of processes. We have two processes to manage together, the user-facing Notes application, and the user authentication service on the back end.

Create a file named `ecosystem.json` containing the following:

```json
{
  "apps" : [
    {
      "name": "User Authentication",
      "script": "user-server.mjs",
      "cwd": "/opt/users",
      "node_args": "--experimental-modules",
      "env": {
        "PORT": "3333",
        "SEQUELIZE_CONNECT": "sequelize-server-mysql.yaml"
      },
      "env_production": { "NODE_ENV": "production" }
    },
    {
      "name": "Notes",
      "script": "app.mjs",
      "cwd": "/opt/notes",
      "node_args": "--experimental-modules",
      "env": {
        "PORT": "3000",
        "SEQUELIZE_CONNECT": "models/sequelize-server-mysql.yaml",
        "NOTES_MODEL": "sequelize",
        "USER_SERVICE_URL": "http://localhost:3333",
        "TWITTER_CONSUMER_KEY": "..",
        "TWITTER_CONSUMER_SECRET": "..",
        "TWITTER_CALLBACK_HOST": "http://45.55.37.74:3000"
      },
      "env_production": { "NODE_ENV": "production" }
    }
  ]
}
```

This file describes the directories containing both services, the script to run each service, the command-line options, and the environment variables to use. It's the same information that is in the `package.json` scripts, but spelled out more clearly. Adjust `TWITTER_CALLBACK_HOST` for the IP address of the server. For documentation, see `http://pm2.keymetrics.io/docs/usage/application-declaration/`.

We then start the services with `npm run start`, which looks like the following on the screen:

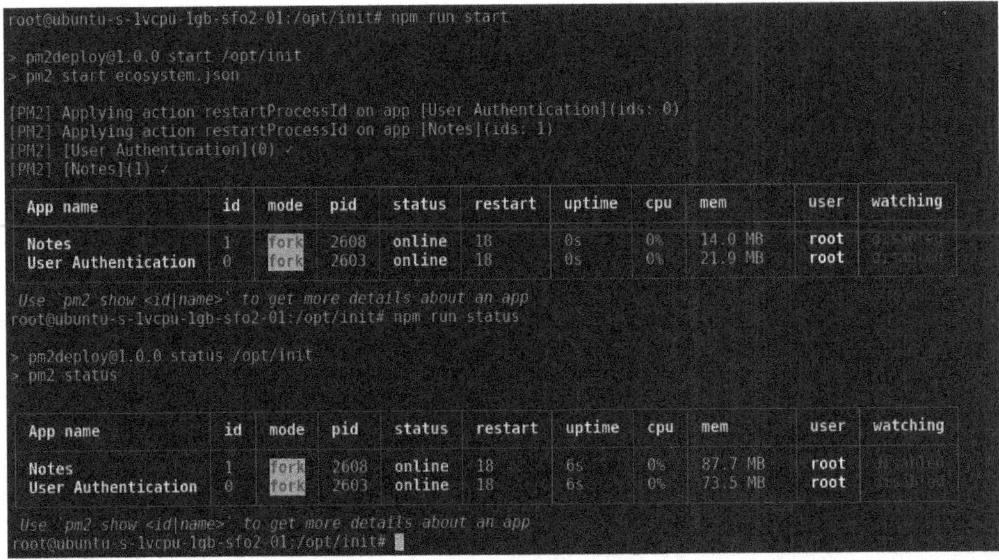

You can again navigate your browser to the URL for your server, such as `http://159.89.145.190:3000`, and check that Notes is working. Once started, some useful commands are as follows:

```
# pm2 list
# pm2 describe 1
# pm2 logs 1
```

These commands let you query the status of the services.

The `pm2 monit` command gives you a pseudo-graphical monitor of system activity. For documentation, see `http://pm2.keymetrics.io/docs/usage/monitoring/`.

The `pm2 logs` command addresses the application log management issue we raised elsewhere. Activity logs should be treated as an event stream, and should be captured and managed appropriately. With PM2, the output is automatically captured, can be viewed, and the log files can be rotated and purged. See `http://pm2.keymetrics.io/docs/usage/log-management/` for documentation.

If we restart the server, these processes don't start with the server. How do we handle that? It's very simple because PM2 can generate an `init` script for us:

```
# pm2 save
```

```
[PM2] Saving current process list...
[PM2] Successfully saved in /root/.pm2/dump.pm2

# pm2 startup
[PM2] Init System found: systemd
Platform systemd
Template
[Unit]
Description=PM2 process manager
Documentation=https://pm2.keymetrics.io/
After=network.target

... more output is printed
```

The pm2 save command saves the current state. Whatever services are running at that time will be saved and managed by the generated start up script.

The next step is to generate the startup script, using the pm startup command. PM2 supports generating start up scripts on several OSes, but when run this way, it autodetects the system type and generates the correct start up script. It also installs the start up script, and starts it running. See the documentation at http://pm2.keymetrics.io/docs/usage/startup/ for more information.

If you look closely at the output, some useful commands will be printed. The details will vary based on your operating system, because each operating system has its own commands for managing background processes. In this case, the installation is geared to use the systemctl command, as verified by this output:

```
Command list
[ 'systemctl enable pm2-root',
  'systemctl start pm2-root',
  'systemctl daemon-reload',
  'systemctl status pm2-root' ]
[PM2] Writing init configuration in /etc/systemd/system/pm2-
root.service
[PM2] Making script booting at startup...
...
[DONE]
>>> Executing systemctl start pm2-root
[DONE]
>>> Executing systemctl daemon-reload
[DONE]
>>> Executing systemctl status pm2-root
```

You are free to run these commands yourself:

```
# systemctl status pm2-root
```

```
● pm2-root.service - PM2 process manager
   Loaded: loaded (/etc/systemd/system/pm2-root.service; enabled;
vendor preset: enabled)
   Active: active (running) since Fri 2018-02-02 22:27:45 UTC; 29min
ago
     Docs: https://pm2.keymetrics.io/
  Process: 738 ExecStart=/opt/init/node_modules/pm2/bin/pm2 resurrect
(code=exited, status=0/SUCCESS)
 Main PID: 873 (PM2 v2.9.3: God)
    Tasks: 30 (limit: 4915)
   Memory: 171.6M
      CPU: 11.528s
   CGroup: /system.slice/pm2-root.service
           ├─873 PM2 v2.9.3: God Daemon (/root/.pm2)
           ├─895 node /opt/users/user-server.mjs
           └─904 node /opt/notes/app.mjs
```

To verify that PM2 starts the services as advertised, reboot your server, then use PM2 to check the status:

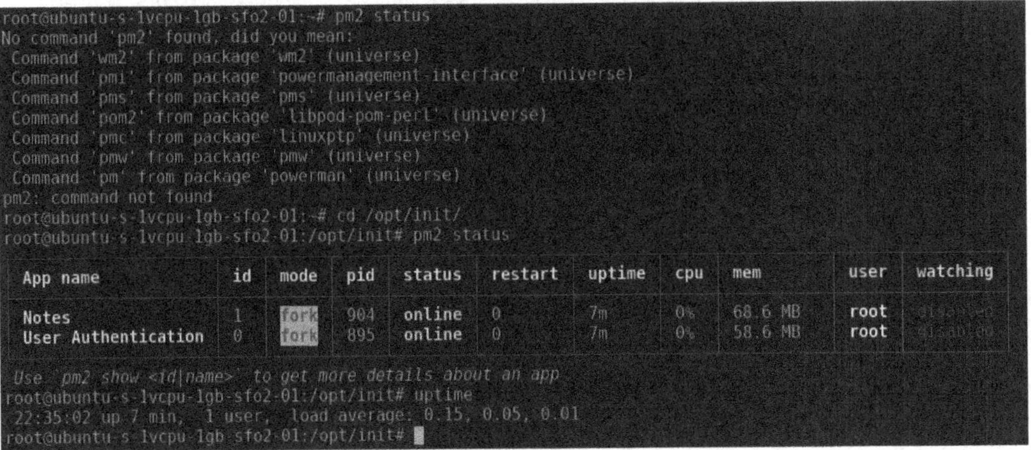

The first thing to notice is that upon initially logging in to the `root` account, the `pm2 status` command is not available. We installed PM2 locally to `/opt/init`, and the command is only available in that directory.

After going to that directory, we can now run the command and see the status. Remember to set the correct IP address or domain name in the `TWITTER_CALLBACK_HOST` environment variable. Otherwise, logging in with Twitter will fail.

We now have the Notes application under a fairly good management system. We can easily update its code on the server and restart the service. If the service crashes, PM2 will automatically restart it. Log files are automatically kept for our perusal.

PM2 also supports deployment from the source on our laptop, which we can push to staging or production environments. To support this, we must add deployment information to the `ecosystem.json` file and then run the `pm2 deploy` command to push the code to the server. See the PM2 website for more information: `http://pm2.keymetrics.io/docs/usage/deployment/`.

While PM2 does a good job at managing server processes, the system we've developed is insufficient for an internet-scale service. What if the Notes application were to become a viral hit and suddenly we need to deploy a million servers spread around the planet? Deploying and maintaining servers one at a time, like this, is not scalable.

We also skipped over implementing the architectural decisions at the beginning. Putting the user authentication data on the same server is a security risk. We want to deploy that data on a different server, under tighter security.

In the next section, we'll explore a new system, Docker, that solves these problems and more.

Node.js microservice deployment with Docker

Docker (`http://docker.com`) is the new attraction in the software industry. Interest is taking off like crazy, spawning many projects, often with names containing puns around shipping containers.

It is described as *an open platform for distributed applications for developers and sysadmins*. It is designed around Linux containerization technology and focuses on describing the configuration of software on any variant of Linux.

Docker automates the application deployment within software containers. The basic concepts of Linux containers date back to `chroot` jail's first implementation in the 1970s, and other systems such as Solaris Zones. The Docker implementation creates a layer of software isolation and virtualization based on Linux cgroups, kernel namespaces, and union-capable filesystems, which blend together to make Docker what it is. That was some heavy geek-speak, so let's try a simpler explanation.

A Docker container is a running instantiation of a Docker image. An image is a given Linux OS and application configuration designed by developers for whatever purpose they have in mind. Developers describe an image using a **Dockerfile**. The Dockerfile is a fairly simple-to-write script showing Docker how to build an image. Docker images are designed to be copied to any server, where the image is instantiated as a Docker container.

A running container will make you feel like you're inside a virtual server running on a virtual machine. But Docker containerization is very different from a virtual machine system such as VirtualBox. The processes running inside the container are actually running on the host OS. The containerization technology (cgroups, kernel namespaces, and so on) create the illusion of running on the Linux variant specified in the Dockerfile, even if the host OS is completely different. Your host OS could be Ubuntu and the container OS could be Fedora or OpenSUSE; Docker makes it all work.

By contrast, with Virtual Machine software (VirtualBox, and VMWare, among others), you're using what feels like a real computer. There is a virtual BIOS and virtualized system hardware, and you must install a full-fledged guest OS. You must follow every ritual of computer ownership, including securing licenses if it's a closed source system such as Windows.

While Docker is primarily targeted at x86 flavors of Linux, it is available on several ARM-based OSes, as well as other processors. You can even run Docker on single-board computers, such as Raspberry Pis, for hardware-oriented Internet of Things projects. Operating systems such as Resin.IO are optimized to solely run Docker containers.

The Docker ecosystem contains many tools, and their number is quickly increasing. For our purposes, we'll be focusing on the following three specific tools:

- **Docker engine**: This is the core execution system that orchestrates everything. It runs on a Linux host system, exposing a network-based API that client applications use to make Docker requests, such as building, deploying, and running containers.
- **Docker machine**: This is a client application performing functions around provisioning Docker Engine instances on host computers.
- **Docker compose**: This helps you define, in a single file, a multi-container application, with all its dependencies defined.

With the Docker ecosystem, you can create a whole universe of subnets and services to implement your dream application. That universe can run on your laptop or be deployed to a globe-spanning network of cloud-hosting facilities around the world. The surface area through which miscreants can attack is strictly defined by the developer. A multicontainer application will even limit access so strongly between services that miscreants who do manage to break into a container will find it difficult to break out of the container.

Using Docker, we'll first design on our laptop the system shown in the previous diagram. Then we'll migrate that system to a Docker instance on a server.

Installing Docker on your laptop

The best place to learn how to install Docker on your laptop is the Docker documentation website. What we're looking for is the Docker **Community Edition (CE)**. There is the Docker **Enterprise Edition (EE)**, with more features and some opportunities to pay support fees:

- macOS installation – `https://docs.docker.com/docker-for-mac/install/`
- Windows installation – `https://docs.docker.com/docker-for-windows/install/`
- Ubuntu installation – `https://docs.docker.com/install/linux/docker-ce/ubuntu/`
- Instructions are available for several other distros. Some useful post-install Linux instructions are at `https://docs.docker.com/install/linux/linux-postinstall/`

Because Docker runs on Linux, it does not run natively on macOS or Windows. Installation on either OS requires installing Linux inside a virtual machine and then running Docker tools within that virtual Linux machine. The days when you had to handcraft that setup yourself are long gone. The Docker team has made this easy by developing easy-to-use Docker applications for Mac and Windows. The Docker for Windows and Docker for Mac bundles package the Docker tools and lightweight virtual machine software. The result is very lightweight, and the Docker containers can be left running in the background with little impact.

You may find references to Docker Toolbox as the method to install Docker on macOS. That application is long gone, and has been replaced by Docker for Windows and Docker for Mac.

Starting Docker with Docker for Windows/macOS

To start Docker for Windows or Mac is very simple. You simply find and double-click on the application icon. It launches as would any other native application. When started, it manages a virtual machine (not VirtualBox) within which is a Linux instance running the Docker Engine. On macOS, a menu bar icon shows up with which you control `Docker.app`, and on Windows, an icon is available in the system tray.

There are settings available so that Docker automatically launches every time you start your laptop.

On both, the CPU must support **Virtualization**. Bundled inside Docker for Windows and Docker for Mac is an ultra-lightweight hypervisor, which, in turn, requires virtualization support from the CPU.

For Windows, this may require BIOS configuration. See `https://docs.docker.com/docker-for-windows/troubleshoot/#virtualization-must-be-enabled`.

For Mac, this requires hardware from 2010 or newer, with Intel's hardware support for **memory management unit** (MMU) virtualization, including **Extended Page Tables** (**EPT**) and Unrestricted Mode. You can check for this support by running `sysctl kern.hv_support`. It also requires macOS 10.11 or later.

Kicking the tires of Docker

With the setup accomplished, we can use the local Docker instance to create Docker containers, run a few commands, and, in general, learn how to use this amazing system.

As in so many software journeys, this one starts with saying `Hello World`:

```
$ docker run hello-world
Unable to find image 'hello-world:latest' locally
latest: Pulling from library/hello-world
ca4f61b1923c: Pull complete
Digest:
sha256:66ef312bbac49c39a89aa9bcc3cb4f3c9e7de3788c944158df3ee0176d32b75
1
Status: Downloaded newer image for hello-world:latest

Hello from Docker!
This message shows that your installation appears to be working
correctly.
```

```
To generate this message, Docker took the following steps:
 1. The Docker client contacted the Docker daemon.
 2. The Docker daemon pulled the "hello-world" image from the Docker
Hub.
    (amd64)
 3. The Docker daemon created a new container from that image which
runs the
    executable that produces the output you are currently reading.
 4. The Docker daemon streamed that output to the Docker client, which
sent it
    to your terminal.

To try something more ambitious, you can run an Ubuntu container with:
 $ docker run -it ubuntu bash

Share images, automate workflows, and more with a free Docker ID:
 https://cloud.docker.com/

For more examples and ideas, visit:
 https://docs.docker.com/engine/userguide/
```

The `docker run` command downloads a Docker image, named on the command line, initializes a Docker container from that image, and then runs that container. In this case, the image, named `hello-world`, was not present on the local computer and had to be downloaded and initialized. Once that was done, the `hello-world` container was executed and it printed out these instructions.

You can query your computer to see that while the `hello-world` container has executed and finished, it still exists:

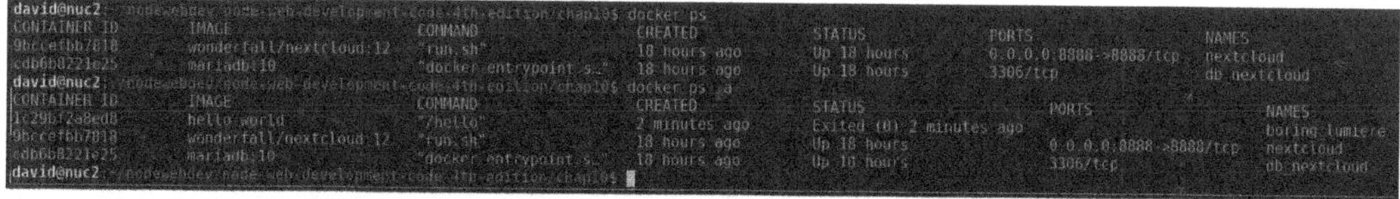

The `docker ps` command lists the running Docker containers. As we see here, the `hello-world` container is no longer running, but with the `-a` switch, `docker ps` also shows those containers that exist but are not currently running. We also see that this computer has a Nextcloud instance installed along with its associated database.

When you're done using a container, you can clean up with the following command:

```
$ docker rm boring_lumiere
boring_lumiere
```

The name `boring_lumiere` is the container name automatically generated by Docker. While the image name was `hello-world`, that's not the container name. Docker generated the container name so you have a more user-friendly identifier for the containers than the hex ID shown in the container ID column. When creating a container, it's easy to specify any container name you like.

Creating the AuthNet for the user authentication service

With all that theory spinning around our heads, it's time to do something practical. Let's start by setting up the user authentication service. In the diagram shown earlier, this will be the box labeled AuthNet containing a MySQL instance and the authentication server.

MySQL container for Docker

To find publicly available Docker images, go to `https://hub.docker.com/` and search. You'll find many Docker images ready to go. For example, Nextcloud, and its associated database, was shown earlier installed alongside the `hello-world` application when we kicked the tires. Both are available from their respective project teams and it's simply (more or less) a matter of typing `docker run nextcloud` to install and run the containers. The process of installing Nextcloud, and its associated database, as well as many other packaged applications, such as GitLab, is very similar to what we're about to do to build AuthNet, so the skills you're about to learn are very practical.

Just for MySQL, there are over 11,000 containers available. Fortunately, the two containers provided by the MySQL team are very popular and easy to use. The `mysql/mysql-server` image is a little easier to configure, so let's use that.

A Docker image name can be specified, along with a *tag* that is usually the software version number. In this case, we'll use `mysql/mysql-server:5.7`, where `mysql/mysql-server` is the container name, and `5.7` is the tag. MySQL 5.7 is the current GA release. Download the image as follows:

```
$ docker pull mysql/mysql-server:5.7
5.7: Pulling from mysql/mysql-server
4040fe120662: Pull complete
d049aa45d358: Pull complete
a6c7ed00840d: Pull complete
853789d8032e: Pull complete
Digest:
sha256:1b4c7c24df07fa89cdb7fe1c2eb94fbd2c7bd84ac14bd1779e3dec79f75f37c
5
Status: Downloaded newer image for mysql/mysql-server:5.7
```

This downloaded four images in total, because this image is built on top of three other images. We'll see later how that works when we learn how to build a Dockerfile.

A container can be started using this image as follows:

```
$ docker run --name=mysql --env MYSQL_ROOT_PASSWORD=f00bar
mysql/mysql-server:5.7
[Entrypoint] MySQL Docker Image 5.7.21-1.1.4
[Entrypoint] Initializing database
[Entrypoint] Database initialized
...
[Entrypoint] ignoring /docker-entrypoint-initdb.d/*
[Entrypoint] Server shut down
[Entrypoint] MySQL init process done. Ready for start up.
[Entrypoint] Starting MySQL 5.7.21-1.1.4
```

We started this service in the foreground. The container name is `mysql`. We set an environment variable, which, in turn (according to the image documentation), initializes the `root` password as shown. In another window, we can get into the container and run the MySQL client as follows:

```
$ docker exec -it mysql mysql -u root -p
Enter password:
Welcome to the MySQL monitor.  Commands end with ; or \g.
Your MySQL connection id is 4
Server version: 5.7.21 MySQL Community Server (GPL)

Copyright (c) 2000, 2018, Oracle and/or its affiliates. All rights
reserved.

Oracle is a registered trademark of Oracle Corporation and/or its
```

```
affiliates. Other names may be trademarks of their respective
owners.

Type 'help;' or '\h' for help. Type '\c' to clear the current input
statement.

mysql> show databases;
+--------------------+
| Database           |
+--------------------+
| information_schema |
| mysql              |
| performance_schema |
| sys                |
+--------------------+
4 rows in set (0.00 sec)

mysql>
```

The `docker exec` command lets you run programs inside the container. The `-it` option says the command is run interactively, on an assigned terminal. Substitute `bash` for `mysql`, and you have an interactive `bash` command shell.

This `mysql` command instance is running inside the container. The container is configured by default to not expose any external port, and it has a default `my.cnf` file.

The database files are locked inside the container. As soon as that container is deleted, the database will go away. Docker containers are meant to be ephemeral, being created and destroyed as needed, while databases are meant to be permanent, with lifetimes measured in decades sometimes.

In other words, it's cool that we can easily install and launch a MySQL instance. But there are several deficiencies:

- Access to the database from other software
- Storing the database files outside the container for a longer lifespan
- Custom configuration, because database admins love to tweak the settings
- It needs to be connected to AuthNet along with the user authentication service

Before proceeding, let's clean up. In a Terminal window, type:

```
$ docker stop mysql
mysql
$ docker rm mysql
mysql
```

This closes out and cleans up the containers. And, to reiterate the point made earlier, the database in that container went away. If that database contained critical information, you just lost it with no chance to recover the data.

Initializing AuthNet

Docker supports creating virtual bridge networks between containers. Remember that a Docker container has many of the features of an installed Linux OS. Each container can have its own IP address(es) and exposed ports. Docker supports creating what amounts to being a virtual Ethernet segment, called a **bridge network**. These networks live solely within the host computer and, by default, are not reachable by anything outside the host computer.

A Docker bridge network, therefore, has strictly limited access. Any Docker container attached to a bridge network can communicate with other containers attached to that network. The containers find each other by hostname, and Docker includes an embedded DNS server to set up the hostnames required. That DNS server is configured to not require dots in domain names, meaning that the DNS/hostname of each container is simply the container name, rather than something such as `container-name.service`. This policy of using hostnames to identify containers is Docker's implementation of service discovery.

Create a directory named `authnet` as a sibling to the `users` and `notes` directories. We'll be working on AuthNet in that directory.

Create a file, `buildauthnet.sh`, containing the following:

```
docker network create --driver bridge authnet
```

Type the following:

```
$ sh -x buildauthnet.sh
+ docker network create --driver bridge authnet
3021e2069278c2acb08d94a2d31507a43f089db1c02eecc97792414b498eb785
```

This creates a Docker bridge network.

Script execution on Windows

Executing scripts on Windows is different because it uses PowerShell rather than `bash`, and a large number of other considerations. For this, and the scripts which follow, make these changes.

Powershell script filenames must end with the `.ps1` extension. For most of these scripts, that's all that is required because the scripts are so simple. To execute the script, simply type `.\scriptname.ps1` in the Powershell window. In other words, on Windows, the script just shown must be named `buildauthnet.ps1`, and is executed as `.\buildauthnet.ps1`.

To execute the scripts, you may need to change the Powershell Execution Policy:

```
PS C:\Users\david\chap10\authnet> Get-ExecutionPolicy
Restricted
PS C:\Users\david\chap10\authnet> Set-ExecutionPolicy Unrestricted
```

Obviously, there are security considerations with this change, so change the Execution Policy back when you're done.

A simpler method on Windows is to simply paste these commands into a PowerShell window.

Linking Docker containers

In the older days of Docker, we were told to link containers using the `--link` option. With that option, Docker would create entries in `/etc/hosts` so that one container can refer to another container by its hostname. That option also arranged access to TCP ports and volumes between linked containers. This allowed the creation of multicontainer services, using private TCP ports for communication that exposed nothing to processes outside the containers.

Today, we are told that the `--link` option is a legacy feature, and that instead we should use `bridge` networks. In this chapter, we'll focus solely on using `bridge` networks.

You can list the networks as follows:

```
$ docker network ls
NETWORK ID          NAME                DRIVER              SCOPE
3021e2069278        authnet             bridge              local
```

Look at details about the network with this command:

```
$ docker network inspect authnet
    ... much JSON output
```

At the moment, this won't show any containers attached to `authnet`. The output shows the network name, the IP range of this network, the default gateway, and other useful network configuration information. Since nothing is connected to the network, let's get started with building the required containers.

The db-userauth container

Now that we have a network, we can start connecting containers to that network. And then we'll explore the containers to see how private they are.

Create a script, `startdb.sh`, containing:

```
docker run --name db-userauth --env MYSQL_RANDOM_ROOT_PASSWORD=true \
    --env MYSQL_USER=userauth --env MYSQL_PASSWORD=userauth \
    --env MYSQL_DATABASE=userauth \
    --volume `pwd`/my.cnf:/etc/my.cnf \
    --volume `pwd`/../userauth-data:/var/lib/mysql \
    --network authnet mysql/mysql-server:5.7
```

On Windows, you will need to name the script `startdb.ps1` instead, and put the text all on one line rather than extend the lines with backslashes. And, the volume mounted on `/var/lib/mysql` must be created separately. Use these commands instead:

```
docker volume create db-userauth-volume

docker run --name db-userauth --env MYSQL_RANDOM_ROOT_PASSWORD=true --env MYSQL_USER=userauth --env MYSQL_PASSWORD=userauth --env MYSQL_DATABASE=userauth --volume $PSScriptRoot\my.cnf:/etc/my.cnf --volume db-userauth-volume:/var/lib/mysql --network authnet mysql/mysql-server:5.7
```

When run, the container will be named `db-userauth`. To give a little bit of security, the `root` password has been randomized. We've instead defined a database named `userauth`, accessed by a user named `userauth`, using the password `userauth`. That's not exactly secure, so feel free to choose better names and passwords. The container is attached to the `authnet` network.

There are two `--volume` options that we must talk about. In Dockerese, a volume is a thing inside a container that can be mounted from outside the container. In this case, we're defining a volume, `userauth-data`, in the host filesystem to be mounted as `/var/lib/mysql` inside the container. And, we're defining a local `my.cnf` file to be used as `/etc/my.cnf` inside the container.

For the Windows version, we have two changes to the `--volume` mounts. We specify the mount for `/etc/my.cnf` as `$PSScriptRoot\my.cnf:/etc/my.cnf`, because that's how you reference a local file in Powershell.

For `/var/lib/mysql`, we referenced a separately created volume. The volume is created using the `volume create` command, and with that command there is no opportunity to control the location of the volume. It's important that the volume lives outside the container, so that the database files survive the destruction/creation cycle for this container.

Taken together, those settings mean the database files and the configuration file live outside the container and will therefore exist beyond the lifetime of one specific container. To get the `my.cnf`, you will have to run the container once without the `--volume `pwd`/my.cnf:/etc/my.cnf` option so you can copy the default `my.cnf` file into the `authnet` directory.

Run the script once without that option:

```
$ sh startdb.sh
... much output
[Entrypoint] GENERATED ROOT PASSWORD: UMyh@q]@j4qijyj@wK4s4SkePIkq
... much output
```

The output is similar to what we saw earlier, but for this newline giving the randomized password:

```
$ docker network inspect authnet
```

This will tell you the `db-userauth` container is attached to `authnet`:

```
$ docker exec -it db-userauth mysql -u userauth -p
Enter password:
Welcome to the MySQL monitor.  Commands end with ; or \g.
    ... much output
mysql> show databases;
+--------------------+
| Database           |
+--------------------+
| information_schema |
```

```
| userauth            |
+---------------------+
2 rows in set (0.00 sec)

mysql> use userauth;
Database changed
mysql> show tables;
Empty set (0.00 sec)
```

We see our database has been created and it's empty. But we did this so we could grab the `my.cnf` file:

```
$ docker cp db-userauth:/etc/my.cnf .
$ ls
my.cnf   mysql-data   startdb.sh
```

The `docker cp` command is used for copying files in and out of containers. If you've used `scp`, the syntax will be familiar.

Once you have the `my.cnf` file, there's a big pile of setting changes you might want to make. The first specific change to make is commenting out the line reading `socket=/var/lib/mysql/mysql.sock`, and the second is adding a line reading `bind-address = 0.0.0.0`. The purpose with these changes is to configure the MySQL service to listen on a TCP port rather than a Unix domain socket. This makes it possible to communicate with the MySQL service from outside the container. The result would be:

```
# socket=/var/lib/mysql/mysql.sock
bind-address = 0.0.0.0
```

Now stop the `db-userauth` service, and remove the container, as we did earlier. Edit the `startdb` script to enable the line mounting `/etc/my.cnf` into the container, and then restart the container:

```
$ docker stop db-userauth
db-userauth
$ docker rm db-userauth
db-userauth
$ sh ./startdb.sh
[Entrypoint] MySQL Docker Image 5.7.21-1.1.4
[Entrypoint] Starting MySQL 5.7.21-1.1.4
```

Now, if we inspect the `authnet` network, we see the following:

```
$ docker network inspect authnet
        "Name": "authnet",
```

```
        . . .
                    "Subnet": "172.18.0.0/16",
                    "Gateway": "172.18.0.1"
        . . .
            "Containers": {
                    "Name": "db-userauth",
                    "MacAddress": "02:42:ac:12:00:02",
                    "IPv4Address": "172.18.0.2/16",

        . . .
```

In other words, the `authnet` network has the network number `172.18.0.0/16`, and
the `db-userauth` container was assigned `172.18.0.2`. This level of detail is rarely
important, but it is useful on our first time through to carefully examine the setup so
we understand what we're dealing with:

```
# cat /etc/resolv.conf
search attlocal.net
nameserver 127.0.0.11
options ndots:0
```

As we said earlier, there is a DNS server running within the Docker bridge network
setup, and domain name resolution is configured to use `nodots`. That's so Docker
container names are the DNS hostname for the container:

```
# mysql -h db-userauth -u userauth -p
Enter password:
Welcome to the MySQL monitor.  Commands end with ; or \g.
Your MySQL connection id is 33
Server version: 5.7.21 MySQL Community Server (GPL)
```

Access the MySQL server using the container name as the hostname.

Dockerfile for the authentication service

In the `users` directory, create a file named `Dockerfile` containing the following:

```
FROM node:10

ENV DEBUG="users:*"
ENV PORT="3333"
ENV SEQUELIZE_CONNECT="sequelize-docker-mysql.yaml"
ENV REST_LISTEN="0.0.0.0"

RUN mkdir -p /userauth
COPY package.json sequelize-docker-mysql.yaml *.mjs *.js /userauth/
WORKDIR /userauth
```

```
RUN apt-get update -y \
    && apt-get -y install curl python build-essential git ca-
certificates \
    && npm install --unsafe-perm

EXPOSE 3333
CMD npm run docker
```

Dockerfiles describe the installation of an application on a server. See `https://docs.docker.com/engine/reference/builder/` for documentation. They document assembly of the bits in a Docker container image, and the instructions in a Dockerfile are used to build a Docker image.

The `FROM` command specifies a pre-existing image from which to derive a given image. We talked about this earlier; you can build a Docker container starting from an existing image. The official Node.js Docker image (`https://hub.docker.com/_/node/`) we're using is derived from `debian:jessie`. Therefore, commands available within the container are what Debian offers, and we use `apt-get` to install more packages. We use Node.js 10 because it supports ES6 modules and the other features we've been using.

The `ENV` commands define environment variables. In this case, we're using the same environment variables defined within the user authentication service, except we have a new `REST_LISTEN` variable. We'll take a look at that shortly.

The `RUN` commands are where we run the shell commands required to build the container. The first thing is to make a `/userauth` directory that will contain the service source code. The `COPY` command copies files into that directory. And then we'll need to run an `npm install` so that we can run the service. But first we use the `WORKDIR` command to move the current working directory into `/userauth` so that the `npm install` is run in the correct place. We also install the requisite Debian packages so that any native code Node.js packages can be installed.

It's recommended that you always combine `apt-get update` with `apt-get install` in the same command line, like this, because of the Docker build cache. When rebuilding an image, Docker starts with the first changed line. By putting those two together, you ensure that `apt-get update` is executed any time you change the list of packages to be installed. For a complete discussion, see the documentation at `https://docs.docker.com/develop/develop-images/dockerfile_best-practices/`.

At the end of this command is `npm install --unsafe-perm`. The issue here is that these commands are being run as `root`. Normally, when `npm` is run as `root`, it changes its user ID to a nonprivileged user. This can cause failure, however, and the `--unsafe-perm` option prevents changing the user ID.

The `EXPOSE` command informs Docker that the container listens on the named TCP port. This does not expose the port beyond the container.

Finally, the CMD command documents the process to launch when the container is executed. The `RUN` commands are executed while building the container, while CMD says what's executed when the container starts.

We could have installed PM2 in the container, then used a PM2 command to launch the service. But Docker is able to fulfill the same function, because it supports automatically restarting a container if the service process dies. We'll see how to do this later.

Configuring the authentication service for Docker

We're using a different file for `SEQUELIZE_CONNECT`. Create a new file named `users/sequelize-docker-mysql.yaml` containing the following:

```
dbname: userauth
username: userauth
password: userauth
params:
    host: db-userauth
    port: 3306
    dialect: mysql
```

The difference is that instead of `localhost` as the database host, we use `db-userauth`. Earlier, we explored the `db-userauth` container and determined that was the hostname of the container. By using `db-userauth` in this file, the authentication service will use the database in the container.

Now we need to take care of the environment variable named `REST_LISTEN`. Previously, the authentication server had listened only to `http://localhost:3333`. We'd done this for security purposes, that is, to limit which processes could connect to the service. Under Docker, we need to connect to this service from outside its container so that other containers can connect to this service. Therefore, it must listen to connections from outside the localhost.

In `users-server.mjs`, we need to make the following change:

```
server.listen(process.env.PORT,
   process.env.REST_LISTEN ? process.env.REST_LISTEN : "localhost",
   () => { log(server.name +' listening at '+ server.url); });
```

That is, if the `REST_LISTEN` variable exists, the REST server is told to listen to whatever it says, otherwise the service is to listen to `localhost`. With the environment variable in the Dockerfile, the authentication service will listen to the world (`0.0.0.0`). Are we throwing caution to the wind and abrogating our fiduciary duty in keeping the sacred trust of storing all this user identification information? No. Be patient. We'll describe momentarily how to connect this service and its database to `AuthNet` and will prevent access to `AuthNet` by any other process.

Building and running the authentication service Docker container

In `users/package.json` add the following line to the `scripts` section:

```
"docker": "node --experimental-modules ./user-server",
"docker-build": "docker build -t node-web-development/userauth ."
```

Previously, we've put the configuration environment variables into `package.json`. In this case, the configuration environment variables are in the Dockerfile. This means we need a way to run the server with no environment variables other than those in the Dockerfile. With this `script` entry, we can do `npm run docker` and then the Dockerfile environment variables will supply all configuration.

We can build the authentication service as follows:

```
$ npm run docker-build

> user-auth-server@0.0.1 docker-build /Users/david/chap10/users
> docker build -t node-web-development/userauth .

Sending build context to Docker daemon 33.8MB
Step 1/11 : FROM node:9.5
 ---> a696309517c6
Step 2/11 : ENV DEBUG="users:*"
 ---> Using cache
 ---> f8cc103432e8
```

```
Step 3/11 : ENV PORT="3333"
 ---> Using cache
 ---> 39b24b8b554e
... more output
```

The `docker build` command builds a container from a Dockerfile. As we said earlier, the process begins with the image defined in the `FROM` command. Then the build proceeds step by step, and the output shows literally each step as it is executed.

Then create a script, `authnet/startserver.sh`, or on Windows call it `startserver.ps1`, containing the following command:

```
docker run -it --name userauth --net=authnet node-web-
development/userauth
```

This launches the newly built container, giving it the name `userauth`, attaching it to `authnet`:

```
$ sh -x startserver.sh
+ docker run -it --name userauth --net=authnet node-web-
development/userauth

> user-auth-server@0.0.1 docker /userauth
> node --experimental-modules ./user-server

(node:17) ExperimentalWarning: The ESM module loader is experimental.
  users:service User-Auth-Service listening at http://0.0.0.0:3333
+0ms
```

That starts the user authentication service. On Windows, start it as `.\startserver.ps1`. You should recall that it's a REST service, and therefore running it through its paces is done with `users-add.js` and the other scripts. But, since we did not expose a public port from the service we must run those scripts from inside the container.

We determine whether a container exposes a public port in one of two ways. The easiest is running `docker ps -a` and viewing the container listing details. There is a column marked PORTS, and for `userauth` we see `3333/tcp`. This is a side effect of the EXPOSE command in the Dockerfile. If that port were exposed, it would appear in the PORTS column as `0.0.0.0:3333->3333/tcp`. Remember the goal for the `userauth` container, and `authnet` overall, was that it would not be publicly accessible because of security concerns.

Exploring Authnet

Let's explore what we just created:

```
$ docker network inspect authnet
```

This prints out a large JSON object describing the network, and its attached
containers, which we've looked at before. If all went well, we'll see there are now two
containers attached to `authnet` where there'd previously been only one.

Let's go into the `userauth` container and poke around:

```
$ docker exec -it userauth bash
root@a29d833287bf:/userauth# ls
node_modules                    user-server.mjs   users-list.js
package-lock.json               users-add.js      users-sequelize.mjs
package.json                    users-delete.js
sequelize-docker-mysql.yaml     users-find.js
```

The `/userauth` directory is inside the container and is exactly the files placed in the
container using the `COPY` command, plus the installed files in `node_modules`:

```
root@a29d833287bf:/userauth# PORT=3333 node users-list.js
List []
root@a29d833287bf:/userauth# PORT=3333 node users-add.js
Created { id: 1, username: 'me', password: 'w0rd', provider: 'local',
  familyName: 'Einarrsdottir', givenName: 'Ashildr',
  middleName: '', emails: '[]', photos: '[]',
  updatedAt: '2018-02-05T01:54:53.320Z', createdAt: '2018-02-
  05T01:54:53.320Z' }
root@a29d833287bf:/userauth# PORT=3333 node users-list.js
List [ { id: 'me', username: 'me', provider: 'local',
    familyName: 'Einarrsdottir', givenName: 'Ashildr', middleName: '',
  emails: '[]', photos: '[]' } ]
```

Our test of adding a user to the authentication service works:

```
root@a29d833287bf:/userauth# ps -eafw
UID          PID  PPID  C STIME TTY          TIME CMD
root           1     0  0 01:52 pts/0    00:00:00 /bin/sh -c npm run
docker
root           9     1  0 01:52 pts/0    00:00:00 npm
root          19     9  0 01:52 pts/0    00:00:00 sh -c node --
experimental-modules ./user-server
root          20    19  0 01:52 pts/0    00:00:01 node --experimental-
modules ./user-server
root          30     0  0 01:54 pts/1    00:00:00 bash
root          70    30  0 01:57 pts/1    00:00:00 ps -eafw
```

```
root@a29d833287bf:/userauth# ping db-userauth
PING db-userauth (172.18.0.2): 56 data bytes
64 bytes from 172.18.0.2: icmp_seq=0 ttl=64 time=0.105 ms
64 bytes from 172.18.0.2: icmp_seq=1 ttl=64 time=0.077 ms
^C--- db-userauth ping statistics ---
2 packets transmitted, 2 packets received, 0% packet loss
round-trip min/avg/max/stddev = 0.077/0.091/0.105/0.000 ms
root@a29d833287bf:/userauth# ping userauth
PING userauth (172.18.0.3): 56 data bytes
64 bytes from 172.18.0.3: icmp_seq=0 ttl=64 time=0.132 ms
64 bytes from 172.18.0.3: icmp_seq=1 ttl=64 time=0.095 ms
^C--- userauth ping statistics ---
2 packets transmitted, 2 packets received, 0% packet loss
```

The process listing is interesting to study. Process PID 1 is the npm run
docker command in the Dockerfile. Processes proceed from there to the node process
running the actual server.

A ping command proves the two containers are available as hostnames matching the
container names.

Then, you can log in to the db-userauth container and inspect the database:

```
$ docker exec -it db-userauth bash
bash-4.2# mysql -u userauth -p
Enter password:
Welcome to the MySQL monitor.  Commands end with ; or \g.
...
mysql> use userauth

Database changed
mysql> show tables;
+---------------------+
| Tables_in_userauth |
+---------------------+
| Users               |
+---------------------+
1 row in set (0.00 sec)

mysql> select * from Users;
+----+----------+----------+----------+----------------+------------+--
...
| id | username | password | provider | familyName     | givenName |
...
+----+----------+----------+----------+----------------+------------+--
...
| 1  | me       | w0rd     | local    | Einarrsdottir  | Ashildr   |
```

```
. . .
+----+----------+----------+----------+----------------+----------+--
. . .
1 row in set (0.00 sec)
```

We have successfully Dockerized the user authentication service in two containers, `db-userauth` and `userauth`. We've poked around the insides of a running container and found some interesting things. But, our users need the fantastic Notes application to be running, and we can't afford to rest on our laurels.

Creating FrontNet for the Notes application

We have the back half of our system set up in a Docker container, as well as the private bridge network to connect the backend containers. We now need to set up another private bridge network, `frontnet`, and attach the other half of our system to that network.

Create a directory, `frontnet`, which is where we'll develop the tools to build and run that network. In that directory, create a file, `buildfrontnet.sh`, or on Windows, `buildfrontnet.ps1`, containing:

```
docker network create --driver bridge frontnet
```

Let's go ahead and create the `frontnet` bridge network:

```
$ sh -x buildfrontnet.sh
+ docker network create --driver bridge frontnet
f3df227d4bfff57bc7aed1e096a2ad16f6cebce4938315a54d9386a42d1ae3ed
$ docker network ls
NETWORK ID NAME DRIVER SCOPE
3021e2069278 authnet bridge local
f3df227d4bff frontnet bridge local
```

We'll proceed from here similarly to how `authnet` was created. However, we can work more quickly because we've already gone over the basics.

MySQL container for the Notes application

From the `authnet` directory, copy the `my.cnf` and `startdb.sh` files into the `frontnet` directory.

The `my.cnf` file can probably be used unmodified, but we have a few changes to make to the `startdb.sh` file:

```
docker run --name db-notes --env MYSQL_RANDOM_ROOT_PASSWORD=true \
  --env MYSQL_USER=notes --env MYSQL_PASSWORD=notes12345 \
  --env MYSQL_DATABASE=notes \
  --volume `pwd`/my.cnf:/etc/my.cnf \
  --volume `pwd`/../notes-data:/var/lib/mysql \
  --network frontnet mysql/mysql-server:5.7
```

On Windows, name the file `startdb.ps1` containing this:

```
docker volume create notes-data-volume

docker run --name db-notes --env MYSQL_RANDOM_ROOT_PASSWORD=true --env
MYSQL_USER=notes --env MYSQL_PASSWORD=notes12345 --env
MYSQL_DATABASE=notes --volume $PSScriptRoot\my.cnf:/etc/my.cnf --
volume notes-data-volume:/var/lib/mysql --network frontnet
mysql/mysql-server:5.7
```

The changes are simple substitutions to transliterate from `userauth` to `notes`. And then run it:

```
$ mkdir ../notes-data
$ sh -x startdb.sh
+ pwd
+ pwd
+ docker run --name db-notes --env MYSQL_RANDOM_ROOT_PASSWORD=true --
env MYSQL_USER=notes --env MYSQL_PASSWORD=notes12345 --env
MYSQL_DATABASE=notes --volume /home/david/nodewebdev/node-web-
development-code-4th-edition/chap10/frontnet/my.cnf:/etc/my.cnf --
volume /home/david/nodewebdev/node-web-development-code-4th-
edition/chap10/frontnet/../notes-data:/var/lib/mysql --network
frontnet mysql/mysql-server:5.7
[Entrypoint] MySQL Docker Image 5.7.21-1.1.4
[Entrypoint] Initializing database
[Entrypoint] Database initialized
[Entrypoint] GENERATED ROOT PASSWORD: 3kZ@q4hBItYGYj3Mes!AdiP83No1
[Entrypoint] ignoring /docker-entrypoint-initdb.d/*
[Entrypoint] Server shut down
[Entrypoint] MySQL init process done. Ready for start up.
[Entrypoint] Starting MySQL 5.7.21-1.1.4
```

For Windows, simply run `.\startdb.ps1`.

This database will be available at the `db-notes` domain name on `frontnet`. Because it's attached to `frontnet`, it won't be reachable by containers connected to `authnet`.

```
$ docker exec -it userauth bash
root@0a2009334b79:/userauth# ping db-notes
ping: unknown host
```

Since `db-notes` is on a different network segment, we've achieved separation.

Dockerizing the Notes application

In the `notes` directory, create a file named `Dockerfile` containing the following:

```
FROM node:10

ENV DEBUG="notes:*,messages:*"
ENV SEQUELIZE_CONNECT="models/sequelize-docker-mysql.yaml"
ENV NOTES_MODEL="sequelize"
ENV USER_SERVICE_URL="http://userauth:3333"
ENV PORT="3000"
ENV NOTES_SESSIONS_DIR="/sessions"
# ENV TWITTER_CONSUMER_KEY="..."
# ENV TWITTER_CONSUMER_SECRET="..."
# Use this line when the Twitter Callback URL
# has to be other than localhost:3000
# ENV TWITTER_CALLBACK_HOST=http://45.55.37.74:3000

RUN mkdir -p /notesapp /notesapp/minty /notesapp/partials
/notesapp/public /notesapp/routes /notesapp/theme /notesapp/views
COPY minty/ /notesapp/minty/
COPY models/*.mjs models/sequelize-docker-mysql.yaml /notesapp/models/
COPY partials/ /notesapp/partials/
COPY public/ /notesapp/public/
COPY routes/ /notesapp/routes/
COPY theme/ /notesapp/theme/
COPY views/ /notesapp/views/
COPY app.mjs package.json /notesapp/

WORKDIR /notesapp
RUN apt-get update -y \
    && apt-get -y install curl python build-essential git ca-
certificates \
    && npm install --unsafe-perm

# Uncomment to build the theme directory
# WORKDIR /notesapp/theme
```

```
# RUN npm run download && npm run build && npm run clean

WORKDIR /notesapp

VOLUME /sessions
EXPOSE 3000
CMD node --experimental-modules ./app
```

This is similar to the Dockerfile we used for the authentication service. We're using the environment variables from `notes/package.json`, plus a new one, and there's a couple of new tricks involved here, so let's take a look.

The most obvious change is the number of `COPY` commands. The Notes application is a lot more involved given the number of subdirectories full of files that must be installed. We start by creating the top-level directories of the Notes application deployment tree. Then, one by one, we copy each subdirectory into its corresponding subdirectory in the container filesystem.

In a `COPY` command, the trailing slash on the destination directory is important. Why? Because the documentation says that the trailing slash is important.

The big question is: Why use multiple `COPY` commands such as this? This would have been trivially simple:

```
COPY . /notesapp
```

But, it is important to avoid copying the `node_modules` directory into the container. The container `node_modules` must be built inside the container, because the container operating system is almost certainly different to the host operating system. Any native code modules must be built for the correct operating system. That constraint led to the question of concisely copying specific files to the destination.

We've developed a process to build a Bootstrap 4 theme, which we developed in Chapter 6, *Implementing the Mobile-First Paradigm*. If you have a Bootstrap 4 theme to build, simply uncomment the corresponding lines in the Dockerfile. Those lines move the working directory to `/notesapp/theme` and then run the scripts to build the theme. A new script is required in `theme/package.json` to remove the `theme/node_modules` directory after the theme has been built:

```
"scripts": {
    ...
    "clean": "rm -rf bootstrap-4.0.0/node_modules"
    ...
}
```

We also have a new SEQUELIZE_CONNECT file. Create `models/sequelize-docker-mysql.yaml` containing the following:

```
dbname: notes
username: notes
password: notes12345
params:
    host: db-notes
    port: 3306
    dialect: mysql
```

This will access a database server on the `db-notes` domain name using the named database, username, and password.

Notice that the USER_SERVICE_URL variable no longer accesses the authentication service at `localhost`, but at `userauth`. The `userauth` domain name is currently only advertised by the DNS server on AuthNet, but the Notes service is on FrontNet. This means we'll have to connect the `userauth` container to the FrontNet bridge network so that its name is known there as well. We'll get to that in a minute.

In Chapter 8, *Multiuser Authentication the Microservice Way* we discussed the need to protect the API keys supplied by Twitter.

We didn't want to commit the keys in the source code, but they have to go somewhere. Placeholders are in the Dockerfile for specifying TWITTER_CONSUMER_KEY and TWITTER_CONSUMER_SECRET.

The value for TWITTER_CALLBACK_HOST needs to reflect where Notes is deployed. Right now, it is still on your laptop, but by the end of the chapter, it will be deployed to the server, and, at that time, it will need the IP address or domain name of the server.

A new variable is NOTES_SESSIONS_DIR and the matching VOLUME declaration. If we were to run multiple Notes instances, they could share session data by sharing this volume.

Supporting the NOTES_SESSIONS_DIR variable requires one change in `app.mjs`:

```
const sessionStore  = new FileStore({
    path: process.env.NOTES_SESSIONS_DIR ?
        process.env.NOTES_SESSIONS_DIR : "sessions"
});
```

Instead of a hardcoded directory name, we can use an environment variable to define the location where session data is stored. Alternatively, there are `sessionStore` implementations for various servers such as REDIS, enabling session data sharing between containers on separate host systems.

In `notes/package.json`, add these scripts:

```
"scripts": {
    . . .
    "docker": "node --experimental-modules ./app",
    "docker-build": "docker build -t node-web-development/notes ."
    . . .
}
```

As for the authentication server, this lets us build the container and then, within the container, we can run the service.

Now we can build the container image:

```
$ npm run docker-build

> notes@0.0.0 docker-build /Users/david/chap10/notes
> docker build -t node-web-development/notes .

Sending build context to Docker daemon 76.27MB
Step 1/22 : FROM node:9.5
 ---> a696309517c6
Step 2/22 : ENV DEBUG="notes:*,messages:*"
 ---> Using cache
 ---> 8628ecad9fa4
```

Next, in the `frontnet` directory, create a file named `startserver.sh`, or, on Windows, `startserver.ps1`:

```
docker run -it --name notes --net=frontnet -p 3000:3000 node-web-development/notes
```

Unlike the authentication service, the Notes application container must export a port to the public. Otherwise, the public will never be able to enjoy this wonderful creation we're building. The -p option is how we instruct Docker to expose a port.

The first number is a TCP port number published from the container, and the second number is the TCP port inside the container. Generally speaking, this option maps a port inside the container to one reachable by the public.

Then run it as follows:

```
$ sh -x startserver.sh
+ docker run -it --name notes --net=frontnet -p 3000:3000 node-web-
development/notes
(node:6) ExperimentalWarning: The ESM module loader is experimental.
  notes:debug-INDEX Listening on port 3000 +0ms
```

On Windows, run `.\startserver.ps1`.

At this point, we can connect our browser to `http://localhost:3000` and start using the Notes application. But we'll quickly run into a problem:

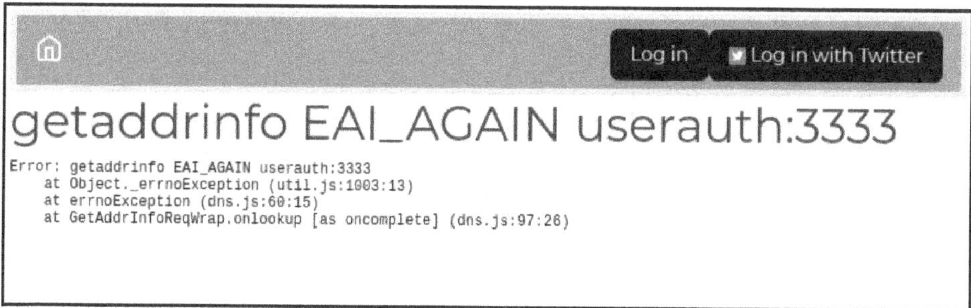

The user experience team is going to scream about this ugly error message, so put it on your backlog to generate a prettier error screen. For example, a flock of birds pulling a whale out of the ocean is popular.

This error means that Notes cannot access anything at the host named `userauth`. That host does exist, because the container is running, but it's not on `frontnet`, and is not reachable from the `notes` container. Namely:

```
$ docker exec -it notes bash
root@125a196c3fd5:/notesapp# ping userauth
ping: unknown host
root@125a196c3fd5:/notesapp# ping db-notes
PING db-notes (172.19.0.2): 56 data bytes
64 bytes from 172.19.0.2: icmp_seq=0 ttl=64 time=0.136 ms
^C--- db-notes ping statistics ---
1 packets transmitted, 1 packets received, 0% packet loss
round-trip min/avg/max/stddev = 0.136/0.136/0.136/0.000 ms
root@125a196c3fd5:/notesapp#
```

If you inspect FrontNet and AuthNet, you'll see the containers attached to each do not overlap:

```
$ docker network inspect frontnet
$ docker network inspect authnet
```

In the architecture diagram at the beginning of the chapter, we showed a connection between the `notes` and `userauth` containers. The connection is required so `notes` can authenticate its users. But that connection does not exist, yet.

Unfortunately, a simple change to `startserver.sh` (`startserver.ps1`) does not work:

```
docker run -it --name notes --net=authnet --net=frontnet -p 3000:3000
node-web-development/notes
```

While it is conceptually simple to specify multiple `--net` options when starting a container, Docker does not support this. It silently accepts the command as shown, but only connects the container to the last network mentioned in the options. Instead, Docker requires that you take a second step to attach the container to a second network:

```
$ docker network connect authnet notes
```

With no other change, the Notes application will now allow you to log in and start adding and editing notes.

There is a glaring architecture question staring at us. Do we connect the `userauth` service to `frontnet`, or do we connect the `notes` service to `authnet`?   To verify that either direction solves the problem, run these commands:

```
$ docker network disconnect authnet notes
$ docker network connect frontnet userauth
```

The first time around, we connected `notes` to `authnet`, then we disconnected it from `authnet`, and then connected `userauth` to `frontnet`. That means we tried both combinations and, as expected, in both cases `notes` and `userauth` were able to communicate.

This is a question for security experts since the consideration is the attack vectors available to any intruders. Suppose Notes has a security hole allowing an invader to gain access. How do we limit what is reachable via that hole?

The primary observation is that by connecting `notes` to `authnet`, `notes` not only has access to `userauth`, but also to `db-userauth`:

```
$ docker network disconnect frontnet userauth
$ docker network connect authnet notes
$ docker exec -it notes bash
root@7fce818e9a4d:/notesapp# ping userauth
PING userauth (172.18.0.3): 56 data bytes
64 bytes from 172.18.0.3: icmp_seq=0 ttl=64 time=0.103 ms
^C--- userauth ping statistics ---
1 packets transmitted, 1 packets received, 0% packet loss
round-trip min/avg/max/stddev = 0.103/0.103/0.103/0.000 ms
root@7fce818e9a4d:/notesapp# ping db-userauth
PING db-userauth (172.18.0.2): 56 data bytes
64 bytes from 172.18.0.2: icmp_seq=0 ttl=64 time=0.201 ms
^C--- db-userauth ping statistics ---
1 packets transmitted, 1 packets received, 0% packet loss
round-trip min/avg/max/stddev = 0.201/0.201/0.201/0.000 ms
root@7fce818e9a4d:/notesapp#
```

This sequence reconnects `notes` to `authnet`, and demonstrates the ability to access both the `userauth` and `db-userauth` containers. Therefore, a successful invader could access the `db-userauth` database, a result we wanted to prevent. Our diagram at the beginning showed no such connection between `notes` and `db-userauth`.

Given that our goal for using Docker was to limit the attack vectors, we have a clear distinction between the two container/network connection setups.
Attaching `userauth` to `frontnet` limits the number of containers that can access `db-userauth`. For an intruder to access the user information database, they must first break into `notes`, and then break into `userauth`. Unless, that is, our amateur attempt at a security audit is flawed.

Controlling the location of MySQL data volumes

The `db-userauth` and `db-notes` Dockerfiles contain VOLUME /var/lib/mysql, and when we started the containers, we gave --volume options, assigning a host directory for that container directory:

```
docker run --name db-notes \
  . . .
  --volume `pwd`/../notes-data:/var/lib/mysql \
  . . .
```

We can easily see this connects a host directory, so it appears within the container at that location. Simply inspecting the host directory with tools such as `ls` shows that files are created in that directory corresponding to a MySQL database.

The `VOLUME` instruction instructs Docker to create a directory outside the container and to map that directory so that it's mounted inside the container on the named path. The `VOLUME` instruction by itself doesn't control the directory name on the host computer. If no `--volume` option is given, Docker still arranges for the content of said directory to be kept outside the container. That's useful, and at least the data is available outside the container, but you haven't controlled the location.

If we restart the `db-notes` container without using the `--volume` option for `/var/lib/mysql`, we can inspect the container to discover where Docker put the volume:

```
$ docker inspect --format '{{json .Mounts}}' db-notes
[{"Type":"bind",
"Source":"/Users/david/chap10/frontnet/my.cnf","Destination":"/etc/my.
cnf",
"Mode":"","RW":true,"Propagation":"rprivate"},{"Type":"volume","Name":
"39f9a80b49e3ecdebc7789de7b7dd2366c400ee7fbfedd6e4df18f7e60bad409",
"Source":"/var/lib/docker/volumes/39f9a80b49e3ecdebc7789de7b7dd2366c40
0ee7fbfedd6e4df18f7e60bad409/_data","Destination":"/var/lib/mysql",
"Driver":"local","Mode":"","RW":true,"Propagation":""}]
```

That's not exactly a user-friendly pathname, but you can snoop into that directory and see that indeed the MySQL database is stored there. The simplest way to use a user-friendly pathname for a volume is with the `--volume` options we showed earlier.

Another advantage we have is to easily switch databases. For example, we could test Notes with pre-cooked test databases full of notes written in Swahili (`notes-data-swahili`), Romanian (`notes-data-romanian`), German (`notes-data-german`) and English (`notes-data-english`). Each test database could be stored in the named directory, and testing against the specific language is as simple as running the notes container with different `--volume` options.

In any case, if you restart the `notes` container with the `--volume` option, you can inspect the container and see the directory is mounted on the directory you specified:

```
$ docker inspect --format '{{json .Mounts}}' db-notes
[{"Type":"bind",
"Source":"/Users/david/chap10/frontnet/my.cnf","Destination":"/etc/my.
cnf",
```

```
"Mode":"","RW":true,"Propagation":"rprivate"},
{"Type":"bind",
"Source":"/Users/david/chap10/notes-
data","Destination":"/var/lib/mysql",
"Mode":"","RW":true,"Propagation":"rprivate"}]
```

With the `--volume` options, we have controlled the location of the host directory corresponding to the container directory.

The last thing to note is that controlling the location of such directories makes it easier to make backups and take other administrative actions with that data.

Docker deployment of background services

With the scripts we've written so far, the Docker container is run in the foreground. That makes it easier to debug the service since you see the errors. For a production deployment, we need the Docker container detached from the terminal, and an assurance that it will restart itself automatically. Those two attributes are simple to implement.

Simply change this pattern:

```
$ docker run -it ...
```

To this pattern:

```
$ docker run --detach --restart always ...
```

The `-it` option is what causes the Docker container to run in the foreground. Using these options causes the Docker container to run detached from your terminal, and if the service process dies, the container will automatically restart.

Deploying to the cloud with Docker compose

This is cool that we can create encapsulated instantiations of the software services we've created. But the promise was to use the Dockerized application for deployment on cloud services. In other words, we need to take all this learning and apply it to the task of deploying Notes on a public internet server with a fairly high degree of security.

We've demonstrated that, with Docker, Notes can be decomposed into four containers that have a high degree of isolation from each other, and from the outside world.

There is another glaring problem: our process in the previous section was partly manual, partly automated. We created scripts to launch each portion of the system, which is a good practice according to the Twelve Factor Application model. But we did not automate the entire process to bring up Notes and the authentication services. Nor is this solution scalable beyond one machine.

Let's start with the last issue first—scalability. Within the Docker ecosystem, several **Docker orchestrator** services are available. An Orchestrator automatically deploys and manages Docker containers over a group of machines. Some examples of Docker Orchestrators are Docker Swarm (which is built into the Docker CLI), Kubernetes, CoreOS Fleet, and Apache Mesos. These are powerful systems able to automatically increase/decrease resources as needed, to move containers from one host to another, and more. We mention these systems for your further study as your needs grow.

Docker compose (`https://docs.docker.com/compose/overview/`) will solve the other problems we've identified. It lets us easily define and run several Docker containers together as a complete application. It uses a YAML file, `docker-compose.yml`, to describe the containers, their dependencies, the virtual networks, and the volumes. While we'll be using it to describe the deployment onto a single host machine, Docker compose can be used for multimachine deployments, especially when combined with Docker Swarm. Understanding Docker compose will provide a basis upon which to understand/use the other tools, such as Swarm or Kubernetes.

Docker machine (`https://docs.docker.com/machine/overview/`) is a tool for installing Docker Engine on virtual hosts, either local or remote, and for managing Docker containers on those hosts. We'll be using this to provision a server on a cloud hosting service, and push containers into that server. It can also be used to provision a virtual host on your laptop within a VirtualBox instance.

Before proceeding, ensure Docker compose and Docker machine are installed. If you've installed Docker for Windows or Docker for Mac, both are installed along with everything else. On Linux, you must install both separately by following the instructions at the links given earlier.

Docker compose files

Let's start by creating a directory, compose, as a sibling to the users and notes directories. In that directory, create a file named `docker-compose.yml`:

```
version: '3'
services:
```

```yaml
db-userauth:
  image: "mysql/mysql-server:5.7"
  container_name: db-userauth
  command: [ "mysqld", "--character-set-server=utf8mb4",
             "--collation-server=utf8mb4_unicode_ci",
             "--bind-address=0.0.0.0" ]
  expose:
    - "3306"
  networks:
    - authnet
  volumes:
    - db-userauth-data:/var/lib/mysql
    - ../authnet/my.cnf:/etc/my.cnf
  environment:
    MYSQL_RANDOM_ROOT_PASSWORD: "true"
    MYSQL_USER: userauth
    MYSQL_PASSWORD: userauth
    MYSQL_DATABASE: userauth
  restart: always

userauth:
  build: ../users
  container_name: userauth
  depends_on:
    - db-userauth
  networks:
    - authnet
    - frontnet
  restart: always

db-notes:
  image: "mysql/mysql-server:5.7"
  container_name: db-notes
  command: [ "mysqld", "--character-set-server=utf8mb4",
             "--collation-server=utf8mb4_unicode_ci",
             "--bind-address=0.0.0.0" ]
  expose:
    - "3306"
  networks:
    - frontnet
  volumes:
    - db-notes-data:/var/lib/mysql
    - ../frontnet/my.cnf:/etc/my.cnf
  environment:
    MYSQL_RANDOM_ROOT_PASSWORD: "true"
    MYSQL_USER: notes
    MYSQL_PASSWORD: notes12345
    MYSQL_DATABASE: notes
```

```
      restart: always

  notes:
    build: ../notes
    container_name: notes
    restart: always
    depends_on:
      - db-notes
    networks:
      - frontnet
    ports:
      - "3000:3000"
    restart: always

networks:
  frontnet:
    driver: bridge
  authnet:
    driver: bridge

volumes:
  db-userauth-data:
  db-notes-data:
```

That's the description of the entire Notes deployment. It's at a fairly high level of abstraction, roughly equivalent to the options on the command-line tools we've used so far. Further details are located inside the Dockerfiles, which are referenced from this compose file.

The `version` line says that this is a version 3 compose file. The version number is inspected by the `docker-compose` command, so it can correctly interpret its content. The full documentation is worth reading at `https://docs.docker.com/compose/compose-file/`.

There are three major sections used here: **services**, **volumes**, and **networks**. The services section describes the containers being used, the networks section describes the networks, and the volumes section describes the volumes. The content of each section matches the intent/purpose of the commands we ran earlier. The information we've already dealt with is all here, just rearranged.

There are two database containers, `db-userauth` and `db-notes`. Both reference the Dockerhub image using the `image` tag. For the databases, we did not create a Dockerfile, but instead built directly from the Dockerhub image. The same happens here in the compose file.

For the `userauth` and `notes` containers, we created a Dockerfile. The directory containing that file is referenced by the `build` tag. To build the container, `docker-compose` looks for a file named `Dockerfile` in the named directory. There are more options for the `build` tag, which are discussed in the official documentation.

The `container_name` attribute is equivalent to the `--name` attribute and specifies a user-friendly name for the container. We must specify the container name in order to specify the container hostname in order to do Docker-style service discovery.

The `command` tag overrides the `CMD` tag in the Dockerfile. We've specified this for the two database containers, so we can instruct MySQL to bind to IP address `0.0.0.0`. Even though we didn't create a Dockerfile for the database containers, there is a Dockerfile created by the MySQL maintainers.

The `networks` attribute lists the networks to which this container must be connected and is exactly equivalent to the `--net` argument. Even though the `docker` command doesn't support multiple `--net` options, we can list multiple networks in the compose file. In this case, the networks are bridge networks. As we did earlier, the networks themselves must be created separately, and in a compose file, that's done in the *networks* section.

Each of the networks in our system is a `bridge` network. This fact is described in the compose file.

The `expose` attribute declares which ports are exposed from the container, and is equivalent to the `EXPOSE` tag. The exposed ports are not published outside the host machine, however. The `ports` attribute declares the ports that are to be published. In the ports declaration, we have two port numbers: the first being the published port number and the second being the port number inside the container. This is exactly equivalent to the `-p` option used earlier.

The `notes` container has a few environment variables, such as `TWITTER_CONSUMER_KEY` and `TWITTER_CONSUMER_SECRET`, that you may prefer to store in this file rather than in the Dockerfile.

The `depends_on` attribute lets us control the start up order. A container that depends on another will wait to start until the depended-upon container is running.

The `volumes` attribute describes mappings of a container directory to a `host` directory. In this case, we've defined two volume names, `db-userauth-data` and `db-notes-data`, and then used them for the volume mapping.

To explore the volumes, start with this command:

```
$ docker volume ls
DRIVER                  VOLUME NAME
...
local                   compose_db-notes-data
local                   compose_db-userauth-data
...
```

The volume names are the same as in the compose file, but with `compose_` tacked on the front.

You can inspect the volume location using the `docker` command line:

```
$ docker volume inspect compose_db-notes-data
$ docker volume inspect compose_db-userauth-data
```

If it's preferable, you can specify a pathname in the `compose` file:

```
db-auth:
  ..
  volumes:
    # - db-userauth-data:/var/lib/mysql
    - ../userauth-data:/var/lib/mysql

db-notes:
  ..
  volumes:
    # - db-notes-data:/var/lib/mysql
    - ../notes-data:/var/lib/mysql
```

This is the same configuration we made earlier. It uses the `userauth-data` and `notes-data` directories for the MySQL data files for their respective database containers.

The `environment` tag describes the environment variables that will be received by the container. As before, environment variables should be used to inject configuration data.

The `restart` attribute controls what happens if, or when, the container dies. When a container starts, it runs the program named in the CMD instruction, and when that program exits, the container exits. But what if that program is meant to run *forever*, shouldn't Docker know it should restart the process? We could use a background process supervisor, such as Supervisord or PM2. But, we can also use the Docker `restart` option.

The `restart` attribute can take one of the following four values:

- `no` – do not restart
- `on-failure:count` – restart up to *N* times
- `always` – always restart
- `unless-stopped` – start the container unless it was explicitly stopped

Running the Notes application with Docker compose

On Windows, we're able to run the commands in this section unchanged.

Before deploying this to a server, let's run it on our laptop using `docker-compose`:

```
$ docker stop db-notes userauth db-auth notesapp
db-notes
userauth
db-auth
notesapp
$ docker rm db-notes userauth db-auth notesapp
db-notes
userauth
db-auth
notesapp
```

We first needed to stop and delete the existing containers. Because the compose file wants to launch containers with the same names as we'd built earlier, we also have to remove the existing containers:

```
$ docker-compose build
Building db-auth
 .. lots of output
$ docker-compose up
Creating db-auth
Recreating compose_db-notes_1
Recreating compose_userauth_1
Recreating compose_notesapp_1
Attaching to db-auth, db-notes, userauth, notesapp
```

Once that's done, we can build the containers, `docker-compose build`, and then start them running, `docker-compose up`.

The first test is to execute a shell in `userauth` to run our user database script:

```
$ docker exec -it userauth bash
root@9972adbbdbb3:/userauth# PORT=3333 node users-add.js
Created { id: 2,
   username: 'me', password: 'w0rd', provider: 'local',
   familyName: 'Einarrsdottir', givenName: 'Ashildr', middleName: '',
   emails: '[]', photos: '[]',
   updatedAt: '2018-02-07T02:24:04.257Z', createdAt:
'2018-02-07T02:24:04.257Z' }
root@9972adbbdbb3:/userauth#
```

Now that we've proved that the authentication service will work, and, by the way, created a user account, you should be able to browse to the Notes application and run it through its paces.

You can also try pinging different containers to ensure that the application network topology has been created correctly.

If you use Docker command-line tools to explore the running containers and networks, you'll see they have new names. The new names are similar to the old names, but prefixed with the string `compose_`. This is a side effect of using Docker compose.

By default, `docker-compose` attaches to the containers so that logging output is printed on the Terminal. Output from all four containers will be intermingled together. Thankfully, each line is prepended by the container name.

When you're done testing the system, simply type *CTRL + C* on the Terminal:

```
^CGracefully stopping... (press Ctrl+C again to force)
Stopping db-userauth ... done
Stopping userauth    ... done
Stopping db-notes    ... done
Stopping notes       ... done
```

To avoid running with the containers attached to the Terminal, use the `-d` option. This says to detach from the Terminal and run in the background.

An alternate way to bring down the system described in the compose file is with the `docker-compose down` command.

The up command builds, recreates, and starts the containers. The build step can be handled separately using the `docker-compose build` command. Likewise, starting and stopping the containers can be handled separately by using the `docker-compose start` and `docker-compose-stop` commands.

In all cases, your command shell should be in the directory containing the `docker-compose.yml` file. That's the default name for this file. This can be overridden with the `-f` option to specify a different filename.

Deploying to cloud hosting with Docker compose

We've verified on our laptop that the services described by the compose file work as intended. Launching the containers is now automated, fixing one of the issues we named earlier. It's now time to see how to deploy to a cloud-hosting provider. This is where we turn to Docker machine.

Docker machine can be used to provision Docker instances inside a VirtualBox host on your laptop. What we'll be doing is provisioning a Docker system on DigitalOcean. The `docker-machine` command comes with drivers supporting a long list of cloud-hosting providers. It's easy to adapt the instructions shown here for other providers, simply by substituting a different driver.

After signing up for a DigitalOcean account, click on the API link in the dashboard. We need an API token to grant `docker-machine` access to the account. Go through the process of creating a token and save away the token string you're given. The Docker website has a tutorial at `https://docs.docker.com/machine/examples/ocean/`.

With the token in hand, type the following:

```
$ docker-machine create --driver digitalocean --digitalocean-size 2gb \
    --digitalocean-access-token TOKEN-FROM-PROVIDER \
    sandbox
Running pre-create checks...
Creating machine...
(sandbox) Creating SSH key...
(sandbox) Creating Digital Ocean droplet...
(sandbox) Waiting for IP address to be assigned to the Droplet...
Waiting for machine to be running, this may take a few minutes...
Detecting operating system of created instance...
```

```
Waiting for SSH to be available...
Detecting the provisioner...
Provisioning with ubuntu(systemd)...
Installing Docker...
Copying certs to the local machine directory...
Copying certs to the remote machine...
Setting Docker configuration on the remote daemon...
Checking connection to Docker...
Docker is up and running!
To see how to connect your Docker Client to the Docker Engine running
on this virtual machine, run: docker-machine env sandbox
```

The `digitalocean` driver is, as we said earlier, used with Digital Ocean. The Docker website has a list of drivers at `https://docs.docker.com/machine/drivers/`.

A lot of information is printed here about things being set up. The most important is the message at the end. A series of environment variables are used to tell the `docker` command where to connect to the Docker Engine instance. As the messages say, run: `docker-machine env sandbox`:

```
$ docker-machine env sandbox
export DOCKER_TLS_VERIFY="1"
export DOCKER_HOST="tcp://45.55.37.74:2376"
export DOCKER_CERT_PATH="/home/david/.docker/machine/machines/sandbox"
export DOCKER_MACHINE_NAME="sandbox"
# Run this command to configure your shell:
# eval $(docker-machine env sandbox)
```

That's the environment variables used to access the Docker host we just created. You should also go to your cloud-hosting provider dashboard and see that the host has been created. This command also gives us some instructions to follow:

```
$ eval $(docker-machine env sandbox)
$ docker-machine ls
NAME         ACTIVE    DRIVER         STATE       URL
SWARM    DOCKER           ERRORS
sandbox     *          digitalocean   Running     tcp://45.55.37.74:2376
v18.01.0-ce
```

This shows that we have a Docker Engine instance running in a host at our chosen cloud-hosting provider.

One interesting test at this point is to run `docker ps -a` on this Terminal, and then to run it in another Terminal that does not have these environment variables. That should show the cloud host has no containers at all, while your local machine may have some containers (depending on what you currently have running):

```
$ docker run hello-world
Unable to find image 'hello-world:latest' locally
latest: Pulling from library/hello-world
ca4f61b1923c: Pull complete
Digest:
sha256:66ef312bbac49c39a89aa9bcc3cb4f3c9e7de3788c944158df3ee0176d32b75
1
Status: Downloaded newer image for hello-world:latest
...
$ docker images
REPOSITORY              TAG             IMAGE ID            CREATED
SIZE
hello-world             latest          f2a91732366c        2 months
ago          1.85kB
```

Here, we've verified that we can launch a container on the remote host.

The next step is to build our containers for the new machine. Because we've switched the environment variables to point to the new server, these commands cause action to happen there rather than inside our laptop:

```
$ docker-compose build
db-userauth uses an image, skipping
db-notes uses an image, skipping
Building notes
Step 1/22 : FROM node:9.5
9.5: Pulling from library/node
f49cf87b52c1: Pull complete
7b491c575b06: Pull complete
b313b08bab3b: Pull complete
51d6678c3f0e: Pull complete
...
```

Because we changed the environment variables, the build occurs on the `sandbox` machine rather than on our laptop, as previously.

This will take a while because the Docker image cache on the remote machine is empty. Additionally, building the `notesapp` and `userauth` containers copies the entire source tree to the server and runs all build steps on the server.

The build may fail if the default memory size is 500 MB, the default on DigitalOcean at the time of writing. If so, the first thing to try is resizing the memory on the host to at least 2 GB.

Once the build is finished, launch the containers on the remote machine:

```
$ docker-compose up
Creating notes ... done
Recreating db-userauth ... done
Recreating db-notes ... done
Creating notes ...
Attaching to db-userauth, db-notes, userauth, notes
```

Once the containers start, you should test the `userauth` container as we've done previously. Unfortunately, the first time you do this, that command will fail. The problem is these lines in the `docker-compose.yml`:

```
 - ../authnet/my.cnf:/etc/my.cnf
...
 - ../frontnet/my.cnf:/etc/my.cnf
```

In this case, the build occurs on the remote machine, and the `docker-machine` command does not copy the named file to the server. Hence, when Docker attempts to start the container, it is unable to do so because that volume mount cannot be satisfied because the file is simply not there. This, then, means some surgery on `docker-compose.yml`, and to add two new Dockerfiles.

First, make these changes to `docker-compose.yml`:

```
...
db-userauth:
  build: ../authnet
  container_name: db-userauth
  networks:
    - authnet
  volumes:
    - db-userauth-data:/var/lib/mysql
  restart: always
...
db-notes:
  build: ../frontnet
  container_name: db-notes
  networks:
    - frontnet
  volumes:
    - db-notes-data:/var/lib/mysql
  restart: always
```

Instead of building the database containers from a Docker image, we're now building them from a pair of Dockerfiles. Now we must create those two Dockerfiles.

In `authnet`, create a file named `Dockerfile` containing the following:

```
FROM mysql/mysql-server:5.7
EXPOSE 3306
COPY my.cnf /etc/
ENV MYSQL_RANDOM_ROOT_PASSWORD="true"
ENV MYSQL_USER=userauth
ENV MYSQL_PASSWORD=userauth
ENV MYSQL_DATABASE=userauth
CMD [ "mysqld", "--character-set-server=utf8mb4", \
    "--collation-server=utf8mb4_unicode_ci", "--bind-address=0.0.0.0" ]
```

This copies certain settings from what had been the `db-userauth` description in `docker-compose.yml`. The important thing is that we now `COPY` the `my.cnf` file rather than use a volume mount.

In `frontnet`, create a `Dockerfile` containing the following:

```
FROM mysql/mysql-server:5.7
EXPOSE 3306
COPY my.cnf /etc/
ENV MYSQL_RANDOM_ROOT_PASSWORD="true"
ENV MYSQL_USER=notes
ENV MYSQL_PASSWORD=notes12345
ENV MYSQL_DATABASE=notes
CMD [ "mysqld", "--character-set-server=utf8mb4", \
    "--collation-server=utf8mb4_unicode_ci", "--bind-address=0.0.0.0" ]
```

This is the same, but with a few critical values changed.

After making these changes, we can now build the containers, and launch them:

```
$ docker-compose build
... much output
$ docker-compose up --force-recreate
... much output
```

Now that we have a working build, and can bring up the containers, let's inspect them and verify everything works.

Execute a shell in `userauth` to test and set up the user database:

```
$ docker exec -it userauth bash
root@931dd2a267b4:/userauth# PORT=3333 node users-list.js
List [ { id: 'me', username: 'me', provider: 'local',
    familyName: 'Einarrsdottir', givenName: 'Ashildr', middleName: '',
    emails: '[]', photos: '[]' } ]
```

As mentioned previously, this verifies that the `userauth` service works, that the remote containers are set up, and that we can proceed to using the Notes application.

The question is: What's the URL to use? The service is not on `localhost`, because it's on the remote server. We don't have a domain name assigned, but there is an IP address for the server.

Run the following command:

```
$ docker-machine ip sandbox
45.55.37.74
```

Docker tells you the IP address, which you should use as the basis of the URL. Hence, in your browser, visit `http://IP-ADDRESS:3000`

With Notes deployed to the remote server, you should check out all the things we've looked at previously. The bridge networks should exist, as shown previously, with the same limited access between containers. The only public access should be port `3000` on the `notes` container.

Remember to set the `TWITTER_CALLBACK_HOST` environment variable appropriately for your server.

Because our database containers mount a volume to store the data, let's see where that volume landed on the server:

```
$ docker volume ls
DRIVER VOLUME NAME
local compose_db-notes-data
local compose_db-userauth-data
```

Those are the expected volumes, one for each container:

```
$ docker volume inspect compose_db-notes-data
[
    {
        "CreatedAt": "2018-02-07T06:30:06Z",
        "Driver": "local",
        "Labels": {
            "com.docker.compose.project": "compose",
            "com.docker.compose.volume": "db-notes-data"
        },
        "Mountpoint": "/var/lib/docker/volumes/compose_db-notes-data/_data",
        "Name": "compose_db-notes-data",
        "Options": {},
        "Scope": "local"
```

```
    }
]
```

Those are the directories, but they're not located on our laptop. Instead, they're on the remote server. Accessing these directories means logging into the remote server to take a look:

```
$ docker-machine ssh sandbox
Welcome to Ubuntu 16.04.3 LTS (GNU/Linux 4.4.0-112-generic x86_64)

 * Documentation:  https://help.ubuntu.com
 * Management:     https://landscape.canonical.com
 * Support:        https://ubuntu.com/advantage

   Get cloud support with Ubuntu Advantage Cloud Guest:
     http://www.ubuntu.com/business/services/cloud

4 packages can be updated.
0 updates are security updates.

Last login: Wed Feb 7 04:00:29 2018 from 108.213.68.139
root@sandbox:~#
```

From this point, you can inspect the directories corresponding to these volumes and see that they indeed contain MySQL configuration and data files:

```
root@sandbox:~# ls /var/lib/docker/volumes/compose_db-notes-data/_data
auto.cnf           client-key.pem   ib_logfile1   mysql.sock.lock
public_key.pem
ca-key.pem         ib_buffer_pool   ibtmp1        notes
server-cert.pem
ca.pem             ibdata1          mysql         performance_schema
server-key.pem
client-cert.pem    ib_logfile0      mysql.sock    private_key.pem     sys
```

You'll also find that the Docker command-line tools will work. The process list is especially interesting:

```
 5044 ?      Ssl    1:33 /usr/bin/dockerd -H tcp://0.0.0.0:2376 -H unix:///var/run/docker.sock --storage-driver aufs --tlsverif
 5051 ?      Ssl    1:04  \_ docker-containerd --config /var/run/docker/containerd/containerd.toml
16770 ?      Sl     0:00      \_ docker-containerd-shim --namespace moby --workdir /var/lib/docker/containerd/daemon/io.container
16798 ?      Ssl    0:00      |   \_ mysqld --character-set-server=utf8mb4 --collation-server=utf8mb4 unicode ci --bind-address
16891 ?      Sl     0:00      \_ docker-containerd-shim --namespace moby --workdir /var/lib/docker/containerd/daemon/io.container
16930 ?      Ssl    0:00      |   \_ mysqld --character-set-server=utf8mb4 --collation-server=utf8mb4 unicode ci --bind-address
17128 ?      Sl     0:00      \_ docker-containerd-shim --namespace moby --workdir /var/lib/docker/containerd/daemon/io.container
17165 ?      Ss     0:00      |   \_ /bin/sh -c npm run docker
17220 ?      Sl     0:00      |       \_ npm
17330 ?      S      0:00      |           \_ sh -c node --experimental-modules ./user-server
17331 ?      Sl     0:01      |               \_ node --experimental-modules ./user-server
17288 ?      Sl     0:00      \_ docker-containerd-shim --namespace moby --workdir /var/lib/docker/containerd/daemon/io.container
17308 ?      Ss     0:00      |   \_ /bin/sh -c node --experimental-modules ./app
17373 ?      Sl     0:02      |       \_ node --experimental-modules ./app
17268 ?      Sl     0:00      \_ /usr/bin/docker-proxy -proto tcp -host-ip 0.0.0.0 -host-port 3000 -container-ip 172.19.0.4 -contai
```

Look closely at this and you see a process corresponding to every container in the system. These processes are running in the host operating system. Docker creates layers of configuration/containment around those processes to create the appearance that the process is running under a different operating system, and with various system/network configuration files, as specified in the container screenshot.

The claimed advantage Docker has over virtualization approaches, such as VirtualBox, is that Docker is very lightweight. We see right here why Docker is lightweight: there is no virtualization layer, there is only a containerization process (`docker-containerd-shim`).

Once you're satisfied that Notes is working on the remote server, you can shut it down and remove it as follows:

```
$ docker-compose stop
Stopping notesapp ... done
Stopping userauth ... done
Stopping db-notes ... done
Stopping db-auth ... done
```

This shuts down all the containers at once:

```
$ docker-machine stop sandbox
Stopping "sandbox"...
Machine "sandbox" was stopped.
```

This shuts down the remote machine. The cloud-hosting provider dashboard will show that the Droplet has stopped.

At this point, you can go ahead and delete the Docker machine instance as well, if you like:

```
$ docker-machine rm sandbox
About to remove sandbox
Are you sure? (y/n): y
Successfully removed sandbox
```

And, if you're truly certain you want to delete the machine, the preceding command does the deed. As soon as you do this, the machine will be erased from your cloud-hosting provider dashboard.

Summary

This chapter has been quite a journey. We went from an application that existed solely on our laptop, to exploring two ways to deploy Node.js applications to a production server.

We started by reviewing the Notes application architecture and how that will affect deployment. That enabled you to understand what you had to do for server deployment.

Then you learned the traditional way to deploy services on Linux using an init script. PM2 is a useful tool for managing background processes in such an environment. You also learned how to provision a remote server using a virtual machine hosting service.

Then you took a long trip into the land of Docker, a new and exciting system for deploying services on machines. You learned how to write a Dockerfile so that Docker knows how to construct a service image. You learned several ways to deploy Docker images on a laptop or on a remote server. And you learned how to describe a multi-container application using Docker compose.

You're almost ready to wrap up this book. You've learned a lot along the way; there are two final things to cover.

In the next chapter, we will learn about both unit testing and functional testing. While a core principle of test-driven development is to write the unit tests before writing the application, we've done it the other way around and put the chapter about unit testing at the end of this book. That's not to say unit testing is unimportant, because it is extremely important.

In the final chapter, we'll explore how to harden our application, and application infrastructure, against attackers.

11
Unit Testing and Functional Testing

nit testing has become a primary part of good software development practice. It is a method by which individual units of source code are tested to ensure proper functioning. Each unit is theoretically the smallest testable part of an application. In a Node.js application, you might consider each module as a unit.

In unit testing, each unit is tested separately, isolating the unit under test as much as possible from other parts of the application. If a test fails, you would want it to be due to a bug in your code rather than a bug in the package that your code happens to use. A common technique is to use mock objects or mock data to isolate individual parts of the application from one another.

Functional testing, on the other hand, doesn't try to test individual components, but instead it tests the whole system. Generally speaking, unit testing is performed by the development team, and functional testing is performed by a **Quality Assurance (QA)** or **Quality Engineering (QE)** team. Both testing models are needed to fully certify an application. An analogy might be that unit testing is similar to ensuring that each word in a sentence is correctly spelled, while functional testing ensures that the paragraph containing that sentence has a good structure.

In this chapter, we'll cover:

- Assertions as the basis of software tests
- The Mocha unit testing framework and the Chai assertions library
- Using tests to find bugs and fixing the bug
- Using Docker to manage test infrastructure
- Testing a REST backend service
- UI testing in a real web browser using Puppeteer
- Improving UI testability with element ID attributes

Assert – the basis of testing methodologies

Node.js has a useful built-in testing tool, the `assert` module. Its functionality is similar to assert libraries in other languages. Namely, it's a collection of functions for testing conditions, and if the conditions indicate an error, the `assert` function throws an exception.

At its simplest, a test suite is a series of `assert` calls to validate the behavior of a thing being tested. For example, a test suite could instantiate the user authentication service, then make an API call, using `assert` methods to validate the result, then make another API call, validating its results, and so on.

Consider a code snippet like this, which you could save in a file named `deleteFile.js`:

```
const fs = require('fs');

exports.deleteFile = function(fname, callback) {
  fs.stat(fname, (err, stats) => {
    if (err) callback(new Error(`the file ${fname} does not exist`));
    else {
      fs.unlink(fname, err2 => {
        if (err) callback(new Error(`could not delete ${fname}`));
        else callback();
      });
    }
  });
};
```

The first thing to notice is this contains several layers of asynchronous callback functions. That presents a couple of challenges:

- Capturing errors from deep inside a callback, to ensure the test scenario fails
- Detecting conditions where the callbacks are never called

The following is an example of using `assert` for testing. Create a file named `test-deleteFile.js` containing the following:

```
const fs = require('fs');
const assert = require('assert');
const df = require('./deleteFile');
```

```
df.deleteFile("no-such-file", (err) => {
    assert.throws(
        function() { if (err) throw err; },
        function(error) {
            if ((error instanceof Error)
              && /does not exist/.test(error)) {
                return true;
            } else return false;
        },
        "unexpected error"
    );
});
```

This is what's called a negative test scenario, in that it's testing whether requesting to delete a nonexistent file throws an error.

If you are looking for a quick way to test, the `assert` module can be useful when used this way. If it runs and no messages are printed, then the test passes. But, did it catch the instance of the `deleteFile` callback never being called?

```
$ node test-deleteFile.js
```

The `assert` module is used by many of the test frameworks as a core tool for writing test cases. What the test frameworks do is create a familiar test suite and test case structure to encapsulate your test code.

There are many styles of assertion libraries available in Node.js. Later in this chapter, we'll use the Chai assertion library (`http://chaijs.com/`) which gives you a choice between three different assertion styles (should, expect, and assert).

Testing a Notes model

Let's start our unit testing journey with the data models we wrote for the Notes application. Because this is unit testing, the models should be tested separately from the rest of the Notes application.

In the case of most of the Notes models, isolating their dependencies implies creating a mock database. Are you going to test the data model or the underlying database? Mocking out a database means creating a fake database implementation, which does not look like a productive use of our time. You can argue that testing a data model is really about testing the interaction between your code and the database, that mocking out the database means not testing that interaction, and therefore we should test our code against the database engine used in production.

With that line of reasoning in mind, we'll skip mocking out the database, and instead run the tests against a database containing test data. To simplify launching the test database, we'll use Docker to start and stop a version of the Notes application stack that's set up for testing.

Mocha and Chai – the chosen test tools

If you haven't already done so, duplicate the source tree to use in this chapter. For example, if you had a directory named `chap10`, create one named `chap11` containing everything from `chap10`.

In the `notes` directory, create a new directory named `test`.

Mocha (`http://mochajs.org/`) is one of many test frameworks available for Node.js. As you'll see shortly, it helps us write test cases and test suites, and it provides a test results reporting mechanism. It was chosen over the alternatives because it supports Promises. It fits very well with the Chai assertion library mentioned earlier. And, we'll need to use ES6 modules from test suites written in CommonJS, and therefore we must use the `esm` module.

You may find references to an earlier `@std/esm` module. That module has been deprecated, with `esm` put in its place.

While in the `notes/test` directory, type this to install Mocha, Chai, and `esm`:

```
$ npm init
... answer the questions to create package.json
$ npm install mocha@5.x chai@4.1.x esm --save
```

Notes model test suite

Because we have several Notes models, the test suite should run against any model. We can write tests using the Notes model API we developed, and an environment variable should be used to declare the model to test.

Because we've written the Notes application using ES6 modules, we have a small challenge to overcome. Mocha only supports running tests in CommonJS modules, and Node.js (as of this writing) does not support loading an ES6 module from a CommonJS module. An ES6 module can use `import` to load a CommonJS module, but a CommonJS module cannot use `require` to load an ES6 module. There are various technical reasons behind this, the bottom line is that we're limited in this way.

Because Mocha requires that tests be CommonJS modules, we're in the position of having to load an ES6 module into a CommonJS module. A module, `esm`, exists which allows that combination to work. If you'll refer back, we installed that module in the previous section. Let's see how to use it.

In the `test` directory, create a file named `test-model.js` containing this as the outer shell of the test suite:

```
'use strict';

require = require("esm")(module,{"esm":"js"});
const assert = require('chai').assert;
const model = require('../models/notes');

describe("Model Test", function() {
  ..
});
```

The support to load ES6 modules is enabled by the `require('esm')` statement shown here. It replaces the standard `require` function with one from the `esm` module. That parameter list at the end enables the feature to load ES6 modules in a CommonJS module. Once you've done this, your CommonJS module can load an ES6 module as evidenced by `require('../models/notes')` a couple of lines later.

The Chai library supports three flavors of assertions. We're using the `assert` style here, but it's easy to use a different style if you prefer. For the other styles supported by Chai, see `http://chaijs.com/guide/styles/`.

Chai's assertions include a very long list of useful assertion functions, see `http://chaijs.com/api/assert/`.

The Notes model to test must be selected with the `NOTES_MODEL` environment variable. For the models that also consult environment variables, we'll need to supply that configuration as well.

With Mocha, a test suite is contained within a `describe` block. The first argument is descriptive text, which you use to tailor the presentation of test results.

Rather than maintaining a separate test database, we can create one on the fly while executing tests. Mocha has what are called hooks, which are functions executed before or after test case execution. The hook functions let you, the test suite author, set up and tear down required conditions for the test suite to operate as desired. For example, to create a test database with known test content:

```
describe("Model Test", function() {
```

```
beforeEach(async function() {
  try {
    const keyz = await model.keylist();
    for (let key of keyz) {
      await model.destroy(key);
    }
    await model.create("n1", "Note 1", "Note 1");
    await model.create("n2", "Note 2", "Note 2");
    await model.create("n3", "Note 3", "Note 3");
  } catch (e) {
    console.error(e);
    throw e;
  }
});

..

});
```

This defines a `beforeEach` hook, which is executed before every test case. The other hooks are `before`, `after`, `beforeEach`, and `afterEach`. The each hooks are triggered before or after each test case execution.

This is meant to be a cleanup/preparation step before every test. It uses our Notes API to first delete all notes from the database (if any) and then create a set of new notes with known characteristics. This technique simplifies tests by ensuring that we have known conditions to test against.

We also have a side effect of testing the `model.keylist` and `model.create` methods.

In Mocha, a series of test cases are encapsulated with a `describe` block, and written using an `it` block. The `describe` block is meant to describe that group of tests, and the `it` block is for checking assertions on a specific aspect of the thing being tested. You can nest the `describe` blocks as deeply as you like:

```
describe("check keylist", function() {
  it("should have three entries", async function() {
    const keyz = await model.keylist();
    assert.exists(keyz);
    assert.isArray(keyz);
    assert.lengthOf(keyz, 3);
  });
  it("should have keys n1 n2 n3", async function() {
    const keyz = await model.keylist();
    assert.exists(keyz);
    assert.isArray(keyz);
    assert.lengthOf(keyz, 3);
```

```
    for (let key of keyz) {
      assert.match(key, /n[123]/, "correct key");
    }
  });
  it("should have titles Node #", async function() {
    const keyz = await model.keylist();
    assert.exists(keyz);
    assert.isArray(keyz);
    assert.lengthOf(keyz, 3);
    var keyPromises = keyz.map(key => model.read(key));
    const notez = await Promise.all(keyPromises);
    for (let note of notez) {
      assert.match(note.title, /Note [123]/, "correct title");
    }
  });
});
```

The idea is to call Notes API functions, then to test the results to check whether they matched the expected results.

This `describe` block is within the outer `describe` block. The descriptions given in the describe and `it` blocks are used to make the test report more readable. The `it` block forms a pseudo-sentence along the lines of *it (the thing being tested) should do this or that.*

It is important with Mocha to not use arrow functions in the `describe` and `it` blocks. By now, you will have grown fond of arrow functions because of how much easier they are to write. But, Mocha calls these functions with a `this` object containing useful functions for Mocha. Because arrow functions avoid setting up a `this` object, Mocha would break.

Even though Mocha requires regular functions for the `describe` and `it` blocks, we can use arrow functions within those functions.

How does Mocha know whether the test code passes? How does it know when the test finishes? This segment of code shows one of the three methods.

Generally, Mocha is looking to see if the function throws an exception, or whether the test case takes too long to execute (a timeout situation). In either case, Mocha will indicate a test failure. That's of course simple to determine for non-asynchronous code. But, Node.js is all about asynchronous code, and Mocha has two models for testing asynchronous code.

In the first (not seen here), Mocha passes in a callback function, and the test code is to call the callback function. In the second, as seen here, it looks for a Promise being returned by the test function, and determines pass/fail on whether the Promise is in the *resolve* or *reject* state.

In this case, we're using `async` functions, because they automatically return a Promise. Within the functions, we're calling asynchronous functions using `await`, ensuring any thrown exception is indicated as a rejected Promise.

Another item to note is the question asked earlier: what if the callback function we're testing is never called? Or, what if a Promise is never resolved? Mocha starts a timer and if the test case does not finish before the timer expires, Mocha fails the test case.

Configuring and running tests

We have more tests to write, but let's first get set up to run the tests. The simplest model to test is the in-memory model. Let's add this to the `scripts` section of `notes/test/package.json`:

```
"test-notes-memory": "NOTES_MODEL=memory mocha test-model",
```

To install dependencies, we must run `npm install` in both the `notes/test` and `notes` directories. That way both the dependencies for the test code, and the dependencies for Notes, are installed in their correct place.

Then, we can run it as follows:

```
$ npm run test-notes-memory

> notes-test@1.0.0 test-notes-memory /Users/david/chap11/notes/test
> NOTES_MODEL=memory mocha test-model

  Model Test
    check keylist
      √ should have three entries
      √ should have keys n1 n2 n3
      √ should have titles Node #

  3 passing (18ms)
```

The `mocha` command is used to run the test suite.

The structure of the output follows the structure of the `describe` and `it` blocks. You should set up the descriptive text strings so it reads nicely.

More tests for the Notes model

That wasn't enough to test much, so let's go ahead and add some more tests:

```
describe("read note", function() {
    it("should have proper note", async function() {
        const note = await model.read("n1");
        assert.exists(note);
        assert.deepEqual({ key: note.key, title: note.title, body:
        note.body }, {
            key: "n1", title: "Note 1 FAIL", body: "Note 1"
        });
    });
    it("Unknown note should fail", async function() {
        try {
            const note = await model.read("badkey12");
            assert.notExists(note);
            throw new Error("should not get here");
        } catch(err) {
            // this is expected, so do not indicate error
            assert.notEqual(err.message, "should not get here");
        }
    });
});

describe("change note", function() {
    it("after a successful model.update", async function() {
        const newnote = await model.update("n1", "Note 1 title
        changed", "Note 1 body changed");
        const note = await model.read("n1");
        assert.exists(note);
        assert.deepEqual({ key: note.key, title: note.title, body:
        note.body }, {
            key: "n1", title: "Note 1 title changed", body: "Note 1 body
        changed"
        });
    });
});

describe("destroy note", function() {
    it("should remove note", async function() {
        await model.destroy("n1");
        const keyz = await model.keylist();
        assert.exists(keyz);
        assert.isArray(keyz);
        assert.lengthOf(keyz, 2);
        for (let key of keyz) {
            assert.match(key, /n[23]/, "correct key");
```

```
        }
    });
    it("should fail to remove unknown note", async function() {
        try {
            await model.destroy("badkey12");
            throw new Error("should not get here");
        } catch(err) {
            // this is expected, so do not indicate error
            assert.notEqual(err.message, "should not get here");
        }
    });
});

after(function() {  model.close(); });
});
```

Notice that for the negative tests – where the test passes if an error is thrown – we run
it in a `try/catch` block. The `throw new Error` line in each case should not execute
because the preceding code should throw an error. Therefore, we can check if the
message in that thrown error is the message which arrives, and fail the test if that's
the case.

Now, the test report:

```
$ npm run test-notes-memory

> notes-test@1.0.0 test-notes-memory /Users/david/chap11/notes/test
> NOTES_MODEL=memory mocha test-model

  Model Test
    check keylist
      √ should have three entries
      √ should have keys n1 n2 n3
      √ should have titles Node #
    read note
      √ should have proper note
      √ Unknown note should fail
    change note
      √ after a successful model.update
    destroy note
      √ should remove note
      √ should fail to remove unknown note


  8 passing (17ms)
```

In these additional tests, we have a couple of negative tests. In each test that we expect to fail, we supply a `notekey` that we know is not in the database, and we then ensure that the model gives us an error.

The Chai Assertions API includes some very expressive assertions. In this case, we've used the `deepEqual` method which does a deep comparison of two objects. In our case, it looks like this:

```
assert.deepEqual({ key: note.key, title: note.title, body: note.body
}, {
   key: "n1", title: "Note 1", body: "Note 1"
});
```

This reads nicely in the test code, but more importantly a reported test failure looks very nice. Since these are currently passing, try introducing an error by changing one of the expected value strings. Upon rerunning the test, you'll see:

```
Model Test
    check keylist
      √ should have three entries
      √ should have keys n1 n2 n3
      √ should have titles Node #
    read note
      1) should have proper note
      √ Unknown note should fail
    change note
      √ after a successful model.update
    destroy note
      √ should remove note
      √ should fail to remove unknown note


  7 passing (42ms)
  1 failing

  1) Model Test
       read note
         should have proper note:
      AssertionError: expected { Object (key, title, ...) } to deeply
      equal { Object (key, title, ...) }
      + expected - actual

       {
          "body": "Note 1"
          "key": "n1"
       -  "title": "Note 1"
       +  "title": "Note 1 FAIL"
       }
```

```
at Context.<anonymous> (test-model.js:53:16)
at <anonymous>
```

At the top is the status report of each test case. For one test, instead of a check mark is a number, and the number corresponds to the reported details at the bottom. Mocha presents test failures this way when the `spec` reporter is used. Mocha supports other test report formats, some of which produce data that can be sent into test status reporting systems. For more information, see `https://mochajs.org/#reporters`.

In this case, the failure was detected by a `deepEqual` method, which presents the detected object inequality in this way.

Testing database models

That was good, but we obviously won't run Notes in production with the in-memory Notes model. This means that we need to test all the other models.

Testing the LevelUP and filesystem models is easy, just add this to the scripts section of `package.json`:

```
"test-notes-levelup": "NOTES_MODEL=levelup mocha",
"test-notes-fs": "NOTES_MODEL=fs mocha",
```

Then run the following command:

```
$ npm run test-notes-fs
$ npm run test-notes-levelup
```

This will produce a successful test result.

The simplest database to test is SQLite3, since it requires zero setup. We have two SQLite3 models to test, let's start with `notes-sqlite3.js`. Add the following to the scripts section of `package.json`:

```
"test-notes-sqlite3": "rm -f chap11.sqlite3 && sqlite3 chap11.sqlite3
--init ../models/chap07.sql </dev/null && NOTES_MODEL=sqlite3
SQLITE_FILE=chap11.sqlite3 mocha test-model",
```

This command sequence puts the test database in the `chap11.sqlite3` file. It first initializes that database using the `sqlite3` command-line tool. Note that we've connected its input to `/dev/null` because the `sqlite3` command will prompt for input otherwise. Then, it runs the test suite passing in environment variables required to run against the SQLite3 model.

Running the test suite does find two errors:

```
$ npm run test-notes-sqlite3

> notes-test@1.0.0 test-notes-sqlite3 /Users/david/chap11/notes/test
> rm -f chap11.sqlite3 && sqlite3 chap11.sqlite3 --init
../models/chap07.sql </dev/null && NOTES_MODEL=sqlite3
SQLITE_FILE=chap11.sqlite3 mocha test-model


  Model Test
    check keylist
      √ should have three entries
      √ should have keys n1 n2 n3
      √ should have titles Node #
    read note
      √ should have proper note
      1) Unknown note should fail
    change note
      √ after a successful model.update (114ms)
    destroy note
      √ should remove note (103ms)
      2) should fail to remove unknown note


  6 passing (6s)
  2 failing

  1) Model Test
       read note
         Unknown note should fail:
     Uncaught TypeError: Cannot read property 'notekey' of undefined
      at Statement.db.get (/home/david/nodewebdev/node-web-
development-
    code-4th-edition/chap11/notes/models/notes-sqlite3.mjs:64:39)
  2) Model Test
       destroy note
         should fail to remove unknown note:

     AssertionError: expected 'should not get here' to not equal
  'should not get here'
      + expected - actual
```

The failing test calls `model.read("badkey12")`, a key which we know does not exist. Writing negative tests paid off. The failing line of code at `models/notes-sqlite3.mjs` (line 64) reads as follows:

```
const note = new Note(row.notekey, row.title, row.body);
```

It's easy enough to insert `console.log(util.inspect(row));` just before this and learn that, for the failing call, SQLite3 gave us `undefined` for `row`, explaining the error message.

The test suite calls the `read` function multiple times with a `notekey` value that does exist. Obviously, when given an invalid `notekey` value, the query gives an empty results set and SQLite3 invokes the callback with both the `undefined` error and the `undefined` row values. This is common behavior for database modules. An empty result set isn't an error, and therefore we received no error and an undefined `row`.

In fact, we saw this behavior earlier with `models/notes-sequelize.mjs`. The equivalent code in `models/notes-sequelize.mjs` does the right thing, and it has a check, which we can adapt. Let's rewrite the `read` function in `models/notes-sqlite.mjs` to this:

```
export async function read(key) {
   var db = await connectDB();
   var note = await new Promise((resolve, reject) => {
      db.get("SELECT * FROM notes WHERE notekey = ?", [ key ], (err,
row)
        => {
           if (err) return reject(err);
           if (!row) { reject(new Error(`No note found for ${key}`)); }
           else {
               const note = new Note(row.notekey, row.title, row.body);
               resolve(note);
           }
        }
     });
   });
   return note;
}
```

This is simple, we just check whether `row` is `undefined` and, if so, throw an error. While the database doesn't see an empty results set as an error, Notes does. Furthermore, Notes already knows how to deal with a thrown error in this case. Make this change and that particular test case passes.

There is a second similar error in the `destroy` logic. The test to destroy a nonexistent note fails to produce an error at this line:

```
await model.destroy("badkey12");
```

If we inspect the other models, they're throwing errors for a nonexistent key. In SQL, it obviously is not an error if this SQL (from `models/notes-sqlite3.mjs`) does not delete anything:

```
db.run("DELETE FROM notes WHERE notekey = ?;", ... );
```

Unfortunately, there isn't a SQL option to make this SQL statement fail if it does not delete any records. Therefore, we must add a check to see if a record exists. Namely:

```
export async function destroy(key) {
    const db = await connectDB();
    const note = await read(key);
    return await new Promise((resolve, reject) => {
        db.run("DELETE FROM notes WHERE notekey = ?;", [ key ], err =>
        {
            if (err) return reject(err);
            resolve();
        });
    });
}
```

Therefore, we read the note and as a byproduct we verify the note exists. If the note doesn't exist, `read` will throw an error, and the `DELETE` operation will not even run.

These are the bugs we referred to in Chapter 7, *Data Storage and Retrieval*. We simply forgot to check for these conditions in this particular model. Thankfully, our diligent testing caught the problem. At least, that's the story to tell the managers rather than telling them that we forgot to check for something we already knew could happen.

Now that we've fixed `models/notes-sqlite3.mjs`, let's also test `models/notes-sequelize.mjs` using the SQLite3 database. To do this, we need a connection object to specify in the `SEQUELIZE_CONNECT` variable. While we can reuse the existing one, let's create a new one. Create a file named `test/sequelize-sqlite.yaml` containing this:

```
dbname: notestest
username:
password:
params:
    dialect: sqlite
    storage: notestest-sequelize.sqlite3
    logging: false
```

This way, we don't overwrite the production database instance with our test suite. Since the test suite destroys the database it tests, it must be run against a database we are comfortable destroying. The logging parameter turns off the voluminous output `Sequelize` produces so that we can read the test results report.

Add the following to the scripts section of `package.json`:

```
"test-notes-sequelize-sqlite": "NOTES_MODEL=sequelize
SEQUELIZE_CONNECT=sequelize-sqlite.yaml mocha test-model"
```

Then run the test suite:

```
$ npm run test-notes-sequelize-sqlite
  ..
  8 passing (2s)
```

We pass with flying colors! We've been able to leverage the same test suite against multiple Notes models. We even found two bugs in one model. But, we have two test configurations remaining to test.

Our test results matrix reads as follows:

- `models-fs`: PASS
- `models-memory`: PASS
- `models-levelup`: PASS
- `models-sqlite3`: 2 failures, now fixed
- `models-sequelize`: with SQLite3: PASS
- `models-sequelize`: with MySQL: untested
- `models-mongodb`: untested

The two untested models both require the setup of a database server. We avoided testing these combinations, but our manager won't accept that excuse because the CEO needs to know we've completed the test cycles. Notes must be tested in a similar configuration to the production environment.

In production, we'll be using a regular database server, of course, with MySQL or MongoDB being the primary choices. Therefore, we need a way that incurs a low overhead to run tests against those databases. Testing against the production configuration must be so easy that we should feel no resistance in doing so, to ensure that tests are run often enough to make the desired impact.

Fortunately, we've already had experience of a technology that supports easily creating and destroying the deployment infrastructure. Hello, Docker!

Using Docker to manage test infrastructure

One advantage Docker gives is the ability to install the production environment on our laptop. It's then very easy to push the same Docker setup to the cloud-hosting environment for staging or production deployment.

What we'll do in this section is demonstrate reusing the Docker Compose configuration defined previously for test infrastructure, and to automate executing the Notes test suite inside the containers using a shell script. Generally speaking, it's important to replicate the production environment when running tests. Docker can make this an easy thing to do.

Using Docker, we'll be able to easily test against a database, and have a simple method for starting and stopping a test version of our production environment. Let's get started.

Docker Compose to orchestrate test infrastructure

We had a great experience using Docker Compose to orchestrate Notes application deployment. The whole system, with four independent services, is easily described in `compose/docker-compose.yml`. What we'll do is duplicate the Compose file, then make a couple of small changes required to support test execution.

Let's start by making a new directory, `test-compose`, as a sibling to the `notes`, `users`, and `compose` directories. Copy `compose/docker-compose.yml` to the newly created `test-compose` directory. We'll be making several changes to this file and a couple of small changes to the existing Dockerfiles.

We want to change the container and network names so our test infrastructure doesn't clobber the production infrastructure. We'll constantly delete and recreate the test containers, so as to keep the developers happy, we'll leave development infrastructure alone and perform testing on separate infrastructure. By maintaining separate test containers and networks, our test scripts can do anything they like without disturbing the development or production containers.

Consider this change to the `db-auth` and `db-notes` containers:

```
db-userauth-test:
  build: ../authnet
  container_name: db-userauth-test
  networks:
    - authnet-test
  environment:
    MYSQL_RANDOM_ROOT_PASSWORD: "true"
    MYSQL_USER: userauth-test
    MYSQL_PASSWORD: userauth-test
    MYSQL_DATABASE: userauth-test
  volumes:
    - db-userauth-test-data:/var/lib/mysql
  restart: always
..
db-notes-test:
  build: ../frontnet
  container_name: db-notes-test
  networks:
    - frontnet-test
  environment:
    MYSQL_RANDOM_ROOT_PASSWORD: "true"
    MYSQL_USER: notes-test
    MYSQL_PASSWORD: notes12345
    MYSQL_DATABASE: notes-test
  volumes:
    - db-notes-test-data:/var/lib/mysql
  restart: always
```

This is the same as earlier, but with `-test` appended to container and network names.

That's the first change we must make, append `-test` to every container and network name in `test-compose/docker-compose.yml`. Everything we'll do with tests will run on completely separate containers, hostnames, and networks from those of the development instance.

This change will affect the `notes-test` and `userauth-test` services because the database server hostnames are now `db-auth-test` and `db-notest-test`. There are several environment variables or configuration files to update.

Another consideration is the environment variables required to configure the services. Previously, we defined all environment variables in the Dockerfiles. It's extremely useful to reuse those Dockerfiles so we know we're testing the same deployment as is used in production. But we need to tweak the configuration settings to match the test infrastructure.

The database configuration shown here is an example. The same Dockerfiles are used, but we also define environment variables in `test-compose/docker-compose.yml`. As you might expect, this overrides the Dockerfile environment variables with the values set here:

```yaml
  userauth-test:
    build: ../users
    container_name: userauth-test
    depends_on:
      - db-userauth-test
    networks:
      - authnet-test
      - frontnet-test
    environment:
      DEBUG: ""
      NODE_ENV: "test"
      SEQUELIZE_CONNECT: "sequelize-docker-test-mysql.yaml"
      HOST_USERS_TEST: "localhost"
    restart: always
    volumes:
      - ./reports-userauth:/reports
  ..
  notes-test:
    build: ../notes
    container_name: notes-test
    depends_on:
      - db-notes-test
    networks:
      - frontnet-test
    ports:
      - "3000:3000"
    restart: always
    environment:
      NODE_ENV: "test"
      SEQUELIZE_CONNECT: "test/sequelize-mysql.yaml"
      USER_SERVICE_URL: "http://userauth-test:3333"
    volumes:
      - ./reports-notes:/reports
  ...
  networks:
    frontnet-test:
```

```
    driver: bridge
  authnet-test:
    driver: bridge

volumes:
  db-userauth-test-data:
  db-notes-test-data:
```

Again, we changed the container and network names to append `-test`. We moved
some of the environment variables from Dockerfile to `test-compose/docker-compose.yml`. Finally, we added some data volumes to mount host directories inside
the container.

Another thing to do is to set up directories to store test code. A common practice in
Node.js projects is to put test code in the same directory as the application code.
Earlier in this chapter, we did so, implementing a small test suite in the `notes/test`
directory. As it stands, `notes/Dockerfile` does not copy that directory into the
container. The test code must exist in the container to execute the tests. Another issue
is it's helpful to not deploy test code in production.

What we can do is to ensure that `test-compose/docker-compose.yml` mounts
`notes/test` into the container:

```
notes-test:
  ...
  volumes:
    - ./reports-notes:/reports
    - ../notes/test:/notesapp/test
```

This gives us the best of both worlds.

- The test code is in `notes/test` where it belongs
- The test code is not copied into the production container
- In test mode, the `test` directory appears where it belongs

We have a couple of configuration files remaining for the `Sequelize` database
connection to set up.

For the `userauth-test` container, the SEQUELIZE_CONNECT variable now refers to a
configuration file that does not exist, thanks to overriding the variable in
`user/Dockerfile`. Let's create that file as `test-compose/userauth/sequelize-docker-mysql.yaml`, containing the following:

```
dbname: userauth-test
username: userauth-test
```

```
password: userauth-test
params:
    host: db-userauth-test
    port: 3306
    dialect: mysql
```

The values match the variables passed to the `db-userauth-test` container. Then we must ensure this configuration file is mounted into the `userauth-test` container:

```
userauth-test:
  ...
  volumes:
    - ./reports-userauth:/reports
    - ./userauth/sequelize-docker-test-mysql.yaml:/userauth/sequelize-docker-test-mysql.yaml
```

For `notes-test` we have a configuration file, `test/sequelize-mysql.yaml`, to put in the `notes/test` directory:

```
dbname: notes-test
username: notes-test
password: notes12345
params:
    host: db-notes-test
    port: 3306
    dialect: mysql
    logging: false
```

Again, this matches the configuration variables in `db-notes-test`. In `test-compose/docker-compose.yml`, we mount that file into the container.

Executing tests under Docker Compose

Now we're ready to execute some of the tests inside a container. We've used a Docker Compose file to describe the test environment for the Notes application, using the same architecture as in the production environment. The test scripts and configuration has been injected into the containers. The question is, how do we automate test execution?

The technique we'll use is to run a shell script, and use `docker exec -it` to execute commands to run the test scripts. This is somewhat automated, and with some more work it can be fully automated.

In `test-compose`, let's make a shell script called `run.sh` (on Windows, `run.ps1`):

```
docker-compose stop

docker-compose build
docker-compose up --force-recreate -d
docker ps
docker network ls

sleep 20
docker exec -it --workdir /notesapp/test -e DEBUG= notes-test npm
install

docker exec -it --workdir /notesapp/test -e DEBUG= notes-test npm run
test-notes-memory
docker exec -it --workdir /notesapp/test -e DEBUG= notes-test npm run
test-notes-fs
docker exec -it --workdir /notesapp/test -e DEBUG= notes-test npm run
test-notes-levelup
docker exec -it --workdir /notesapp/test -e DEBUG= notes-test npm run
test-notes-sqlite3
docker exec -it --workdir /notesapp/test -e DEBUG= notes-test npm run
test-notes-sequelize-sqlite
docker exec -it --workdir /notesapp/test -e DEBUG= notes-test npm run
test-notes-sequelize-mysql

docker-compose stop
```

It's common practice to run tests out of a continuous integration system such as Jenkins. Continuous integration systems automatically run builds or tests against software products. The build and test results data is used to automatically generate status pages. Visit `https://jenkins.io/index.html`, which is a good starting point for a Jenkins job.

That makes the first real step to building the containers, followed by bringing them up. The script sleeps for a few seconds to give the containers time to fully instantiate themselves.

The subsequent commands all follow a particular pattern that is important to understand. The commands are executed in the `/notesapp/test` directory thanks to the `--workdir` option. Remember that directory is injected into the container by the Docker Compose file.

Using `-e DEBUG=` we've disabled the `DEBUG` options. If those options are set, we'd have excess unwanted output in the test results, so using this option ensures that debugging output doesn't occur.

Now that you understand the options, you can see that the subsequent commands are all executed in the `test` directory using the `package.json` in that directory. It starts by running `npm install`, and then running each of the scenarios in the test matrix.

To run the tests, simply type:

```
$ sh -x run.sh
```

That's good, we've got most of our test matrix automated and pretty well squared away. There is a glaring hole in the test matrix and plugging that hole will let us see how to set up MongoDB under Docker.

MongoDB setup under Docker and testing Notes against MongoDB

In `Chapter 7`, *Data Storage and Retrieval*, we developed MongoDB support for Notes, and since then we've focused on `Sequelize`. To make up for that slight, let's make sure we at least test our MongoDB support. Testing on MongoDB would simply require defining a container for the MongoDB database and a little bit of configuration.

Visit `https://hub.docker.com/_/mongo/` for the official MongoDB container. You'll be able to retrofit this to allow deploying the Notes application running on MongoDB.

Add this to `test-compose/docker-compose.yml`:

```
db-notes-mongo-test:
  image: mongo:3.6-jessie
  container_name: db-notes-mongo-test
  networks:
    - frontnet-test
  volumes:
    - ./db-notes-mongo:/data/db
```

That's all that's required to add a MongoDB container to a Docker Compose file. We've connected it to `frontnet` so that the `notes` (`notes-test`) container can access the service.

Then in `notes/test/package.json` we add a line to facilitate running tests on MongoDB:

```
"test-notes-mongodb": "MONGO_URL=mongodb://db-notes-mongo-test/
MONGO_DBNAME=chap11-test NOTES_MODEL=mongodb mocha --no-timeouts test-
model"
```

Simply by adding the MongoDB container to `frontnet-test`, the database is available at the URL shown here. Hence, it's simple to now run the test suite using the Notes MongoDB model.

The `--no-timeouts` option was necessary to avoid a spurious error while testing the suite against MongoDB. This option instructs Mocha to not check whether a test case execution takes too long.

The final requirement is to add this line in `run.sh` (or `run.ps1` for Windows):

```
docker exec -it --workdir /notesapp/test -e DEBUG= notes-test npm run
test-notes-mongodb
```

That, then, ensures MongoDB is tested during every test run.

We can now report to the manager the final test results matrix:

- `models-fs`: PASS
- `models-memory`: PASS
- `models-levelup`: PASS
- `models-sqlite3`: Two failures, now fixed, PASS
- `models-sequelize` with SQLite3: PASS
- `models-sequelize` with MySQL: PASS
- `models-mongodb`: PASS

The manager will tell you "good job" and then remember that the Models are only a portion of the Notes application. We've left two areas completely untested:

- The REST API for the user authentication service
- Functional testing of the user interface

Let's get on with those testing areas.

Testing REST backend services

It's now time to turn our attention to the user authentication service. We've
mentioned tests of this service, saying that we'll get to them later. We had developed
some scripts for ad hoc testing, which have been useful all along. But later is
now, and it's time to get cracking on some real tests.

There's a question of which tool to use for testing the authentication service. Mocha
does a good job of organizing a series of test cases, and we should reuse it here. But
the thing we have to test is a REST service. The customer of this service, the Notes
application, uses it through the REST API, giving us a perfect rationalization to test at
the REST interface. Our ad hoc scripts used the SuperAgent library to simplify
making REST API calls. There happens to be a companion library, SuperTest, that is
meant for REST API testing. Read its documentation here: `https://www.npmjs.com/`
`package/supertest`.

We've already made the `test-compose/userauth` directory. In that directory, create
a file named `test.js`:

```
'use strict';

const assert = require('chai').assert;
const request = require('supertest')(process.env.URL_USERS_TEST);
const util = require('util');
const url = require('url');
const URL = url.URL;

const authUser = 'them';
const authKey = 'D4ED43C0-8BD6-4FE2-B358-7C0E230D11EF';

describe("Users Test", function() {
    ... Test code follows
});
```

This sets up Mocha and the SuperTest client. The `URL_USERS_TEST` environment
variable specifies the base URL of the server to run the test against. You'll almost
certainly be using `http://localhost:3333` given the configuration we've used
earlier in the book. SuperTest initializes itself a little differently to SuperAgent. The
SuperTest module exposes a function that we call with
the `URL_USERS_TEST` environment variable, then we use THAT `request` object
throughout the rest of the script to make REST API requests.

This variable was already set in `test-compose/docker-compose.yml` with the required value. The other thing of importance is a pair of variables to store the authentication user ID and key:

```
beforeEach(async function() {
  await request.post('/create-user')
      .send({
          username: "me", password: "w0rd", provider: "local",
          familyName: "Einarrsdottir", givenName: "Ashildr",
          middleName: "",
          emails: [], photos: []
      })
      .set('Content-Type', 'application/json')
      .set('Acccept', 'application/json')
      .auth(authUser, authKey);
});
afterEach(async function() {
  await request.delete('/destroy/me')
      .set('Content-Type', 'application/json')
      .set('Acccept', 'application/json')
      .auth(authUser, authKey);
});
```

If you remember, the `beforeEach` function is run immediately before every test case, and `afterEach` is run afterward. These functions use the REST API to create our test user before running the test, and then afterward to destroy the test user. That way our tests can assume this user will exist:

```
describe("List user", function() {
    it("list created users", async function() {
        const res = await request.get('/list')
            .set('Content-Type', 'application/json')
            .set('Acccept', 'application/json')
            .auth(authUser, authKey);
      assert.exists(res.body);
      assert.isArray(res.body);
      assert.lengthOf(res.body, 1);
      assert.deepEqual(res.body[0], {
          username: "me", id: "me", provider: "local",
          familyName: "Einarrsdottir", givenName: "Ashildr",
          middleName: "",
          emails: [], photos: []
      });
    });
});
```

Now, we can turn to testing some API methods, such as the /list operation.

We have already guaranteed that there is an account, in the beforeEach method, so /list should give us an array with one entry.

This follows the general pattern for using Mocha to test a REST API method. First, we use SuperTest's request object to call the API method, and await its result. Once we have the result, we use assert methods to validate it is what is expected:

```
describe("find user", function() {
  it("find created users", async function() {
    const res = await request.get('/find/me')
            .set('Content-Type', 'application/json')
            .set('Acccept', 'application/json')
            .auth(authUser, authKey);
    assert.exists(res.body);
    assert.isObject(res.body);
    assert.deepEqual(res.body, {
            username: "me", id: "me", provider: "local",
            familyName: "Einarrsdottir", givenName: "Ashildr",
            middleName: "",
            emails: [], photos: []
    });
  });
  it("fail to find non-existent users", async function() {
    var res;
    try {
      res = await request.get('/find/nonExistentUser')
            .set('Content-Type', 'application/json')
            .set('Acccept', 'application/json')
            .auth(authUser, authKey);
    } catch(e) {
      return; // Test is okay in this case
    }
    assert.exists(res.body);
    assert.isObject(res.body);
    assert.deepEqual(res.body, {});
  });
});
```

We are checking the `/find` operation in two ways:

- Looking for the account we know exists – failure is indicated if the user account is not found
- Looking for the one we know does not exist – failure is indicated if we receive something other than an error or an empty object

Add this test case:

```
describe("delete user", function() {
  it("delete nonexistent users", async function() {
    var res;
    try {
      res = await request.delete('/destroy/nonExistentUser')
             .set('Content-Type', 'application/json')
             .set('Acccept', 'application/json')
             .auth(authUser, authKey);
    } catch(e) {
      return; // Test is okay in this case
    }
    assert.exists(res);
    assert.exists(res.error);
    assert.notEqual(res.status, 200);
  });
});
```

Finally, we should check the `/destroy` operation. We already check this operation in the `afterEach` method, where we `destroy` a known user account. We need to also perform the negative test and verify its behavior against an account we know does not exist.

The desired behavior is that either an error is thrown, or the result shows an HTTP `status` indicating an error. In fact, the current authentication server code gives a 500 status code along with some other information.

In `test-compose/docker-compose.yml`, we need to inject this script, `test.js`, into the `userauth-test` container. We'll add that here:

```
userauth-test:
  ...
  volumes:
    - ./reports userauth:/reports
    - ./userauth/sequelize-docker-test-mysql.yaml:/userauth/sequelize-
docker-test-mysql.yaml
    - ./userauth/test.js:/userauth/test.js
```

We have a test script, and have injected that script into the desired container (`userauth-test`). The next step is to automate running this test. One way is to add this to `run.sh` (aka `run.ps1` on Windows):

```
docker exec -it -e DEBUG= userauth-test npm install supertest mocha
chai
docker exec -it -e DEBUG= userauth-test ./node_modules/.bin/mocha
test.js
```

Now, if you run the `run.sh` test script you'll see the required packages get installed, and then this test suite execution.

Automating test results reporting

It's cool we have automated test execution, and Mocha makes the test results look nice with all those check marks. What if the management wants a graph of test failure trends over time? Or there could be any number of reasons to report test results as data rather than a user-friendly printout on the console.

Mocha uses what's called a Reporter to report test results. A Mocha Reporter is a module that prints data in whatever format it supports. Information is on the Mocha website: `https://mochajs.org/#reporters`.

You will find the current list of available `reporters` like so:

```
# mocha --reporters

    dot - dot matrix
    doc - html documentation
    spec - hierarchical spec list
    json - single json object
    progress - progress bar
    list - spec-style listing
    tap - test-anything-protocol
...
```

Then you use a specific `reporter` like so:

```
# mocha --reporter tap test
1..4
ok 1 Users Test List user list created users
ok 2 Users Test find user find created users
ok 3 Users Test find user fall to find non-existent users
ok 4 Users Test delete user delete nonexistent users
# tests 4
```

```
# pass 4
# fail 0
```

Test Anything Protocol (TAP) is a widely used test results format, increasing the possibility of finding higher level reporting tools. Obviously, the next step would be to save the results into a file somewhere, after mounting a host directory into the container.

Frontend headless browser testing with Puppeteer

A big cost area in testing is manual user interface testing. Therefore, a wide range of tools have been developed to automate running tests at the HTTP level. Selenium is a popular tool implemented in Java, for example. In the Node.js world, we have a few interesting choices. The *chai-http* plugin to Chai would let us interact at the HTTP level with the Notes application, while staying within the now-familiar Chai environment.

However, for this section, we'll use Puppeteer (`https://github.com/GoogleChrome/puppeteer`). This tool is a high-level Node.js module to control a headless Chrome or Chromium browser, using the DevTools protocol. That protocol allows tools to instrument, inspect, debug, and profile Chromium or Chrome.

Puppeteer is meant to be a general purpose test automation tool, and has a strong feature set for that purpose. Because it's easy to make web page screenshots with Puppeteer, it can also be used in a screenshot service.

Because Puppeteer is controlling a real web browser, your user interface tests will be very close to live browser testing without having to hire a human to do the work. Because it uses a headless version of Chrome, no visible browser window will show on your screen, and tests can be run in the background, instead. A downside to this attractive story is that Puppeteer only works against Chrome. Meaning that an automated test against Chrome does not test your application against other browsers, such as Opera or Firefox.

Setting up Puppeteer

Let's first set up the directory and install the packages:

```
$ mkdir test-compose/notesui
$ cd test-compose/notesui
$ npm init
... answer the questions
$ npm install puppeteer@1.1.x mocha@5.x chai@4.1.x --save
```

During installation, you'll see that Puppeteer causes the download of Chromium like
so:

```
Downloading Chromium r497674 - 92.5 Mb [====================] 100%
0.0s
```

The `puppeteer` module will launch that Chromium instance as needed, managing it
as a background process, and communicating with it using the DevTools protocol.

In the script we're about to write, we need a user account that we can use to log in
and perform some actions. Fortunately, we already have a script to set up a test
account. In `users/package.json`, add this line to the scripts section:

```
"setupuser": "PORT=3333 node users-add",
```

We're about to write this test script, but let's finish the setup, the final bit of which is
adding these lines to `run.sh`:

```
docker exec -it userauth-test npm run setupuser
docker exec -it notesapp-test npm run test-docker-ui
```

When executed, these two lines ensure that the test user is set up, and it then runs the
user interface tests.

Improving testability in the Notes UI

While the Notes application displays well in the browser, how do we write test
software to distinguish one page from another? The key requirement is for test
scripts to inspect the page, determine which page is being displayed, and read the
data on the page. That means each HTML element must be easily addressable using a
CSS selector.

While developing the Notes application, we forgot to do that, and the **Software Quality Engineering** (SQE) manager has requested our assistance. At stake is the testing budget, which will be stretched further the more the SQE team can automate their tests.

All that's necessary is to add a few `id` or `class` attributes to HTML elements to improve testability. With a few identifiers, and a commitment to maintain those identifiers, the SQE team can write repeatable test scripts to validate the application.

In `notes/partials/header.hbs,` change these lines:

```
...
<a id="btnGoHome" class="navbar-brand" href='/'>
...
{{#if user}}
...
<a class="nav-item nav-link btn btn-dark col-auto" id="btnLogout"
href="/users/logout">...</a>
<a class="nav-item nav-link btn btn-dark col-auto" id="btnAddNote"
href='/notes/add'>...</a>
{{else}}
...
<a class="nav-item nav-link btn btn-dark col-auto" id="btnloginlocal"
href="/users/login">..</a>
<a class="nav-item nav-link btn btn-dark col-auto"
                          id="btnLoginTwitter"
href="/users/auth/twitter">...</a>
...
{{/if}}
...
```

In `notes/views/index.hbs,` make these changes:

```
<div id="notesHomePage" class="container-fluid">
  <div class="row">
    <div id="notetitles" class="col-12 btn-group-vertical"
role="group">
      {{#each notelist}}
      <a id="{{key}}" class="btn btn-lg btn-block btn-outline-dark"
         href="/notes/view?key={{ key }}">...</a>
      {{/each}}
    </div>
  </div>
</div>
```

In `notes/views/login.hbs`, make these changes:

```
<div id="notesLoginPage" class="container-fluid">
...
<form id="notesLoginForm" method='POST' action='/users/login'>
...
<button type="submit" id="formLoginBtn" class="btn btn-
default">Submit</button>
</form>
...
</div>
```

In `notes/views/notedestroy.hbs`, make these changes:

```
<form id="formDestroyNote" method='POST'
action='/notes/destroy/confirm'>
...
<button id="btnConfirmDeleteNote" type="submit" value='DELETE'
                class="btn btn-outline-dark">DELETE</button>
...
</form>
```

In `notes/views/noteedit.hbs`, make these changes:

```
<form id="formAddEditNote" method='POST' action='/notes/save'>
...
<button id='btnSave' type="submit" class="btn btn-
default">Submit</button>
...
</form>
```

In `notes/views/noteview.hbs`, make these changes:

```
<div id="noteView" class="container-fluid">
...
<p id="showKey">Key: {{ notekey }}</p>
...
<a id="btnDestroyNote" class="btn btn-outline-dark"
    href="/notes/destroy?key={{notekey}}" role="button"> ...  </a>
<a id="btnEditNote" class="btn btn-outline-dark"
    href="/notes/edit?key={{notekey}}" role="button"> ... </a>
<button id="btnComment" type="button" class="btn btn-outline-dark"
    data-toggle="modal" data-target="#notes-comment-modal"> ...
</button>
...
</div>
```

What we've done is add `id=` attributes to selected elements in the templates. We can now easily write CSS selectors to address any element. The engineering team can also start using these selectors in UI code.

Puppeteer test script for Notes

In `test-compose/notesui`, create a file named `uitest.js` containing the following:

```
const puppeteer = require('puppeteer');
const assert = require('chai').assert;
const util = require('util');
const { URL } = require('url');

describe('Notes', function() {
    this.timeout(10000);
    let browser;
    let page;

    before(async function() {
        browser = await puppeteer.launch({ slomo: 500 });
        page = await browser.newPage();
        await page.goto(process.env.NOTES_HOME_URL);
    });

    after(async function() {
        await page.close();
        await browser.close();
    });
});
```

This is the start of a Mocha test suite. In the `before` function, we set up Puppeteer by launching a Puppeteer instance, starting a new Page object, and telling that Page to go to the Notes application home page. That URL is passed in using the named environment variable.

It's useful to first think about scenarios we might want to verify with the Notes applications:

- Log into the Notes application
- Add a note to the application
- View an added note
- Delete an added note
- Log out
- And so on

Here's code for an implementation of the Login scenario:

```
describe('Login', function() {
    before(async function() { ... });
    it('should click on login button', async function() {
        const btnLogin = await page.waitForSelector('#btnloginlocal');
        await btnLogin.click();
    });
    it('should fill in login form', async function() {
        const loginForm = await page.waitForSelector('#notesLoginPage
        #notesLoginForm');
        await page.type('#notesLoginForm #username', "me");
        await page.type('#notesLoginForm #password', "w0rd");
        await page.click('#formLoginBtn');
    });
    it('should return to home page', async function() {
        const home = await page.waitForSelector('#notesHomePage');
        const btnLogout = await page.waitForSelector('#btnLogout');
        const btnAddNote = await page.$('#btnAddNote');
        assert.exists(btnAddNote);
    });
    after(async function() { ... });
});
```

This test sequence handles the Login Scenario. It shows you a few of the Puppeteer API methods. Documentation of the full API is at `https://github.com/ GoogleChrome/puppeteer/blob/master/docs/api.md`. The Page object encapsulates the equivalent of a browser tab in Chrome/Chromium.

The `waitForSelector` function does what it says – it waits until an HTML element matching the CSS selector appears, and it will wait over one or more page refreshes. There are several variants of this function to allow waiting for several kinds of things. This function returns a Promise, making it worth our time to use async functions in our test code. The Promise will resolve to an `ElementHandle`, which is a wrapper around an HTML element, or else throw an exception, which would conveniently make the test fail.

The named element, `#btnloginlocal`, is in `partials/header.hbs`, and will show up only when a user is not logged in. Hence, we will have determined that the browser is currently displaying a Notes page, and that it is not logged in.

The `click` method does what it suggests, and causes a mouse button click on the referenced HTML element. If you want to emulate a tap, such as for a mobile device, there is a `tap` method for that purpose.

The next stage of the test sequence picks up from that click. The browser should have gone to the Login page, and therefore this CSS selector should become valid: `#notesLoginPage #notesLoginForm`. What we do next is type text for our test user ID and password into the corresponding form elements, and then click on the **Log In** button.

The next test stage picks up from there, and the browser should be on the home page as determined by this CSS selector: `#notesHomePage`. If we were logged in successfully, the page should have **Log Out** (`#btnLogout`) and **ADD Note** buttons (`#btnAddNote`).

In this case, we've used a different function, `$`, to check if the **ADD Note** button exists. Unlike the `wait` functions, `$` simply queries the current page without waiting. If the named CSS Selector is not in the current page, it simply returns `null` rather than throwing an exception. Therefore, to determine that the element exists, we use `assert.exists` rather than relying on the thrown exception.

Running the login scenario

Now that we have one test scenario entered, let's give it a whirl. In one window, start the Notes test infrastructure:

```
$ cd test-compose
$ docker-compose up --force-rebuild
```

Then in another window:

```
$ docker exec -it userauth bash
userauth# PORT=3333 node ./users-add.js
userauth# exit
$ cd test-compare/notesui
$ NOTES_HOME_URL=http://localhost:3000 mocha --no-timeouts uitest.js

  Notes
    Login
      √ should click on login button
      √ should fill in login form (72ms)
      √ should return to home page (1493ms)

  3 passing (3s)
```

The NOTES_HOME_URL variable is what the script looks for to direct the Chromium
browser to use the Notes application. To run the tests, we should use Docker
Compose to launch the test infrastructure, and then ensure the test user is installed in
the user database.

The Add Note scenario

Add this to uitest.js:

```
describe('Add Note', function() {
    // before(async function() { ... });
    it('should see Add Note button', async function() {
        const btnAddNote = await page.waitForSelector('#btnAddNote');
        await btnAddNote.click();
    });
    it('should fill in Add Note form', async function() {
        const formAddEditNote = await
        page.waitForSelector('#formAddEditNote');
        await page.type('#notekey', 'key42');
        await page.type('#title', 'Hello, world!');
        await page.type('#body', 'Lorem ipsum dolor');
        await page.click('#btnSave');
    });
    it('should view note', async function() {
        await page.waitForSelector('#noteView');
        const shownKey = await page.$eval('#showKey', el =>
        el.innerText);
        assert.exists(shownKey);
```

```
            assert.isString(shownKey);
            assert.include(shownKey, 'key42');
            const shownTitle = await page.$eval('#notetitle', el =>
            el.innerText);
            assert.exists(shownTitle);
            assert.isString(shownTitle);
            assert.include(shownTitle, 'Hello, world!');
            const shownBody = await page.$eval('#notebody', el =>
            el.innerText);
            assert.exists(shownBody);
            assert.isString(shownBody);
            assert.include(shownBody, 'Lorem ipsum dolor');
        });
        it('should go to home page', async function() {
            await page.waitForSelector('#btnGoHome');
            await page.goto(process.env.NOTES_HOME_URL);
            // await page.click('#btnGoHome');
            await page.waitForSelector('#notesHomePage');
            const titles = await page.$('#notetitles');
            assert.exists(titles);
            const key42 = await page.$('#key42');
            assert.exists(key42);
            const btnLogout = await page.$('#btnLogout');
            assert.exists(btnLogout);
            const btnAddNote = await page.$('#btnAddNote');
            assert.exists(btnAddNote);
        });
        // after(async function() { ... });
    });
```

This is a more involved scenario, in which we:

- Click on the **ADD Note** button
- Wait for the note edit screen to show up
- Fill in the text for the note and click the **Save** button
- Validate the note view page to ensure that's correct
- Validate the home page to ensure that's correct.

Most of this is using the same Puppeteer functions as before, but with a couple of additions.

The `$eval` function looks for the element matching the CSS selector, and invokes the callback function on that element. If no element is found an error is thrown instead. As used here, we are retrieving the text from certain elements on the screen, and validating that it matches what the test entered as the note. That's an end-to-end test of adding and retrieving notes.

The next difference is using `goto` instead of clicking on `#btnGoHome`.

As you add test scenarios to the test script, you'll find it easy for Puppeteer to have a spurious timeout, or for the login process to mysteriously not work, or other spurious errors.

Rather than go over the remaining scenarios, we'll spend the next section discussing how to mitigate such issues. But first we need to prove the scenario does work even if we have to run the test 10 times to get this result:

```
$ NOTES_HOME_URL=http://localhost:3000 ./node_modules/.bin/mocha --no-
timeouts uitest3.js

  Notes
    Login
      √ should click on login button (50ms)
      √ should fill in login form (160ms)
      √ should return to home page (281ms)
    Add Note
      √ should see Add Note button
      √ should fill in Add Note form (1843ms)
      √ should view note
      √ should go to home page (871ms)

  7 passing (5s)
```

Mitigating/preventing spurious test errors in Puppeteer scripts

The goal is to fully automate the test run, in order to avoid having to hire a human to babysit the test execution and spend time rerunning tests because of spurious errors. To do so, the tests need to be repeatable without any spurious errors. Puppeteer is a complex system – there is a Node.js module communicating with a Chromium instance running Headless in the background – and it seems easy for timing issues to cause a spurious error.

Configuring timeouts

Both Mocha and Puppeteer allow you to set timeout values, and a long timeout value can avoid triggering an error, if some action simply requires a long time to run. At the top of the test suite, we used this Mocha function:

```
this.timeout(10000);
```

That gives 10 seconds for every test case. If you want to use a longer timeout, increase that number.

The `puppeteer.launch` function can take a timeout value in its options object. By default, Puppeteer uses a 30-second timeout on most operations, and they all take an options object with a setting to change that timeout period. In this case, we've added the `slowMo` option to slow down operations on the browser.

Tracing events on the Page and the Puppeteer instance

Another useful tactic is to generate a trace of what happened so you can puzzle away. Inserting `console.log` statements is tedious and makes your code look a little ugly. Puppeteer offers a couple of methods to trace the actions and to dynamically turn off tracing.

In `uitest.js`, add this code:

```
function frameEvent(evtname, frame) {
    console.log(`${evtname} ${frame.url()} ${frame.title()}`);
}

function ignoreURL(url) {
    if (url.match(/\/assets\//) === null
      && url.match(/\/socket.io\//) === null
      && url.match(/fonts.gstatic.com/) === null
      && url.match(/fonts.googleapis.com/) === null) {
        return false;
    } else {
        return true;
    }
}
...
before(async function() {
    browser = await puppeteer.launch({ slomo: 500 });
    page = await browser.newPage();
```

```
    page.on('console', msg => {
        console.log(`${msg.type()} ${msg.text()} ${msg.args().join('
')}`);
    });
    page.on('error', err => {
        console.error(`page ERROR ${err.stack}`);
    });
    page.on('pageerror', err => {
        console.error(`page PAGEERROR ${err.stack}`);
    });
    page.on('request', req => {
        if (ignoreURL(req.url())) return;
        console.log(`page request ${req.method()} ${req.url()}`);
    });
    page.on('response', async (res) => {
        if (ignoreURL(res.url())) return;
        console.log(`page response ${res.status()} ${res.url()}`);
    });
    page.on('frameattached', async (frame) =>
frameEvent('frameattached', await frame));
    page.on('framedetached', async (frame) =>
frameEvent('framedetached', await frame));
    page.on('framenavigated', async (frame) =>
frameEvent('framenavigated', await frame));
    await page.goto(process.env.NOTES_HOME_URL);
});
...
```

That is, the Page object offers several event listeners in which we can output details
about various events, including HTTP requests and responses. We can even print out
the HTML text of the response. The `ignoreURL` function lets us suppress a few select
URLs so we're not inundated with unimportant requests and responses.

You can trace Puppeteer itself using its DEBUG environment variable. See the
README for more information: `https://github.com/GoogleChrome/puppeteer`.

Inserting pauses

It can be useful to insert a long pause at certain points to give the browser time to do
something. Try this function:

```
function waitFor(timeToWait) {
    return new Promise(resolve => {
      setTimeout(() => { resolve(true); }, timeToWait);
    });
};
```

This is how we implement the equivalent of a `sleep` function using Promises. Using `setTimeOut` this way, along with a timeout value, simply causes a delay for the given number of milliseconds.

To use this function, simply insert this into the test scenarios:

```
await waitFor(3000);
```

A variant on this is to wait for things to fully render in the browser. For example, you might have seen a pause before the **Home** icon in the upper-left corner fully renders. That pause can cause spurious errors, and this function can wait until that button fully renders itself:

```
async function waitForBtnGoHome() {
    return page.waitForSelector('#btnGoHome');
}
```

To use it:

```
await waitForBtnGoHome();
```

If you don't want to maintain this extra function, it's easy enough to add the `waitForSelector` call into your test cases instead.

Avoiding WebSockets conflicts

An error, `Cannot find context with specified id undefined`, can be thrown by Puppeteer. According to an issue in the Puppeteer issue queue, this can arise from unplanned interactions between Puppeteer and WebSockets: `https://github.com/GoogleChrome/puppeteer/issues/1325` This issue in turn affects the Socket.IO support in the Notes application, and therefore it may be useful to disable Socket.IO support during test runs.

It's fairly simple to allow disabling of Socket.IO. In `app.mjs`, add this exported function:

```
export function enableSocketio() {
  var ret = true;
  const env = process.env.NOTES_DISABLE_SOCKETIO;
  if (!env || env !== 'true') {
    ret = true;
  }
  return ret;
}
```

This looks for an environment variable to cause the function to return `true` or `false`.

In `routes/index.mjs` and `routes/notes.mjs`, add this line:

```
import { enableSocketio, sessionCookieName } from '../app';
```

We do this to import the preceding function. It also demonstrates some of the flexibility we get from ES6 Modules, because we can import just the required functions.

In `routes/index.mjs` and `routes/notes.mjs`, for every router function that calls `res.render` to send results, use the `enableSocketio` function as so:

```
res.render('view-name', {
   ...
   enableSocketio: enableSocketio()
});
```

Hence, we've imported the function and for every view we pass `enableSocketio` as data to the view template.

In `views/index.hbs` and `views/noteview.hbs`, we have a section of JavaScript code to implement SocketIO-based semi-real-time features. Surround each such section like so:

```
{{#if enableSocketio}}
...   JavaScript code for SocketIO support
{{/if}}
```

By eliminating the client-side SocketIO code, we ensure the user interface does not open a connection to the SocketIO service. The point of this exercise was to avoid using WebSockets to avoid issues with Puppeteer.

Similarly, in `views/noteview.hbs` support disabling the **Comment** button like so:

```
{{#if enableSocketio}}
    <button id="btnComment" type="button" class="btn btn-outline-dark"
        data-toggle="modal" data-target="#notes-comment-
modal">Comment</button>
{{/if}}
```

The final step would be to set the environment variable, `NOTES_DISABLE_SOCKETIO`, in the Docker Compose file.

Taking screenshots

One of Puppeteer's core features is to take screenshots, either as PNG or PDF files. In our test scripts, we can take screenshots to track what was on the screen at any given time during the test. For example, if the Login scenario spuriously fails to log in, we can see that in the screenshots:

```
await page.screenshot({
    type: 'png',
    path: `./screen/login-01-start.png`
});
```

Simply add code snippets like this throughout your test script. The filename shown here follows a convention where the first segment names the test scenario, the number is a sequence number within the test scenario, and the last describes the step within the test scenario.

Taking screenshots also provides another stage of validation. You may want to do visual validation of your application as well. The `pixelmatch` module can compare two PNG files, and therefore a set of so-called Golden Images can be maintained for comparison during test runs.

For an example of using Puppeteer this way, see: `https://meowni.ca/posts/2017-puppeteer-tests/`.

Summary

We've covered a lot of territory in this chapter, looking at three distinct areas of testing: unit testing, REST API testing, and UI functional tests. Ensuring that an application is well tested is an important step on the road to software success. A team that does not follow good testing practices is often bogged down with fixing regression after regression.

We've talked about the potential simplicity of simply using the assert module for testing. While the test frameworks, such as Mocha, provide great features, we can go a long way with a simple script.

There is a place for test frameworks, such as Mocha, if only to regularize our test cases, and to produce test results reports. We used Mocha and Chai for this, and these tools were quite successful. We even found a couple of bugs with a small test suite.

When starting down the unit testing road, one design consideration is mocking out dependencies. But it's not always a good use of our time to replace every dependency with a mock version.

To ease the administrative burden of running tests, we used Docker to automate setting up and tearing down the test infrastructure. Just as Docker was useful in automating deployment of the Notes application, it's also useful in automating test infrastructure deployment.

Finally, we were able to test the Notes web user interface in a real web browser. We can't trust that unit testing will find every bug; some bugs will only show up in the web browser. Even so, we've only touched the beginning of what could be tested in Notes.

In this book, we've covered the gamut of Node.js development, giving you a strong foundation from which to start developing Node.js applications.

In the next chapter, we'll explore RESTful web services.

12
REST – What You Did Not Know

Over the last few years, we have started taking for granted that data sources feeding for content, mobile device service feeds, or cloud computing are all driven by modern technologies, such as RESTful web services. Everybody has been talking about how their stateless model allows applications to scale easily and how it emphasizes on clear decoupling between data provisioning and data consumption. Nowadays, architects have started introducing the concept of microservices, aiming to reduce the complexity in systems by splitting their core components into small independent pieces that simply do a single task. So, enterprise-grade software is about to become a composite of such microservices. This makes it easy to maintain, and allows better life cycle management when new parts need to be introduced. Unsurprisingly, most of the microservices are serviced by RESTful frameworks. This fact may leave the impression that REST was invented sometime in the last decade, but that is far from the truth. In fact, REST has been around since the last decade of the previous century!

This chapter will walk you through the foundation of **Representational State Transfer (REST)** and will explain how REST couples with the HTTP protocol. You will look into five key principles that have to be considered while turning any HTTP application into a RESTful service-enabled application. You will also look at the differences between describing RESTful and classic **Simple Object Access Protocol (SOAP)**-based web services. Finally, you will learn how to utilize already-existing infrastructure for your benefit.

In this chapter, we will cover the following topics:

- REST fundamentals
- REST with HTTP
- Essential differences in the description, discovery, and documentation of RESTful services compared to classical SOAP-based services
- Taking advantage of existing infrastructure

REST fundamentals

It actually happened back in 1999, when a request for comments was submitted to the **Internet Engineering Task Force (IETF;** `http://www.ietf.org/`**)** via RFC 2616: *Hypertext Transfer Protocol-HTTP/1.1*. One of its authors, Roy Fielding, later defined a set of principles built around the HTTP and URI standards. This gave birth to REST as we know it today.

These definitions were given in `https://www.ics.uci.edu/ ~fielding/pubs/dissertation/fielding_dissertation.pdf` in the fifth chapter, *Representational State Transfer (REST)*, of Fielding's dissertation called *Architectural Styles and the Design of Network-Based Software Architectures*. The dissertation is still available at `http://www.ics.uci.edu/~fielding/pubs/dissertation/rest_arc h_style.htm`.

Let's look at the key principles around the HTTP and URI standards, sticking to which will make your HTTP application a RESTful service-enabled application:

1. Everything is a resource
2. Each resource is identifiable by a **unique identifier** (URI)
3. Resources are manipulated via standard HTTP methods
4. Resources can have multiple representations
5. Communicate with resources in a stateless manner

Principle 1 – Everything is a resource

To understand this principle, one must conceive of the idea of representing data by a specific format and not by a physical file containing a bunch of bytes. Each piece of data available on the internet has a format that describes it, known as the content type; for example, JPEG images, MPEG videos, HTML, XML, text documents, and binary data are all resources with the following content types: image/jpeg, video/mpeg, text/html, text/xml, and application/octet-stream.

Principle 2 – Each resource is identifiable by a unique identifier

Since the internet contains so many different resources, they all should be accessible via URIs and should be identified uniquely. Furthermore, the URIs can be in a human-readable format, despite the fact that their consumers are more likely to be software programs rather than ordinary humans.

Human-readable URIs keep data self-descriptive and ease further development against it. This helps you to keep the risk of logical errors in your programs to a minimum.

Here are a few sample examples of such URIs representing different resources in a catalog application:

- `http://www.mycatalog.com/categories/watches`
- `http://www.mycatalog.com/categories/watches?collection=2018`
- `http://www.mycatalog.com/categories/watches/model-xyz/image`
- `http://www.mycatalog.com/categories/watches/model-xyz/video`
- `http://www.mycatalog.com/archives/2017/categories/watches.zip`

These human-readable URIs expose different types of resources in a straightforward manner. In the preceding example URIs, it is quite clear the data is items in a catalog, which are categorized watches. The first link shows all the items in the category. The second shows only the ones that are part of the 2018 collection. Next is a link pointing to the image of the item, followed by a link to a sample video. The last link points to a resource containing items from the previous collection in a ZIP archive. The media types served per each URI are rather easy to identify, with the assumption that the data format of an item is either JSON or XML, so we can easily map the media type of a self-described URL to one of the following:

- JSON or XML documents describing the items
- Images
- Videos
- Binary archive documents

Principle 3 – Manipulate resources via standard HTTP methods

The native HTTP protocol (RFC 2616) defines eight actions, also known as HTTP verbs:

- GET
- POST
- PUT
- DELETE
- HEAD
- OPTIONS

- TRACE
- CONNECT

The first four of them just feel natural in the context of resources, especially when defining actions for data manipulation. Let's make a parallel with relative SQL databases where the native language for data manipulation is **CRUD** (short for **Create, Read, Update, and Delete**), originating from the different types of SQL statements, INSERT, SELECT, UPDATE, and DELETE, respectively. In the same manner, if you apply the REST principles correctly, the HTTP verbs should be used as shown here:

HTTP verb	Action	HTTP response status code
GET	Retrieves an existing resource.	200 OK if the resource exists, 404 Not Found if it does not exist, and 500 Internal Server Error for other errors.
PUT	Updates a resource. If the resource does not exist, the server can either decide to create it with the provided identifer or return the appropriate status code.	200 OK if successfully updated, 201 Created if a new resource is created, 404 Not found if the resource to be updated does not exist, and 500 Internal Server Error for other unexpected errors.

POST	Creates a resource with an identifier generated at server side or updates a resource with an existing identifier provided from the client. If this verb is to be used only for creating but not for updating, return the appropriate status code.	`201 CREATED` if a new resource is created, `200 OK` if the resource has been updated successfully, `409 Conflict` if the resource already exists and update is not allowed, `404 Not Found` if the resource to be updated does not exist, and `500 Internal Server Error` for other errors.
DELETE	Deletes a resource.	`200 OK` or `204 No Content` if the resource has been deleted successfully, `404 Not Found` if the resource to be deleted does not exist, and `500 Internal Server Error` for other errors.

Note that a resource might be created by either the POST or PUT HTTP verbs, based on the policy of an application. However, if a resource has to be created under a specific URI with an identifier provided by the client, then PUT is the appropriate action:

```
PUT /categories/watches/model-abc HTTP/1.1
Content-Type: text/xml
Host: www.mycatalog.com

<?xml version="1.0" encoding="utf-8"?>
<Item category="watch">
    <Brand>...</Brand>
    </Price></Price>
</Item>

HTTP/1.1 201 Created
Content-Type: text/xml
Location: http://www.mycatalog.com/categories/watches/model-abc
```

However, in your application, you may want to leave it up to the backend RESTful service to decide where to expose the newly created resource, and thus create it under an appropriate but still unknown or non-existent location.

For instance, in our example, we might want the server to define the identifier of newly created items. In such cases, just use the POST verb to a URL without providing an identifier parameter. Then it is up to the service itself to provide a new unique and valid identifier for the new resource and to expose back this URL via the Location header of the response:

```
POST /categories/watches HTTP/1.1
Content-Type: text/xml
Host: www.mycatalog.com
```

```
<?xml version="1.0" encoding="utf-8"?>
<Item category="watch">
    <Brand>...</Brand>
    </Price></Price>
</Item>


HTTP/1.1 201 Created
Content-Type: text/xml
Location: http://www.mycatalog.com/categories/watches/model-abc
```

Principle 4 – Resources can have multiple representations

A key feature of a resource is that it may be represented in a different format from the one in which it is stored. Thus, it can be requested or created in different representations. As long as the specified format is supported, the REST-enabled endpoint should use it. In the preceding example, we posted an XML representation of a watch item, but if the server had supported the JSON format, the following request would have been valid as well:

```
POST /categories/watches HTTP/1.1
Content-Type: application/json
Host: www.mycatalog.com

{
  "watch": {
    "id": ""watch-abc"",
    "brand": "...",
    "price": {
      "-currency": "EUR",
      "#text": "100"
    }
  }
}
HTTP/1.1 201 Created
Content-Type: application/json
Location: http://mycatalog.com/categories/watches/watch-abc
```

Principle 5 – Communicate with resources in a stateless manner

Resource manipulation operations through HTTP requests should always be considered atomic. All modifications of a resource should be carried out within an HTTP request in an isolated manner. After the request execution, the resource is left in a final state; this implicitly means that partial resource updates are not supported. You should always send the complete state of the resource.

Back to our catalog example, updating the price field of a given item would mean making a PUT request with a complete document (JSON or XML) that contains the entire data, including the updated price field. Posting only the updated price is not stateless, as it implies that the application is aware that the resource has a price field, that is, it knows its state.

Another requirement for your RESTful application to be stateless is that once the service gets deployed on a production environment, it is likely that incoming requests are served by a load balancer, ensuring scalability and high availability. Once exposed via a load balancer, the idea of keeping your application state at server side gets compromised. This doesn't mean that you are not allowed to keep the state of your application. It just means that you should keep it in a RESTful way. For example, keep a part of the state within the URI, or use HTTP headers to provide additional state-related data

The statelessness of your RESTful API isolates the caller against changes at the server side. Thus, the caller is not expected to communicate with the same server in consecutive requests. This allows easy application of changes within the server infrastructure, such as adding or removing nodes.

Remember that it is your responsibility to keep your RESTful APIs stateless, as the consumers of the APIs would expect them to be.

Now that you know that REST is around 18 years old, a sensible question would be, "Why has it become so popular just quite recently?" Well, we the developers usually reject simple, straightforward approaches and, most of the time, prefer spending more time on turning already-complex solutions into even more complex and sophisticated ones.

Take classical SOAP web services, for example. Their various WS-* specifications are so many, and sometimes so loosely defined, that in order to make different solutions from different vendors interoperable, a separate specification, WS-Basic Profile, has been introduced. It defines extra interoperability rules in order to ensure that all WS-* specifications in SOAP-based web services can work together.

When it comes to transporting binary data with classical web services over HTTP, things get even more complex, as SOAP-based web services provide different ways of transporting binary data. Each way is defined in other sets of specifications, such as **SOAP with Attachment References (SwaRef)** and **Message Transmission Optimization Mechanism (MTOM).** All this complexity was caused mainly because the initial idea of the web service was to execute business logic remotely, not to transport large amounts of data.

The real world has shown us that, when it comes to data transfer, things should not be that complex. This is where REST fits into the big picture—by introducing the concept of resources and a standard means for manipulating them.

The REST goals

Now that we've covered the main REST principles, it is time to dive deeper into what can be achieved when they are followed:

- Separation of the representation and the resource
- Visibility
- Reliability
- Scalability
- Performance

Separation of the representation and the resource

A resource is just a set of information, and as defined by principle 4, it can have multiple representations; however, its state is atomic. It is up to the caller to specify the desired media type with the `Accept` header in the HTTP request, and then it is up to the server application to handle the representation accordingly, returning the appropriate content type of the resource together with a relevant HTTP status code:

- `HTTP 200 OK` in the case of success
- `HTTP 400 Bad Request` if an unsupported format is given or for any other invalid request information
- `HTTP 406 Not Acceptable` if an unsupported media type is requested
- `HTTP 500 Internal Server Error` when something unexpected happens during the request processing

Let's assume that, at server side, we have items resources stored in an XML format. We can have an API that allows a consumer to request the item resources in various formats, such as `application/xml`, `application/json`, `application/zip`, `application/octet-stream`, and so on.

It would be up to the API itself to load the requested resource, transform it into the requested type (for example, JSON or XML), and either use ZIP to compress it or directly flush it to the HTTP response output.

The caller would make use of the `Accept` HTTP header to specify the media type of the response they expect. So, if we want to request our item data inserted in the previous section in XML format, the following request should be executed:

```
GET /category/watches/watch-abc HTTP/1.1
Host: my-computer-hostname
Accept: text/xml

HTTP/1.1 200 OK
Content-Type: text/xml
<?xml version="1.0" encoding="utf-8"?>
<Item category="watch">
    <Brand>...</Brand>
    </Price></Price>
</Item>
```

To request the same item in JSON format, the `Accept` header needs to be set to `application/json`:

```
GET /categoery/watches/watch-abc HTTP/1.1
Host: my-computer-hostname
Accept: application/json

HTTP/1.1 200 OK
Content-Type: application/json
{
  "watch": {
    "id": ""watch-abc"",
```

```
      "brand": "...",
      "price": {
        "-currency": "EUR",
        "#text": "100"
      }
    }
  }
```

Visibility

REST is designed to be visible and simple. Visibility of the service means that every aspect of it should self-descriptive and follow the natural HTTP language according to principles 3, 4, and 5.

Visibility in the context of the outer world would mean that monitoring applications would be interested only in the HTTP communication between the REST service and the caller. Since the requests and responses are stateless and atomic, nothing more is needed to flow the behavior of the application and to understand whether anything has gone wrong.

Remember that caching reduces the visibility of your RESTful applications and in general should be avoided, unless needed for serving resources subject to large amounts of callers. In such cases, caching may be an option, after carefully evaluating the possible consequences of serving obsolete data.

Reliability

Before talking about reliability, we need to define which HTTP methods are safe and which are idempotent in the REST context. So, let's first define what safe and idempotent methods are:

- An HTTP method is considered to be safe provided that, when requested, it does not modify or cause any side effects on the state of the resource
- An HTTP method is considered to be idempotent if its response stays the same, regardless of the number of times it is requested, am idempotent request always gives back the same request, if repeated identically.

The following table lists which HTTP methods are safe and which are idempotent:

HTTP method	Safe	Idempotent
GET	Yes	Yes
POST	No	No
PUT	No	Yes
DELETE	No	Yes

Consumers should consider operation's safety and the idempotence features in order to be served reliably.

Scalability and performance

So far, we stressed the importance of having stateless behavior for a RESTful web application. The **World Wide Web (WWW)** is an enormous universe, containing huge amount of data and a lot of users, eager to get that data. The evolution of the WWW has brought the requirement that applications should scale easily as their load increases. Scaling applications that have a state is difficult to achieve, especially when zero or close-to-zero operational downtime is expected.

That's why staying stateless is crucial for any application that needs to scale. In the best-case scenario, scaling your application would require you to put another piece of hardware for a load balancer, or bring another instance in your cloud environment. There would be no need for the different nodes to sync between each other, as they should not care about the state at all. Scalability is all about serving all your clients in an acceptable amount of time. Its main idea is to keep your application running and to prevent **Denial of Service (DoS)** caused by a huge amount of incoming requests.

Scalability should not be confused with the performance of an application. Performance is measured by the time needed for a single request to be processed, not by the total number of requests that the application can handle. The asynchronous non-blocking architecture and event-driven design of Node.js make it a logical choice for implementing an application that scales and performs well.

Working with WADL

If you are familiar with SOAP web services, you may have heard of the **Web Service Definition Language** (**WSDL**). It is an XML description of the interface of the service and defines an endpoint URL for invocation. It is mandatory for a SOAP web service to be described by such a WSDL definition.

Similar to SOAP web services, RESTful services can also make use of a description language, called WADL. **WADL** stands for **Web Application Definition Language**. Unlike WSDL for SOAP web services, a WADL description of a RESTful service is optional, that is, consuming the service has nothing to do with its description.

Here is a sample part of a WADL file that describes the GET operation of our catalog service:

```xml
<?xml version="1.0" encoding="UTF-8"?>
<application xmlns="http://wadl.dev.java.net/2009/02"
xmlns:service="http://localhost:8080/catalog/"
xmlns:xsd="http://www.w3.org/2001/XMLSchema">
  <grammer>
    <include href="items.xsd" />
    <include href="error.xsd" />
  </grammer>
  <resources base="http://localhost:8080/catalog/categories">
    <resource path="{category}">
      <method name="GET">
        <request>
          <param name="category" type="xsd:string" style="template" />
        </request>
        <response status="200">
          <representation mediaType="application/xml"
element="service:item" />
          <representation mediaType="application/json" />
        </response>
        <response status="404">
          <representation mediaType="application/xml"
element="service:item" />
        </response>
      </method>
    </resource>
  </resources>
</application>
```

This extract of a WADL file shows how application, exposing resources is described. Briefly, each resource must be part of an application. The resource provides a, where it is located with the `base` attribute, and describes each of its supported HTTP methods in a method. Additionally, an optional `doc` element can be used at resource and application to provide additional documentation about the service and its operations.

Though WADL is optional, it significantly reduces the efforts of discovering RESTful services.

Documenting RESTful APIs with Swagger

Public APIs exposed on the web should be well documented, otherwise it would be difficult for developers to use them in their applications. While WADL definitions might be considered a source of documentation, they address a different problem—the discovery of the service. They serve metadata for the services to machines, not to humans. The Swagger project (`https://swagger.io/`) addresses the need for neat documentation of RESTful APIs. It defines a meta description of an API from an almost human-readable JSON format. The following is a sample `swagger.json` file, partially describing the catalog service:

```
{
  "swagger": "2.0",
  "info": {
    "title": "Catalog API Documentation",
    "version": "v1"
  },
  "paths": {
    "/categories/{id}" : {
      "get": {
        "operationId": "getCategoryV1",
        "summary": "Get a specific category ",
        "produces": [
          "application/json"
        ],
        "responses": {
          "200": {
            "description": "200 OK",
            "examples":
              {"application/json": {
                "id": 1,
                "name": "Watches",
                "itemsCount": 550
```

```
                    }
                }
            },
            "404": {"description" : "404 Not Found"},
            "500": {"description": "500 Internal Server Error"}
          }
        }
      }
    },
    "consumes": ["application/json"]
  }
```

The `swagger.json` file is really straightforward: it defines a name and version of your API and gives a brief description of each operation it exposes, nicely coupled with a sample payload. But the real benefit from it comes in another subproject of Swagger, called `swagger-ui` (`https://swagger.io/swagger-ui/`), which actually renders this data from `swagger.json` nicely into an interactive web page that only provides documentation, but also allows interaction with the service:

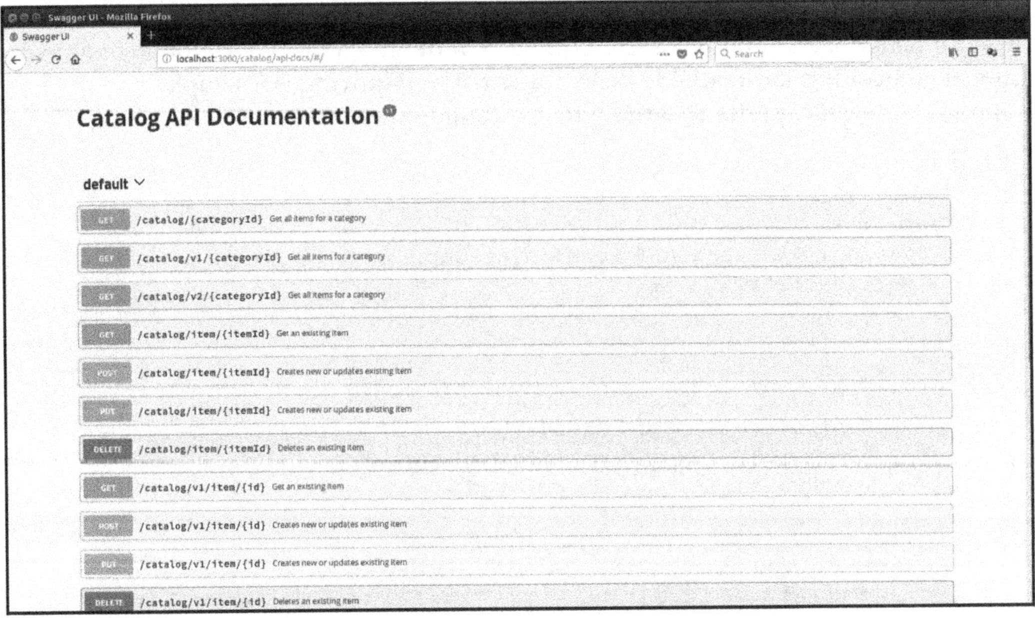

We will have a look at and utilize the `swagger-ui` Node.js module to provide the API that we will develop later in the book, with up-to-date documentation.

Taking advantage of the existing infrastructure

The best part of developing and distributing RESTful applications is that the infrastructure needed is already out there, available to you. As RESTful applications use the existing web space heavily, you need to do nothing more than follow the REST principles when developing. In addition, there are plenty of libraries available out there for any platform, and I do mean any platform. This eases the development of RESTful applications, so you just need to choose your preferred platform and start developing.

Summary

In this chapter, you learned about foundation of a REST, looking at five key principles that transform a web application into a REST-enabled application. We made a brief comparison between RESTful services and classical SOAP web services, and finally took a look at how RESTful services are documented and how we can simplify the discovery of the services we develop.

Now that you know the basics, we are ready to dive into the Node.js way of implementing RESTful services. In the next chapter, you will learn about the essentials of Node.js and the accompanying tools that it is necessary to use and understand in order to build a real-life fully-fledged web service.

Building a Typical Web API 13

Our first draft API will be a read-only version and will not support creating or updating items in the catalog as real-world applications do. Instead, we will concentrate on the API definition itself, and will worry about data storage later on. Of course, using file storage for data exposed to millions of users is anything but an option, so a database layer will be provided to our application further in the book, after we have looked into modern NoSQL database solutions.

We will also cover the topic of content negotiation, a mechanism that allows consumers to specify the expected format of requested data. Finally, we will take a look at several ways to expose different versions of a service, in case it evolves in a backward-incompatible way.

To sum up, in this chapter, you will learn the following:

- How to specify a web API
- How to implement routes
- How to query your API
- Content negotiation
- API versioning

After this chapter, you should be able to completely specify a RESTful API and will be almost ready to start implementing real-life Node.js RESTful services.

Specifying the API

The very first thing a project usually starts with is a definition of the operations the API will expose. According to the REST principles, an operation is exposed by an HTTP method and a URI. The action performed by each operation should not contradict the natural meaning of its HTTP method. The following table specifies the operations of our API in detail:

Method	URI	Description
GET	`/category`	Retrieves all available categories in the catalog.
GET	`/category/{category-id}/`	Retrieves all the items available under a specific category.
GET	`/category/{category-id}/{item-id}`	Retrieves an item by its ID under a specific category.
POST	`/category`	Creates a new category; if it exists, it will update it.
POST	`/category/{category-id}/`	Creates a new item in a specified category. If the item exists, it will update it.
PUT	`/category/{category-id}`	Updates a category.
PUT	`/category/{category-id}/{item-id}`	Updates an item in a specified category.
DELETE	`/category/{category-id}`	Deletes an existing category.
DELETE	`/category/{category-id}/{item-id}`	Deletes an item in a specified category.

The second step is to choose an appropriate format for our catalog application's data. JSON objects are natively supported by JavaScript. They are easy to extend during the evolution of an application and are consumable by almost any platform available. Thus, the JSON format seems to be our logical choice for us. Here is the JSON representation of an item, and category objects that will be used throughout this book:

```
{
    "itemId": "item-identifier-1",
    "itemName": "Sports Watch",
    "category": "Watches",
    "categoryId": 1,
    "price": 150,
    "currency": "EUR"
}
```

```
{
    "categoryName" : "Watches",
    "categoryId" : "1",
    "itemsCount" : 100,
    "items" : [{
            "itemId" : "item-identifier-1",
            "itemName":"Sports Watch",
            "price": 150,
            "currency" : "EUR"
    }]
}
```

So far, our API has defined a set of operations and the data format to be used. The next step is to implement a module that will export functions serving each of the operations in the route.

To begin with, let's create a new Node.js Express project. Select a directory where your projects will be stored and from your shell Terminal, execute `express chapter3`. If you are using Windows, you will need to install the `express-generator` module before generating the project. The `express-generator` will create your an initial express project layout in the selected directory. This layout provides the default project structure for you, ensuring that your Express project follows the standard project structure. It makes your project easier to navigate.

The next step is to import the project into the Atom IDE. Right-click anywhere in the **Projects** tab and select **Add project folder** then select the directory Express generated for you.

As you can see, Express has done some background work for us and has created a starting point for our application: `app.js`. It has also created the `package.json` file for us. Let's take a look at each of these files, starting with `package.json`:

```
{
  "name": "chapter3",
  "version": "1.0.0",
  "description": "",
  "main": "app.js",
  "scripts": {
    "test": "test"
  },
  "author": "",
  "license": "ISC",
  "dependencies": {
  "dependencies": {
    "body-parser": "~1.13.2",
    "cookie-parser": "~1.3.5",
```

```
        "debug": "~2.2.0",
        "express": "~4.16.1",
        "jade": "~1.11.0",
        "morgan": "~1.6.1",
        "serve-favicon": "~2.3.0"


    }
}
```

As we created a blank Node.js Express project, we initially have dependencies only to the Express framework, some middleware modules such as `morgan`, `body-parser`, and `cookie-parser`, and the Jade template language. Jade is a straightforward template language used to produce HTML code inside templates. If you are interested in it, you can find out more about it at `http://www.jade-lang.com`.

The current version of the Express framework at the time of writing is 4.16.1; to update it, execute `npm install express@4.16.1 --save` from the `chapter3` directory. This command will update the dependency of the application to the desired version. The `--save` option will update and save the new version of the dependency in the project's `package.json` file.

When you introduce new module dependencies, it is up to you to keep the `package.json` file up to date in order to maintain an accurate state of the modules your application depends on.

We will come to what middleware modules are a bit later in the chapter.

For now, we will ignore the content of the `public` and `view` directories as it is not relevant to our RESTful service. They contain the auto-generated stylesheets and template files that might be helpful, if we decide to develop a web-based consumer of the services at a later stage.

We've already mentioned that the Express project created a starting point for our web application in `app.js`. Let's take a deeper look at it:

```
var express = require('express');
var path = require('path');
var favicon = require('serve-favicon');
var logger = require('morgan');
var cookieParser = require('cookie-parser');
var bodyParser = require('body-parser');

var routes = require('./routes/index');
var users = require('./routes/users');

var app = express();

// view engine setup
app.set('views', path.join(__dirname, 'views'));
app.set('view engine', 'jade');

// uncomment after placing your favicon in /public
//app.use(favicon(path.join(__dirname, 'public', 'favicon.ico')));
app.use(logger('dev'));
app.use(bodyParser.json());
app.use(bodyParser.urlencoded({ extended: false }));
app.use(cookieParser());
app.use(express.static(path.join(__dirname, 'public')));

app.use('/', routes);
app.use('/users', users);

// catch 404 and forward to error handler
app.use(function(req, res, next) {
  var err = new Error('Not Found');
  err.status = 404;
  next(err);
});

// error handlers

// development error handler
// will print stacktrace
if (app.get('env') === 'development') {
  app.use(function(err, req, res, next) {
    res.status(err.status || 500);
    res.render('error', {
      message: err.message,
      error: err
    });
```

```
    });
  }

  // production error handler
  // no stacktraces leaked to user
  app.use(function(err, req, res, next) {
    res.status(err.status || 500);
    res.render('error', {
      message: err.message,
      error: {}
    });
  });
```

```
  module.exports = app;
```

Obviously, the Express generator has done a lot for us as it has instantiated the
Express framework and has assigned a complete development environment around
it. It has done the following:

- Configured the middleware to be used in our application, `body-parser`,
  the default router, as well as error handler middleware for our
  development environment
- Injected a logger instance of the morgan middleware module
- Configured the Jade template, as it has been selected as the default
  template for our application
- Configured the default URI that our Express application will be listening
  to, `/` and `/users`, and created dummy handle functions for them

You will have to install all the modules used in `app.js` in order to start the generated
application successfully. Also, make sure you update the dependencies of your
`package.json` file using the `--save` option after installing them.

The Express generator also created a starting script for the application. It is under
the `bin/www` directory of your project and looks like the following snippet:

```
#!/usr/bin/env node

/**
 * Module dependencies.
 */

var app = require('../app');
var debug = require('debug')('chapter3:server');
var http = require('http');
```

```
/**
 * Get port from environment and store in Express.
 */

var port = normalizePort(process.env.PORT || '3000');
app.set('port', port);

/**
 * Create HTTP server.
 */

var server = http.createServer(app);

/**
 * Listen on provided port, on all network interfaces.
 */

server.listen(port);
server.on('error', onError);
server.on('listening', onListening);

/**
 * Normalize a port into a number, string, or false.
 */

function normalizePort(val) {
  var port = parseInt(val, 10);

  if (isNaN(port)) {
    // named pipe
    return val;
  }

  if (port >= 0) {
    // port number
    return port;
  }

  return false;
}

/**
 * Event listener for HTTP server "error" event.
 */

function onError(error) {
  if (error.syscall !== 'listen') {
    throw error;
```

```
  }

  var bind = typeof port === 'string'
    ? 'Pipe ' + port
    : 'Port ' + port;

  // handle specific listen errors with friendly messages
  switch (error.code) {
    case 'EACCES':
      console.error(bind + ' requires elevated privileges');
      process.exit(1);
      break;
    case 'EADDRINUSE':
      console.error(bind + ' is already in use');
      process.exit(1);
      break;
    default:
      throw error;
  }
}

/**
 * Event listener for HTTP server "listening" event.
 */

function onListening() {
  var addr = server.address();
  var bind = typeof addr === 'string'
    ? 'pipe ' + addr
    : 'port ' + addr.port;
  debug('Listening on ' + bind);
}
```

To start the application, execute `node bin/www`; this will execute the script above and will start the Node.js application. So requesting `http://localhost:3000` in your browser will result in calling the default `GET` handler, which gives a warm welcome response:

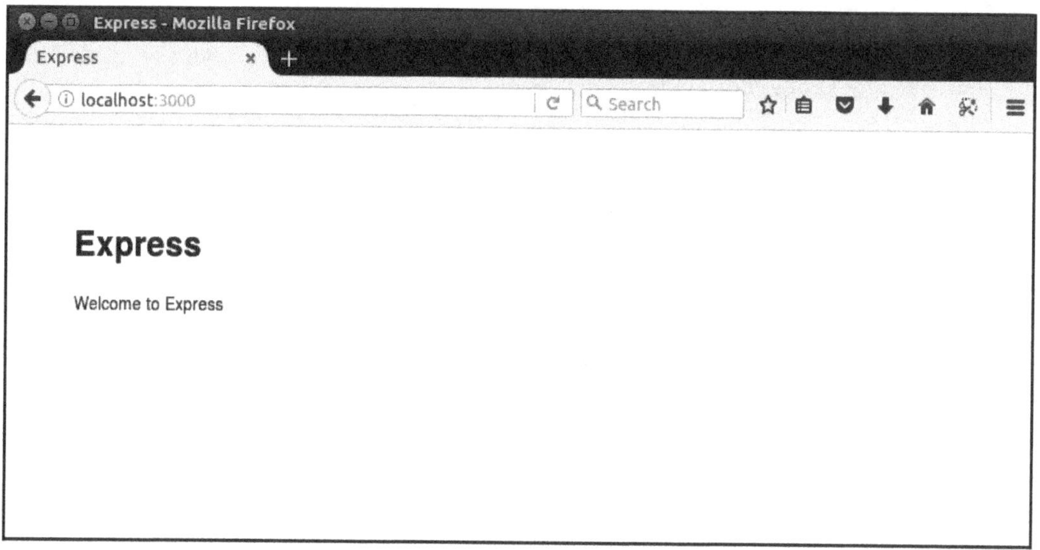

Default welcome message from an Express application

The generator created a dummy `routes/users.js`; it exposes a route linked to a dummy module available at the `/users` location. Requesting it will result in calling the `list` function of the user's route, which outputs a static response: `respond with a resource`.

Our application will not be using a template language and style sheets, so let's get rid of the lines that set the views and view engine properties in the application configuration. In addition, we will be implementing our own routes. Thus, we don't need the binding of the `/` and `/users` URIs for our app, neither do we need the `user` module; instead, we will utilize a `catalog` module and from a route:

```
var express = require('express');
var path = require('path');
var favicon = require('serve-favicon');
var logger = require('morgan');
var cookieParser = require('cookie-parser');
var bodyParser = require('body-parser');

var routes = require('./routes/index');
var catalog = require('./routes/catalog')
var app = express();

//uncomment after placing your favicon in /public
//app.use(favicon(path.join(__dirname, 'public', 'favicon.ico')));
app.use(logger('dev'));
```

```
app.use(bodyParser.json());
app.use(bodyParser.urlencoded({ extended: false }));
app.use(cookieParser());
app.use(express.static(path.join(__dirname, 'public')));

app.use('/', routes);
app.use('/catalog', catalog);


// catch 404 and forward to error handler
app.use(function(req, res, next) {
  var err = new Error('Not Found');
  err.status = 404;
  next(err);
});

//development error handler will print stacktrace
if (app.get('env') === 'development') {
  app.use(function(err, req, res, next) {
    res.status(err.status || 500);
    res.render('error', {
      message: err.message,
      error: err
    });
  });
}

// production error handler no stacktraces leaked to user
app.use(function(err, req, res, next) {
  res.status(err.status || 500);
  res.render('error', {
    message: err.message,
    error: {}
  });
});

module.exports = app;
```

So after this cleanup, our application looks a lot cleaner and we are ready to move forward.

Before doing that, though, there is one term that needs further explanation: middleware. It is a subset of chained functions called by the Express.js routing layer before a user-defined handler is invoked. Middleware functions have full access to the `request` and `response` objects and can modify either of them. The middleware chain is always called in the exact order in which it has been defined, so it is vital for you to know exactly what a specific piece of middleware is doing. Once a middleware function finishes, it calls the next function in the chain by invoking its next argument as a function. After the complete chain gets executed, the user-defined request handler is called.

Here are the basic rules that apply to the middleware chain:

- A middleware function has the following signature: `function (request, response, next)`.
- Middleware functions are executed in the exact order in which they have been added to the application chain. This means that if you want your middleware function to be called before a specific route, you need to add it before declaring the route.
- Middleware functions use their third parameter, `next`, as a function to indicate that they have completed their work and to exit. When the `next()` parameter of the last function in the chain has been called, the chained execution is completed and the `request` and the `response` objects reach the defined handlers, in the state set by the middleware.

Now that we know what a middleware function is, let's clarify what the currently used middleware functions provide our application with. The `body-parser` middleware is the Express framework built in a parser. It parses the `request` body and populates the `request` object after the middleware execution finishes, that is, it provides JSON payload handling.

Now it is time to move on and implement our user module that will be mapped to our URIs. The module will be named `modules/catalog.js`:

```
var fs = require('fs');

function readCatalogSync() {
    var file = './data/catalog.json';
    if (fs.existsSync(file)) {
        var content = fs.readFileSync(file);
        var catalog = JSON.parse(content);
        return catalog;
```

```javascript
    }
    return undefined;
  }

exports.findItems = function(categoryId) {
  console.log('Returning all items for categoryId: ' + categoryId);
  var catalog = readCatalogSync();
  if (catalog) {
    var items = [];
    for (var index in catalog.catalog) {
        if (catalog.catalog[index].categoryId === categoryId) {
            var category = catalog.catalog[index];
            for (var itemIndex in category.items) {
              items.push(category.items[itemIndex]);
            }
        }
    }
    return items;
  }
  return undefined;
}

exports.findItem = function(categoryId, itemId) {
  console.log('Looking for item with id' + itemId);
  var catalog = readCatalogSync();
  if (catalog) {
    for (var index in catalog.catalog) {
        if (catalog.catalog[index].categoryId === categoryId) {
          var category = catalog.catalog[index];
          for (var itemIndex in category.items) {
            if (category.items[itemIndex].itemId === itemId) {
              return category.items[itemIndex];
            }
          }
        }
    }
    return undefined;
}

exports.findCategoryies = function() {
  console.log('Returning all categories');
  var catalog = readCatalogSync();
  if (catalog) {
    var categories = [];
    for (var index in catalog.catalog) {
        var category = {};
        category["categoryId"] = catalog.catalog[index].categoryId;
```

```
        category["categoryName"] =
catalog.catalog[index].categoryName;

        categories.push(category);
    }
    return categories;
  }
  return [];
}
```

The catalog module is built around the `catalog.json` file, stored in the `data` directory. The content of the source file is read synchronously using the File System module, `fs`, within the `readCatalogSync` function. The File System module provides multiple useful filesystem operations such as functions for creating, renaming, or deleting files or directories; truncating; linking; `chmod` functions; as well as synchronous and asynchronous file access for reading and writing data. In our sample application, we aim to use the most straightforward approach, so we implement functions that read the `catalog.json` file by utilizing the `readFileSync` function of the File System module. It returns the content of a file as a string, within a synchronous call. All other functions of the module are exported and can be used to query the content of the source file, based on different criteria.

The catalog module exports the following functions:

- `findCategories`: This returns an array of JSON objects containing all the categories in the `catalog.json` file
- `findItems (categoryId)`: This returns an array JSON objects representing all the items in a given category
- `findItem(categoryId, itemId)`: This returns a JSON object representing a single item in a given category

Now that we have three complete functions, let's see how to bind them to our Express application.

Implementing routes

In Node.js terms, a route is a binding between a URI and function. The Express framework provides built-in support for routing. An `express` object instance contains functions named after each HTTP verb: `get`, `post`, `put`, and `delete`. They have the following syntax: `function(uri, handler);`.

They are used to bind a handler function to a specific HTTP action executed over a URI. The handler function usually takes two arguments: `request` and `response`. Let's see it with a simple `Hello route` application:

```
var express = require('express');
var app = express();

app.get('/hello', function(request, response){
  response.send('Hello route');
});

app.listen(3000);
```

Running this sample at localhost and accessing `http://localhost:3000/hello` will result in calling your handler function and it will respond saying `Hello route`, but routing can give you much more. It allows you to define a URI with parameters; for example, let's use `/hello/:name` as a routing string. It tells the framework that the URI used consists of two parts: a static part (`hello`) and a variable part (the `name` parameter).

Furthermore, when the routing string and the handler function are defined in line with the `get` function of an Express instance, a parameter collection is made available directly in the `request` argument of the handler function. To demonstrate this, let's modify our previous example a bit:

```
var express = require('express');
var app = express();

app.get('/hello:name', function(request, response){
  response.send('Hello ' + request.params.name);
});

app.listen(3000);
```

As you can see in the preceding code snippet, we used a colon (`:`) to separate the parameter part of the URI from the static part. You can have multiple parameters in an Express route; for example, `/category/:category-id/items/:item-id` defines a route for displaying an item that belongs to a category, where the `category-id` and `item-id` are parameters.

Now let's try it out. Requesting `http://localhost:3000/hello/friend` will result in the following output:

```
hello friend
```

This is how we can provide parameterized URIs with Express. It is a nice feature, but it is often not enough. In web applications, we are used to providing additional parameters with GET parameters.

Unfortunately, the Express framework is not so good with GET parameters. Thus, we have to utilize the url module. It is built into Node.js to provide an easy way of using URL parsing. Let's use our hello result with other parameters in the application again, but extend it in a way that it outputs hello all when /hello is requested and hello friend when the requested URI is /hello?name=friend:

```
var express = require('express');
var url = require('url');
var app = express();

app.get('/hello', function(request, response){
    var getParams = url.parse(request.url, true).query;

    if (Object.keys(getParams).length == 0) {
        response.end('Hello all');
    } else {
        response.end('Hello ' + getParams.name);
    }
});

app.listen(3000);
```

There are a few things worth mentioning here. We used the url module's function parse. It takes a URL as its first argument and a Boolean as an optional second argument, which specifies whether the query string should be parsed or not. The url.parse function returns an associative object. We used Object.keys with it to transform the keys in these associative objects into an array so that we can check its length. This will help us check whether our URI has been called with GET parameters or not. In addition to the routing functions named after each HTTP verb, there is also a function named all. When used, it routes all the HTTP actions to the specified URI.

Now that we know how routing and the GET parameters work within Node.js and the Express environment, we are ready to define a route for the catalog module and bind it in our application. The following is the route as defined in routes/catalog.js.

```
var express = require('express');
var catalog = require('../modules/catalog.js')

var router = express.Router();
```

```javascript
router.get('/', function(request, response, next) {
  var categories = catalog.findCategoryies();
  response.json(categories);
});

router.get('/:categoryId', function(request, response, next) {
  var categories = catalog.findItems(request.params.categoryId);
  if (categories === undefined) {
    response.writeHead(404, {'Content-Type' : 'text/plain'});
    response.end('Not found');
  } else {
    response.json(categories);
  }
});

router.get('/:categoryId/:itemId', function(request, response, next) {
  var item = catalog.findItem(request.params.categoryId,
request.params.itemId);
  if (item === undefined) {
    response.writeHead(404, {'Content-Type' : 'text/plain'});
    response.end('Not found');
  } else {
  response.json(item);
  }
});
module.exports = router;
```

First, a `Router` instance is created from the Express module. Here is a table that nicely describes the routing we just implemented. This will be helpful later when we test our API:

HTTP method	Route	Catalog's module function
GET	/catalog	findCategories()
GET	/catalog/:categoryId	findItems(categoryId)
GET	/catalog/:categoryId/:itemId	findItem(categoryId, itemId)

Querying the API using test data

We need some test data in order to test our service, so let's use the `catalog.json` file in the `data` directory of our project. This data will allow us to test all our three functions, but to do that, we would need a client that can send REST requests against an endpoint. If you still haven't created a Postman project for testing your application, now is an appropriate time to create it.

Requesting `/catalog` should return all the categories in the `test` file:

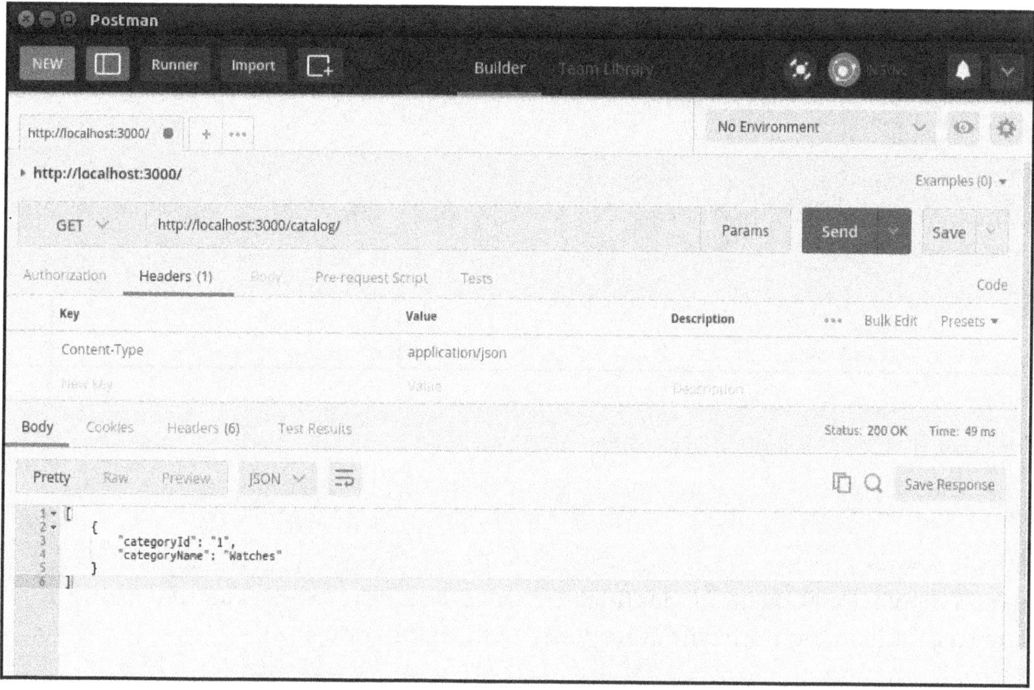

Thus, requesting `/catalog/1` should result in returning a list with all the items under the `Watches` category:

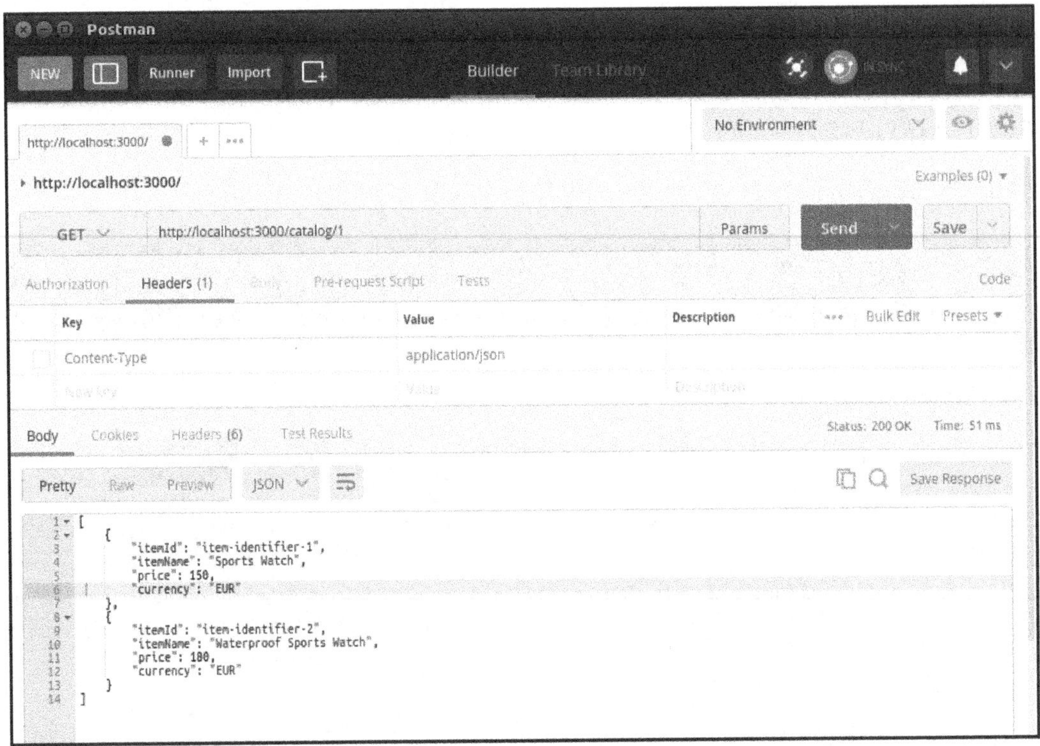

Finally, requesting `http://localhost:3000/catalog/1/item-identifier-1` would display only the item identified by `item-identifier-1`, and requesting a nonexistent item would result in response with status code `404`:

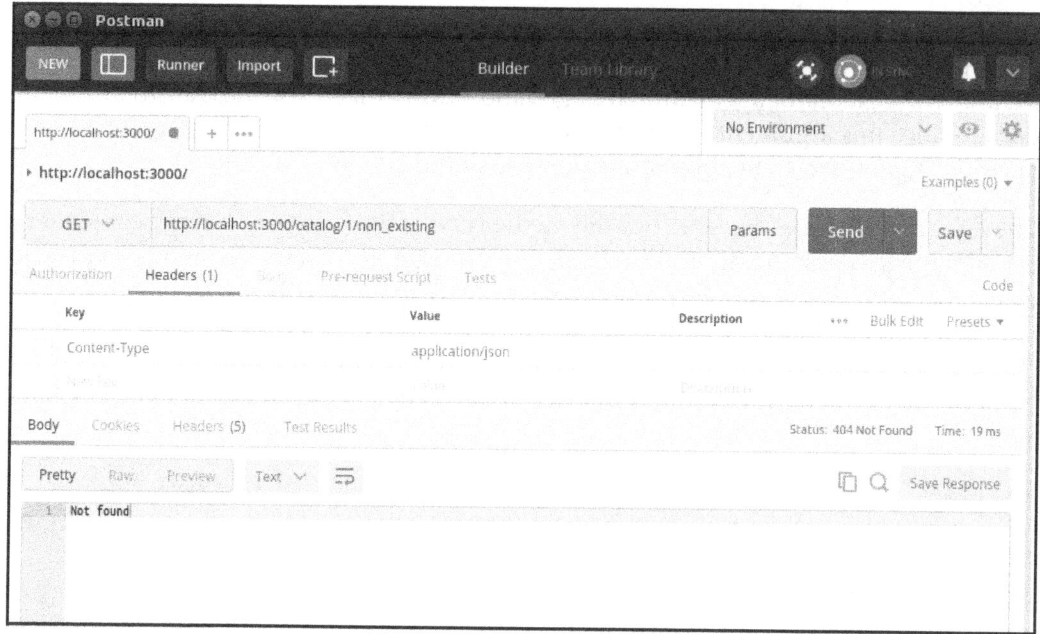

Content negotiation

So far, the catalog service supports only the JSON format, and thus works only with the media type `application/json`. Let's assume our service has to offer data in different formats, for example, both JSON and XML. Then, the consumer needs to explicitly define the data format they need. The best way to carry out content negotiation in REST has been a very debatable subject for a long time.

In his famous discussion on implementing content negotiation correctly, Roy Fielding states the following:

> *All important resources must have URIs.*

However, that leaves a gap on how to expose the same resource in a different data format, so Roy continues with the following:

> *Agent-driven negotiation is far more effective, but there was a huge disagreement between myself and the chair of the HTTP working group and my original agent-driven design for HTTP/1.1 was effectively buried in committee. To do negotiation right, the client needs to be aware of all the alternatives and what it should use as a bookmark.*

While one can still choose to stick with a URI-driven negotiation by providing the desired format with custom `GET` parameters, the REST community has chosen to stick to Roy's suggestion for agent-driven negotiation. Now that it has been almost a decade since this argument was initiated, it has been proven that they took the right decision. Agent-driven negotiation makes use of the `Accept` HTTP header.

The `Accept` HTTP header specifies the media type of the resource that the consumer is willing to process. In addition to the `Accept` header, the consumer may also make use of the `Accept-Language` and `Accept-Encoding` headers to specify what language and encoding the results should be provided in. If the server fails to provide the results in the expected format, it can either return a default value or make use of `HTTP 406 Not acceptable` in order not to cause data confusion errors on the client side.

The Node.js HTTP `response` object contains a method, `format`, that performs content negotiation based on the `Accept` HTTP header if set in the `request` object. It uses the built-in `request.accepts()` to select an appropriate handler for the request. If that is not found, the server invokes the default handler, which responds with `HTTP 406 Not acceptable`. Let's create a demo on how to use the `format` method within one of our routes. For that purpose, let's assume we have implemented a function within our `catalog` module, named `list_groups_in_xml`, that provides the group data in XML format:

```
app.get('/catalog', function(request, response) {
    response.format( {
      'text/xml' : function() {
        response.send(catalog.findCategoiesXml());
      },
      'application/json' : function() {
        response.json(catalog.findCategoriesJson());
      },
      'default' : function() {.
        response.status(406).send('Not Acceptable');
      }
    });
});
```

This is how you can implement content negotiation in a clear and straightforward way.

API versioning

It is an inevitable fact that all application APIs evolve. However, the evolution of public APIs with an unknown number of consumers, such as RESTful services, is a sensitive topic. As consumers may not be able to handle the modified data appropriately and there is no way of notifying all of them, we need to keep our APIs as backward-compatible as possible. One way to do so is to use different URIs for different versions of our application. Currently, our catalog API is available at `/catalog`.

When the time is right for a new version, for example, Version 2, we may need to keep the previous version available at another URI for backward-compatibility. Best practice is to encode the version number in the URI, such as `/v1/catalog`, and keep `/catalog` mapped to the latest version. Thus, requesting `/catalog` will cause a redirect to `/v2/catalog` and will make use of the HTTP `3xx` status codes to indicate the redirection to the latest version.

Another option for versioning would be to keep the URI of your API stable and rely on custom HTTP headers that will specify the version. But that's not very stable approach concerning backward-compatibility as it is much more natural to modify a URL of a request in an application rather than modify the headers that are sent within the request.

Self-test questions

To get additional confidence, go through this set of statements and state whether they are true or false:

1. A REST-enabled endpoint must support all HTTP methods relevant to the REST principles
2. When content negotiation fails, due to an unsupported media type passed as a value of the accepts header, 301 is the appropriate status code.
3. When using parameterized routes, the developer can specify the type of the parameter, for example, whether it is a numeric or a literal type.

Summary

In this chapter, we dived into some more complex topics. Let's sum up what we covered. We started by specifying the operations of our web API and defined that an operation is a combination of a URI and HTTP action. Next, we implemented routes and bound them to an operation. Then, we requested each operation using the Postman REST client to request the URIs that we routed. In the content negotiation section, we handled the `Accept` HTTP header to provide the results in the format requested by consumers. Finally, we covered the topic of API versions, which allow us to develop backward-compatible APIs.

We used old-fashioned filesystem storage for our data in this chapter. This is not suitable for a web application. Thus, we will look into modern, scalable, and reliable NoSQL storage in the next chapter.

Using NoSQL Databases

In the last chapter, we implemented a sample application exposing a read-only service that provided catalog data. For the sake of simplicity, we introduced a performance bottleneck in this implementation by using file storage. This storage is not suitable for web applications. It relies on 33 physical files, preventing our application from servicing heavy loads, as file storage lacks multitenant support due to disc I/O operations. In other words, we definitely need to look for a better storage solution, which scales easily, when needed, following the demands of our REST-enabled application. NoSQL databases are now heavily used in web and in cloud environments, ensuring zero downtime and high availability. They have the following advantages over traditional transactional SQL databases:

- They **support schema versions**; that is, they can work with object representations rather than filling the object state based on definitions of one or several tables.
- They are **extensible**, because they store an actual object. Data evolution is supported implicitly, so all you need to do is call the operation that stores the modified object.
- They are designed to be **highly distributed** and **scalable**.

Nearly all modern NoSQL solutions out there support clustering and can scale further, along with the load of your application. Additionally, most of them have REST-enabled interfaces over HTTP, which eases their usage over a load balancer in high-availability scenarios. Classical database drivers are usually not available for traditional client-side languages, such as JavaScript, because they require native libraries or drivers. However, the idea of NoSQL originated from using document data stores. Thus, most of them support the JSON format, which is native to JavaScript. Last but not least, most NoSQL solutions are open source and are available for free, with all the benefits that open source projects offer: community, examples, and freedom!

In this chapter, we will take a look at the MongoDB NoSQL database and the Mongoose module that interacts with it. We will see how to design and implement automated tests for the database models. Finally, at the end of the chapter, we will remove the file storage bottleneck and will move our application to an almost ready for production state.

MongoDB – a document store database

MongoDB is an open source document database with built-in support for the JSON format. It provides a full index support, based on any of the available attributes in a document. It is ideal for high-availability scenarios due to its scalability features. MongoDB, available at `https://mms.mongodb.com`, is cloud-ready with its management services, **MongoDB Management Services** (**MMS**). They utilize and automate most development operations that need to be carried out to keep your cloud database in good shape, taking care of upgrades, further scaling, backups, recovery, performance, and security alerts.

Let's move forward and install MongoDB. Installers for Windows, Linux, macOS, and Solaris are available at `http://www.mongodb.org/downloads`. Linux users can find MongoDB in all popular distribution repositories, while Windows users can make use of a user-friendly wizard which will guide you through the installation steps, where, for a typical installation, all you need to do is accept the license agreement and provide an installation path.

After a successful installation, execute the following command to start MongoDB. If you want to specify a custom location for your data, you have to use the `--dbpath` argument. Optionally, you can start the MongoDB HTTP console via the `--rest` argument:

```
mongod --dbpath ./data --rest
```

The default port for communicating with MongoDB is `27017`, and its HTTP console is implicitly configured to use a port higher than the data port by a value of 1,000. Therefore, the default port of the console will be `28017`. The HTTP console provides useful information about the database, such as logs, health status, available databases, and so on. I strongly advise you to spend some time with it. The console can also be used as a RESTful health check service of the database, because it provides JSON-encoded information about the running database services and the last error that occurred:

```
GET /replSetGetStatus?text=1 HTTP/1.1
```

```
Host: localhost:28017
Connection: Keep-Alive
User-Agent: RestClient-Tool
HTTP/1.0 200 OK
Content-Length: 56
Connection: close
Content-Type: text/plain;charset=utf-8
{
"ok": 0,
"errmsg": "not running with --replSet"
}
```

This REST interface can be used in a script or an application to automate altering notifications providing the current state of the database engine and so on.

The log section of the console shows that your server is running successfully (if it is). Now we are ready to move further and see how to connect Node.js to MongoDB.

Database modeling with Mongoose

Mongoose is a module that connects Node.js to MongoDB in an **object document mapper** (ODM) style. It offers the **Create, Read, Update, and Delete** (also known as **CRUD**) functionalities for documents stored in the database. Mongoose defines the structure of the used documents using schemas. The schema is the smallest unit of data definition in Mongoose. A model is built out of a schema definition. It is a constructor-like function that can be used to create or query documents. Documents are instances of a model and represent one-to-one mapping to the documents stored in MongoDB. The schema-model-document hierarchy provides a self-descriptive way of defining objects and allows easy data validation.

Let's start by installing Mongoose with npm:

```
npm install mongoose
```

Now that we have the Mongoose module installed, our first step will be to define a schema that will represent an item in the catalog:

```
var mongoose = require('mongoose');
var Schema = mongoose.Schema;
var itemSchema = new Schema ({
    "itemId" : {type: String, index: {unique: true}},
    "itemName": String,
    "price": Number,
    "currency" : String,
```

```
    "categories": [String]
});
```

The preceding code snippet creates a schema definition of an item. Defining a schema is straightforward and is quite similar to JSON schema definition; you have to describe and attribute with its type and optionally provide additional properties for each key. In the case of the catalog application, we need to use the `itemId` as a unique index in order to avoid having two different items with the same ID. Thus, apart from defining its type as `String`, we also use the `index` attribute to describe that the value of the `itemId` field must be unique for each individual item.

Mongoose introduces the term **model**. A model is a constructor-like function compiled out of a schema definition. An instance of a model represents a document that can be saved to or read from the database. Creating a model instance is done by calling the `model` function of a `mongoose` instance and passing the schema that the model should use:

```
var CatalogItem = mongoose.model('Item', itemSchema);
```

A model also exposes functions for querying and data manipulations. Assuming that we have initialized a schema and created a model, storing a new item to MongoDB is as simple as creating a new `model` instance and invoking its `save` function:

```
var mongoose = require('mongoose');

mongoose.connect('mongodb://localhost/catalog');
var db = mongoose.connection;

db.on('error', console.error.bind(console, 'connection error:'));
db.once('open', function() {
  var watch = new CatalogItem({
    itemId: 9 ,
    itemName: "Sports Watch1",
    brand: 'A1',
    price: 100,
    currency: "EUR",
    categories: ["Watches", "Sports Watches"]
  });

  watch.save((error, item, affectedNo)=> {
    if (!error) {
      console.log('Item added successfully to the catalog');
    } else {
      console.log('Cannot add item to the catlog');
    }
  });
```

```
});

db.once('open', function() {
  var filter = {
    'itemName' : 'Sports Watch1',
    'price': 100
  }

  CatalogItem.find(filter, (error, result) => {
    if (error) {
      consoloe.log('Error occured');
    } else {
      console.log('Results found:'+ result.length);
      console.log(result);
    }
  });
});
```

Here is how to use the model in order to query for documents representing a sports watch belonging to the `Watches` group named `Sports Watches`:

```
db.once('open', function() {
  var filter = {
    'itemName' : 'Sports Watch1',
    'price': 100
  }
  CatalogItem.findOne(filter, (error, result) => {
    if (error) {
      consoloe.log('Error occurred');
    } else {
      console.log(result);
    }
  });
});
```

The model also exposes a `findOne` function, a convenient way of finding an object by its unique index and then performing some data manipulation on it, that is, for delete or update operations. The following example deletes an item:

```
CatalogItem.findOne({itemId: 1 }, (error, data) => {
  if (error) {
    console.log(error);
    return;
  } else {
    if (!data) {
    console.log('not found');
      return;
```

```
    } else {
      data.remove(function(error){
        if (!error) { data.remove();}
        else { console.log(error);}
        });
      }
    }
});
```

Testing a Mongoose model with Mocha

Mocha is one of the most popular testing frameworks for JavaScript; its main goal is to provide an easy way to test asynchronous JavaScript code. Let's install Mocha globally so that we can make it available to any Node.js application that we may develop in the future:

```
npm install -g mocha
```

We will also need an assertion library that can be used together with Mocha. The assertion library provides functions for validating actual values, against expected ones, when they are not equal, the assertion library will cause test failure. `Should.js` assertion library module is easy to use and it will be our choice, so let's install it globally too:

```
npm install -g should
```

Now that we have our testing modules installed, we need to specify our `testcase` file path in the `package.json` file. Let's modify it by adding a `test` element pointing to Mocha and the `testcase` file in the script node:

```
{
"name": "chapter4",
"version": "0.0.0",
"private": true,
"scripts": {
"start": "node ./bin/www",
"test": "mocha test/model-test.js"
  },
"dependencies": {
"body-parser": "~1.13.2",
"cookie-parser": "~1.3.5",
"debug": "~2.2.0",
"express": "~4.16.0",
"jade": "~1.11.0",
"morgan": "~1.6.1",
```

```
"serve-favicon": "~2.3.0"
  }
}
```

This will tell the npm package manager to trigger Mocha when the npm test is executed.

Automation of Mongoose tests must not be affected by the current state of the database. To ensure that the results are predictable at each test run, we need to ensure that the database state is exactly as we would expect it. We will implement a module called `prepare.js` in the `test` directory. It will clear the database before each test run:

```javascript
var mongoose = require('mongoose');
beforeEach(function (done) {
  function clearDatabase() {
    for (var i in mongoose.connection.collections) {
      mongoose.connection.collections[i].remove(function()
      {});
    }
    return done();
  }
  if (mongoose.connection.readyState === 0) {
    mongoose.connect(config.db.test, function (err) {
      if (err) {
        throw err;
      }
      return clearDatabase();
    });
  } else {
    return clearDatabase();
  }
});
afterEach(function (done) {
  mongoose.disconnect();
  return done();
});
```

Next, we will implement a Mocha test, which creates a new item:

```javascript
var mongoose = require('mongoose');
var should = require('should');
var prepare = require('./prepare');

const model = require('../model/item.js');
const CatalogItem = model.CatalogItem;
```

```
mongoose.createConnection('mongodb://localhost/catalog');

describe('CatalogItem: models', function () {
  describe('#create()', function () {
    it('Should create a new CatalogItem', function (done) {

      var item = {
        "itemId": "1",
        "itemName": "Sports Watch",
        "price": 100,
        "currency": "EUR",
        "categories": [
          "Watches",
          "Sports Watches"
        ]

      };

      CatalogItem.create(item, function (err, createdItem) {
        // Check that no error occured
        should.not.exist(err);
        // Assert that the returned item has is what we expect

        createdItem.itemId.should.equal('1');
        createdItem.itemName.should.equal('Sports Watch');
        createdItem.price.should.equal(100);
        createdItem.currency.should.equal('EUR');
        createdItem.categories[0].should.equal('Watches');
        createdItem.categories[1].should.equal('Sports Watches');
        //Notify mocha that the test has completed
        done();
      });
    });
  });
});
```

Executing the `npm test` now results in a call against the MongoDB database creating an item out of the passed JSON object. After insertion, the assert callback will be executing, ensuring that values passed to by Mongoose are the same as the returned ones from the database. Give it a try and break the test—simply change the expected value in the assert with an invalid one—you will see the test failing.

Creating a user-defined model around a Mongoose model

After seeing how a model works, it is time to create a user-defined module that wraps all CRUD operations for the catalog. Since we intend to use that module in a RESTful web application, it seems logical to leave the schema definition and the model creation outside the module and have them provided as arguments of each module function. The same schema definition is used in the unit tests, ensuring stability of the module. Now let's add an implementation for each CRUD function, starting with a `remove()` function. It looks up an item based on its `id` and deletes it from the database, if it exists:

```
exports.remove = function (request, response) {
    console.log('Deleting item with id: '    + request.body.itemId);
    CatalogItem.findOne({itemId: request.params.itemId}, function(error,
data) {
        if (error) {
            console.log(error);
            if (response != null) {
                response.writeHead(500, contentTypePlainText);
                response.end('Internal server error');
            }
            return;
        } else {
            if (!data) {
                console.log('Item not found');
                if (response != null) {
                    response.writeHead(404, contentTypePlainText);
                    response.end('Not Found');
                }
                return;
            } else {
                data.remove(function(error){
                    if (!error) {
                        data.remove();
                        response.json({'Status': 'Successfully
deleted'});
                    }
                    else {
                        console.log(error);
                        response.writeHead(500, contentTypePlainText);
                        response.end('Internal Server Error');
                    }
                });
            }
```

```
            }
      });
    }
```

The `saveItem()` function takes the request body payload as an argument. A valid
update request will contain the new state of an `item` object, represented in JSON
format. First, the `itemId` is parsed out of the JSON object. Next, lookup is done. If an
item exists, it gets updated. Otherwise, a new one gets created:

```
exports.saveItem = function(request, response)
{
  var item = toItem(request.body);
  item.save((error) => {
    if (!error) {
      item.save();
      response.writeHead(201, contentTypeJson);
      response.end(JSON.stringify(request.body));
    } else {
      console.log(error);
      CatalogItem.findOne({itemId : item.itemId    },
      (error, result) => {
        console.log('Check if such an item exists');
            if (error) {
                console.log(error);
                response.writeHead(500, contentTypePlainText);
                response.end('Internal Server Error');
            } else {
                if (!result) {
                    console.log('Item does not exist. Creating a new
one');
                    item.save();
                    response.writeHead(201, contentTypeJson);
                    response.
                    response.end(JSON.stringify(request.body));
                } else {
                    console.log('Updating existing item');
                    result.itemId = item.itemId;
                    result.itemName = item.itemName;
                    result.price = item.price;
                    result.currency = item.currency;
                    result.categories = item.categories;
                    result.save();
                    response.json(JSON.stringify(result));
                }
            }
      });
```

```
    }
  });
};
```

The `toItem()` function converts the JSON payload to a `CatalogItem` model instance, that is, an item document:

```
function toItem(body) {
    return new CatalogItem({
        itemId: body.itemId,
        itemName: body.itemName,
        price: body.price,
        currency: body.currency,
        categories: body.categories
    });
}
```

We will also need to provide a means of querying data, so let's implement a function that queries for all items in a category:

```
exports.findItemsByCategory = function (category, response) {
    CatalogItem.find({categories: category}, function(error, result) {
        if (error) {
            console.error(error);
            response.writeHead(500, { 'Content-Type': 'text/plain' });
            return;
        } else {
            if (!result) {
                if (response != null) {
                    response.writeHead(404, contentTypePlainText);
                    response.end('Not Found');
                }
                return;
            }

            if (response != null){
                response.setHeader('Content-Type',
'application/json');
                response.send(result);
            }
            console.log(result);
        }
    });
}
```

Similar to `findItemsByCategory`, the following is a function that finds an item by its ID:

```
exports.findItemById = function (itemId, response) {
    CatalogItem.findOne({itemId: itemId}, function(error, result) {
        if (error) {
            console.error(error);
            response.writeHead(500, contentTypePlainText);
            return;
        } else {
            if (!result) {
                if (response != null) {
                    response.writeHead(404, contentTypePlainText);
                    response.end('Not Found');
                }
                return;
            }

            if (response != null){
                response.setHeader('Content-Type',
'application/json');
                response.send(result);
            }
            console.log(result);
        }
    });
}
```

Finally, there's a function that lists all the catalog items stored in the database. It uses the Mongoose model `find` function that looks for all documents of the model, and uses its first arguments as a filter. We want a function that returns all existing documents; that's why we provide an empty object. This will return all available items. The results are available in the `callback` function, which is the second argument of the model's `find` function:

```
exports.findAllItems = function (response) {
    CatalogItem.find({}, (error, result) => {
        if (error) {
            console.error(error);
            return null;
        }
        if (result != null) {
            response.json(result);
        } else {
```

```
      response.json({});
    }
  });
};
```

The `catalog` module will be the foundation of our RESTful service. It is responsible for all data manipulation operations, as well as for different kinds of queries. It encapsulates all operations in a reusable way.

Wiring up a NoSQL database module to Express

Now we have automated tests for the model and a user-defined module which makes use of them. This ensures the stability of the module and makes it ready for wider adoption.

It is time to build a new Express-based application and add a route, exposing the new module to it:

```
const express = require('express');
const router = express.Router();

const catalog = require('../modules/catalog');
const model = require('../model/item.js');

router.get('/', function(request, response, next) {
  catalog.findAllItems(response);
});

router.get('/item/:itemId', function(request, response, next) {
  console.log(request.url + ' : querying for ' +
request.params.itemId);
  catalog.findItemById(request.params.itemId, response);
});
```

```
router.get('/:categoryId', function(request, response, next) {
  console.log(request.url + ' : querying for ' +
request.params.categoryId);
  catalog.findItemsByCategory(request.params.categoryId, response);
});

router.post('/', function(request, response, next) {
  console.log('Saving item using POST method);
  catalog.saveItem(request, response);
});

router.put('/', function(request, response, next) {
  console.log('Saving item using PUT method');
  catalog.saveItem(request, response);
});

router.delete('/item/:itemId', function(request, response, next) {
  console.log('Deleting item with id: request.params.itemId);
  catalog.remove(request, response);
});

module.exports = router;
```

To sum up, we routed each function of the catalog data service module to an operation of a RESTful service:

- `GET /catalog/item/:itemId`: This calls `catalog.findItemById()`
- `POST /catalog`: This calls `catalog.saveItem()`
- `PUT /catalog`: This calls `catalog.saveItem()`
- `DELETE / catalog/item/:id`: This calls `catalog.remove()`
- `GET /catalog/:category`: This calls `catalog.findItemsByCategory()`
- `GET /catalog/`: This calls `catalog.findAllItems()`

As we have our operations exposed, we are ready to perform some more serious REST testing. Let's start Postman and test the newly exposed endpoints:

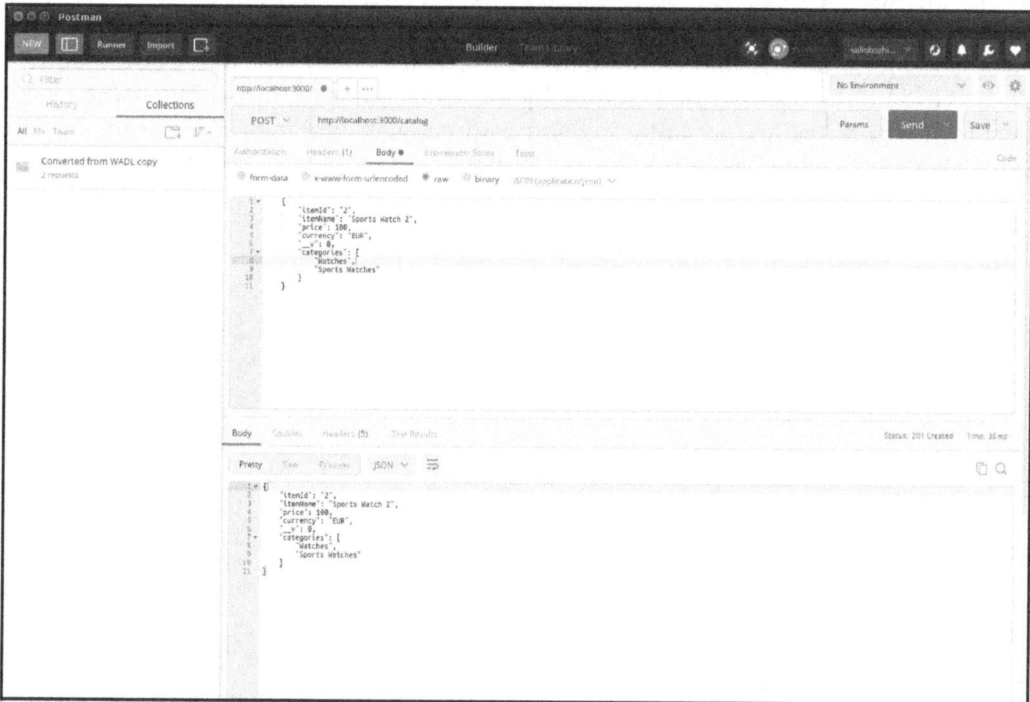

Spend some time testing each operation thoroughly. This will help you gain confidence that the catalog data service module really works, and also will make you more comfortable with how HTTP responses are served and read. As a RESTful API developer, you should be able to read HTTP dumps, which show different request payloads and status codes, fluently.

Self-test questions

Go through the following questions:

- How would you perform a query with Mongoose for a single value of a multivalued attribute?
- Define a strategy for testing a Node.js module manipulating a NoSQL database.

Summary

In this chapter, we looked at MongoDB, a powerful document-oriented database. We utilized it and made use of Mocha to implement an automated test for the database layer. Now it is time to build a fully-fledged RESTful web service. In the next chapter, we will extend the user-defined module by including support for searching via document attributes, and add filtering and pagination capabilities that will finally evolve into full-fledged RESTful service implementation.

15 Restful API Design Guidelines

In the previous chapter, we implemented a catalog module that exposed functions for data manipulation for the items in the catalog application. These functions made use of the `express.js` **request** object to parse the incoming data in the body and then to carry out the appropriate database operation. Each function populated the **response** object with a relevant status code and response body payload, if needed. Finally, we bound each function to a route, accepting HTTP requests.

Now, it's time to look closer into the URLs of the routes and into the returned HTTP status codes per operation.

In this chapter, we will cover the following topics:

- Endpoint URLs and HTTP status codes best practices
- Extensibility and versioning
- Linked data

Endpoint URLs and HTTP status codes best practices

Each RESTful API operation is a combination of an HTTP request against a URL and an appropriate HTTP method.

When executed, each operation will return a status code, indicating whether the invocation has been successful or not. Successful invocation is indicated by a HTTP 2XX status code, while operations that are not executed correctly indicate this with erroneous status code—4XX if the error is at client side, or 5xx when the server fails to process a valid request.

Having a well-specified API is vital for its adoption. Such specification should not only completely enumerate the status codes of each operation, but should also specify the expected data format, that is, its supported media types.

The following table defines how the Express.js Router will expose the API operations, and it should serve as a reference specification for it:

Method	URI	Media type	Description	Status Code
GET	/catalog	application/json	Returns all the items in the catalog.	200 OK 500 Internal Server Error
GET	/catalog/{categoryId}	application/json	Returns all items for the selected category. If the category does not exist, it returns 404.	200 OK, 404 NOT FOUND 500 Internal Server Error
GET	/item/{itemId}	application/json	Returns a single item for the selected itemId. If there is no such item, it returns 404.	200 OK, 404 NOT FOUND 500 Internal Server Error
POST	/item/	application/json	Creates a new item; if an item with the same identifier exists, it will be updated. When an item is created, a **Location** header is returned. It provides the URL where the newly created item can be accessed.	201 Created 200 OK 500 Internal Server Error
PUT	/item/{itemId}	application/json	Updates an existing item; if an item with the provided identifier does not exist, it creates it. When an item is created, a **Location** header is returned. It provides the URL where the newly created item can be accessed.	201 Created 200 OK 500 Internal Server Error

DELETE	/item/{itemId}	application/json	Deletes an existing item; if an item with the provided identifier does not exist, it returns 404.	200 OK, 404 NOT FOUND 500 Internal Server Error

The catalog application handles two types of entities: items and categories. Each item entity contains a collection of categories where it belongs. As you can see, the category is just a logical entity in our application; it will exist as long as there is at least one item referencing it, and will cease to exist when no items refer it. This is why the application exposes routes for exposing data manipulation functions only for resources of type items, while the operations for categories are more or less read only. Looking more carefully into the URLs exposing the data manipulation operations for the items, we can see a clear pattern aligning the URL to the REST fundamental principles—a resource is exposed by a single URL, and it supports resource manipulation actions that are determined by the HTTP method of the request. To sum up, listed here are the generally accepted rules that a well-defined API should follow. They are semantically related to each resource manipulation operation:

- When a **new** resource is created, the service makes use of the **201 Created** status code, followed by a location header that specifies the URL where the newly created resource can be accessed.
- Operation that creates resources may be implemented to gracefully reject creation of resources, which unique identifiers already use; in such cases, the operation should indicate a non-successful invocation with an appropriate status code **409 Conflict**, or a more general **400 BAD REQUEST**. However, a general status code should always be followed by a meaningful explanation of what has gone wrong. In our implementation, we choose a different approach—we update the resource from the create operation, if it exists, and notify the caller that the resource was updated by returning the **200 OK** status code instead of **201 Created**.

- The **Update** operation resembles the create operation; however, it always expects a resource identifier as a parameter, if a resource with this identifier exists—it gets updated with a new state provided in the body of the HTTP PUT request. The **200 OK** status code indicates successful invocation. The implementation may decide to reject handling of non-existent resources with the **404 Not Found** status code or creating a new resource with the passed identifier. In that case, it would return the **201 Created** status code, followed by a location header that specifies the URL where the newly created resource can be accessed. Our API makes use of the second option.

- While successful **deletion** can be indicated with the **204 No Content** status and further payload, most user agents would expect the **2xx** HTTP status to be followed by a body. Thus, to stay compatible with most of the agents, our API will indicate successful deletion with the **200 OK** status code, followed by a JSON payload:`{'Status': 'Successfully deleted'}`. Status code **404 Not found** will indicate that a resource with the provided identifier does not exist.

- As a general rule, **5XX** should not indicate application state errors but more severe errors, such as application server or database failures.

- It is best practice that `update` and `create` operations should return as a payload to the entire state of the resource. For instance, if a resource is created with a minimum set of attributes, all non specified attribute will get default values; the response body should contain the full state of the object. The same is valid for updates; even if an update operation updates the resource restate partially, the response should return the complete state. This may save the user-agent an additional GET request if they needed to check the new state.

Now that we have defined some general recommendations on how operations should behave, it's time to implement them in a new version of the API.

Extensibility and versioning

We've already defined a few basic versioning rules in `Chapter 13`, *Building a Typical Web API*. Let's apply them to the MongoDB database-aware module we implemented in the previous chapter. Our starting point would be to enable the current consumers of the API to continue using the same version on a different URL. This will keep them backward-compatible until they adopt and successfully test the new version.

Keeping a REST API stable is not a question of only moving one endpoint from one URI to another. It makes no sense to perform redirection and afterward have an API that behaves differently. Thus, we need to ensure that the behavior of the moved endpoint stays the same. To ensure that we don't change the previously implemented behavior, let's move the current behavior from the `catalog.js` module to a new module by renaming the file to `catalogV1.js`. Then, make a copy of it to the `catalogV2.js` module, where we will introduce all new functionality; but before doing that, we have to reroute Version 1 from `/`, `/{categoryId}`, `/{itemId}` to `/v1`, `/v1/{categoryId}`, `/v1/{itemId}`:

```
const express = require('express');
const router = express.Router();

const catalogV1 = require('../modules/catalogV1');
const model = require('../model/item.js');

router.get('/v1/', function(request, response, next) {
  catalogV1.findAllItems(response);
});

router.get('/v1/item/:itemId', function(request, response, next) {
  console.log(request.url + ' : querying for ' +
request.params.itemId);
  catalogV1.findItemById(request.params.itemId, response);
});

router.get('/v1/:categoryId', function(request, response, next) {
  console.log(request.url + ' : querying for ' +
request.params.categoryId);
  catalogV1.findItemsByCategory(request.params.categoryId, response);
});

router.post('/v1/', function(request, response, next) {
  catalogV1.saveItem(request, response);
});

router.put('/v1/', function(request, response, next) {
  catalogV1.saveItem(request, response);
});

router.delete('/v1/item/:itemId', function(request, response, next) {
  catalogV1.remove(request, response);
});

router.get('/', function(request, response) {
  console.log('Redirecting to v1');
```

```
    response.writeHead(301, {'Location' : '/catalog/v1/'});
    response.end('Version 1 is moved to /catalog/v1/: ');
});

module.exports = router;
```

Since Version 2 of our API is not yet implemented, executing a `GET` request against `/` will result in receiving a `301 Moved Permanently` HTTP status, which will then redirect to `/v1/`. This will notify our consumers that the API is evolving and that they will soon need to decide whether to continue using Version 1 by explicitly requesting its new URI or prepare for adopting Version 2.

Go ahead and give it a try! Start the modified node application and, from Postman, make a GET request to `http://localhost:3000/catalog`:

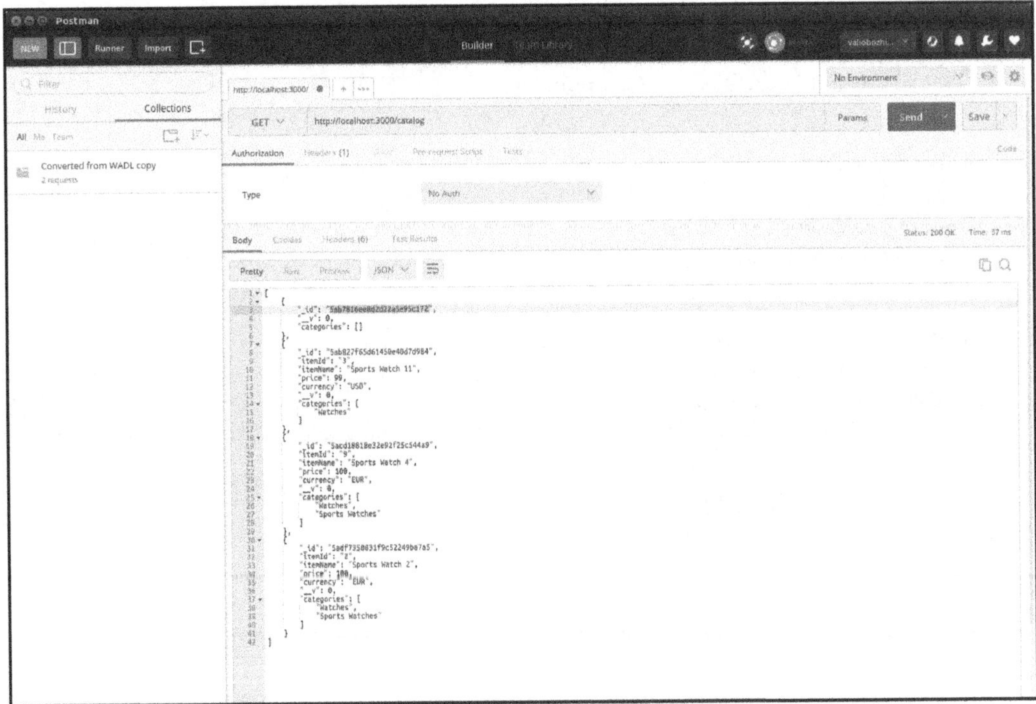

You will see that your request is redirected to the newly routed location at `http://localhost:3000/catalog/v1`.

Now that we have finalized Version 1 of the catalog, it's time to think of further extensions that we can add in Version 2. Currently, the catalog service supports listing of all items in a category and fetching an item by its ID. It's about time to take full advantage of MongoDB, being a document-oriented database, and implement a function that will enable our API consumer to query for items based on any of their attributes. For instance, list all items for a specific category with an attribute that matches a query parameter, such as price or color, or search by item name. RESTful services usually expose document-oriented data. However, their usage is not limited to documents only. In the next chapter, we will extend the catalog in a way that it also stores binary data—an image that can be linked to each item. For that purpose, we will use a MongoDB binary format called **Binary JSON (BSON)** in the *Working with arbitrary data* section in `Chapter 16`, *Implementing a Full Fledged RESTful Service*.

Getting back to the searching extension, we've already used the `Mongoose.js` model's `find()` and `findOne()` functions. So far, we used them to provide the name of the document attribute to be searched with, statically, in our JavaScript code. However, this filtering parameter of `find()` is just a JSON object where the key is the document attribute and the value is the attribute's value to be used in the query. Here is the first new function we will add to Version 2. It queries MongoDB by an arbitrary attribute and its value:

```
exports.findItemsByAttribute = function (key, value, response) {
    var filter = {};
    filter[key] = value;
    CatalogItem.find(filter, function(error, result) {
        if (error) {
            console.error(error);
            response.writeHead(500, contentTypePlainText);
            response.end('Internal server error');
            return;
        } else {
            if (!result) {
                if (response != null) {
                    response.writeHead(200, contentTypeJson);
                    response.end({});
                }
                return;
            }
            if (response != null){
                response.setHeader('Content-Type',
'application/json');
                response.send(result);
            }
```

```
        }
    });
  }
```

This function calls find on the model with the provided attribute and value as parameters. We will bind this function to the router's `/v2/item/` GET handler.

At the end, our aim is to have `/v2/item/?currency=USD` that returns only records for items that are sold in USD currency, as indicated by the value of the passed GET parameter. That way, if we modify the model with additional attributes, such as color and size, we can query for all items having the same color or any other attribute that an item can have.

We will keep the old behavior of returning a list of all available items when no parameters are provided within the query string, but we will also parse the query string for the first provided GET parameter and use it as a filter in the `findItemsByAttribute()` function:

```
router.get('/v2/items', function(request, response) {
    var getParams = url.parse(request.url, true).query;
    if (Object.keys(getParams).length == 0) {
      catalogV2.findAllItems(response);
    } else {
      var key = Object.keys(getParams)[0];
      var value = getParams[key];
      catalogV2.findItemsByAttribute(key, value, response);
    }
});
```

Perhaps the most interesting part in this function is the URL parsing. As you can see, we keep using the same old strategy to check whether any GET parameters are supplied. We parse the URL in order to get the query string, and then we use the built-in `Object.keys` function to check whether the parsed key/value list contains elements. If it does, we take the first element and extract its value. Both the key and the value are passed to the `findByAttribute` function.

You may want to improve Version 2 further by providing search support by multiple arguments that are provided by more than one GET parameters. I will leave that to you as an exercise.

Linked data

Every catalog application supports an image or set of images bound to this item. For that purpose, in the next chapter, we will see how to work with binary objects in MongoDB. However, now is the time to decide how to semantically link the binary data to an item document. Extending the model schema in such a way that it contains binary base64 representation of binary data in the document is anything but a good idea, as mixing literally encoded and binary data in one format is never a good idea. It increases the complexity of the application and makes it error-prone:

```
{
  "_id": "5a4c004b0eed73835833cc9a",
  "itemId": "1",
  "itemName": "Sports Watch",
  "price": 100,
  "currency": "EUR",
  "categories": [
    "Watches",
    "Sports Watches"
  ],
  "image":"
iVBORw0KGgoAAAANSUhEUgAAAJEAAACRCAMAAAD0BqoRAAAAGXRFWHRTb2Z0d2FyZQBBZG
9iZSBJbWFnZVJlYWR5ccllPAAAAyJpVFh0WE1MOmNvbS5hZG9iZS54bXAAAAAAADw/eHBh
Y2tldCBiZWdpbj0i77u/IiBpZD0iVzVNME1wQ2VoaUh6cmVTek5UY3prYzlkIj8+IDx4On
htcG1ldGEgeG1sbnM6eD0iYWRvYmU6bnM6bWV0YS8iIHg6eG1wdGs9IkFkb2JlIFhNUCBD
b3JlIDUuMC1jMDYwIDYxLjEzNDc3NywgMjAxMC8wMi8xMi0xNzozMjowMCAgICAgICAgIj
4gPHJkZjpSREYgeG1sbnM6cmRmPSJodHRwOi8vd3d3LnczLm9yZy8xOTk5LzAyLzIyLXJk
Zi1zeW50YXgtbnMjIj4gPHJkZjpEZXNjcmlwdGlvbiByZGY6YWJvdXQ9IiIgeG1sbnM6
eG1wPSJodHRwOi8vbnMuYWRvYmUuY29tL3hhcC8xLjAvIiB4bWxuczp4bXBNTT0iaHR0cD
ovL25zLmFkb2JlLmNvbS94YXAvMS4wL21tLyIgeG1sbnM6c3RSZWY9Imh0dHA6Ly9ucy5h
ZG9iZS5jb20veGFwLzEuMC9zVHlwZS9SZXNvdXJjZVJlZiMiIHhtcDpDcmVhdG9yVG9vbD
0iQWRvYmUgUGhvdG9zaG9wIENTNSBNYWNpbnRvc2giIHhtcE1OOkluc3RhbmNlSUQ9Inht
cC5paWQ6MjMwNjQ1NDdFNjJCMTFERkI5QzU4OTFCMjJCQzEzM0EiIHhtcE1OOkRvY3VtZW
50SUQ9InhtcC5kaWQ6MjMwNjQ1NDhFNjJCMTFERkI5QzU4OTFCMjJCQzEzM0EiPiA8eG1w
TU06RGVyaXZlZEZyb20gc3RSZWY6aW5zdGFuY2VJRD0ieG1wLmlpZDoyMzA2NDU0NUU2Mk
IxMURGQjlDNTg5MUIyMkJDMTMzQSIgc3RSZWY6ZG9jdW1lbnRJRD0ieG1wLmRpZDoyMzA2
NDU0NkU2MkIxMURGQjlDNTg5MUIyMkJDMTMzQSIvPiA8L3JkZjpEZXNjcmlwdGlvbj4gPC
9yZGY6UkRGPiA8L3g6eG1wbWV0YT4gPD94cGFja2V0IGVuZD0iciI/Px5Xq1XXhWFY1+v1
51/b3ij5tI/GPEVP0e8U/SPAABPLjHnaJ6XvAAAAAElFTkSuQmCC
"}
```

Imagine how large a result for a non-filtered query can become just for a few hundred items, if all of them had an image binary representation as a value of a JSON attribute. To avoid that, we will return the image for each item at a URL that is logically linked to the resource's URL—`/catalog/v2/item/{itemId}/image`.

That way, if there is an image assigned to an item, it will be served at a known location. This approach, however, does not semantically link the binary item to its corresponding resource, as when accessing the item at `/catalog/v2/item/{itemId}`, there would be no indication of whether it has an image assigned or not. To solve this, let's use a custom HTTP header in response of the item route:

```
GET http://localhost:3000/catalog/v2/item/1 HTTP/1.1
Host: localhost:3000
Connection: Keep-Alive
User-Agent: Apache-HttpClient/4.1.1 (java 1.5)

HTTP/1.1 200 OK
X-Powered-By: Express
Content-Type: application/json; charset=utf-8
Content-Length: 152
Image-Url: http://localhost:3000/catalog/v2/item/1/image
ETag: W/"98-2nJj2mZdLV2YDME3WYCyEwIXfuA"
Date: Thu, 01 Feb 2018 13:50:43 GMT
Connection: keep-alive

{
   "_id": "5a4c004b0eed73835833cc9a",
   "itemId": "1",
   "itemName": "Sports Watch",
   "price": 100,
   "currency": "EUR",
   "__v": 0,
   "categories": [
     "Watches",
     "Sports Watches"
   ]
}
```

When present in the response, the `Image-Url` header indicates that the item has an additional resource bound to it, and the header value provides the address where it is available. Using this approach, we linked a binary resource semantically to our document.

In the next chapter, we will implement the routes that will handle the manipulation of arbitrary items bound to the items in the catalog.

Summary

In this chapter, we discussed in detail how resources should be exposed via a RESTful API; we paid close attention to URL best practices and looked into appropriate usage of the HTTP status codes indicating each state of our operations.

We covered the topics of versioning and extensibility, where we used the `301 Moved Permanently` status code to automatically redirect API calls to different URLs.

Finally, we figured out how to semantically link our resource items to arbitrary binary represented data.

Implementing a Full Fledged RESTful Service

16

So far, we have created a second version of our RESTful service, and we had the two versions exposed by different URLs, ensuring backward compatibility. We implemented unit tests for its database layer and discussed how to use HTTP status codes appropriately. In this chapter, we will extend that implementation—by providing handling of non-document—binary data to the second version of the service and linking it accordingly to the documents it relates to.

We will look at a convenient way of presenting large result sets to consumers. For that purpose, we will introduce pagination as well as further filtering capabilities to our API.

There are cases when caching data responses should be considered as an option. We will look at its benefits and drawbacks and also decide to enable caching when necessary.

Finally, we will dive into the discovery and exploration of REST services.

To sum up, here's what should be further implemented to turn the catalog data service into a full-fledged RESTful service:

- Working with arbitrary data
- Working with Linked data in the real world
- Paging and filtering
- Caching
- Discovery and exploration

Working with arbitrary data

MongoDB utilizes BSON (Binary JSON) as the primary data format. It is a binary format that stores key/value pairs in a single entity called **document.** For example, a sample JSON, `{"hello":"world"}`, becomes `\x16\x00\x00\x00\x02hello\x00\x06\x00\x00\x00world\x00\x00` when encoded in BSON.

BSON stores data rather than literals. For instance, if an image is to be part of the document, it will not have to be converted to a base64-encoded string; instead, it will be directly stored as binary data, unlike plain JSON, which will usually represent such data as base64-encoded bytes, but that is obviously not the most efficient way.

Mongoose schemas enable storing binary content in the BSON format via the schema type—**buffer**. It stores binary content (image, ZIP archive, and so on) up to 16 MB. The reason behind the relatively small storage capacity is to prevent excessive usage of memory and bandwidth during transmission.

The **GridFS** specification addresses this limitation of BSON and enables you to work with data larger than 16 MB. GridFS divides data into chunks stored as separate document entries. Each chunk, by default, has a size of up to 255 KB. When data is requested from the data store, the GridFS driver retrieves all the required chunks and returns them in an assembled order, as if they had never been divided. Not only does this mechanism allow storage of data larger than 16 MB, it also enables consumers to retrieve data in portions so that it doesn't have to be loaded completely into the memory. Thus, the specification implicitly enables streaming support.

GridFS actually offers more—it supports storing metadata for the given binary data, for example, its format, a filename, size, and so on. The metadata is stored in a separate file and is available for more complex queries. There is a very usable Node.js module called `gridfs-stream`. It enables easy streaming of data in and out of MongoDB, as on all other modules it is installed as an npm package. So, let's install it globally and see how it is used; we will also use the `-s` option to ensure that the dependencies in the project's `package.json` are updated:

```
npm install -g -s gridfs-stream
```

To create a `Grid` instance, you are required to have a connection opened to the database:

```
const mongoose = require('mongoose')
const Grid = require('gridfs-stream');

mongoose.connect('mongodb://localhost/catalog');
var connection = mongoose.connection;
var gfs = Grid(connection.db, mongoose.mongo);
```

Reading and writing into the stream is done through the `createReadStream()` and `createWriteStream()` functions. Each piece of data streamed into the database must have an `ObjectId` attribute set. The `ObjectId` identifies binary data entry uniquely, just as it would have identified any other document in MongoDB; using this `ObjectId`, we can find or delete it from the MongoDB collection by this identifier.

Let's extend the catalog service with functions for fetching, adding, and deleting an image assigned to an item. For simplicity, the service will support a single image per item, so there will be a single function responsible for adding an image. It will overwrite an existing image each time it is invoked, so an appropriate name for it is `saveImage`:

```
exports.saveImage = function(gfs, request, response) {

    var writeStream = gfs.createWriteStream({
            filename : request.params.itemId,
            mode : 'w'
        });

    writeStream.on('error', function(error) {
        response.send('500', 'Internal Server Error');
        console.log(error);
        return;
    })

    writeStream.on('close', function() {
        readImage(gfs, request, response);
    });

    request.pipe(writeStream);
}
```

As you can see, all we need to do to flush the data in MongoDB is to create a GridFS write stream instance. It requires some options that provide the `ObjectId` of the MongoDB entry and some additional metadata, such as a title as well as the writing mode. Then, we simply call the pipe function of the request. Piping will result in flushing the data from the request to the write stream, and, in this way, it will be safely stored in MongoDB. Once stored, the `close` event associated with the `writeStream` will occur, and this is when our function reads back whatever it has stored in the database and returns that image in the HTTP response.

Retrieving an image is done the other way around—a `readStream` is created with options, and the value of the `_id` parameter should be the `ObjectId` of the arbitrary data, optional file name, and read mode:

```
function readImage(gfs, request, response) {

    var imageStream = gfs.createReadStream({
        filename : request.params.itemId,
        mode : 'r'
    });

    imageStream.on('error', function(error) {
      console.log(error);
      response.send('404', 'Not found');
      return;
    });
    response.setHeader('Content-Type', 'image/jpeg');
    imageStream.pipe(response);
  }
```

Before piping the read stream to the response, the appropriate `Content-Type` header has to be set so that the arbitrary data can be presented to the client with an appropriate image media type, `image/jpeg`, in our case.

Finally, we export from our module a function for fetching the image back from MongoDB. We will use that function to bind it to the express route that reads the image from the database:

```
exports.getImage = function(gfs, itemId, response) {
    readImage(gfs, itemId, response);
};
```

Deleting arbitrary data from MongoDB is also straightforward. You have to delete the entry from two internal MongoDB collections, the `fs.files`, where all the files are kept, and from the `fs.files.chunks`:

```
exports.deleteImage = function(gfs, mongodb, itemId, response) {
  console.log('Deleting image for itemId:' + itemId);

    var options = {
            filename : itemId,
    };

    var chunks = mongodb.collection('fs.files.chunks');
    chunks.remove(options, function (error, image) {
        if (error) {
            console.log(error);
            response.send('500', 'Internal Server Error');
            return;
        } else {
            console.log('Successfully deleted image for item: ' +
itemId);
        }
    });

    var files = mongodb.collection('fs.files');
    files.remove(options, function (error, image) {
        if (error) {
            console.log(error);
            response.send('500', 'Internal Server Error');
            return;
        }

        if (image === null) {
            response.send('404', 'Not found');
            return;
        } else {
            console.log('Successfully deleted image for primary item: '
+ itemId);
            response.json({'deleted': true});
        }
    });
}
```

Let's bind the new functionality to the appropriate item route and test it:

```
router.get('/v2/item/:itemId/image',
  function(request, response){
    var gfs = Grid(model.connection.db, mongoose.mongo);
    catalogV2.getImage(gfs, request, response);
});

router.get('/item/:itemId/image',
  function(request, response){
    var gfs = Grid(model.connection.db, mongoose.mongo);
    catalogV2.getImage(gfs, request, response);
});

router.post('/v2/item/:itemId/image',
  function(request, response){
    var gfs = Grid(model.connection.db, mongoose.mongo);
    catalogV2.saveImage(gfs, request, response);
});

router.post('/item/:itemId/image',
  function(request, response){
    var gfs = Grid(model.connection.db, mongoose.mongo);
    catalogV2.saveImage(gfs, request.params.itemId, response);
});

router.put('/v2/item/:itemId/image',
  function(request, response){
    var gfs = Grid(model.connection.db, mongoose.mongo);
    catalogV2.saveImage (gfs, request.params.itemId, response);
});

router.put('/item/:itemId/image',
function(request, response){
  var gfs = Grid(model.connection.db, mongoose.mongo);
  catalogV2.saveImage(gfs, request.params.itemId, response);
});

router.delete('/v2/item/:itemId/image',
function(request, response){
  var gfs = Grid(model.connection.db, mongoose.mongo);
  catalogV2.deleteImage(gfs, model.connection,
  request.params.itemId, response);
});

router.delete('/item/:itemId/image',
function(request, response){
  var gfs = Grid(model.connection.db, mongoose.mongo);
```

```
catalogV2.deleteImage(gfs, model.connection,  request.params.itemId,
response);
});
```

Since, at the time of writing, Version 2 is the latest version of our API, any new functionality exposed by it should be available at both locations: `/catalog` and `/v2/catalog`.

Let's start Postman and post an image to an existing item, assuming that we have an item with ID 14 `/catalog/v2/item/14/image`:

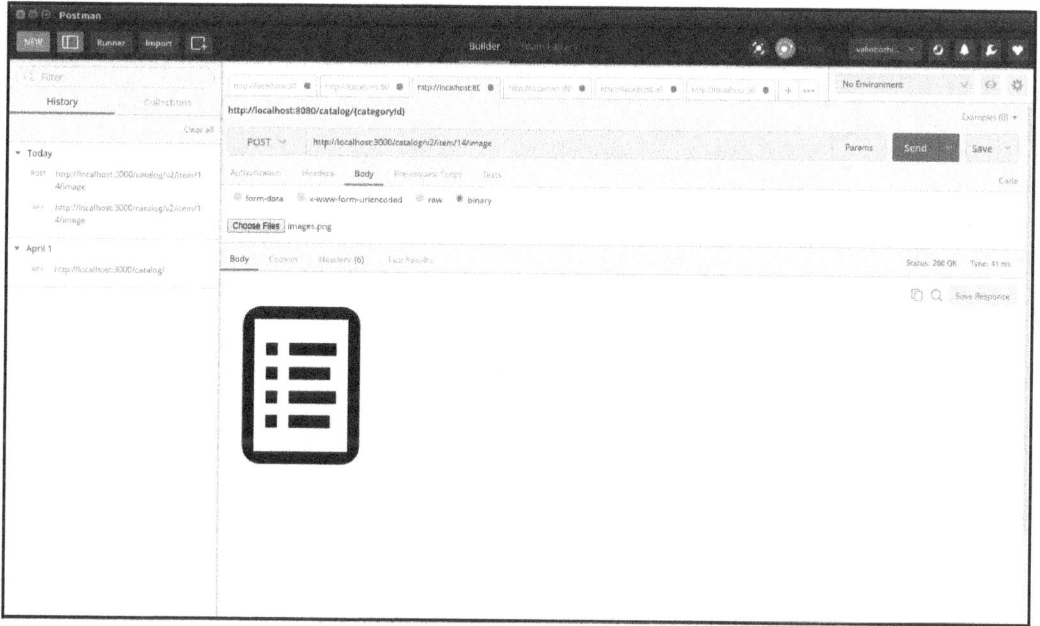

Post request assigning an image to an item using Postman. This is a screenshot for Postman. The individual settings are not important here. The purpose of the image is just to show how the window looks.

After the request is processed, the binary data is stored in the grid datastore and the image is returned in the response.

Linking

In the Linked data section of the previous chapter, we defined that if an item in the catalog has an image assigned to it, this will be indicated with an HTTP header named **Image-URL**.

Let's modify the `findItemById` function in the V2 of the catalog. We will use the GridFS's existing function to check whether there is an image bound to the selected item; in case there is an image assigned to the item, its URL will be available to the response with the Image-Url header:

```
exports.findItemById = function (gfs, request, response) {
    CatalogItem.findOne({itemId: request.params.itemId},
function(error, result) {
        if (error) {
            console.error(error);
            response.writeHead(500,     contentTypePlainText);
            return;
        } else {
            if (!result) {
                if (response != null) {
                    response.writeHead(404, contentTypePlainText);
                    response.end('Not Found');
                }
                return;
            }

            var options = {
                filename : result.itemId,
            };
            gfs.exist(options, function(error, found) {
                if (found) {
                    response.setHeader('Content-Type',
'application/json');
                    var imageUrl = request.protocol + '://' +
request.get('host') + request.baseUrl + request.path + '/image';
                    response.setHeader('Image-Url', imageUrl);
                    response.send(result);
                } else {
                    response.json(result);
                }
            });
        }
    });
}
```

So far, we linked an item to its image; however, that leaves our data partially linked, as there is a link from an item to its image but not the other way around. Let's change that and supply a header Item-Url to the image response by modifying the `readImage` function:

```
function readImage(gfs, request, response) {

  var imageStream = gfs.createReadStream({
      filename : request.params.itemId,
      mode : 'r'
  });

  imageStream.on('error', function(error) {
    console.log(error);
    response.send('404', 'Not found');
    return;
  });

  var itemImageUrl = request.protocol + '://' + request.get('host') +
request.baseUrl+ request.path;
  var itemUrl = itemImageUrl.substring(0,
itemImageUrl.indexOf('/image'));
  response.setHeader('Content-Type', 'image/jpeg');
  response.setHeader('Item-Url', itemUrl);

  imageStream.pipe(response);
}
```

Now requesting the item at `http://localhost:3000/catalog/v2/item/3/` will return the item encoded in the JSON format:

```
GET http://localhost:3000/catalog/v2/item/3/image HTTP/1.1
Accept-Encoding: gzip,deflate
Host: localhost:3000

HTTP/1.1 200 OK
X-Powered-By: Express
Content-Type: application/json; charset=utf-8
Image-Url: http://localhost:3000/catalog/v2/item/3/image
Content-Length: 137
Date: Tue, 03 Apr 2018 19:47:41 GMT
Connection: keep-alive

{
    "_id": "5ab827f65d61450e40d7d984",
    "itemId": "3",
    "itemName": "Sports Watch 11",
```

```
      "price": 99,
      "currency": "USD",
      "__v": 0,
      "categories": ["Watches"]
  }
```

Looking into the response headers, we find the `Image-Url` header its value, `http://localhost:3000/catalog/v2/item/3/image` provides the URL of the image linked to the item.

Requesting that image results in the following:

```
GET http://localhost:3000/catalog/v2/item/3/image HTTP/1.1
Host: localhost:3000
Connection: Keep-Alive

HTTP/1.1 200 OK
X-Powered-By: Express
Content-Type: image/jpeg
Item-Url: http://localhost:3000/catalog/v2/item/3
Connection: keep-alive
Transfer-Encoding: chunked

<BINARY DATA>
```

This time, the response provides the payload of the image linked to the item and a special header **Item-Url**. Its value—`http://localhost:3000/catalog/v2/item/3`—is the address where the item resource is available. Now if the item image appears, for instance, in image search results, the URL of the item linked with the image will also be part of the result. In this way, we linked the two data semantically without modifying or compromising their payload.

Implementing paging and filtering

Once deployed to the web, each service becomes available to an enormous number of consumers. They will not only use it to get data but also to insert new data. At some point of time, this will inevitably lead to a large amount of data being available in the database. To keep the service user-friendly and maintain a reasonable response time, we need to take care of providing big data in reasonable portions, assuring that it does not need to return a few hundred thousand items when the `/catalog` URI is requested.

Web data consumers are used to having various pagination and filtering capabilities. Earlier in this chapter, we implemented the `findIfindItemsByAttribute()` function, which enabled filtering by any of the attributes of an item Now, it's time to introduce pagination capabilities to enable navigation within the `resultset` with the help of a URI parameter.

The `mongoose.js` models can make use of different plugin modules to provide additional functionality on top of them. Such a plugin module is `mongoose-paginate`. The Express framework also provides a piece of pagination middleware named `express-paginate`. It provides out-of-the-box linking and navigation with Mongoose's result pages:

1. Before starting to develop the pagination mechanism, we should install these two useful modules:

   ```
   npm install -g -s express-paginate
   npm install -g -s mongoose-paginate
   ```

2. The next step will to be to create instances of the `express-paginate` middleware in our application:

   ```
   expressPaginate = require('express-paginate');
   ```

3. Initialize the pagination middleware in the application by calling its `middleware()` function. Its parameters specify a default limit and a maximum limit of results per page:

   ```
   app.use(expressPaginate.middleware(limit, maxLimit);
   ```

4. Then, provide the `mongoose-pagination` instance as a plugin to the `CatalogItem` schema before creating a model. Here's how the `item.js` module will export that along with the model:

   ```
   var mongoose = require('mongoose');
   var mongoosePaginate = require('mongoose-paginate');
   var Schema = mongoose.Schema;

   mongoose.connect('mongodb://localhost/catalog');

   var itemSchema = new Schema ({
       "itemId" : {type: String, index: {unique: true}},
       "itemName": String,
       "price": Number,
       "currency" : String,
       "categories": [String]
   ```

```
});
console.log('paginate');
itemSchema.plugin(mongoosePaginate);
var CatalogItem = mongoose.model('Item', itemSchema);

module.exports = {CatalogItem : CatalogItem, connection :
mongoose.connection};
```

5. Finally, call the `paginate()` function of the model to fetch the requested
    entries in a paginated manner:

```
CatalogItem.paginate({}, {page:request.query.page,
limit:request.query.limit},
    function (error, result){
        if(error) {
            console.log(error);
            response.writeHead('500',
                {'Content-Type' : 'text/plain'});
            response.end('Internal Server Error');
        } else {
            response.json(result);
        }
});
```

The first parameter is the filter that Mongoose should use for its query. The second
parameter is an object specifying which page is requested and the entries per page.
The third parameter is a callback-handler function, providing the result and any
available error information via its parameters:

- `error`: This specifies whether the query was executed successfully
- `result`: This is the retrieved data from the database

The `express-paginate` middleware enables seamless integration of the `mongoose-paginate` module in the web environment by enriching the `request` and `response` objects of an Express handler function.

The `request` objects get two new attributes: `query.limit`, which tells the middleware the number of entries on the page, and `query.page`, which specifies the requested page. Note that the middleware will ignore values of `query.limit` that are larger than the `maxLimit` value specified at the middleware's initialization. This prevents the consumer from overriding the maximum limit and gives you total control over your application.

Here's the implementation of the `paginate` function in the second version of the catalog module:

```javascript
exports.paginate = function(model, request, response) {
    var pageSize = request.query.limit;
    var page = request.query.page;
    if (pageSize === undefined) {
        pageSize = 100;
    }
    if (page === undefined) {
        page = 1;
    }


    model.paginate({}, {page:page, limit:pageSize},
            function (error, result){
                if(error) {
                    console.log(error);
                    response.writeHead('500',
                        {'Content-Type' : 'text/plain'});
                    response.end('Internal Server Error');
                }
                else {
                    response.json(result);
                }
            });
}
```

The following is the response from querying a dataset containing 11 items with a limit
of five items per page:

```json
{
  "docs": [
    {
      "_id": "5a4c004b0eed73835833cc9a",
      "itemId": "1",
      "itemName": "Sports Watch 1",
      "price": 100,
      "currency": "EUR",
      "__v": 0,
      "categories": [
        "Watches",
        "Sports Watches"
      ]
    },
    {
      "_id": "5a4c0b7aad0ebbce584593ee",
      "itemId": "2",
      "itemName": "Sports Watch 2",
      "price": 100,
      "currency": "USD",
      "__v": 0,
```

```
        "categories": [
          "Sports Watches"
        ]
      },
      {
        "_id": "5a64d7ecfa1b585142008017",
        "itemId": "3",
        "itemName": "Sports Watch 3",
        "price": 100,
        "currency": "USD",
        "__v": 0,
        "categories": [
          "Watches",
          "Sports Watches"
        ]
      },
      {
        "_id": "5a64d9a59f4dc4e34329b80f",
        "itemId": "8",
        "itemName": "Sports Watch 4",
        "price": 100,
        "currency": "EUR",
        "__v": 0,
        "categories": [
          "Watches",
          "Sports Watches"
        ]
      },
      {
        "_id": "5a64da377d25d96e44c9c273",
        "itemId": "9",
        "itemName": "Sports Watch 5",
        "price": 100,
        "currency": "USD",
        "__v": 0,
        "categories": [
          "Watches",
          "Sports Watches"
        ]
      }
    ],
    "total": 11,
    "limit": "5",
    "page": "1",
    "pages": 3
  }
```

The `docs` attribute contains all the items that are part of the results. Its size is the same as the selected limit value. The `pages` attribute provides the total number of pages; in the example here, its value is 3, as 11 items are accommodated in three pages, each containing five items. The `Total` attribute gives us the total number of items.

The final step to enable pagination is to modify the `/v2/` route to start making use of the newly created function:

```
router.get('/v2/', function(request, response) {
  var getParams = url.parse(request.url, true).query;
  if (getParams['page'] !=null) {
    catalogV2.paginate(model.CatalogItem, request, response);
  } else {
    var key = Object.keys(getParams)[0];
    var value = getParams[key];
    catalogV2.findItemsByAttribute(key, value, response);
  }
});
```

We will use the HTTP `302 Found` status for the default route, `/catalog`. In this way, all incoming requests will be redirected to `/v2/`:

```
router.get('/', function(request, response) {
  console.log('Redirecting to v2');
  response.writeHead(302, {'Location' : '/catalog/v2/'});
  response.end('Version 2 is is available at /catalog/v2/: ');
});
```

Using an appropriate status code for redirection here is vital to the life cycle of any RESTful web service. Returning `302 Found`, followed by a redirection, ensures that the consumer of the API will always have its latest version available at that location. Furthermore, it is also a good practice from the development point of view to use redirection instead of code duplication here.

When you are between two versions, you should always consider using the HTTP `301 Moved Permanently` status to show where the previous version has been moved and the HTTP `302 Found` status to show the actual URI of the current version.

Now, getting back to pagination, as the requested page and the limit number are provided as GET parameters and we don't want to mix that up with the filtering capabilities, there is an explicit check for them. Pagination will be used only when either the page or the limit GET parameters, are available in the request. Otherwise, searching will be carried out.

Initially, we set the maximum limit of 100 results and a default limit of 10, so, before trying the new pagination functionality, ensure that you insert more items than the default limit into the database. This will make the test results more obvious.

Now, let's give it a try. Requesting `/catalog?limit=3` will result in returning a list containing only two items, as shown:

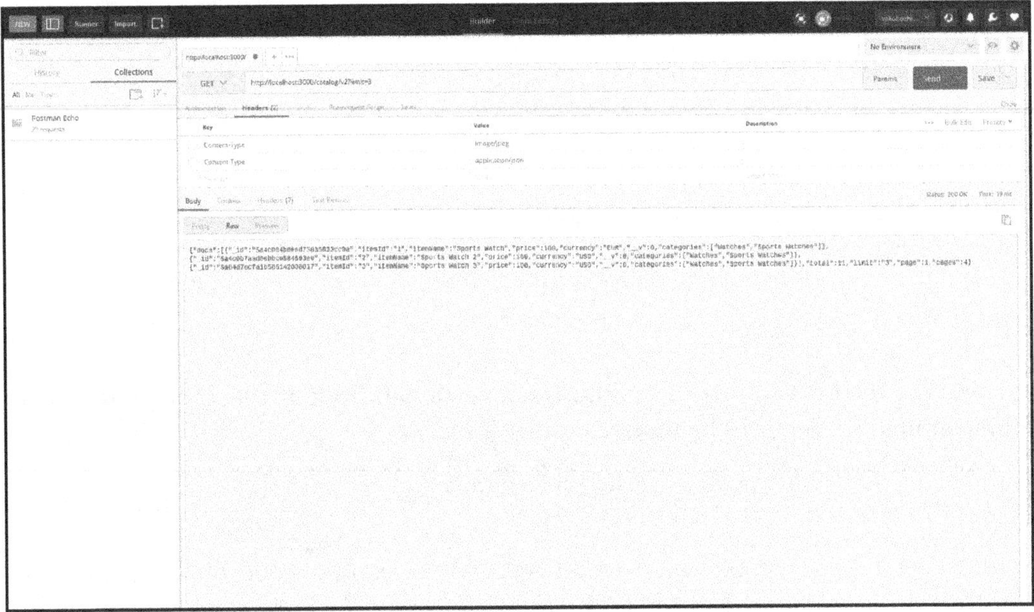

Pagination enabled results. This is a screenshot for Postman. The individual settings are not important here. The purpose of the image is just to show how the window looks.

As you can see from the example, the total number of pages is four. The total number of items is stored in the database 11. Since we didn't specify a page parameter in the request, the pagination implicitly returned the first page. To navigate to the next page, simply add `&page=2` to the URI.

Also, try changing the `limit` attribute, requesting `/catalog/v2?limit=4`. This will return the first four items, and the response will show that the total number of pages is three.

Caching

When we discussed the REST principles defined by Roy Fielding, we mentioned that caching was a rather sensitive topic. In the end, our consumers will expect up-to-date results when executing a query. However, from a statistical point of view, data exposed in the web is more likely to be read rather than updated or deleted.

So, it is reasonable that some resources exposed by a public URL become a subject of millions of requests, considering taking off part of the load from the server to a cache. The HTTP protocol allows us to cache some responses for a given period of time. For instance, when multiple requests are received in a short period of time, querying for all items in the catalog of a given group, such as `/catalog/v2`, our service can utilize special HTTP headers that would force the HTTP server to cache the response for a defined time period. This would prevent redundant requests to the underlying database server.

Caching at the HTTP server level is achieved via special response headers. The HTTP server uses a `Cache-Control` header to specify how long a given response should be cached for. The period before the cache needs invalidation is set via its `max-age` attribute, and its value is provided in seconds. Of course, there is a nice Node.js module that provides a middleware function for caching, called `express-cache-control`.

Supplying the Cache-Control header in Express applications

Let's install it with the NPM package manager; once again, we will install it globally and make use of the `-s` option, which will update the `package.json` file with the new `express-cache-control` dependency automatically:

```
npm install -g -s express-cache-control
```

Enabling caching with the `express-cache-control` middleware requires three straightforward steps:

1. Get the module:

   ```
   CacheControl = require("express-cache-control")
   ```

2. Create an instance of the `CacheControl` middleware:

   ```
   var cache = new CacheControl().middleware;
   ```

3. To bind the middleware instance to the routes you want to enable caching for:

   ```
   router.get('/v2/', cache('minutes', 1), function(request,
   response) {
       var getParams = url.parse(request.url, true).query;
       if (getParams['page'] !=null || getParams['limit'] !=
   null) {
           catalogV2.paginate(model.CatalogItem, request,
   response);
       } else {
           var key = Object.keys(getParams)[0];
           var value = getParams[key];
           catalogV2.findItemsByAttribute(key, value, response);
       }
   });
   ```

Usually, common URIs that provide many result entries should be the subject of caching, rather than URIs providing data for a concrete entry. In our application, only the `/catalog` URI will make use of caching. The `max-age` attribute must be selected according to the load of your application to minimize inaccurate responses.

Let's test our changes by requesting `/catalog/v2` in Postman:

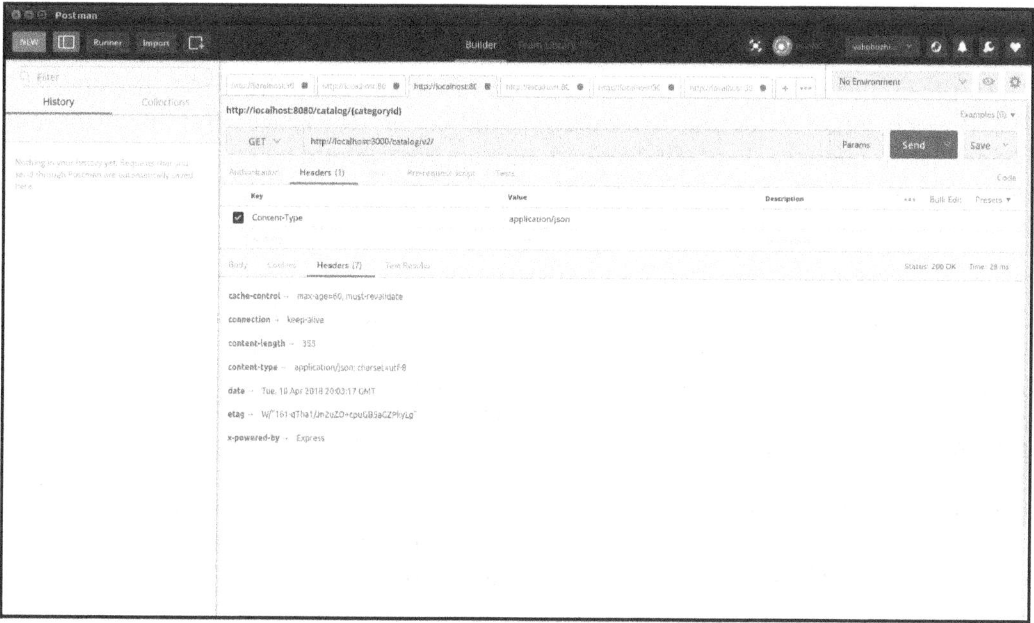

Cache-control header indicating that caching is enabled. This is a screenshot for Postman. The individual settings are not important here. The purpose of the image is just to show how the window looks.

As expected, the `express-cache-control` middleware has done its job—the `Cache-Control` header is now included in the response. The `must-revalidate` option ensures that the cache content is invalidated after the `max-age` interval expires. Now, if you make another request for a specific item, you will see that the response does not make use of the `express-cache-control` middleware, which is because it needs to be explicitly provided in each individual route. It will not be used in URIs deriving from one another.

Responses from `GET` requests against any route `/v1/` will not contain the `Cache-Control` header, as it is supported only in Version 2 of our API, and the `Cache-Control` middleware is used only in the main catalog routes: `/catalog/v2/` or `/catalog`.

Discovering and exploring RESTful services

The topic of discovering RESTful services has a long and complicated history. The HTTP specification states that a resource should be self-descriptive and that it should be identified uniquely by a URI. Dependent resources should be linked by the dependency using their own unique URIs. Discovering a RESTful service means navigating from one service to another, following the links it provides.

In the year 2009, a specification called **Web Application Discovery Language (WADL)** was invented. It aims to document every URI exposed from a web application, along with the HTTP methods it supports and the parameter it expects. The response media type of the URI is also described. This is very useful for documenting purposes, and it's all that a WADL file can provide us in terms of RESTful service provisioning.

Unfortunately, there is currently no Node.js module that can automatically generate a WADL file for a given express route. We will have to manually create a WADL file to demonstrate how it is used by other clients for discovery.

The following listing shows a sample WADL file describing the resources available at `/catalog, /catalog/v2/{categoryId}`:

```xml
<?xml version="1.0" encoding="UTF-8"?>
<application xmlns="http://wadl.dev.java.net/2009/02"
xmlns:service="http://localhost:8080/catalog/"
xmlns:xsd="http://www.w3.org/2001/XMLSchema">
    <grammer>
        <include href="items.xsd" />
        <include href="error.xsd" />
    </grammer>
    <resources base="http://localhost:8080/catalog/">
        <resource path="{categoryId}">
            <method name="GET">
                <request>
                    <param name="category" type="xsd:string"
style="template" />
                </request>
                <response status="200">
                    <representation mediaType="application/xml"
element="service:item" />
                    <representation mediaType="application/json" />
                </response>
                <response status="404">
```

```
                <representation mediaType="text/plain"
element="service:item" />
            </response>
        </method>
    </resource>
    <resource path="/v2/{categoryId}">
        <method name="GET">
            <request>
                <param name="category" type="xsd:string"
style="template" />
            </request>
            <response status="200">
                <representation mediaType="application/xml"
element="service:item" />
                <representation mediaType="application/json" />
            </response>
            <response status="404">
                <representation mediaType="text/plain"
element="service:item" />
            </response>
        </method>
    </resource>
  </resources>
</application>
```

As you can see, the WADL format is very straightforward. It basically describes the URI of each resource, providing information about the media types it uses and the status codes that are expected at that URI. Many third-party RESTful clients understand the WADL language and can generate request messages out of a given WADL file.

Let's import the WADL file in Postman. Click on the **Import** button and select your
WADL file:

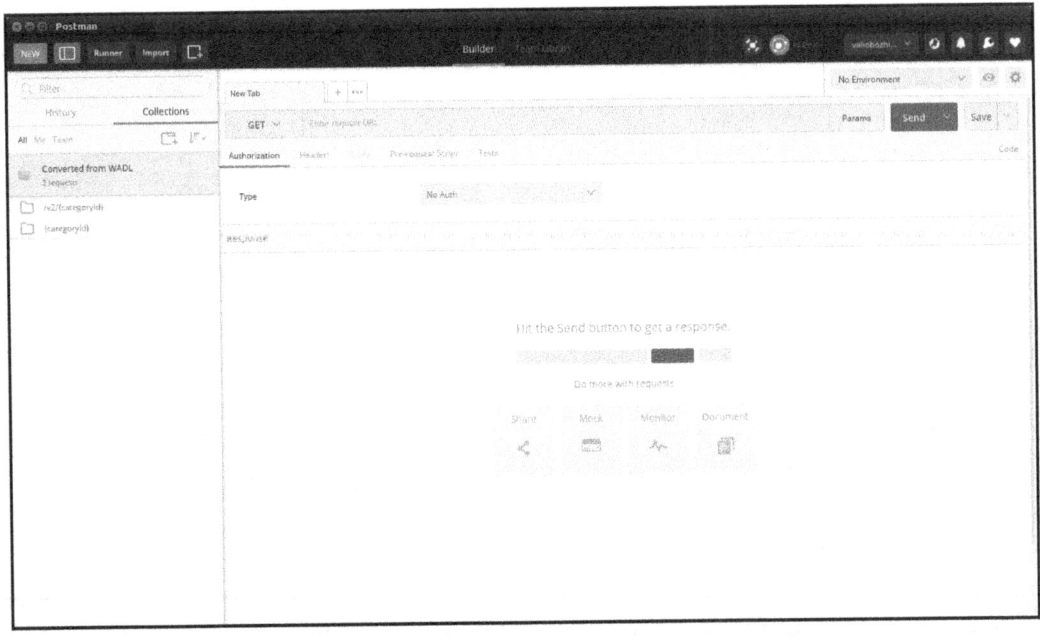

Import a WADL in Postman to get a stub of the service. This is a screenshot for Postman. The individual settings are not important here. The purpose of the image is
just to show how the window looks.

As you can see, the result of importing the WADL file is that we have a project ready
to test each aspect of a REST service in the nick of time. All the routes defined in the
WADL file are now conveniently available as separate request entities on the right
menu. That's not all; apart from the WADL standard, currently the swagger
documentation format is heavily adopted and has become an informal standard for
describing RESTful services, so we can also use it to ease the adoption and discovery
of our service. In the next chapter, we will bind these description files to our service.
This is an important step in the phase of production preparation.

Summary

Congratulations! In this chapter, you succeeded in transforming a sample REST-enabled endpoint into a full-fledged RESTful web service that supports filtering for usability and paging for easy navigation. The service delivers both arbitrary and JSON data, and it is ready for high-load scenarios, as it enables caching in its critical parts. One thing that should draw your attention is the appropriate usage of the HTTP status codes when it comes to redirection between new and obsolete versions of any public API.

Implementing appropriate HTTP status is really important for the REST application, so we made use of rather exotic statuses, such as `301 Moved Permanently` and `302 Found`.

Consuming a RESTful API

To demonstrate some more advanced topics related to the consumption of our API, we will implement a really simple web client. It will help us cover those topics, and it can serve as a reference implementation for the catalog's consumers. For this frontend client, we will use the famous JavaScript library, jQuery. Utilizing it will help us cover the following:

- Consuming RESTful services with jQuery
- Content Delivery Network
- Troubleshooting and identifying problems on the wire
- Cross-Origin Resource Sharing policy
- Client-side handling of different HTTP status codes

Consuming RESTful services with jQuery

JQuery is a fast, light, and powerful JavaScript library; it eliminates DOM-related complexity by providing direct access to HTML elements once the DOM three has been loaded. To use jQuery within an HTML document, you have to import it:

```
<script type="text/javascript"
src="https://code.jquery.com/jquery-3.3.1.min.js "></script>
```

Assume that somewhere within an HTML document, there is a button defined as `<input type="button" id="btnDelete" value="Delete"/>`.

To assign a function to the click event of this button with JQuery means we need to do the following:

1. Import the jquery library in the HTML document
2. Assure that the DOM document of the HTML document is completely loaded
3. Access the button using the identifier defined by the ID attribute
4. Provide a handler function as an argument to the `click` event:

```
$(document).ready(function() {
    $('#btn').click(function () {
        alert('Clicked');
    });
});
```

The `$('#identifier')` expression provides direct access to elements in DOM three, `$` states that an object is referenced, and the value within the bracket, prefix by # specifies its identifier. jQuery will have access to the element only after the entire document has been loaded; that's why elements should be accessed within `${document).ready()` block scope.

Similarly, you can access the value of a text input with an identifier `txt`:

```
$(document).ready(function() {
  var textValue = $('#txt').val();
  });
});
```

The `$(document)` object is predefined in jQuery and represents the entire DOM document of the HTML page. In a similar way, jQuery predefines a function for AJAX-enabled communication, that is, for sending HTTP request to an HTTP endpoint. This function is named after **Asynchronous JavaScript + XML-** AJAX, which was the de facto standard that enabled a JavaScript application to communicate with HTTP-enabled backends. Nowadays, **JSON** is being widely used; however, naming conversion for AJAX is still used as a term for asynchronous communication, regardless of the data format; that is why the predefined function in jQuery is called `$.ajax(options, handlers)`.

To send an http request with the `$.ajax` function, invoke it by providing the endpoint URL, http method for the request, and its content type; the result will be returned in a callback function. The following example shows how an item with identifier 3 is requested from our catalog:

```
$.ajax({
    contentType: 'application/json',
    url: 'http://localhost:3000/catalog/v2/item/3',
    type: 'GET',
    success: function (item, status, xhr) {
        if (status === 'success') {
            //the item is successfully retrieved load & display its
details here
        }
    }
    ,error: function (xhr, options, error) {
      //Item was not retrieved due to an error handle it here
    }
  });
});
```

Posting data to an endpoint is rather similar:

```
$.ajax({
  url: "http://localhost:3000/catalog/v2/",
  type: "POST",
  dataType: "json",
  data: JSON.stringify(newItem),
   success: function (item, status, xhr) {
     if (status === 'success') {
       //item was created successfully
     }
   },
   error: function(xhr, options, error) {
     //Error occurred while creating the iteam
   }
  });
```

Simply use the appropriate options `type` set to POST, and the `dateType` set to JSON. Those will specify that a POST request is to be sent to the endpoint in the JSON format. The payload of the object is provided as a value to the `data` attribute.

Invoking a `delete` method is quite similar:

```javascript
$.ajax({
  contentType: 'application/json',
  url: 'http://localhost:3000/catalog/v2/item/3',
  type: 'DELETE',
  success: function (item, status, xhr) {
      if (status === 'success') {
        //handle successful deletion
      }
  }
  ,error: function (xhr, options, error) {
      //handle errors on delete
  }
});
```

A basic understanding of how jQuery works is just about fine for the scope of this book. Now, let's glue all this together and create two HTML pages; that way, we will handle creating, displaying, and deleting an item in our catalog, starting with the page that displays an item and allows its deletion. This page loads an item from the catalog using GET request, and then displays the item's attributes in the HTML page in a table-like manner:

```html
<html>
<head><title>Item</title></head>
<body>
    <script type="text/javascript"
src="https://code.jquery.com/jquery-3.3.1.min.js "></script>
  <script>
  $(document).ready(function() {
    $('#btnDelete').click(function () {
      $.ajax({
        contentType: 'application/json',
        url: 'http://localhost:3000/catalog/v2/item/3',
        type: 'DELETE',
        success: function (item, status, xhr) {
            if (status === 'success') {
              $('#item').text('Deleted');
              $('#price').text('Deleted');
              $('#categories').text('Deleted');
            }
        }
        ,error: function (xhr, options, error) {
          alert('Unable to delete item');
        }
      });
    });
```

```
    $.ajax({
      contentType: 'application/json',
      url: 'http://localhost:3000/catalog/v2/item/3',
      type: 'GET',
      success: function (item, status, xhr) {
          if (status === 'success') {
            $('#item').text(item.itemName);
            $('#price').text(item.price + ' ' + item.currency);
            $('#categories').text(item.categories);
          }
      }
      ,error: function (xhr, options, error) {
        alert('Unable to load details');
      }
    });
  });
  </script>
  <div>
    <div style="position: relative">
      <div style="float:left; width: 80px;">Item: </div>
      <div><span id="item"/>k</div>
    </div>
    <div style="position: relative">
      <div style="float:left; width: 80px;">Price: </div>
      <div><span id="price"/>jjj</div>
    </div>
    <div style="position: relative">
      <div style="float:left; width: 80px;">Categories: </div>
      <div><span id="categories"/>jjj</div>
    </div>
    <div><input type="button" id="btnDelete" value="Delete"/></div>
  </div>
</body>
</html>
```

The page that handles creation is quite similar. However, it provides text inputs instead of span labels for an item's fields, where the view page will display the data for the attributes of the loaded item. JQuery provides a simplified access model to the input controls, rather than DOM—simply access the input element as follows:

```
<html>
<head><title>Item</title></head>
<body>
  <script type="text/javascript"
src="https://code.jquery.com/jquery-3.3.1.min.js "></script>
  <script>
  $(document).ready(function() {
    $('#btnCreate').click(function(){
```

```javascript
          var txtItemName = $('#txtItem').val();
          var txtItemPrice = $('#txtItemPrice').val();
          var txtItemCurrency = $('#txtItemCurrency').val();
          var newItem = {
            itemId: 4,
            itemName: txtItemName,
            price: txtItemPrice,
            currency: txtItemCurrency,
            categories: [
              "Watches"
            ]
          };
          $.ajax({
            url: "http://localhost:3000/catalog/v2/",
            type: "POST",
            dataType: "json",
            data: JSON.stringify(newItem),
            success: function (item, status, xhr) {
                alert(status);
              }
          });
        })
    });
  </script>
  <div>
    <div style="position: relative">
      <div style="float:left; width: 80px;">Id: </div>
      <div><input type="text" id="id"/></div>

      <div style="float:left; width: 80px;">Item: </div>
      <div><input type="text" id="txtItem"/></div>
    </div>
    <div style="position: relative">
      <div style="float:left; width: 80px;">Price: </div>
      <div><input type="text" id="price"/></div>
    </div>
    <div style="position: relative">
      <div style="float:left; width: 80px;">Categories: </div>
      <div><input type="text" id="categories"/></div>
    </div>
    <div><input type="button" id="btnCreate" value="Create"/></div>
  </div>
</body>
</html>
```

Let's give that a try and load an existing item in the view page by opening our static page directly from the filesystem in a browser of your choice. It looks as if we have some kind of a problem, as nothing gets displayed. Enabling client-side debugging using the browser's developer suite doesn't give much more information either:

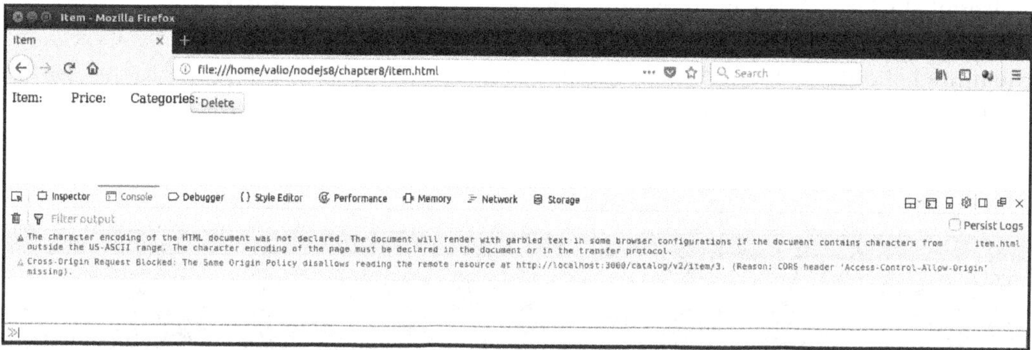

It states that the content is partially blocked; however, it is not quite clear whether this is due to a backend-related error, or something has gone wrong on the client side. We will look at how to troubleshoot such problematic situations in the next section.

Troubleshooting and identifying problems on the wire

Sometimes the interaction between the client and the server fails, and the reason for such failures often requires analysis; otherwise, their root cause stays unknown. We spotted that our client application does not load and thus doesn't display data for an existing item. Let's try to investigate the root cause for that by setting up an `http` tunnel between the client and the server. This will be a kind of MiM (man-in-the-middle)-based investigation, as we will listen to one port and redirect the incoming request to another, to see whether the server returns correct responses or its pipe gets broken somewhere in the middle. There are various TCP tunnels available out there; I have been using a simple open source one available on GitHub at `https://github.com/vakuum/tcptunnel`. Its author also maintains a separate website where you can download prebuilt binaries for the most common operating system; they are available at `http://www.vakuumverpackt.de/tcptunnel/`.

After you have built or downloaded a copy of the tunnel, start it as follows:

```
./tcptunnel --local-port=3001 --remote-port=3000 --remote-host=localhost --log
```

This will start the application listening on port 3001 and will forward each incoming request to location port 3000; the `--log` option specifies that all the data flow passing the tunnel should be logged in the console. Finally, modify HTML pages to use port 3001 instead of 3000, and let's see what the tunnel would show us after firing new GET request for the item with id 3, this time on port 3001: `http://localhost:3001/catalog/v2/item/3`:

```
valio@G771JW: ~/git/tcptunnel
valio@G771JW:~/git/tcptunnel$ ./tcptunnel --local-port=3001 --remote-port=3000 --remote-host=localhost --log
> 2018-03-26 01:57:40 tcptunnel: request from 127.0.0.1
> 2018-03-26 01:57:40 > GET /catalog/v2/item/3 HTTP/1.1
Host: localhost:3001
Connection: keep-alive
Cache-Control: no-cache
Content-Type: application/json
User-Agent: Mozilla/5.0 (X11; Linux x86_64) AppleWebKit/537.36 (KHTML, like Gecko) Chrome/67.0.3377.1 Safari/537.36
Postman-Token: 917e1dfd-b00b-fb5b-3019-1e47bda13708
Accept: */*
Accept-Encoding: gzip, deflate, br
Accept-Language: en-US,en;q=0.9

HTTP/1.1 200 OK
X-Powered-By: Express
Content-Type: application/json; charset=utf-8
Image-Url: http://localhost:3001/catalog/v2/item/3/image
Content-Length: 137
ETag: W/"89-onqoMr/67e303rbPFZKMhCIQ+fU"
Date: Sun, 25 Mar 2018 22:57:40 GMT
Connection: keep-alive

{"_id":"5ab827f65d61450e40d7d984","itemId":"3","itemName":"Sports Watch 11","price":99,"currency":"USD","__v":0,"categor
ies":["Watches"]}valio@G771JW:~/git/tcptunnel$ 
```

Surprisingly, the tunnel shows that the server responds normally with `200 OK` and a relevant payload. So it seems as if the problem is not on the server side.

Well, since the error is obviously not on the server side, let's try to investigate deeper what has happened on the client side. Nowadays, all popular browsers have so-called web developer tools. They provide access to `http` logs, dynamically-rendered code, the DOM three of the HTML document, and so on. Let's invoke our RESTful GET operation with Mozillas Firefox and see what its web console will log about our request. Open the Mozilla Firefox menu and select `Web Developer`, and then select `Browser Console`:

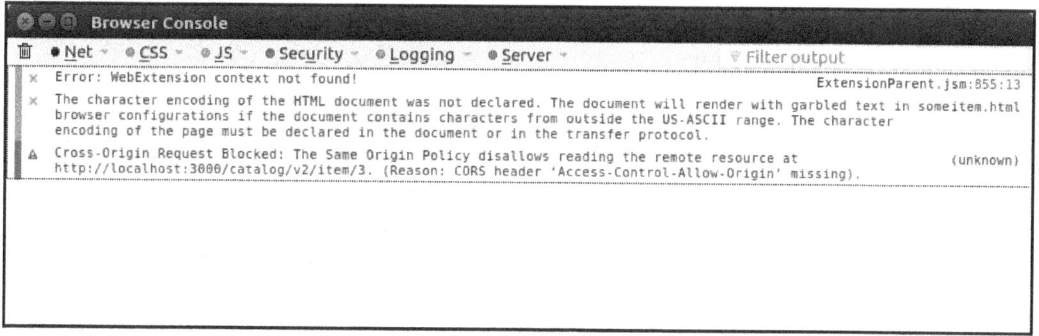

Aha! Seems like we found it: `Cross-Origin Request Blocked: The Same Origin Policy disallows reading the remove resource at....`
This error is blocking the server-side response at client level. In the next section, we will see what this actually means.

Cross Origin Resource Sharing

Cross-site HTTP requests are requests that refer to resources to be loaded from a domain different from the one that initially requested them. In our case, we started the client from our filesystem, and it requested resources from a network address. This is considered a potential **Cross-site scripting** request, which, according to the **W3C recommendation** at `http://w3.org/cors/TR/cors`, should be carefully handled. This means that if an external resource is requested, the domain where it is requested from—its Origin—should be explicitly specified in a header, as long as an external resource loading is not allowed in general. This mechanism prevents Cross-Side Scripting (XSS) attacks, and it is based on HTTP headers.

The following HTTP request headers specify how external resources should be handled on the client side:

- `Origin` defines where the request originated from
- `Access-Control-Request-Method` defines the HTTP method that was used to request the resource
- `Access-Control-Request-Header` defines any headers that will be allowed in combination with the external resource request

On the server side, the following headers indicate whether a response is eligible for a CORS-enabled client request:

- `Access-Control-Allow-Origin`: This header either, if exists, specifies that the requester's host is allowed by repeating it, or it could specify that all remote origins are allowed by returning a wildcard: '*'
- `Access-Control-Allow-Methods`: This header specifies the HTTP methods that the server would allow from cross-side's domain
- `Access-Control-Allow-Headers`: This header specifies the HTTP headers that the server would allow from cross-side's domain

There are some more `Access-Control-*` headers that can be used for further granularity when incoming XSS requests are to be served, or not, based on credentials and request's max-age, but basically, the most important ones are for the allowed origin, allowed methods, and allowed headers.

There is a node module that handles `CORS` configuration at server side; it is installed by `npm install -g cors` and is easily enabled in our application via a middleware module. Simply use it in all the exposed routes by passing it to the application:

```
app.use(cors());
```

Use the tunnel after you enabled the `cors` middleware to see that the server would now gracefully handle requests from different origins by serving the "Access-Control-Allow-Origin' header set to '*'":

```
valio@G771JW: ~/git/tcptunnel
valio@G771JW:~/git/tcptunnel$
valio@G771JW:~/git/tcptunnel$ ./tcptunnel --local-port=3001 --remote-port=3000 --remote-host=localhost --log
> 2018-03-26 01:51:54 tcptunnel: request from 127.0.0.1
> 2018-03-26 01:51:54 > GET /catalog/v2/item/3 HTTP/1.1
Host: localhost:3001
Connection: keep-alive
Cache-Control: no-cache
Content-Type: application/json
User-Agent: Mozilla/5.0 (X11; Linux x86_64) AppleWebKit/537.36 (KHTML, like Gecko) Chrome/67.0.3377.1 Safari/537.36
Postman-Token: 100ae78b-b8f8-353f-f5f8-6c0b5e9a9ec2
Accept: */*
Accept-Encoding: gzip, deflate, br
Accept-Language: en-US,en;q=0.9

HTTP/1.1 200 OK
X-Powered-By: Express
Access-Control-Allow-Origin: *
Content-Type: application/json; charset=utf-8
Image-Url: http://localhost:3001/catalog/v2/item/3/image
Content-Length: 137
ETag: W/"89-onqoMr/67e303rbPFZKMhCIQ+fU"
Date: Sun, 25 Mar 2018 22:51:54 GMT
Connection: keep-alive

{"_id":"5ab827f65d61450e40d7d984","itemId":"3","itemName":"Sports Watch 11","price":99,"currency":"USD","__v":0,"categories":["Watches"]}valio@G771JW:~/git/tcptunnel$
```

Content Delivery Networks

When we imported the jQuery library into our client application, we directly referred to its optimized source from its vendor as `<script type="text/javascript" src="https://code.jquery.com/jquery-3.3.1.min.js "/>`.

Now, imagine that for some reason this site goes down either temporarily or for good; this will make our application unusable, as the import wouldn't work.

Content Delivery Networks come to help in these cases. They serve as a repository for libraries or other static media content, assuring that the needed resources will be available without downtime, even when something goes wrong with their vendors. One of the most popular JavaScript CDNs is `https://cdnjs.com/`; it provides the most common JS libraries available out there. We will switch our clients to refer to the jquery library from this CDN rather than from its vendors' website at `<script type="text/javascript" src="https://code.jquery.com/jquery-3.3.1.min.js "/>`.

While there is hardly anything wrong with directly downloading your JS libraries and placing them in the static directory of your node.js project, it may lead to having local changes and fixes directly in your library dependencies. This can easily result in incompatible changes and can prevent your application from easily switching to newer versions in the future. As long as your dependencies are open source, you should strive to improve them by contributing fixes or reporting bugs rather than having fixes in your own local fork. Still, if you are unfortunate enough to run into a bug that you can easily fix, you can fork the library to resolve your problem faster. However, always consider contributing the fix back to the community. After it is accepted, switch back to the official version; otherwise, you will find yourself in a difficult situation the next time with another issue, and the community would track it much harder if reported from a forked version. That is the beauty of open source, and that is why you should always consider consuming JavaScript APIs' Content Delivery Networks. They will provide you with the stability and support you may need at any point in the life of your application.

Handling HTTP status codes on the client side

We spent quite some time addressing how RESTful services should represent each state, including erroneous ones, gracefully. A well-defined API should demand from its consumers to handle all its errors gracefully and to provide as much information per state as required, rather than just stating "An error has occurred". That is why it should look up the returned status code and clearly distinguish between client requests such as `400 Bad Request` or `415 Unsupported media types` caused by faulty payload, caused by wrong media types, or authentication-related errors, such as `401 Unauthorized`.

The status code of an erroneous response is available in the `error` callback of the jQuery callback function and should be used to provide detailed information back to the request:

```
$.ajax({
    url: "http://localhost:3000/catalog/v2/",
    type: "POST",
    dataType: "json",
    data: JSON.stringify(newItem),
    success: function (item, status, jqXHR) {
        alert(status);
    },
    error: function(jqXHR, statusText, error) {
        switch(jqXHR.status) {
            case 400: alert('Bad request'); break;
            case 401: alert('Unauthroizaed'); break;
            case 404: alert('Not found'); break;
            //handle any other client errors below
            case 500: alert('Internal server error); break;
            //handle any other server errors below
        }
    }
});
```

Unsuccessful requests are handled by the error callback function. It provides `jqXHR` - the `XmlHttpRequest` JavaScript—object as its first argument. It carries across all the request/response related information, such as status code and headers. Use it to determine what the requested server has returned so that your application can handle different errors more granularly.

Summary

In this chapter, we implemented a simple web-based client with the jQuery library. We utilized this client to demonstrate how the Cross-Origin Resource Sharing policy works, and we used a man in the middle means to troubleshoot issues on the wire. Finally, we looked at how errors should be handled on the client side. This chapter brings us one step closer to the end of our journey, as we got the first consumer of our service. In the next chapter, we will walk you through the final step before bringing a service to production—choosing its security model.

18
Securing the Application

Once deployed in production, an application is exposed to a large number of requests. Inevitably, some of them will be malicious. This brings the requirement of granting explicit access permissions only to authenticated users, that is, authenticating a selected number of consumers to have access to your service. Most of the consumers will use the service only for data provisioning. However, a few will need to be able to provide new, or modify the existing, catalog data. To ensure that only appropriate consumers will be able to execute the POST, PUT, and DELETE requests, we will have to introduce the concept of authorization into our application, which will grant only explicitly selected users modification permissions.

Data services may provide sensitive private information, such as email addresses; the HTTP protocol, being a text protocol, may not be secure enough. The information transmitted through it is subject to **man-in-the-middle** attacks, which can lead to data leakage. To prevent such cases, **Transport Layer Security (TLS)** should be used. The HTTPS protocol encrypts the transmitted data, ensuring that only appropriate consumers who have the right decryption key will be able to consume the data exposed by the service.

In this chapter, we will look at how Node.js enables the following security features:

- Basic authentication
- Passport-based basic authentication
- Passport-based third-party authentication
- Authorization
- Transport layer security

Authentication

An application considers a user authenticated when their identity has been successfully validated against a trusted store. Such trusted stores can either be any kind of specially maintained database, storing the credentials of the application (basic authentication), or a third-party service that checks a given identity against its own trusted store (third-party authentication).

Basic authentication

HTTP basic authentication is one of the most popular and straightforward authentication mechanisms available out there. It relies on HTTP headers in the request, which provide the user's credentials. Optionally, the server may reply with a header, forcing the clients to authenticate themselves. The following diagram shows a client-server interaction when basic authentication is carried out:

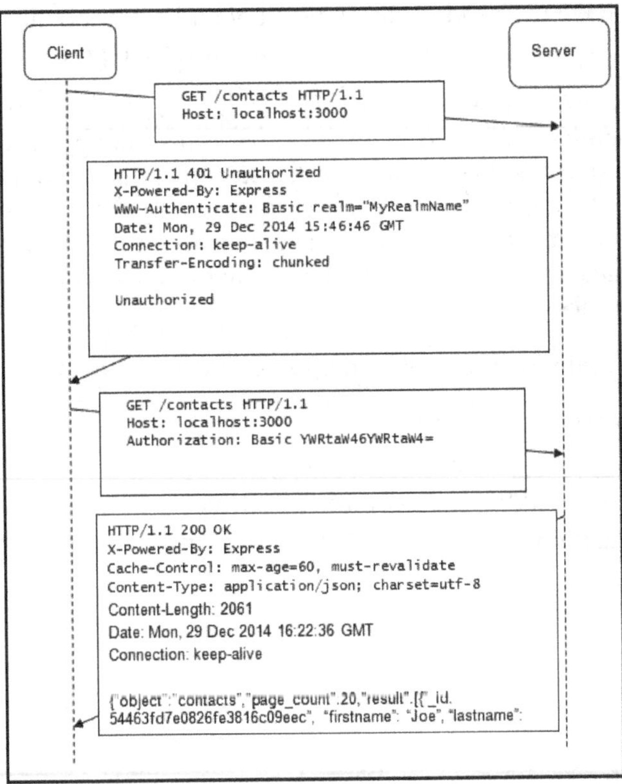

Whenever an HTTP request is sent to an endpoint secured by HTTP basic authentication, the server replies with an HTTP `401 Unauthorized` status code, and, optionally, with a `WWW-Authenticate` header. This header forces the client to send another request, containing the `Authorization` header, which specifies that the authentication method is `basic`. This request is followed by a base64-encoded key/value pair, providing the username and the password to authenticate with. Optionally, the server can specify a message to the client with the `realm` attribute.

This attribute specifies that resources sharing the same `realm` value should support the same authentication means. In the preceding diagram, the `realm` message is `MyRealmName`. The client authenticates by sending the `Authentication` header with the value of `Basic YWRtaW46YWRtaW4`, specifying that `Basic` authentication is used, followed by the base64-encoded value. In the diagram, the literal `YWRtaW46YWRtaW4` decoded in base64 represents the `admin:admin` literal. In case such a username/password combination is successfully authenticated, the HTTP server will respond with the JSON payload of the requested items. If the authentication fails, the server will respond with the `401 Unauthorized` status code, but this time without including the `WWW-Authenticate` header.

Passport

There are plenty of authentication methods to choose from nowadays. Perhaps the most popular methods are basic authentication, where each user has their own username and password, and third-party authentication, where users can identify themselves with their already-existing account for an external public service, such as personal social services such as LinkedIn, Facebook, and Twitter.

Choosing the most appropriate type of authentication for a web API depends mainly on its consumers. Apparently, an application consuming an API to fetch data is not likely to authenticate with a personal social account. This approach is more suitable when the API is used via a frontend directly by a human being.

Implementing a solution capable of switching between different authentication methods easily is a complex and time-consuming task. In fact, it can become hardly possible if not considered at the initial design phase of an application.

Passport is a piece of authentication middleware for Node.js, created especially for use-cases where the means of authentication should be easily switched from one to another. It has modular architecture that enables the usage of a specific authentication provider, called **strategy**. The strategy takes care of implementing a chosen authentication approach.

There are plenty of authentication strategies to choose from, for example, a regular basic authentication strategy or social platform-based strategies for services such as Facebook, LinkedIn, and Twitter. Refer to the official Passport website, `http://www.passportjs.org/`, for a complete list of the available strategies.

Passport's basic authentication strategy

Now it is time to look at how to utilize Passport's strategies; we will start with the basic authentication strategy; it is a logical choice now that we know how basic authentication works.

As usual, we will start by installing the relevant modules with the NPM package manager. We will need the `passport` module, which provides the base functionality that allows you to plug in different authentication strategies, and a concrete strategy for basic authentication, provided by the `passport-http` module:

```
npm install passport
npm install passport-http
```

Next, we have to instantiate both the Passport middleware and the basic authentication strategy. `BasicStrategy` takes as an argument a callback function, which checks whether the provided username/password combination is valid. Finally, passport's authenticate method is provided as a middleware function to the express route, assuring that unauthenticated requests will be rejected with an appropriate `401 Unauthorized` status:

```
const passport = require('passport');
const BasicStrategy = require('passport-http').BasicStrategy;

passport.use(new BasicStrategy(function(username, password, done) {
  if (username == 'user' && password=='default') {
    return done(null, username);
  }
}));

router.get('/v1/',
  passport.authenticate('basic', { session: false }),
    function(request,    response, next) {
      catalogV1.findAllItems(response);
});
router.get('/v2/',
  passport.authenticate('basic', { session: false }),
    function(request,    response, next) {
      catalogV1.findAllItems(response);
```

```
});

router.get('/',
  passport.authenticate('basic', { session: false }),
    function(request,     response, next) {
      catalogV1.findAllItems(response);
});
```

The `BasicStrategy` constructor takes a handler function as an argument. It gives us access to the username and password supplied by the client, and to the Passport middleware's `done()` function, which notifies Passport with whether the user has been successfully authenticated. Invoke the `done()` function with `user` as an argument in order to grant authentication, or pass the `error` argument to it to revoke the authentication:

```
passport.use(new BasicStrategy(
function(username, password, done) {
  AuthUser.findOne({username: username, password: password},
    function(error, user) {
      if (error) {
        return done(error);
      } else {
        if (!user) {
          console.log('unknown user');
          return done(error);
        } else {
          console.log(user.username + '
          authenticated successfully');
          return done(null, user);
        }
      }
    });
  })
);
```

Finally, use the `passort authenticate()` function in the router middleware to attach it to a specific HTTP method-handler function.

In our case, we specify that we don't want to store any authentication details in a session. This is because, when using basic authentication, there is no need to store any user information in a session, as each request contains the `Authorization` header that provides the login details.

Passport's OAuth Strategy

OAuth is an open standard for third party authorization, it defines a delegation protocol used fer authorizing against a third party authentication providers. OAuth uses special tokens, once issued, identify the user instead of user credentials. Let's look closer at OAuth workflow, with a sample scenario. The main actors in the scenario are - a **user** interacting with a **web application,** which consumes a restful service from a **back-end** system providing some kind of data. The web application delegates its authorization to a separate **third-party authorization server.**

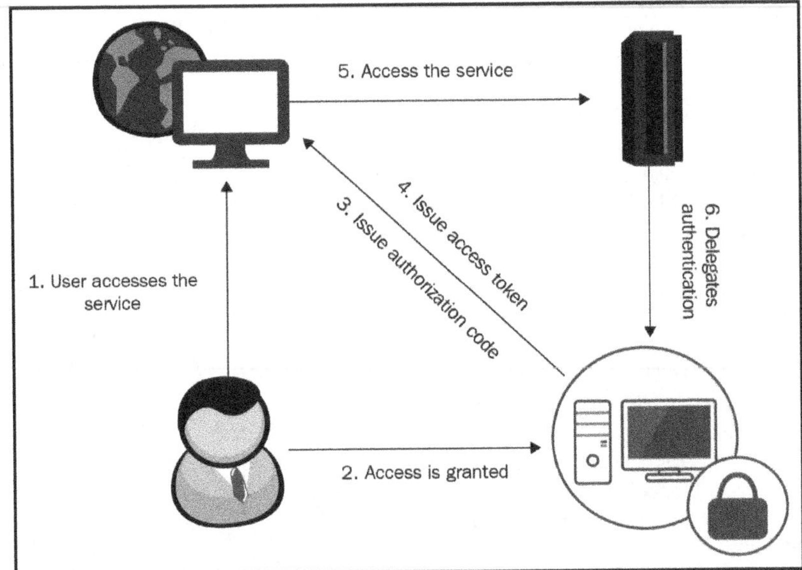

1. The user requests a web application which requires authentication to establish communication with the back-end service. This is the initial request thus the user is still not authenticated, so they get redirected to a login page asking for their credentials for the relevant third party account.

2. After a successful authentication an authorization code is issued by the authentication server to the web application. This authorization code is a composite combination between an issued client-id and a secret issued by the provider. They should be sent from a web application to the authentication server and is exchanged for an access token that has a limited lifetime.

3. The Web application uses the authentication token for authentication until it gets expired. Afterwards it has to request a new token using the authorization code.

Passport.js hides the complexity behind this process with a separate strategy module automating the OAuth workflow. It is available in the npm repository

```
npm install passport-oauth
```

Create an instance of the strategy and supply it with the urls for requesting tokens and for authenticating it together, it is your personal consumer key and a secret phrase of your choice.

```
var passport = require('passport')
  , OAuthStrategy = require('passport-oauth').OAuthStrategy;

passport.use('provider', new OAuthStrategy({
    requestTokenURL: 'https://www.provider.com/oauth/request_token',
    accessTokenURL: 'https://www.provider.com/oauth/access_token',
    userAuthorizationURL: 'https://www.provider.com/oauth/authorize',
    consumerKey: '123-456-789',
    consumerSecret: 'secret'
    callbackURL: 'https://www.example.com/auth/provider/callback'
  }, function(token, tokenSecret, profile, done) {
    //lookup the profile and authenticate   and call done
  }
));
```

Passport.js provides separate strategy wrapping different providers, like linkedin or github. They ensure that your application stays up to date with the token issuing URLs. Once you have made up your mind about the provider you want to support, you should check for specific strategies for them.

Passport's third-party authentication strategies

Today, almost everyone owns at least one personal public social media account, such as Twitter, Facebook, and LinkedIn. Recently, it has become really popular for websites to allow their visitors to authenticate themselves via one of their social accounts by just clicking on an icon to bind their social service account to a service-internal automatically generated account.

This approach is very convenient for web users who are usually permanently logged into at least one of their accounts. If they are not currently logged in, clicking on an icon will redirect them to their social service login page, and, after a successful login, another redirection takes place, ensuring that the user gets the content they originally requested. When it comes to exposing data via a web API, this approach is not really an option.

Publicly exposed APIs cannot predict whether they are to be consumed by a human or by an application. Also, APIs aren't usually consumed directly by humans. Thus, third-party authentication is the only option when you, as API authors, are convinced that the exposed data will be directly available to the end users who have requested it manually through a frontend from an internet browser. Once they have successfully logged into their social account, a unique user identifier will be stored in a session, so your service will need to be able to handle such sessions appropriately.

To enable session support for storing user login information with Passport and Express, you have to initialize the Express session middleware before initializing Passport and its session middleware:

```
app.use(express.session());
app.use(passport.initialize());
app.use(passport.session());
```

Then, specify the user whose details Passport should serialize/deserialize into or out of the session. For that purpose, Passport provides the `serializeUser()` and `deserializeUser()` functions, which store complete user information in a session:

```
passport.serializeUser(function(user, done) { done(null, user); });
passport.deserializeUser(function(obj, done) { done(null, obj); });
```

The order of initializing the session handling of the Express and Passport middleware is important. The Express session should be passed to the application first and should be followed by the Passport session.

After enabling session support, you have to decide which third-party authentication strategy to rely on. Basically, third-party authentication is enabled via a plugin or application created by the third-party provider, for example, a social service site. We will briefly look at creating a LinkedIn application that allows authentication via the OAuth standard.

Usually, this is done via a pair of public key and a secret (token) associated with the social media application. Creating a LinkedIn application is easy—you just have to log into `http://www.linkedin.com/secure/developer` and fill out a brief application information form. You will be given a secret key and a token to enable the authentication. Perform the following steps to enable LinkedIn authentication:

1. Install the `linkedin-strategy` module—`npm install linkedin-strategy`

2. Get an instance of the LinkedIn strategy and initialize it to the Passport middleware by the `use()` function after session support has been enabled:

```
var passport = require('passport')
  , LinkedInStrategy = require('passport-
  linkedin').Strategy;

  app.use(express.session());
  app.use(passport.initialize());
  app.use(passport.session());

passport.serializeUser(function(user, done) {
  done(null, user);
});

passport.deserializeUser(function(obj, done) {
  done(null, obj);
});

  passport.use(new LinkedInStragety({
    consumerKey: 'api-key',
    consumerSecret: 'secret-key',
    callbackURL: "http://localhost:3000/catalog/v2"
  },
    function(token, tokenSecret, profile, done) {
      process.nextTick(function () {
        return done(null, profile);
      });
    })
  );
```

3. Explicitly specify that the LinkedIn strategy should be used as Passport for each individual route, ensuring that session handling is enabled:

```
router.get('/v2/',
  cache('minutes',1),
  passport.authenticate('linked', { session: true}),
  function(request, response) {
    //...
  }
});
```

4. Provide a means for a user to log out by exposing a logout URI, making use of `request.logout`:

```
router.get('/logout', function(req, res){
request.logout();
  response.redirect('/catalog');
});
```

The given third-party URLs and service data are subject to change. You should always refer to the service policy when providing third-party authentication.

Authorization

So far, the catalog data service uses basic authentication to protect its routes from unknown users; however, a catalog application should allow only few white-listed users to modify the items inside the catalog. To restrict access to the catalog, we will introduce the concept of authorization, that is, a subset of authenticated users, with appropriate permission allowed.

When Passport's `done()` function is invoked to authenticate a successful login, it takes as an argument a `user` instance of the user that has been granted authentication. The `done()` function adds that user model instance to the `request` object, and, in this way, provides access to it via the `request.user` property, after successful authentication. We will make use of that property to implement a function performing the authorization check after successful authentication:

```
function authorize(user, response) {
   if ((user == null) || (user.role != 'Admin')) {
     response.writeHead(403, { 'Content-Type' :
     'text/plain'});
     response.end('Forbidden');
     return;
   }
}
```

The HTTP 403 Forbidden status code can be easily confused with 405 Not allowed. However, the 405 Not Allowed status code indicates that a specific HTTP verb is not supported by the requested resource, so it should be used only in that context.

The `authorize()` function will close the `response` stream, returning the `403 Forbidden` status code, which indicates that the logged-in user is recognized but has insufficient permissions. This revokes access to the resource. This function has to be used in each route that carries out data manipulation.

Here's an example of how a `post` route implements authorization:

```
app.post('/v2',
  passport.authenticate('basic', { session: false }),
    function(request, response) {
      authorize(request.user, response);
      if (!response.closed) {
        catalogV2.saveItem(request, response);
      }
    }
);
```

After `authorize()` is invoked, we check whether the `response` object still allows writing to its output by checking the value of the closed property of the `response` object. It will return `true` once the end function of the `response` object has been called, which is exactly what the `authorize()` function does when the user lacks admin permissions. Thus, we can rely on the closed property in our implementation.

Transport layer security

Publicly available information in the web easily becomes the subject of different types of cyber attacks. Often it is not enough just to keep the so-called "bad guys" out. Sometimes, they won't bother gaining authentication at all and may prefer to carry out a **man-in-the-middle (MiM)** attack, pretending to be the final receiver of a message and sniffing the communication channel that transmits the data—or, even worse, altering the data while it flows.

Being a text-based protocol, HTTP transfers data in a human-readable format, which makes it an easy victim of MiM attacks. Unless transferred in an encrypted format, all the catalog data of our service is vulnerable to MiM attacks. In this section, we will switch our transport from an insecure HTTP protocol to the secure HTTPS protocol.

HTTPS is secured by asymmetric cryptography, also known as **public-key encryption**. It is based on a pair of keys that are mathematically related. The key used for encryption is called **public key**, and the key used for decryption is called **private key**. The idea is to freely provide the encryption key to partners who have to send encrypted messages and to perform decryption with the private key.

A typical public-key encryption communication scenario between two parties, *A* and *B*, will be the following:

1. Party *A* composes a message, encrypts it with Party B's public key, and sends it

2. Party *B* decrypts the message with its own private key and processes it

3. Party *B* composes a response message, encrypts it with Party *A*'s public key, and then sends it

4. Party *A* decrypts the response message with its own private key

Now that we know how public-key encryption works, let's go through a sample of HTTPS client-server communication, as shown in this diagram:

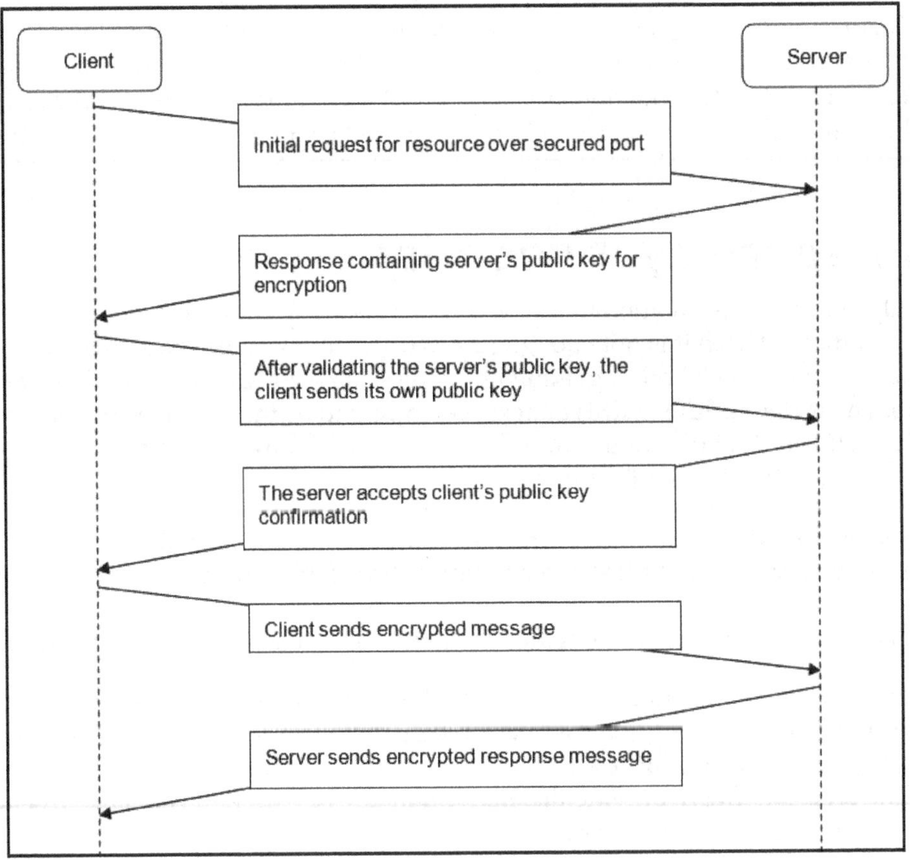

The client sends an initial request against an SSL-secured endpoint. The server responds to that request by sending its public key to be used for encrypting further incoming requests. Then, the client has to check the validity and verify the identity of the received key. After successful verification of the server's public key, the client has to send its own public key back to the server. Finally, after the key exchange procedure is complete, the two parties can start communicating securely.

HTTPS relies on trust; thus, it is vital to have a reliable way of checking whether a specific public key belongs to a specific server. Public keys are exchanged within an X.509 certificate, which has a hierarchical structure. This structure enables clients to check whether a given certificate has been generated from a trusted root certificate. Clients should trust only certificates that have been issued by a known **certificate authority (CA)**.

Before switching our service to use the HTTPS transport, we need a public/private key pair. Since we are not a certificate authority, we will have to use OpenSSL tooling to generate test keys for us.

OpenSSL is available for download at `http://www.openssl.org/`, where source code distributions are available for all popular operating systems. OpenSSL can be installed as follows:

1. Binary distribution is available for download for Windows, and Debian and Ubuntu users can make use of the packaged distribution by executing the following:

    ```
    sudo apt-get install openssl
    ```

     Windows users will have to set an environment variable, OPENSSL_CNF, specifying the location of the `openssl.cnf` configuration file, typically located in the share directory in the installation archive.

2. Now let's generate a test key/value pair with OpenSSL:

    ```
    opensslreq -x509 -nodes -days 365 -newkey rsa:2048-
    keyoutcatalog.pem -out catalog.crt
    ```

OpenSSL will prompt some details required for generating the certificate, such as country code, city, and fully qualified domain name. Afterward, it will generate a private key in the `catalog.pem` file and a public key certificate that will be valid for a year in the `catalog.crt` file. We will be using these newly generated files, so copy them into a new subdirectory, called `ssl`, in the catalog data service directory.

Now we have everything needed to modify our service to use HTTPS:

1. First, we need to switch and use the HTTPS module instead of HTTP and specify the port that we want to use to enable HTTPS communication:

```
var https = require('https');
var app = express();
app.set('port', process.env.PORT || 3443);
```

2. Then, we have to read the private key from the `catalog.cem` file and the certificate from `catalog.crt` into an array:

```
var options = {key : fs.readFileSync('./ssl/catalog.pem'),
               cert : fs.readFileSync('./ssl/catalog.crt')
};
```

3. Finally, we pass the array containing the key pair to the HTTPS instance when creating the server and start listening through the specified port:

```
https.createServer(options, app).listen(app.get('port'));
```

That's all you need to do to enable HTTPS for an Express-based application. Save your changes and give it a try by requesting `https://localhost:3443/catalog/v2` in a browser. You will be shown a warning message informing you that the server you are connecting to is using a certificate that is not issued by a trusted certificate authority. That's normal, as we generated the certificate on our own, and we are not a CA for sure, so just ignore that warning.

Before deploying a service on a production environment, you should always ensure that you use a server certificate issued by a trusted CA.

Self-test questions

Go through the following questions:

- Is HTTP basic authentication secure against man-in-the-middle attacks?

- What are the benefits of Transport Layer Security?

Summary

In this chapter, you learned how to protect exposed data by enabling a means of authentication and authorization. This is a critical aspect of any publicly available data service. In addition, you learned how to prevent man-in-the-middle attacks using the secured layer transport protocol between a service and its users. As a developer of such services, you should always consider the most appropriate security features that your application should support.

I hope this was a useful experience! You gained enough knowledge and practical experience, which should have made you much more confident in understanding how RESTful APIs work and how they are designed and developed. I strongly encourage you to go through the code evolution chapter by chapter. You should be able to further refactor it, adopting it to your own coding style. Of course, some parts of it can be further optimized, as they repeat quite often. That is an intentional decision rather than good practice, as I wanted to emphasize their importance. You should always strive to improve your code-base, making it easier to maintain.

Finally, I would like to encourage you to always follow the development of the `Node.js` modules you use in your applications. Node.js has an extraordinary community that is eager to grow rapidly. There is always something exciting going on there, so ensure that you don't miss it. Good luck!

19
The Age of Microservices

Decades ago, more specifically in 1974, Intel introduced 8080 to the world, which is an 8-bit processor with a 2 MHz clock speed and 64 KB of memory. This processor was used in Altair and began the revolution in personal computers.

It was sold pre-assembled or as a kit for hobbyists. It was the first computer to have enough power to actually be used for calculations. Even though it had some poor design choices and needed an engineering major to be able to use and program it, it started the spread of personal computers to the general public.

The technology evolved rapidly and the processor industry followed Moore's law, almost doubling speed every two years. Processors were still single core, with a low-efficiency ratio (power consumption per clock cycle). Because of this, servers usually did one specific job, called a service, like serving HTTP pages or managing a **Lightweight Directory Access Protocol (LDAP)** directory. Services were the monolith, with very few components, and were compiled altogether to be able to take the most out of the hardware processor and memory.

In the 90s, the internet was still only available for the few. Hypertext, based on HTML and HTTP, was in its infancy. Documents were simple and browsers developed language and protocol as they pleased. Competition for market share was ferocious between Internet Explorer and Netscape. The latter introduced JavaScript, which Microsoft copied as JScript:

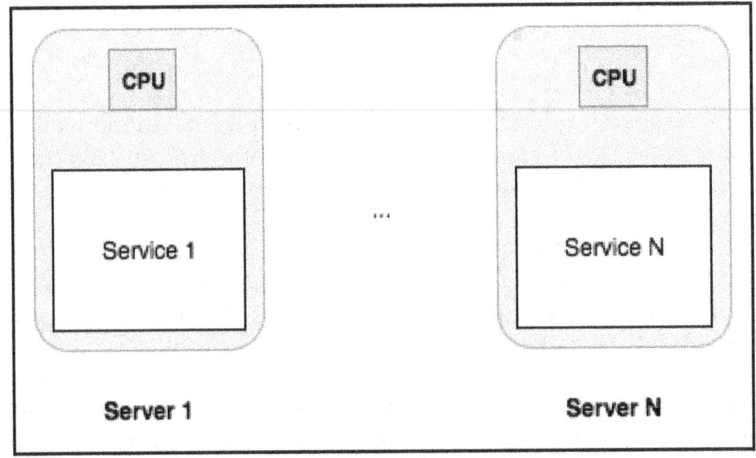

Simple single-core servers

After the turn of the century, processor speed continued to increase, memory grew to generous sizes, and 32-bit became insufficient for allocating memory addresses. The all-new 64-bit architecture appeared and personal computer processors hit the 100 W consumption mark. Servers gained muscle and were able to handle different services. Developers still avoided breaking the service into parts. Interprocess communication was considered slow and services were kept in threads, inside a single process.

The internet was starting to become largely available. Telcos started offering triple play, which included the internet bundled with television and phone services. Cellphones became part of the revolution and the age of the smartphone began.

JSON appeared as a subset of the JavaScript language, although it's considered a language-independent data format. Some web services began to support the format.

The following is an example of servers with a couple of services running, but still having only one processor.

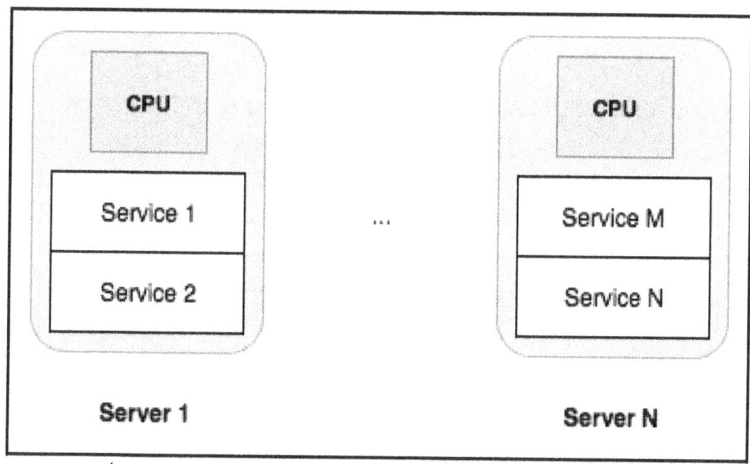

Powerful but single-core servers

Processor evolution then shifted. Instead of the increased speed that we were used to, processors started to appear with two cores, and then four cores. Eight cores followed, and it seemed the evolution of the computer would follow this path for some time.

This also meant a shift in architecture in the development paradigms. Relying on the system to take advantage of all processors is unwise. Services started to take advantage of this new layout and now it's common to see services having at least one processor per core. Just look at any web server or proxy, such as Apache or Nginx.

The internet is now widely available. Mobile access to the internet and its information corresponds to more or less half of all internet access.

In 2012, the **Internet Engineering Task Force (IETF)** began its first drafts for the second version of HTTP or HTTP/2, and **World Wide Web Consortium (W3C)** did the same for HTML/HTML5, as both standards were old and needed a remake. Thankfully, browsers agreed on merging new features and specifications and developers no longer have the burden of developing and testing their ideas on the different browser edge cases.

The following is an example of servers with more services running as we reach a point where each server has more than one processor:

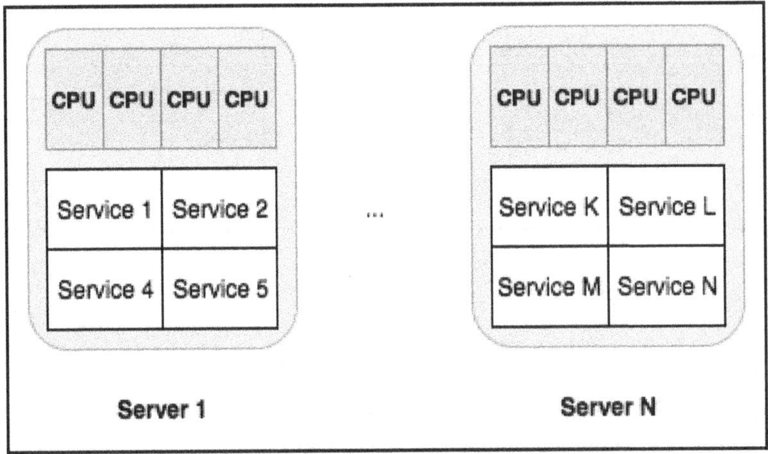

Powerful multi-core servers

Access to information in real time is a growing demand. The **Internet of Things (IoT)** multiplies the number of devices connected to the internet. People now have a couple of devices at home, and the number will just keep rising. Applications need to be able to handle this growth.

On the internet, HTTP is the standard protocol for communication. Routers usually do not block it, as it is considered a low traffic protocol (in contrast with video streams). This is actually not true nowadays, but it's now so widely used that changing this behavior would probably cause trouble.

Nowadays, it's actually so common to have the HTTP serving developer API working with JSON that most programming languages that release any version after 2015 probably support this data format natively.

As a consequence of processor evolution, and because of the data-demanding internet we now have, it's important to not only be able to scale a service or application to the several available cores, but also to scale outside a single hardware machine.

Many developers started using and following the **Service-Oriented Architecture (SOA)** principle. It's a principle where the architecture is focused on services, and each service presents itself to others as an application component and provides information to other application components, passing messages over some standard communication protocol.

From monolith to microservices

As we described previously, a microservices architecture is based on a loosely coupled set of services that work together to achieve a specific target application. At the end of the spectrum, there are monolith applications.

A monolith application is composed of a set of components that are tightly coupled. These components are usually developed using the same language and the application runs as a whole. The first noticeable difference is probably the slow start. Deploying might also be slow since you might need a couple of dependencies before having anything up and running.

Let's imagine an event application, a simple one, an application that lets users define events and be notified when those events are about to start.

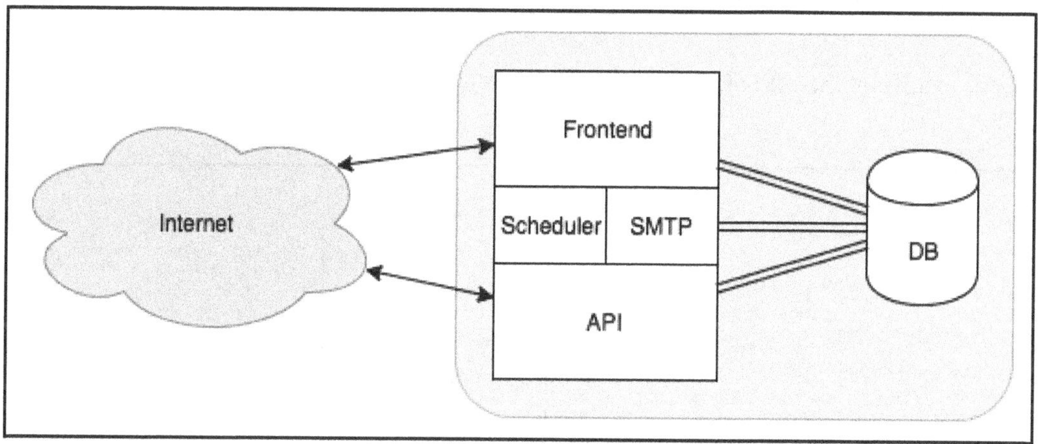

A monolith event application

Let's describe what the event application does:

- It allows users to register themselves and add events to a calendar
- A few minutes before the event starts (that's what the **Scheduler** component is for), the users receive an email with the event information (that's the **SMTP** component)
- Users can use the frontend interface or the **API** interface

Imagine the preceding application as being a monolith (the greyed out area on the right).

Imagine that all four parts are part of the same process, even though they could be in separate threads. Imagine that the database is accessed directly across the application. Sound good?

Well, it sounds terrible, perhaps not for a small application, but for a medium one, this would be a representation of chaos. Having a group of developers making new features or improvements would be a nightmare, and for new developers entering the group, it would take some time before having the base knowledge to make some changes.

The first principle that you should follow is the **Don't Repeat Yourself (DRY)** principle. Avoiding multiple components from accessing a data source helps developers in the future. Later on, if there's a need to change the data source or part of its structure, it will be easier if only one component manipulates it. This is not always possible, but if it is possible, you should keep the data source access to a minimum.

In our example, the API should probably have access, and all others should use the API.

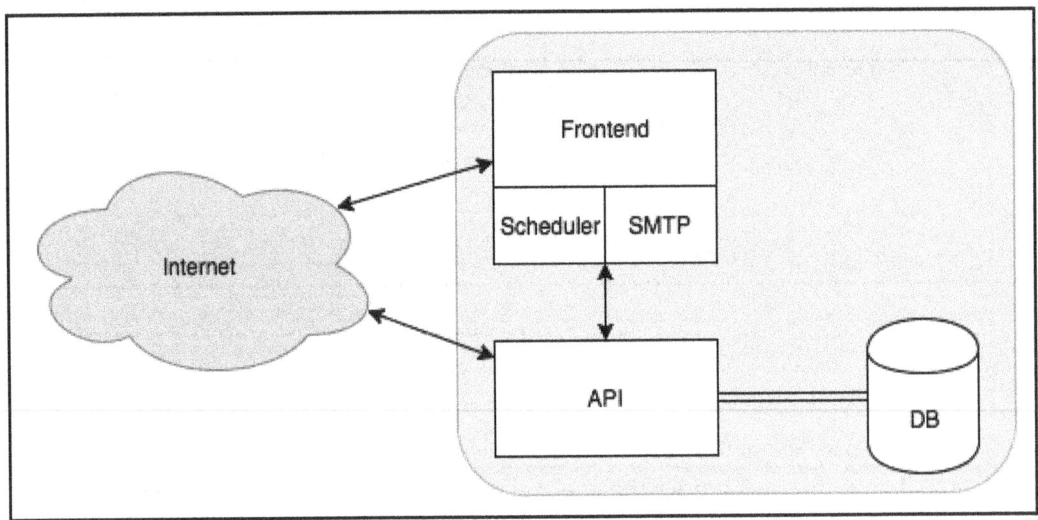

A single service accessing a data source

We now have two services:

- The API, which is the only service accessing the data source
- The frontend, which is the user's interface to change the data source

Although the frontend is used to manage events, it uses the API service to manipulate data sources. Besides having only one service managing data sources, it forces you to think of the API for external developers. It's a win-win.

There is still room for improvement. The **Frontend** could be in a separate service, allowing you to scale the interface according to user traffic, and have the other parts on separate services. **Scheduler** and **SMTP** are both candidates for separate services. **SMTP** should be thought of as a reusable service for other applications you might develop later on.

Let's take a look at how we could build the same application using the microservices approach:

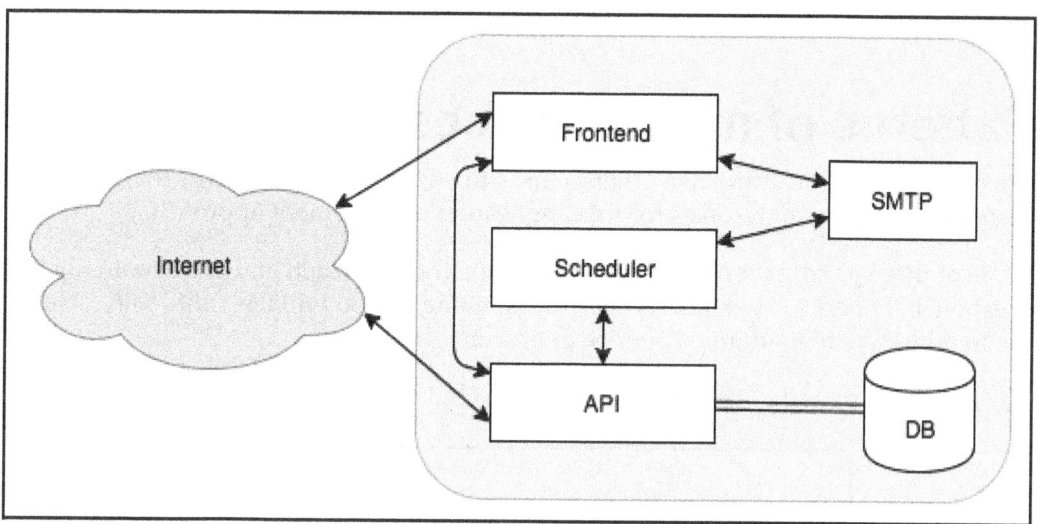

A microservices event application

It looks more complex. Well, the architecture is more complex. The difference is that now, we have loosely coupled components, and each one of them is easily understandable and maintainable. Summing up the changes and advantages:

- The **API** is the only one accessing the database so it can change from SQLite, MongoDB, MySQL, or anything else, and no other component is affected
- **SMTP** can be used from the **Frontend** and **Scheduler**, and if you decide to change it from using a local service to using a third-party email sending **API**, you can make the change easily

- **SMTP** is a candidate for being a reusable service in other applications, meaning you can use it in other applications or event share the same service between multiple applications

You can think of these components as capabilities of your application. They can be swapped, upgraded, maintained, and scaled, all without affecting other components or your application.

A commonly underestimated advantage of using this approach is that your application is much more resilient to failures. In a monolith application, any part can bring your application offline. In this microservices approach, this application might not send emails but can still be running and accessible. Add caching into the mixture and the API can restart in moments.

Patterns of microservices

Microservices architecture, like other archicectures, has a set of patterns that are easily identifiable and form the basis for this application development approach.

Some of these patterns can make the initial bootstrap a burden and can eventually be postponed. Others are essential from the beginning or you will have difficulty, later on, in migrating to a full microservice approach.

The following patterns are not an extensive list but they represent a solid foundation:

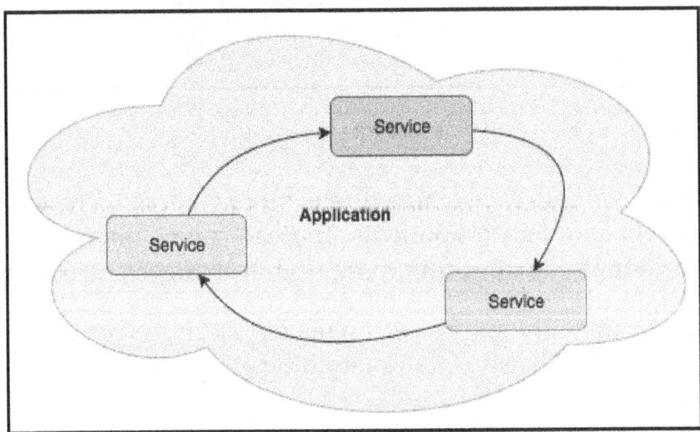

An example of services working together to form an application

Decomposable

The main pattern behind a microservice architecture is the ability to have loosely coupled services. These services are decomposed, separated into smaller parts. This decomposition should create a set of services that implement a set of strongly related functions.

Each service should be small but complete, meaning it should run a set of functions in a given context. Those functions should represent all the functions you need or need to support for that context. What this means is that if you have a service that handles meeting events, all meeting event functions should be done using that service, whether it's creating an event, changing, removing, or getting information about a specific event. This ensures that an implementation change to events will affect that service only.

Decomposing an application can take one of two main approaches:

- By capability, when a service has a specific power or set of powers, such as sending emails, regardless of its content
- By subdomain, when a service has the complete knowledge of a subdomain or module of your application domain

In our previous event application, a service that was decomposed by capability is, for example, the SMTP service. A service decomposed by the domain could be the API service, assuming the application only manages events:

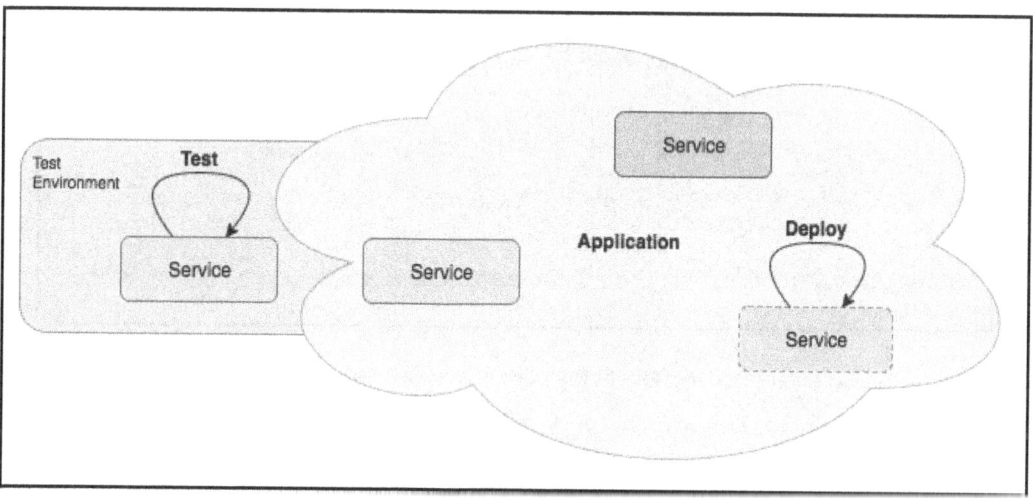

An example of services being tested and deployed autonomously, instead of the whole application

Autonomous

In a microservice architecture, each service should be autonomous. A small team should be able to run it without the other services that make your application. That team should also be able to develop autonomously and make changes to implementation without affecting the application.

The development team should be able to:

- Test, creating business logic and unit tests to ensure the service functions work as expected
- Deploy, upgrading functionality, without restarting other services in the process

Services should be able to evolve regardless of others, keeping backward compatibility, adding new functions, and scaling to several locations, with minimal changes to the architecture:

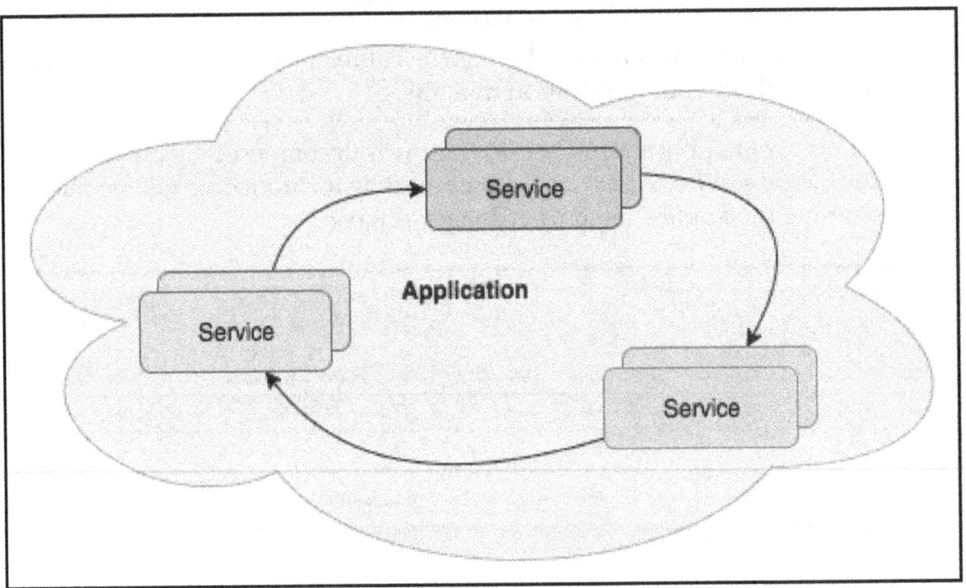

An example of an application with two instances per service, making it fault-tolerant

Scalable

A service should be scalable. At least two instances should be able to run in parallel, enabling failure tolerance and maintenance downtime. A service can also, later on, scale geographically, be near your customers, and improve apparent performance and application response.

For this scaling to be effective, the application platform will need service discovery and routing, a service that could be used by other services to register themselves and expose their capabilities. Other services could, later on, inquire this service directory and know how to reach these capabilities.

To reduce complexity for other services, a service router can redirect requests to service instances. For example, to send emails, you could have three instances and one central router that would redirect requests in a round-robin manner. If any of those instances go offline, the router will stop redirecting to it and the rest of the application doesn't need to care about it.

Another approach could be to use a DNS approach. The name service is capable of handling registrations to a subdomain, and then, when another service makes simple requests, it will receive one or all of the addresses and connect it as if there was only one service operating:

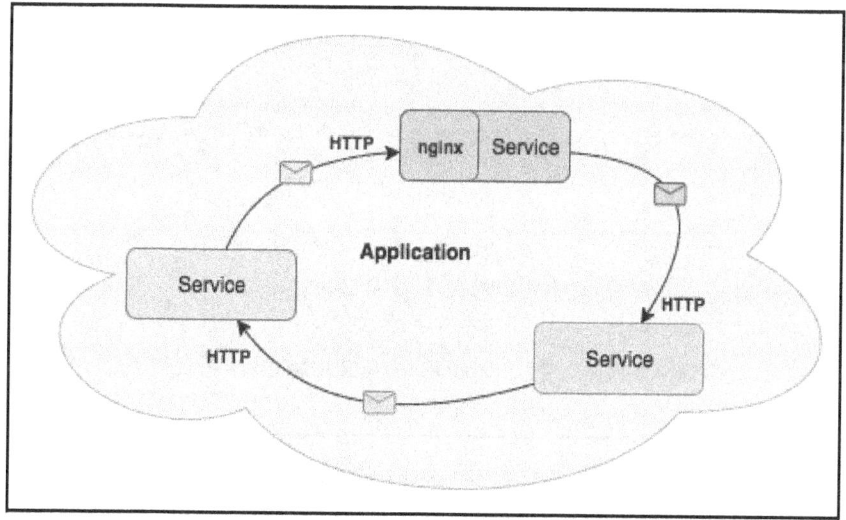

An example of communication between services of an application

Communicable

Usually, services communicate over HTTP using a REST-compliant API. This is not a pattern that you must follow, but it's something that comes naturally based on how common HTTP is nowadays, making it an obvious choice.

There are plenty of HTTP servers out there, making it easy to expose a non-HTTP service with minimum effort.

HTTP is also a mature communication transport layer. It's a stateless protocol, giving developers and operations many features, such as:

- Caching commonly used and often updated resources
- Proxying and routing requests
- Securing communication over TLS

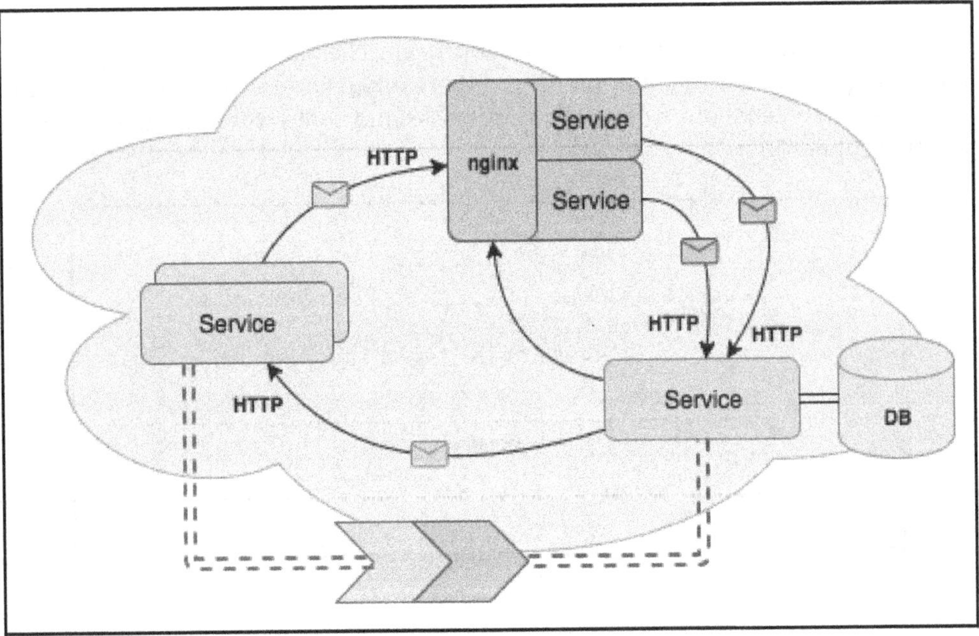

A complex application with several services and streams of communication

Summary

In conclusion, microservices architecture is a good, clear pattern that helps tackle more complex projects. In the long term, it reduces the complexity associated with new projects by appealing to service reuse. It helps to structure an application into loosely coupled services that can be independently developed and tested by small, different teams. It comes at the cost of initial proper planning and a more complex deployment.

Before creating your first microservice, let's look at some Node.js tools that could eventually help you leverage your next big project. This is what we'll be covering in the next chapter.

20
Modules and Toolkits

Now that we have reviewed what Node.js's new features are, and now that we know what a microservice is, it's time to see what tools or modules we can we to create one. We'll review a couple of options and build a more or less simple microservice so that we can point out advantages and disadvantages for each approach.

We'll look at different modules:

- **Seneca**: A microservice toolkit based on property matching
- **Hydra**: A package that bundles a couple of modules to help you resolve many microservices concerns, such as distribution and monitoring

Seneca

Let's look at framework called Seneca which was designed to help you develop message-based microservices. It has two distinct characteristics:

- **Transport agnostic**: Communication and message transport is separated from your service logic and it's easy to swap transports
- **Pattern matching**: Messages are JSON objects and each function exposes what sort of messages they can handle based on object properties

What is really interesting about Seneca is its ability to expose functions based on object patterns. Let's start by installing Seneca:

```
npm install seneca
```

For now, let's forget the transport and create a producer and consumer in the same file. Let's look at an example:

```
const seneca  = require("seneca");
const service = seneca();

service.add({ math: "sum" }, (msg, next) => {
    next(null, {
        sum : msg.values.reduce((total, value) => (total + value), 0)
    });
});

service.act({ math: "sum", values: [ 1, 2, 3 ] }, (err, msg) => {
    if (err) return console.error(err);

    console.log("sum = %s", msg.sum);
});
```

We first include the `seneca` module and create a new service. We then expose a producer function that matches an object that has `math` equal to `sum`. This means that any request object to the service that has the property `math` and that is equal to `sum` will be passed to this function. This function accepts two arguments. The first, which we called `msg`, is the request object. The second argument, `next`, is the callback that the function should invoke when finished or in case of an error. In this particular case, we're expecting an object that also has a `values` list and we're returning the sum of all values by using the `reduce` method that's available in arrays. Finally, we invoke `act`, expecting it to consume our producer. We pass an object with the `math` equal to `sum` and a list of `values`. Our producer should be invoked and should return the sum.

Assuming you have this code in `app.js`, if you run this in the command line, you should see something like this:

```
$ node app

sum = 6
```

Let's try and replicate our previous stack example. This time, instead of having the consumer and producer in the code, we'll use `curl` as the consumer, just like we did previously.

First, we need to create our `service`. We do that, as we've seen before, by loading Seneca and creating an instance:

```
const seneca  = require("seneca");
const service = seneca({ log: "silent" });
```

We explicitly tell it that we don't care about logging for now. Now, let's create a variable to hold our stack:

```
const stack = [];
```

We then create our producers. We'll create three of them: one for adding an element to the stack, called push; one to remove the last element from the stack, called pop; and one to see the stack, called get. Both push and pop will return the final stack result. The third producer is just a helper function so that we can see the stack without performing any operations.

To add elements to the stack, we define:

```
service.add("stack:push,value:*", (msg, next) => {
    stack.push(msg.value);

    next(null, stack);
});
```

There are a few new things to see here:

- We defined our pattern as a string instead of an object. This action string is a shortcut to the extended object definition.
- We explicitly indicate that we need a value.
- We also indicate that we don't care what the value is (remember, this is pattern matching).

We now define a simpler function to remove the last element of the `stack`:

```
service.add("stack:pop", (msg, next) => {
    stack.pop();

    next(null, stack);
});
```

This one is simpler as we don't need a value, we're just removing the last one. We're not addressing the case where the stack is empty already. An empty array won't throw an exception, but perhaps, in a real scenario, you would want another response.

Our third function is even simpler as we just return the `stack`:

```
service.add("stack:get", (msg, next) => {
    next(null, stack);
});
```

Finally, we need to tell our `service` to listen for messages. The default transport is HTTP and we just indicate port 3000 as we did in our previous examples:

```
service.listen(3000);
```

Wrap all this code in a file and try it out. You can use curl or just try it in your browser. Seneca won't differentiate between HTTP verbs in this case. Let's begin by checking our `stack`. The URL describes an action (`/act`) we want to perform and the query parameter gets converted to our pattern:

We can then try adding the value `one` to our `stack` and see the final `stack`:

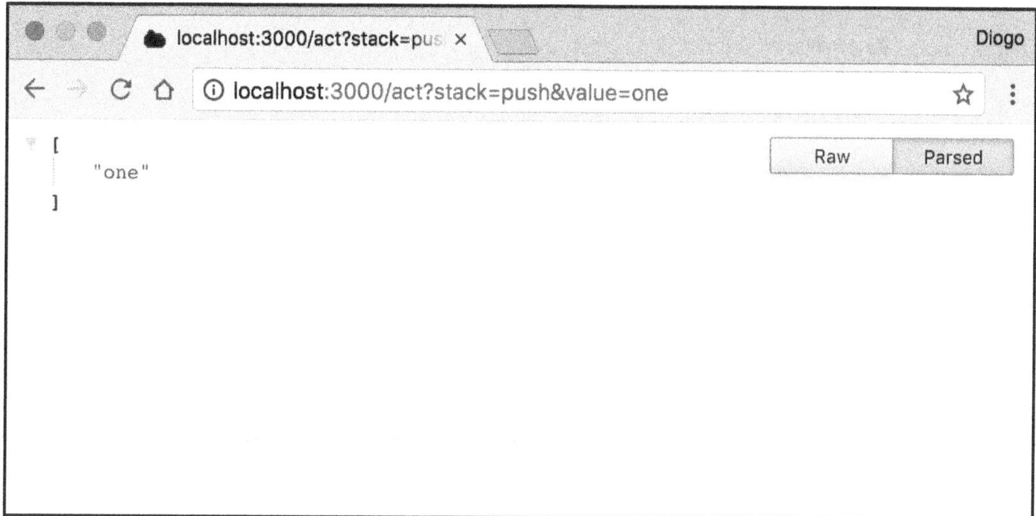

We can continue and add the value `two` and see how the `stack` grows:

If we then try to remove the last element, we'll see the `stack` shrinking:

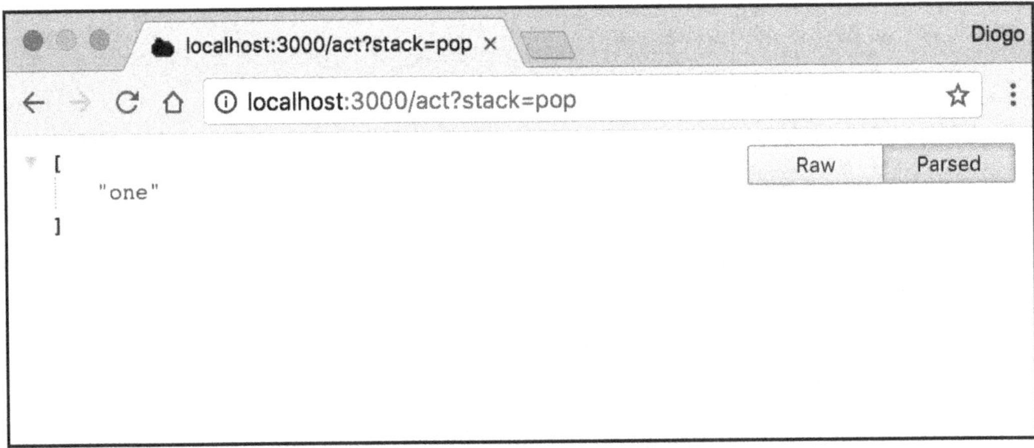

As in Express, Seneca also has middleware that you can install and use. In this case, the middleware is called plugins. By default, Seneca includes a number of core plugins for transport, and both HTTP and TCP transports are supported. There are more transports available, such as **Advanced Message Queuing Protocol (AMQP)** and Redis.

There are also storage plugins for persistent data and there's support for several database servers, both relational and non-relational. Seneca exposes an **object-relational mapping (ORM)**-like interface to manage data entities. You can manipulate entities and use a simple storage in development and then move to production storage later on. Let's see a more complex example of this:

```javascript
const async   = require("async");
const seneca  = require("seneca");
const service = seneca();

service.use("basic");
service.use("entity");
service.use("jsonfile-store", { folder : "data" });

const stack = service.make$("stack");

stack.load$((err) => {
    if (err) throw err;

    service.add("stack:push,value:*", (msg, next) => {
        stack.make$().save$({ value: msg.value }, (err) => {
            return next(err, { value: msg.value });
```

```
        });
    });

    service.add("stack:pop,value:*", (msg, next) => {
        stack.list$({ value: msg.value }, (err, items) => {
            async.each(items, (item, next) => {
                item.remove$(next);
            }, (err) => {
                if (err) return next(err);

                return next(err, { remove: items.length });
            });
        });
    });

    service.add("stack:get", (msg, next) => {
        stack.list$((err, items) => {
            if (err) return next(err);

            return next(null, items.map((item) => (item.value)));
        });
    });

    service.listen(3000);
});
```

Just run this new code and we'll see how this code behaves by making some requests
to test it. First, let's see how our `stack` is by requesting it:

Nothing different. Now, let's add the value one to the stack:

Well, we haven't received the final stack. We could, but instead we changed the service to return the exact item that was added. It's actually a good way to confirm what we just did. Let's add another one:

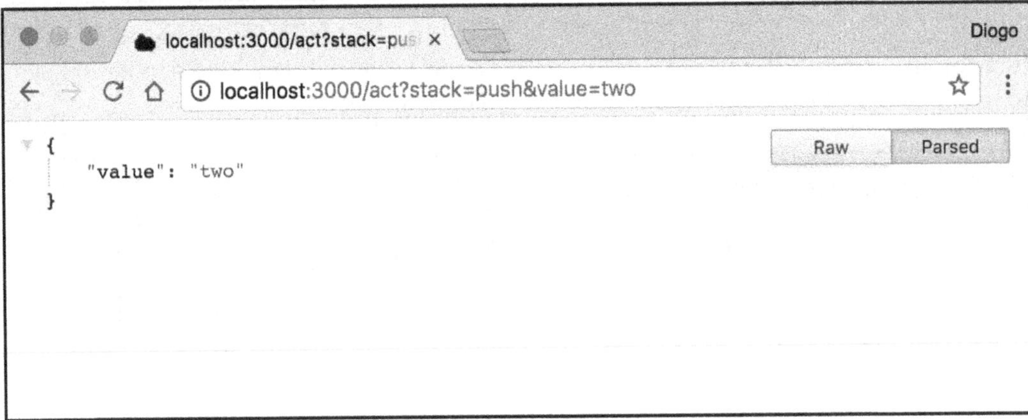

Again, it returns the value we just added. Now, let's see how our stack is:

Our `stack` now has our two values. Now comes one big difference compared with the previous code. We're using *entities*, an API exposed by Seneca, which helps you store and manipulate data objects using a simple abstraction layer similar to an ORM, or to people who are familiar with Ruby, an `ActiveRecord`.

Our new code, instead of just popping out the last value, removes a value we indicate. So, let's remove the value `one` instead of `two`:

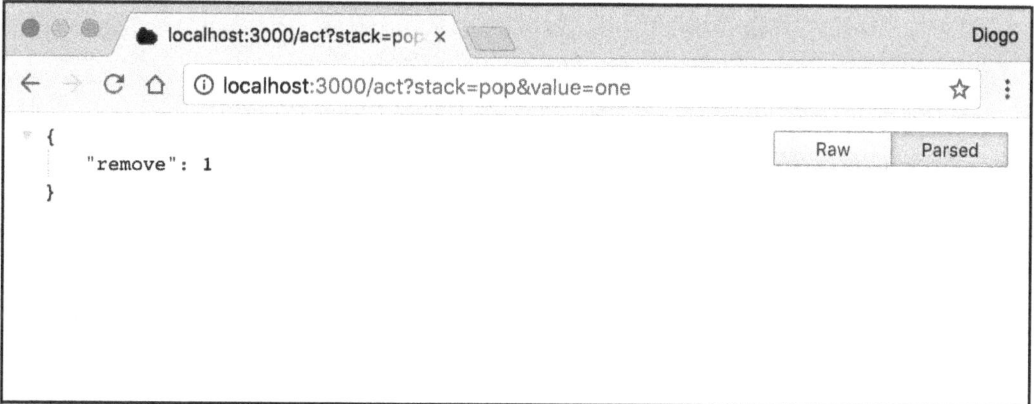

Success! We removed exactly one item. Our code will remove all items from the `stack` that match the value (it has no duplication check so you can have repeated items). Let's try to remove the same item again:

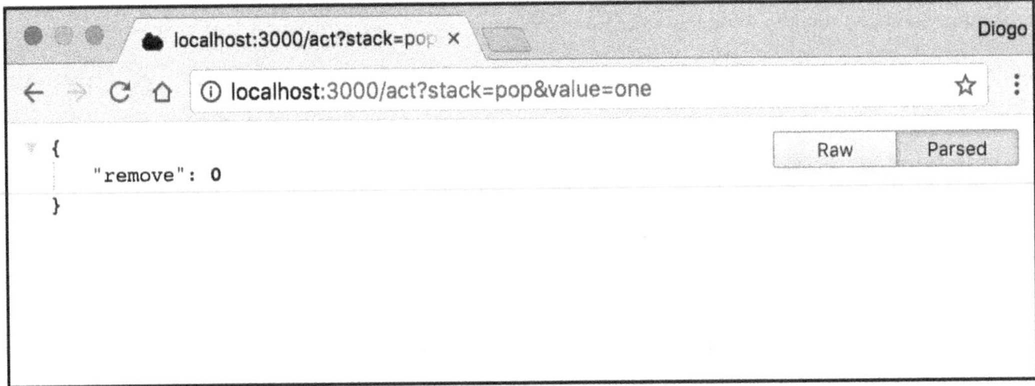

No more items match `one`, so it didn't remove anything. We can now check our `stack` and confirm that we still have the value `two`:

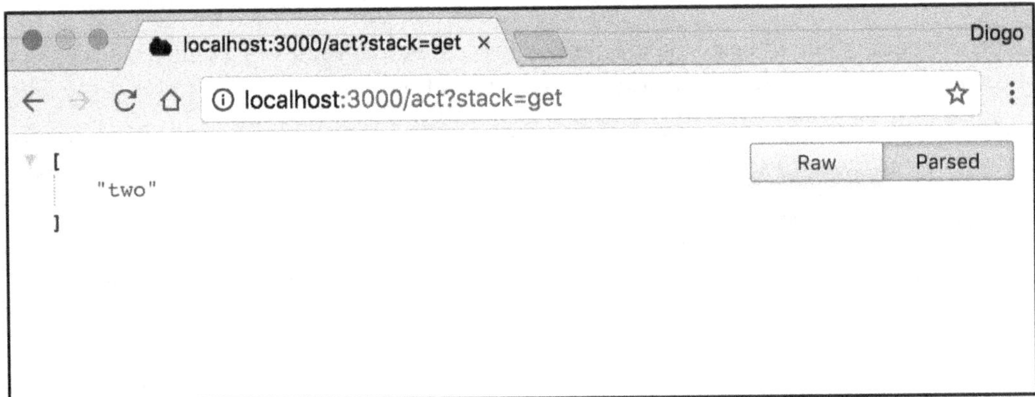

Correct! And, as a bonus, you can stop and restart the code and your stack will still have the value `two`. That's because we're using the JSON file store plugin.

When testing using Chrome or any other browser, be aware that sometimes, browsers make requests in advance while you're typing. Because we already tested our first code, which had the same URL addresses, the browser might duplicate requests and you might get a stack with duplicated values without knowing why. This is why.

Hydra

Let's get back to Express. As you've seen before, it's a rock-solid layer on top of the `http` module. Although it adds an important base layer in the somewhat raw module, it still lacks many features you need to make a good microservice.

As there are lots of plugins out there to extend Express, it can be hard to pick a useful list for us to use.

After picking the right list, you'll still need to make other decisions:

- How can I distribute my service with multiple instances?
- How can the service be discovered?
- How can I monitor whether my service is running properly?

Enter Hydra, a framework that facilitates building distributed microservices. Hydra leverages the power of Express and helps you create microservices or communicate with microservices.

It will, out of the box, enable you to:

- Do service registration and service discovery, allowing your microservices to discover and be discoverable
- Communicate with microservices and load balance communication between multiple instances, taking care of failed instances and automatically rerouting requests to other running instances
- Monitor instances, checking whether the microservice is available and operating normally

Unlike the other modules we've reviewed so far, Hydra has a dependency that is not installable directly using the NPM. Hydra uses Redis to accomplish its goal. Look for information on the Redis website at `https://redis.io/` to install it on your operating system before continuing. If you have macOS and use Homebrew, type the following to install `redis`:

```
1. nazgul.home: /Users/dresende (bash)
~ > brew install redis
==> Downloading https://homebrew.bintray.com/bottles/redis-4.0.6.high_sierra.bottle.tar.gz
Already downloaded: /Users/dresende/Library/Caches/Homebrew/redis-4.0.6.high_sierra.bottle.tar.gz
==> Pouring redis-4.0.6.high_sierra.bottle.tar.gz
==> Caveats
To have launchd start redis now and restart at login:
  brew services start redis
Or, if you don't want/need a background service you can just run:
  redis-server /usr/local/etc/redis.conf
==> Summary
🍺 /usr/local/Cellar/redis/4.0.6: 13 files, 2.8MB
~ >
```

Now, let's make sure `redis` has successfully started:

```
1. nazgul.home: /Users/dresende (bash)
~ > brew services start redis
==> Successfully started `redis` (label: homebrew.mxcl.redis)
~ >
```

After that, we need to install Hydra command-line tools:

```
sudo npm install -g yo generator-fwsp-hydra hydra-cli
```

We now need to configure the connection to Redis. We do this by creating a configuration. Type in the command and follow the instructions. If you installed it locally (or used the preceding instructions), you should answer something similar to the following screenshot:

```
● ● ●                    1. nazgul.home: /Users/dresende (bash)
~ > hydra-cli config local
redisUrl: 127.0.0.1
redisPort: 6379
redisDb: 15
~ > _
```

Now, let's create a very simple microservice, just to see what the workflow is like. Hydra has a scaffolding tool using `yeoman`. To create a service, type the following command and follow the instructions:

```
● ● ●                    1. nazgul.home: /Users/dresende (bash)
~ > yo fwsp-hydra
fwsp-hydra generator v0.3.1    yeoman-generator v2.0.2    yo v2.0.0
? Name of the service (`-service` will be appended automatically) hello
? Your full name?
? Your email address?
? Your organization or username? (used to tag docker images)
? Host the service runs on?
? Port the service runs on? 0
? What does this service do?
? Does this service need auth? No
? Is this a hydra-express service? Yes
? Set up a view engine? No
? Set up logging? No
? Enable CORS on serverResponses? No
? Run npm install? No
   create hello-service/specs/test.js
   create hello-service/specs/helpers/chai.js
   create hello-service/.editorconfig
   create hello-service/.eslintrc
   create hello-service/.gitattributes
   create hello-service/.nvmrc
   create hello-service/.gitignore
   create hello-service/package.json
   create hello-service/README.md
   create hello-service/hello-service.js
   create hello-service/config/sample-config.json
   create hello-service/config/config.json
   create hello-service/scripts/docker.js
   create hello-service/routes/hello-v1-routes.js

Done!
'cd hello-service' then 'npm install' and 'npm start'

~ > _
```

On the name of the service, just type **hello**. Just hit *Enter* to the rest of the questions to use the defaults. In the end, enter the folder that was created and install the dependencies:

```
1. nazgul.home: /Users/dresende/hello-service (bash)
~ > cd hello-service/
~/hello-service > npm i
added 338 packages in 6.56s
~/hello-service >
```

The service is now ready to start. You might have already seen the instructions when scaffolding the service. Let's start the service:

```
1. nazgul.home: /Users/dresende/hello-service (node)
~/hello-service > npm start

> hello-service@0.0.1 start /Users/dresende/hello-service
> node hello-service.js

INFO
{ event: 'start',
  message: 'hello-service (v.0.0.1) server listening on port 45394' }
INFO
{ event: 'info', message: 'Using environment: development' }
serviceInfo { serviceName: 'hello-service',
  serviceIP: '192.168.1.108',
  servicePort: 45394 }
```

As we can see from the preceding screenshot, the service has started and has been attached to a local IP (**192.168.1.108**) and port (**45394**). Open up the folder in your code editor:

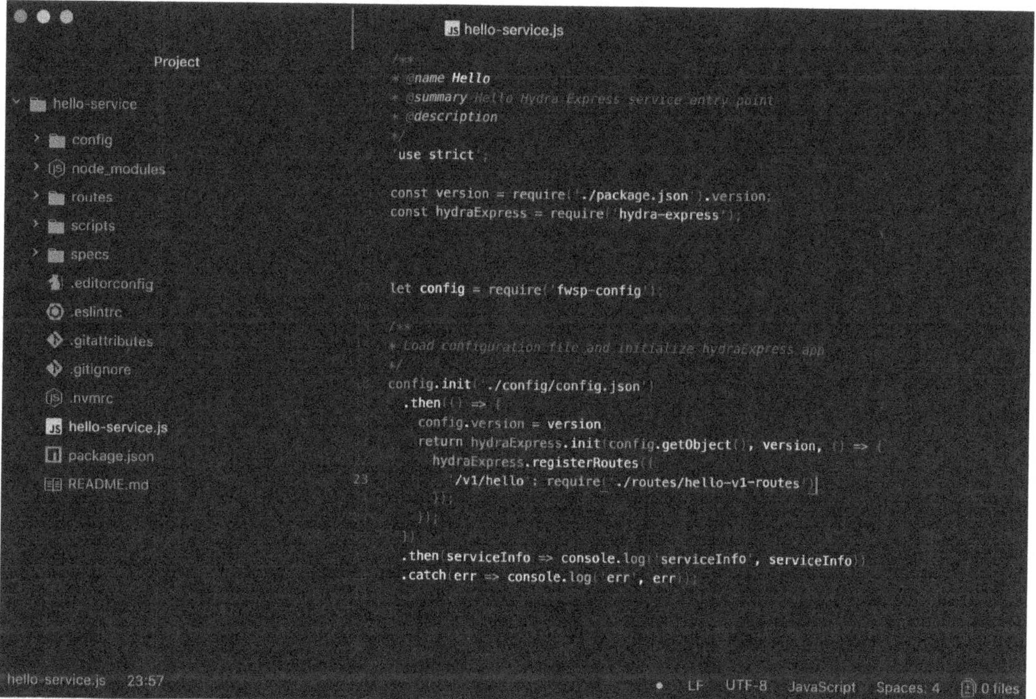

You'll see a file in the base folder called `hello-service.js`, which has the service routes inside it. You'll find the `/v1/hello` route, which points to another file in `routes/hello-v1-routes.js`:

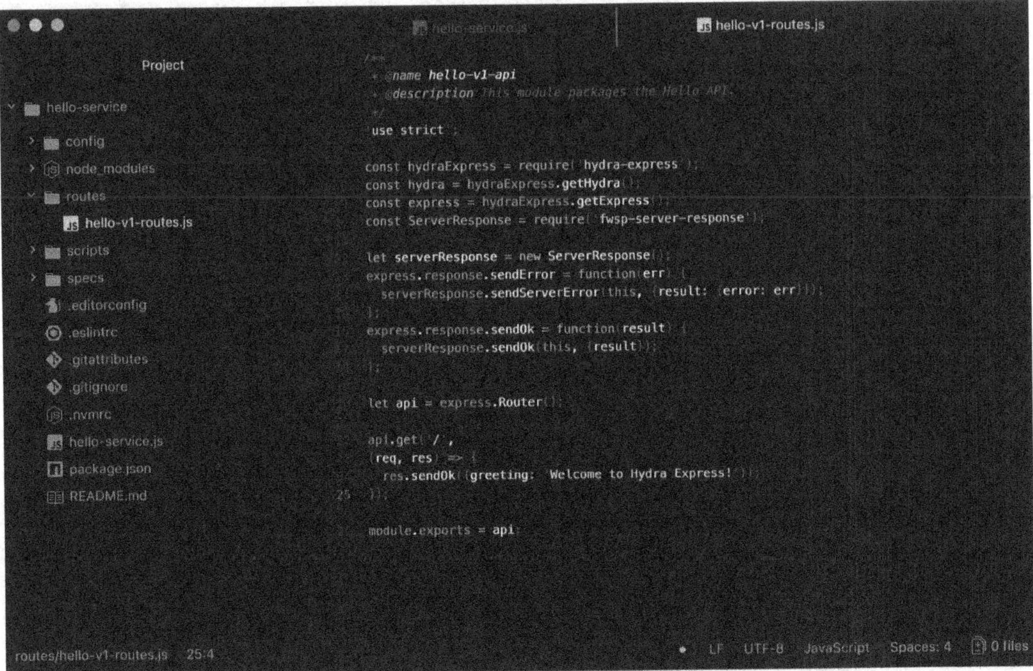

Inside that file, you'll see the response to that route. Now, let's jump to a web browser and see if it's up and running:

What we saw in the file is inside the result property of the JSON response. We just deployed our first Hydra microservice without writing a single line of code!

Summary

We've just covered a range of different modules and toolkits to help develop microservices. From patterns in Seneca, to the Hydra bundle, many approaches are available.

They all target different audiences and fill different needs. I would advise you to experiment with some of them to help you make a better choice instead of just picking one.

Let's dig into some of these tools and start creating a more complete microservice. In the next chapter, we'll be making a useful microservice, covering different use cases, while we develop a fully functional and distributed microservice.

21
Building a Microservice

Now that we've seen some examples of building microservices using some tools, let's dig deeper and create a microservice from scratch using these tools. To accomplish our goal, we'll first use Hydra, and then, we'll create our microservice using the Seneca approach.

There are many microservices we could create, but some are more interesting than others. More specifically, a microservice that you can use in several applications is obviously more useful.

Let's create an image processing microservice. We'll start with a simple thumbnail service, and then we'll evolve to make some simple image transformations. We'll be covering how to:

- Use external modules to manipulate images
- Build our microservice in Hydra and Seneca

The microservice name is very important, as it gives identity. Let's name it *imagini*, the Latin name for image.

Using Hydra

As you may remember, Hydra has a scaffolding command that helps to bootstrap our service quickly. Let's use it, and prepare our base layout. Run `yo fwsp-hydra` and answer the questions. You can leave most of them as default. Depending on the versions you'll use, you should get something similar to the lines shown here:

```
fwsp-hydra generator v0.3.1   yeoman-generator v2.0.2   yo v2.0.1
? Name of the service (`-service` will be appended automatically)
imagini
? Your full name? Diogo Resende
? Your email address? dresende@thinkdigital.pt
? Your organization or username? (used to tag docker images) dresende
? Host the service runs on?
? Port the service runs on? 3000
? What does this service do? Image thumbnail and manipulation
? Does this service need auth? No
? Is this a hydra-express service? Yes
? Set up a view engine? No
? Set up logging? No
? Enable CORS on serverResponses? No
? Run npm install? No
   create imagini-service/specs/test.js
   create imagini-service/specs/helpers/chai.js
   create imagini-service/.editorconfig
   create imagini-service/.eslintrc
   create imagini-service/.gitattributes
   create imagini-service/.nvmrc
   create imagini-service/.gitignore
   create imagini-service/package.json
   create imagini-service/README.md
   create imagini-service/imagini-service.js
   create imagini-service/config/sample-config.json
   create imagini-service/config/config.json
   create imagini-service/scripts/docker.js
   create imagini-service/routes/imagini-v1-routes.js

Done!

'cd imagini-service' then 'npm install' and 'npm start'
```

Well, let's do just that. Let's enter our service folder and install dependencies. If you then start it using `npm start`, and open the browser and point it to our service, you should get something like this:

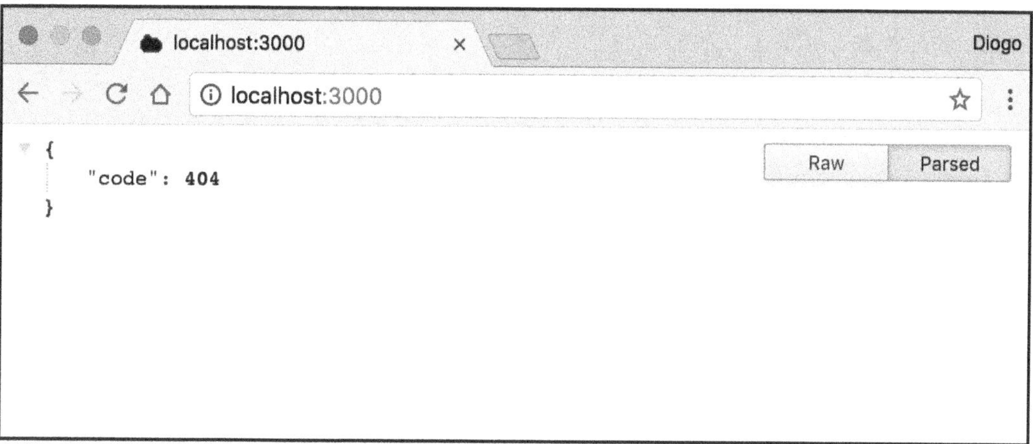

Not surprising, because Hydra created a different base route. To enable versioning and having different services running on the same HTTP backend, Hydra scaffolding created a route under the `/v1/imagini` prefix. Remember, we scaffolded Hydra with Express integration, so many of the terms we discussed earlier will be the same here:

Before we pick our previous code and integrate into Hydra, we need to add our Sharp dependency to `package.json`. Look up the `dependencies` property and add `sharp`. You should end up with something along these lines:

```
(...)
"dependencies": {
    "sharp"                 : "^0.19.0",
    "body-parser"           : "^1.18.2",
    "fwsp-config"           : "1.1.5",
    "hydra-express"         : "1.5.5",
    "fwsp-server-response"  : "2.2.6"
},
(...)
```

Now, run `npm install` to install Sharp. Then, open the `imagini-v1-routes.js` file, which is under the `routes` folder. Basically, what it does is get a handler for Hydra and Express, prepare a generic JSON server response (that's what the `fwsp-server-response` module is), create an Express router, attach the / route, and then export it.

We'll keep this structure for now. I refactored the file as I'm a bit picky about indentation and quotes. I added our image route parameter and added the image upload route. I changed our previous route code to drop the /uploads route prefix, and use the new `sendOk` and `sendError` functions you see in the preceding code:

```
/**
 * @name          imagini-v1-api
 * @description   This module packages the Imagini API.
 */
"use strict";

const fs                = require("fs");
const path              = require("path");
const sharp             = require("sharp");
const bodyparser        = require("body-parser");
const hydraExpress       = require("hydra-express");
const ServerResponse    = require("fwsp-server-response");
const hydra             = hydraExpress.getHydra();
const express           = hydraExpress.getExpress();

let serverResponse = new ServerResponse();

express.response.sendError = function (err) {
    serverResponse.sendServerError(this, { result : { error : err }});
};
```

```javascript
express.response.sendOk = function (result) {
    serverResponse.sendOk(this, { result });
};

let api = express.Router();

api.param("image", (req, res, next, image) => {
    if (!image.match(/\.(png|jpg)$/i)) {
        return res.sendError("invalid image type/extension");
    }

    req.image     = image;
    req.localpath = path.join(__dirname, "../uploads", req.image);

    return next();
});

api.post("/:image", bodyparser.raw({
    limit : "10mb",
    type  : "image/*"
}), (req, res) => {
    let fd = fs.createWriteStream(req.localpath, {
        flags    : "w+",
        encoding : "binary"
    });

    fd.end(req.body);

    fd.on("close", () => {
        res.sendOk({ size: req.body.length });
    });
});

module.exports = api;
```

Then, we restart our microservice, create the `uploads` folder under the `imagini-service` folder, and try to upload an image. Like before, I used `curl` to test it:

```
curl -X POST -H 'Content-Type: image/png' \
    --data-binary @example.png \
    http://localhost:3000/v1/imagini/example.png
```

As expected, I received a JSON response with our `size` property:

```json
{
    "statusCode"        : 200,
    "statusMessage"     : "OK",
    "statusDescription" : "Request succeeded without error",
```

```
    "result" : {
        "size" : 55543
    }
}
```

We can have our uploaded file in our `uploads` folder. We're getting there; just two more routes:

```javascript
api.head("/:image", (req, res) => {
    fs.access(req.localpath, fs.constants.R_OK , (err) => {
        if (err) {
            return res.sendError("image not found");
        }

        return res.sendOk();
    });
});
```

Our check route is very similar. We just changed the return methods to use the methods defined previously:

```javascript
api.get("/:image", (req, res) => {
    fs.access(req.localpath, fs.constants.R_OK , (err) => {
        if (err) {
            return res.sendError("image not found");
        }

        let image      = sharp(req.localpath);
        let width      = +req.query.width;
        let height     = +req.query.height;
        let blur       = +req.query.blur;
        let sharpen    = +req.query.sharpen;
        let greyscale = [ "y", "yes", "true", "1",
        "on"].includes(req.query.greyscale);
        let flip       = [ "y", "yes", "true", "1",
        "on"].includes(req.query.flip);
        let flop       = [ "y", "yes", "true", "1",
        "on"].includes(req.query.flop);

        if (width > 0 && height > 0) {
            image.ignoreAspectRatio();
        }

        if (width > 0 || height > 0) {
            image.resize(width || null, height || null);
        }

        if (flip)        image.flip();
```

```
if (flop)        image.flop();
if (blur > 0)    image.blur(blur);
if (sharpen > 0) image.sharpen(sharpen);
if (greyscale)   image.greyscale();

res.setHeader("Content-Type", "image/" +
path.extname(req.image).substr(1));

image.pipe(res);
  });
});
```

Our image download method is equally similar. For this route, we're not using the JSON responses, and instead just return our image directly. This allows us to try it out on our browser:

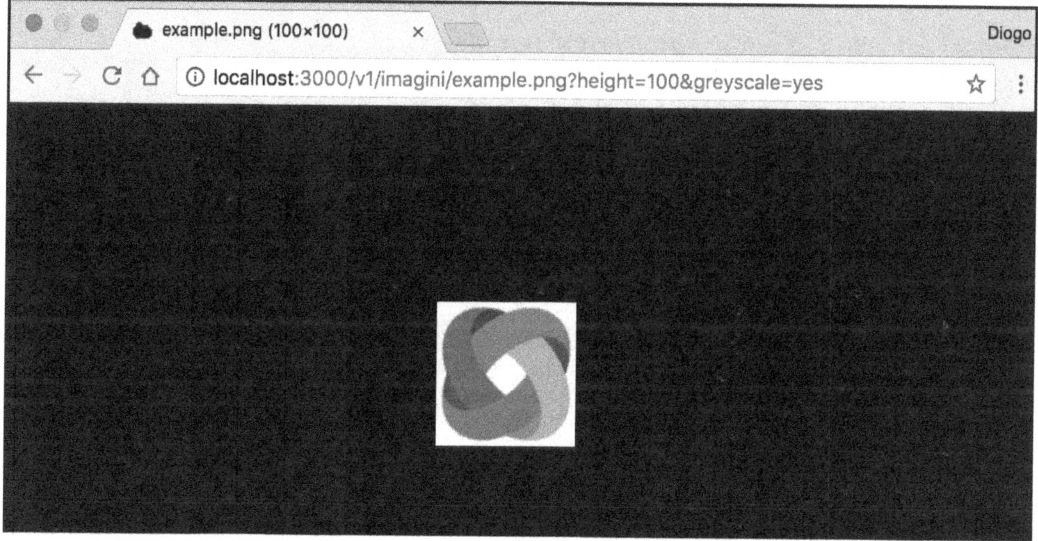

We just migrated our service from Express to Hydra. Not much of a difference, but Hydra gives you a more robust layout, about which we'll find out more later on. Let's take a look at our third framework: Seneca.

Using Seneca

Remember that routing on this framework is all about patterns. Let's keep it simple for now and use a role property to indicate what we want to do (upload, check, or download).

By default, every message should be JSON-encoded, so we'll encode the image in `base64` to pass it as a string inside the JSON messages to upload and download.

Create a folder for our Seneca service, and then create a child folder called `uploads`. Then, install `seneca` and `sharp` on that folder by running the following command:

```
npm install seneca sharp --save
```

Then, create a file called `imagini.js` with the following content:

```javascript
const seneca  = require("seneca");
const sharp   = require("sharp");
const path    = require("path");
const fs      = require("fs");
const service = seneca();

service.add("role:upload,image:*,data:*", function (msg, next) {
    let filename = path.join(__dirname, "uploads", msg.image);
    let data = Buffer.from(msg.data, "base64");

    fs.writeFile(filename, data, (err) => {
        if (err) return next(err);

        return next(null, { size : data.length });
    });
});

service.listen(3000);
```

What this does is initiate a simple service with a route for uploading. Since we're receiving all the image content directly on an object property, I used `fs.writeFile`. It's a simpler method and gives me an error whether something incorrect happens, which we can pass on to the route response.

I also used `Buffer.from` to convert our image data, which we'll be uploading in `base64`.

So, let's just start it as we did with the others. I included the same `example.png` image and used `curl` to test this out.

```
curl -H "Content-Type: application/json" \
--data '{"role":"upload","image":"example.png","data":"'"$( base64
example.png)"'"}' \
http://localhost:3000/act
```

Seneca promptly replied with the following:

```
{"size":55543}
```

This is the image size. Notice I'm taking advantage of bash interpolation (variable substitution) to directly convert the image file to `base64` and pass it to `curl`, which then sends that JSON piece of data to our service:

```
service.add("role:check,image:*", function (msg, next) {
    let filename = path.join(__dirname, "uploads", msg.image);

    fs.access(filename, fs.constants.R_OK , (err) => {
        return next(null, { exists : !err });
    });
});
```

Our check route is very similar. Instead of just replying with an HTTP 404 response code, we reply with a stringified JSON object with a boolean property exists, which will indicate if the image was found.

Here, we are checking for our image using `curl`:

```
curl -H "Content-Type: application/json" \
    --data '{"role":"check","image":"example.png"}' \
    http://localhost:3000/act
```

We will respond with the following:

```
{"exists":true}
```

If you change the image name, it will respond with `false`:

```
service.add("role:download,image:*", function (msg, next) {
    let filename = path.join(__dirname, "uploads", msg.image);

    fs.access(filename, fs.constants.R_OK , (err) => {
        if (err) return next(err);

        let image     = sharp(filename);
        let width     = +msg.width;
        let height    = +msg.height;
        let blur      = +msg.blur;
        let sharpen   = +msg.sharpen;
```

```
let greyscale = !!msg.greyscale;
let flip      = !!msg.flip;
let flop      = !!msg.flop;

if (width > 0 && height > 0) {
    image.ignoreAspectRatio();
}

if (width > 0 || height > 0) {
    image.resize(width || null, height || null);
}

if (flip)         image.flip();
if (flop)         image.flop();
if (blur > 0)     image.blur(blur);
if (sharpen > 0)  image.sharpen(sharpen);
if (greyscale)    image.greyscale();

image.toBuffer().then((data) => {
    return next(null, { data: data.toString("base64") });
});
    });
});
```

Our downloaded route has some changes:

- Instead of query parameters, we check directly on `msg`. One noticeable advantage is that we have types and not just strings, so we can use Boolean and numbers directly.
- Instead of returning the image in binary, so that we could just open in the browser, we convert it to `base64` and pass it on the JSON response.

We need some tools to test this on the command line. Since I use JSON a lot, I have `jq` installed. I strongly recommend you install it too and take a look at the tutorials. It will make your life easier. Using the `base64` command we previously used to encode, we can decode the content and pipe the data to a local file:

We can then open the folder and see the image is there. Notice I added `greyscale` and resized the image just by passing two more JSON parameters:

Plugins

In the spirit of Seneca, we should make a plugin for our `imagini` service. Let's split our code into two parts:

- The `imagini` plugin, a service that manipulates images
- A Seneca microservice, which exposes the `imagini` plugin, and possibly others later on

There's lot of room for improvement on our code, starting with code we repeated constantly. It's important to detect repetitions while our service is still very small.

The most repeated part is the local filename. This is actually something you might want to configure when starting the service, so let's change that to a function. Start by changing our `imagini.js` file to be a plugin. Clear all content and write this code:

```
const sharp    = require("sharp");
const path     = require("path");
const fs       = require("fs");

module.exports = function (settings = { path: "uploads" }) {
    // plugin code goes here
};
```

This is the basis of our plugin. We're loading the modules we need, but not Seneca, because our plugin will have access to the service directly. Seneca itself will load the plugin by calling our exported function. Following the idea of being able to configure the local image folder, we define an optional `settings` parameter, which will default to an object with the property `path` equal to `uploads`, which is the folder we've been using so far.

Now, let's add the content of our plugin, inside the preceding function:

```
const localpath = (image) => {
    return path.join(settings.path, image);
}
```

We start by defining a function that will convert our image parameter to the local path. We can actually reduce the function to be written in one single line:

```
const localpath = (image) => (path.join(settings.path, image));
```

Then, let's create another function that will check whether we have access to a local file, and return a Boolean (if it exists or not) and the filename we provided:

```
const access = (filename, next) => {
    fs.access(filename, fs.constants.R_OK , (err) => {
        return next(!err, filename);
    });
};
```

We can use this for our image check, and for our image download. This way, we can improve or even cache the results for greater performance, avoiding excessive filesystem hits. Our image check route can now be written in a very concise way:

```
this.add("role:check,image:*", (msg, next) => {
    access(localpath(msg.image), (exists) => {
        return next(null, { exists : exists });
    });
});
```

Notice that we're referring to the `this` object. Our Seneca service will call our plugin function and reference itself to `this`. Again, we can write it in a more concise way:

```
this.add("role:check,image:*", (msg, next) => {
    access(localpath(msg.image), (exists) => (next(null, { exists
}))));
});
```

Our upload route is fairly simple and has no changes:

```
this.add("role:upload,image:*,data:*", (msg, next) => {
    let data = Buffer.from(msg.data, "base64");

    fs.writeFile(localpath(msg.image), data, (err) => {
        return next(err, { size : data.length });
    });
});
```

The download route uses our previously created helper functions to avoid storing our local filename. We also made some tweaks to how `width` and `height` were treated:

```
this.add("role:download,image:*", (msg, next) => {
    access(localpath(msg.image), (exists, filename) => {
        if (!exists) return next(new Error("image not found"));

        let image      = sharp(filename);
        let width      = +msg.width  || null;
        let height     = +msg.height || null;
        let blur       = +msg.blur;
```

```
let sharpen   = +msg.sharpen;
let greyscale = !!msg.greyscale;
let flip      = !!msg.flip;
let flop      = !!msg.flop;

if (width && height) image.ignoreAspectRatio();
if (width || height) image.resize(width, height);
if (flip)            image.flip();
if (flop)            image.flop();
if (blur > 0)        image.blur(blur);
if (sharpen > 0)     image.sharpen(sharpen);
if (greyscale)       image.greyscale();

image.toBuffer().then((data) => {
    return next(null, { data: data.toString("base64") });
});
    });
});
```

There are actually a lot of variables we're using where we could just check the
message parameter instead. We can rewrite our download function and get one-third
reduction:

```
this.add("role:download,image:*", (msg, next) => {
    access(localpath(msg.image), (exists, filename) => {
        if (!exists) return next(new Error("image not found"));

        let image   = sharp(filename);
        let width   = +msg.width || null;
        let height  = +msg.height || null;

        if (width && height) image.ignoreAspectRatio();
        if (width || height) image.resize(width, height);
        if (msg.flip)        image.flip();
        if (msg.flop)        image.flop();
        if (msg.blur > 0)    image.blur(blur);
        if (msg.sharpen > 0) image.sharpen(sharpen);
        if (msg.greyscale)   image.greyscale();

        image.toBuffer().then((data) => {
            return next(null, { data: data.toString("base64") });
        });
    });
});
```

In the end, you should have an `imagini.js` file with the following content:

```
const sharp   = require("sharp");
```

```javascript
const path     = require("path");
const fs       = require("fs");

module.exports = function (settings = { path: "uploads" }) {
    const localpath = (image) => (path.join(settings.path, image));
    const access    = (filename, next) => {
        fs.access(filename, fs.constants.R_OK , (err) => {
            return next(!err, filename);
        });
    };

    this.add("role:check,image:*", (msg, next) => {
        access(localpath(msg.image), (exists) => (next(null, { exists
}))));
    });

    this.add("role:upload,image:*,data:*", (msg, next) => {
        let data = Buffer.from(msg.data, "base64");

        fs.writeFile(localpath(msg.image), data, (err) => {
            return next(err, { size : data.length });
        });
    });

    this.add("role:download,image:*", (msg, next) => {
        access(localpath(msg.image), (exists, filename) => {
            if (!exists) return next(new Error("image not found"));

            let image      = sharp(filename);
            let width      = +msg.width || null;
            let height     = +msg.height || null;

            if (width && height) image.ignoreAspectRatio();
            if (width || height) image.resize(width, height);
            if (msg.flip)        image.flip();
            if (msg.flop)        image.flop();
            if (msg.blur > 0)    image.blur(blur);
            if (msg.sharpen > 0) image.sharpen(sharpen);
            if (msg.greyscale)   image.greyscale();

            image.toBuffer().then((data) => {
                return next(null, { data: data.toString("base64") });
            });
        });
    });
};
```

We just need to create our Seneca service and use our plugin. This is actually very straightforward. Create a file called `seneca.js`, and add the following:

```
const seneca  = require("seneca");
const service = seneca();

service.use("./imagini.js", { path: __dirname + "/uploads" });

service.listen(3000);
```

What the code does, line by line, is as follows:

1. Loads the `seneca` module
2. Creates a Seneca `service`
3. Loads the `imagini.js` plugin and passes our desired path
4. Starts `service` on port `3000`

That's it, our service is now a plugin and could be used by any Seneca service! You should now start our `service` by running the new file and not `imagini.js` directly:

```
node seneca
```

Summary

As you can see, writing a service does not change much between frameworks. Our code is very similar, with minor changes. Seneca is stricter about message format and content, so we used `base64` to encode our image inside the JSON message. Other than that, everything is the same.

You get the advantage of being able to choose everything about the service, but you need to write a lot of code. To facilitate the task, Hydra might be a good start for an initial set of plugins.

For other tools such as Seneca, some aspects of the microservice (for instance, the communication using JSON messages and service composition) are already packed. This comes at the price of a stricter service definition.

In the next chapter, we will discuss the security of our three service versions, and how we can store state.

Now that we have created our microservice base layout on different frameworks, it's time to read our code more carefully and see if everything looks good. It's easy to just keep writing code and stop thinking about what we're doing, but later on, when we do stop for a while, we'll be wasting time deleting repeated code and reorganizing our service.

It's always better to think before we code. This is something you'll learn with time, to value the time you dedicate to plan your service or think about a new feature. It's never a good idea to just start coding. In theory, your **Service** should be inside a **Security** layer, with a good and stable connection to **State**:

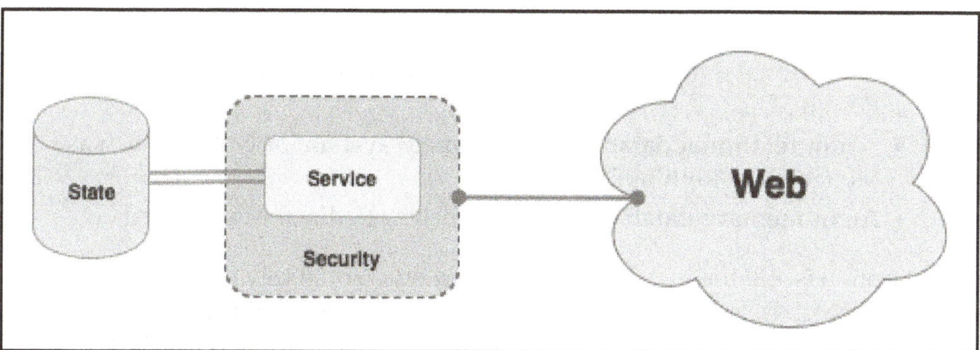

State

Think of state as a person's memory. Usually, a service has state, which means it has memory of actions and information it's serving. The idea is that our service will run indefinitely, but sometimes we're forced to restart it or even stop it for some time because of maintenance or an upgrade.

Ideally, a service should resume without losing state, giving its users the perception that it never stopped. This is achieved by doing one of two things:

- Having state stored in a persistent storage
- Saving state in a persistent storage before stopping and loading that state after restarting

The first option will make your service a bit slower (nothing is faster than state in system memory) but should give you a more consistent state across restarts.

The second option is trickier, because sometimes our service might stop abruptly and be unable to save that state, but for those use cases, you may not care about the state. It's up to you.

There are a lot of options to store state; it will depend on what you want to store. For a microservice, you should avoid the filesystem so as to make your service more compatible with multiple operating systems.

Storing state

Depending on your service, you can store state using:

- A **relational database management system (RDBMS)**, such as MySQL or PostgreSQL
- A **non-relational database management system**, or NoSQL, such as MongoDB or RethinkDB
- An **in-memory database (IMDB)**, such as Redis or Memcached

The first option is still the most commonly used one. You'll rely on stable and more than proven database systems that run in multiple systems and that you can find on any cloud service where you might want to deploy your microservice. Apart from the maturity of most solutions, a relational database, if properly set up, should give you consistency.

The second option is more recent compared to the first one. Usually, there are no fixed tables as in RDBMS, and you normally work with collections of documents that are just common JSON structures. It's more agile as there are usually no restrictions, and each document might have a different structure. The more agile, the less consistent.

All three options, depending on the specific system you choose, support replication, which should enable fault tolerance and improve speed in geographically spaced instances.

Let's try each of the three options using one of the suggested systems. Let's begin with the relational database, and use MySQL.

MySQL

Installing MySQL is very simple. Just head to the official website and follow the instructions. You'll usually be asked for a password for the root user, which you can use later on to manage the server settings and user accounts.

There are some options to connect to a MySQL server using Node.js, but the best tools are the `mysql` and `mysql2` modules. They both serve the required purpose, and neither is the next version of the other, they're just a bit different in design and supported features.

First, let's add the dependency to our service. On the terminal, go to our service folder and type:

```
npm install mysql --save
```

We can now include our dependency and configure a connection to the database. To avoid having the credentials in our code, we can create a separate file and put settings there that we may change in the future, and that shouldn't belong in the code. We can take advantage of Node.js being able to include JSON files, and just write our settings in JSON.

Create a file called `settings.json`, and add the following content:

```
{
    "db": "mysql://root:test@localhost/imagini"
}
```

We defined a setting called `db` that has a database URI, which is a handy way of defining our database access and credentials using an address similar to any website address. Our database uses `mysql`; it's at `localhost` (using the default port), which can be accessed using the username `root` and the password `test`, and our database name is called `imagini`.

We can now include the module and settings, and create the connection:

```
const settings = require("./settings");
const mysql    = require("mysql");
const db       = mysql.createConnection(settings.db);
```

This module only connects to the database when you make a query. This means the service would start and you wouldn't know whether your connection settings are correct until you make the first query. We don't want to figure out we can't connect to the database only when the service is used later on, so let's force a connection and check if the server is running and accepts our connection:

```
db.connect((err) => {
    if (err) throw err;

    console.log("db: ready");

    // ...
    // the rest of our service code
    // ...

    app.listen(3000, () => {
        console.log("app: ready");
    });
});
```

This way, if anything is wrong with the database, the service won't start and will throw an exception, which will notify you to check what's wrong. Here's an example of a possible error:

```
Error: ER_ACCESS_DENIED_ERROR: Access denied for user
'root'@'localhost' (using password: YES)
```

This indicates you probably typed the password incorrectly, or the user doesn't match, or even the hostname or database may be wrong. Ensuring you connect to the database before setting up the service means your service won't be exposed to the public without a proper state.

Our microservice has a very simple state, so to speak. Our state is the images previously uploaded. Instead of using the filesystem, we can now use the database and create a table to store them all:

```
db.query(
    `CREATE TABLE IF NOT EXISTS images
    (
        id INT(11) UNSIGNED NOT NULL AUTO_INCREMENT,
        date_created TIMESTAMP NOT NULL DEFAULT CURRENT_TIMESTAMP,
```

```
        date_used TIMESTAMP NULL DEFAULT NULL,
        name VARCHAR(300) NOT NULL,
        size INT(11) UNSIGNED NOT NULL,
        data LONGBLOB NOT NULL,

        PRIMARY KEY (id),
        UNIQUE KEY name (name)
    )
    ENGINE=InnoDB DEFAULT CHARSET=utf8`
);
```

We can issue this query every time the service starts because it will create the images table only if it doesn't exist already. If we don't change its structure, it's fine to always do this.

You can see we're creating a table with a unique identification number (`id`), a creation date (`date_created`), a date to know when our image has been used(`date_used`), the `name` of the image, the `size` of it in bytes, and the image `data`. The size is a little redundant here as we could just check the data length, but bear with me, this is just an example.

We also defined our name as a unique key, meaning it has an index for quickly finding images by name, and also ensures our name does not repeat and that no one can overwrite an image (without removing it first).

Having the images stored this way on a database table gives you several advantages, such as regarding:

- How many images you have
- The size of every image and the total size
- When the images were created and last used

It also enables you to improve your service; for example, you can delete images that are not used for longer than a specific time period. You can also make this dependent on the image sizes. Later, you can add authentication (mandatory or not) and have user-specific rules.

It's also easy to back up and replicate the state to another site. There are plenty of tools for backing up databases, and you can have another MySQL server acting as a slave to this one and have your images replicated in real time to another geographical location.

Let's change our service from the previous chapter to use our table instead of the previously used folder on our filesystem.

We can remove our `fs` module dependency (don't remove the path dependency for now):

```
app.param("image", (req, res, next, image) => {
    if (!image.match(/\.(png|jpg)$/i)) {
        return res.status(403).end();
    }

    db.query("SELECT * FROM images WHERE name = ?", [ image ], (err,
    images) => {
        if (err || !images.length) {
            return res.status(404).end();
        }

        req.image = images[0];

        return next();
    });
});
```

Our `app.param` is completely different. We now validate the `image` against our `image` table. If it doesn't find it, it returns code `404`. If it does find it, it stores the `image` information in `req.image`. We can now change our `image` upload to store the `image` on our table:

```
app.post("/uploads/:name", bodyparser.raw({
    limit : "10mb",
    type : "image/*"
}), (req, res) => {
    db.query("INSERT INTO images SET ?", {
        name : req.params.name,
        size : req.body.length,
        data : req.body,
    }, (err) => {
        if (err) {
            return res.send({ status : "error", code: err.code });
        }

        res.send({ status : "ok", size: req.body.length });
    });
});
```

Uploading images no longer use the filesystem and instead creates a new row on our table. We don't need to specify the `id` as it's automatic. Our creation date is also automatic as it defaults to the current timestamp. Our use date defaults to `NULL`, which means we haven't used the `image` yet:

```
app.head("/uploads/:image", (req, res) => {
    return res.status(200).end();
});
```

Our `image` check method now gets extremely simple as it relies on the previous `app.param` to check whether the `image` exists, so, if we get to this point, we already know the image exists (it's on `req.image`), so we just need to return the code `200`.

Before updating our image `fetch` method, let's try our service. If you start it on the console, you can immediately open any MySQL administration tool and check our database. I'm using Sequel Pro for macOS. Although there's a Pro in the name, it's free software and it's damn good:

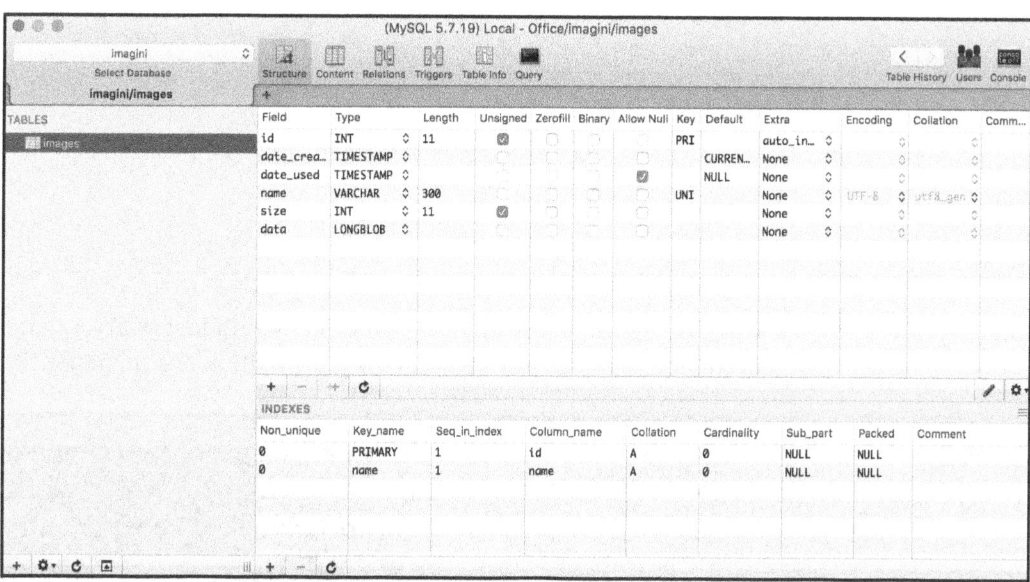

Our table was created, and you can check it has all the properties and indexes we defined. Let's now upload an `image` once again:

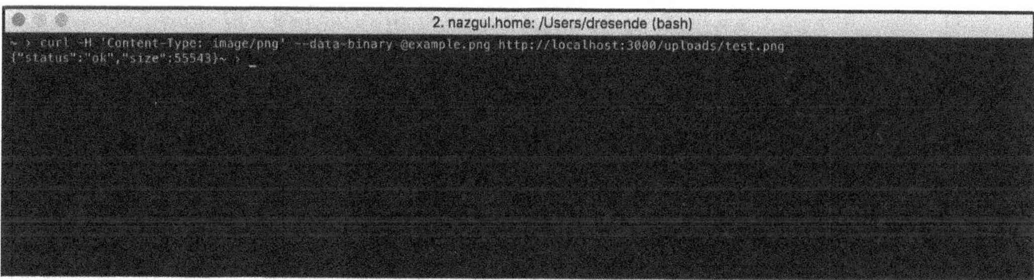

As before, it returns a JSON response with a success status and the size of the `image`. If you look at Sequel again, on the content separator, you'll see our **images** data:

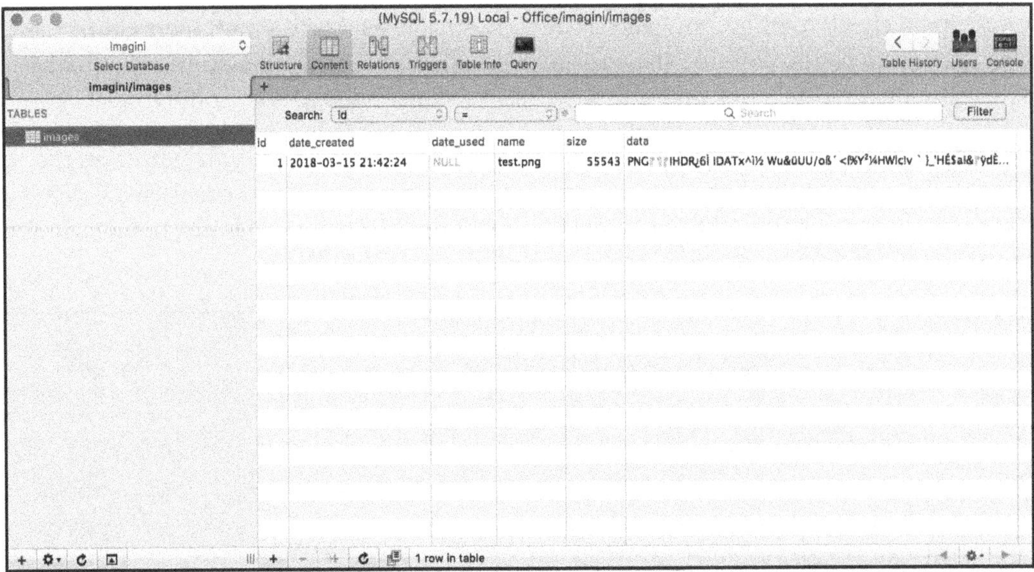

Let's try and upload the `image` again. Previously, our service would just overwrite it. Now, because of our unique index, it should deny an `INSERT` with the same name:

Great! The `ER_DUP_ENTRY` is the MySQL code for duplicate insertion. We can rely on that and deny overwriting images.

We can also check whether our `image` exists using the `check` method:

```
2. nazgul.home: /Users/dresende (bash)
~ > curl --head http://localhost:3000/uploads/test.png
HTTP/1.1 200 OK
X-Powered-By: Express
Date: Thu, 15 Mar 2018 21:56:32 GMT
Connection: keep-alive

~ > _
```

If we use another name, we'll get a code `404`:

```
2. nazgul.home: /Users/dresende (bash)
~ > curl --head http://localhost:3000/uploads/test.png
HTTP/1.1 200 OK
X-Powered-By: Express
Date: Thu, 15 Mar 2018 21:56:40 GMT
Connection: keep-alive

~ > curl --head http://localhost:3000/uploads/other.png
HTTP/1.1 404 Not Found
X-Powered-By: Express
Date: Thu, 15 Mar 2018 21:56:44 GMT
Connection: keep-alive

~ > _
```

It looks like everything is working great. Let's now change our final method, the `image` manipulation one. This method is almost the same; we just don't have to read the `image` file, as it's already available:

```
app.get("/uploads/:image", (req, res) => {
    let image     = sharp(req.image.data);
    let width     = +req.query.width;
    let height    = +req.query.height;
    let blur      = +req.query.blur;
    let sharpen   = +req.query.sharpen;
    let greyscale = [ "y", "yes", "true", "1",
    "on"].includes(req.query.greyscale);
    let flip      = [ "y", "yes", "true", "1",
    "on"].includes(req.query.flip);
    let flop      = [ "y", "yes", "true", "1",
    "on"].includes(req.query.flop);

    if (width > 0 && height > 0) {
        image.ignoreAspectRatio();
    }
```

```
if (width > 0 || height > 0) {
    image.resize(width || null, height || null);
}

if (flip)        image.flip();
if (flop)        image.flop();
if (blur > 0)    image.blur(blur);
if (sharpen > 0) image.sharpen(sharpen);
if (greyscale)   image.greyscale();

db.query("UPDATE images " +
        "SET date_used = UTC_TIMESTAMP " +
        "WHERE id = ?", [ req.image.id ]);

res.setHeader("Content-Type", "image/" +
path.extname(req.image.name).substr(1));

image.pipe(res);
});
```

You can see how we used the path dependency to get the extension of the `image` name. The rest is the same. We just add an update to our image every time we request this method.

We can use a web browser to test our method and see our previously uploaded image:

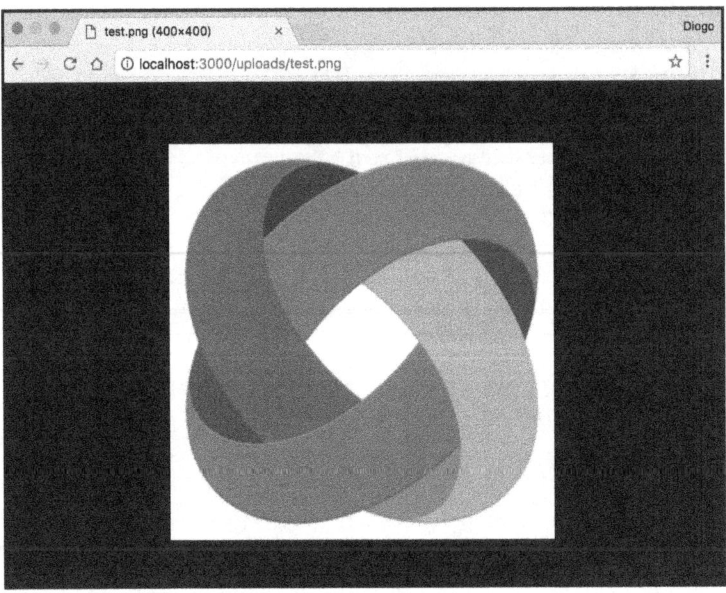

Everything should just work as before because we haven't changed our image manipulation dependency, so blurring and the other actions should work as expected:

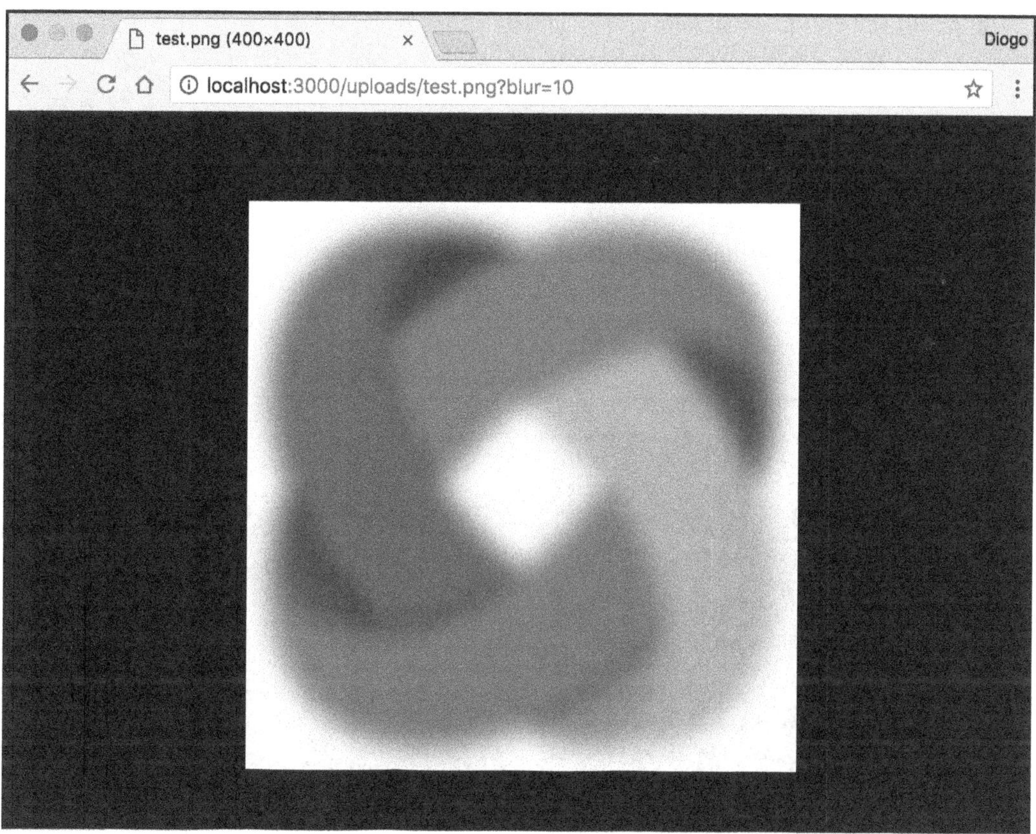

We can now improve our service and add a method we didn't expose before: deleting an `image`. To do that, we can use the `DELETE` verb from HTTP and just remove the `image` from our table:

```
app.delete("/uploads/:image", (req, res) => {
    db.query("DELETE FROM images WHERE id = ?", [ req.image.id ],
(err)
    => {
        return res.status(err ? 500 : 200).end();
    });
});
```

We just have to check whether the query resulted in an error. If so, we respond with a code `500` (internal server error). If not, we respond with the usual code `200`.

Let's restart our microservice and try to delete our `image`:

```
2. nazgul.home: /Users/dresende (bash)
~ > curl -v -X DELETE http://localhost:3000/uploads/test.png
*   Trying ::1...
* TCP_NODELAY set
* Connected to localhost (::1) port 3000 (#0)
> DELETE /uploads/test.png HTTP/1.1
> Host: localhost:3000
> User-Agent: curl/7.54.0
> Accept: */*
>
< HTTP/1.1 200 OK
< X-Powered-By: Express
< Date: Fri, 16 Mar 2018 22:44:08 GMT
< Connection: keep-alive
< Content-Length: 0
<
* Connection #0 to host localhost left intact
~ >
```

It looks like it worked; it responded with a code 200. If we try to open our image in the web browser, we should see something like this:

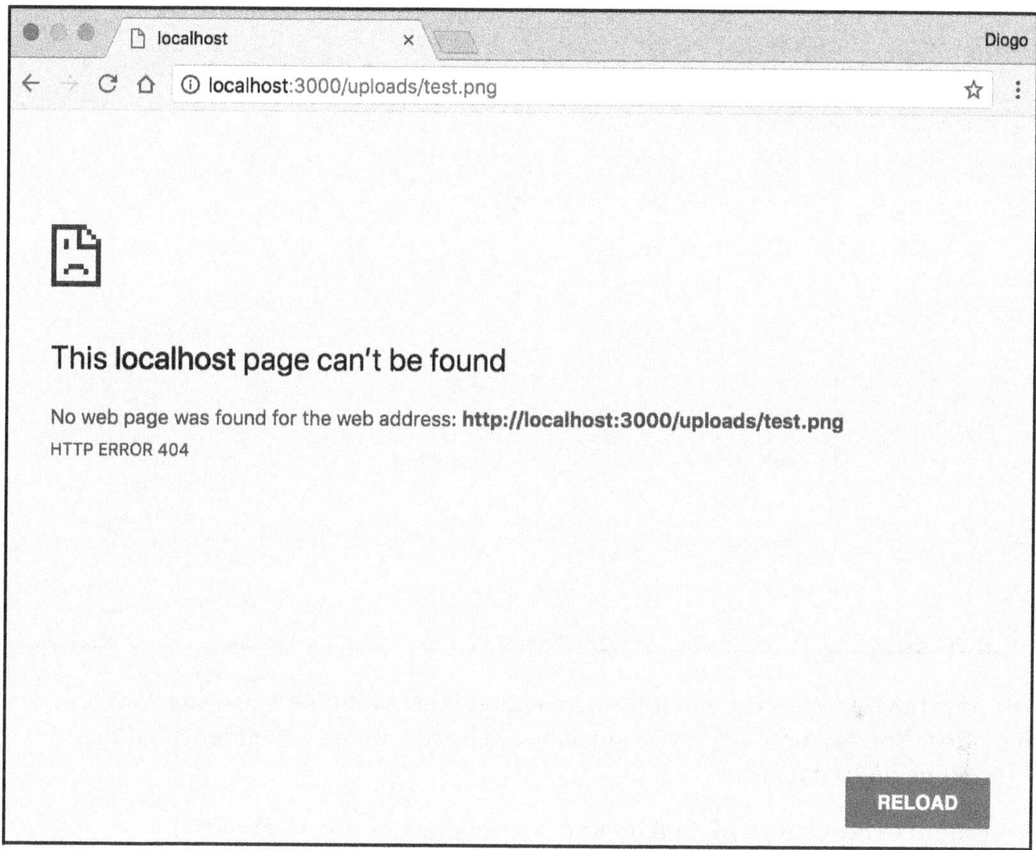

On Sequel, the table should now be empty too:

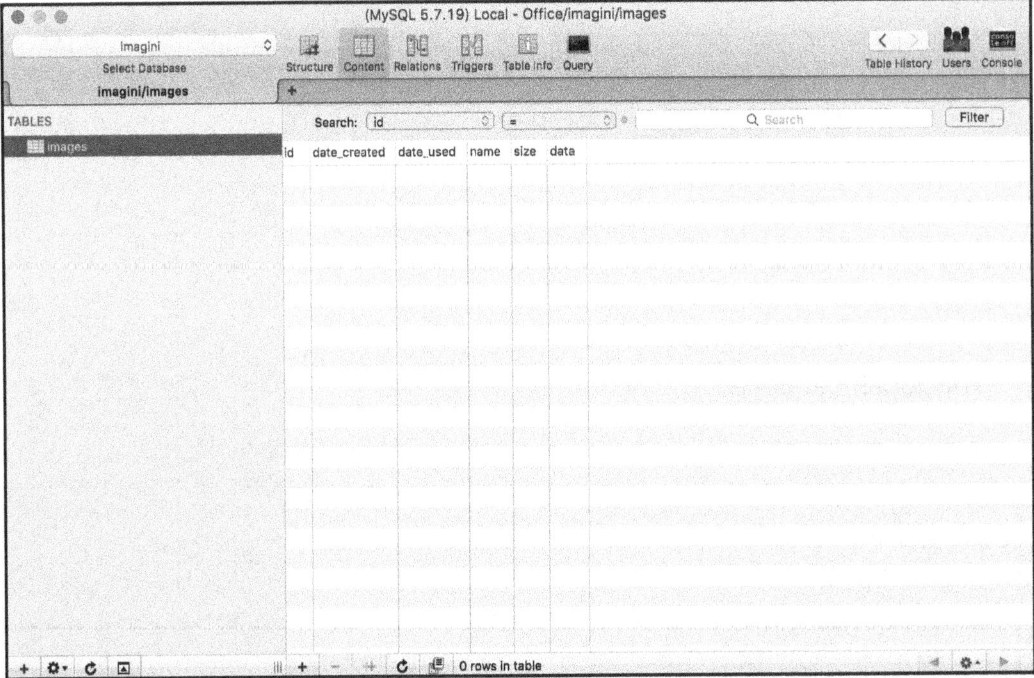

We now have a functional microservice with a state that persists across restarts, as we intended. You can now deploy to any cloud service with no dependency on the filesystem, just a database.

You could easily change MySQL to another database or use an **object relational mapping** (**ORM**) module to enable you to change database server without changing your code. An ORM is a library that allows you to use a common interface to access different types of databases. Usually, this kind of abstraction involves not using SQL at all and reducing your interaction with the databases to simpler queries (to allow for interoperability between database servers).

Let's take this opportunity to go a little further and add a few methods that got simplified by this migration to the database. Let's create a method that exposes statistics about our database, and let's remove old images.

Our first statistics method should just return a JSON structure with some useful information. Let's expose the following:

- The total number of images
- The total size of the images
- How long our service is running
- When the last time was that we uploaded an image

Here's an example of how our statistics method could look:

```
app.get("/stats", (req, res) => {
    db.query("SELECT COUNT(*) total" +
            ", SUM(size) size " +
            ", MAX(date_created) last_created " +
            "FROM images",
    (err, rows) => {
        if (err) {
            return res.status(500).end();
        }

        rows[0].uptime = process.uptime();

        return res.send(rows[0]);
    });
});
```

Restart the service, and let's try it:

As we can see, we have no images as we just removed our image previously. There's no size because we have no images. There's also no used date, and the service uptime is 5 seconds.

If we upload our previous image, we will get different results, something like the following screenshot:

Now, for our second task, deleting old images, we need to check our database periodically. We'll use an interval timer and just run a `DELETE` query. The intervals mentioned in the following query are just an example; you can write the conditions you want.

```
setInterval(() => {
    db.query("DELETE FROM images " +
             "WHERE (date_created < UTC_TIMETSTAMP - INTERVAL 1 WEEK
             AND date_used IS NULL) " +
             " OR (date_used < UTC_TIMETSTAMP - INTERVAL 1 MONTH)");
}, 3600 * 1000);
```

This query deletes `images` that were not used in the past month (but were used before) or images that were not used in the past week (and never used before). This means that images uploaded need to be used at least once or they will get removed quickly.

You can think of a different strategy, or use no strategy and delete manually if you want. Now that we've seen MySQL, let's move on and look at another kind of database server.

RethinkDB

Let's see the differences for a non-relational database using RethinkDB. If you don't have it, just install it by following the official documentation (`https://www.rethinkdb.com/docs/`). Let's just start the server:

```
rethinkdb
```

This will start the server, which comes with a very nice administration console on port `8080`. You can open it in the web browser:

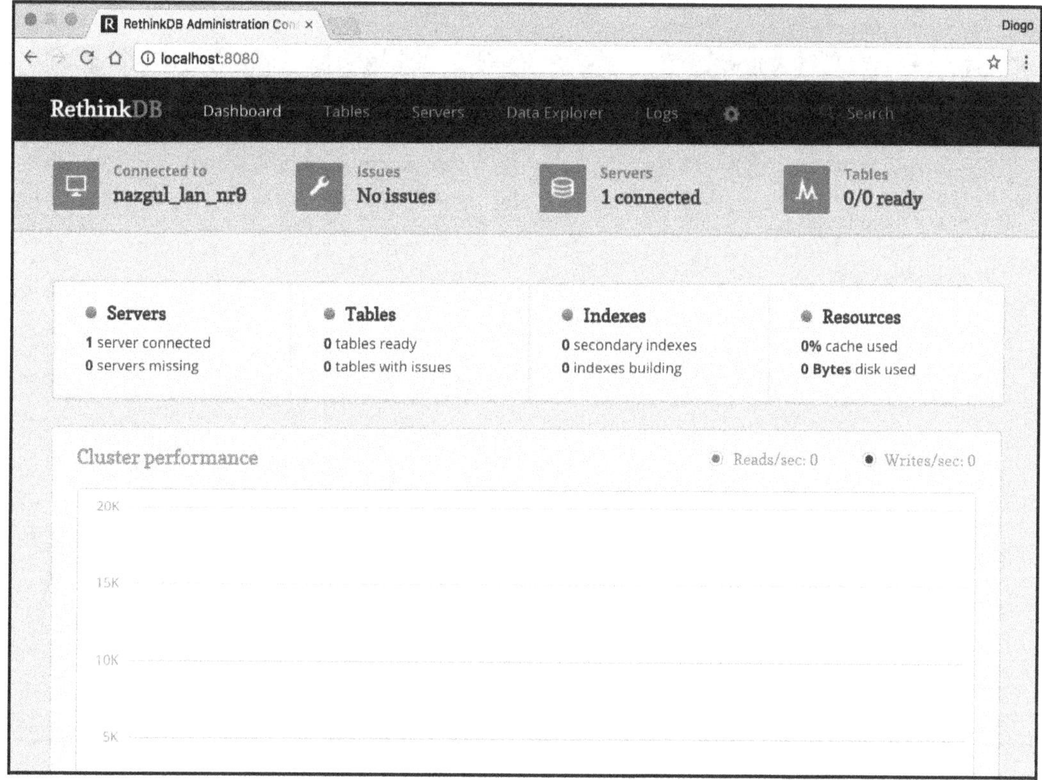

Go to the **Tables** section on top to see the databases:

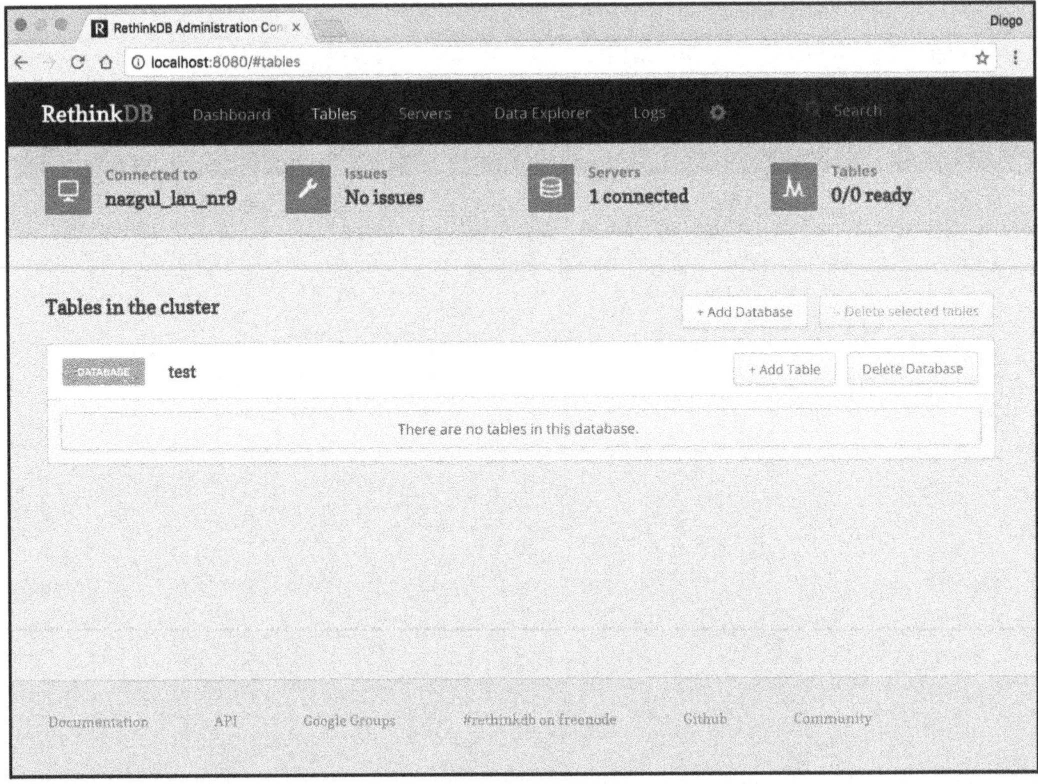

Create a database called `imagini` using the **Add Database** button. You should now have our database ready. You need nothing else here:

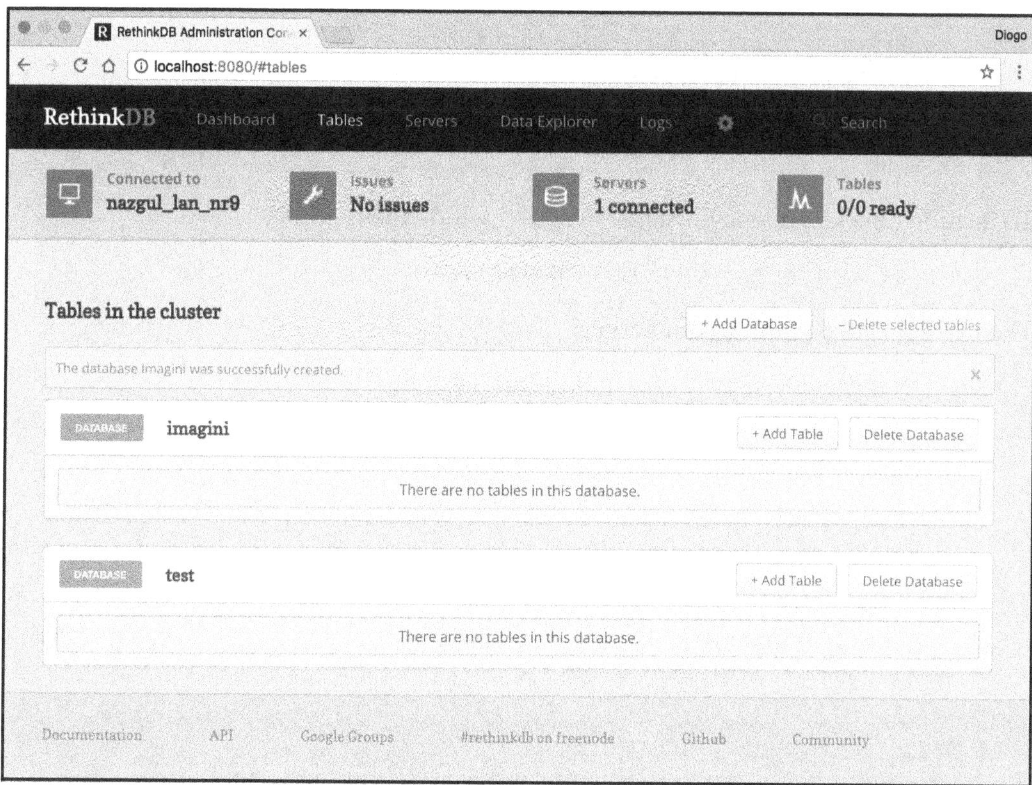

To use our new database, we need to install the `rethinkdb` dependency. You can remove the MySQL dependency:

```
npm uninstall mysql --save
npm install rethinkdb --save
```

Now, let's change our `settings` file. This module doesn't accept a connection string, so we'll use a JSON structure:

```json
{
    "db": {
        "host" : "localhost",
        "db" : "imagini"
    }
}
```

To include our dependency, we just need to include the module:

```
const rethinkdb = require("rethinkdb");
```

Then, use this to connect to our server:

```
rethinkdb.connect(settings.db, (err, db) => {
    if (err) throw err;

    console.log("db: ready");

    // ...
    // the rest of our service code
    // ...

    app.listen(3000, () => {
        console.log("app: ready");
    });
});
```

After connecting, we can create our table as we did before. This time, we don't need to specify any structure:

```
rethinkdb.tableCreate("images").run(db);
```

The `rethinkdb` object is the one we'll use to manipulate our table, and the `db` object is a connection object used to reference the connection and to indicate where to run our manipulations.

If you restart our service just like this, you'll see a new table on our previously created database:

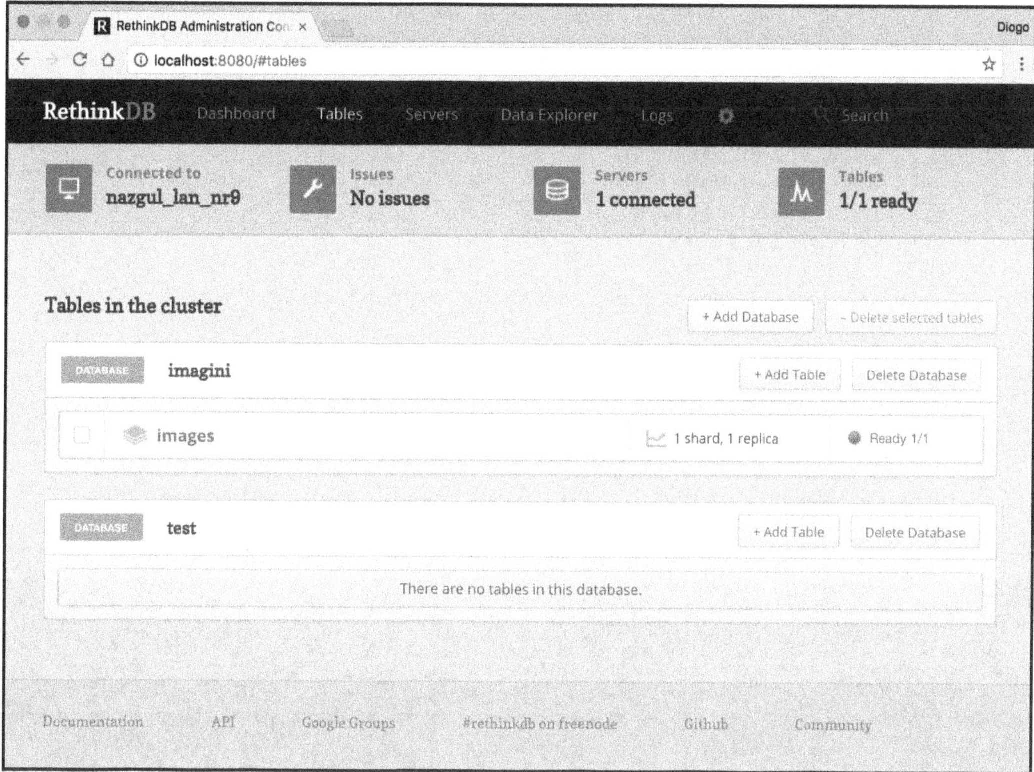

If you restart our service again, you'll get an error trying to create the table that already exists. We need to check whether it already exists, and only issue the command if not:

```
rethinkdb.tableList().run(db, (err, tables) => {
    if (err) throw err;

    if (!tables.includes("images")) {
        rethinkdb.tableCreate("images").run(db);
    }
});
```

Moving on, our upload method should be changed slightly to something like the following:

```
app.post("/uploads/:name", bodyparser.raw({
    limit : "10mb",
    type : "image/*"
}), (req, res) => {
    rethinkdb.table("images").insert({
        name : req.params.name,
        size : req.body.length,
        data : req.body,
    }).run(db, (err) => {
        if (err) {
            return res.send({ status : "error", code: err.code });
        }

        res.send({ status : "ok", size: req.body.length });
    });
});
```

If you restart the server just like this, you should be able to upload an `image`:

```
2. nazgul.lan: /Users/dresende (bash)
~ > curl -H 'Content-Type: image/png' --data-binary @example.png http://localhost:3000/uploads/test.png
{"status":"ok","size":55543}~ > 
```

We receive the same response, just like with MySQL. We can go to the **Data Explorer** section in the administration console and get our record to see whether it's there:

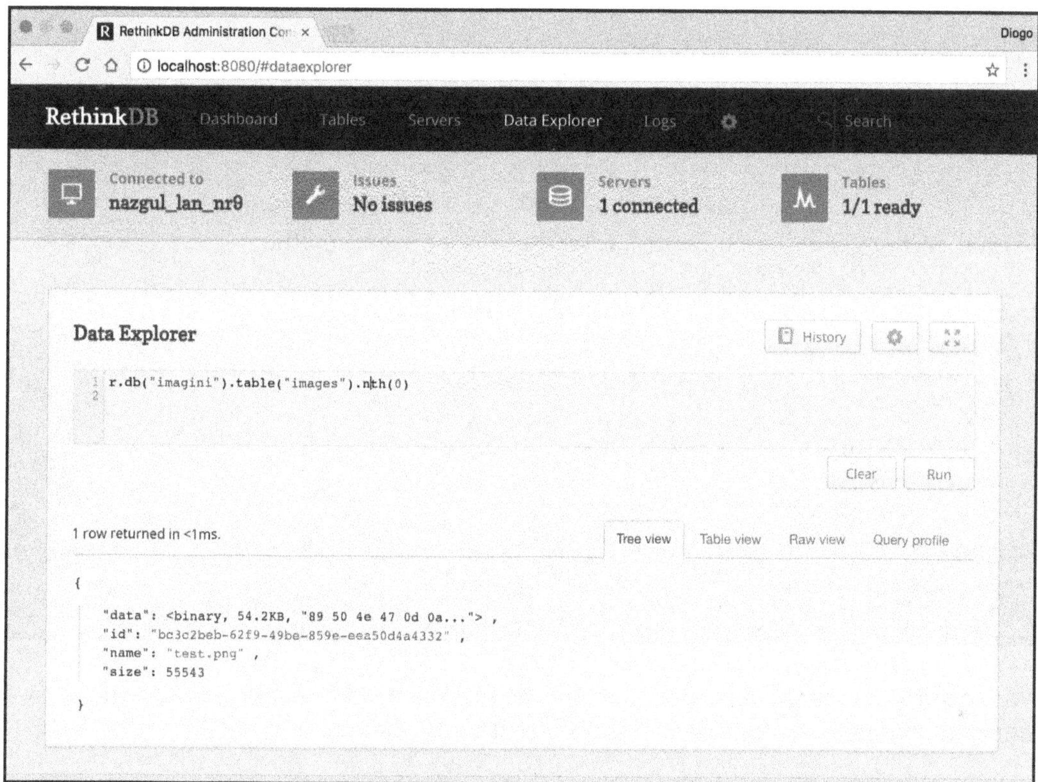

Looks good. Notice our record ID is not a number, it's a **Universally Unique Identifier** (UUID). This is because RethinkDB has support for sharding (our table is sharded by default if there was more than one server) and it's easier to shard unique identifiers than an incremental number.

Moving on to our Express parameter:

```
app.param("image", (req, res, next, image) => {
    if (!image.match(/\.(png|jpg)$/i)) {
        return res.status(403).end();
    }

    rethinkdb.table("images").filter({
        name : image
    }).limit(1).run(db, (err, images) => {
        if (err) return res.status(404).end();
```

```
        images.toArray((err, images) => {
            if (err) return res.status(500).end();
            if (!images.length) return res.status(404).end();

            req.image = images[0];

            return next();
        });
    });
});
```

With this change, we can now restart our service and see whether our `image` exists:

```
2. nazgul.lan: /Users/dresende (bash)
~ > curl --head http://localhost:3000/uploads/test.png
HTTP/1.1 200 OK
X-Powered-By: Express
Date: Sat, 17 Mar 2018 22:04:07 GMT
Connection: keep-alive

~ >
```

We need to change the download just a little bit. We need to remove the previous query to update our usage date and replace it with a new one:

```
app.get("/uploads/:image", (req, res) => {
    let image       = sharp(req.image.data);
    let width       = +req.query.width;
    let height      = +req.query.height;
    let blur        = +req.query.blur;
    let sharpen     = +req.query.sharpen;
    let greyscale   = [ "y", "yes", "true", "1",
    "on"].includes(req.query.greyscale);
    let flip        = [ "y", "yes", "true", "1",
    "on"].includes(req.query.flip);
    let flop        = [ "y", "yes", "true", "1",
    "on"].includes(req.query.flop);

    if (width > 0 && height > 0) {
        image.ignoreAspectRatio();
    }

    if (width > 0 || height > 0) {
```

```
        image.resize(width || null, height || null);
    }

    if (flip)         image.flip();
    if (flop)         image.flop();
    if (blur > 0)     image.blur(blur);
    if (sharpen > 0)  image.sharpen(sharpen);
    if (greyscale)    image.greyscale();

    rethinkdb.table("images").get(req.image.id).update({ date_used :
    Date.now() }).run(db);

    res.setHeader("Content-Type", "image/" +
    path.extname(req.image.name).substr(1));

    image.pipe(res);
});
```

We can now download our image using the web browser:

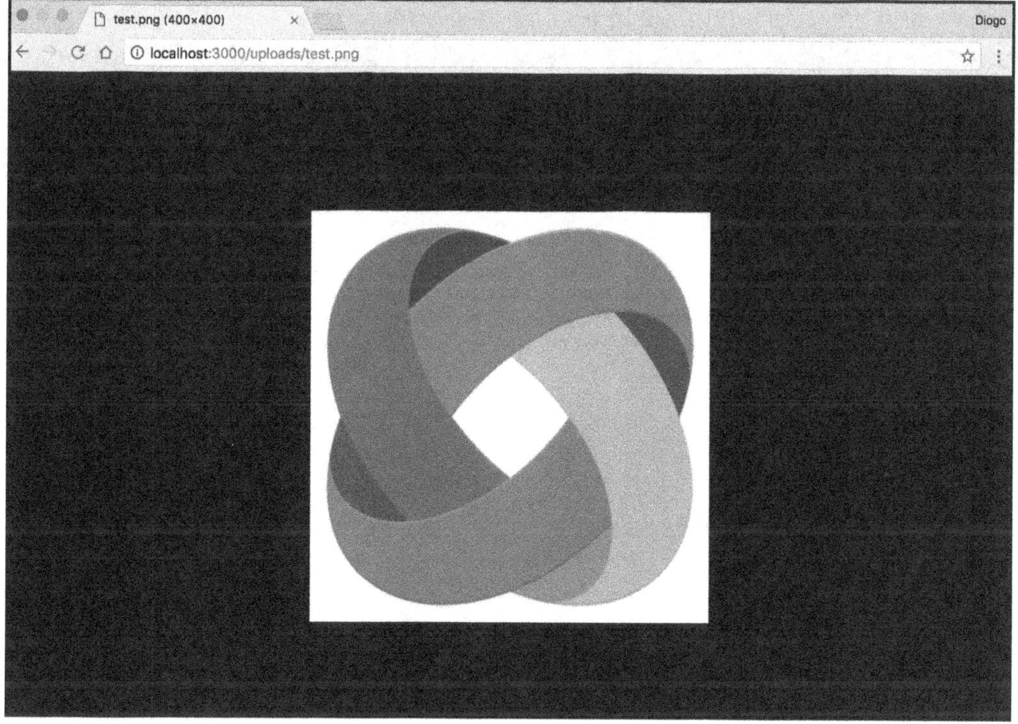

Next, we need to update our image removal method. It's as easy as our upload:

```
app.delete("/uploads/:image", (req, res) => {
    rethinkdb.table("images").get(req.image.id).delete().run(db, (err)
    => {
        return res.status(err ? 500 : 200).end();
    });
});
```

This time, we used the image unique ID to remove it. If we try again using the `curl` command, we'll receive a code `200`:

```
2. nazgul.lan: /Users/dresende (bash)
~ > curl -v -X DELETE http://localhost:3000/uploads/test.png
*   Trying ::1...
* TCP_NODELAY set
* Connected to localhost (::1) port 3000 (#0)
> DELETE /uploads/test.png HTTP/1.1
> Host: localhost:3000
> User-Agent: curl/7.54.0
> Accept: */*
>
< HTTP/1.1 200 OK
< X-Powered-By: Express
< Date: Sun, 18 Mar 2018 19:07:50 GMT
< Connection: keep-alive
< Content-Length: 0
<
* Connection #0 to host localhost left intact
~ > _
```

If we try to get the first record of our table, we'll see there's nothing there:

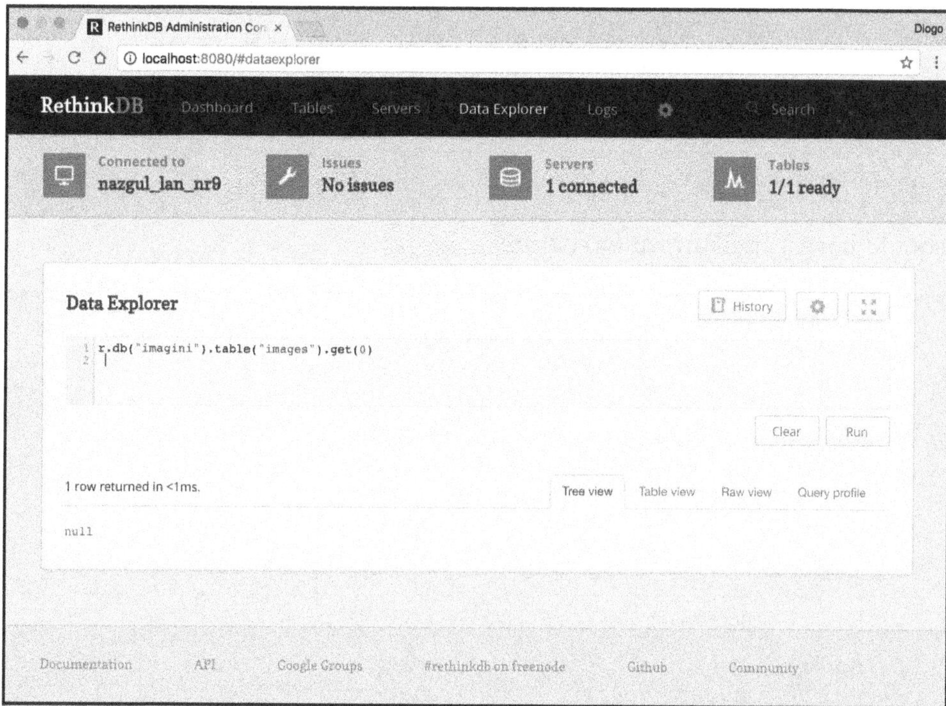

Finally, there are our two extra features that we added after introducing MySQL: the statistics and removing old unused images.

Our statistics method is not so simple as running an SQL query with aggregations. We must calculate each of our statistics:

```
app.get("/stats", (req, res) => {
    let uptime = process.uptime();

    rethinkdb.table("images").count().run(db, (err, total) => {
        if (err) return res.status(500).end();

        rethinkdb.table("images").sum("size").run(db, (err, size) => {
            if (err) return res.status(500).end();

            rethinkdb.table("images").max("date_created").run(db,
(err,
            last_created) => {
                if (err) return res.status(500).end();
```

```
                last_created = (last_created ? new
                Date(last_created.date_created) : null);

                return res.send({ total, size, last_created, uptime
  });
          });
      });
    });
  });
```

We should have a similar result to before:

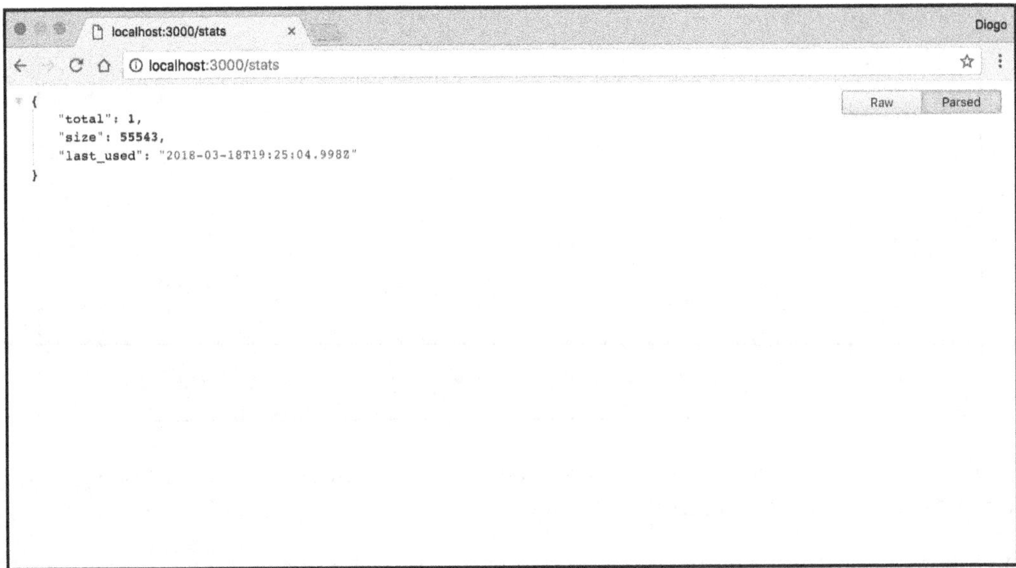

Removing old images is more or less easy; we just need to filter the images we want
to remove, and then remove them:

```
setInterval(() => {
    let expiration = Date.now() - (30 * 86400 * 1000);

    rethinkdb.table("images").filter((image) => {
        return image("date_used").lt(expiration);
    }).delete().run(db);
}, 3600 * 1000);
```

I simplified the previous strategy and am just removing images older than 1 month
(30 days, times 86,400 seconds a day, times 1,000 milliseconds).

Redis

In-memory databases are different from the previous two types, as they're usually not structured, which means you have no tables. What you have is normally lists of some kind that you can look up and manipulate, or simple hash tables.

Taking advantage of the Redis instance we installed previously for Hydra, let's see another drawback, or actually feature, of this kind of database. Let's connect to our Redis instance and make the following sequence of instructions:

```
1. nazgul.home: /Users/dresende (redis-cli)
~ > redis-cli
127.0.0.1:6379> get counter
(nil)
127.0.0.1:6379> incr counter
(integer) 1
127.0.0.1:6379> incr counter
(integer) 2
127.0.0.1:6379> get counter
"2"
127.0.0.1:6379> shutdown
not connected>
~ > redis-server --daemonize yes
20676:C 19 Mar 21:14:28.654 # o000o000o000o Redis is starting o000o000o000o
20676:C 19 Mar 21:14:28.655 # Redis version=4.0.6, bits=64, commit=00000000, modified=0, pid=20676, just started
20676:C 19 Mar 21:14:28.655 # Configuration loaded
~ > redis-cli
127.0.0.1:6379> get counter
(nil)
127.0.0.1:6379> _
```

What we did here was to:

1. Connect to the Redis service using `redis-cli`.
2. Get the content of the counter, which is nil (nothing), because we haven't defined it yet.
3. Increment the counter, which is now automatically defined and set to 1.
4. Increment the counter again, which is now 2.
5. Get the content of the counter, which is of course 2.
6. Shut down the Redis service.
7. Start the Redis service.
8. Connect to the Redis service again.
9. Get the content of the counter, which is nil (nothing).

Where's our counter? Well, this is an in-memory database, so everything is gone when we shut down the Redis service. This is the design of almost all kinds of in-memory databases.

They're designed to be fast and in-memory. Their purpose is normally to cache data that is expensive to get, such as some complex calculations, or extensive to download, and we want that to be available faster (in-memory).

I wasn't completely fair with Redis as it actually allows your data to be saved between service restarts. So, let's see how far we can go in using it to save our microservice state.

As before, let's uninstall `rethinkdb` and install the `redis` module:

```
npm uninstall rethinkdb --save
npm install redis --save
```

Let's ignore our `settings.json` file (you can remove it if you prefer) and assume Redis will be on our local machine.

First, we need to include the `redis` module and create a `Client` instance:

```
const redis = require("redis");
const db    = redis.createClient();
```

We then need to wait until it connects:

```
db.on("connect", () => {
    console.log("db: ready");

    // ...
    // the rest of our service code
    // ...

    app.listen(3000, () => {
        console.log("app: ready");
    });
});
```

There are a couple of ways we can use Redis to store our data. To make it simple, as we don't have tables, let's use hashes to store our images. Each image will have a different hash, and the name of the hash will be the name of the image.

As there are no tables in this kind of database, our initialization code can just be removed.

Next, let's change our upload method to store data on Redis. As I mentioned, let's store it in a hash with the name of the `image`:

```
app.post("/uploads/:name", bodyparser.raw({
    limit : "10mb",
    type : "image/*"
}), (req, res) => {
    db.hmset(req.params.name, {
        size : req.body.length,
        data : req.body.toString("base64"),
    }, (err) => {
        if (err) {
            return res.send({ status : "error", code: err.code });
        }

        res.send({ status : "ok", size: req.body.length });
    });
});
```

The `hmset` command lets us set multiple fields of a hash, in our case, `size` and `data`. Notice we're storing our image content in `base64` encoding, otherwise we'll lose data. If we restart our service and try to upload our test `image`, it should work fine:

```
2. nazgul.home: /Users/dresende (bash)
~ › curl -H 'Content-Type: image/png' --data-binary @example.png http://localhost:3000/uploads/test.png
{"status":"ok","size":55543}~ ›
```

We can then use `redis-cli` and see whether our image is there. Well, we're checking to see whether our hash has the field size and matches our image size:

```
2. nazgul.home: /Users/dresende (redis-cli)
~ › redis-cli
127.0.0.1:6379> hget test.png size
"55543"
127.0.0.1:6379>
```

Great! We can now change our Express parameter to look for the `image` hash:

```
app.param("image", (req, res, next, name) => {
    if (!name.match(/\.(png|jpg)$/i)) {
        return res.status(403).end();
    }

    db.hgetall(name, (err, image) => {
        if (err || !image) return res.status(404).end();

        req.image      = image;
        req.image.name = name;

        return next();
    });
});
```

Our `image` check method should work now. And, for our download method to work, we just need to change the image loading to decode our previous `base64` encoding:

```
app.get("/uploads/:image", (req, res) => {
    let image     = sharp(Buffer.from(req.image.data, "base64"));
    let width     = +req.query.width;
    let height    = +req.query.height;
    let blur      = +req.query.blur;
    let sharpen   = +req.query.sharpen;
    let greyscale = [ "y", "yes", "true", "1",
"on"].includes(req.query.greyscale);
    let flip      = [ "y", "yes", "true", "1",
"on"].includes(req.query.flip);
    let flop      = [ "y", "yes", "true", "1",
"on"].includes(req.query.flop);

    if (width > 0 && height > 0) {
        image.ignoreAspectRatio();
    }

    if (width > 0 || height > 0) {
        image.resize(width || null, height || null);
    }

    if (flip)          image.flip();
    if (flop)          image.flop();
    if (blur > 0)      image.blur(blur);
    if (sharpen > 0)   image.sharpen(sharpen);
    if (greyscale)     image.greyscale();

    db.hset(req.image.name, "date_used", Date.now());
```

```
    res.setHeader("Content-Type", "image/" +
path.extname(req.image.name).substr(1));

    image.pipe(res);
});
```

Our images are now being served from Redis. As a bonus, we're adding/updating a `date_used` field in our `image` hash to indicate when it was last used:

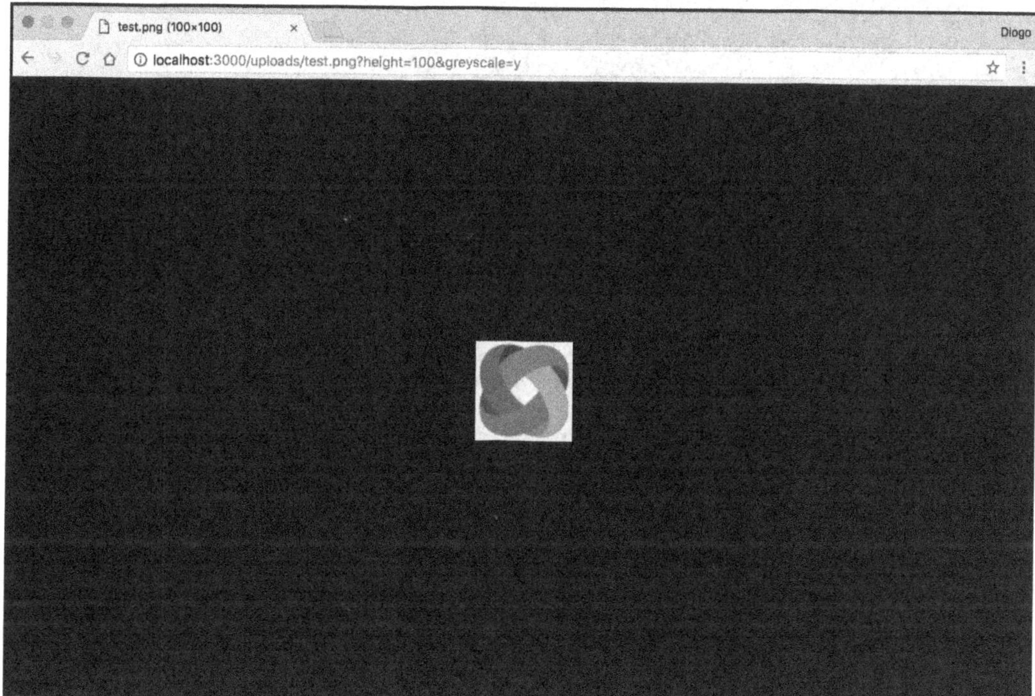

Removing our `image` is as simple as removing our hash:

```
app.delete("/uploads/:image", (req, res) => {
    db.del(req.image.name, (err) => {
        return res.status(err ? 500 : 200).end();
    });
});
```

We can then try to remove our `test` image:

```
3. nazgul.home: /Users/dresende (bash)
~ > curl -v -X DELETE http://localhost:3000/uploads/test.png
*   Trying ::1...
* TCP_NODELAY set
* Connected to localhost (::1) port 3000 (#0)
> DELETE /uploads/test.png HTTP/1.1
> Host: localhost:3000
> User-Agent: curl/7.54.0
> Accept: */*
>
< HTTP/1.1 200 OK
< X-Powered-By: Express
< Date: Mon, 19 Mar 2018 22:07:52 GMT
< Connection: keep-alive
< Content-Length: 0
<
* Connection #0 to host localhost left intact
~ >
```

Using `redis-cli` to check whether the hash exists, we see that it's gone:

```
3. nazgul.home: /Users/dresende (redis-cli)
~ > redis-cli
127.0.0.1:6379> get test.png
(nil)
127.0.0.1:6379>
```

The only two features missing are the statistics and removing old images.

For the statistics, that could be hard as we're using generic hash tables and we can't be sure how many hash tables are defined, and if all or any have image data. We would have to scan all hash tables, which is complex for large sets.

To remove old images, the problem is the same as there's no way of looking for hash tables with a specific condition, such as a field value.

There are still other paths available to tackle this problem. For example, we could have another hash table with just our image names and use dates. But, the complexity would increase, and the integrity could be at risk as we're splitting information through different hash tables with no certainty of making **Atomicity**, **Consistency**, **Isolation**, and **Durability (ACID)** operations.

Conclusion

As we've seen, there are plenty of options to store our microservice state. Depending on the type of information we're manipulating, there are databases better-prepared to handle our data.

It all depends on a few different questions we should ask ourselves:

- Is our data integrity important?
- Is our data structure complex?
- How and what type of information do we need to acquire?

If our data integrity is important or the data structure is complex, do not use in-memory databases. Depending on the complexity, see if you need a non-relational database, or whether you can go with a relational database that can handle more complex manipulation and data aggregation operations, which will help you to achieve the last point.

Security

One good practice is to write code iteratively, testing every time we make a new small feature or improvement, and always write code thinking of all the features we envision for our service.

Thinking about the service roadmap allows you to prepare the service for future improvements, reducing the amount of code wasted or replaced later on.

For instance, in terms of security:

- Is our service secure? Is it prepared for some types of malicious attacks?
- Is our service private? Should it have some kind of authentication or authorization mechanism?

Luckily, our frameworks allow our code to be composed and allow us to add layers of security later. For example, using Express or Hydra, we can add a precedent routing function that will run before any of our service methods, allowing us to enforce, for example, authentication.

Looking at our service, since it exposes its methods using HTTP, there are a couple of improvements we can add to it, for example:

- **Authentication**: Forcing anyone that uses it to identify themselves. Or, just the upload and removal methods. It's up to you. There could also be user accounts, and each user would see their respective list of images.
- **Authorization**: Restricting, for example, what networks could access the service, independently of having a valid authentication or not.
- **Confidentiality**: Giving your users protection against prying eyes over the network traffic.
- **Availability**: Restricting the maximum usage frequency of the service, per client, to ensure a single client cannot block your entire service.

To introduce these improvements, you may add an authentication module such as the Passport module, and use a certificate to give your users a more secure HTTPS experience.

Other types of insecurity come directly from your code and don't improve by adding a certificate or forcing authentication. I'm referring to:

- Bugs, programming logic flaws, and use cases not properly tested, which can lead to minor or serious problems
- Dependency bugs, which you might not be aware of but can still ruin your service and may force you to look for alternative dependencies, which is never a pleasant task

To minimize these events, you should always keep evolving your test suite, adding use cases as they show up, ensuring a new bug that is solved does not reappear later. Regarding dependency bugs, you can subscribe to the Node Security Project and even integrate it with your code to always know when one of your dependencies is a risk.

If there were source code commandments, the next four would surely be on the list:

- Keep the code simple. If the code is getting complex, stop, look back, and split the code into simpler parts.
- Validate external input, whether it's the user or another service. Never trust data from the outside.
- Deny by default and not the opposite, checking whether someone has access to a resource and denying anyone that is not.
- Add test cases from the beginning of the project.

Summary

The state is part of any service, and state is built upon data. For a more cloud-native experience, a service cannot depend on a traditional filesystem and needs to use other kinds of storage structures to store data. Databases are a natural progress, and there are some types of databases to choose from, depending on how important and complex our data is.

Assuming our state is securely stored in a database service of some kind, it's also important to ensure our data cannot be corrupted using our service. There can be security flaws and bugs in our service that may put our data at risk, so it's important to write simple code, validate input, and think about security in general when planning the service roadmap.

To progress our service, let's introduce something we haven't done yet, and should, which is a proper test suite. In the next chapter, we'll see some good options and create a test suite, establishing whether anything needs to change in order to make our service as secure as possible.

23
Testing

When you're developing an application, it will eventually form a structure and evolve into a stable product that you can use in production and sell to your customers. In the beginning, everything may seem simple and many tend to postpone the construction of a proper test suite.

"Debugging is twice as hard as writing the code in the first place."

—Brian W. Kernighan and P. J. Plauger in The Elements of Programming Style

Later on, the application may become just sufficiently complex for you to hesitate to begin testing. You may eventually give up and never test your application. It may be frustrating, especially if you have never seen or used any test suite before.

Proper testing gives you more than a little bit of quality assurance. Proper testing gives you:

- **Predictability**: This means that your code execution, no matter if it's an application or just a module, will have an expected result. As you evolve the tests and introduce different test cases, you begin to fulfill all the uses for your code, and you ensure its results were as intended.

- **Feature coverage**: This means that you can measure what parts of your code are tested or not. There are plenty of tools to inspect your code and tell you what parts of it haven't been used in your test suite, which helps you create specific tests for specific parts of the code that are not yet covered.

- **Safe evolution**: This is a side effect. When your code gets complex, if your test suite has good code coverage, you can make changes and add features without compromising stability, as you can continuously run the test suite and see if it breaks anything.

There's a developing methodology that involves first creating a test for a new feature and then making sure the test passes. This way, you can focus on how you think your code should be used (in the new test) and then evolve it (actually develop it) so the test stops failing and gives proper results.

Let's see how code coverage can help in the testing process. Finally, we'll look at how you can mock parts of your code.

Integrating tests

We will create our first integration tests. Each of our tests will run separately, meaning they should not depend on any other test and should follow a predictable workflow. First, we need to change our `run.js` file to run all test files. For that, we'll use `mocha` and add all files found in the `integration` folder:

```js
const fs    = require("fs");
const path  = require("path");
const mocha = require("mocha");
const suite = new mocha();

fs.readdir(path.join(__dirname, "integration"), (err, files) => {
    if (err) throw err;

    files.filter((filename) =>
    (filename.match(/\.js$/))).map((filename) => {
        suite.addFile(path.join(__dirname, "integration", filename));
    });

    suite.run((failures) => {
        process.exit(failures);
    });
});
```

Then, let's create the `integration` folder inside our `test` folder, and let's create our first test file, called `image-upload.js`. Add this content to the file:

```
describe("Uploading image", () => {
    it("should accept only images");
});
```

If we now run the tests again, we should see the default `mocha` response with no tests passing and no tests failing:

```
npm test
> imagini@1.0.0 test /Users/dresende/imagini
> node test/run

0 passing (2ms)
```

To avoid repeating code, let's create a `tools.js` file inside the `test` folder, so we can export common tasks that every test file can use. Out of the box, I'm thinking about our microservice location and a sample image:

```
const fs   = require("fs");
const path = require("path");

exports.service = require("../imagini.js");
exports.sample  = fs.readFileSync(path.join(__dirname, "sample.png"));
```

Create a `sample.png` image in the `test` folder. When a test needs to upload an image, it will use that sample. In the future, we could have different kinds of samples, such as huge images, to test performance and limitations.

Using chai

We also need to make a little change to our microservice. We need to export its app so that the HTTP plugin from `chai` can load it and were able to test it without the need to run in a separate console. Add this to the end of our microservice file:

```
module.exports = app;
```

You should have a folder hierarchy similar to the following screenshot:

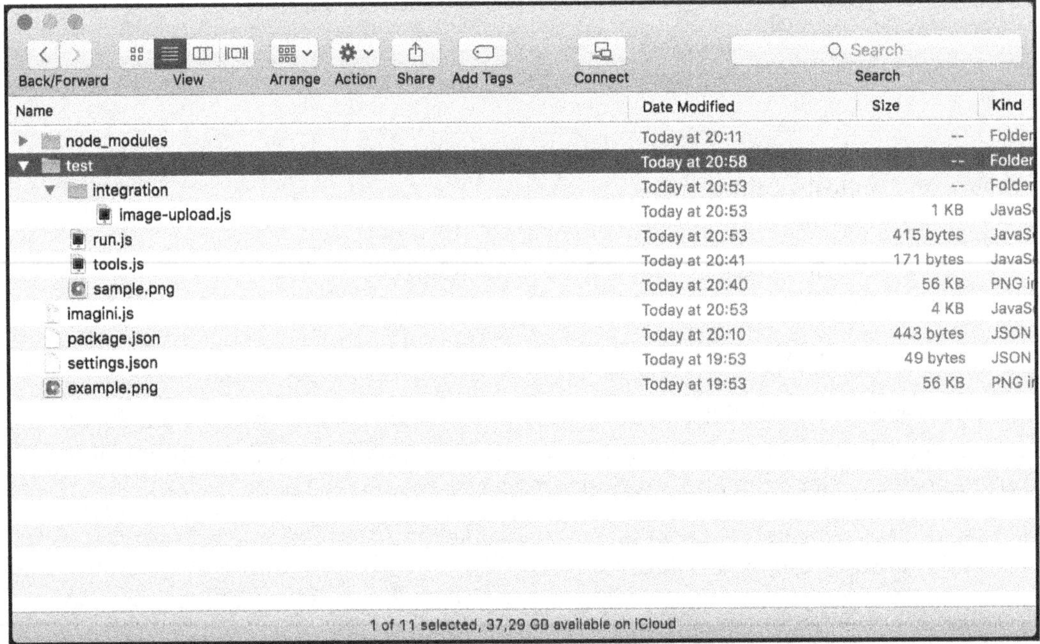

We should now change our `image-upload.js` test file to create our first real test:

```javascript
const chai  = require("chai");
const http  = require("chai-http");
const tools = require("../tools");

chai.use(http);

describe("Uploading image", () => {
    beforeEach((done) => {
        chai
        .request(tools.service)
        .delete("/uploads/test_image_upload.png")
        .end(() => {
            return done();
        });
    });

    it ("should accept a PNG image", function (done) {
        chai
        .request(tools.service)
        .post("/uploads/test_image_upload.png")
```

```
                .set("Content-Type", "image/png")
                .send(tools.sample)
                .end((err, res) => {
                    chai.expect(res).to.have.status(200);
                    chai.expect(res.body).to.have.status("ok");

                    return done();
                });
        });
    });
});
```

We start by first including the `chai` modules and our `tools` file:

```
const chai  = require("chai");
const http  = require("chai-http");
const tools = require("../tools");

chai.use(http);
```

Then, we describe our test file as `Uploading image`:

```
describe("Uploading image", () => {
```

We'll add the different use cases we can think of, related to the uploading of images.

Inside, we use `beforeEach`, which is a `mocha` method that will be called before every test in this file. Remember, we want our tests to be consistent, so we add this method to remove our image before running every test. We don't care whether the image exists:

```
beforeEach((done) => {
    chai
    .request(tools.service)
    .delete("/uploads/test_image_upload.png")
    .end(() => {
        return done();
    });
});
```

Look how we use the `tools.service`, which points to our microservice. If, later on, we change the name or somehow make it more complex, we just need to change the `tools` file, and everything should work.

Then, we add our first `integration` file's test – a simple image upload:

```
it("should accept a PNG image", (done) => {
    chai
```

```
        .request(tools.service)
        .post("/uploads/test_image_upload.png")
        .set("Content-Type", "image/png")
        .send(tools.sample)
        .end((err, res) => {
            chai.expect(res).to.have.status(200);
            chai.expect(res.body).to.have.status("ok");

            return done();
        });
    });
```

It checks whether the HTTP response code is `200` and if the response body, which is a JSON structure, has the status property set to `ok`. And we're done!

Let's run our test suite again and see how it goes.

```
1. nazgul.local: /Users/dresende/imagini (bash)
~/imagini > npm test

> imagini@1.0.0 test /Users/dresende/imagini
> node test/run

Uploading image
  ✓ should accept a PNG image

1 passing (59ms)

~/imagini >
```

Adding code coverage

Now that our test suite is working and has one test, let's introduce code coverage. Adding this from the beginning of development is very easy and will help us focus on parts of the code that need to be tested, especially some use cases that involve specific conditions (such as `if-then-else` statements in our code). Having it all set up from the start of development is easy. On the other hand, if you have a fully working code and want to add tests and coverage, it will be harder and will take quite some time.

To add code coverage, we'll introduce another module. We'll install it globally to be able to run the tests with it directly:

```
npm install -g nyc
```

We can now run our tests with the following instrumentation:

```
nyc npm test
```

This should run our tests with the instrumentation installed. In the end, you'll get a nice console report.

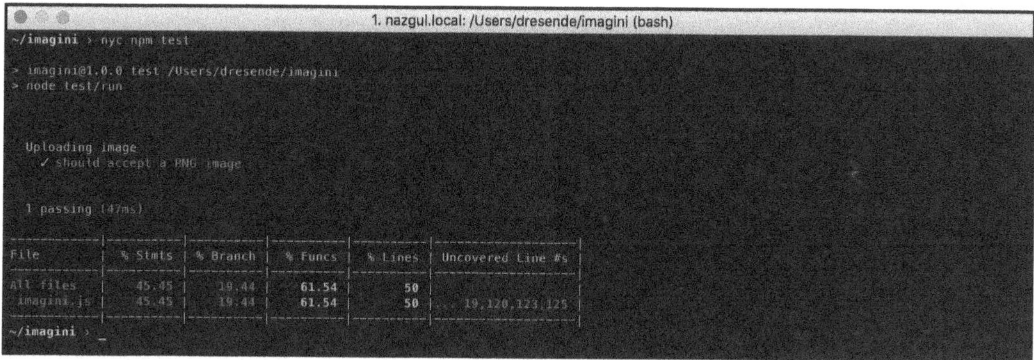

The coverage results are stored inside in a `.nyc_output` folder. This enables you to look at the last test results without running tests again. This is useful if your test suite is big and takes some time to finish.

To see the results, you just run `nyc report`:

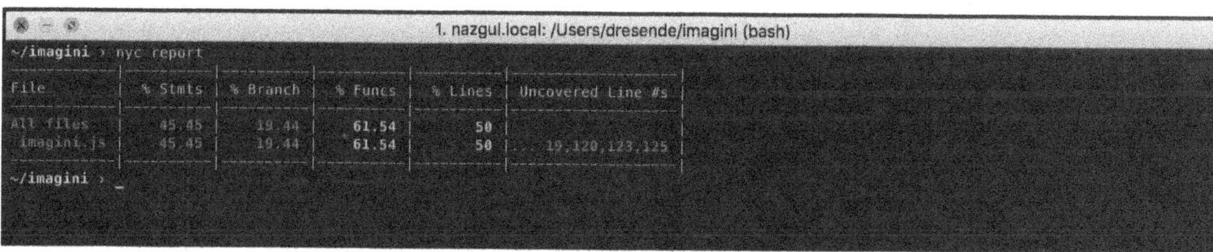

The result is a console report. There are several other styles of reports. One particularly useful one is the `html` report. Let's generate it:

```
nyc report --reporter=html
```

You should now have a `coverage` folder with an `index.html` file. Open that in your browser, and you should see something like the following screenshot:

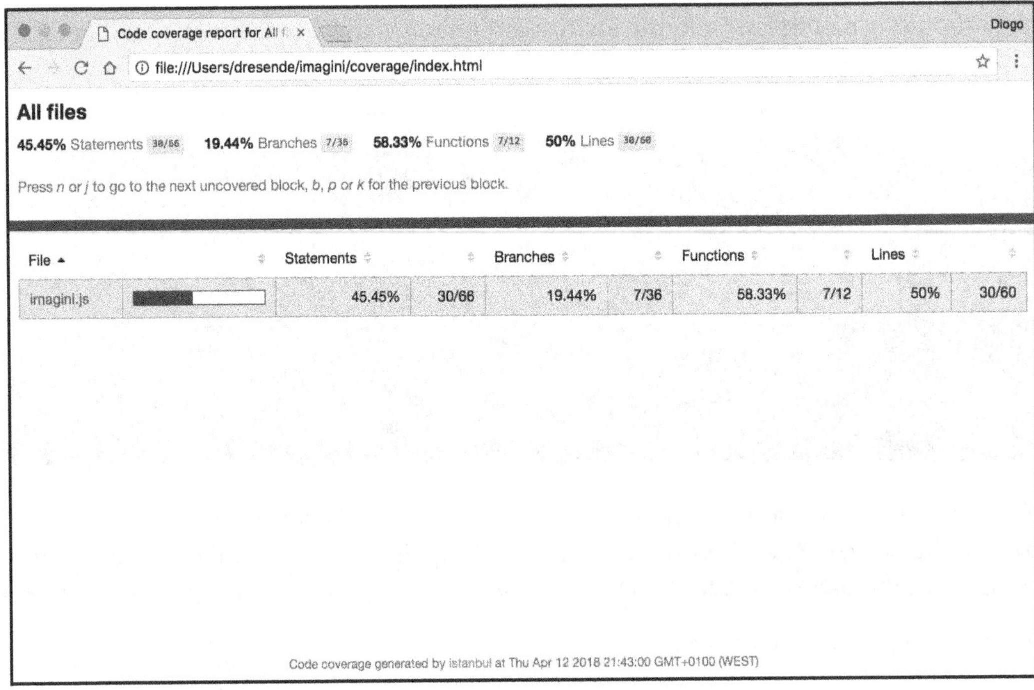

We only have one file that represents our microservice. If we had more, they would be listed hierarchically. There are global average statistics for every file.

There are three important groups of columns:

- **Statements**: Which represent code statements (conditions, assignments, assertions, calls, and so on)
- **Branches**: Which represent possible code control workflows, such as if-then-else or switch-case statement possibilities
- **Functions**: Which represent our actual code functions and callbacks

You can click in our file, look at the specific details of it and, more specifically, see the code and information line by line:

```
●  ●  ●        🗋  Code coverage report for ima   ×                                                              Diogo
←  →  C  ⌂    ① file:///Users/dresende/imagini/coverage/imagini.js.html                                    ☆  ⋮

All files imagini.js

45.45% Statements 30/66     19.44% Branches 7/36     58.33% Functions 7/12     50% Lines 30/60

Press n or j to go to the next uncovered block, b, p or k for the previous block.


  1  2x   const settings    = require("./settings");
  2  2x   const bodyparser = require("body-parser");
  3  2x   const express     = require("express");
  4  2x   const mysql       = require("mysql");
  5  2x   const path        = require("path");
  6  2x   const sharp       = require("sharp");
  7
  8  2x   const app = express();
  9  2x   const db  = mysql.createConnection(settings.db);
 10
 11  2x   db.connect((err) => {
 12  2x       I if (err) throw err;
 13
 14  2x       db.query(
 15           `CREATE TABLE IF NOT EXISTS images
 16           (
 17               id            INT(11)       UNSIGNED NOT NULL AUTO_INCREMENT,
 18               date_created  TIMESTAMP     NOT NULL DEFAULT CURRENT_TIMESTAMP,
 19               date_used     TIMESTAMP     NULL DEFAULT NULL,
 20               name          VARCHAR(300)  NOT NULL,
 21               size          INT(11)       UNSIGNED NOT NULL,
 22               data          LONGBLOB      NOT NULL,
 23           PRIMARY KEY (id),
 24           UNIQUE KEY name (name)
 25           ) ENGINE=InnoDB DEFAULT CHARSET=utf8`
 26           );
```

To the right of every line number, you see a gray area and, in this case, you see 2x in some of the lines. This is the execution count for that line. The execution has passed by that line twice. This is actually not that important, unless you're looking for bits of code that get largely executed and you want to do some kind of optimization.

You can also see that *line 12* has two changes. First, there's a pinkish background in the back of `throw err`. That means that statement never got executed, which is normal for now as we always successfully connected to the database. The mark before the `if` statement means that the condition never got executed:

```
Code coverage report for ima ×
← → C ⌂  ⓘ file:///Users/dresende/imagini/coverage/imagini.js.html

54
55  2x    app.post("/uploads/:name", bodyparser.raw({
56          limit : "10mb",
57          type  : "image/*"
58        }), (req, res) => {
59  2x      db.query("INSERT INTO images SET ?", {
60            name : req.params.name,
61            size : req.body.length,
62            data : req.body,
63          }, (err) => {
64  2x        I if (err) {
65              return res.send({ status : "error", code: err.code });
66            }
67
68  2x        res.send({ status : "ok", size: req.body.length });
69          });
70        });
71
72  2x    app.head("/uploads/:image", (req, res) => {
73          return res.status(200).end();
74        });
75
76  2x    app.delete("/uploads/:image", (req, res) => {
77  2x      db.query("DELETE FROM images WHERE id = ?", [ req.image.id ], (err) => {
78  2x        return res.status(err ? 500 : 200).end();
79          });
80        });
81
82  2x    app.get("/uploads/:image", (req, res) => {
83          let image    = sharp(req.image.data);
84          let width    = +req.query.width;
85          let height   = +req.query.height;
86          let blur     = +req.query.blur;
87          let sharpen  = +req.query.sharpen;
88          let greyscale = [ "y", "yes", "true", "1", "on"].includes(req.query.greyscale);
89          let flip      = [ "y", "yes", "true", "1", "on"].includes(req.query.flip);
```

If you scroll a few lines down, we'll see more lines with marks. For example, we can see our image upload method got almost completely covered. The only statement missing is the error handling.

As we delete our test image before running the tests, our image deletion method is also covered. Again, the only missing branch is if the database returns an error to our `DELETE` query.

Before going any further with the image upload, let's add another `integration` test
file called `image-parameter.js`, and add some tests to increase our coverage:

```
const chai = require("chai");
const http = require("chai-http");
const tools = require("../tools");

chai.use(http);

describe("The image parameter", () => {
    beforeEach((done) => {
        chai
        .request(tools.service)
        .delete("/uploads/test_image_parameter.png")
        .end(() => {
            return done();
        });
    });

    it("should reply 403 for non image extension", (done) => {
        chai
        .request(tools.service)
        .get("/uploads/test_image_parameter.txt")
        .end((err, res) => {
            chai.expect(res).to.have.status(403);

            return done();
        });
    });

    it("should reply 404 for non image existence", (done) => {
        chai
        .request(tools.service)
        .get("/uploads/test_image_parameter.png")
        .end((err, res) => {
            chai.expect(res).to.have.status(404);

            return done();
        });
    });
});
```

Let's run our test suite and see how it goes:

```
1. nazgul.local: /Users/dresende/imagini (bash)

~/imagini > nyc npm test

> imagini@1.0.0 test /Users/dresende/imagini
> node test/run


  The image parameter
    ✓ should reply 403 for non image extension
    ✓ should reply 404 for non image existance

  Uploading image
    ✓ should accept a PNG image


  3 passing (70ms)

----------|----------|----------|----------|----------|-------------------|
File      | % Stmts  | % Branch | % Funcs  | % Lines  | Uncovered Line #s |
----------|----------|----------|----------|----------|-------------------|
All files |   48.48  |    25    |   58.33  |   53.33  |                   |
 imagini.js |  48.48 |    25    |   58.33  |   53.33  | 17,118,121,123    |
----------|----------|----------|----------|----------|-------------------|
~/imagini > nyc report --reporter=html
~/imagini > _
```

Refresh the HTML report page and look at our parameter method:

```
Code coverage report for ima…  ×                                          Diogo

←  →  C  ⌂   ⓘ file:///Users/dresende/imagini/coverage/imagini.js.html      ☆  ⋮

14  2x   db.query(
15       `CREATE TABLE IF NOT EXISTS images
16       (
17           id           INT(11)      UNSIGNED NOT NULL AUTO_INCREMENT,
18           date_created TIMESTAMP    NOT NULL DEFAULT CURRENT_TIMESTAMP,
19           date_used    TIMESTAMP    NULL DEFAULT NULL,
20           name         VARCHAR(300) NOT NULL,
21           size         INT(11)      UNSIGNED NOT NULL,
22           data         LONGBLOB     NOT NULL,
23         PRIMARY KEY (id),
24         UNIQUE KEY name (name)
25       ) ENGINE=InnoDB DEFAULT CHARSET=utf8`
26       );
27
28  2x   setInterval(() => {
29         db.query("DELETE FROM images " +
30               "WHERE (date_created < UTC_TIMETSTAMP - INTERVAL 1 WEEK AND date_used IS NULL) " +
31               "  OR (date_used < UTC_TIMETSTAMP - INTERVAL 1 MONTH)");
32       }, 3600 * 1000);
33
34  2x   app.param("image", (req, res, next, image) => {
35  10x     if (!image.match(/\.(png|jpg)$/i)) {
36  2x        return res.status(403).end();
37         }
38
39  8x     db.query("SELECT * FROM images WHERE name = ?", [ image ], (err, images) => {
40  8x       if (err || !images.length) {
41  6x          return res.status(404).end();
42         }
43
44  2x       req.image = images[0];
45
46  2x       return next();
47       });
48     });
49
```

As you can see, we now cover the following condition:

```
if (!image.match(/\.(png|jpg)$/i)) {
```

The following condition:

```
if (err || !images.length) {
```

We now have full coverage on this method.

There are other coverage lines that are harder to test, such as timers (you can see one on *line 28*), `catch` statements, or external errors coming from databases or other storage sources. There are ways of mocking those events, and we'll cover them later on.

Covering all code

For now, let's focus on adding coverage to our code. It's important to have it covered as much as possible when it's still just a small service. If we start adding tests and coverage when it's already big, you'll be frustrated, and it will be hard to find the motivation to cover it all.

This way, you'll find it rewarding to cover it in the beginning and keep the coverage percentage as high as possible along with code evolution.

Let's get back to our image upload test, and add another test:

```
it("should deny duplicated images", (done) => {
    chai
    .request(tools.service)
    .post("/uploads/test_image_upload.png")
    .set("Content-Type", "image/png")
    .send(tools.sample)
    .end((err, res) => {
        chai.expect(res).to.have.status(200);
        chai.expect(res.body).to.have.status("ok");

        chai
        .request(tools.service)
        .post("/uploads/test_image_upload.png")
        .set("Content-Type", "image/png")
        .send(tools.sample)
        .end((err, res) => {
            chai.expect(res).to.have.status(200);
            chai.expect(res.body).to.have.status("error");
```

```
            chai.expect(res.body).to.have.property("code",
            "ER_DUP_ENTRY");

            return done();
        });
    });
});
```

This will upload the same image twice in a row and we should receive an error from the database saying there's a duplicate. Let's run the tests again:

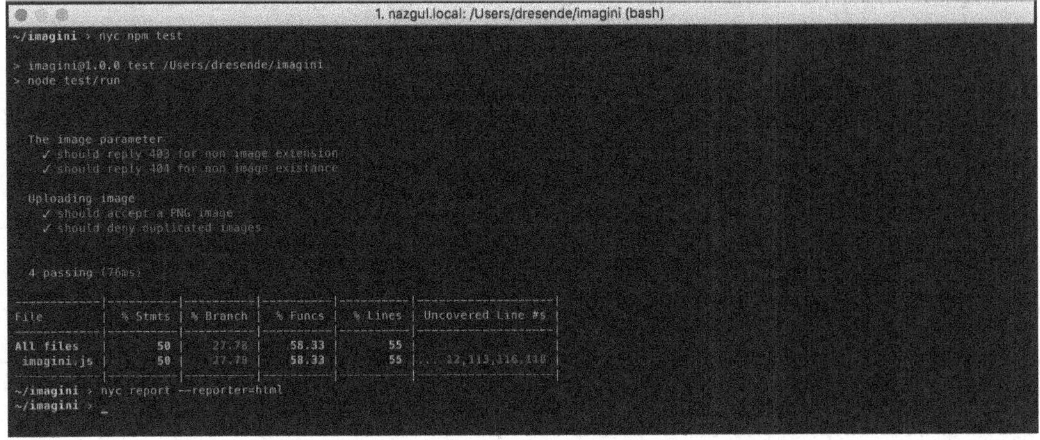

Now, let's open the initial page of the coverage report:

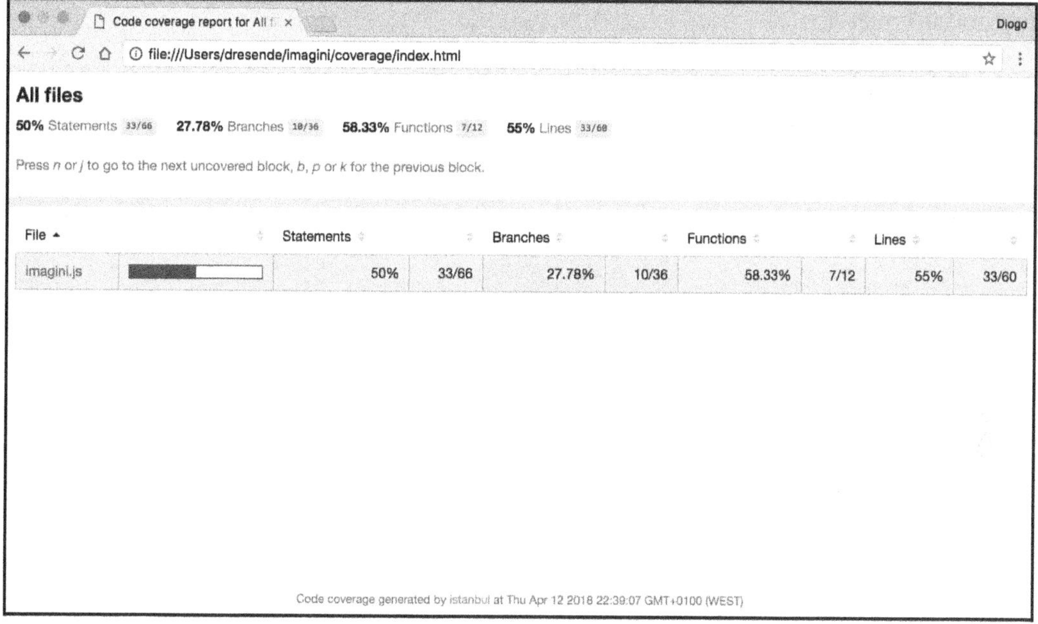

Notice that our file is no longer in a red background. This means the statement coverage has reached *50%*. Let's click on our file and see how our image upload method is covered:

```
45
46   4x          return next();
47              });
48          });
49
50   2x      app.post("/uploads/:name", bodyparser.raw({
51              limit : "10mb",
52              type  : "image/*"
53          }), (req, res) => {
54   6x          db.query("INSERT INTO images SET ?", {
55                  name : req.params.name,
56                  size : req.body.length,
57                  data : req.body,
58              }, (err) => {
59   6x              if (err) {
60   2x                  return res.send({ status : "error", code: err.code });
61                  }
62
63   4x              res.send({ status : "ok", size: req.body.length });
64              });
65          });
66
67   2x      app.head("/uploads/:image", (req, res) => {
68              return res.status(200).end();
69          });
70
71   2x      app.delete("/uploads/:image", (req, res) => {
72   4x          db.query("DELETE FROM images WHERE id = ?", [ req.image.id ], (err) => {
73   4x              return res.status(err ? 500 : 200).end();
74              });
75          });
76
77   2x      app.get("/uploads/:image", (req, res) => {
78              let image     = sharp(req.image.data);
```

It's complete! We can now move on. Just a reminder before we move to another method: having full coverage does not mean there are no bugs. That's something you need to understand. You might have a use case that you're not expecting, and so, you have no code for it, so there's no obvious coverage.

For example, the `bodyparser` module will not limit the type of content. If we upload a text file with an image name on it, our code will accept it and store it in the database without noticing. Think of this use case as your homework, and try to create a test to cover that use case and then fix the code.

Let's move to the next method we see after our upload method: the image check on *line 67*. Let's create a new integration test file called `image-check.js`, and add a simple test:

```
const chai = require("chai");
const http = require("chai-http");
const tools = require("../tools");

chai.use(http);
```

```javascript
describe("Checking image", () => {
    beforeEach((done) => {
        chai
        .request(tools.service)
        .delete("/uploads/test_image_check.png")
        .end(() => {
            return done();
        });
    });

    it("should return 404 if it doesn't exist", (done) => {
        chai
        .request(tools.service)
        .head("/uploads/test_image_check.png")
        .end((err, res) => {
            chai.expect(res).to.have.status(404);

            return done();
        });
    });

    it("should return 200 if it exists", (done) => {
        chai
        .request(tools.service)
        .post("/uploads/test_image_check.png")
        .set("Content-Type", "image/png")
        .send(tools.sample)
        .end((err, res) => {
            chai.expect(res).to.have.status(200);
            chai.expect(res.body).to.have.status("ok");

            chai
            .request(tools.service)
            .head("/uploads/test_image_check.png")
            .end((err, res) => {
                chai.expect(res).to.have.status(200);

                return done();
            });
        });
    });
});
```

Let's run the test suite:

```
1. nazgul.local: /Users/dresende/imagini (bash)
~/imagini > nyc npm test

> imagini@1.0.0 test /Users/dresende/imagini
> node test/run


  Checking image
    ✓ should return 404 if it doesn't exist
    ✓ should return 200 if it exists

  The image parameter
    ✓ should reply 403 for non image extension
    ✓ should reply 404 for non image existance

  Uploading image
    ✓ should accept a PNG image
    ✓ should deny duplicated images


  6 passing (90ms)

----------|---------|----------|---------|---------|-------------------|
File      | % Stmts | % Branch | % Funcs | % Lines | Uncovered Line #s |
----------|---------|----------|---------|---------|-------------------|
All files |   51.52 |    27.78 |   66.67 |   56.67 |                   |
 imagini.js|  51.52 |    27.78 |   66.67 |   56.67 |  12,113,116,118   |
----------|---------|----------|---------|---------|-------------------|
~/imagini > nyc report --reporter=html
~/imagini > _
```

We can see our console report is getting bigger. As we're creating new integration test files and having a description for each one, `mocha` writes a nice tree view showing how the tests run. On the bottom, we can see the coverage report:

```
64        });
65      });
66
67  2x  app.head("/uploads/:image", (req, res) => {
68  2x    return res.status(200).end();
69      });
70
71  2x  app.delete("/uploads/:image", (req, res) => {
72  6x    db.query("DELETE FROM images WHERE id = ?", [ req.image.id ], (err) => {
73  6x      return res.status(err ? 500 : 200).end();
74        });
75      });
76
77  2x  app.get("/uploads/:image", (req, res) => {
78        let image     = sharp(req.image.data);
79        let width     = +req.query.width;
80        let height    = +req.query.height;
81        let blur      = +req.query.blur;
82        let sharpen   = +req.query.sharpen;
83        let greyscale = [ "y", "yes", "true", "1", "on"].includes(req.query.greyscale);
84        let flip      = [ "y", "yes", "true", "1", "on"].includes(req.query.flip);
85        let flop      = [ "y", "yes", "true", "1", "on"].includes(req.query.flop);
86
87        if (width > 0 && height > 0) {
88          image.ignoreAspectRatio();
89        }
90        if (width > 0 || height > 0) {
91          image.resize(width || null, height || null);
92        }
93        if (flip)        image.flip();
94        if (flop)        image.flop();
95        if (blur > 0)    image.blur(blur);
96        if (sharpen > 0) image.sharpen(sharpen);
97        if (greyscale)   image.greyscale();
```

Looking at the check method, we see it's now fully covered. This one was very simple.

We're still in the middle of statement coverage as our top method; the image manipulation one is almost half of our code. This means that when we start covering it, the coverage will significantly rise.

Let's create an `integration` test for it:

```javascript
const chai = require("chai");
const http = require("chai-http");
const tools = require("../tools");

chai.use(http);

describe("Downloading image", () => {
    beforeEach((done) => {
        chai
        .request(tools.service)
        .delete("/uploads/test_image_download.png")
        .end(() => {
            chai
            .request(tools.service)
            .post("/uploads/test_image_download.png")
            .set("Content-Type", "image/png")
            .send(tools.sample)
            .end((err, res) => {
                chai.expect(res).to.have.status(200);
                chai.expect(res.body).to.have.status("ok");

                return done();
            });
        });
    });

    it("should return the original image size if no parameters given",
    (done) => {
        chai
        .request(tools.service)
        .get("/uploads/test_image_download.png")
        .end((err, res) => {
            chai.expect(res).to.have.status(200);
            chai.expect(res.body).to.have.length(tools.sample.length);

            return done();
        });
    });
});
```

Before each test, we're deleting the image (if it exists) and then uploading a fresh sample one. Then, for each test, we'll download it and test the output according to what we asked for.

Let's try and run it:

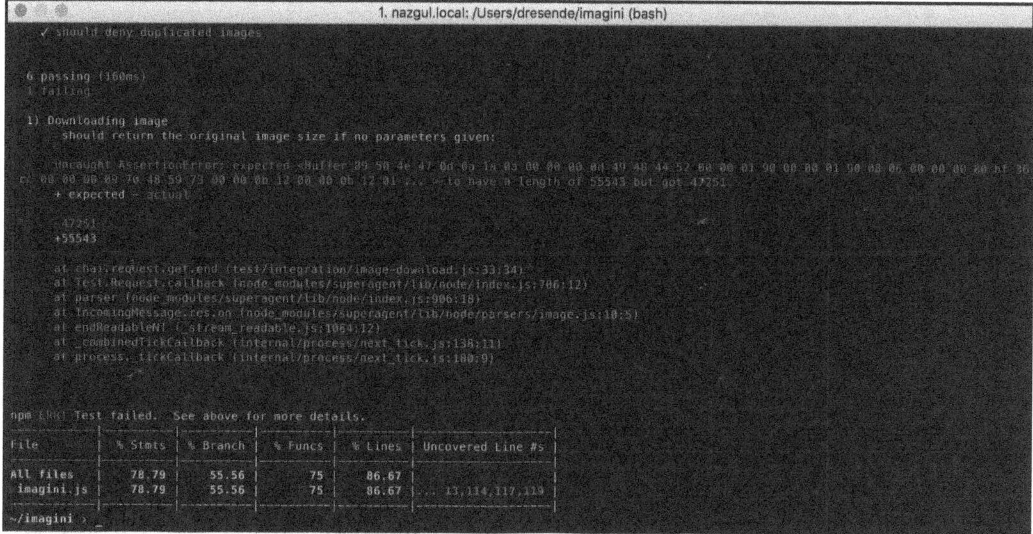

Well, that was unexpected. The test fails because our length check does not match. This is actually a good example of something we just notice when we start to execute testing.

What happens is that, when we request an image, we use the `sharp` module to make any manipulation on the image, according to query parameters. In this case, we're not asking for any manipulation, but when we output the image (through `sharp`), it actually returns the same image in size, but perhaps with a little bit less quality, or maybe it just knows how to better encode our image and remove data from the file that is not needed.

We don't know exactly, but let's assume we want the original image, untouched. We need to change our download method. Let's assume that if no query parameters are defined at all, we just return the original image. Let's add a condition to the top of our method:

```
if (Object.keys(req.query).length === 0) {
    db.query("UPDATE images " +
             "SET date_used = UTC_TIMESTAMP " +
             "WHERE id = ?",
             [ req.image.id ]);

    res.setHeader("Content-Type", "image/" +
    path.extname(req.image.name).substr(1));

    return res.end(req.image.data);
}
```

If we run it now, we should have no failures:

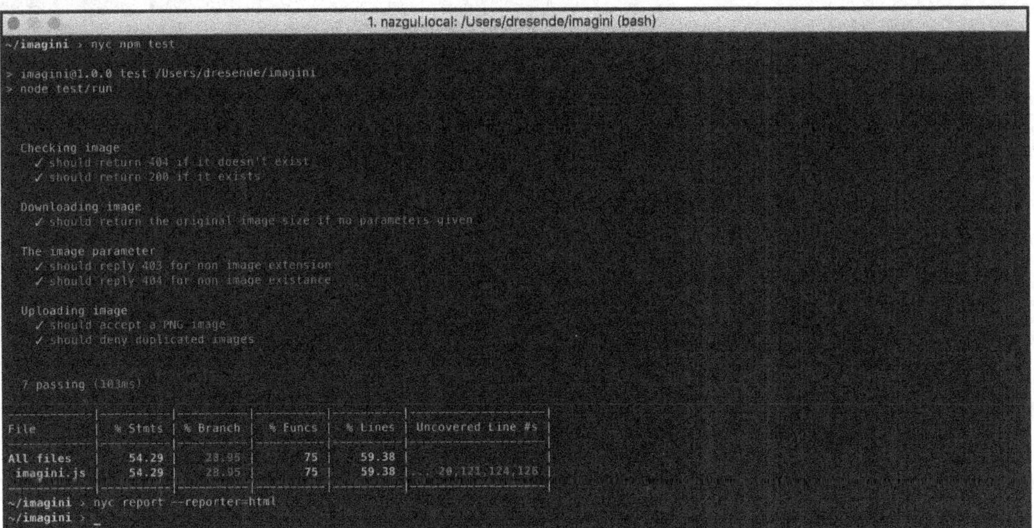

Our statement coverage did not rise much because we actually created a condition on top of the method and returned immediately, so our previous method is still untested:

```
71  2x    app.delete("/uploads/:image", (req, res) => {
72  8x      db.query("DELETE FROM images WHERE id = ?", [ req.image.id ], (err) => {
73  8x        return res.status(err ? 500 : 200).end();
74          });
75        });
76
77  2x    app.get("/uploads/:image", (req, res) => {
78  2x    E if (Object.keys(req.query).length === 0) {
79  2x        db.query("UPDATE images SET date_used = UTC_TIMESTAMP WHERE id = ?", [ req.image.id ]);
80
81  2x        res.setHeader("Content-Type", "image/" + path.extname(req.image.name).substr(1));
82
83  2x        return res.end(req.image.data);
84        }
85
86        let image     = sharp(req.image.data);
87        let width     = +req.query.width;
88        let height    = +req.query.height;
89        let blur      = +req.query.blur;
90        let sharpen   = +req.query.sharpen;
91        let greyscale = [ "y", "yes", "true", "1", "on"].includes(req.query.greyscale);
92        let flip      = [ "y", "yes", "true", "1", "on"].includes(req.query.flip);
93        let flop      = [ "y", "yes", "true", "1", "on"].includes(req.query.flop);
94
95        if (width > 0 && height > 0) {
96          image.ignoreAspectRatio();
97        }
98        if (width > 0 || height > 0) {
99          image.resize(width || null, height || null);
100       }
101       if (flip)        image.flip();
102       if (flop)        image.flop();
103       if (blur > 0)    image.blur(blur);
104       if (sharpen > 0) image.sharpen(sharpen);
```

Looking at *line 78,* you should see a new mark, an `E` that means that the condition in that line never executed the `else` statement, which is the rest of our code. Let's add a test to this integration and resize our image.

We will need `sharp` to help us check whether the results are correct. Let's include it on the top of our file:

```
const sharp = require("sharp");
```

Then, add a resize test:

```
it("should be able to resize the image as we request", (done) => {
    chai
    .request(tools.service)
    .get("/uploads/test_image_download.png?width=200&height=100")
    .end((err, res) => {
        chai.expect(res).to.have.status(200);

        let image = sharp(res.body);

        image
        .metadata()
        .then((metadata) => {
            chai.expect(metadata).to.have.property("width", 200);
            chai.expect(metadata).to.have.property("height", 100);

            return done();
        });
    });
});
```

Let's run our test suite:

```
~/imagini > nyc npm test

> imagini@1.0.0 test /Users/dresende/imagini
> node test/run


  Checking image
    ✓ should return 404 if it doesn't exist
    ✓ should return 200 if it exists

  Downloading image
    ✓ should return the original image size if no parameters given
    ✓ should be able to resize the image as we request

  The image parameter
    ✓ should reply 403 for non image extension
    ✓ should reply 404 for non image existance

  Uploading image
    ✓ should accept a PNG image
    ✓ should deny duplicated images


  8 passing (145ms)

----------|---------|----------|---------|---------|-------------------
File      | % Stmts | % Branch | % Funcs | % Lines | Uncovered Line #s
----------|---------|----------|---------|---------|-------------------
All files |   82.86 |    63.16 |      75 |   90.63 |
 imagini.js |  82.86 |    63.16 |      75 |   90.63 | 20,121,124,126
----------|---------|----------|---------|---------|-------------------
~/imagini > nyc report --reporter=html
~/imagini > _
```

It now looks very good. From the console report, we can see some green. Let's look at the front page of the coverage report:

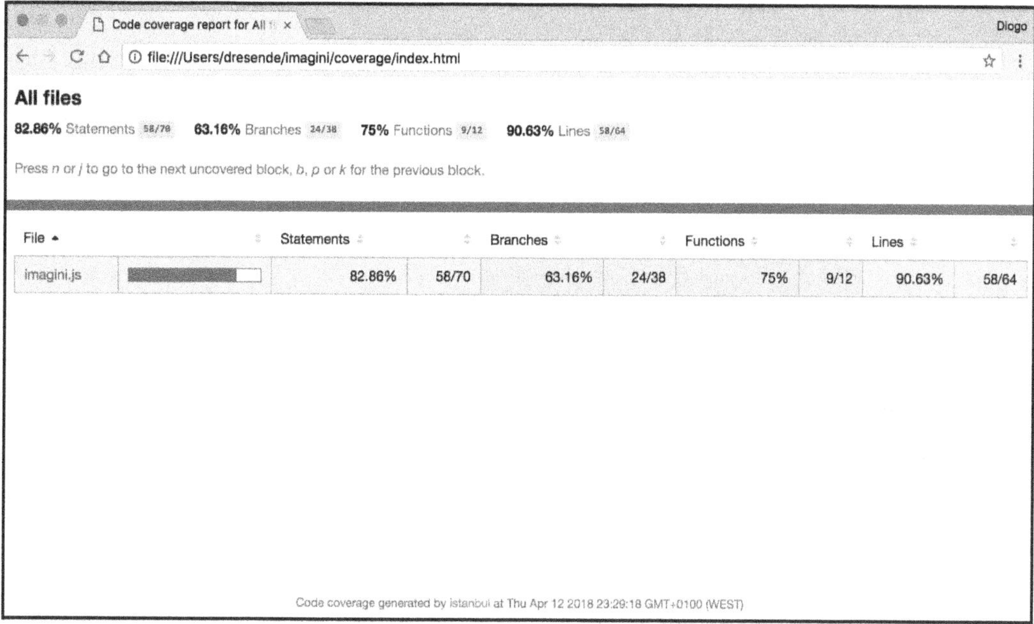

We see green here as well. Having more than *80%* coverage is good, but we can still go further. Let's see the file:

```
 Code coverage report for ima… ×                                                                    Diogo
 ←  →  C  ⌂   ⓘ file:///Users/dresende/imagini/coverage/imagini.js.html                         ☆  ⋮
 79  2x        db.query("UPDATE images SET date_used = UTC_TIMESTAMP WHERE id = ?", [ req.image.id ]);
 80
 81  2x        res.setHeader("Content-Type", "image/" + path.extname(req.image.name).substr(1));
 82
 83  2x        return res.end(req.image.data);
 84        }
 85
 86  2x    let image    = sharp(req.image.data);
 87  2x    let width    = +req.query.width;
 88  2x    let height   = +req.query.height;
 89  2x    let blur     = +req.query.blur;
 90  2x    let sharpen  = +req.query.sharpen;
 91  2x    let greyscale = [ "y", "yes", "true", "1", "on"].includes(req.query.greyscale);
 92  2x    let flip     = [ "y", "yes", "true", "1", "on"].includes(req.query.flip);
 93  2x    let flop     = [ "y", "yes", "true", "1", "on"].includes(req.query.flop);
 94
 95  2x    E if (width > 0 && height > 0) {
 96  2x        image.ignoreAspectRatio();
 97        }
 98  2x    E if (width > 0 || height > 0) {
 99  2x        image.resize(width || null, height || null);
100        }
101  2x    I if (flip)         image.flip();
102  2x    I if (flop)         image.flop();
103  2x    I if (blur > 0)     image.blur(blur);
104  2x    I if (sharpen > 0)  image.sharpen(sharpen);
105  2x    I if (greyscale)    image.greyscale();
106
107  2x    db.query("UPDATE images SET date_used = UTC_TIMESTAMP WHERE id = ?", [ req.image.id ]);
108
109  2x    res.setHeader("Content-Type", "image/" + path.extname(req.image.name).substr(1));
110
111  2x    image.pipe(res);
112    });
113
```

It's more or less covered. We still need to cover all the effects. We can actually run them all at once. The first two conditions also have an E marker, but that should disappear after adding a test without resizing. Let's add it:

```
it("should be able to add image effects as we request", (done) => {
    chai
    .request(tools.service)
    .get("/uploads/test_image_download.png?
flip=y&flop=y&greyscale=y&blur=10&sharpen=10")
    .end((err, res) => {
        chai.expect(res).to.have.status(200);

        return done();
    });
});
```

Looking at our report now, we see the coverage is almost complete:

```
Code coverage report for ima… ×                                          Diogo
←   C  ⌂  ⓘ file:///Users/dresende/imagini/coverage/imagini.js.html        ☆  ⋮

 83  2x       return res.end(req.image.data);
 84        }
 85
 86  4x     let image    = sharp(req.image.data);
 87  4x     let width    = +req.query.width;
 88  4x     let height   = +req.query.height;
 89  4x     let blur     = +req.query.blur;
 90  4x     let sharpen  = +req.query.sharpen;
 91  4x     let greyscale = [ "y", "yes", "true", "1", "on"].includes(req.query.greyscale);
 92  4x     let flip     = [ "y", "yes", "true", "1", "on"].includes(req.query.flip);
 93  4x     let flop     = [ "y", "yes", "true", "1", "on"].includes(req.query.flop);
 94
 95  4x     if (width > 0 && height > 0) {
 96  2x       image.ignoreAspectRatio();
 97        }
 98  4x     if (width > 0 || height > 0) {
 99  2x       image.resize(width || null, height || null);
100        }
101  4x     if (flip)        image.flip();
102  4x     if (flop)        image.flop();
103  4x     if (blur > 0)    image.blur(blur);
104  4x     if (sharpen > 0) image.sharpen(sharpen);
105  4x     if (greyscale)   image.greyscale();
106
107  4x     db.query("UPDATE images SET date_used = UTC_TIMESTAMP WHERE id = ?", [ req.image.id ]);
108
109  4x     res.setHeader("Content-Type", "image/" + path.extname(req.image.name).substr(1));
110
111  4x     image.pipe(res);
112      });
113
114  2x   app.get("/stats", (req, res) => {
115        db.query("SELECT COUNT(*) total" +
116             ", SUM(size) size " +
```

To cover those yellow nulls there, we need to resize the image with only `width` or
`height`. We can add two tests for those:

```
it("should be able to resize the image width as we request", (done) =>
{
    chai
    .request(tools.service)
    .get("/uploads/test_image_download.png?width=200")
    .end((err, res) => {
        chai.expect(res).to.have.status(200);

        let image = sharp(res.body);

        image
        .metadata()
        .then((metadata) => {
            chai.expect(metadata).to.have.property("width", 200);

            return done();
        });
    });
});
```

Add a similar one for the `height`, and run the test suite. You should not see the statement coverage go up, only the branch coverage:

```
  ●  ●  ●      🗋 Code coverage report for ima   ✕                                              Diogo
  ←  →  C  ⌂   ⓘ file:///Users/dresende/imagini/coverage/imagini.js.html                    ☆   ⋮

  87  8x      let width    = +req.query.width;
  88  8x      let height   = +req.query.height;
  89  8x      let blur     = +req.query.blur;
  90  8x      let sharpen  = +req.query.sharpen;
  91  8x      let greyscale = [ "y", "yes", "true", "1", "on"].includes(req.query.greyscale);
  92  8x      let flip     = [ "y", "yes", "true", "1", "on"].includes(req.query.flip);
  93  8x      let flop     = [ "y", "yes", "true", "1", "on"].includes(req.query.flop);
  94
  95  8x      if (width > 0 && height > 0) {
  96  7x        image.ignoreAspectRatio();
  97          }
  98  8x      if (width > 0 || height > 0) {
  99  6x        image.resize(width || null, height || null);
 100          }
 101  8x      if (flip)        image.flip();
 102  8x      if (flop)        image.flop();
 103  8x      if (blur > 0)    image.blur(blur);
 104  8x      if (sharpen > 0) image.sharpen(sharpen);
 105  8x      if (greyscale)   image.greyscale();
 106
 107  8x      db.query("UPDATE images SET date_used = UTC_TIMESTAMP WHERE id = ?", [ req.image.id ]);
 108
 109  8x      res.setHeader("Content-Type", "image/" + path.extname(req.image.name).substr(1));
 110
 111  8x      image.pipe(res);
 112          });
 113
 114  2x    app.get("/stats", (req, res) => {
 115          db.query("SELECT COUNT(*) total" +
 116                  ", SUM(size) size " +
 117                  ", MAX(date_used) last_used " +
 118                  "FROM images",
 119          (err, rows) => {
 120            if (err) {
```

The only method missing is the statistics method. This one is simple. We could eventually run a more specific test, by asking statistics, making a change such as an upload, and asking for statistics again to compare. I'll leave that to you. Let's just add a simple request test:

```
const chai = require("chai");
const http = require("chai-http");
const tools = require("../tools");

chai.use(http);

describe("Statistics", () => {
    it("should return an object with total, size, last_used and
    uptime", (done) => {
        chai
        .request(tools.service)
        .get("/stats")
        .end((err, res) => {
            chai.expect(res).to.have.status(200);
            chai.expect(res.body).to.have.property("total");
            chai.expect(res.body).to.have.property("size");
```

```
        chai.expect(res.body).to.have.property("last_used");
        chai.expect(res.body).to.have.property("uptime");

        return done();
      });
    });
  });
```

Now, running our test suite should give all green:

We see there are only two lines uncovered: `29.121`. The first one is our timer and the second one is on the statistics method. Let's refresh our HTML report:

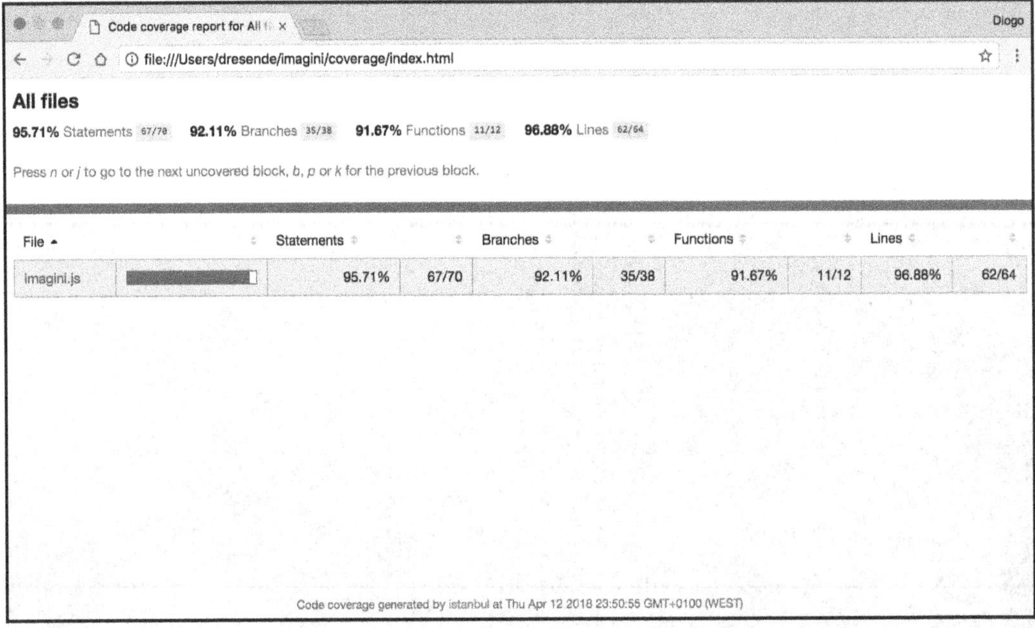

This is rewarding; we have almost *100%* coverage. There's only one function not covered, which is our timer. And, there are only tree statements, which also represent the three branches, that aren't covered, but those aren't actually that important.

What is important is to keep this high coverage mark during the course of our development.

Mocking our services

It's not at all uncommon to have parts of your service that are harder to test. Some, or most, of those parts are error-related conditions, where it's hard to make an external service such as a database engine return an error that will rarely occur during normal execution.

To be able to test, or at least simulate these kinds of events, we need to mock our services. There are a couple of options around, and Sinon is the most commonly used one in the Node.js ecosystem. This framework provides more than mocking; it also provides the following:

- **Spies**: Which monitor function calls and record arguments passed, the returned value and other properties
- **Stubs**: Which are enhanced spies with a pre-programmed behavior, helping us drive the execution into a pre-determined path (allowing us to mock a behavior)

Sinon also allows us to bend time, by virtually changing the service perception of time, and to be able to test timed interval calls (remember our interval timer?). With this in mind, let's see if we can make our microservice reach *100%* test coverage.

Let's start by installing the framework, as we did with `chai`:

```
npm install --save-dev sinon
```

Now, let's add a test for the image deletion. This method is tested through the other tests and that's why we didn't need to add it before, but now that we want to fully test it, let's add a basic test file called `image-delete.js`, with the following content:

```js
const chai = require("chai");
const sinon = require("sinon");
const http = require("chai-http");
const tools = require("../tools");

chai.use(http);

describe.only("Deleting image", () => {
    beforeEach((done) => {
        chai
        .request(tools.service)
        .delete("/uploads/test_image_delete.png")
        .end(() => {
            return done();
        });
    });
});

it("should return 200 if it exists", (done) => {
    chai
    .request(tools.service)
    .post("/uploads/test_image_delete.png")
    .set("Content-Type", "image/png")
    .send(tools.sample)
```

```
        .end((err, res) => {
            chai.expect(res).to.have.status(200);
            chai.expect(res.body).to.have.status("ok");

            chai
            .request(tools.service)
            .delete("/uploads/test_image_delete.png")
            .end((err, res) => {
                chai.expect(res).to.have.status(200);

                return done();
            });
        });
    });
});
```

Notice that I added the Sinon dependency on top, although I'm not using it just yet. You may run the tests again, but you shouldn't notice any difference.

We'll need to change the database behavior, so let's export a reference to it, so as to be able to access it from the tests. Add the following line in our microservice file before connecting to the database:

```
app.db = db;
```

Now, add another test to that file:

```
it("should return 500 if a database error happens", (done) => {
    chai
    .request(tools.service)
    .post("/uploads/test_image_delete.png")
    .set("Content-Type", "image/png")
    .send(tools.sample)
    .end((err, res) => {
        chai.expect(res).to.have.status(200);
        chai.expect(res.body).to.have.status("ok");

        let query = sinon.stub(tools.service.db, "query");

        query
        .withArgs("DELETE FROM images WHERE id = ?")
        .callsArgWithAsync(2, new Error("Fake"));

        query
        .callThrough();

        chai
        .request(tools.service)
```

```
            .delete("/uploads/test_image_delete.png")
            .end((err, res) => {
                chai.expect(res).to.have.status(500);

                query.restore();

                return done();
            });
        });
    });
```

What we're doing is uploading an image, but, before requesting to delete it, we create a `stub` on the `db.query` method. We then inform Sinon that when the `stub` is called with the first argument with `DELETE`, we want it to asynchronously call the third argument (counting starts at 0) with a fake error. For any other call, we want it to just pass through.

Then, after deleting the image, we check that we received an HTTP 500 error code and restore the `stub` to the original function, ensuring that the other tests pass.

We're able to test this because `mocha` runs tests in serial; otherwise, we would need to do some gymnastics to ensure that we wouldn't interfere with the other tests.

Now, open the previously created test file, `image-stats.js`, include Sinon on the top, and add the following test:

```
it("should return 500 if a database error happens", (done) => {
    let query = sinon.stub(tools.service.db, "query");

    query
    .withArgs("SELECT COUNT(*) total, SUM(size) size, MAX(date_used)
    last_used FROM images")
    .callsArgWithAsync(1, new Error("Fake"));

    query
    .callThrough();

    chai
    .request(tools.service)
    .get("/stats")
    .end((err, res) => {
        chai.expect(res).to.have.status(500);

        query.restore();

        return done();
    });
```

```
});
```

We're now over 97% coverage. Let's bend time and test our timer. Create a new test file called `image-delete-old.js`, and add the following content:

```javascript
const chai = require("chai");
const sinon = require("sinon");
const http = require("chai-http");
const tools = require("../tools");

chai.use(http);

describe("Deleting older images", () => {
    let clock = sinon.useFakeTimers({ shouldAdvanceTime : true });

    it("should run every hour", (done) => {
        chai
        .request(tools.service)
        .get("/stats")
        .end((err, res) => {
            chai.expect(res).to.have.status(200);

            clock.tick(3600 * 1000);
            clock.restore();

            return done();
        });
    });
});
```

In this test, we're replacing the global timer functions (`setTimeout` and `setInterval`) with fake timers. We then make a simple call to statistics, and then advance time by one hour (the tick call), and then finish.

Now, run the tests and see the results:

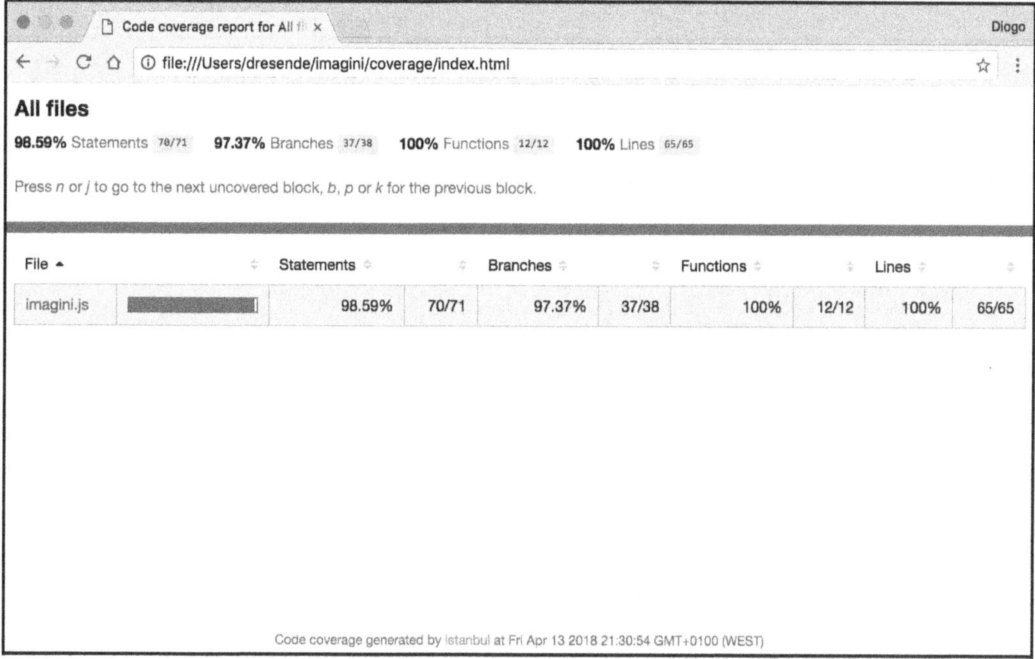

We now reach *100% coverage* on functions and lines. There's only one branch, with one statement missing. It's the possibility of a connection error:

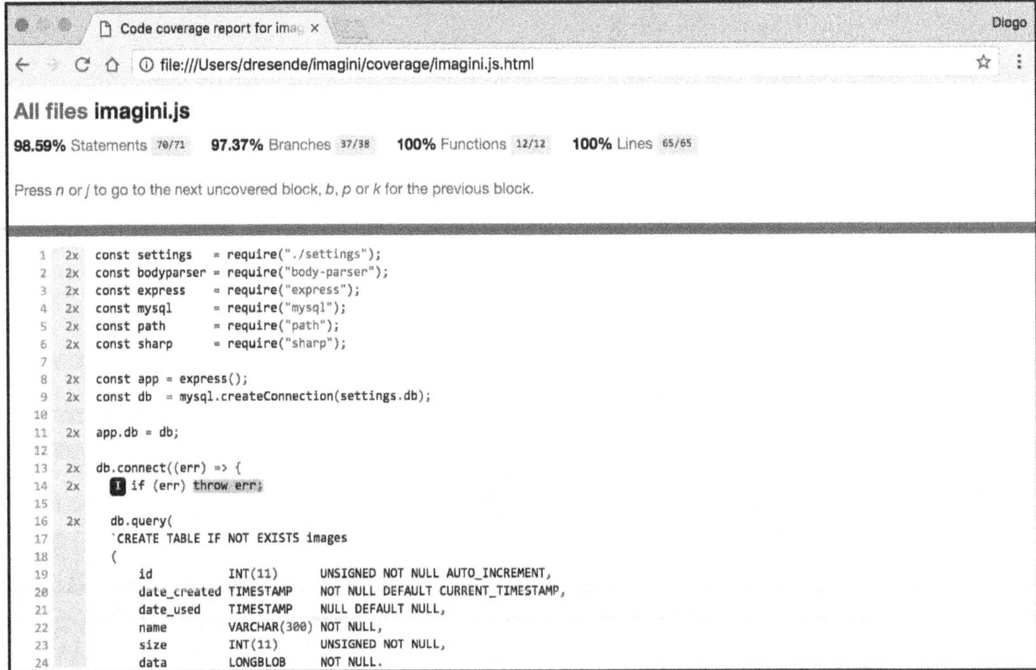

I'll leave it to you to figure it out how to mock that.

Remember that if you successfully mock the `connect` method, you'll also need to handle the throw.

Summary

Tests allow us to ensure a certain code quality level. It's very important to include tests from the very beginning, while the code is simple, to ensure that we keep tests updated and avoid regressions to the expected behavior.

It's very rewarding when we see that our code has a very high test coverage. This feeling forces you to keep that high mark and indirectly maintains good code quality.

24
Design Patterns

In the previous chapter, we successfully deployed our service to a cloud provider without having to fundamentally change our code. We used a database to store our data, and the only thing we needed to do was to point to the new location.

It's common, during the specification and development process, to have challenging problems with one or more ways of solving them. The ways, or paths, you choose throughout the development are called design patterns, as they're part of your design.

Some design patterns are more common than others. Some are well-known, others, not so much. Some are good design patterns and you should follow them. Others are bad because of the disadvantages they bring in the short or long term.

In this chapter, we're going to take a look at the importance of choosing good patterns; we will look at some common architectural patterns and review the continuous integration we followed through the entire book until we successfully deployed to the cloud.

Choosing patterns

Patterns are not libraries or classes, they're concepts, reusable solutions to common programming problems, tested and optimized for specific use cases. As they're just concepts to solve specific problems, they have to be implemented in every language.

Every pattern has its advantages and disadvantages, and choosing a wrong pattern for a problem can cause you a big headache.

Patterns can speed up the development process because they provide well-tested and well-proven development paradigms. Reusing patterns helps prevent issues and improves code readability between developers that are familiar with the patterns.

Patterns have major importance in high-performance applications. Sometimes, in order to achieve some flexibility, patterns introduce a new level of indirection in the code, which may reduce performance. You should choose when to introduce a pattern or when that introduction will hurt the performance metric you're targeting.

Knowing good patterns is essential for avoiding the opposite: anti-patterns. An anti-pattern is something that looks good in the beginning but later on turns out to look like the worst decision you ever made. Anti-patterns are not specific patterns but are more like common errors, seen by the majority as strategies you shouldn't use. Some of the most common and frequent anti-patterns seen out there are:

- **Repeating yourself**: Don't repeat excessive parts of the code. Lean back, look at the big picture and refactor it. Some developers tend to look at this refactoring as a complexity of the application, but it can actually turn your application simpler. If you think you won't be able to understand the simplicity of your refactoring, don't forget to add a couple of introductory comments to the code.
- **Golden hammer or silver bullet**: Don't think your favorite language or framework is universally applicable. Most of the languages can actually do practically anything, at least the mature ones, and with a huge community. That doesn't mean a language performs some tasks well. If your goal is performance, try to have a couple of hammers in your belt.
- **Coding by exception**: Don't add new code to handle new cases as they appear. By new cases, I don't mean new features; I mean behavior your code was not expecting. For example, when you're making a file upload feature of some kind, remember an error might happen during transfer, the file can be empty, have weird content, be huge, and so on.
- **Programming by accident**: Don't program by trial and error until you succeed. This is something you should really avoid. Programming by accident can sometimes make your code work in some cases (by accident) and produce erroneous behaviors in others.

Architectural patterns

When developing microservices and, more specifically, an ecosystem of microservices, some patterns become very obvious, and you'll use them without knowing. Just looking at the architectural patterns, here are some that you might find interesting. Perhaps you have already used them before.

Front Controller

The **Front Controller** pattern is when all requests go for a single point in your architecture, called the handler, which then processes and dispatches the requests to other handlers. This is the pattern used by, for example, load balancers and reverses proxies:

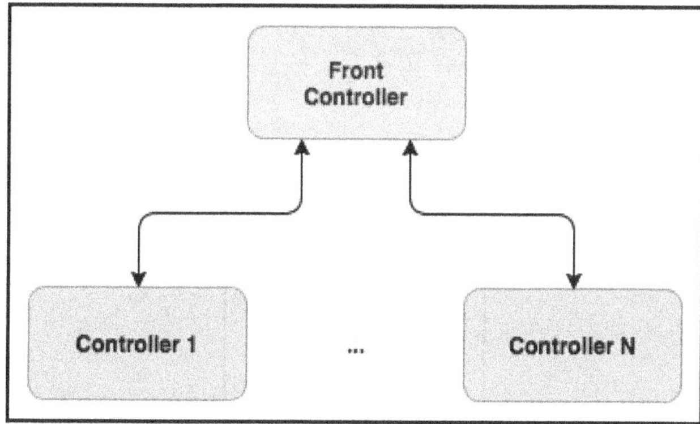

It's useful to scale horizontally, especially when the **Front Controller** is just routing requests, so it can handle a lot more requests than each separate controller, which need, some time to actually process each request.

This pattern is also very useful in helping other services not having to know where the controllers are and choosing the one with the lowest load that should handle the request faster.

Layered

The layered pattern is common in filesystems and operative systems (and virtual machines for that matter). This pattern consists of creating different layers that go from the raw data through to the data seen by a user:

The idea is to separate the complexity of the different layers, each one not having to know how the others do their tasks:

- Handling the data structures and storing them in a fast and secure way
- Manipulating the data structures and adding business logic to them
- Handling user requests and showing the data in a localised format

Service Locator

The **Service Locator** pattern is actually an anti-pattern. It's not considered a good practice because it adds much more complexity to an ecosystem. The pattern consists of a central registry, called a **Service Locator**, where services register their abilities, and other services can consult the registry and know where the services they need are located:

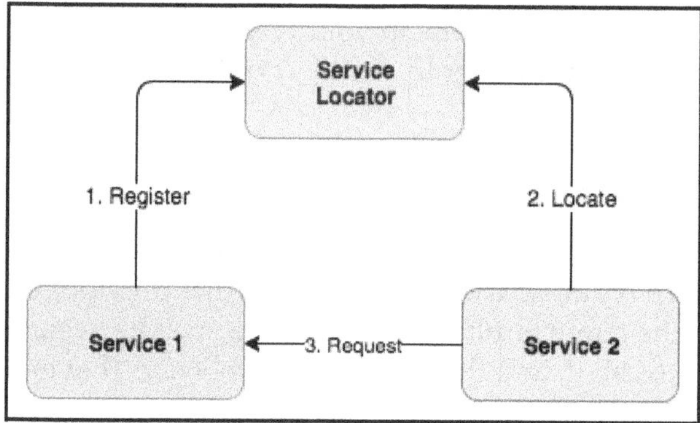

The **Service Locator** is similar to the Front Controller, but with added complexity, as you need to contact the Service Locator and the service you need, instead of just making a simple request to a Front Controller.

Observer

The Observer pattern is used every day in Node.js. It consists of a **Subject**, which maintains a list of dependents, called Observers, which get notified of any state change happening on the **Subject**:

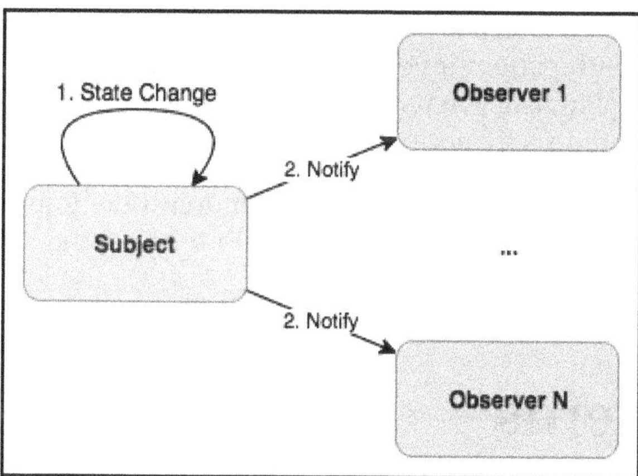

You can see this happening every time in your web browser when some code (**Observer**) attaches an event listener to an object or interface element (**Subject**).

Publish-Subscribe

Another very similar pattern is the Publish-Subscribe pattern, usually abbreviated as **Pub-Sub**. This pattern is almost exactly the same as the previous one. You have Subscribers that, as the name implies, subscribe to a specific event, or topic, or whatever you want to call it, and then you have Publishers that emit those events or send information to those topics:

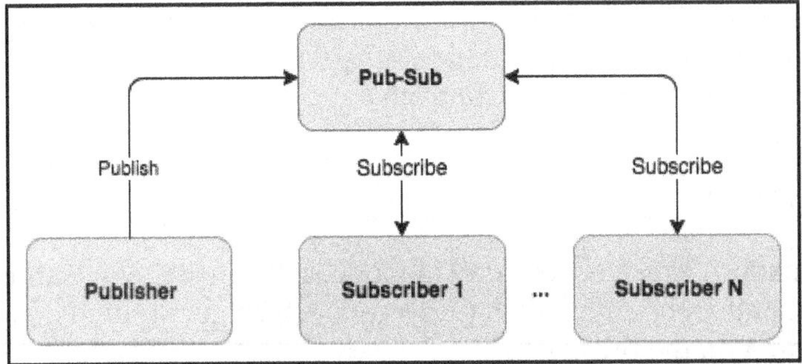

The difference to the previous pattern may look very thin but is actually very important. The **Pub-Sub** pattern involves a third-party service and, unlike the Observer pattern, the Publishers have no knowledge of the Subscribers. This removes the need to handle and directly notify the Subscribers, thereby simplifying your code.

This pattern is quite useful for microservice communication. It involves a third party that abstracts the state change notification. Also, Publishers and Subscribers have no knowledge of each other.

Using patterns

Choosing good design patterns is essentially choosing best practices. Not all design patterns fit every purpose, but for many scenarios, they'll make your life easier. Perhaps you may not notice any difference in the beginning, but you should in the long-term.

Good design patterns also have indirect advantages. You'll find more documentation and examples online, as well as a broader set of options to choose from, for example, when using the Publish-Subscribe pattern, where you'll find many types of implementations to integrate with your services.

Choosing the pattern that fits your needs also involves planning and knowing what you need and what you'll need in the future. Think of the edge cases and see if the pattern is capable of handling them.

Planning your microservice

Developing a microservice may look like a simple task. As the name implies, it is a micro service. But that is not necessarily true, as sometimes we tend to complexify something that should be simple.

This does not mean a service should be simple, it can be quite complex. What should be simple is the goal and the properties of the service. There shouldn't be any doubt regarding what it does and what it shouldn't do.

Before writing any line of code, you should start by knowing a couple of what I call characteristics of the service, such as:

- What is it for? What tasks will it do?
- What other services will use it? What protocol will it speak?
- Will it replace another service? Will it cover the same tasks?

This can be summed in one word—purpose. If you don't clearly define its purpose and just start developing tasks it can handle, you'll end up having a mixed service that deviates from the main goal of a microservice.

After having a proper purpose, you can then choose the best pattern and plan the individual tasks. The first task will probably take longer to develop, as you're creating the base layout for the service.

Don't forget to add tests, coverage, and documentation as soon as possible. I know this is something most developers tend to ignore, but it will bite you later. It's easier to add a simple test for a first simple task. Code coverage is easier at this point. Adding documentation should also be easier if you're planning the individual tasks.

After having your first task, with a proper test, you should set your first deploy. This will end your first development cycle and bring you back to planning. If you keep this loop going, with small tasks, you'll develop faster, and deploy faster:

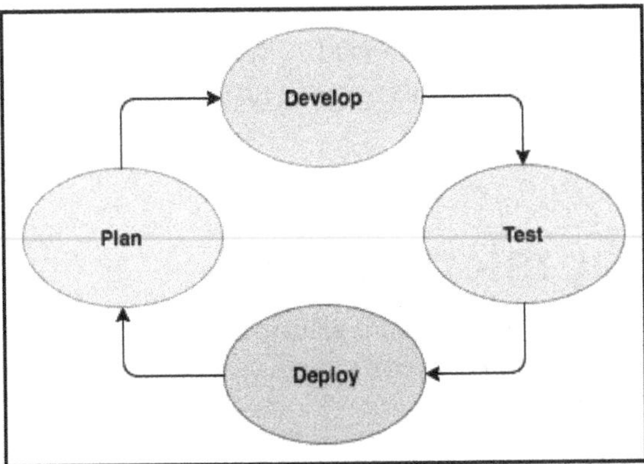

This type of simple loop with small tasks will allow you to do what is called **continuous integration** and **continuous deployment**, where you're able to develop and deploy to a testing cluster. The change can be automatically tested and deployed if everything passes the tests.

Obstacles when developing

As we saw previously, a microservice architecture has many advantages, such as splitting code into smaller isolated projects, where it becomes easier to develop or even delegate responsibility.

These advantages come at a cost, which is the build of a more complex system or application. Because of how microservices are supposed to work, an information barrier is intrinsic. A microservice responsible for a type of information should be the only one manipulating it, forcing any other service to communicate with it to have access to information.

This gives you a finer control over the information because you know the service responsible for it, and you can force service or user authentication, with authorization or even rate-access limits. But, this means that a complex application will tend to penalize the network as there will be significant inter-service messaging.

Inter-service messaging means network traffic and latency. If the services are not on the same local network, this will eventually create noticeable latency. Adding some kind of cache service to accelerate access will also add more complexity.

Although testing and development for each microservice should be easier than a monolith application, looking at the microservice test frameworks all together, and having two or more services test together, is more complicated.

Finally, avoid something called a nanoservice. This is considered an anti-pattern, and it's when you exaggerate on fine-graining your architecture and create overly small services, complexifying your development to the extreme.

Find a good balance between the number of microservices and what each will do. Think of them as a person that will handle a specific task. Is the task too simple to have one person allocated to do just that? Shouldn't the person have a broader set of tasks from the same context?

Summary

Today's applications have space for microservices. Applications are no longer monolith and left the traditional computer architecture long ago. Users constantly demand integrations and interoperability between applications.

Microservices help developers to reduce the complexity of applications by separating different contexts, such as frontend, backend, mobile, or a simple API. They're a concept, or a pattern, that, when used well, can give you great power, and split complexity and responsibility.

But, microservices are more than that. Microservices help you scale horizontally by just replicating the services you need and not a complete monolith application, saving resources and, ultimately, money.

There's a lot to explore out there; we have just scratched the surface. There are plenty of cloud providers and tools for you to experiment with and choose what fits you best. Remember, practice makes perfect, so head to your work desk, and good luck!

Other Books You May Enjoy

If you enjoyed this book, you may be interested in these other books by Packt:

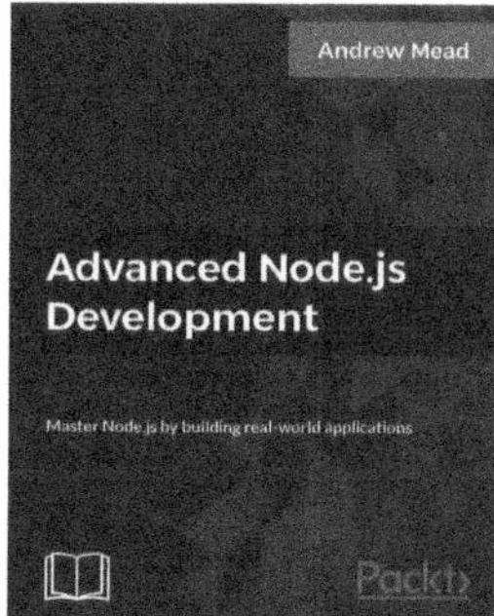

Advanced Node.js Development

Andrew Mead

ISBN: 9781788393935

- Develop, test, and deploy real-world Node.js applications
- Master Node.js by building practical, working examples
- Use awesome third-party Node modules such as MongoDB, Mongoose, Socket.io, and Express
- Create real-time web applications
- Explore async and await in ES7

Learning Node.js for Mobile Application Development
Stefan Buttigieg, Milorad Jevdjenic

ISBN: 9781785280498

- Develop an API from scratch
- Set up a MongoDB Database as part of your mobile application backend
- Deploy a cross-platform mobile application from the command line
- Incorporate features within your mobile application that use native phone features such as a gyroscope, GPS, and accelerometer
- Implement mobile applications that use web-enabled APIs
- Build a mobile application with real-time chat messaging features
- Develop a secure mobile application that is capable of functioning with real-time data

Building Bots with Node.js
Stefan Buttigieg, Milorad Jevdjenic

ISBN: 9781786465450

- Create a bot template that responds to e-mails based on certain ruling criteria

- Interact with SMS and perform some basic Natural Language Processing using the Twilio API for Node.js
- Work with the Skype Web SDK and Node.js to create a bot that works with SQL Server and Skype
- Build an automated Flight Information Agent bot using the Twitter and Air France KLM APIs
- Create a scheduling bot for teams using the Facebook Messenger API
- Interact with BotKit along with and MongoDB Amazon S3 to create a document management bot in Node.js
- Leverage ICR and Azure Table Storage from Node.js to create a bug tracking bot
- Integrate Force.com API and Kik to create a Salesforce CRM bot

Leave a review - let other readers know what you think

Please share your thoughts on this book with others by leaving a review on the site that you bought it from. If you purchased the book from Amazon, please leave us an honest review on this book's Amazon page. This is vital so that other potential readers can see and use your unbiased opinion to make purchasing decisions, we can understand what our customers think about our products, and our authors can see your feedback on the title that they have worked with Packt to create. It will only take a few minutes of your time, but is valuable to other potential customers, our authors, and Packt. Thank you!

Index

O

P

used, for Node.js installation 32
paging
    implementing 524, 525, 526, 529, 530
PaperCSS
    URL 193
Passport
    about 555, 556
    basic authentication strategy 556
    OAuth Strategy 558, 559
    third-party authentication strategies 559,
        560, 561, 562
    URL 261, 266, 556
PATH variable
    configuring, for commands installed by
        modules 95
    configuring, on Windows 96
    modifications, avoiding 96
pathname 77, 79
patterns, microservices
    autonomous 578
    communicable 580
    decomposable 577
    scalable 579
patterns
    architectural patterns 692
    selecting 691, 692
    using 696
Picnic CSS
    URL 193
PM2
    reference 350
    setting up, for management of Node.js
        processes 350
POSIX-like systems
    developer tools, installing on macOS 38
    installing, from source 37, 40
    Node.js, compiling from source 39
    prerequisites, installing 37
private key 563
Promise objects, states
    Fulfilled 155
    Pending 155
    Rejected 155
Promise
    about 51, 153, 154

asynchronous code, flattening 156
    error handling 155
    generators 156, 157, 158, 159, 160
public key 563
public-key encryption
    about 563
    scenario 564
Publish-Subscribe pattern 696
Puppeteer API
    reference 437
Puppeteer
    about 432
    Add Note scenario, testing 439, 440
    frontend headless browser, testing 432
    login scenario, executing 438
    reference 443, 446
    setting up 433
    spurious test errors, mitigating 441
    spurious test errors, preventing 441
    test script, for Notes 436, 437, 438
    testability, improving for Notes 436
    testability, improving in Notes UI 433
    URL 432
Pure.css
    URL 193
Pyramid of Doom 153
Python
    reference 32, 41

Q

Quality Assurance (QA) team 403
Quality Engineering (QE) team 403
queries
    reference 257

R

Read-Eval-Print Loop (REPL) 11
real-time updates, on Notes home page
    executing 322
    execution, while viewing note 326
    home page, modifying 320, 321
    implementing 316
    layout template, modifying 320, 321
    managing 318, 319
    note view template, modifying 324, 325

Printed in March 2021
by Rotomail Italia S.p.A., Vignate (MI) - Italy